Front-Bench Opposition

Front-Bench Opposition

The Role of the Leader of the
Opposition, the Shadow
Cabinet and Shadow
Government in British Politics

R. M. PUNNETT

Lecturer in Politics in the University of Strathclyde

HEINEMANN . LONDON

Heinemann Educational Books Ltd

LONDON EDINBURGH MELBOURNE TORONTO
AUCKLAND JOHANNESBURG SINGAPORE
IBADAN NAIROBI HONG KONG NEW DELHI

ISBN 0 435 83734 6
HEB paperback ISBN 0 435 83735 4

Published by Heinemann Educational Books Ltd
48 Charles Street, London W1X 8AH

Printed in Great Britain by
Butler and Tanner Ltd Frome and London

To Marjory

'*Political opposition is an eternal paradox. It postulates the principle that impediments to political action may be wholesome and are therefore to be protected. But what is the chance of institutionalizing such limitations?*'

OTTO KIRCHHEIMER

Contents

page

Preface

PART ONE: INTRODUCTION

1. Her Majesty's Opposition   3

    *Parliamentary Opposition in Britain. The Opposition
    and other 'Oppositions'. The Limitations of Official
    Opposition.*

PART TWO: THE OPPOSITION FRONT-BENCH TEAM

2. The Evolution of the Opposition Team   35

    *Coordinating Opposition in the Eighteenth and Nine-
    teenth Centuries. The Conservatives in Opposition this
    Century. Labour's Elected Shadow Cabinet. The Emer-
    gence of a Shadow Government. Opposition in the
    Modern Parliament.*

3. The Leader of the Opposition   74

    *The Status of the Leader of the Opposition. The Emer-
    gence of Leaders of the Opposition. The Power of the
    Leader of the Opposition. The Leader of the Opposition
    and the Public. The Leader, the Shadow Cabinet and
    the Spokesmen.*

4. The Election of Labour's Parliamentary Com-   110
    mittee

    *Structure of the Parliamentary Committee of the PLP.
    Voting Behaviour in the Parliamentary Committee Ballot.
    The Committee and the Front-Bench Spokesmen.*

5. The Selection of Opposition Spokesmen   137

    *The Size of the Front-Bench Team. Horses for Courses.
    A Shadow of the Past or a Cabinet of the Future? The
    Selection of Experts. The Re-allocation of Duties.*

page

PART THREE: THE OPPOSITION TEAM
AT WORK

6. The Activities of the Opposition   179
   *The Compensations of Opposition. Opposition Pre-
   occupations. Opposing the Government. Preparing for
   Office.*

7. The Role and Organisation of the Shadow Cabinet   216
   *Meetings of the Shadow Cabinet. The Shadow Cabinet
   in Action. Group and Individual Roles within the
   Shadow Cabinet. Shadow Cabinet Committees.*

8. Spokesmen as Parliamentary Critics and Policy   250
   Makers
   *The Spokesman's Duties. Spokesmen and Policy Making.
   The Opposition Civil Service. Other Sources of Infor-
   mation.*

9. Spokesmen and Their Parliamentary Colleagues   286
   *Spokesmen and Collective Responsibility. Resignations
   and Dismissals. Spokesmen and their Backbench Colleagues: the Conservative Party. Spokesmen and their
   Backbench Colleagues: the Labour Party.*

10. Spokesmen and Their Parliamentary Subject   315
    Specialisations
    *Index of Specialisation 1900–70. Degree of Specialisa-
    tion and Level of Activity. Individual Spokesmen and
    their Specialisations. Patterns of Behaviour.*

PART FOUR: CONCLUSION

11. From Opposition to Office   365
    *The Overlap Between Opposition and Office 1964 and
    1970. Spokesmen and Ministers. Towards a More
    Formal Opposition.*

Appendices

A. Coalitions, Liberals and Peers   403
   *Parliamentary Opposition in Wartime. The Liberal
   Party in Opposition. The Opposition Front Bench in
   the House of Lords.*

B. The Cross-National Context   431

C. Standing Orders for the Election of the Officers of   450
   the Parliamentary Labour Party

page

D. Parliamentary Committee Ballot Results and Lists   453
   of Opposition Spokesmen
E. A Note on Sources and Methods   468
   Interviews. Index of Specialisation. The Index to The
   Times. The Gallup Political Index. Bibliographical
   Note.

Index of Names   489

Subject Index   495

List of Tables

page

1 Parliamentary Roles of the Conservative, Labour and Liberal Parties this Century   7
2 Government Performance in By-Elections 1922–70   12
3 Main Subject Areas of Activity in Parliament for Members of the Parliamentary Committee 1952–3 Session   64
4 Leaders of the Opposition 1900–70   83
5 Coverage of Cabinet and Shadow Cabinet by *The Times* in 1961 and 1968   101
6 Coverage of Cabinet and Shadow Cabinet by *The Times* during the 1964, 1966 and 1970 General Election Campaigns   102
7 Parliamentary Committee Ballots November 1952   116
8 Timetable of the 1971 Ballots for the PLP Officers and the Parliamentary Committee   117
9 MPs Serving Concurrently on NEC and Parliamentary Committee 1951–64 and 1970   126
10 Average Ages of the Front-Bench Teams 1951–70   153
11 New MPs Elected at General Elections 1945–70   155
12 Overlap between the Attlee Government in October 1951 and the Opposition Front-Bench Team of 1951–64   156
13 Overlap between the Douglas-Home Government in October 1964 and the Opposition Front-Bench Team 1964–70   159
14 Overlap between the Wilson Government in June 1970 and the Opposition Front-Bench Team in December 1970   160
15 Former Ministers Covering in Opposition the Departments in which they Served at the Dissolution   165
16 Main Area of Parliamentary Activity of Backbenchers in the Session before Their Appointments as Spokesmen   168
17 Spokesmen and Membership of House of Commons Standing Committees   254

xi

page

18 Study Groups, Sub-Committees and Working Parties of the Labour Party NEC 1963–4 and 1970–1   269
19 House of Commons Division on the Principle of Common Market Entry 28 October 1971, Voting of Labour MPs   288
20 Conservative Backbench Subject Committees 1969–1970 Session   304
21 PLP Subject Groups 1970–1 Session   311
22 Index of Specialisation 1900–70   318
23 Index of Specialisation: Labour Spokesmen who served throughout the 1955–64 Period   322
24 Index of Specialisation: Conservative Spokesmen who served throughout the 1964–70 Period   323
25 Index of Specialisation: Debates, Oral Questions and Written Questions   325
26 Average Number of Policy Areas Covered by Front Benchers in Debates and Questions   328
27 Main Topic related to Assigned Duty   330
28 Level of Activity in Main Area compared with Other Areas   333
29 Index of Specialisation related to Level of Activity 337
30 Index of Specialisation by Subject Area   340
31 Specialisation in Assigned Area before and after Appointment as Spokesman   342
32 Index of Specialisation: Labour Backbenchers Appointed as Spokesmen in 1961–2 Session   343
33 Index of Specialisation: Conservative Backbenchers Appointed as Spokesmen in 1967–8   344
34 Specialisation in Assigned Area Before and After Change of Duty   346
35 Index of Specialisation: Labour Spokesmen involved in a Change of Duty at Beginning or End of 1961–2 Session   347
36 Index of Specialisation: Conservative Spokesmen involved in a Change of Duty at Beginning or End of 1967–8 Session   348
37 Index of Specialisation: Mrs Thatcher   349
38 Index of Specialisation: Members of the Shadow Cabinet without any Ministerial Experience Compared with Shadow Cabinet and Team as a Whole   353

page

39 Former Spokesmen holding Ministerial Posts in the Wilson Government, 1964–70, and in the Heath Government in July 1970 and April 1972 — 371

40 Former Spokesmen as Proportion of MPs in the Wilson Cabinet and Government 1964–70, and in the Heath Cabinet and Government, July 1970 and April 1972 — 374

41 Liberal Party Spokesmen in the Commons and the Lords 1969–70 Session — 417

42 Conservative Opposition Spokesmen in the House of Lords 1969–70 Session — 423

43 Labour Opposition Spokesmen in the House of Lords 1970–1 Session — 424

44 Results of the Parliamentary Committee Ballot 1923, 1924–9 and 1931–9 — 454

45 Results of the Parliamentary Committee Ballot 1951–64 — 456

46 Labour Opposition Front-Bench Spokesmen 1955–9 Parliament — 458

47 Labour Opposition Front-Bench Spokesmen 1959–1964 Parliament — 460

48 Conservative Opposition Front-Bench Spokesmen 1964–6 Parliament — 462

49 Conservative Opposition Front-Bench Spokesmen 1966–70 Parliament — 464

50 Labour Opposition Front-Bench Spokesmen 1970 Parliament — 466

51 Results of the Parliamentary Committee Ballot 1970–2 — 467

List of Figures

		page
A	Gallup Poll: Voting Intention 1960–9	11
B	Relationship between Government and Opposition in Britain 1900–70	17
C	Percentage Seats won by Government and Opposition Parties at British General Elections 1900–70	19
D	The Context of Front-Bench Opposition	26
E	The Structure of the Opposition Front-Bench Team	75
F	Gallup Poll: Leader of the Opposition's Rating compared with that of His Party 1961–70	104
G	Gallup Poll: Leader of the Opposition's Rating compared with that of the Prime Minister	106
H	Number of Opposition Spokesmen and Ministers in the Commons 1955–70	144
I	Index of Specialisation 1900–70 (Shadow Cabinet)	320
J	Index of Specialisation 1945–70: Debates, Oral and Written Questions	326
K	Average Number of Policy Areas covered by Spokesmen in Debates and Questions	329
L	Number of References per Spokesman per Day in Main and Other Areas	334
M	Patterns of Government–Opposition Relationships in Western Parliamentary Systems 1945–70	447

Preface

This book examines the role of the Leader of the Opposition, the Shadow Cabinet, and Opposition Spokesmen in British politics. The prime concern is with the years 1951–70, spanning the 1951–64 period of Labour Opposition, and the 1964–1970 period of Conservative Opposition, but to give a fuller perspective reference is also made to the historical background to modern practices, and to developments in the post-1970 period of Labour Opposition. Throughout, emphasis is placed on comparing the two parties in terms of their front-bench organisation and behaviour when in opposition, and in comparing the practices of opposition with those of office. The book is in four parts. Part One introduces the subject and examines the main features, merits, and defects of the principle of a loyal, office-seeking, Parliamentary Opposition. Part Two deals with the structure and composition of the Opposition front-bench team, and Part Three deals with the Opposition at work, examining the functions that are performed by the Shadow Cabinet, Opposition spokesmen, and the Opposition as a whole. Part Four examines the transfer from opposition to office. Some topics which are outside the main themes of the study, but which are of associated interest, are presented in Appendices.

The sources and methods used in the study are discussed in some detail in an Appendix. It may be noted here, however, that the bulk of the information on contemporary practices was obtained from a series of eighty non-attributable interviews with MPs, peers, party officials, and officers of Parliament. Through these interviews a detailed picture was built up of Labour and Conservative patterns of organisation and behaviour in the 1951–64 and 1964–70 periods, and this forms the basis of the study. The knowledge of contemporary practices that was obtained from these interviews was supplemented by information gleaned from newspapers, particularly *The Times* and *The Guardian*, and from political biographies and auto-biographies. There is an abundance of such biographies and autobiographies, and these were also used to build up a picture of Opposition practices in the earlier years of this century, and in the eighteenth and nineteenth centuries. Other secondary sources were used, such as the standard books and articles on Parliament, the political parties, the Cabinet, and the theory of opposition. More specific information came from sources like Hansard, House of Commons Select and Standing Committee reports, the index to *The Times*, the opinion polls, and various Parliamentary reference books. In particular, the Hansard sessional index was used as the basis of a statistical analysis of Opposition front benchers' Parliamentary behaviour. Whenever information or quotations have a written source, this is acknowledged in a footnote, but material obtained from the interviews has to remain unacknowledged, as this was a condition on which almost all of the interviewees insisted.

The research on which the study is based was financed by a grant from the Nuffield Foundation, through its Social Sciences Small Grants Scheme. I am extremely grateful for this assistance. I am also indebted to a number of individuals for giving me help and advice. Special thanks are due to my colleague, A. L. M. Smith, for his help and encouragement over a long period. He commented on various drafts, and preserved his patience and sense of humour through numerous changes of plan. Professor Richard Rose, Professor William Pickles and Bruce Headey read most of the chapters at one stage or another, and William Miller, John Barnes, Eddie Oram, and Derek Urwin commented on individual chapters. Ian Chalmers helped with the preparation of the graphs and diagrams, and Mrs M. P. Chalmers prepared the Index of Names. I am indebted to them all for sound advice on innumerable points. Sir Michael Fraser, James Douglas, and Geoffrey Block for the Conservative Party, Terry Pitt for the Labour Party, and Richard Moore for the Liberals, checked an earlier draft of the manuscript. Their diligence enabled me to correct a number of errors of fact and emphasis. Any errors that remain are, of course, my own responsibility.

I am obliged to Mrs G. Buchanan, Mrs D. C. Elder, and

Mrs J. Mal for typing parts of the final draft, and to Mrs C. Ryburn for helping with earlier drafts. The bulk of the typing of the several drafts, however, was done by my wife: my debt to her as a typist, adviser, and comforter is incalculable. The dedication of the book to her is only a small acknowledgement of this debt.

Glasgow, 1973   R. M. PUNNETT

part one

Introduction

1

Her Majesty's Opposition

THERE ARE essentially two ways in which a political system gains from the toleration of opposition to the established government. In the first place, a number of benefits can flow from subjecting the activities of those in power to regular scrutiny. Criticism can help to make rulers alert and aware of their limitations: thus John Stuart Mill points out that 'Both teachers and learners go to sleep at their post, as soon as there is no enemy in the field.'[1] Criticism may lead to the improvement of policies, and certainly provides those in power with a reaction to their activities. As expressed by David Apter,

> Just as the fluctuations in the glass of a barometer indicate information about the weather, so the rise and fall of support to an opposition indicates to government the effectiveness of its policies.[2]

Even where those in power choose to ignore this 'barometer', the exposure of government actions and intentions provides a release for the public's frustrations with their rulers, while such exposure serves also to educate the public and keep them aware of the deficiencies of those in power.

In addition to all the benefits that flow from subjecting the rulers to scrutiny, the toleration of critics of those in power can provide the public with a choice of rulers—always assuming that the system provides for elections, or for some other process, to enable the Government to be replaced by its critics. These two functions of criticising those in power and seeking

[1] J. S. Mill, *On Liberty*, London 1910 (Everyman edition), p. 102.
[2] D. E. Apter, 'Some Reflections on the Role of Political Opposition in New Nations', *Comparative Studies in Society and History*, 1961–2, pp. 154–68.

to replace them do not necessarily have to be performed by the same individuals or institutions. In ancient Rome the Tribunes were a medium through which citizens could oppose decisions taken by the government, in that Tribunes had the right to veto measures initiated by the Senate.[1] This role, however, was purely a negative one: the Tribunes could oppose, but had no power to propose measures, and in no sense at all were they an 'alternative government'. Medieval English Parliaments opposed the Monarch, but did not seek to wrest executive power from him, other than in a civil war situation. In the modern British Parliamentary system, however, Her Majesty's Opposition does perform both roles: it seeks to expose the deficiencies of Her Majesty's Government, and ultimately to replace it. It is thus an 'office-seeking Opposition', with the Leader of the Opposition posing as an alternative Prime Minister, and his leading colleagues as alternative Ministers. This situation is illustrated well by a comment made by Lord Balfour, to the effect that in Britain

> . . . a General Election which brings about the fall of a Government may not only modify national policy but will certainly change the functions of the great majority of individual Members of Parliament. With regard to Ministers and ex-Ministers this is plain enough. They invert their roles when they exchange their Benches. Those who formerly criticised have now to administer. Those who formerly administered have now to criticise.[2]

Balfour was writing in the context of the Parliamentary situation of almost one hundred years ago, but his comment is even more valid today because the inversion of the roles of the Government and the Opposition in Britain is now institutionalised through the development of the system of an Opposition Shadow Cabinet, and Opposition Spokesmen, assigned by the Leader of the Opposition to cover the work of specific Ministers and Departments. The role of Opposition leaders as a potential Government is thereby emphasised. The seeds of this modern institutionalised Opposition existed in the nineteenth century

[1] For the role of the Tribunes, see M. Cary, *The History of Rome*, London 1954, pp. 116–7. For a comment, see Bertrand de Jouvenel, 'The Means of Contestation', *Government and Opposition*, 1965–6, pp. 155–74.

[2] A. J. Balfour, *Chapters of Autobiography* (edited by Blanche E. C. Dugdale), London 1930, p. 133.

with the practice of former Ministers continuing to meet together in opposition as the 'ex-Cabinet'. In this century, however, and particularly over the last twenty years or so, the organisation of the Shadow Cabinet has become increasingly formalised, and a considerable number of the arrangements and practices of Cabinet and Ministerial organisation have been adopted in the organisation of the Shadow Cabinet in opposition. In effect, since 1955 there has existed a 'Shadow Government', with the Ministerial hierarchy reflected in the Shadow Cabinet and in the various categories of senior and assistant Spokesmen. The party, the press, and the public are made aware of this in various ways. On first going into opposition, and at the beginning of each subsequent session, the Leader of the Opposition announces the composition of his Opposition front bench 'team', together with the duties they have been allocated. The news media note any changes from the previous session and comment upon these in the same way that they comment upon Ministerial changes. Within Parliament a Minister is faced across the floor of the House, and in committees, by an Opposition Spokesman who answers him in debates and leads the attack in Question Time. The news media recognise this situation and refer to Opposition leaders as 'the Opposition Spokesman for Defence' or 'the Shadow Foreign Secretary'. The Chancellor of the Exchequer's annual television appearance to explain his Budget proposals is followed the next night by that of the Opposition's Treasury Spokesman, while during election campaigns radio and television confrontations are often arranged between a Minister and his 'shadow'. Although Shadow Cabinet meetings are less newsworthy than Cabinet meetings, they will attract comment at times of crisis for the Opposition party, or when significant stories are 'leaked' to the press.

In these and many other ways press and public today are made aware that the leaders of the Opposition party have organised themselves into a team that constitutes a Shadow Government. This raises a number of general questions about Opposition front-bench organisation and behaviour.

How and why has the contemporary situation evolved, and in what respects are modern Opposition front-bench practices different from those in the past?

How is the structure, organisation and behaviour of the modern Shadow Government affected by the dual nature of the role of Her Majesty's Opposition?

How close to the organisational and behavioural patterns of office are those of a modern Shadow Government?

By what procedures are members of the Shadow Government chosen, and what criteria are used in their selection?

Precisely what functions are performed by Opposition Spokesmen individually, and by the Shadow Cabinet and the Shadow Government collectively?

What are the consequences of the increased formalisation of Opposition practices in recent years, and how suitable are the overall arrangements as a means of achieving both effective Opposition and a preparation for office?

The answers to these questions, of course, may be different for each of the two main parties. The two parties have contrasting origins. The Conservative Party emerged first as a Parliamentary force, and the extra-Parliamentary organisation grew from this, while with the Labour Party Parliamentary representation came after the emergence of the Labour Movement outside Parliament. Because of these different histories it might be expected that in party organisation in opposition Labour would give a more influential role to the extra-Parliamentary wing of the party than would the Conservatives. Further, many of the Conservative Party's opponents argue that the Conservatives' view of themselves as the 'natural ruling party' in Britain means that whenever they do lose an election and go into opposition they *think* that they are still in power, and *behave* as though they are still in charge of the nation's destiny. Such an attitude, if it is indeed characteristic of the Conservative Party, might be expected to lead to a copying when in opposition of the organisational and behavioural patterns of government. Conversely, it is often said of the Labour Party that by inclination it is primarily a party of dissent and opposition, with a philosophy and attitude to authority that makes it more comfortable in opposition than in office. Such an outlook, again if truly characteristic of the Labour Party, would not be expected to lead to a copying in opposition of governmental patterns of behaviour and organisation.

Whether or not these 'cultural stereotypes' are still, or ever were, accurate reflections of Labour and Conservative attitudes, it is certainly the case that there is a major contrast between the two parties in terms of the amount of time spent in office. This is illustrated in Table 1, which shows the status (Government party, main Opposition party, or third party) of the

TABLE I

Parliamentary Roles of the Conservative,[a] *Labour, and Liberal Parties this Century*

	Government Party	Main Opposition Party	Third Party[b]
1900–05	Con.	Lib.	Lab.
1905–15	Lib.	Con.	Lab.
1915–22[c]	Wartime and then post-war Coalition		
1922	Con.	Lib.	Lab.
1922–4	Con.	Lab.	Lib.
1924	Lab.	Con.	Lib.
1924–9	Con.	Lab.	Lib.
1929–31	Lab.	Con.	Lib.
1931–40[d]	Con.	Lab.	Lib.
1940–5	Wartime Coalition		
1945	Con.	Lab.	Lib.
1945–51	Lab.	Con.	Lib.
1951–64	Con.	Lab.	Lib.
1964–70	Lab.	Con.	Lib.
1970	Con.	Lab.	Lib.

Source: Based on Figure C., p. 19

(a) Includes the Unionists.
(b) This excludes the Irish Party (which had more MPs than Labour in the 1900–22 period) and the various other minor parties that have secured representation in the Commons at different times.
(c) For a comment on the confused situation that applied between 1918 and 1922 see below, p. 80.
(d) Some Labour and Liberal members served in the Conservative-dominated National Government formed in 1931, but the bulk of the Labour Party, and a minority of Liberals, remained outside the Government. The Liberals left the Government in 1932.

Conservative, Labour, and Liberal parties during this century. In the first seventy years of this century, the Conservatives, alone or in coalition, spent forty-five years in office, and since 1918 they have not been in opposition for more than six and a half years at any one time. Given this good electoral record, with the expectations of success that such a record brings, the Conservatives have been able legitimately to think of their periods in opposition as likely to be brief, providing merely a short respite between long periods in office. In contrast Labour has spent a total of only twenty years in office, and five of these were in the 1940–5 Churchill coalition, when a section of the party regarded itself as still being in opposition. Even since 1924, when Labour first formed a Government, the party has spent more time out of office than in office, and each of the four occasions when Labour Governments have been formed (1924, 1929–31, 1945–51, and 1964–70) has been sandwiched between longer spells in opposition, although it remains to be seen how long the current period in opposition will last. The occasions when the Labour Party has been subjected directly to the influences of office, therefore, have been considerably more brief than have those of the Conservative Party. In the short periods of Conservative Opposition former Cabinet Ministers have remained dominant, numerically and practically, within the Parliamentary party. The much longer periods of Labour Opposition, on the other hand, allowed many of the ex-Ministers to be superseded in the positions of authority within the PLP by newer and younger MPs who had not experienced Ministerial office. Given these factors, the influence of Ministerial practices on behaviour and organisation in opposition might be expected to be considerably less for Labour than for the Conservative Party.

There is a further fundamental distinction between the two parties in this context. The Conservatives' Shadow Cabinet evolved from the nineteenth-century practice of the 'ex-Cabinet' continuing to meet after the party had left office, in order to manage the party's affairs in opposition. It thus developed as an off-shoot from the institutions of government. In contrast, the organisational structure of the PLP was established before any but a handful of the party had gained experience of government. It was essentially a product of years spent in opposition, and the basis of the structure remained broadly unchanged after the party's brief forays into government before 1939.

Thus in the context of the general issues that were raised

earlier about Opposition front-bench organisation and behaviour, it may be questioned whether the two parties' contrasting historical patterns produce major differences in their
respective practices in opposition. Before examining in subsequent chapters the detailed organisation and behaviour of
Labour and Conservative Shadow Governments, however, it
is necessary to look more closely at the general context in
which Opposition leaders operate in Britain. In the rest of this
chapter, then, a look will be taken at the basis of British Parliamentary Opposition, with its requirement that Ministers and
their Parliamentary critics automatically be able to 'invert their
roles when they exchange their benches'.[1]

Parliamentary Opposition in Britain

What are the main features of the role and status of Her
Majesty's Opposition? Perhaps the basic characteristics are
that it is an *office-seeking, loyal, single-party, Parliamentary* Opposition. It is *Parliamentary*, in that the main arena of its operations is the House of Commons, and to a lesser extent the House
of Lords. The retention of the constitutional principle that
evolved in the eighteenth century, that Ministers be drawn
from Parliament, means that Her Majesty's Government and
Her Majesty's Alternative Government confront each other
daily in Parliament. The Prime Minister is faced by the Leader
of the Opposition, and individual Ministers by Opposition
Spokesmen. This system is thus the precise reverse of the principle of the physical separation of the legislative and executive
branches of the government, such as applied in the Medieval
Constitution. The Opposition's Parliamentary role is formally
recognised in various aspects of procedure. Although the Government has ultimate control over the Parliamentary timetable, the Government whips consult regularly with their
Opposition counterparts. The Opposition chooses the subjects
for debate on the twenty-nine 'Supply Days' each session.[2]
Members of the Opposition are always chairmen of the Select
Committees for Public Accounts, Statutory Instruments, and
the Parliamentary Commissioner. The front bench on the

[1] Balfour's phrase, quoted above, p. 4.
[2] See below, p. 217, footnote 1.

Opposition side of the House is formally acknowledged in Erskine May to be the preserve of 'the leading members of the Opposition'.[1] The Leader of the Opposition, and some other members of the Opposition, are paid salaries additional to their remuneration as MPs. The Leader of the Opposition, and many of his senior colleagues, are frequently given access to state secrets. In these and many other ways the presence of Her Majesty's Opposition is formally recognised within the machinery of Government: the Opposition recognises the Government's right to govern, and in turn the Government officially recognises the Opposition and provides opportunities for the Opposition to function.

The Opposition is *office-seeking*, in that its role is not merely to criticise those who are in power, but is also to seek to replace them. The Opposition's role as critic of the activities of Her Majesty's current Ministers is inseparably bound up with its own desire to gain office. There can be, of course, a vast difference between hope and fulfilment, and to seek office is not necessarily to attain it. There can exist virtual one-party rule within a two-party or multi-party system, and in Northern Ireland the Unionist Party remained in power at Stormont continuously for fifty years. Indeed, the operation of the principle of majority rule means that even with a perfectly 'legitimate' electoral system, in which the principle of proportional representation operates fully, a party could remain permanently in opposition, despite commanding up to 49 per cent of the electorate, provided that the electoral support of the ruling party remained sufficiently cohesive and consistent. As noted earlier, the parties in Britain have not shared office equally. Since 1922, when Labour became one of the two main parties, the Conservatives have spent fifteen years in opposition and thirty-five in office, whereas Labour has spent thirty years in opposition, and just twenty in office (with five of these being in a wartime coalition). Labour was out of office for nine years after 1931, and for thirteen years after 1951. Many Conservatives after the 1945 election, and many Labour supporters after 1959, thought in terms of being out of office for decades.[2]

[1] Sir T. Erskine May, *The Law, Privileges, Proceedings and Usage of Parliament*, London 1964, pp. 233-4.

[2] See, for example, J. D. Hoffman, *The Conservative Party in Opposition*

Nevertheless, in contrast to many countries Britain 'enjoys' fairly regular changes of Government. Of the fourteen British general elections since 1922, seven led to a change of Government, while on two other occasions (1931 and 1940) Coalition Governments were formed between elections. Although the pattern of Governments since 1922 has been that of long periods of Conservative rule interspaced with shorter periods of Labour rule, this alternation of Governments has been sufficiently

FIGURE A

Gallup Poll: Voting Intention 1960–69[*]

Conservative Government | Labour Government
1961   1963   1965   1967   1969,

Source: Gallup Political Index (see appendix C)

[*]The figures represent a quarterly average

regular to enable successive Oppositions to enjoy reasonable expectations of office.

There is a further point here. Between general elections Governments in Britain invariably experience periods of acute unpopularity, so that the Opposition party's hopes of office are preserved. This Government unpopularity in most Parliaments is reflected in the opinion polls, and in the results of by-elections and local government elections.[1] Figure A shows that according to the Gallup Poll throughout the 1960s the Opposition invariably had a lead in popularity over the Government. Similarly,

---

1945–51, London 1964; M. Abrams and R. Rose, *Must Labour Lose?* London 1960. See also below, p. 180.

as Table 2 indicates, in almost all of the Parliaments over the last fifty years the Government of the day has lost more seats than it has gained in by-elections, with the Government receiving a particularly large number of by-election setbacks in the 1924–9 and 1966–70 Parliaments. Only four seats have

TABLE 2

Government Performance in By-elections 1922–71

Parl.	Govt.	Total By-elections	Gained by the Govt.	Gained from the Govt.	Net Gain from the Govt. as % of Total By-elections
1922–3	Con.	16	1	4	18·7
1923–4	Lab.	10	1	1	—
1924–9	Con.	63	1	16	23·8
1929–31	Lab.	36	2	4	5·5
1931–5	Nat.	62	—	9	14·5
1935–9*	Nat.	78	—	17	21·8
1945–50	Lab.	52	—	—	—
1950–1	Lab.	16	—	—	—
1951–5	Con.	48	1	—	−2·1
1955–9	Con.	52	1	4	5·8
1959–64	Con.	62	2	7	8·1
1964–6	Lab.	13	—	1	7·7
1966–70	Lab.	38	—	15	39·5
1970–1	Con.	12	—	1	8·3
TOTAL (1922–71)		558	9	79	12·5

Source: Based on information in D. E. Butler and J. Freeman, *British Political Facts*, London 1969, pp. 151–4.

* By-elections in the 1939–45 war years are excluded, as a 'truce' was agreed between the main parties in this period (see Appendix A).

been gained by Governments in by-elections since 1945, and only nine since 1922. Government unpopularity in mid-Parliament, of course, does not necessarily lead to a change of Government at the general election. Nevertheless, whether or

[1] Some indication of Government unpopularity in the 1950s and 1960s, as reflected in local government election results, is given in D. E. Butler and M. Pinto-Duschinsky, *The British General Election of 1970*, London 1971, p. 21.

not a Government recovers its standing with the electorate before a general election, it is clear that in most Parliaments the Opposition, the Government, and the electorate are made aware by the opinion polls, by-elections, and other means, that a change of Government at the next election is a distinct possibility. In these circumstances, Her Majesty's Opposition, as well as being office-*seeking*, is also office-*expecting*, and its role is different from that of opposition parties in situations where the alternation of parties in office has not been as regular as in the United Kingdom.

Her Majesty's Opposition is *loyal*, in that it is concerned with achieving office within the established constitutional framework. The Opposition is thus essentially non-revolutionary. It strives to gain office, and the Government seeks to retain office, but both are dedicated to the preservation of the basic features of the Constitution. Thus the notion of a loyal Opposition rests on the assumption that there are two levels of authority, firstly the basis of the established system, or 'the Constitution', which is accepted both by those in power and those in opposition as the framework in which they will operate, and to which they will be 'loyal'; and secondly, details within the system, which are not accepted by those in opposition, and which are 'opposed' by the means permitted by the agreed rules of the game. Her Majesty's Loyal Opposition, therefore, provides 'limited opposition', or 'opposition-up-to-a-point', in that it is concerned with criticising and seeking to change some aspects of the established system, while at the same time accepting its main features. The precise distinctions, however, between 'details' and 'main features' inevitably will be somewhat arbitrary, and there remains considerable scope for conflicting interpretations as to the exact limits of 'limited opposition'. Nevertheless, the essence of the position of Her Majesty's Opposition is that of (as described by A. L. Lowell)

> . . . a party out of power which is recognised as perfectly loyal to the institutions of the state, and ready at any moment to come into office without a shock to the political traditions of the nation.[1]

Here, however, it should be emphasised that there are degrees of loyalty. The Labour and Conservative Parties are

[1] A. L. Lowell, *The Government of England*, London 1920 (2 vols) I, p. 451.

both 'loyal' in the sense that they accept the existing constitutional system in Britain. They may seek constitutional reforms of one kind or another, like the reform of Parliament or of aspects of the local government system, but they accept the basis of the established constitution. For the most part, the Conservatives also accept the basis of the socio-economic structure, whereas Labour's traditional aims have been to achieve major social and economic changes in Britain. Conservatives might argue that this underestimates their party's commitment to social and economic reform, while critics of the Labour Party might claim that it over-estimates Labour's current commitment, but the traditions of the two parties certainly put them in different camps as regards the extent of their loyalty to the socio-economic system. Thus it is clearly possible to be loyal to the Constitution, while at the same time seeking to alter the established economic structure of society. Nevertheless, more extreme reformist groups will reject both the constitutional system and the socio-economic system, because they see attempts to reform the socio-economic system, without first reforming the constitutional framework, as being doomed to failure (or if not to complete failure, at least to an unacceptably long-drawn-out process of piecemeal reform). Thus militant left-wing groups condemn bourgeois Parliamentary institutions as the agencies through which the capitalist system is maintained, while many Scottish and Welsh social and economic reformers see the break-up of the United Kingdom constitution, and the achievement of Scottish and Welsh home rule, as a necessary first step to the achievement of fundamental socio-economic changes in their countries. Conversely, extreme right-wing groups might accept the basic socio-economic structure of society, but seek to change the constitutional structure, perhaps by creating a one-party Fascist state or a military dictatorship, because they see the socio-economic structure as being undermined by decadent, destructive forces that are tolerated, misguidedly, within the established liberal democratic constitution.

Thus it needs to be acknowledged that an Opposition's commitment of loyalty to the Constitution does not necessarily commit it to accept the basis of the socio-economic system. Indeed, throughout the history of the Labour Movement in

Britain, and of social democracy throughout the world, there has been constant conflict between those who reject both the constitutional and socio-economic systems, and those who are content to strive to achieve Socialism within the established constitutional system. The latter element has always been dominant among the Labour Party's Parliamentary leadership, and has been content to accept the role of a loyal Parliamentary Opposition, seeking office by constitutional means, and attempting to achieve social and economic reforms within the constitutional and political rules of the game.

The Opposition is a *single-party Opposition*, in that throughout the period since 1945, Britain has been ruled by single-party majority Governments, and these Governments have been faced by an Opposition side of the House on which one party has held almost all of the seats. Thus the Opposition has been readily identifiable, in party political terms, in that it could be equated with the second party in what is essentially a two-party system. Clearly, however, in theoretical terms, both Government and Opposition can consist of various possible party bases, depending on whether Parliament operates within the context of a two-party, three-party, or multi-party system. In this respect in a Parliamentary system six main possible bases for a Government can be identified. There is an initial distinction between a single-party majority situation (where the Government is formed from a party that has at least half the seats in the Commons), a single-party minority situation (where the Government is dependent upon the support of another party or parties), and a Coalition situation (where the Government is drawn from more than one party). Each of these categories can be further sub-divided, according to the numerical balance that obtains between Government and Opposition. Within the single-party majority situation a distinction can be drawn according to the size of the Government's majority. What constitutes a 'large' or a 'small' majority is clearly arguable, but a distinction (albeit somewhat arbitrary) can be made between a situation in which the Government party holds twice as many seats as the other parties, and one in which it holds less than this. Within the minority Government situation, a distinction can be made between a Government that is drawn from the largest party in the House, and

one that is drawn from a party other than the largest. Within
the Coalition situation there is a distinction between an all-
party Government, and one which is not so all-embracing,
with one or more parties remaining outside the Government.

These sub-divisions produce six categories of Governments.
On the Opposition side of the House, assuming that the Government does not monopolise the seats, four main possible situations can be identified. Basically, a single-party or a multi-
party situation can apply, but within a multi-party situation
a distinction can be drawn between a situation where one of
the opposition parties is numerically dominant, and one where
the opposition parties are fairly evenly balanced. Again, the
definition as to what constitutes a 'dominant' situation has to
be somewhat arbitrary, but a reasonable definition of dominance in this context would be where one party constitutes at
least two-thirds of the Opposition side of the House. A fourth
possible Opposition situation is where, in face of an all-party
Coalition Government, the role of opposition is performed only
by small groups of disaffected MPs. These possible Opposition
situations (excluding the single-party Opposition situation,
which has not operated in Britain this century), are depicted in
Figure B, together with the six possible Government situations.
The periods and total number of years that each situation has
applied in Britain this century are indicated.[1]

For twenty-two of the thirty-five years between 1910 and
1945, minority or Coalition Governments of one kind or
another were in office in Britain, but for most of the century
Britain has experienced single-party majority Governments.
At the same time, on no occasion in Britain this century has
there been a Parliamentary confrontation between the Government party and only *one* Opposition party: there have always
been at least two parties in opposition, other than the periods
of the Asquith and Churchill all-party wartime Coalitions
when 'the Opposition' consisted merely of individuals and
groups.[2] Nevertheless, invariably one of the Opposition parties
in Britain has been clearly dominant. In the first twenty-five
years of the century, the emergence of the Labour Party, the

[1] See Appendix B, and especially Figure M, for a similar analysis in a
cross-national context.
[2] See below, Appendix A.

FIGURE B

Relationship between Government and Opposition in Britain 1900–70

Government Situation	Opposition Situation: Multi-party Opposition: One Party 'Dominant'†	Opposition Situation: Multi-party Opposition: No One Party 'Dominant'†	Opposition Situation: Opposition From Groups Only	Total Number of Years
Single-Party Majority Govt.				
'Overwhelming' Majority*	9 (1924–9 1935–40)	3 (1932–5)		12
Not 'Overwhelming' Majority*	31 (1900–6 1945–70)	5 (1906–10 1922–4)		36
Single-Party Minority Govt.				
Largest Party	3½ (1910 1929–31)			3½
Other Than Largest Party	4½ (1910–15)	½ (1924)		5
Coalition Govt.				
All-Party			6 (1915–16 1940–5)	6
Multi-Party	1 (1931–2)	6½ (1916–22)		7½
Total Number of Years	49	15	6	70

* As defined here, an 'overwhelming' majority is one where the Government holds at least two-thirds of the seats in the Commons.
† As defined here, one party is 'dominant' where it holds at least two-thirds of the seats on the Opposition side of the House.

decline of the Liberal Party, and the presence (until 1922) of
the Irish Party, meant that for much of the time no one party
dominated the Opposition side of the House, in the sense of
holding at least two-thirds of the Opposition seats. Since the
1930s, however, one or other of the two main parties has
dominated the Opposition benches. Other than when Coalition
Governments have been in office, the numerical balance between Government and Opposition sides of the House has been
reasonably close, and there have been few 'overwhelming'
majorities (as defined here). A more precise indication of this
is given in Figure C which shows graphically the proportion of
seats won by Government and Opposition parties in the
general elections this century. The general absence of overwhelming majorities is clear.

Thus this century in Britain there have been various combinations of Government and Opposition situations, although
the situation that has applied continuously since 1945 has been
that of a single-party majority Government faced by more than
one opposition party, but with one of the Opposition parties
being clearly dominant. Although a multiplicity of parties and
independents have contested recent British elections, in real
terms these have been a 'straight fight' between the Government party and *the* Opposition party, and the Labour and
Conservative parties between them have won at least 95 per
cent of the seats at each of the elections since 1945 (as Figure C
indicates). After a general election, therefore, the Opposition
is readily identifiable as the second party in the Commons. In
a different party situation, with three or more parties of
roughly equal strength, or with a different electoral system that
gave even the existing minor parties representation in Parliament in proportion to the votes they receive, there would not
be the simple relationship that exists at present between the
Government, drawn from one of the two main parties, and the
Opposition, drawn from the other main party. Equally, the
situation would be altered if there operated a system of looser
internal party discipline, allowing independent factions to
flourish within the two parties more readily than at present.
As our party and electoral system operates at present, however,
the Government and Opposition can be equated with the two
parties that together almost monopolise representation in the

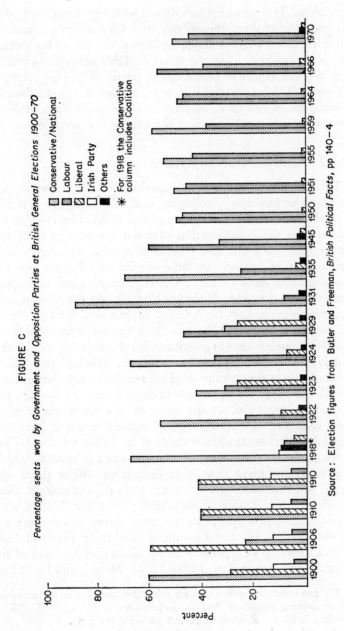

FIGURE C

Percentage seats won by Government and Opposition Parties at British General Elections 1900-70

Conservative/National
Labour
Liberal
Irish Party
Others

✳ For 1918 the Conservative column includes Coalition

Source: Election figures from Butler and Freeman, *British Political Facts*, pp 140-4

Commons. This situation, combined with the strength of internal party discipline, means that the Opposition's chance of attaining office today is dependent upon 'the will of the electorate' as expressed in a general election. Thus although Westminster, and the House of Commons in particular, is the centre of the Opposition's operations, its activities are directed primarily towards the electorate in an attempt to persuade them to throw out the Government and elect the Opposition to office.

The Opposition and other 'Oppositions'

The official 'Westminster Opposition' is not alone in performing the function of opposing and criticising the activities of the incumbent Ministry. One of the dangers inherent in the principle of the confrontation between the Government and the Opposition is the implication that these two forces have a monopoly of wisdom, to the exclusion of all other forces of opposition. In reality there are many other centres of opposition additional to Her Majesty's Opposition: the Westminster Opposition represents the 'official' Opposition (that is, Opposition with a capital 'O'), but there are numerous centres of unofficial opposition (opposition with a small 'o').[1] The fact that Her Majesty's Opposition is 'loyal', 'official', and 'office-seeking' means that groups bent on revolutionary change have to look elsewhere for the means of expressing their dissent. The Opposition has to court the votes of 'the silent majority' in order to secure its ultimate goal of coming to office. It cannot afford to alienate moderate opinion by being seen to be too sympathetic to the cause of revolutionary elements within society. At any given time, therefore, there will be those who regard the Westminster Opposition as providing merely token opposition over details rather than the more fundamental 'opposition of principle'.[2] In the early eighteenth century the Jacobite faction in the Commons saw their Parliamentary activities merely as a prelude to revolution in the form of the restoration of the Stuarts. In the 1930s, Mosley and his British

---

[1] For more detailed comments on this distinction between Opposition and opposition, see Allen Potter's contribution in R. A. Dahl, *Political Opposition in Western Democracies*, New York 1966, pp. 3-33.

[2] Otto Kirchheimer's phrase: see *Social Research*, 1957.

Union of Fascists rejected Parliamentary Opposition as a means to power, while revolutionaries today see Parliament and Parliamentary elections as largely irrelevant in the 'real' power struggle. For them, and for any group dedicated to the destruction of the established political system, the activities of the Westminster Opposition are irrelevant, concerned as is Her Majesty's Opposition with achieving power within the accepted Constitution.[1]

More than this, however, there are many elements within society that are like the Opposition in being loyal to the Constitution, and are dedicated to gradual reform rather than to total revolution, but who nevertheless choose to pursue their cause other than through the channels of dissent provided at Westminster. Opposition to the Government can be expressed through the extra-Parliamentary activities of individual citizens, pressure groups, or political parties that are not represented in Parliament. Bodies like Shelter, or the Child Poverty Action Group, which seek major social reform, for the most part ignore the political parties and the channels of opposition represented by the Westminster Opposition, and choose instead to work directly upon public opinion. Equally, workers' leaders exercise another form of extra-Parliamentary opposition when they resist Government policies by means of strikes, mass demonstrations, or the take-over of shipyards or factories that are threatened with closure. They reject purely 'verbal opposition' through Parliament in favour of 'direct action' outside Parliament. A very effective form of 'verbal opposition', of course, can be expressed by and through the news media, and indeed it is sometimes argued that the Parliamentary process is merely an extension of the 'real' centre of opposition in Fleet Street.[2] The *Daily Express*, for example, conducted a long and intense campaign against British entry into the EEC, and throughout the 1960s was more consistent and outspoken in its condemnation of the Market than were the parties represented at Westminster. Similarly, in the 1930s, the Beaverbrook and Rothermere 'Press Lords', fought a consistent campaign in favour of the principle of Imperial trade

[1] See below, pp. 29–32.
[2] See, for example, John Whale, *Journalism and Government*, London 1972, especially Chapter 4.

preference, and against the free trade policies of successive Governments and successive Oppositions. The more the State extends its activities in the areas of economic and social policies, the more the Government comes in contact with pressure groups of one form or another who seek to influence the Government directly, as well as, or rather than, through the traditional Parliamentary channels of expression.

Again, in some political systems 'institutional opposition' is found. In a federal system, for example, the State or Provincial levels of government serve as an opposition to the power of the Federal government, while in a Constitution that embraces the principle of the separation of powers between the executive, legislative, and judicial branches of government, the power of the executive is checked by the legislature and the judiciary. The fact that the United Kingdom is a unitary state, and one in which Constitutional authority is concentrated in the hands of the executive at Whitehall–Westminster, means that there does not exist here the degree of institutional opposition that is to be found in the USA, the Constitution of which is federal and emphasises the principle of the separation of powers. Nevertheless, there are some forms of institutional opposition in Britain, as through the House of Lords, where a Government that is dominant in the Commons can be faced by a hostile majority,[1] or at the level of local government, with Labour-controlled councils resisting the implementation of a Conservative Government's concepts of educational or housing reform.

The Parliamentary scene is thus only one of many forums that exist for the expression of dissent, and there are many centres of 'non-Westminster opposition'. The activities of the Parliamentary Opposition, of course, are not confined to the House of Commons, and Opposition leaders are not divorced from contact with extra-Parliamentary oppositions. They may choose to co-operate with those fighting the Government from outside Parliament, and indeed the ability to harness extra-Parliamentary support can be of great importance in the Parliamentary battle. At the same time, however, those opposing the Government in Parliament may well be embarrassed by the activities of some of those conducting the battle outside

[1] See Appendix A.

Parliament: the 'respectability' of Her Majesty's Opposition, and its quest for votes as an alternative Government, can be undermined by extra-Parliamentary opposition that is concerned with criticism but not with the role of an alternative Government. In this respect, in periods of Labour Opposition, Labour's involvement with seemingly irresponsible trade unions has been an embarrassment in the party's attempts to present itself to the electorate as a respectable, moderate party of government.

Even at Westminster, opposition to the Government can be voiced other than through the Leader of the Opposition and his senior colleagues. Within the main opposition party a distinction has to be made between, on the one hand, the Leader of the Opposition and his leading colleagues who constitute the 'official' Opposition front-bench team, and on the other hand backbench members of the party who may quarrel with the way the party leaders are conducting the fight against the Government. Backbench MPs will often form a 'ginger group' within the main Opposition party, and will pursue tactics and policies of their own. A party leader who is seen to be too mild in his attitude to the Government will often face dissent within his own party ranks. In the 1880–5 Parliament the 'Fourth Party' emerged as an 'unofficial opposition' within the Unionist Party in opposition. In the 1940s there was a group of largely backbench Conservative MPs, who called themselves the Progress Trust, who operated as a research group, seeking to invigorate the Churchill Opposition.[1] In the 1964–70 Parliament members of the right-wing Monday Club often took a more vigorous line in opposing the Labour Government's immigration and Rhodesian policies than did the Conservative Party leaders. Groups like PEST (Pressure for Economic and Social Toryism) or the Bow Group also operate within the Conservative Party, in opposition or in office, seeking to guide party attitudes in particular directions. Whenever the Labour Party has been in opposition there has invariably been a group of left-wing backbenchers, like the Clydesiders,[2] the Bevanites

---

[1] Kenneth Young, *Sir Alec Douglas-Home*, London 1970, pp. 65, 75.

[2] For the activities of the Clydeside MPs between the wars see R. E. Dowse, *Left in the Centre*, London 1966; R. K. Middlemas, *The Clydesiders*, London 1966.

of the Tribune Group,[1] who have seen it as their function to press opposition to the Government more vigorously than have their front-bench colleagues. Thus there may be 'oppositions' within *the* Opposition, and Emmanuel Shinwell has commented about the Labour Party in the 1951–5 Parliament that, 'Bevan's supporters began forming a definite group, which after the [1951] election, became virtually a second Opposition to the Shadow Cabinet'.[2] In these circumstances the Government will be faced by the official Leader of the Opposition and his front-bench colleagues, and also by independent criticism from Opposition backbenchers—although the Government will often welcome this situation as a chance to expose divisions in the ranks of the Opposition.

There are also invariably some independent MPs and representatives of minor parties who will attack the Government from their own particular standpoint, and who may be more consistent and virulent in their criticism than is the main Opposition party. The Irish Party in the 1880s and 1890s is a clear example of this. Since 1945 the Liberals have been the only minor party to secure a consistent representation in the Commons, and the Liberal leader is officially recognised in the House in that he is given precedence, after the Prime Minister and the Leader of the Opposition, in some aspects of Parliamentary business. He and his colleagues thus exist as an independent group, sitting on the Opposition side of the House, but outside the main Opposition party.[3]

It is also the case that some MPs do not cease to oppose when their party goes into office. Indeed, very often the most effective resistance to the Government comes from within the Government's own party.[4] Government backbenchers who are dissatisfied with party policies, and who are prepared to campaign within the party for changes in these policies, can often be far

---

[1] For the left-wing groups in the 1951–64 period, and their clashes with the leadership, see S. Haseler, *The Gaitskellites*, London 1969. See also below, p. 123, footnote 2.

[2] E. Shinwell, *The Labour Story*, London 1963, p. 193.

[3] See Appendix A.

[4] See R. E. Dowse, 'The Left-Wing Opposition during the First Two Labour Governments', *Parliamentary Affairs 1960–1*, pp. 80–93, 229–43. For an example of rather ineffective intra-party opposition, see Neville Thompson, *The Anti-Appeasers*, London 1971.

more effective than the Leader of the Opposition and his side of the House, partly because clear divisions within the Government party can be electorally embarrassing, but more particularly because the Government depends upon the support of its backbenchers for the maintenance of its Parliamentary majority. Thus an open revolt by Government backbenchers, carried to the extent of abstaining or voting against the Government in a division, can be a particularly effective form of opposition. In 1969 the Labour Government was forced to drop its proposal for a full-scale reform of the House of Lords (after achieving agreement on the measure with the Opposition front bench) when Government and Opposition backbenchers formed an 'unholy alliance' to fight the proposal.[1] Even without open revolt, however, the behind-the-scenes contacts between a Government and its own backbenchers can cause the Government to make more concessions than can hours of open conflict with the official Opposition across the floor of the House. Discreet meetings between Ministers and individual backbenchers, comments made to the whips, and (rather less discreetly) opinions expressed at meetings of the Parliamentary party or backbench committees, are all means through which Government party MPs can make known their opposition to policies. There are an infinite number of occasions when a Government does not bring forward proposals in the first place, because its backbenchers have succeeded in persuading the Government to revise its plans.

Thus the official Leader of the Opposition clearly has no monopoly over the role of opposition, either in or out of Parliament. As depicted in Figure D, the Opposition front-bench team in the Commons is only the 'inner circle' among those practising opposition to the Government within Parliament, while in its turn Parliamentary Opposition is only one of the many forms of political opposition that exist within British society today. It has to be emphasised, therefore, that this study, specifically concerned as it is with the organisation and behaviour of those who constitute the Opposition front-bench team in the British House of Commons, deals with only one fairly small aspect of the broad circle of political opposition in Britain. Nevertheless the importance of the subject is

[1] See *The Times*, 16 and 18 April 1969.

undoubted. Unlike all of the others who are engaged in opposing the activities of the Government, the Leader of the Opposition and his leading colleagues are alone in performing the second main function of opposition—that of presenting the electorate with a choice of Government. Above all else it is this role as a potential Government that distinguishes the leaders of the official Opposition from the other oppositions referred to above

FIGURE D

The Context of Front Bench Opposition

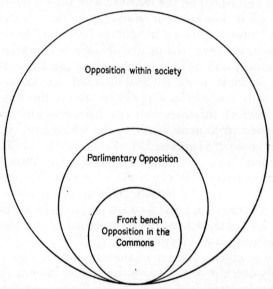

Opposition within society

Parlimentary Opposition

Front bench
Opposition in the
Commons

and gives them a special significance. Many backbench MPs, of course, and many of those who are prominent in opposition outside Parliament, may see themselves as future Prime Ministers. The Liberal Party may have dreams of office at some distant time in the future, or, as in the past, may be called upon to serve in an all-party coalition. Given a rise in support for the Liberals, or for some other minor party, the electorate might again have a choice of three potential Governments, as they had for a short period between the wars. As the party and electoral system has operated since the 1930s, however, with the Labour and Conservative parties alternating in office, and dominating the House of Commons, the electorate has been faced only with a choice between re-electing the established Prime Minister and his Government, or replacing them with the Leader of the Opposition and his alternative Government. This particular role as the team poised to take over the chief executive offices gives the Leader of the Opposition and his senior colleagues a special place among the many individuals and groups who are engaged in opposing the activities of the Government in and out of Parliament. It is this unique combination of functions by Opposition front benchers, as critics of the Government and as alternative Ministers, that forms the basis of this study.

The Limitations of Official Opposition

What are the limitations of the system that has been described in the previous two sections? This chapter began with some comments on the benefits that flow from the toleration of opposition within a political system, and it is reasonable to conclude by pointing to some of the criticisms that are levelled at the concept of political opposition, and in particular at the British system of a loyal, office-seeking, Parliamentary Opposition. Three main sources of criticism can be identified. In the first place, there are a number of disadvantages that follow from the active encouragement of dissent within a political system. Undoubtedly in Britain somewhat artificial divisions over policy are encouraged by the recognition of an official Opposition, with the consequent daily encounters across the floor of the House between Ministers and those who seek to replace them. The Opposition leaders often have to strike false attitudes, and condemn things they might be doing themselves were they in office. This system, as seen by Disraeli, represents

. . . a disguised civil war . . . Each section of the State affects to regard its rivals as public enemies, while it admits that their existence is essential to the Constitution; it misrepresents their actions, thwarts their proposals even if it may know them to be good, and by all means, fair or foul, endeavours to supplant them in the favour of the people . . . The modern politician has often to oppose what in his heart he believes to be useful, and defend what he does not wholly approve. He has to affect to be in

desperate earnest when he is talking of things which are not
worth a second's serious thought.[1]

Such sham warfare, and the impression that it can produce that
party leaders say one thing in office, and an entirely different
thing in opposition, can be damaging not only to the specific
individuals concerned, but to politicians in general, and the
political system as a whole.

The presence in Parliament of ambitious critics, many of
whom will be former Ministers, and thus familiar with the
workings of government, means that Ministers of the Crown
have to perform their duties in an atmosphere that is considerably more hostile than that surrounding almost any other
occupation. While everyone has to contend with difficulties
inherent in his job, the Minister has the added problem of
having to cope with these difficulties while at the same time
defending his actions against constant public attacks by official
critics. Up to half of the electors are likely to condemn Government policies unquestioningly, because they take their cue from
the attitudes of 'their' party leaders in opposition. This encourages a rigidity in outlook among the electorate, and helps to
stimulate the attitude, perhaps particularly prevalent in Britain
in recent years, that the Government is to blame for all ills, and
that Her Majesty's Ministers are incurably incompetent. Certainly, Opposition leaders are purveyors of gloom. Like
prosecuting counsel, they have to cast doubts on all actions and
motives, refusing to give the Government the benefit of any
doubt. They are obliged to highlight a Government's failures
and ignore its successes, greeting bad trade figures, a run on
the pound, a rise in unemployment, a failure to meet housing
targets, or any policy failure or national setback, as further
ammunition for an attack upon the Government. The Government, of course, can make capital from this aspect of the
Opposition's role. This is well illustrated in a speech by Harold
Wilson, then Prime Minister, to the Labour Party Conference
in 1969, when he declared that,

> We shall await with interest statements made from this rostrum
> next week. We shall see whether the National Misery Party will
> join with us and with those who comment on Britain from abroad

[1] J. A. Froude, *Life of the Earl of Beaconsfield*, London 1914, pp. 153–4.

in applauding the achievements of Britain, or whether there will still be a last despairing attempt to present Britain to the world through the distorting mirrors of Tory propaganda.[1]

Even though the Leader of the Opposition could riposte that, '. . . I am not going to take lessons in patriotism from anybody at a Labour Conference . . .',[2] the general role of the Opposition as a critic must inevitably cast it as something of a 'National Misery Party' and make its leaders seem negative and generally slow to applaud national success.

Inevitably, therefore, the Opposition encourages the British national sport of self-denigration. Thus Christopher Mayhew has pointed out recently that

> Possibly our greatest need in Britain today is for pride in ourselves, our homes, our jobs and our country. So far from giving us this pride, many of our leaders owe their positions and power to their skill in destroying it.[3]

The fact that the Opposition is ready to seize on any errors can also discourage enterprise on the part of Ministers, on the basis that the amount of political capital that the Opposition would be able to make in the event of the failure of a policy, often outweighs, in the Minister's eyes, any possible benefits that might flow from its success. When it does not actually discourage enterprise, it can produce excessive secrecy in the affairs of Government, in that Ministers are likely to be wary about revealing any information which might be seized upon and 'used in evidence' by the Opposition.

These, then, are all somewhat undesirable consequences of the encouragement of opposition, although they have to be accepted if the benefits of opposition are to be enjoyed. It can be argued, of course, that because the Opposition is office-seeking, and many of its leaders will previously have held office, its dissent will be tempered by moderation and responsibility, so that some of the more divisive effects of organised opposition will not be felt. Indeed, a second and entirely different line of criticism of the British system is that a loyal and official Opposition which accepts the basis of the political system, and

---

[1] *1969 Labour Party Conference Reports*, p. 356.
[2] *1969 Conservative Party Conference Report*.
[3] C. Mayhew, *Party Games*, London 1969, p. 148.

which is concerned only with 'limited' opposition, is largely valueless as a force for fundamental change. Precisely because the Opposition seeks office it alienates those who are opposed wholeheartedly to the existing system, and for whom a mere change of government is not enough. Thus revolutionaries regard Parliamentary conflicts as sham battles in a largely private war fought by political mercenaries who are far removed from contact with real forces of discontent. They see the Opposition as being preoccupied with trivia rather than with ideology, and confined by the strait-jacket of seeking to operate within the established Constitution.

Clearly, however, opposition has to be non-revolutionary if it is to be given an official status within the Constitution. A society can afford to foster within its ranks 'reformist' groups that are concerned with achieving changes within the fundamental principles on which the society rests. Only a society that is bent on self-destruction, however, will encourage a 'revolutionary' element that is so alienated that it is dedicated to the complete destruction of the basis of the society—unless the alienated group is so small and weak as to be merely part of an ineffectual 'lunatic fringe'. Thus for opposition to be tolerated, let alone encouraged and provided with an official status and machinery to enable it to pursue its ends, it *has* to be loyal and content to channel its activities within the accepted basis of the system. This means, however, that revolutionaries have to look beyond the official Opposition for the means through which to operate, so that the official Opposition is likely to have to co-exist with various other oppositions, be they other political parties or pressure groups, which are not loyal and official, and which are concerned with more than just limited opposition.

Thus the concept of a loyal Opposition is attacked on the one hand by those who see dangers in the official encouragement of dissent, and on the other by those who see any Opposition which is 'loyal' as being inevitably too tame to be a voice of real protest. A third line of criticism can be noted, however (and one that is particularly relevant to the main theme of this study). This criticism is that there is a basic weakness in a system that requires the leaders of Her Majesty's Opposition to be themselves an alternative Government as well as critics of the established Government. Even if one rejects the criticism of revolutionaries, and accepts that even a limited and loyal Opposition is of some value, it has still to be recognised that the dual nature of the Opposition's role complicates the general approach that it has to adopt. The constant highlighting of Government failures in Parliament, of course, can help towards an electoral victory for the Opposition. Equally, the very fact that the Opposition is led by potential Ministers, who are probably also ex-Ministers, gives added weight to its criticisms, raising them above the level of mere uninformed carping by irresponsible demagogues. Nevertheless, a very real danger for Opposition leaders is that one aspect of their role will impede the successful execution of the other. There are two facets of this. On the one hand, there is the possibility that in striving to pose as a responsible body of potential Ministers, the Opposition leaders may be too muted in their criticisms. If a party were permanently in opposition, and were not seeking to replace the Government, the Government could be attacked on all fronts, without a thought for electoral popularity, or of the consequences for its own period in office. Bertrand de Jouvenel, for example, has pointed out that the great strength of the Roman Tribunes (who were quoted previously as an early example of a non-office-seeking opposition)[1] was that '. . . the people were defended by those who did not aspire to become masters. The role of exercising power is widely different from that of combatting abuses: and the two should be kept separate.'[2] The leaders of Her Majesty's Opposition, however, do 'aspire to become masters', and their critical activities inevitably will be conditioned by considerations of how they will affect the party's chances of regaining office. As an alternative Government the Opposition has to consider carefully the effect its criticisms will have on the electorate's view of it as Ministerial potential, while as an ex-Government it is likely to be censured if it criticises in opposition policies which are similar to those it pursued itself when in office. If, however, the Opposition leaders attack only those aspects of Government policy that they themselves would have handled differently had they been in office (or did handle differently when they were in office), the result will be that Government activities will not be scrutinised with the fervour that perhaps they merit, and the

---

[1] See p. 4.   [2] *Government and Opposition*, 1965–6, p. 161.

Opposition leaders may be seen as being part of a 'front-bench conspiracy of silence'.

The second facet of the Opposition's dilemma is the possibility that the pursuit of a highly critical role in Parliament will inhibit the party's ability to think constructively about the future, and damage the party's image as a potential Government. If the Opposition leaders adopt a very hostile approach, and attack Government policies at all times, regardless of what they did when they themselves were in office, or are likely to do when they are next in office, they are liable to be accused of applying one standard in office and a different one in opposition. They risk being dubbed as an effective body of critics who do well in opposition, but who cannot really be trusted with office. The general dilemma is illustrated by the Labour Opposition's position on British entry to the EEC. In 1971 Labour chose to mount a vigorous Parliamentary campaign against the terms on which the Conservative Government sought to take Britain into the EEC. At the same time, the Labour leaders had to acknowledge, at least in private, that the opposition to British entry probably would not succeed, and that a future Labour Government would almost certainly have to face a situation in which Britain was an EEC member. As a potential Government they had to consider how they would deal with the post-entry situation, while, as an Opposition, they resisted the Government's attempts to secure entry. While it is certainly not impossible to pursue one particular line while preparing an entirely different line for action in the future, such an exercise has clear dangers, not least the risk that the performance of one duty will be weakened by the performance of the other. For the vast majority of Opposition front benchers the prime ambition will be to obtain office as soon as possible, rather than to be a success as a permanent opposition. Their activities in opposition, therefore, are likely to be determined mainly by what they see as the most electorally rewarding stance at any given time. This, however, touches on the much broader question of the tactics of Opposition, which will be considered in detail in Part Three of the study. First of all, though, it is necessary to look more closely at the structure and composition of the Opposition team, and this is done in Part Two.

part two

The Opposition
Front-Bench Team

2

The Evolution of the
Opposition Team

THE WAY in which Her Majesty's Opposition executes its role
will be determined largely by its leadership, which today means
the Leader of the Opposition, the Shadow Cabinet, and what
amounts to a 'Shadow Government' of senior party figures who
have duties as Opposition Spokesmen for particular subject
areas. How has this system evolved? The modern Shadow
Cabinet can be defined as a group of leading figures of the
Opposition party, selected by the Leader of the Opposition in
the case of the Conservative Party, or elected by the Parliamentary party in the case of the Labour Party, who meet
together as a committee on a regular basis to assist the Leader
of the Opposition in the task of managing the business of
Opposition.[1] Defined in this way, the Shadow Cabinet has a
comparatively short history. The origins of the Conservative
Party's appointed Shadow Cabinet can be found in the practice
that emerged in the nineteenth century of Liberal and Conservative Ministerial Cabinets continuing to meet after the
party had left office, in order to manage the party's affairs in
opposition. Labour did not emerge as a Parliamentary party
until the early years of this century, and the party's elected
Shadow Cabinet dates only from the nineteen-twenties, when
Labour replaced the Liberals as the main Opposition party.
The tendency of many ex-Ministers when in opposition to
concern themselves particularly with the affairs of their old
departments, or with the affairs of the departments to which

[1] Just what comprises the 'business of opposition' is considered in detail
in Part Three of the study.

they hoped to be appointed in the future, dates from the nineteenth century. The practice, however, of creating a 'Shadow
Government', in the sense of giving Opposition MPs formally
announced posts as 'Opposition Spokesmen' for particular
policy areas, is very recent, dating only from the 1951–64
period of Labour Opposition. For the most part, therefore, the
seeds of the current practices are to be found in this century
or the late nineteenth century. At the same time, instances of
leading figures of out-of-office factions meeting together to
coordinate their activities against the Ministry of the day can
be found in the eighteenth century, and indeed the practice is
as old as the Cabinet itself.

What were the detailed stages in the emergence of the modern
system? What was the nature of the eighteenth- and early
nineteenth-century gatherings of leading figures in opposition?
When did it become the practice of the members of the 'ex-
Cabinet' to meet together in opposition, and how important a
role did this body play in the affairs of opposition? What was
the effect of the emergence of the Labour Party on the practices developed by the two older parties? What factors under-
lay the greater formalisation of the system during this century,
and in particular why has the Shadow Cabinet system been
augmented by a system of Opposition Spokesmen in recent
years? These various themes will be considered in the five
sections of this chapter.

Coordinating Opposition in the Eighteenth and Nineteenth Centuries[1]

For much of the eighteenth and early nineteenth centuries,
the task of leading the often disconnected groups opposed to
the Ministry tended to be in the hands of a cabal. A. S. Foord,
in his study of eighteenth-century Parliamentary Opposition
points out that

> The final triumph of an Opposition did not yet require a parlia-
> mentary leader who would take over the first post in government
> and from thence distribute the spoils. Management of a malcon-
> tent coalition usually lay in the hands of a junto or partnership,

[1] For general histories of the Shadow Cabinet, see J. P. Mackintosh, *The
British Cabinet*, London, 1968, pp. 259–61, 524–9, and D. R. Turner, *The
Shadow Cabinet in British Politics*, London 1969.

composed of the chief figures in the combined interests, in which no one necessarily stood pre-eminent.[1]

If the factions opposed to those currently in office were to succeed either in overthrowing Ministers or in influencing their policies, they had to co-operate to a certain degree. Thus meetings were held of the leading figures of the out-of-office factions. In the Parliament of 1715–22, the 'Leicester House opposition' (so named from the siting of its headquarters in the Prince of Wales' house in Leicester Square) developed a directing council to make its policy decisions and plan its tactics.[2] Also in this Parliament, and before he became First Lord of the Treasury and 'Prime Minister' in 1721, Sir Robert Walpole led a Whig faction in opposition to the Ministry of Stanhope and Sunderland.[3] Walpole, Charles Townshend and other prominent members of the faction met at times as a cabal to plan their Parliamentary tactics. It is clearly a long step from the directing council of the Leicester House opposition, and Walpole's opposition cabal, to a modern Shadow Cabinet, but these bodies nevertheless remain as early examples of groups of Parliamentary leaders forming and meeting regularly to plan and lead opposition to the Ministers of the day.

There are further examples later in the eighteenth century. For most of Walpole's reign as First Lord of the Treasury (1721–43), opposition to him was managed by a junto made up of the chief figures of the three or four groups opposed to the Ministry.[4] After the 1741 election, Dodington, who was a recent defector from the Ministry, proposed a meeting of eight or ten leading figures drawn from the out of office groups in order to plan tactics before the new Parliament met.[5] After the fall of Walpole there was formed in the autumn of 1743 an 'anti-ministerial cabinet' of six members, each representing an out-of-office group.[6] This body later grew into a junto of nine members, led by Lord Chesterfield, and a degree of unity was

[1] A. S. Foord, *His Majesty's Opposition 1740–1830*, London, 1964, p. 163.
[2] Ibid., p. 92.
[3] Ibid., p. 92.
[4] Ibid., p. 164. See also K. Feiling, *The Second Tory Party 1715–1832*, London 1959.
[5] Foord, *His Majesty's Opposition*, p. 200.
[6] Ibid., pp. 240–2.

brought to the opposition groups. Again, in the 1760s Rockingham was leader of the groups in opposition to George III's Ministries, and in order to strengthen his forces Rockingham formed a 'conciliabulum', or inner council of prominent opposition figures.[1] Meetings of this body were held regularly when Parliament was in session, although only when Rockingham summoned them, and the venue was generally one of the town houses of the nobility.[2] There were no rigid rules of composition, and membership depended upon availability, but numbers were kept low to try and avoid divisions. The conciliabulum laid down the broad lines of policy for the opposition groups, and then larger meetings of twenty or thirty members, generally over dinner, worked out detailed tactics. These arrangements gave to the Rockingham group more uniformity than any previous Parliamentary opposition faction had enjoyed.

A very different form of Shadow Cabinet may also be noted in the eighteenth and early nineteenth century. When the fall of a Ministry seemed imminent, opposition leaders would often form a 'Shadow Cabinet', in the sense of a list of possible Ministerial appointments. Such a Tory 'Shadow Cabinet' was formed in 1741,[3] while for the 1747 election 'the Prince of Wales' Shadow Cabinet' framed a list of proposed policies, which included a limitation on the civil list.[4] This programme was duly submitted to, and approved by, a meeting of fourteen leading Tories at Carlton House. Again, in 1788,[5] 1809[6] and 1811,[7] the Whigs prepared detailed lists of appointments in expectation (unfulfilled on these occasions) that the Tory Ministry would soon fall. This form of 'Shadow Cabinet', however, in the sense of a list of potential Ministers, drawn up in anticipation of *imminent* office, clearly differs from a modern Shadow Cabinet, which operates throughout a party's period in opposition and is not created merely when office seems

---

[1] Foord, *His Majesty's Opposition*, pp. 339–43.

[2] For examples see D. A. Winstanley, *Lord Chatham and the Whig Opposition*, London 1966, pp. 79, 97, 156, 160, 167, 325, 340.

[3] Feiling, *The Second Tory Party*, p. 36.

[4] Ibid., p. 52.

[5] For a full account, see J. W. Derry, *The Regency Crisis and the Whigs 1788–9*, London 1963.

[6] M. Roberts, *The Whig Party 1807–12*, London 1965, p. 317.

[7] Ibid., p. 324.

imminent. It also differs from Rockingham's conciliabulum, Chesterfield's junto, Walpole's cabal, and the Leicester House directing council, which, like a modern Shadow Cabinet, were bodies formed to provide leadership, coordination, and more effective organisation among groups which were out of office, and which had no immediate prospects of office.

Social contacts between political colleagues were closer in the eighteenth and nineteenth centuries than they are today.[1] In that more leisured age, political clubs and dinner parties provided informal media for the discussion of tactics and policies. These 'coffee cup contacts' were something of a substitute for the more formal processes of consultation that exist today. In their long period in opposition in the early years of the nineteenth century, the Whigs developed these informal processes of consultation. In 1820 Duncannon proposed regular dinners of Whig leaders, and Lord John Russell supported the idea 'as a beginning of something else'.[2] Russell's 'something else' was a scheme for a 'sort of cabinet to be made up of seven to ten members to put business into some form previously to general meetings'.[3] Nothing seems to have come of Russell's proposal, but the informal social contacts remained. Similarly, the attitude and tactics of the Tory Party to the 1830–2 Reform Bills were worked out by Peel, Wellington and other Tory leaders in semi-social gatherings at the Carlton Club or at Peel's or Wellington's home.[4] Later in the century it became Conservative practice when in opposition to hold an annual eve of session dinner, attended by the party's leading figures, at which the impending Speech from the Throne was discussed, and the party's tactics towards it worked out.[5]

---

[1] See, for example, accounts of gatherings at the country estates of the Whig leaders in the early nineteenth century: A. Mitchell, *The Whigs in Opposition 1815–30*, London 1967, p. 42; Sir H. L. Bulwer, *Life of Viscount Palmerston* (3 vols), London 1870–4, III, pp. 109, 130.

[2] Mitchell, *The Whigs in Opposition*, p. 36.

[3] Ibid.

[4] For details see Feiling, *The Second Tory Party*, pp. 386, 393; G. Kitson Clark, *Peel and the Conservative Party 1832–41*, London 1929, pp. 51, 61, 81; C. S. Parker, *Sir Robert Peel* (3 vols), London 1899, II, p. 188.

[5] For examples see Sir A. Hardinge, *The Fourth Earl of Carnarvon 1831–90* (3 vols), London 1925, I, p. 277; W. A. Monypenny and G. E. Buckle, *Life of Benjamin Disraeli* (5 vols), London 1912–20, V, p. 270.

As well as these semi-social contacts, however, more formal gatherings were held. In the 1835–41 Parliament there were instances of 'a sort of Cabinet' and a 'party Cabinet' being held by Peel to coordinate Tory tactics in the two Houses of Parliament.[1] Also in the 1830s, the 'Stanleyites' who resigned from the Whig Ministry, formed a third party for a while, ' . . . holding 'Cabinets' to concert their line of action.'[2] Later, when the Stanleyites joined forces with the Tories, Graham records that he was more and more involved in Parliamentary work through attendance at 'the planning meetings of the increasingly organised Conservative party . . .'.[3]

In the second half of the nineteenth century, after the long years of Tory rule up to 1830, and then the Whig domination of the 1830–41 period, there was a fairly regular alternation of Ministries, with Conservative, Whig, Whig–Peelite and Liberal Governments succeeding each other in fairly rapid succession. The practice developed of the 'ex-Cabinet' (or 'late Cabinet' or 'old Cabinet') continuing to meet in the period out of office in order to arrange the affairs of opposition, and to plan for a return to office. In particular, in the period of alternating Liberal and Conservative Governments between 1868 and 1886, the ex-Cabinet became a regular feature of party organisation out of office, although even before this the ex-Cabinet was increasingly evident in opposition. After the fall of Peel's Government in 1846 the Peelites at first could not operate successfully in Parliament because Peel was reluctant to hold meetings of his former colleagues.[4] After Peel's death, however, Gladstone, Aberdeen, and other former members of Peel's 1841–6 Ministry met together more regularly.[5] Similarly, when the Conservatives were out of office in the 1852–8 period, there

---

[1] Clark, *Peel and the Conservative Party*, pp. 350, 420. For other references to such gatherings, see ibid., pp. 185, 270, 279, 345; Parker, *Sir Robert Peel*, II, pp. 319 and 335–6; J. Morley, *Life of Gladstone* (2 vols), London 1908, I, p. 103.

[2] C. S. Parker, *Life and Letters of Sir James Graham* (2 vols), London 1907, I, p. 219. See also pp. 214, 224.

[3] J. T. Ward, *Sir James Graham*, London 1967, p. 163.

[4] See Mackintosh, *The British Cabinet*, p. 141; Morley, *Life of Gladstone*, I, p. 260; Parker, *Sir Robert Peel*, III, p. 454.

[5] Parker, *Life and Letters of Sir James Graham*, pp. 185, 191. See also Morley, *Life of Gladstone*, I, pp. 410, 430.

is evidence of meetings of 'the 1852 Cabinet',[1] while in the 1859–66 period of Conservative opposition, Gathorne-Hardy reveals that, 'the inner circle of leaders of the Opposition met in consultation as a sort of informal Cabinet . . .'.[2] Nevertheless, in this Parliament, as in previous and subsequent periods of Conservative Opposition, there were complaints about the infrequency of meetings of the Conservative leaders,[3] and Lord Malmesbury complained that there was insufficient contact between Lord Derby, as the overall party leader, and Disraeli, the leader in the Commons.[4] Contacts between Conservative leaders in the two Houses were again a problem in the 1868–74 Parliament,[5] although Disraeli, then overall party leader, did hold meetings of the ex-Cabinet from time to time.[6]

Gatherings of Liberal ex-Cabinets also took place when the party was in opposition. After the fall of the Liberal Government in 1866, meetings of the ex-Cabinet were summoned by Lord John Russell,[7] and then by Gladstone when he succeeded Russell as Liberal leader.[8] Similarly, in the 1874–80 Parliament, when Gladstone went into semi-retirement, Lord Hartington often consulted with his colleagues of the late Cabinet.[9] It is

---

[1] Monypenny and Buckle, *Life of Benjamin Disraeli*, III, p. 63. See also ibid., III, pp. 523, 528; ibid., IV, pp. 42, 59, 82; Earl of Malmesbury, *Memoirs of an Ex-Minister*, London 1885, pp. 317, 396–8.

[2] A. E. Gathorne Hardy, *Gathorne Hardy: A Memoir* (2 vols), London 1910, I, p. 137. For examples see I, pp. 165, 188; Malmesbury, *Memoirs of an Ex-Minister*, pp. 598, 602, 616; Monypenny and Buckle, *Life of Benjamin Disraeli*, IV, pp. 264, 366, 441; Hardinge, *The Fourth Earl of Carnarvon*, I, p. 277.

[3] For a comment on this problem in the 1846–52 period see Monypenny and Buckle, *Life of Benjamin Disraeli*, III, p. 247. See, however, pp. 31, 83, 204, 229, 239, 293, for references to meetings.

[4] Hardinge, *The Fourth Earl of Carnarvon*, I, pp. 272–3.

[5] Malmesbury, *Memoirs of an Ex-Minister*, p. 660; Monypenny and Buckle, *Life of Benjamin Disraeli*, V, p. 175.

[6] Gathorne Hardy, *A Memoir*, I, pp. 304, 316; Monypenny and Buckle, *Life of Benjamin Disraeli*, V, pp. 173, 203.

[7] Lord Edmond Fitzmaurice, *Life of Lord Granville 1815–91* (2 vols), London 1906, I, p. 516.

[8] R. A. J. Walling (ed.), *The Diaries of John Bright*, London 1930, pp. 315–16, 320–2; T. Wemyss Reid, *Life of W. E. Forster* (2 vols), London 1888, I, p. 401; Morley, *Life of Gladstone*, I, p. 648.

[9] Fitzmaurice, *Life of Lord Granville*, II, pp. 138, 141, 160; A. G. Gardiner, *Life of Sir William Harcourt* (2 vols), London 1923, I, pp. 287, 317; Reid,

easy, of course, to exaggerate the frequency of these gatherings of the 'ex-Cabinet', or the importance that the members and other MPs attached to them. For the most part, informal social contacts, of the type referred to above, or individual meetings or regular correspondence between the leader and his senior colleagues, remained as the most usual means of conducting party business in opposition. The 'ex-Cabinet' was certainly not universally accepted as an 'institution of opposition', even in the last quarter of the nineteenth century, and its importance can be easily over-emphasised. For the most part its meetings were infrequent, and were dependent largely on the whim of the Leader of the Opposition. In the twentieth century this pattern was to change, with formal meetings of the Shadow Cabinet gradually coming to replace informal social contacts as the medium through which business was transacted in opposition. In the late nineteenth century, however, the status of the Shadow Cabinet was still in doubt. Thus Sir William Harcourt could declare in 1876 that

> For my part I know nothing of the 'late Cabinet'. They were dissolved at the election of 1874 which was their last great work. They have ceased to exist. I cannot recognise them as a body of *vieux émigrés* sitting *en permanence* on the banks of opposition longing to return having learned nothing and forgotten nothing'.[1]

Gladstone was also unwilling to accept the ex-Cabinet as a body that he was obliged to consult in opposition. In 1885 and 1886, for example, his colleagues sought to persuade him to summon a meeting of the ex-Cabinet to discuss the party's attitude to the vital question of Irish home rule. Gladstone, however, was unwilling to call the ex-Cabinet together because

---

Life of W. E. Forster, I, pp. 165, 192–5; Walling, *The Diaries of John Bright*, pp. 362, 377, 388–91, 402, 406; A. Ramm, *The Political Correspondence of Mr. Gladstone and Lord Granville 1876–86* (2 vols), London 1962, I, pp. 35–6, 45, 47, 90; Morley, *Life of Gladstone*, II, pp. 83, 128, 157. For gatherings of the Conservative ex-Cabinet in the eighteen-eighties see Gathorne Hardy, *A Memoir*, II, pp. 142–3, 148, 155–6, 161, 176, 199, 217, 247–9; Monypenny and Buckle, *Life of Benjamin Disraeli*, VI, pp. 578, 588, 607, 609; Hardinge, *The Fourth Earl of Carnarvon*, III, pp. 55, 77, 117, 141, 156; A. Long, *Life and Letters of Sir Stafford Northcote*, London 1891, pp. 329 and 358; Lord Chilston, *Chief Whip: The Political Life and Times of Aretas Akers-Douglas*, London 1961, pp. 71–2.

[1] Gardiner, *Life of Sir William Harcourt*, I, p. 298.

this would limit his own freedom to decide Liberal Party policy
on the issue. He declared to Lord Granville that

> A Cabinet does not exist out of office, and no-one in his senses
> could covenant to call *the late cabinet* together, I think, even if
> there *were* something on which it was ready to take counsel, which
> at this moment there is not.[1]

Thus the Liberal commitment to grant home rule to Ireland,
one of the most crucial decisions of the nineteenth century, was
made by Gladstone in opposition, after he had persistently
refused to consult his colleagues collectively in the winter of
1885–6.[2]

This episode illustrates very well the power of a Leader of the
Opposition in the late nineteenth century to dispense with
meetings of the ex-Cabinet if he so desired. The Leader of the
Opposition, of course, did not necessarily choose to work in
isolation. In the 1892–5 period of Unionist Opposition, for
example, A. J. Balfour met with his House of Commons colleagues fairly regularly: in a memo to Balfour, Walter Long
later commented that

> . . . [in 1892–5] *you* decided *everything*, taking counsel whenever
> you thought fit (which happily for us was very frequently, often
> two or three times a week) with your chief colleagues.[3]

There was an increasing tendency at this time for Leaders of
the Opposition to summon to meetings of the party leaders
some who had not served in the late Cabinet, and to exclude
some of those who had. The split in Liberal ranks over the

---

[1] Morley, *Life of Gladstone*, II, p. 382.

[2] The episode is worth exploring in detail as an example of the ability
of the Leader of the Opposition in the late nineteenth century to act
independently of his colleagues. See Fitzmaurice, *Life of Lord Granville*,
II, pp. 462–77; Peter Fraser, *Joseph Chamberlain*, London 1966, pp. 73–80;
Lord Crewe, *Lord Rosebury* (2 vols), London 1931, I, pp. 250–7; J. L.
Garvin and J. Amery, *Life of Joseph Chamberlain* (3 vols), London 1932–69,
II, pp. 160–5; Ramm, *The Political Correspondence of Mr. Gladstone and Lord
Granville*, II, pp. 393–4, 401, 405, 415–18; Morley, *Life of Gladstone*, II,
pp. 371–85; Gardiner, *Life of Sir William Harcourt*, I, pp. 551–8.

[3] Sir Charles Petrie, *Walter Long and His Times*, p. 149. For examples
of these meetings see Lord George Hamilton, *Parliamentary Reminiscences
and Reflections 1868–1906* (2 vols), London 1917–22, p. 240; Garvin and
Amery, *Life of Joseph Chamberlain*, II, pp. 537, 577, 618, 623.

Irish home rule issue in 1886 meant that Gladstone's 1886 Cabinet could not meet as a unit in opposition in the 1886–92 Parliament. Gladstone continued to consult with those of his leading colleagues who had not joined the ranks of the Liberal Unionists, but those who attended these gatherings did not coincide with the membership of the ex-Cabinet.[1] Again, at the general election of 1895 a large number of Liberal MPs, including many Cabinet Ministers, were defeated, and in 1906 the Unionists lost an even larger number of Cabinet Ministers. In the circumstances, the ex-Cabinet could not exist as a viable unit in opposition. In 1897 Morley complained to the retired Gladstone that

> . . . on our bench in the H. of C. nobody had a Cabinet life of more than three years, except Harcourt, C.B. [Campbell-Bannerman] and me, and C.B. and I were hardly three and a half years. None of the others quite equal to three.[2]

Also, the Liberals remained in opposition for a decade after 1895, so that by the end of this period the 1892–5 Cabinet was even less meaningful as a basis for providing leadership in opposition. Nevertheless, Campbell-Bannerman sought to create a sense of unity among his senior colleagues, and he maintained contact through what Asquith called 'the formal councils' of the Liberals in the Commons.[3] By 1900, however, after Morley and Harcourt had retired, there were only four ex-Cabinet Ministers available for regular consultation in the Commons, so that these 'formal councils' embraced Grey and others who were not ex-Cabinet Ministers.[4] Thus by the turn of the century the Shadow Cabinet had become much more

[1] Crewe, *Lord Rosebery*, I, pp. 257, 318, 333; II, p. 520; R. R. James, *Rosebery*, London 1963, pp. 177, 201–2, 229; Fitzmaurice, *Life of Lord Granville*, II, p. 496; Gardiner, *Life of Sir William Harcourt*, II, pp. 153 and 160; John Morley, *Recollections* (2 vols), London 1917, I, p. 259.

[2] Morley, *Recollections*, II, p. 70.

[3] Lord Oxford and Asquith, *Fifty Years of Parliament* (2 vols), London 1926, I, p. 265.

[4] Roy Jenkins, *Asquith*, London 1964, p. 92; G. M. Trevelyan, *Grey of Falloden*, London 1937, p. 75; Oxford and Asquith, *Fifty Years of Parliament*, I, p. 265. For examples of meetings see Crewe, *Lord Rosebery*, II, p. 520; Oxford and Asquith, *Fifty Years of Parliament*, II, p. 30; J. A. Spender and C. Asquith, *Life of Lord Oxford and Asquith* (2 vols), London 1932, II, pp. 169–70.

than just the 'ex-Cabinet', and in the first half of this century this was to become even more clearly the case.

The Conservatives in Opposition this Century

This century the Conservative Party has been in opposition on five separate occasions, for a total of twenty-five years— 1905–15 under Balfour and Bonar Law, 1924 and 1929–31 under Baldwin, 1945–51 under Churchill, and 1964–70 under Douglas-Home and Heath. On each occasion the party's affairs in Parliament have been managed by a group of leaders, selected by the Leader of the Opposition, who met as a committee, known at various times as the Shadow Cabinet, the Business Committee, the Leader's Committee and (most recently) the Leader's Consultative Committee. Precisely what arrangements were made regarding the membership and meetings of these bodies? How formalised have the procedures become in this century? The nature of the arrangements in the 1966–70 period is examined in detail in Chapter 7, but the situation in the earlier periods of Conservative Opposition is looked at in this section.

After their ten years in power from 1895 to 1905, the Unionists were routed at the 1906 general election, and many former Ministers lost their seats. In April 1906, Lord Lansdowne, the Unionist leader in the Lords, sent Balfour a memo calling for the creation of some machinery to establish contact between the Opposition leaders in each House.[1] Lansdowne pointed out that the Opposition was numerically weak in the Commons, but strong in the Lords, and he suggested that the two should thus work very closely together. He proposed the formation of a 'not too numerous Committee, including, say, four or five members of each House' to meet at least weekly in Balfour's room.[2] He suggested that it could create various sub-committees for policy areas. Balfour replied to the memo, agreeing in principle. He pointed out, however, that

> if we are to have, as you suggest, a Committee consisting of members selected from the Front Bench in both Houses, I think it would be very difficult to exclude any member of the late Cabinet

[1] Lord Newton, *Lord Lansdowne*, London 1929, pp. 353–4.
[2] Ibid.

who had a seat in the present Parliament, and, if that be so, what
we should really have would be a shadow Cabinet once a week.
This, however, is all a question of detail.[1]

In the event, Shadow Cabinet meetings were held less regularly
than once per week during the 1906–10 Parliament, although
there are numerous instances of meetings being held to deal
with particular issues. On 17 December 1906, for example,
Lansdowne and Balfour met with a dozen or so of their colleagues to discuss the tactics of the Unionist Peers towards the
Education Bill,[2] and on 12 and 13 February 1907, there were
meetings at which the tariff issue was discussed at length.[3]

Under Balfour the Shadow Cabinet became much more
than just the 'ex-Cabinet', and there were included some who
had not served in the Unionist Cabinet in 1905. Henry Chaplin,
who had left the Unionist Government in 1900, was often
summoned to the Shadow Cabinet after 1906, and the Chief
Whip (Lord Balcarres), the Law Officers, and the party chairman (Sir Arthur Steel-Maitland) also often attended, even
though they had not been in the late Cabinet.[4] Bonar Law had
been Parliamentary Secretary at the Board of Trade up to
1905, and at first in opposition he was not seen as being
sufficiently prestigeous to consult on high policy matters. He
came to be consulted more and more on financial and economic
issues, however, and by the end of 1908 he had become one
of the recognised party leaders. In 1911 he was made a Privy
Councillor, and this coincided with his entry into the Shadow
Cabinet.[5] In June 1914 Lord Milner also joined the Shadow
Cabinet, after he had become accepted as a leading opponent
of Irish home rule.[6]

During 1909 and 1910 the meetings of the Shadow Cabinet
were generally rancorous, as the Unionists argued over their

[1] Newton, *Lord Lansdowne*, p. 354.

[2] Sir Charles Petrie, *Life and Letters of Sir Austen Chamberlain* (2 vols),
London 1939–40, I, p. 193.

[3] Sir Austen Chamberlain, *Politics From the Inside*, London 1936, pp. 50–2.
For other examples early in this Parliament, see ibid., pp. 84, 143.

[4] Blanche E. C. Dugdale, *Arthur James Balfour* (2 vols), London 1939, II,
p. 49.

[5] R. Blake, *The Unknown Prime Minister*, London 1955, p. 69.

[6] Chamberlain, *Politics From the Inside*, p. 368; A. M. Gollin, *Proconsul
in Politics*, London 1964, p. 218.

attitude towards the controversial 1909 Finance Bill, and towards the issue of House of Lords reform. Lord Midleton records that

> ... constant meetings were held of the ex-Cabinet, in which the divisions of opinion as to throwing out the Budget were only less acrimonious than those which ensued on the Parliament Act ... meeting after meeting developed hopeless and inharmonious divisions.[1]

The pattern persisted in the short 1910 Parliament, and at meetings in March and April 1910 the Shadow Cabinet failed to agree on a policy towards the Liberal Government's proposals for House of Lords reform.[2] Balfour eventually surrendered the leadership in November 1911, after the Shadow Cabinet had met without him to discuss the whole leadership issue.[3]

Bonar Law succeeded Balfour as Leader of the Opposition in the Commons,[4] but the Conservatives did not have an overall party leader until Bonar Law became Prime Minister in 1922. Until then Bonar Law (1911–21) and Austen Chamberlain (1921–2) served only as leaders of the Conservatives in the Commons. Thus in the 1911–15 period, the House of Commons members of the Shadow Cabinet were selected by Bonar Law, and the Peers by Lord Lansdowne.[5] By 1911, the Unionist Cabinet of 1905 was remote, and many new party figures had emerged. There were no clear rules as to who should attend Shadow Cabinet meetings, and in a memo to Bonar Law soon after he became leader, the chief whip (Balcarres) stated about the Shadow Cabinet, 'Constitution. There is no particular qualification and no definite membership.'[6] Bonar Law and Lansdowne summoned the Shadow Cabinet as infrequently as

---

[1] Earl of Midleton, *Records and Reactions 1856–1939*, London 1939, p. 270.

[2] Chamberlain, *Politics From the Inside*, pp. 219, 263, 295–7; Newton, *Lord Lansdowne*, pp. 402, 413; K. Young, *Arthur James Balfour*, London 1963, p. 299.

[3] Fraser, *Joseph Chamberlain*, p. 307; Dugdale, *Arthur James Balfour*, II, pp. 63–5, 85; Newton, *Lord Lansdowne*, p. 413. See also below, p. 91.

[4] See below, p. 85.

[5] Blake, *The Unknown Prime Minister*, p. 102.

[6] Ibid., p. 103.

possible: Austen Chamberlain commented that it was 'inordinately big, is also extraordinarily useless, and BL rightly avoids summoning it as much as possible'.[1] Nevertheless, some meetings of the party leaders were held. On 12 February 1912, for example, Bonar Law, Austen Chamberlain, Walter Long, Lord Curzon, and Lord Lansdowne met at Lansdowne House to discuss plans for the new session,[2] and on 29 February 1912 there was a Shadow Cabinet meeting which Austen Chamberlain described as 'the best meeting of the kind that I have ever attended'.[3] Again, on 13 March 1913, a smaller group of leaders met at Lansdowne House to discuss Parliamentary tactics over the coal strike.[4] In the crises of 1914 over Ireland and the European war, Bonar Law kept his leading colleagues informed of the regular contacts he had with the Prime Minister. In August 1914, however, the Unionist decision to support the Government in its attitude to the European crisis,[5] and then in May 1915 the decision to participate in a Coalition Government,[6] were taken by Bonar Law and only a handful of his closest colleagues. With the formation of the wartime Coalition the Unionists again became a party of government, and remained so until the first Labour Government was formed in February 1924.

In 1924 Stanley Baldwin became Leader of the Opposition and sought to make use of the period in opposition to reunify and revivify the Conservative Party. Austen Chamberlain and Lord Birkenhead had left the Baldwin Government in 1923, but on 6 February 1924, Baldwin invited them to dinner, and there invited them to 'join our councils', which they agreed to do.[7] The 'councils' into which Chamberlain and Birkenhead were invited, amounted to the Shadow Cabinet, which in this

---

[1] Chamberlain, *Politics From the Inside*, p. 527.

[2] Ibid., p. 409.   [3] Ibid., pp. 432–6.

[4] Ibid., p. 446. For other examples, see pp. 605, 626; Garvin and Amery, *Life of Joseph Chamberlain*, VI, p. 979; Blake, *The Unknown Prime Minister*, p. 177.

[5] Petrie, *Life and Letters of Sir Austen Chamberlain*, I, p. 370; Petrie, *Walter Long and His Times*, p. 187.

[6] Blake, *The Unknown Prime Minister*, pp. 243, 249; Lord Beaverbrook, *Politicians and the War 1914–16*, (2 vols), London 1928–32, I, p. 114. See also below, Appendix A.

[7] Iain Macleod, *Neville Chamberlain*, London 1961, p. 102.

period in opposition consisted of the members of Baldwin's 1923–4 Cabinet, plus Austen Chamberlain, Lord Birkenhead, Lord Crawford, and Lord Balfour.[1] Baldwin's biographers point out that for this period of Conservative Opposition

> Some much more substantial organisation was needed than had satisfied them in opposition before 1915 . . . Baldwin instituted what came to be called the Shadow Cabinet, as a formal body with a secretariat. The invitations to Austen Chamberlain and Birkenhead were phrased as requests to join that body, just as if they had been appointed to a Government.[2]

The first meeting of the Shadow Cabinet, which was held on February 7, was divided over the tariffs issue, and Baldwin declared that he would 'have to do some skilful tight-rope walking' when he met the Conservative backbench MPs.[3] The divisions in the party were revealed again when, on February 11, Baldwin met the junior Ministers of his late Government, who were not members of the Shadow Cabinet, and outlined to them the party policies for opposition.[4] The Conservative leaders were also divided over the proposal, championed by Winston Churchill, that a new anti-Socialist 'Centre Party' should be formed by the Conservative and Liberal parties. In face of these divisions, and to try and avoid criticism after the 1923 election setback, Baldwin avoided formal meetings with his colleagues as far as possible. Austen Chamberlain tried to persuade him to call more Shadow Cabinet meetings, and complained that Baldwin 'struggles like a bronco to avoid them'.[5]

When the Conservatives were next in opposition, after the 1929 election defeat, Baldwin set up a Shadow Cabinet on the same lines as in 1924. Not all the members of the late Cabinet were included. In 1929 Joynson-Hicks, who had been Home Secretary 1924–9, accepted a Peerage in the Dissolution Honours, but he had not intended that this should indicate his retirement, and he expected to become a member of the

---

[1] Lord Birkenhead, *F. E.: The Life of F. E. Smith*, London 1965, p. 449; R. S. Churchill, *Lord Derby: King of Lancashire*, London 1959, p. 565.

[2] K. Middlemas and J. Barnes, *Baldwin*, London 1969, p. 264.

[3] L. S. Amery, *My Political Life* (3 vols), London 1953–5, II, p. 289.

[4] Earl Winterton, *Orders of the Day*, London 1953, p. 125.

[5] K. Feiling, *The Life of Neville Chamberlain*, London 1947, p. 114.

Shadow Cabinet.[1] In fact, he was not invited to Shadow Cabinet meetings, nor did he receive a Ministerial post in 1931. As in 1924, Baldwin had to try to hold together a divided party, and the Shadow Cabinet revealed divisions on a number of issues.[2] Because of this, Baldwin again tried to avoid summoning it. In March 1930 he set up a small 'Business Committee' of half-a-dozen or so senior Shadow Cabinet members. The Business Committee was originally designed to meet weekly in order to make Shadow Cabinet meetings unnecessary, but often Baldwin was reluctant to summon even this body.[3] There were Business Committee meetings on 7 and 14 October 1930, however, to discuss the tariff issue,[4] and at another Business Committee meeting on 11 March 1931 Austen Chamberlain asked Baldwin to release Neville Chamberlain from his duties as Chairman of the Conservative Research Department (which had been set up in this period of opposition), so as to strengthen the front bench in the Commons.[5]

After returning to power in 1931, the Conservatives remained in office for fourteen years, until defeated in 1945. A large number of Conservative Ministers and junior Ministers lost their seats at the 1945 election, and although some of them were soon returned in by-elections, the party was inevitably weakened and dispirited at the beginning of the Parliament. Thus Sir Henry Channon recorded in his diary for 21 August 1945 that

> Winston, accompanied by Anthony Eden, addressed the 1922 Committee. He seemed totally unprepared, indifferent and deaf, and failed to stir the crowded audience. I came away fearing that the Tory Party was definitely dead.[6]

---

[1] H. A. Taylor, *Jix: Viscount Brentford*, London 1933, p. 290.

[2] See Amery, *My Political Life*, II, p. 508; G. M. Young, *Stanley Baldwin*, London 1952, p. 146; Garvin and Amery, *Life of Joseph Chamberlain*, VI, p. 1019; Middlemas and Barnes, *Baldwin*, pp. 533, 538, 541.

[3] Macleod, *Neville Chamberlain*, p. 134; Viscount Templewood, *Nine Troubled Years*, London 1954, p. 48; Feiling, *Life of Neville Chamberlain*, p. 177.

[4] Macleod, *Neville Chamberlain*, pp. 137–8.

[5] R. R. James, *Memoirs of a Conservative: J. C. C. Davidson's Memoirs and Papers 1910–27*, London 1969, p. 360. For the history of the Conservative Research Department, see below, pp. 263–4 and 272–4.

[6] R. R. James, *Chips: The Diaries of Sir Henry Channon*, London 1967, p. 412.

Business had to continue, however, and in September the Conservative arrangements for opposition were announced. These included a series of committees in the Commons, each dealing with a departmental subject area, and a Shadow Cabinet. This was selected by Churchill, and the usual members for most of the Parliament were Churchill, Anthony Eden, Oliver Stanley, Oliver Lyttelton, R. A. Butler, W. S. Morrison, Harold Macmillan, Harry Crookshank, Earl Winterton, R. Assheton, Walter Elliot, David Maxwell-Fyfe, James Stuart (as chief whip) and Lords Salisbury, Swinton, and Woolton.[1] Sir John Anderson generally attended, although he was an Independent MP. Earl Winterton was included, despite not having served in the Coalition or Caretaker Governments, and he was the only one in this position. Anthony Eden was 'second in command', and Lord Salisbury was Leader of the Opposition in the Lords, with Lord Woolton standing in for him on occasions. Stuart was Opposition chief whip in the Commons, and as such attended Shadow Cabinet meetings without being a full member. When he was succeeded as chief whip by Patrick Buchan-Hepburn in 1948, Stuart joined the Shadow Cabinet in his own right.

The Shadow Cabinet met weekly at 6.00 p.m. on Wednesdays, in the Leader of the Opposition's room in the Commons. In the tradition of the 'coffee cup contacts' of the nineteenth century, there were also fortnightly Shadow Cabinet luncheons at the Savoy, although here social talk, or Churchill monologues, often took precedence over business.[2] A 'Business Committee' was also set up in this period of opposition, although it was very different from Baldwin's small Business Committee of the 1929–31 Parliament.[3] Under Churchill, the Business Committee was made up of the 1922 Committee's officers, together with the officers of the backbench subject committees. It was designed to serve as a link between the Shadow Cabinet and

[1] Harold Macmillan, *Tides of Fortune 1945–55*, London 1969, pp. 43–6. For comments on the membership, see Lord Kilmuir, *Political Adventure*, London 1964, p. 148; Winterton, *Orders of the Day*, p. 321; Lord Woolton, *Memoirs*, London 1959, p. 326; James Stuart, *Within The Fringe*, London 1967, p. 147.

[2] Kilmuir, *Political Adventure*, p. 149.

[3] See also below, p. 241.

the 1922 Committee, and it met before Shadow Cabinet meetings, with Eden in the chair. The Shadow Cabinet, and the Conservative Party as a whole, were divided over a number of issues, so that even the great Churchill had difficulties with his colleagues in opposition.[1] His attendance at the Commons was not as regular as it might have been, and the effectiveness of the Opposition suffered because of this. He left most Parliamentary business in the hands of the chief whip, and often did not even attend meetings of the Shadow Cabinet. Consequently there were 'murmurings' against him, but the discontent subsided towards the end of the 1945–50 Parliament, as office again seemed a possibility.[2] By 1950 Churchill was firmly in control of the party, and Sir Henry Channon records in his diary for 16 March 1950 (in clear contrast to his entry for 21 August 1945, quoted above), 'Winston spoke today in the Defence Debate for over an hour and seemed in the highest spirits. No extinct volcano he.'[3]

After the 1950 election Lord Cherwell offered to resign from the Shadow Cabinet 'on the grounds of its size', and because he was the oldest member and felt himself too old for office in any subsequent Churchill Government.[4] Churchill was not prepared to accept his resignation, however, and Cherwell continued to attend Shadow Cabinet meetings. Sir John Anderson also remained a member, even though he was not then in the Commons, as his University seat had been abolished.[5] Following the formation of the Churchill Government in 1951, the Conservatives remained in office for thirteen years. When they were next in opposition, between 1964 and 1970, they were to adopt more elaborate and formal procedures for covering Ministers and departments, similar to practices pioneered by Labour in opposition in the 1951–64 period.

---

[1] See, for example, Macmillan, *Tides of Fortune*, pp. 77, 149, 286; Hoffman, *The Conservative Party in Opposition*, pp. 227, 252; Young, *Sir Alec Douglas-Home*, p. 75.

[2] Stuart, *Within the Fringe*, p. 145.

[3] James, *Chips*, p. 442.

[4] Lord Birkenhead, *The Prof in Two Worlds*, London 1961, p. 269.

[5] J. W. Wheeler Bennett, *John Anderson: Viscount Waverley*, London 1962, p. 348.

Labour's Elected Shadow Cabinet

What arrangements did the emerging Labour Party make for the management of its Parliamentary affairs? At the 1906 general election thirty Labour Party members were elected, and after this election they organised themselves as a party within Parliament.[1] They held a regular Thursday meeting to discuss tactics and select speakers for all the important debates, and there was an annual ballot to select a chairman, vice-chairman, chief whip, and secretary. At this time, however, there was no executive committee for the Parliamentary party. A number of Labour MPs objected to the principle of 'Cabinet rule' which, they claimed, suppressed the voices of the individual MPs. At the 1914 Independent Labour Party Conference, for example, the 'Bradford Resolution' was passed, emphasising the desirability of internal party democracy.[2] In the spirit of this resolution organisational matters were decided at the weekly meetings of all the Labour MPs. The debating tasks were shared among all Labour MPs, and in order that the party might present a united front to Parliament, all speeches by Labour MPs were regarded as official statements of Party attitudes, and as such had to be approved by the MPs as a whole.

The number of Labour MPs increased at the general elections of 1910 (January and December) and 1918, but it was only as a result of the 1922 election, when 142 Labour MPs were elected, that Labour became recognised undisputedly as the main Opposition party.[3] In February 1923 Ramsay MacDonald was elected chairman of the PLP. He thus became Leader of the Opposition, and for the first time the chairman of the PLP was accorded the title of 'party leader'. J. R. Clynes, who had been chairman of the PLP in the previous Parliament, became deputy leader, and Arthur Henderson chief whip.[4] In

[1] For details see D. E. McHenry, *The Labour Party in Transition 1931–8*, London 1938, p. 165; J. Scanlon, *Decline and Fall of the Labour Party*, London 1933, p. 36; Philip Snowden, *An Autobiography* (2 vols), London 1934, I, pp. 122, 133, 211.   [2] 1914 ILP Conference Report, pp. 111–18.

[3] See below, p. 80, for the confusing situation that had emerged after the 1918 election.

[4] See Colin Cross, *Philip Snowden*, London 1966, p. 185; R. Postgate, *The Life of George Lansbury*, London 1951, p. 220. See also below, p. 87.

addition, for the first time, a 'Parliamentary Committee' was formed,[1] made up of the three officers, plus an additional twelve members elected by the PLP. Those elected to the Committee in the inter-war period are shown in Table 44 in Appendix D. In this Parliament the Committee met two or three times a week in MacDonald's room in the House of Commons, to manage the day to day affairs of the PLP, and to prepare proposals on policy and organisation for submission to the full meetings of the PLP.[2] It thus represents the creation of a Labour Shadow Cabinet.

The emergence of Labour's Shadow Cabinet contrasts with that of Conservative and Liberal Shadow Cabinets in two fundamental respects. In the first place, the Shadow Cabinets that have been discussed in the preceding sections grew out of the practices of office, and indeed they were known in the nineteenth century as the 'ex-Cabinet' or the 'late Cabinet'. Labour's Shadow Cabinet, on the other hand, was essentially a product of opposition, emerging *before* the party held office. It was thus in no sense an 'ex-Cabinet'. Secondly in the democratic traditions of the party, and in line with the practice of electing the leader, deputy leader, and chief whip, the Parliamentary Committee was an elected body. This represented a basic contrast with the Liberal and Conservative concept of an appointed Shadow Cabinet. It also removed Labour's Shadow Cabinet even further from the concept of the 'ex-Cabinet', in that even in later periods of Labour Opposition, after the party had gained experience of office, the process of election by the PLP meant that there was no guarantee that ex-Cabinet Ministers would be elected to the Shadow Cabinet.

With the return to opposition following Labour's brief taste of office in 1924, the Parliamentary Committee was revived. Ramsay MacDonald and his four principal lieutenants, Arthur Henderson, J. R. Clynes, J. H. Thomas and Philip Snowden, dined at the Webbs' home on 21 and 28 November 1924, to

[1] It was known at first as the 'Parliamentary Executive Committee', but this was later changed to 'Parliamentary Committee'. In the interests of consistency I have used the title of 'Parliamentary Committee' throughout.

[2] M. Cole (ed.), *Beatrice Webb's Diaries 1912–24 and 1924–32* (2 vols), London 1952–6, I, p. 237.

discuss the organisation of the PLP for the new Parliament.[1] There were no Standing Orders covering the Parliamentary Committee, and there was some doubt as to what machinery should be set up. Some Labour MPs felt that in opposition the PLP should have an executive committee, but that former Cabinet Ministers should be excluded.[2] Had this been implemented, there would have developed two bodies within the PLP—an elected backbench Parliamentary Committee, and an appointed 'Shadow Cabinet' made up of former Cabinet Ministers. This pattern was not adopted, however, and in December 1924 a Parliamentary Committee was formed on the same lines as in 1923.[3] The 'ex-Cabinet' was still recognised as an entity, however, and the members dined together before the session began in December 1924.[4] Also, it may be noted that even today the Labour 'ex-Cabinet' might still meet when the party first goes into opposition. While a Conservative leader can appoint his Consultative Committee within a few hours of going into opposition, as did Sir Alec Douglas-Home in 1964, the business of electing Labour's Parliamentary Committee is a more lengthy process. There is, therefore, an inevitable time lag between a Labour Government leaving office and a Parliamentary Committee coming into being,[5] and in these circumstances the ex-Cabinet may continue to meet in order to manage party affairs in the first weeks in opposition. Thus in July 1970 the ex-Cabinet met on a number of occasions, although not during the actual week of balloting for the Parliamentary Committee in case this was interpreted as indicating a claim by the members of the ex-Cabinet for election, *en bloc*, to the Committee.[6]

Other than this, however, the principle was established in 1924 that the elected Parliamentary Committee, and not the ex-Cabinet, is the body that serves as the 'executive committee' for the PLP in opposition. As described in the 1925 Labour Party Conference Report, the function of the Committee was ' . . . to discuss business coming before the House, and to settle

[1] Ibid., II, p. 52.   [2] Ibid., II, p. 53.
[3] Ibid., II, p. 54.
[4] Ibid.
[5] The precise time scale involved is indicated in Chapter IV.
[6] See also below, p. 57, for the ex-Cabinet meeting in August 1931.

Party policy, subject to the decisions of the weekly Party meetings'.[1] Beatrice Webb recorded the opinion that although the
Parliamentary Committee was not markedly pro-MacDonald
in composition, it would be the dominating force within the
PLP, and this would seem to have been the case in the 1924–9
Parliament.[2] Initially, no provision was made on the Committee for any representation of the Labour Peers. Early in
1925, however, the Labour whip in the Lords began to attend,
and then a further 'representative' of the Labour Peers was
provided for. In this Parliament, however, the leader of the
Labour Peers did not serve on the Committee, and this led to
some difficulty in coordinating the work of the Opposition in
the two Houses.[3]

The emergence of Labour as the main Opposition party in
the 1920s created problems regarding the seating arrangements
on the Opposition side of the House. In the eighteenth century
the practice had developed of the opposition groups sitting on
the benches to the left of the Speaker, with the leading figures
and orators occupying the front row of benches, partly because
from the front bench they would have a good chance of catch-
ing the Speaker's eye.[4] They thus directly faced the 'Treasury
bench' on the Speaker's right, occupied by members of the
Ministry. By the second half of the eighteenth century the term
'Opposition bench', meaning the front bench on the Speaker's
left, was in common use.[5] In the nineteenth century the convention was established that seats on the Opposition front
bench were the preserve of Opposition MPs who were Privy
Councillors.[6] Then, as now, a seat on the front bench carried
practical advantages as well as prestige, as the Speaker normally
gives precedence in debates to anyone rising to speak from the
front bench. When Labour became the main Opposition party

[1] 1925 Labour Party Conference Report, p. 90.

[2] Cole, *Beatrice Webb's Diaries*, II, p. 54.

[3] See, for example, D. Sommer, *Haldane of Cloan: His Life and Times
1856–1928*, London 1960, pp. 339 and 419.

[4] P. D. G. Thomas, *The House of Commons in the Eighteenth Century*, London
1971, pp. 130–2, 192.   [5] Ibid., p. 132.

[6] Erskine May, *The Law, Privileges, Proceedings and Usage of Parliament*:
the 1964 edition reads (p. 233), 'The front bench on the opposite side,
though other members occasionally sit there, is reserved for the leading
members of the Opposition.'

in 1922, the Speaker ruled that the Labour leaders could sit
on the Opposition front bench, even though very few of them
were Privy Councillors.[1] The Speaker also ruled, however,
that the Liberal Party's Privy Councillors could continue to
sit there, although few chose to exercise the privilege, and
Sir John Simon was the only one to do so with any regularity.[2]
Until 1926, however, membership of Labour's Parliamentary
Committee did not necessarily coincide with a place on the
front bench, as MacDonald reserved the right to decide which
Committee members, or non-Committee members, would join
him on the front bench. Philip Snowden, for example, was a
member of the Parliamentary Committee, but MacDonald
'invited' him to sit on the front bench only after he had made a
particularly effective speech on the unemployment situation
early in the session.[3] Similarly, Sidney Webb had to await an
invitation to sit on the front bench, despite the fact that he was
a member of the Committee.[4] In February 1926, however, the
PLP voted that the Parliamentary Committee should occupy
the Opposition front bench, 'as of right', rather than Mac-
Donald's former Cabinet Ministers. Thus, George Lansbury, a
classic anti-establishment figure, had to leave the back benches
and sit on the front bench (an event which led Stanley Baldwin
to comment that he 'looked like an old watch-dog brought
into the drawing-room').[5]

Labour returned to opposition in August 1931, with the fall
of the second Labour Government. On 27 August the former
members of the Labour Cabinet (minus MacDonald, Snowden,
and Thomas, who remained as members of the National Government) met and agreed that Labour should form the official
Opposition to the National Government.[6] The next day, the
PLP chose Arthur Henderson to succeed MacDonald as leader,
with Clynes as his deputy and Willie Graham as whip. Arrangements were made for the election of a Parliamentary Committee. The Committee was short-lived, however, as Parliament

---

[1] J. MacNeill Weir, *The Tragedy of Ramsay MacDonald*, London 1935, p. 105.

[2] Snowden, *An Autobiography*, II, p. 575.

[3] Ibid., II, p. 580; Cross, *Philip Snowden*, p. 185.

[4] Cole, *Beatrice Webb's Diaries*, II, p. 231.

[5] Postgate, *The Life of George Lansbury*, p. 237.

[6] Ibid., p. 273; Hugh Dalton, *Memoirs* (3 vols), London 1953–5, I, p. 276.

was dissolved within six weeks, and of the members of the Parliamentary Committee, only George Lansbury, Charles Edwards, and David Grenfell were returned in the general election which followed. After the election, Lansbury was appointed Chairman of the PLP, with Clement Attlee as his deputy, and Charles Edwards as whip. A new Parliamentary Committee was elected, but as there were now only fifty-two Labour MPs, it was decided to elect only seven members to the Committee.[1] The seven selected in November 1931 were re-elected for each session of the 1931–5 Parliament. When the House was sitting, they met daily before Question Time to plan tactics for the day's business. George Lansbury, Clement Attlee, and Stafford Cripps bore the brunt of the Parliamentary labours and one of them was always present on the front bench.[2] Arthur Henderson remained as party leader during the 1931–2 session, even though he had lost his seat at the 1931 election. At the beginning of the next session, however, Lansbury became party leader as well as chairman of the PLP.

At the 1935 election, some of Labour's former Ministers regained seats in the Commons. In this Parliament, therefore, the Parliamentary Committee returned to its normal size. Five of the seven who had served throughout the 1931–5 Parliament were re-elected to the Committee in November 1935, together with seven former Ministers who had returned to Parliament. Attlee, who had taken over the leadership from Lansbury at the end of the 1934–5 session, was re-elected leader. In 1937, in an attempt to strengthen the front-bench team, a body known as the 'second eleven' (although, in fact, there were twelve of them) was elected by the PLP.[3] They sat on the front bench and assisted the members of the Parliamentary Committee in the official duties of Opposition. Most of those elected to the second eleven, like Sir Stafford Cripps, J. R. Clynes, and Josiah Wedgwood, were former members of the Parliamentary Committee, but in November 1938 James Griffiths joined the second eleven, even though he had entered Parliament only

---

[1] Postgate, *Life of George Lansbury*, pp. 227–8.

[2] C. Cooke, *The Life of Richard Stafford Cripps*, London 1957, p. 136; C. R. Attlee, *As It Happened*, London 1954, p. 77; McHenry, *The Labour Party in Transition*, p. 167.

[3] James Griffiths, *Pages From Memory*, London 1969, pp. 56, 332.

in 1936, while in November 1939 George Hall and J. J. Lawson 'graduated' from the second eleven to membership of the Parliamentary Committee.

After joining the Churchill Coalition in 1940[1] the Labour leaders remained in government for eleven years, first of all in the Coalition and then in the Attlee Government of 1945–51. With the return to opposition in 1951, a Parliamentary Committee was once again formed to manage the affairs of the PLP. The composition of the Committee in the 1951–64 period, and the factors that Labour MPs consider when electing the Parliamentary Committee, are looked at in Chapter 4. During the 1951–64 period, however, a major change was made in Labour's arrangements for Opposition, the nature and significance of which will now be considered.

The Emergence of a Shadow Government

On 14 July 1955, following a meeting of the PLP, the Leader of the Opposition, Clement Attlee announced that members of the Parliamentary Committee and other leading Opposition figures were to be allocated to cover specific policy areas.[2] Those named were to specialise in their assigned subjects, normally take the lead for the Opposition in debates in their area, and maintain close contact with the appropriate backbench subject groups. Attlee appointed thirty-nine members of the PLP as Spokesmen, with individual or shared responsibilities, grouped around twenty-four subject areas, with a senior Spokesman for each area. Arthur Woodburn, for example, was Spokesman for Scottish Affairs, with Tom Fraser and Margaret Herbison as assistant Spokesmen. Harold Wilson was Spokesman for Trade, assisted by Arthur Bottomley. George Brown was named for Supply, while James Callaghan had a dual responsibility for Fuel and Power and for the Admiralty. The thirty-nine Spokesmen included the twelve elected members of the Parliamentary Committee, but excluded Attlee and the other ex officio members of the Committee. The Spokesmen, together with the ex officio members of the Parliamentary Committee, thus made up a 'front-bench

---

[1] See Appendix A for details of the wartime arrangements.
[2] See *The Times*, 15 July 1955.

team' of forty-five members. Attlee denied that he was attempting to create a full 'Shadow Government', although it was interpreted as such by many commentators.[1] The system was followed, with minor modifications, throughout the remainder of Labour's term in opposition, and when the Conservatives went into opposition in 1964, they also adopted a system of officially named Opposition Spokesmen, rather than the much more informal system that had operated when they were in opposition before 1951.

To what extent is the post-1955 system different from that which had applied until then? Before 1955 parties in opposition had made some arrangements for ex-Ministers and other leading party figures to supervise the affairs of specific departments. For particular debates former Ministers or other prominent MPs would be given the task of making the opening and closing speeches for the Opposition, and in a more general way leading members of the Opposition would develop particular policy interests, and would lead attacks for the Opposition in these areas. Sometimes the Leader of the Opposition would ask a member of the party to specialise in a particular area and become the Opposition's 'expert' in that field. More generally, former Ministers would maintain an interest in the affairs of their former departments, or would develop a new departmental interest, perhaps with a view to subsequent Ministerial office in that area. This was the case even in the nineteenth century. When the Conservatives were in opposition to the Gladstone and Rosebery Governments of 1892–5, for example, many ex-Ministers continued their departmental interests. Lord George Hamilton, who had been First Lord of the Admiralty in the 1886–92 Government, continued to cover the affairs of his old department.[2] On occasions he also spoke on Indian affairs, and when the Conservatives returned to power in 1895 he was appointed Secretary of State for India. This surprised him, however, as he expected to return to the Admiralty because, as he records in his autobiography, 'I had done all the work of representing during Opposition the naval policy of the Unionist Party.'[3] Similarly, W. S. J. Brodrick was Financial

[1] See *The Times*, 15 July 1955.
[2] Hamilton, *Parliamentary Reminiscences and Reflections*, II, pp. 219, 242.
[3] Ibid., II, p. 251.

Secretary at the War Office until 1892, and in opposition he was put 'in charge of the Army business on the front Opposition bench'.[1] Not all topics were covered in this way, however, and for a debate on the Home Rule Bill on 13 February 1893, the Opposition, perhaps not surprisingly, had difficulty in finding someone to follow Gladstone's opening speech (although eventually Edward Clarke was nominated, and he seems to have acquitted himself reasonably well).[2] In the 1905–15 period of Conservative Opposition, many former Ministers continued to specialise in the affairs of their old departments. As the late Chancellor of the Exchequer, Austen Chamberlain led the attack on Lloyd George's controversial Finance Bill in 1909.[3] As a former Irish Secretary, Walter Long led the Opposition's attack on the Irish Home Rule Bill, and Austen Chamberlain referred to him as the Unionist spokesman on Irish affairs.[4] Again, under Baldwin in the nineteen-twenties, Conservative ex-Ministers in opposition tended to shadow their old departments. In 1924 L. S. Amery, as the former First Lord of the Admiralty, spoke on naval matters,[5] while Joynson-Hicks, who was Minister of Health until 1924, led the attack on the first Labour Government's housing policy.[6]

It was not always the case, however, that former Ministers in opposition would cover the affairs of their old departments. Among Conservative leaders in the 1924 Parliament, for example, Baldwin, Austen Chamberlain, and Sir Robert Horne were all former Chancellors of the Exchequer, so that there was an excess of economic expertise on the Opposition front bench. In the 1895–1900 Parliament, in contrast, Asquith was one of only six surviving Cabinet Ministers in the Commons, so that he had a number of varying tasks to perform from the

---

[1] Middleton, *Records and Reactions*, p. 87.

[2] Hamilton, *Parliamentary Reminiscences and Reflections*, II, p. 209. For other examples see Petrie, *Walter Long and His Times*, London 1936, p. 55; Turner, *The Shadow Cabinet in British Politics*, p. 26.

[3] Chamberlain, *Politics From the Inside*, pp. 136, 176.

[4] Petrie, *Life and Letters of Sir Austen Chamberlain*, p. 189; Petrie, *Walter Long and His Times*, p. 175. For Long's comments on the situation in this period, see ibid., p. 151.

[5] Amery, *My Political Life*, I, p. 294.

[6] Taylor, *Jix*, p. 172. See also James, *Memoirs of a Conservative*, p. 192.

Opposition front bench.[1] When Labour became the official Opposition after 1922, the party's leaders soon developed their own specialisations, even though nearly all were without Ministerial experience. John Wheatley, for example, spoke mainly on housing policy, Tom Johnston on colonial affairs, Emanuel Shinwell on the mines, and Philip Snowden on finance.[2] After their brief spell in office in 1924, the leaders tended to specialise in the affairs of their former departments. William Adamson, the Scottish Secretary in 1924 and again in 1929, continued to specialise in Scottish affairs in the 1924–9 Parliament, while Willie Graham, Financial Secretary to the Treasury in 1924, specialised in economic affairs and was Chairman of the Public Accounts Committee.[3] Philip Snowden was essentially 'shadow' to Churchill as Chancellor of the Exchequer, although Snowden resented MacDonald's tendency to 'encroach' on financial and economic affairs.[4] In the 1931–5 Parliament, after Labour's disaster at the 1931 election, there were so few experienced Labour MPs in the House that Lansbury had to ask leading figures to develop subjects that were unfamiliar to them.[5] Tom Williams (Minister of Agriculture 1945–51), David Grenfell, and others were brought into prominence this way, and Tom Williams' interest in agriculture stemmed from his enforced specialisation in this Parliament.[6] After the 1935 election a number of Labour's ex-Ministers returned to the House and revived their former specialisations. In the 1935–9 period Hugh Dalton spoke mainly on foreign affairs,[7] while Pethick-Lawrence was widely seen as Labour's financial spokesman.[8]

In the post-1945 period the pre-war pattern again emerged and under Churchill in the 1945–51 period of Conservative Opposition, Shadow Cabinet members developed particular

[1] Jenkins, *Asquith*, p. 92. See also Trevelyan, *Grey of Falloden*, p. 68.

[2] See Chapter 10 for the behaviour and specialisations of Labour MPs in the inter-war period.

[3] T. N. Graham, *Willie Graham*, London 1948, p. 155.

[4] Snowden, *An Autobiography*, II, p. 722; Cross, *Philip Snowden*, p. 217; Dalton, *Memoirs*, I, p. 173.

[5] Herbert Morrison, *An Autobiography*, London 1960, p. 131.

[6] Roy Jenkins, *Mr. Attlee*, London 1948, p. 149. See also Attlee, *As It Happened*, p. 77.

[7] Dalton, *Memoirs*, II, p. 84.

[8] Vera Brittain, *Pethick-Lawrence*, London 1963, p. 110.

specialisations. Eden in the Commons, and Salisbury in the Lords, concentrated on foreign affairs.[1] Oliver Stanley dealt mainly with financial matters, and after his death in 1950 he was succeeded as the main financial expert by Oliver Lyttelton.[2] Harold Macmillan tended to concentrate on foreign and economic policy. He has pointed out, however, that although in this period ex-Ministers tended to specialise in the affairs of their old departments, there was certainly no official allocation to specific duties.[3] Of general Conservative practice in opposition before 1951 Macmillan says, 'There were a number of advisers to the leader (often a former Prime Minister), which the Press had christened after 1929 by the name of "Shadow Cabinet". But its members were not—as in a real cabinet—allocated to particular posts.' In the 1945–51 period, says Macmillan, no one was given the title of ' . . . "Shadow" Minister of this or that . . . there was no precise or exclusive designation. The incongruity of calling someone "Shadow" Minister of Transport or "Shadow" Postmaster-General was avoided.'[4] The same general principle applied for Labour in the 1951–5 Parliament. Ex-Ministers tended to devote more of their Parliamentary time to their former departments than to any others. Some indication of this is given in Table 3, which shows that, in the 1952–3 session, ten of thirteen members of the Parliamentary Committee devoted most of their activity in questions or debates (or both) to the affairs of the department in which they had last held office.

In this Parliament, however, as in the pre-1945 period, members of the Parliamentary Committee, and other leading PLP figures, were not officially named as Spokesmen for particular policy areas. Until 1955, Labour and Conservative arrangements in opposition for covering the work of particular departments and Ministers were unofficial and largely unannounced, and were essentially informal and casual. The

---

[1] Macmillan, *Tides of Fortune*, p. 43.

[2] Lord Chandos, *Memoirs*, London 1962, pp. 334, 338; Macmillan, *Tides of Fortune*, p. 43. See also Wheeler Bennett, *John Anderson*, p. 342; Birkenhead, *The Prof In Two Worlds*, p. 270; Woolton, *Memoirs*, p. 341; Winterton, *Orders of the Day*, p. 330.

[3] Macmillan, *Tides of Fortune*, p. 43.

[4] Ibid., pp. 43–4.

significance of the change that Attlee made in 1955 was two-fold. Firstly, the responsibilities of the leading Opposition figures were made much more specific and watertight than had been usual until then. Secondly, the responsibilities were formally and officially announced to the PLP and to the public.

TABLE 3

Main Subject Areas of Activity in Parliament for Members of the Parliamentary Committee, 1952–3 Session

Parliamentary Committee Members*	Last Post Held in the Attlee Government	Main Subject Area of Activity in the 1952–3 Session	
		Debates	Questions
Bevan	Health†	Health	Health
Callaghan	Admiralty	Transport	Transport
Dalton	Local Govt.	Local Govt.	Treasury
Ede	Home Office	Education	Home Office
Gaitskell	Treasury	Treasury/Trade	Treasury/Trade
Griffiths	Colonies	Colonies	Colonies
Hall	Treasury†	Treasury	Home Office
Morrison	Foreign Office	Transport	Foreign Office
Noel Baker	Fuel and Power	Foreign Office	Foreign Office
Robens	Labour	Labour	Labour
Shinwell	Defence	Defence	Defence
Soskice	Attorney General	Colonies	(No Questions)
Dr Summerskill	National Insurance	Health	Health

Source: Hansard (see Appendix E).

* Excluding the Leader of the Opposition, chief whip, and the three Peers.
† Bevan and Glenvil Hall left the Government before October 1951, but these are the last Ministerial posts that they held.

The consequence was that a considerable number of Labour MPs (thirty-nine in 1955, and almost double this number in 1970) were officially and publicly identified as senior or assist-ant Spokesmen for the Opposition in particular policy areas. In interview, Labour MPs who had been among the Spokes-men named in 1955 emphasised that the new system involved a change of status rather than any fundamental change in their activities. The effect, however, was that from the meetings in the eighteenth century of leaders of out-of-office factions, to coordinate opposition to the Ministers of the day, there had evolved by 1955 a system of official Opposition Spokesmen amounting virtually to the creation of a 'Shadow Government'.

Opposition in the Modern Parliament

How was Attlee's innovation received, and what factors lay behind its introduction and then its retention by successive Leaders of the Opposition? The system of official Spokesmen was subjected to considerable criticism in 1955 and subsequently. Some critics attacked the creation of official 'Shadow Ministers' as an unnecessarily flamboyant formalisation of the processes of Opposition, and as a rather futile attempt to make the tasks of Opposition seem more significant and grand than they really were. As one backbench MP expressed it in interview, it was a case of putting 'paper crowns on the heads of little tin Gods'. Harold Macmillan has been a critic of the post-1955 system, his main objection being that it is detrimental to a party in opposition to have its leaders cast into watertight subject compartments.[1] For Macmillan, the post-1955 pattern of a quite rigid allocation of Spokesmen to particular posts was much less desirable than the system that applied in the 1945–51 period of Conservative Opposition, when former Ministers ranged over a number of topics without necessarily being tied to one area. As was noted above, Macmillan regarded it as incongruous that someone should be labelled 'Shadow Postmaster General', and that he should thereby be required to devote the bulk of his Parliamentary activity to the somewhat routine Post Office affairs. He argues that the main compensation for being out of office is that it offers an opportunity for former Ministers to diversify their interests, and that this advantage of being in opposition is lost through a rigid copying of Ministerial patterns. Says Macmillan, 'Out of office let them wander free and unencumbered. This at least was Churchill's plan'.[2]

When Herbert Morrison left Parliament he became another critic of Attlee's innovation, condemning it as an unnecessary rigidification of Opposition responsibilities. He also attacked the system because it gave the Leader of the Opposition too

[1] Macmillan, *Tides of Fortune*, p. 44.
[2] Ibid.

much patronage power: he pointed out that, ' . . . the enormous patronage which as a whole is properly exercised by a Prime Minister in forming a Government is thereby duplicated in the selection of Shadow Ministers in Opposition'.[1] He further suggested that this new power of patronage in opposition could re-bound on the Leader when he became Prime Minister, in that the existence of official 'shadows' could limit the incoming Prime Minister's freedom of appointment. While nominally the Prime Minister would retain complete freedom to appoint whomsoever he wished, he would not be able to ignore the considerable claims that Spokesmen would have to particular posts. In a sense, a large slice of the Prime Minister's traditional power of patronage would be used up in opposition, long before the party came to office, and this, claimed Morrison, was bad both for the Prime Minister and for the Opposition.[2] Morrison's fears about a Prime Minister's loss of patronage power as a result of the greater formalisation of the system of Spokesmen, were not new. As early as 1910 A. J. Balfour had argued in much the same way when resisting a suggestion from Walter Long that Unionist MPs should be allocated to specific duties to improve the efficiency of the Opposition in the Commons.[3] Like Morrison, Balfour argued that too rigid an allocation of Opposition duties would cause difficulties when the party came to power, although Long denied that such problems need arise.

Another of Morrison's criticisms of the system of Spokesmen was that the naming of a small, select band of Opposition MPs to specific posts could produce a feeling of resentment and exclusion among those MPs who were not given posts.[4] So long as the arrangements in opposition were fairly informal, the distinction between front- and back benchers was not too precise, and thus it was possible to spread Opposition duties among a number of MPs. With a rigid system of official Spokesmen, however, the distinction between the front-bench 'team' and the rest of the Opposition MPs could become much clearer. It was possible that back benchers could feel excluded from official Opposition duties in almost the same way as they were ex-

---

[1] Lord Morrison, *Government and Parliament*, London 1959, p. 350.
[2] Ibid.
[3] Petrie, *Walter Long and His Times*, pp. 151–2.
[4] Morrison, *Government and Parliament*, p. 350.

cluded from the activities of government when their party was in office. As Morrison expressed it, ' . . . the system tends to spread a feeling among other Members of the Party that they are outside the sphere of consideration . . .'.[1]

In this same general context of backbench resentment of the Spokesmen, it may be noted that in the 1970–1 session a dispute arose within the PLP because it was felt by Labour MPs that some Spokesmen were abusing their status by raising constituency issues from the Opposition front bench. As was noted earlier in the chapter, contributions made from the front bench are seen as committing the Opposition party in a way that backbench contributions do not, and those who rise from the front bench are generally given precedence in debates by the Speaker. Thus the question of who sits on the front bench is of practical importance, and is not merely a question of prestige and tradition. The creation of a large front-bench team complicated the whole question of who has the right to sit on, and speak from, the Opposition front bench. Both parties now apply the same broad rules to the issue. Members of the Shadow Cabinet (that is, Labour's Parliamentary Committee and the Conservatives' Consultative Committee) will always sit there. Privy Councillors are also entitled to sit on the front bench, regardless of whether or not they are Shadow Cabinet members or Spokesmen, although in practice Privy Councillors who are no longer members of the team tend not to sit there, as any contributions they then make might be interpreted as committing the party. Thus when Selwyn Lloyd left the Conservative team in 1966 he moved to the back benches, as did Michael Stewart in 1970, despite the fact that they were both Privy Councillors. Spokesmen or assistant Spokesmen who are not members of the Shadow Cabinet, and are not Privy Councillors, will normally sit on the back benches, and will occupy the front bench only when they are to make an official contribution for the Opposition in debates or questions, or when the front bench is so thinly occupied that, for the sake of appearances, the presence in the Chamber of senior Opposition figures needs to be emphasised. In 1970, however, some assistant Spokesmen were thought to be taking advantage of their position, in that they were not confining their front-bench contributions purely

[1] Ibid.

to official party matters. Accordingly, Harold Wilson had to emphasise to his junior Spokesmen the principle that their front-bench contributions were restricted to the expression of official Opposition attitudes, and that for the raising of constituency problems the Spokesmen had to speak from the back benches.[1]

In 1955 there was apprehension among some Labour MPs that the authority of the PLP's subject groups would be undermined to some extent by the Spokesmen.[2] Until 1955 the chairmen of the subject groups, who were *elected* to their posts by the groups, had some claim to be regarded as the party's 'experts' in their particular areas, but an essential aspect of Attlee's innovation in 1955 was that the Spokesmen, who were *appointed* to their posts by the leader, would become the acknowledged experts in their fields. In fact, there developed in the 1955–64 period some overlap of personnel between the Spokesmen and the chairmen of the subject groups. In some instances it was the chairman of the group who was appointed to be the Spokesman for that subject, but more often the Spokesman for a particular topic was later elected by the appropriate group to be its chairman. In this way conflict between Spokesmen and chairmen of the subject groups was largely avoided, although discordance did emerge at times. In the case of the Conservative backbench groups in the 1964–70 period, the Spokesmen were automatically made chairmen. A number of Conservative Spokesmen and backbench MPs who were interviewed acknowledged that there was some jealousy of the Spokesmen's role by the other officers and leading figures of the groups, particularly in the months before the 1966 election when a very large team of Spokesmen was appointed. Again, however, this issue is examined in detail later.[3]

There were also fears by some Labour MPs in 1955 that the appointment of Spokesmen would undermine the status of the elected Parliamentary Committee. For the Conservatives, this problem does not arise, as the leader appoints the Consultative Committee as well as the lesser Spokesmen. With the PLP's

[1] See *The Guardian*, 28 November 1970.
[2] For details of the relationship between Spokesmen and the subject groups see below, pp. 301–14.
[3] See below, pp. 142–6.

practice of electing the Parliamentary Committee, however, the introduction of Attlee's system of appointed Spokesmen raised the question of whether the Parliamentary Committee would retain its dominant position within the PLP, or whether this would be weakened by the new concept of an appointed shadow 'team', made up in part of people who were not members of the Committee. In general, however, it is probably fair to say that the status of the Parliamentary Committee was not weakened after 1955 (although again, the precise nature of the relationship between the Spokesmen and the Parliamentary Committee is looked at in Chapter 4).

Thus the system of Spokesmen introduced in 1955 has had its critics, but Leaders of the Opposition of both parties have chosen to retain it. Attlee adopted the system of officially named Spokesmen largely in response to a desire within the PLP for greater clarity and precision in Opposition arrangements. Towards the end of the 1951–5 Parliament there had emerged among many Labour MPs a feeling that there should be a clearer demarcation of responsibilities among Labour's leaders. It was felt that too often the party appeared to speak with two or more voices on policy matters, because it was not always clear who was empowered to express official party policy in a particular field. In particular, demands for a clearer allocation of front-bench duties increased after the April 1954 'SEATO incident', when Aneurin Bevan made a dramatic speech from the front bench against the official Opposition line of supporting the Churchill Government's involvement with the South East Asia Treaty Organisation.[1] After this incident it was argued by a number of Labour MPs that if *official* party Spokesmen were appointed, and were announced to the press and public as well as to the PLP, there would be less confusion over who was authorised to speak for the party in the various policy areas. Hugh Gaitskell and Harold Wilson were particularly influential in persuading Attlee to accept this view, and the system of official Spokesmen emerged as a result.

Gaitskell, when he succeeded Attlee in 1956, and Wilson, when he succeeded Gaitskell in 1963, or when he returned to Opposition in 1970, could have given up the system of official Spokesmen on the basis of a new Leader of the Opposition,

[1] 526 H.C. Debs. 5s cols. 969–75. See also below, Chapter 9.

with new plans, abandoning his predecessor's practices. They chose, however, to retain the system and develop it further. Again, when the Conservatives went into Opposition in 1964 it would have been possible for them to ignore the Labour system, and return to the much more informal practices that Churchill and previous Conservative Leaders of the Opposition had used. Neither Douglas-Home nor Heath chose to do this, however. By 1964, of course, the system had been in use for nine years, and had become a recognised part of the machinery of Opposition. In some ways, therefore, the easiest course was to accept the existing system rather than attempt to revive old practices. More than this, however, there are various practical reasons why the system has been seen as desirable by successive Leaders of the Opposition since 1955. The immediate reason for the introduction of the system of Spokesmen in July 1955 (as noted above) was the 'SEATO' incident, and the confusion that it caused within the ranks of the Labour Party, and in the minds of the electorate, as to what was the Labour Party's *official* attitude on the issue. This incident, however, merely highlights a general problem that, to varying degrees, faces all parties when in opposition. If it is to appear credible as an alternative Government, the Opposition has to avoid seeming to speak with many conflicting voices on policy matters. This was perhaps especially important for Labour in the mid-1950s, given the particularly acute problem of disunity that the party then faced, but it is something that even a relatively united Opposition party has to guard against. Thus for all Leaders of the Opposition since 1955 there has been an incentive to copy Attlee's system of official Spokesmen in order to clarify just who was empowered to express the official party point of view in particular policy areas.

The need for this clarity is all the greater now than in the 'pre-television age', because there is a demand by the mass media for instant reactions from the Opposition on the currently topical issues. It is in the Opposition's interests to have official Spokesmen who are seen as being responsible for particular policy areas, and who, at short notice, can provide the media with authoritative interviews and comments on their assigned topics. There are, of course, numerous back benchers ready to provide the media with comment, but the particular advantage (for the media and for the Opposition) of having an official Spokesman available for interview is that he can readily provide the official party attitude on an issue within his assigned area. What is more, there is almost certainly an electoral advantage for the Opposition in being seen to have a team of recognised Spokesmen who can be presented as potential Ministers. In general the Opposition has difficulty in competing with the Government for news coverage. On radio and TV the Government and Opposition parties are allocated the same amount of time for party political broadcasts, but in daily news coverage and current affairs programmes, and in the press, the Government inevitably dominates. The more formal the organisation of the Opposition front bench, the more publicity the arrangements are likely to be given, and thus the more easily the Opposition leaders can be identified by the electorate as a *team* of possible Ministers.

There is a further vital factor that operates today. People now come in contact with government much more directly and frequently than was the case in the pre-1945 world. There is, therefore, a greater need now than in the past for a readily recognisable machinery of Parliamentary Opposition with which those who feel abused by the power of the state can identify. Further, the technicality of much of the business of modern government demands expertise on the part of those who are faced with the task of criticising Government policies, and offering alternatives. In the post-war period the content of legislation, and the nature of Government business in general, has become increasingly complex. Much more so than in a more leisured and 'amateur' world, it is difficult and dangerous today for ex-Ministers to rely merely on their vague recollections of their own experiences in office in order to mount an effective attack upon Government policies. Opposition leaders have to be well-informed on technical matters if they are to oppose the Government with any conviction, particularly at the committee stage of legislation. The Opposition has no civil service on which to rely for expert guidance in these respects. Although, as is discussed in Chapter 8, Opposition leaders can get assistance from numerous sources, they have to be much more self-reliant than have Ministers. Thus the somewhat casual approach to the tasks of opposition, as advocated by

Macmillan and Morrison, is hardly possible today. The wealth of ability and Ministerial experience among Conservative and Labour leaders in the immediate post-war decade perhaps made it possible for a fairly informal system to operate successfully then. At the same time, as some MPs pointed out in interview, it is even arguable whether particularly effective opposition did emerge in that period, given the talent available and the acute problems with which the Governments were faced. Today, certainly, the arrangements for opposition have to be much more 'professional' than they were before the second world war, and one way of developing the expertise required for effective opposition is by allocating Opposition leaders to specialise in particular policy areas.

Another consideration that will weigh with the Leader of the Opposition today is that, much more so than with the informal and often haphazard distribution of duties that applied in opposition before 1955, the formation of a team of official Spokesmen provides status and a recognised role for at least some Opposition MPs. For many MPs with Ministerial experience, or Ministerial ambitions, a major problem in opposition is what to do with their time. Without a place in an official 'Shadow Government' the more active Opposition MPs, and particularly those who would be holding Ministerial posts if the party were in office, might suffer frustration on the Opposition benches. This factor is perhaps of growing importance because of the greater number of active, full-time MPs now than in the past, and the generally greater desire by back benchers for active participation in Parliamentary procedures (of which the demands for the extention of the Select Committee system in the 1960s is perhaps another example).[1] Clearly, the bigger the team, and the more elaborate and formal its structure, the greater the chances of combating the frustrations of Opposition.[2] What is more, from the point of view of the Leader of the Opposition the allocation of his colleagues to posts as Spokesmen has the added advantage of providing him

[1] For the factors involved see B. Crick, *The Reform of Parliament*, London 1964.

[2] It is debatable, however, whether it is better to have a large team with well defined boundaries, or a small team backed by numerous unofficial and 'temporary' Spokesmen. This issue is considered below, pp. 142–6.

with a certain amount of patronage power, although Morrison's and Balfour's reservations about this have been noted.[1] This is perhaps especially important for a Labour Leader of the Opposition, who does not enjoy the Conservative Leader's freedom to select his own immediate colleagues in the Shadow Cabinet. Further, the allocation of his colleagues to specific policy areas leaves the Leader of the Opposition as the supreme generalist in a team of specialists. In so far as the Spokesmen concern themselves with their assigned topics, the Leader of the Opposition is unique in not being tied to one departmental area, and he alone is free to concern himself with the full range of policy areas. His particular role as leader of the team is thereby emphasised.

These several factors underlie the continuation by successive Leaders of the Opposition of the system of Spokesmen introduced in 1955. Despite the criticisms that have been levelled against the system it is probably fair to conclude that the Opposition can now function most effectively only through the degree of precision that has existed since 1955 in the arrangements for covering the activities of the various departments of state. Having said this, however, there still remains considerable room for variation in the organisation of the team, and different Leaders of the Opposition can have contrasting approaches to the detailed operation of the system. The size, structure, and general make-up of the team, the frequency with which changes are made in its personnel, the balance that is achieved between ex-Ministers and back benchers, the extent to which ex-Ministers are asked to cover their old departments, the interpretation that is put on the nature and extent of a Spokesman's duties, the extent to which Spokesmen concentrate on their assigned duties —these and many other aspects of the system are liable to variation from one party to another, and from one Leader of the Opposition to another. In Section Three of the book the working of the contemporary system, and the nature of the relationship that exists between the Spokesmen, the Shadow Cabinet and the Leader of the Opposition, will be considered at length, but in the next three chapters the structure and general composition of the modern Opposition front-bench team will be looked at in more detail.

[1] See above, pp. 65–7.

3

The Leader of the Opposition

A MODERN Shadow Government has a complex structure. At the top of the structure (as depicted in Figure E) is the Leader of the Opposition. He presides over the Shadow Cabinet (Labour's Parliamentary Committee and the Conservatives' Consultative Committee), which meets regularly as an executive committee to manage the affairs of the Opposition. The members of the Shadow Cabinet normally will be given duties as 'senior' or 'principal' Opposition Spokesmen, covering the most important subjects, although, as is discussed later,[1] there may be exceptions to this general rule in the case of members of Labour's Parliamentary Committee, while for both the Parliamentary Committee and the Consultative Committee, the party officers normally are not given specific posts as Spokesmen. Within the Shadow Cabinet there may be an inner group, or 'Inner Shadow Cabinet', of figures particularly close to the Leader. Outside the Shadow Cabinet there will be other senior Spokesmen, roughly equivalent in a Ministerial team to full Ministers who are not included in the Cabinet. Also outside the Shadow Cabinet are the 'junior Spokesmen', who are assistants to the senior Spokesmen and are broadly equivalent to Parliamentary Secretaries and Under-Secretaries in a Ministerial team. There may also be in the Opposition team some 'deputy Spokesmen', whose status is mid-way between that of the senior Spokesman for a subject and his junior Spokesmen. In 1970, for example, Roy Hattersley was appointed as 'Deputy Spokesman for Foreign Affairs', with Denis Healey as the senior

[1] See below, pp. 129–36.

Spokesman, and three other junior Spokesmen subordinate to them both. Healey and Hattersley assumed joint overall responsibility for the full range of foreign affairs, with Healey undertaking the Parliamentary aspects of a Spokesman's role, and Hattersley the non-Parliamentary duties. In Government there is no precise equivalent to this type of appointment,

FIGURE E

The Structure of the Opposition Front-Bench Team

Opposition Front-Bench Team	Ministerial Equivalent
Leader of the Opposition	Prime Minister
Shadow Cabinet:	Cabinet
Labour's Parliamentary Committee elected by the PLP. Conservatives' Consultative Committee, appointed by the party leader.	
Senior Spokesmen not serving in the Shadow Cabinet	Ministers outside the Cabinet (Ministers of State, the Law Officers, some departmental heads)
Deputy Spokesmen (in some instances only)	
Junior Spokesmen (assistants to the senior Spokesmen for particular subjects)	Junior Ministers (Parliamentary Secretaries and Under-Secretaries)
Temporary Assistant Spokesmen brought on to the front bench for some debates	
Assistant Opposition Whips	Assistant Government Whips
Parliamentary Private Secretaries to some leading Opposition figures	Parliamentary Private Secretaries to Ministers

although the closest parallel perhaps would be a senior Minister of State, or the post of Chief Secretary to the Treasury, which is effectively a second full Ministerial post at the Treasury.

Some commentators use the term 'Shadow Cabinet' quite loosely, and it is sometimes used to describe the whole structure of the Opposition front-bench team of Spokesmen. Throughout this study, however, references to the Shadow Cabinet mean the Parliamentary Committee or the Consultative Committee, while the references to the 'Shadow Government', or 'Opposition team as a whole', or 'front-bench team as a whole', mean the Shadow Cabinet plus the other senior, deputy, and junior Spokesmen who are outside the Shadow Cabinet. Outside the 'team as a whole', however, there is a further category of 'temporary assistant Spokesmen', which again has no equivalent in a Ministerial team. Such temporary assistant Spokesmen are brought on to the front bench occasionally, to lead for the Opposition in particular debates, but they are not permanent members of the team. Although they may swell the ranks of the team on occasions, their names and numbers generally are not made public, and thus they cannot be included in any calculations that may be made about the precise size of the Opposition team. The confusion that such appointments can cause was well illustrated in January 1972, when, as part of a re-organisation of duties, it was announced to the press that David Marquand had been dropped from the team. This came as a surprise to Marquand, however, as he was unaware that he had been a member of the team: he had been given certain duties in relation to the 1971 Finance Bill, but he had assumed that this was merely a temporary role which lapsed once the Bill has passed through the House.[1] Thus the Opposition team can have very blurred edges.

Also outside the main structure of the team, and also excluded from any calculations as to the size of the team, are the assistant Opposition Whips and the Parliamentary Private Secretaries of the senior party figures, although in opposition the number of front-bench MPs with PPSs is considerably less than is the case in Government. In the House of Lords there is a further team of Opposition Spokesmen. This study, however, is concerned primarily with the House of Commons, and references to the 'team as a whole' include the two or three Peers who are members of the Consultative Committee or the Parliamentary Committee, but exclude the other members of the House of Lords team, whose role is considered in Appendix A.

Within this general structure what is the particular position of the Leader of the Opposition? What is the nature of his constitutional and political status? Who fills the role and how does

[1] See *The Guardian*, 21 January 1972.

a new Leader emerge? What factors determine the extent of his political power? In comparison with the Prime Minister, how secure is he in his post, and how dominant is he in relation to his Shadow Cabinet and Parliamentary party colleagues? To what extent, in the eyes of the public, is Her Majesty's Opposition epitomised by the Leader? The subsequent sections of this chapter will examine these questions.

The Status of the Leader of the Opposition

The Leader of the Opposition personifies the two basic functions of Her Majesty's Loyal Opposition: firstly, he acts as a public watchdog by keeping the actions of the Government under scrutiny, and secondly he provides an element of choice for the electorate by posing as an alternative Prime Minister at the head of an alternative Government. Like so many aspects of the British Constitution, the Leader of the Opposition's functions are not governed by statute, but his role is officially recognised in a number of ways. In the Commons he is allocated a special place on the front bench on the Opposition side of the House, directly opposite the Prime Minister. He has a large 'gloomy Gothic cavern'[1] of a room in the Palace of Westminster, and he had this when Parliamentary accommodation was considerably more scarce than it is now. He is recognised in the procedure of the Commons as the person who leads the attack on the Government. He normally leads the questioning when the Prime Minister answers in Question Hour on Tuesdays and Thursdays, and he takes part with the Whips in the discussions 'behind the Speaker's chair' to settle points of dispute between Government and Opposition. He also has an accepted place at official functions and Parliamentary ceremonies.

In recognition of his role, the Leader of the Opposition is now paid a salary. The Ministers of the Crown Act 1937 provided him with £2,000 a year (additional to his salary as an MP). This was raised to £3,000 by the Ministerial Salaries Act 1957, to £4,500 by the Ministerial Salaries Consolidation Act 1965, and to £9,500 by the Ministerial and Other Salaries Act 1972. He also receives £3,000 of the £4,500 salary that is

---

[1] Anthony Howard's phrase, *The Observer*, 17 January 1971.

paid to all MPs. Parliament also provides him with a car and a chauffeur, while the party will generally meet many of his expenses. Nevertheless, a considerable decline in income is involved in the transition from the post of Prime Minister (salary £20,000) to that of Leader of the Opposition. The 1965 Act also provided salaries for the Leader of the Opposition in the Lords (now £3,500) and the Opposition chief whips in each House (now £7,500 in the Commons and £2,500 in the Lords), and the 1972 Act introduced salaries (£4,000) for two assistant whips in the Commons. These various salaries are paid as a service on the Consolidated Fund, and thus do not require annual Parliamentary approval. In these as in so many other matters, however, the 'Mother of Parliaments' lagged behind other Commonwealth Parliaments.[1] In Canada the Leader of the Opposition in the federal Parliament was given a salary as early as 1905, and even before this had been given a grant towards his clerical and administrative costs. In the New South Wales legislature the Leader was first paid a salary in 1912, and in the Australian federal Parliament in 1920. In addition, in Australia and Canada the leaders of the minor parties are paid a salary, although in Britain the leader of the Liberal Party has not yet been given this privilege.

The most significant aspect of the Leader of the Opposition's official role is that he is formally recognised as the person for whom the Monarch will send in the event of the resignation of the Government. Thus in 1945, 1951, 1964, and 1970, when the Government party was clearly defeated at the polls, the Prime Minister tendered his resignation to the Monarch as soon as the election result was clear, and the Monarch at once sent for the Leader of the Opposition. Sir Ivor Jennings, in *Cabinet Government*, discusses the various changes of Government since the eighteen-thirties, and he suggests that there are three basic conventions regarding the rights and obligations of the Leader of the Opposition in the event of the resignation of the Government.[2] Firstly, when the Monarch receives the Prime Minister's resignation, she must first of all send for the

---

[1] D. E. McHenry, 'Formal Recognition of the Leader of the Opposition in Parliaments of the British Commonwealth', *Political Science Quarterly*, 1954, pp. 438–52.

[2] Sir Ivor Jennings, *Cabinet Government*, London 1969, pp. 32–40.

Leader of the Opposition: as Jennings expresses it, 'Where there is a Leader of the Opposition the Queen must send for him.'[1] Further, the Monarch must not take any other advice before seeing the Leader of the Opposition, as this could only serve to deprive the Leader of the Opposition of his constitutional rights. Thus the existence of the Leader of the Opposition is an essential part of the neutrality of the Monarch. Finally, for his part, the Leader of the Opposition must agree to become Prime Minister, or at least to attempt to form a Government if invited to do so, or he must suggest an alternative. Thus of all the members of the party in opposition, only the Leader of the Opposition can be sure of the post he will fill if his party comes to power.

In party political terms the Leader of the Opposition is readily identifiable as the person who leads the largest out-of-office party in the House of Commons. His position has been statutorily defined by the Ministers of the Crown Act 1937, and more recently by the Ministerial Salaries Consolidation Act 1965. The 1965 Act declares that:

> 'The Leader of the Opposition' means, in relation to either House of Parliament, that Member of that House who is for the time being the Leader in that House of the party in opposition to Her Majesty's Government having the greatest numerical strength in the House of Commons.[2]

Thus the Act recognises that there is a Leader of the Opposition in each House, but specifies that it is the party composition in the *Commons* that determines which party will provide the Leader of the Opposition in *both* Houses. The Leader of the Opposition in the Lords, therefore, might find his party outnumbered, not only by the Government, but also by another Opposition party. Thus between the wars, the Labour Party, though the main Opposition party by virtue of its numbers in the Commons, had a smaller representation in the Lords than either the Conservative or Liberal parties, just as all Labour Governments have been in a minority in the Lords. It is the party strength in the House of Commons that is

---

[1] Ibid., p. 40.
[2] 13 & 14 Eliz. 2 ch. 58 s4.

the vital factor, however, and it is the Leader of the Opposition in the Commons who is the centre of this study.[1]

In a Parliamentary situation where there were a number of evenly balanced parties, there could be confusion over which party was entitled to provide the Leader of the Opposition. The dominance of the Labour and Conservative parties in Britain over the past forty years has meant that no such problem has arisen, although there was a period of confusion between the wars, as Labour grew to outnumber the Liberals in the Commons. At the 1918 general election, of the parties ranged against the Lloyd George Coalition, Labour won sixty-three seats and the Asquith Liberals twenty-eight, while Sinn Fein won seventy-eight, all of them in Ireland. There was thus some doubt as to which was the principal Opposition party, and who was to be the Leader of the Opposition.[2] William Adamson, then Chairman of the PLP, pressed Labour's claim, but the Speaker pointed out that on a strictly numerical basis Sinn Fein had the best claim, while the Liberals also had a claim in that their status as the second party could be revived at a subsequent election if the Coalition Government broke up and the Coalition Liberals re-united with the Asquith Liberals. The Speaker therefore worked out a compromise, whereby Adamson for the Labour Party, and Sir Donald Maclean (who was acting leader of the Liberals in Asquith's temporary absence from the Commons) took weekly turns to ask the Business Questions on Thursdays, and to open and wind up in the major debates. At the next general election, in 1922, Labour won 142 seats and thereby became unquestionably the main Opposition party, with its newly chosen leader, Ramsay MacDonald, filling the post of Leader of the Opposition. Subsequently, the Ministers of the Crown Act 1937 specified that in the event of a confused situation, the Speaker should determine which was the largest out-of-office party, and, if necessary, who was the leader of that party.

Since 1945 there has been no such problem, as the Labour and Conservative parties have alternated in office, and the

---

[1] See Appendix A for comments on the role of the Opposition in the House of Lords.

[2] See Cole (ed.), *Beatrice Webb's Diaries*, I, pp. 141–3; J. W. Lowther, *A Speaker's Commentaries* (2 vols), London 1925, II, pp. 251–2.

Liberals have not had a large enough representation to challenge them. Nevertheless, the main Opposition party shares the Opposition side of the House with the Liberals, and with the other minor parties and independent MPs who regard themselves as being opposed to the Government. Thus a Labour or Conservative party leader when in opposition is generally at great pains to emphasise that he is not just leader of *an* Opposition party, but that he is *the* Leader of the Opposition, and as the only real alternative Prime Minister is entitled to more prestige and public recognition than is the leader of the Liberal Party, or any other minor party leader. Whether at a wreath-laying ceremony at the Cenotaph, or in a series of TV interviews, the Leader of the Opposition strives to be equated with the Prime Minister rather than with the Liberal leader. For his part, the Prime Minister usually seeks to downgrade the Leader of the Opposition, and thereby reduce his credibility as an alternative Prime Minister, whenever possible treating the main and minor Opposition party leaders as equals. Thus during the 1966 general election campaign, when the Leader of the Opposition sought a TV confrontation with the Prime Minister to discuss the election issues, the Prime Minister agreed to appear only if the leader of the Liberal Party was also involved. This condition proved to be unacceptable to the Leader of the Opposition, and no TV confrontation materialised.[1]

Today it is assumed that whoever serves as Leader of the Opposition in the Commons will also be the overall party leader. Since 1945 (which is the main period under consideration here) this has always been the case. Thus Winston Churchill, Sir Alec Douglas-Home and Edward Heath for the Conservatives, and Clement Attlee, Hugh Gaitskell and Harold Wilson for the Labour Party, have been leaders of their party as well as Leaders of the Opposition. Before 1945, however, the Leader of the Opposition in the Commons was at times someone other than the overall leader of the party. In the nineteenth century, Liberal and Conservative leaders were often Peers. Indeed, in the whole of the second half of the nineteenth century, from 1846 to 1902, the overall leader of the Conservative

[1] For a comment see D. E. Butler and A. King, *The British General Election of 1966*, London 1966, p. 99.

Party sat in the Commons for only twelve years (1868–80). In such circumstances the Leader of the Opposition in the Commons remained subservient to the acknowledged party leader. The Liberal Party leader was more generally drawn from the Commons, but Lord Rosebery remained leader of the party for a while when the Liberals went into opposition in 1895, with Harcourt serving as Leader of the Opposition in the Commons.[1]

In the exceptional wartime situations of 1914–18 and 1939–1945, the Leader of the Opposition was not leader of his party. When the leading Unionists joined the Asquith Coalition in 1915, Henry Chaplin became a token Unionist Leader of the Opposition, while Bonar Law remained leader of the Unionist Party in the Commons.[2] During the second world war, H. B. Lees-Smith, Pethick-Lawrence, and Arthur Greenwood served successively as Leader of the Opposition, although they did not draw the Leader's salary, while the Labour Party leader, Attlee, was a member of the Coalition Government.[3] There have been other occasions in this century when the party leader has lost his seat in the Commons but has remained as leader of the party while one of his colleagues served as Leader of the Opposition. Balfour was defeated in the Unionist rout of 1906, and for a few weeks, until he re-entered the House in a by-election, Joseph Chamberlain carried out the functions of Leader of the Opposition.[4] Similarly, Asquith was beaten in the 1918 election, and did not return to the House until 1920. Although Asquith remained leader of the Liberal Party, or at least the 'Asquithian' half of the party, Sir Donald Maclean led the Liberals in the Commons in his absence, and performed the functions of Leader of the Opposition.[5] Arthur Henderson

[1] For the complications that arose, see Jenkins, *Asquith*, p. 96; James, *Rosebery*, p. 386.

[2] See Gollin, *Proconsul in Politics*, pp. 276 and 307; Beaverbrook, *Politicians and the War*, II, p. 87. For more comments on the wartime situation see below, Appendix A.

[3] See Brittain, *Pethick-Lawrence*, p. 117; Dalton, *Memoirs*, II, pp. 332, 365. For the situation with regard to the non-payment of the Leader's salary, see 361 H.C. Debs. 5s cols. 20–1; 413 H.C. Debs. 5s col. 801.

[4] See Garvin and Amery, *Life of Joseph Chamberlain*, VI, pp. 801, 812, 845–60.

[5] See Jenkins, *Asquith*, p. 483.

became leader of the Labour Party after the fall of the Labour Government in 1931, and the 'defection' of Ramsay Mac-Donald, but Henderson was defeated at the 1931 election. He remained party leader for a year, while Lansbury carried out the functions of Leader of the Opposition, but in 1932 Henderson retired and Lansbury became party leader as well as Leader of the Opposition.[1]

TABLE 4

Leaders of the Opposition 1900–70

Period	Leader of the Opposition	Party	Reason for Relinquishing Post
1899–1905	Campbell-Bannerman	Liberal	Became Prime Minister
1905–11	Balfour	Unionist	Retired as party leader
1911–15	Bonar Law	Unionist	Joined Coalition Government
1915–16	Chaplin	Unionist	Asquith Liberals left Coalition Government
1916–18	Asquith	Liberal	Lost seat in the Commons
1918–20	Maclean	Liberal	Asquith returned to Commons
1920–22	Asquith	Liberal	Liberals replaced as second party by Labour
1922–4	MacDonald	Labour	Became Prime Minister
1924	Baldwin	Con.	Became Prime Minister
1924–9	MacDonald	Labour	Became Prime Minister
1929–31	Baldwin	Con.	Joined Coalition Government
1931	Henderson	Labour	Retired as party leader
1931–5	Lansbury	Labour	Retired as party leader
1935–40	Attlee	Labour	Joined Coalition Government
1940–1	Lees-Smith	Labour	Death
1941–2	Pethick-Lawrence	Labour	Greenwood left the Coalition
1942–5	Greenwood	Labour	End of Coalition Government
1945	Attlee	Labour	Became Prime Minister
1945–51	Churchill	Con.	Became Prime Minister
1951–6	Attlee	Labour	Retired as party leader
1956–63	Gaitskell	Labour	Death
1963–4	Wilson	Labour	Became Prime Minister
1964–5	Douglas-Home	Con.	Retired as party leader
1965–70	Heath	Con.	Became Prime Minister
1970	Wilson	Labour	—

[1] See McHenry, *The Labour Party in Transition*, p. 168.

There were other occasions in the past when the party in opposition did not have an acknowledged party leader at all: a leader was chosen in each House, but not an overall party leader. Thus Bonar Law became Unionist leader in the Commons in 1911, with Lord Lansdowne serving as leader of the Unionist Peers, but the post of overall party leader remained vacant until just before Bonar Law became Prime Minister in 1922. Since 1945, however, none of these somewhat exceptional situations has emerged. It has been clear which was the main party in opposition, there has been no doubt as to who was leader of the party, and that leader has been a member of the House of Commons. Since 1945, therefore, the office of Leader of the Opposition has coincided with that of leader of the second main party in the Commons.

The Emergence of Leaders of the Opposition

How does a new Leader of the Opposition emerge, and once established, how secure is he in his post? Apart from exceptional circumstances, such as were described in the preceding section, a new Leader of the Opposition will emerge either when the Government and Opposition parties exchange their roles, or when the Opposition party changes its leader. On eight occasions this century there has been such a straight switch of parties in office, with the vanquished Prime Minister taking over the role of Leader of the Opposition. In six of these cases (MacDonald in 1924, Baldwin in 1929, Churchill in 1945, Attlee in 1951, Douglas-Home in 1964, and Wilson in 1970) the new Leader of the Opposition took up his post following the general election result. In 1905, however, conflict within the Balfour Unionist Government caused its downfall towards the end of the Parliament, but before an election had been held, while in 1924, following the indecisive general election of December 1923, Baldwin met Parliament before resigning as Prime Minister.

On these eight occasions the new Leader of the Opposition came directly from 10 Downing Street. On seven other occasions this century he emerged from the ranks of the Opposition party, following the death, retirement, or overthrow of the previous Leader. This century the Conservatives have changed their overall party leader, or their leader in the Commons, on eleven occasions, but only twice has the change been made while the party has been in opposition.[1] In 1911, following Balfour's retirement,[2] Walter Long and Austen Chamberlain seemed the most likely candidates to succeed him, and there was the prospect of a close contest which could have added to the party's existing divisions over policy and personalities.[3] In an effort to avoid this, Long and Chamberlain agreed to support Andrew Bonar Law as a compromise candidate. Accordingly, at a meeting of Conservative and Unionist MPs at the Carlton Club on 13 November 1911, Bonar Law's candidacy was proposed by Walter Long and seconded by Austen Chamberlain, and was accepted unanimously by the meeting, although with reservations expressed in private by many of the supporters of Long and Chamberlain. Bonar Law thus became leader of the Conservative Party in the Commons, and thereby Leader of the Opposition.

The second Conservative leadership change in opposition this century was in July 1965, following Sir Alec Douglas-Home's retirement as leader.[4] As with Bonar Law in 1911, the new leader was elected, but this time by a secret ballot of Conservative MPs.[5] This process had been devised only in February 1965, largely as a reaction to the criticism of the 'informal processes of consultation within the party' through which Lord Home (as he then was) had 'emerged' as leader in 1963.[6] In July 1965 Edward Heath, Reginald Maudling, and Enoch Powell announced their candidacies, and in the ballot Heath got 150 votes, Maudling 133 and Powell 15. Heath thus had an

---

[1] For a more detailed review of party leadership changes see R. T. McKenzie, *British Political Parties*, London 1963, pp. 21–55, 295–364.

[2] See below, p. 91, for comments on Balfour's retirement.

[3] For details of this leadership change see Blake, *The Unknown Prime Minister*, pp. 71–86; Chamberlain, *Politics From the Inside*, pp. 384–400; Petrie, *Life and Letters of Sir Austen Chamberlain*, I, pp. 295–302.

[4] See below, p. 92, for comments on Douglas-Home's retirement.

[5] For details see Young, *Sir Alec Douglas-Home*, pp. 220–34; Roth, *Enoch Powell*, pp. 327–32.

[6] See R. S. Churchill, *The Fight for the Tory Leadership*, London 1964 (and Iain Macleod's review of the book in *The Spectator*, 17 January 1964); Humphry Berkeley, *Crossing the Floor*, London 1972. See also interview with Martin Redmayne, then Conservative chief whip, in *The Listener*, 19 December 1963.

overall majority, but did not have the 15 per cent lead over his nearest rival that was required by the rules of the contest. A second ballot would have been necessary, in which only a simple majority would have been enough to produce a result, but in the event Maudling and Powell withdrew from the contest, and no new candidates entered, so that Edward Heath emerged as the winner. He was then formally presented for approval to a meeting of Conservative MPs, Peers, candidates, and members of the executive committee of the National Union, and thereby became party leader and new Leader of the Opposition.

Labour Party leaders are also elected through a secret ballot of the party's MPs, although the procedure is somewhat less complicated than that which the Conservatives adopted in 1965. Labour's method requires that, in order to be elected, a candidate has to receive an overall majority of votes, and if this is not achieved on the first ballot, further ballots are held at weekly intervals.[1] If Labour had to select a new leader while in government, the same system would be used, although the necessary ballots would all be held on one day. Once chosen by this process, the leader, and the other officers, are subject to annual re-election. In practice, however, re-election of the leader has never been challenged when the party has been in office, and only rarely has it been challenged in opposition. In all, Labour has had five leaders since it became the main Opposition party in 1922, and, in contrast to the Conservative Party pattern, all have been chosen while the party was in opposition, although not all have been selected by a contested secret ballot election. The 1922 general election gave the Labour Party the undisputed status of main Opposition party. It also transformed the composition of the PLP, in that a number of new Labour MPs were elected, together with some prominent party figures who had lost seats in 1918.[2] Among these was Ramsay MacDonald, who had been chairman of the PLP prior to 1914. In the previous Parliament it had been

[1] See Appendix C.

[2] See MacNeill Weir, *The Tragedy of Ramsay MacDonald*, pp. 104–8; Snowden, *An Autobiography*, II, pp. 573–4; J. R. Clynes, *Memoirs* (2 vols), London 1937, I, pp. 330–1; Mary A. Hamilton, *Arthur Henderson*, London 1938, p. 229; David Kirkwood, *My Life in Revolt*, London 1935, pp. 194–7.

decided that the party officers should be elected at the end of a session rather than at the beginning, and accordingly J. R. Clynes had been elected chairman of the PLP in 1921. At the first PLP meeting after the 1922 election, however, it was agreed that in view of the changed composition of the PLP, the offices should be contested again, and on a show of hands MacDonald defeated Clynes for the leadership. MacDonald thus became Leader of the Opposition, and was accorded the title of chairman and leader of the PLP.

Ramsay MacDonald remained leader until the fall of the second Labour Government in 1931, when the bulk of the party declined to follow MacDonald in the formation of a National Government.[1] The party leadership thereby became vacant, and the Labour MPs met on 28 August 1931 and, without a contest, chose Arthur Henderson to succeed MacDonald as leader, and thus to serve as the new Leader of the Opposition.[2] Henderson, however, was defeated at the general election that came in October 1931, and George Lansbury took his place as Leader of the Opposition (although, as noted earlier,[3] Henderson remained as *party* leader for a year, even though he was outside Parliament). Lansbury led the party for most of the Parliament, but following his retirement in October 1935,[4] Clement Attlee, who had been deputy leader since 1931, was elected, unopposed, to succeed him.[5] At that time there were only some fifty Labour MPs, following the party's crushing defeat at the 1931 general election. At the general election which came in November 1935, the Labour representation increased to 154, and at the beginning of the new session Attlee's re-election was contested by Herbert Morrison and Arthur Greenwood.[6] It was thought that Attlee, like Clynes after the 1922 election, might be rejected in favour of one of his more experienced colleagues, but in the first ballot Attlee received fifty-eight votes, Morrison forty-four, and Greenwood

[1] For details see R. Bassett, *1931 Political Crisis*, London 1958.

[2] Hamilton, *Arthur Henderson*, p. 389; Dalton, *Memoirs*, I, pp. 274–9, 296–7; Clynes, *Memoirs*, II, p. 198; Postgate, *George Lansbury*, p. 276.

[3] See p. 83.

[4] See below, p. 92, for comments on Lansbury's retirement.

[5] Jenkins, *Mr. Attlee*, pp. 134–62; Dalton, *Memoirs*, II, pp. 64–83.

[6] Clynes, *Memoirs*, II, p. 228; Jenkins, *Mr. Attlee*, p. 167; Morrison, *An Autobiography*, p. 162.

thirty-two. Attlee did not have the required overall majority, but in the second ballot, with the bottom candidate eliminated, Attlee defeated Morrison by eighty-eight votes to forty-four.

Attlee remained party leader, in office and in opposition, for twenty years without his re-election ever again being opposed. He eventually retired voluntarily at the end of 1955, when he was seventy-two. In the contest for his successor, Herbert Morrison again entered the ballot, together with Aneurin Bevan and Hugh Gaitskell.[1] Bevan sought to persuade Gaitskell to allow the ageing Morrison to become leader unopposed, in recognition of his services to the party, but Gaitskell declined. No doubt Bevan and Gaitskell both assumed that the chances of Bevan defeating Gaitskell were probably less in January 1956 than they might have been at some time in the future. In the event, Gaitskell won easily on the first ballot, with 157 votes to Bevan's 70 and Morrison's 40. Although Gaitskell's re-election as leader was opposed by Harold Wilson in 1960, and by Anthony Greenwood in 1961, these challenges were un-successful, and Gaitskell remained as party leader, and Leader of the Opposition, until his death, when only fifty-six, in 1963. Harold Wilson, George Brown, and James Callaghan contested the succession,[2] and on the first ballot Wilson obtained 115 votes, Brown 88, and Callaghan 41. Wilson subsequently triumphed on the second ballot by 144 votes to Brown's 103, and served as Leader of the Opposition for eighteen months before becoming Prime Minister in October 1964.

Thus for the most part the Leader of the Opposition will either be a vanquished former Prime Minister, or else a 'new boy' who has not yet served as Prime Minister. As a 'new boy' (like Attlee in the nineteen-thirties or Heath before 1970) he will lack the prestige that goes with being a former Prime Minister. A major problem will be for him to make himself known to the electorate, while he also has to seek to lead those who until recently were his equals in the Shadow Cabinet and Parliament. Indeed, it may be that, like Bonar Law in 1911, he is presiding over colleagues who have more prestige within the party than he has. In this respect a Leader of the Opposition

---

[1] Dalton, *Memoirs*, III, p. 429; Krug, *Aneurin Bevan*, p. 231; Morrison, *An Autobiography*, p. 292.

[2] See *The Observer*, 17 February 1963; Haseler, *The Gaitskellites*, pp. 240-6.

who is an ex-Prime Minister (like Churchill, Attlee after 1951, Douglas-Home, and Wilson after 1970) has an advantage over a Leader who has not been Prime Minister (like Gaitskell), and perhaps has not even held one of the two or three top Cabinet posts (like Wilson before 1964 and Heath before 1970). In interview, however, a number of Shadow Cabinet members argued that being a former Prime Minister counts for much more in the Leader's dealings with the House of Commons than in his dealings with his Shadow Cabinet colleagues. Equally, if the Leader of the Opposition is a former Prime Minister, he can be regarded as a 'loser', in the sense that he has just been rejected by the electorate, and therefore carries the stigma that goes with electoral failure. Thus a number of Conservative Spokesmen who were interviewed commented on the fall in Sir Alec Douglas-Home's status within the Consultative Committee after the 1964 election defeat, as compared with his position within the Cabinet only a few weeks previously, and some Labour Spokesmen made similar comments about Harold Wilson's position in the Cabinet and Shadow Cabinet in 1970. It is debatable, of course, whether it is easier for a 'new boy' to build a reputation than it is for a 'loser' to live one down. Perhaps worst of all, however, the Leader of the Opposition may be a 'new boy' who has just lost an election (as with Gaitskell after the 1959 election, and Heath after 1966), and whose task it is to live down the defeat while at the same time attempting to build a positive image.

The job of Leader of the Opposition is considerably less wearing, in the physical sense, than that of Prime Minister, so that in terms of preservation of health and sanity, the post can be retained for longer periods than can that of Prime Minister. At the same time, the change-round of Leaders of the Opposition has been greater than that of Prime Ministers this century, and (as shown in Table 4) the only Leaders of the Opposition who have held the post for more than five years at a stretch have been Campbell-Bannerman (1899–1905), Balfour (1905–11), Churchill (1945–51) and Gaitskell (1956–1963). To some extent, however, this merely reflects the fact that general election victories have translated Leaders of the Opposition into Prime Ministers on eight occasions this century. Nevertheless, the post of Leader of the Opposition has certain built-in hazards that make the occupant's position less secure than that of the Prime Minister. The Leader of the Opposition is much more exposed to party criticism, although perhaps not to public criticism, than is the Prime Minister. As an election approaches, it becomes less feasible for a party to change its leader, and the incumbent leader gains more status among his colleagues as the possibility of office looms ahead. Leaders of the Opposition, however, often run into trouble from party colleagues after an electoral setback. A Conservative Leader of the Opposition suffers in particular from the fact that his party expects its leaders to be successful. The usual reaction of the Conservatives to electoral defeat has been graphically described by Robert Rhodes James:

> [The Conservative Party] is a Confederation that does not flourish and is not seen to best advantage in Opposition. Deprived of office, it becomes fractious and querulous, and casts around for an explanation of the calamity. The burden of censure naturally falls upon its leader.[1]

The Labour Party, with more experience of electoral defeat, and with a tradition of dissent within the Movement, is prepared to make the party leader the subject of regular attack without necessarily wanting to overthrow him. A Conservative Party leader, however, if he is not Prime Minister, at least has to be seen to be leading the party to victory in by-elections and local government elections and in the battles of Parliament. Failure to appear as a likely election winner makes a Conservative Leader of the Opposition extremely vulnerable. Thus Baldwin's position was in peril in the 1924 and 1929–31 Parliaments,[2] and even Churchill had his difficulties after 1945.[3] Heath survived defeat in 1966, but might have had difficulty in surviving a further defeat in 1970.

Nevertheless, few Leaders of the Opposition in this century have been overthrown, and the vast majority gave up the post only by becoming Prime Minister, as with Campbell-Bannerman in 1905, MacDonald in 1924 and 1929, Baldwin in 1924,

---

[1] R. R. James, *Churchill: A Study in Failure 1900–39*, London 1970, p. 192.

[2] See, for example, Middlemas and Barnes, *Baldwin*, pp. 264–8, 533–41.

[3] See, for example, Stuart, *Within the Fringe*, p. 145.

Attlee in 1945, Churchill in 1951, Wilson in 1964, and Heath in 1970. In addition, three others (Bonar Law in 1915, Baldwin in 1931, and Attlee in 1940) joined Coalition Governments in some post other than Prime Minister. The other Leaders of the Opposition of this century were replaced whilst in opposition, but for a variety of reasons. Gaitskell died in 1963, and Lees-Smith in 1941, both while still serving as Leader of the Opposition, although Lees-Smith was not party leader. Attlee retired in 1955 because of his age, and in 1931 Arthur Henderson was Leader of the Opposition for only a few weeks, as he was defeated at the 1931 general election. In the somewhat exceptional wartime situation in 1916, Chaplin gave way to Asquith when he was replaced as Prime Minister, and in 1922 Asquith gave way to MacDonald when Labour succeeded the Liberals as the second main party. During the second world war, Pethick-Lawrence was replaced by the more senior Arthur Greenwood when he became available on leaving the Coalition Government in 1941, although neither was party leader. In his turn, Greenwood gave way to Attlee when the Coalition Government was replaced by the Conservative 'Caretaker' Government in 1945.

This leaves, in this century, only Balfour in 1911, Lansbury in 1935, and Douglas-Home in 1965, who were replaced as Leader of the Opposition as a result of pressure (gentle or otherwise) from their colleagues. Balfour retired as Unionist leader in November 1911, after there had been much dissatisfaction over the quality of his leadership.[1] He lost the confidence of many Unionists, in and out of Parliament, through what they saw as his over-cautious handling of the resistance to the Parliament Bill in 1910 and 1911. In October 1911 the 'Halsbury Club' was formed, made up of those Unionists, led by Lord Halsbury, who sought a more rigorous handling of Opposition affairs. A 'Balfour Must Go' campaign was launched, and some of Balfour's senior Parliamentary colleagues expressed the feeling that the party outside Parliament was restless, and sought a new and more aggressive leader. Balfour bowed to this pressure, and although he claimed that age and health factors

[1] For details see Dugdale, *Arthur James Balfour*, II, pp. 85–8; Chamberlain, *Politics From the Inside*, pp. 348–59; A. W. Fox, *The Earl of Halsbury*, London 1919, p. 286.

had persuaded him that it was time to go, it seems clear that his retirement was a response to the attacks to which he had been subjected by his party colleagues.

The same is also true of George Lansbury's retirement as Labour party leader in 1935.[1] In the context of the rise of Fascism in the nineteen-thirties, a section of the Labour Party objected strongly to Lansbury's pacifist views. Previously he had offered to resign if the PLP or Party Conference felt that he was out of step with majority opinion in the party, but his offers had been declined. In October 1935, however, at the annual Party Conference, a speech by Lansbury on the subject of collective security was followed by one from Ernest Bevin, in which Lansbury's attitude was attacked bitterly. Although Lansbury had contemplated resigning for some time, Bevin's attack upon him, and the absence of any support from his colleagues at the Conference after Bevin's speech, finally convinced Lansbury that he should retire, and he submitted his resignation to the PLP a few days later.

In the case of Sir Alec Douglas-Home's retirement as Conservative leader in 1965, there was not such dramatic evidence of dissatisfaction as the 'Balfour Must Go' campaign, or Bevin's conference attack on Lansbury, but the pressures for his retirement nonetheless were considerable.[2] The feeling that Sir Alec was too mild to be effective as Leader of the Opposition, and that he could not compete with Harold Wilson as a Parliamentary or television performer, served to produce pressure for a change of leader in the summer of 1965. Many Conservatives felt that a more youthful and dynamic leader was necessary before the general election, which was expected in the autumn of 1965 or early in 1966. Douglas-Home subsequently announced his retirement in July 1965, and although, as with Balfour and Lansbury, technically he retired voluntarily, in reality his resignation, like theirs, came as a result of the criticism to which he had been subjected. These three cases, however, are untypical of the fate of Leaders of the Opposition in Britain this century, the majority of whom have not been forced

[1] For details see Postgate, *The Life of George Lansbury*, ch. 22; A. Bullock, *The Life and Times of Ernest Bevin*, London 1960, p. 564; Cooke, *The Life of Richard Stafford Cripps*, pp. 144–77.

[2] See Young, *Sir Alec Douglas-Home*, pp. 220–34.

from office, but have retired for health or similar reasons, or have died in harness, or have graduated to the office of Prime Minister.

The Power of the Leader of the Opposition

Regardless of the degree of security of tenure, how much power does the Leader of the Opposition enjoy within the structure of the Opposition team? In particular, how many of the factors that contribute towards the Prime Minister's powerful position within the machinery of government are mirrored in the case of the Leader of the Opposition?[1] Many of these factors have no parallel at all in opposition. The Leader of the Opposition lacks the mystique that is associated with the office of Prime Minister. The Downing Street network and the 'trappings of office' have an aura and a glamour that contribute to a Prime Minister's authority over his colleagues, for which the Leader of the Opposition has no parallel, although an ex-Prime Minister may carry some of this aura with him into opposition. In the wartime situations, like those of 1914–18 and 1939–45, the prestige and power of the Prime Minister increases as he is given wide authority to deal with the national emergency. Thus Lloyd George in the first world war, and Churchill in the second, acquired 'presidential' status, and to a considerable extent came to personify the national image. The reverse is true of the Leader of the Opposition, however, as in wartime, criticism and dissent becomes unpatriotic, and during both world wars the Leader of the Opposition became little more than a token figure.[2] Whether or not the wartime authority of the office of Prime Minister carries over into peacetime, it is clear

---

[1] For discussions of the power of the Prime Minister see Mackintosh, *The British Cabinet* (especially pp. 610–27); Walter Bagehot, *The English Constitution*, London 1963 (Fontana Library edition, introduction by R. H. S. Crossman); A. King (ed.), *The British Prime Minister*, London 1969; A. H. Brown, 'Prime Ministerial Power', *Public Law 1968*, pp. 28–51, 96–118; G. W. Jones, 'The Prime Minister's Power', *Parliamentary Affairs* 1964–5, pp. 167–85; R. W. K. Hinton, 'The Prime Minister as an Elected Monarch', *Parliamentary Affairs* 1959–60, pp. 297–303; D. J. Heasman, 'The Prime Minister and the Cabinet', *Parliamentary Affairs* 1961–2, pp. 461–84.

[2] For comments on the nature of Opposition in wartime, see Appendix A.

that the Leader of the Opposition enjoys no such wartime boost to his status, and if anything, the whole concept of the legitimacy of Opposition is weakened by an emergency situation.

The Prime Minister's constitutional right to advise the Monarch as to the date for a general election gives him an influence over the careers of his colleagues that is in no way reflected in the powers of the Leader of the Opposition. Also, while the Prime Minister is head of the Civil Service organisation, as well as of the Ministerial and party structures, the Opposition has no parallel bureaucracy. An Opposition party is served by its own Research Department, and a Conservative Leader of the Opposition retains ultimate control of this, but his Labour counterpart does not even have this power, as the Labour Party Research Department is answerable to the NEC rather than directly to the leader of the party.[1] Also, in office or in opposition, the leader of the Labour Party is subject to annual re-election. In fact, even in opposition he is rarely challenged, although Gaitskell's re-election was opposed in 1960 and 1961, and the possibility of a contest is always there. When the party is in office, the re-election requirement remains, but it is unlikely that the re-election of a Labour Prime Minister would be challenged in the way that that of a Labour Leader of the Opposition might be. A Conservative leader, of course, is free from any requirement of annual re-election, although all of the Conservative Leaders of the Opposition this century have been faced at some stage with discontent over their leadership.

In these vital respects, therefore, the Prime Minister has clear advantages over the Leader of the Opposition. Other aspects of Prime Ministerial authority, however, are reflected to some extent in the position of the Leader of the Opposition. The Prime Minister is sometimes presented as being at the apex of the Ministerial power structure, being the focal point of an organisation that embraces the Cabinet, other Ministers and junior Ministers outside the Cabinet, the Civil Service, and the party in and out of Parliament. To some extent the Leader of the Opposition also stands at the top of a pyramid structure, with below him the Shadow Cabinet, the Spokesmen, the backbench MPs, and the party outside Parliament. Like the

[1] See below, pp. 272–8.

Prime Minister, the Leader of the Opposition is normally leader of his party, with all the power and prestige that flows from this. For a Conservative Leader of the Opposition this includes the power to appoint personally the deputy leader (if he wants one), the chief whip, the party chairman and deputy chairmen, and, of course, the Consultative Committee and the Opposition Spokesmen. For a Labour Leader of the Opposition the powers of appointment are not as extensive, as whether the party is in office or in opposition, the Labour Party chairman is elected by the NEC, and the deputy leader by the PLP, and in opposition, although not in office, the Labour chief whip is elected by the PLP. A Labour Leader of the Opposition is also faced by an elected Parliamentary Committee, so that he does not share the Conservative Leader of the Opposition's power of selecting his immediate colleagues on the party's Parliamentary 'executive committee'. This factor represents a major difference between Labour and Conservative Leaders of the Opposition (and the full implications of this are discussed in the next chapter).

A Labour Leader of the Opposition, like his Conservative counterpart, does appoint the Parliamentary Committee members and other MPs to duties as Opposition Spokesmen, and for both parties this is a valuable patronage power. The job of Spokesman, of course, carries no salary, and is generally seen as a poor substitute for Ministerial office, especially by those with Cabinet experience. There is no guarantee that the party will win the next election and thereby return to office, or that the Spokesmen will receive Ministerial posts if the party does form the Government. Nonetheless, an opposition appointment is generally regarded as something of a step towards Ministerial office, especially by young backbench MPs. Opposition can be used as an opportunity to rebuild a front-bench team, and recruit new and young MPs from the back benches. In the 1966–70 Parliament particularly, Heath brought a number of new Spokesmen into his team, and in these circumstances the Leader's power over the careers of young MPs is considerable. His power is perhaps all the greater as a general election approaches, and if the Leader of the Opposition looks like becoming Prime Minister, he enjoys something of a foretaste of the power that stems from the control of appointments to a Ministerial team. The Leader of the Opposition also supplies some names for the annual Honours Lists.[1]

These various powers of appointment enjoyed by the Leader of the Opposition are very much less extensive than those of a Prime Minister, and the Leader of the Opposition cannot hope to match the vast patronage power that a Prime Minister commands. This difference between the power of the Prime Minister and the Leader of the Opposition is a major one, and in interview Shadow Cabinet members emphasised this factor more than any other as marking a contrast between the power of the two men. Nevertheless, the leader of the Opposition's patronage powers do amount to a degree of influence over the careers of some of his colleagues, and especially his young backbench colleagues who are hoping for a career on the front bench. This is much more the case now than in the past, because of the increased number of full-time MPs today, and because of the much greater formalisation of the role of Spokesmen in opposition. As noted in the previous chapter, the introduction of the system of Spokesmen in 1955 was criticised in some quarters as being likely to increase the Leader of the Opposition's patronage power, giving him almost Prime Ministerial powers of appointment. Many of these assumptions may have been exaggerated, but the Leader's powers of appointment are nonetheless considerable.

In the allocation of Opposition duties, the Leader of the Opposition can 'shuffle the pack' so as to reduce the status of a possible emerging rival: just as a potential rival to the Prime Minister can be given Ministerial posts which will do his career more harm than good, so in opposition a similar principle can apply with regard to shadow duties. Also, if he is due to retire, the Leader of the Opposition can influence the succession through the duties that he allocates to the various contenders for his post. Whether deliberately or not, Douglas-Home probably increased Heath's chances of succeeding him, when, in a general re-shuffle of duties early in 1965, he moved Reginald Maudling from the Treasury to Foreign Affairs, and gave Heath responsibility for Treasury, as well as Economic Affairs. Heath thus received a lot of publicity during the spring and summer of 1965, as he led the attack on the Finance Bill, and his support

[1] See P. G. Richards, *Patronage in British Government*, London 1963.

within the party rose at the vital time before Douglas-Home's retirement from the leadership in July 1965.[1]

The Leader of the Opposition is chairman of the Shadow Cabinet, it meets on his territory, and (as is discussed in more detail in Chapter 7) he enjoys the special authority in its deliberations that accrues to the chairman of any committee. He normally does not take on any specific shadow duties himself. In 1960 Gaitskell took over Foreign Affairs for a while after Aneurin Bevan's death, and in 1971 Harold Wilson assumed responsibility for Ulster affairs, but these are exceptions to the general rule. Normally, of course, the Leader of the Opposition will have a particular area of interest: for Churchill and Douglas-Home this was external affairs, and for Wilson and Heath it was the economy. Generally, however, the Leader of the Opposition, like the Prime Minister, remains free from specific departmental responsibilities, and serves as 'co-ordinator in chief' of the front-bench team, taking the broad view of policy and strategy as a whole, and acting as the 'supreme generalist' in a team of specialists. In office, Ministers tend to be so bound up with their own departmental affairs that the task of coordinating separate departmental policies is left to Cabinet committees, and to a few non-departmental Ministers, with the Prime Minister being the chief of these. The duties of Opposition Spokesmen are considerably less time-consuming and watertight than are those of Ministers, and Spokesmen have much more freedom than have Ministers to range into broader policy considerations than those covered by their specific shadow duties. As is discussed below,[2] however, there is evidence that Spokesmen are becoming considerably more specialised, at least in their Parliamentary activities, and some Spokesmen even approach in opposition the level of specialisation that they would practise in office. To this end the Leader of the Opposition may encourage specialisation among his colleagues, and potential rivals. In such a situation, the Leader of the Opposition's position is enhanced as the chief figure in opposition capable of taking the broad non-departmental view of policy. Thus in 1955 Attlee was eager that Aneurin Bevan's public utterances should be confined to an

[1] For a comment see Young, *Sir Alec Douglas-Home*, p. 229.
[2] See below, Chapter 10.

area for which he was specifically responsible,[1] while before Enoch Powell's dismissal from the Conservative Shadow Cabinet in 1968, Heath sought to restrict him to his specific shadow 'brief'.[2] In so far as the Leader of the Opposition can involve his colleagues in narrow specialisations, he alone is able to emulate the Prime Minister in posing as a truly 'national' figure, who, like the Medieval Monarch, rises above the particular to concern himself with the national well-being as a whole.[3]

The Leader of the Opposition has a small personal staff. In the 1945–51 period Churchill had a private office next to his home at Hyde Park Gate, and he also operated from a suite in the Savoy Hotel. Heath had a small private office staff which operated from an outer office of the Leader's room in the House. It was headed by John MacGregor and then Douglas Hurd, and consisted of two Parliamentary Private Secretaries (Anthony Kershaw and James Prior) to deal with House of Commons matters, a senior assistant, two junior assistants, and a number of secretaries, making less than ten in all. This team was financed almost exclusively out of Conservative Party funds, although Heath himself paid the salary of a personal secretary.[4] As Leader of the Opposition until 1963, Hugh Gaitskell had the services of only two secretaries and a press officer. Soon after Labour returned to Opposition in 1970, however, Transport House agreed to finance a larger personal staff for Harold Wilson. This now extends to two administrative assistants, a Transport House liaison officer, and four junior assistants or secretaries. He also has two Parliamentary Private Secretaries (Frank Judd and Charles Morris), so that his 'staff' is now much the same size as was Heath's in the 1966–70 Parliament. The Leader's private office, of course, is a poor substitute for the Cabinet Office and the Downing Street network that surrounds the Prime Minister.[5] Nevertheless, even the Leader's small personal staff is more than his colleagues in opposition possess,

---

[1] See above, p. 69.

[2] See below, p. 296.

[3] For comments on the Prime Minister's role in this respect see Hinton, *Parliamentary Affairs* 1959–60, pp. 297–303.

[4] G. Hutchison, *Edward Heath*, London 1970, p. 170.

[5] See R. K. Mosley, *The Story of the Cabinet Office*, London 1969.

and Opposition Spokesmen are very much alone in the performance of their duties, except for perhaps a secretary and, for Conservative Spokesmen, the assistance of a Research Department officer. While a Minister has a department behind him in any policy clash with the Prime Minister, an Opposition Spokesman has no such backing: while a Minister can 'speak for the department', an Opposition Spokesman is essentially an individual performing duties on his own initiative. He is thus 'on his own' in any clash with the Leader of the Opposition.

Finally in this section it may be noted that unlike most of his colleagues in opposition the Leader of the Opposition has some international standing, and he will be received by foreign governments in an official capacity. In 1971 Harold Wilson visited the USA and the Soviet Union for talks with political leaders, and was duly seen with them on television and in press photographs.[1] In 1969 Edward Heath visited the USA and south-east Asia, as well as some European capitals, and as Leader of the Opposition he was regarded by foreign newsmen and politicians as a political figure of some significance.[2] Overseas political leaders who are visiting Britain often arrange to meet the Leader of the Opposition to hear his party's views on current issues. In November 1971 the Prime Minister of Northern Ireland flew to London specifically to meet the Leader of the Opposition to discuss Labour's attitude to the Ulster situation,[3] and when Harold Wilson visited Ulster and Eire in 1971 his visit was treated by his hosts and by the press almost with the importance of a Prime Ministerial mission.[4] Compared with the serving Prime Minister, of course, the Leader of the Opposition's international standing is usually slight, although some ex-Prime Ministers, like Winston Churchill in the 1945–51 period, may be exceptionally well known on the world scene. For the most part, however, it is his role as a potential Prime Minister that gives him some recognition abroad, and the impact that he makes on the international scene will depend in large part upon the imminence of a general election, and his party's chances of winning it.

[1] See *The Times*, 1 and 4 May 1971.
[2] See *The Times*, 30 May 1969 and 22 October 1969.
[3] See *The Times*, 5 November 1971.
[4] See *The Times*, 20 November 1971.

The Leader of the Opposition and the Public

In terms of contacts with the public through the press, the Government has a distinct advantage over the Opposition. The news media are interested in 'action' rather than 'opinion', and only the Government 'acts'. Also, while the Prime Minister appears as a national leader, grappling with the nation's problems, the Leader of the Opposition can all too easily appear carping and even unpatriotic in his attacks upon the Government's performance. Within this general situation, to what extent is press and public awareness of the work of the Opposition centred on the activities of the Leader of the Opposition? The Leader of the Opposition receives considerably more news coverage than do his colleagues, and in general, public awareness of front-bench personalities (in office or in opposition) does not extend beyond the party leaders. Aneurin Bevan in the nineteen-fifties, and George Brown and Enoch Powell in the sixties, are perhaps exceptions to this, but a *Sunday Times* survey in 1962 found that the majority of people interviewed were unable to even name any front benchers, other than the party leaders themselves, on either side of the House.[1] D. E. Butler and D. Stokes, as part of their analysis of the factors determining voting behaviour in Britain, found much the same thing in surveys in 1963 and 1964.[2] While George Brown and Quintin Hogg did produce clear reactions, favourable or unfavourable, among interviewers in 1964 (no doubt as a result of their controversial contributions to the 1964 election campaign), something like two-thirds of Butler and Stokes' respondents had 'neutral or no feelings' about the party front benchers, other than the Leader of the Opposition and the Prime Minister.

Opposition front benchers are at a particular disadvantage in this respect. While Ministers receive some attention through their departmental work, and thus can compete with the Prime Minister for publicity to at least some extent, the Leader of the Opposition is almost alone among Opposition figures in receiving regular coverage by the news media. Some indication

[1] D. E. Butler and D. Stokes, *Political Change in Britain*, London 1969, p. 26.

[2] Ibid., p. 377.

of this is given in Table 5, which indicates the amount of coverage given to the Government and the Opposition by *The Times* newspaper in 1961 and 1968. These two years were chosen as the middle years of the 1959–64 Parliament (Conservative Government in office) and the 1966–70 Parliament (Labour Government in office). The figures represent the number of references contained in the Index to *The Times* for the members

TABLE 5

Coverage of Cabinet and Shadow Cabinet by 'The Times' in 1961 and 1968*

	1961	Shadow	1968	Shadow
	Cab.	Cab.	Cab.	Cab.
N	20	18	18	18
Total References	3,135	1,077	1,967	708
Average for all Members	156	59	77	39
Leader's References	569	329	563	242
Average for Other Members	135	44	78	27
Leader's Share of Total (%)	19·8	30·5	28·0	34·1

Source: Index to *The Times* (see Appendix E).

* In each case only those who served in the Cabinet or the Shadow Cabinet throughout the year are included.

of the Cabinet and Shadow Cabinet in the two years in question.[1] In both years, the Cabinet received two to three times as much coverage as the Shadow Cabinet, as indicated by the average number of references for the members of the two bodies. In each case the Leader of the Opposition had only about half the coverage of the Prime Minister, although Gaitskell in 1961 received more coverage than did Heath in 1968, perhaps because 1961 was a critical year for Gaitskell in his post-1959 fight to retain the party leadership. Excluding the Leader of the Opposition and the Prime Minister, the other members of the Shadow Cabinet had only about one third of the coverage given to the other Cabinet members. The Leader of the Opposition's share of the Shadow Cabinet's coverage was

[1] For a comment on the method used in this analysis, see Appendix E.

thus higher than was the Prime Minister's share of the Cabinet's coverage, although for both the Prime Minister and the Leader of the Opposition their share was greater in 1968 than in 1961.

A rather different pattern emerges for the coverage given to Government and Opposition in election campaigns. Table 6 shows the number of references contained in the Index to *The Times* for the members of the Cabinet and Shadow Cabinet in the 1964, 1966, and 1970 election campaign periods. In each case Cabinet Ministers received slightly more coverage than

TABLE 6

Coverage of Cabinet and Shadow Cabinet by 'The Times' during the 1964, 1966 and 1970 General Election Campaigns

	1964 Cab.	1964 Shadow Cab.	1966 Cab.	1966 Shadow Cab.	1970 Cab.	1970 Shadow Cab.
N	23	18	23	21	21	16
Total References	248	172	218	163	219	151
Average for all Members	10·7	9·5	9·4	7·7	10·4	9·4
Leader's References	74	101	67	90	81	72
Average for Other Members	7·9	4·1	6·7	3·4	6·9	5·3
Leader's Share of Total (%)	30·0	59·0	39·2	55·2	36·9	47·0

Source: Index to *The Times* (see Appendix E).

did the members of the Shadow Cabinet, although the Shadow Cabinet came considerably closer to the Cabinet figures than was the case in Table 5. When the figures for the leaders are considered separately from the others, however, clear differences emerge. In 1964 and 1966, the Leader of the Opposition received about 25 per cent *more* coverage than did the Prime Minister, while the rest of the Shadow Cabinet received only about half of the coverage given to the rest of the Cabinet. In 1970 Harold Wilson as Prime Minister received slightly more coverage than did Edward Heath as Leader of the Opposition, but Heath still accounted for about half of the Shadow Cabinet's total references. Thus, in all three years, *The Times'* coverage of the Opposition's election campaign was concentrated very much on the Leader of the Opposition. In the Government's campaign the Prime Minister was also the centre of *The Times'* attention, but he did not dominate their coverage to the same extent as did the Leader of the Opposition. The same broad picture applies in the case of the radio and television coverage of the two parties in the 1970 election campaign. Butler and Pinto-Duschinsky calculated that Heath received 60 per cent of the Conservative party's news coverage, compared with Wilson's 56 per cent of Labour's coverage.[1] In general, few Cabinet or Shadow Cabinet figures were covered at all in the news, and Butler and Pinto-Duschinsky concluded about the Conservatives' 1970 campaign that '[Heath's] colleagues attracted little publicity and there was no evidence of any effort to promote the collective leadership of the party.'[2]

Thus, although he is surrounded by his team of Shadow Cabinet colleagues and other Spokesmen, each with a specific responsibility for a policy area, general responsibility for the conduct of opposition is seen by press and public to rest very much on the shoulders of the Leader of the Opposition. Much more than any of his Opposition colleagues, then, the Leader of the Opposition has 'responsibility without power'. When things go badly in opposition he receives more than his fair share of the blame—just as when things go well he receives most of the credit. Nevertheless, it is clear that the public can distinguish between the Leader of the Opposition and his party, and between the Prime Minister and the Government party, and can have a favourable attitude to the one, but an unfavourable attitude to the other. Thus the opinion poll rating of the party and its leader can diverge considerably—as is indicated in Figure F, which compares the Leader of the Opposition's Gallup Poll rating with that of his party in the 1961–70 period.[3] Edward Heath, as Leader of the Opposition, lagged well behind his party in popularity (at least as indicated by the Gallup Poll) for most of the 1966–70 Parliament, and his

[1] Butler and Pinto-Duschinsky, *The British General Election of 1970*, p. 207.
[2] Ibid., p. 146.
[3] For a comment on the method used in this analysis, see Appendix E.

rating declined in periods when his party's rating was improving. Harold Macmillan, on the other hand, as Prime Minister ran ahead of his party in the early nineteen-sixties, as did Harold Wilson at the end of the decade. In a detailed analysis of opinion poll ratings, C. A. E. Goodhart and R. J. Bhansali found that major changes in the level of popularity of the leader might have a small effect upon the party's rating, but that on the whole the relationship between the two was only slight.[1]

FIGURE F

Gallup Poll: Leader of the Opposition's Rating compared with that of His Party 1961-70*

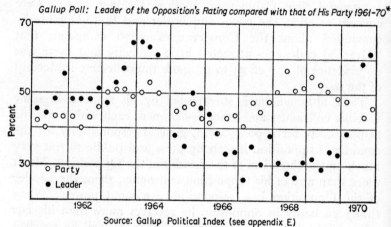

Source: Gallup Political Index (see appendix E)

*The figures represent a quarterly average

Clearly, however, an electorally attractive figure can enjoy considerable prestige within the Opposition party, whereas an electorally unattractive figure can pay the price for being a liability to the party—as did Sir Alec Douglas-Home in 1965.

Butler and Stokes show that the British elector perceives the party leaders in personalised terms:[2] that is, the elector forms an image of a leader which is based on his personal characteristics, be they favourable or unfavourable, and which is not merely an extension of his party's image. Nevertheless, Butler

[1] See C. A. E. Goodhart and R. J. Bhansali, 'Political Economy', *Political Studies* 1970, pp. 43–106.
[2] Butler and Stokes, *Political Change in Britain*, p. 378.

and Stokes suggest that while the elector may differentiate clearly between the party and its leader, the elector's attitude to the party is a better indication of how he will vote than is his attitude to the leader: despite the news media's concentration on the party leaders, British general elections remain much less personalised contests than are American Presidential elections.[1] Thus, while the elections of 1959 and 1966 may have been decided to some extent by the personal prestige of the serving Prime Minister, the elections of 1945 and 1970 can perhaps be cited as examples of the Opposition coming to power despite suffering from the 'disadvantage' of having less prestigious leaders than their opponents.[2] In these elections, Winston Churchill and Harold Wilson discovered to their cost that (to adapt Bagehot) the British electorate could 'damn the Government but cheer the Prime Minister'.

Finally, it may be noted that while the Prime Minister and the Leader of the Opposition undoubtedly are competing with each other for public favour, this situation is not necessarily reflected in opinion poll findings. In terms of voting or voting intention, the elector can favour only one party at a time. If, for example, the Labour Party commands 55 per cent of electoral support, or opinion poll preferences, this leaves only 45 per cent to be shared among its opponents. The response, however, to the Gallup Poll's questions of whether the respondent is satisfied with X as Prime Minister and Y as Leader of the Opposition can be the same in each case: the Leader of the Opposition can be regarded as performing competently in opposition by the same electors who are satisfied with the Prime Minister's performance in office.[3] Some evidence of this is provided by Figure G, which indicates the levels of satisfaction with the Leader of the Opposition and the Prime Minister as reflected by the Gallup Poll in the 1961–70 period. There were, of course, occasions when a high level of satisfaction with

[1] Ibid.

[2] For details of these elections, see R. B. McCallum and A. Readman, *The British General Election of 1945*, London 1947; D. E. Butler and R. Rose, *The British General Election of 1959*, London 1960; Butler and King, *The British General Election of 1966*: Butler and Pinto-Duschinsky, *The British General Election of 1970*.

[3] This, of course, depends on the precise wording of the questions used by the various polls to measure the leaders' popularity. See Appendix E.

one leader mirrored a low level of satisfaction with the other. Thus for much of the 1963–6 period, a consistently high rating for Harold Wilson, in opposition and in office, was accompanied by a low rating for successive Conservative leaders (Macmillan, Douglas-Home, and then Heath). Similarly, there were occasions when a rise in one leader's rating was accompanied by a fall in the other leader's rating, as in 1961 when Macmillan's and Gaitskell's graphs drew towards each other,

FIGURE G

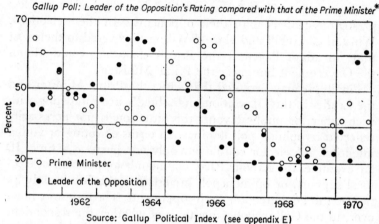

*Gallup Poll: Leader of the Opposition's Rating compared with that of the Prime Minister**

Source: Gallup Political Index (see appendix E)

*The figures represent a quarterly average

after Gaitskell had long trailed behind his rival. There were many other occasions, however, when the leaders' ratings moved in the same direction, or when they were both regarded as being equally satisfactory or equally unsatisfactory. For example, for much of 1961 and 1962 both Macmillan and Gaitskell enjoyed comparatively high ratings, while in 1968 and 1969 Wilson and Heath both had very low ratings.[1] It is clear, therefore, that the electorate does not have a fixed amount of goodwill to be divided between the Prime Minister and the Leader of the Opposition, but can have the same low

[1] See also R. Rose, 'Voters Show Their Scepticism of Politicians', *The Times*, 9 April 1968.

opinion, or the same high opinion, of the Leader of the Opposition in the performance of his role, as it has of the Prime Minister in the performance of his.

The Leader, the Shadow Cabinet, and the Spokesmen

It is clear from the preceding two sections that most of the important factors upon which the power and prestige of the Leader of the Opposition depend are consequent upon his role as the alternative Prime Minister. The Leader of the Opposition's security of tenure depends to a very considerable extent upon his prospects of becoming Prime Minister: a Leader who looks like an election winner will generally be fairly secure in his post, whereas a Leader who has just lost an election, or who seems unlikely to win the next one, will normally be in a much less secure position. The ability of the Leader of the Opposition to compete with the Prime Minister for press and television coverage during election campaigns, unlike at other times, is in great part because he may be on the point of becoming Prime Minister. Similarly, any recognition he may receive abroad is based largely on the fact that he may be Britain's next Prime Minister, or on his reputation as a former Prime Minister. The patronage power that the Leader enjoys through the appointment of Spokesmen is dependent upon the fact that allocation to a post as Spokesman is seen widely as a step towards a Ministerial post. Indeed, without the possibility of future office, the time-consuming but unpaid job of Spokesman would be a thankless one. At meetings of the Shadow Cabinet the Leader's authority will be all the greater if he seems capable of leading the party to victory at an imminent general election, and thereby having Cabinet posts at his disposal. In these various ways, it is the Leader of the Opposition's role as a potential Prime Minister that is the key to his position in relation to his colleagues: for those with whom he comes in contact the important consideration is what he may become, rather than what he is.

Although in most of the factors discussed so far the Prime Minister has clear advantages over the Leader of the Opposition, there is one respect in which the advantage is with the Leader of the Opposition: the arrangements surrounding the

Shadow Government are much more flexible, and much more subject to the whims of the Leader than is the case with the machinery of government. The Cabinet is indispensable to the modern constitutional system in Britain. Although its status may have declined in favour of the personal authority of the Prime Minister (as Mackintosh and Crossman argue)[1] or in favour of 'Partial Cabinets' (as Gordon Walker argues),[2] it is still very far from being relegated to what Bagehot refers to as the 'dignified' parts of the Constitution.[3] It remains as one of the very real limitations on the power of the Prime Minister and of individual Ministers. The Shadow Cabinet, on the other hand, has no such indispensable place in the Constitution or in the machinery of opposition, despite the fact that its history can be traced back as far as that of the Cabinet itself.

The Conservative Shadow Cabinet is the creation of the party leader, and Conservatives properly refer to it as the Consultative Committee or the Leader's Committee. The Shadow Cabinet, of course, has to be *seen* to be active if the Opposition is to avoid the accusation that it is a 'one-man band'. Thus the press is kept informed of special Shadow Cabinet meetings, and of important Shadow Cabinet 'decisions', and before a general election, photographs sometimes appear of the Shadow Cabinet at work in the Leader of the Opposition's room, thereby emphasising that the Opposition is equipped with an 'alternative Cabinet', ready to take office. Nevertheless, although the Shadow Cabinet has acquired a recognised place in contemporary patterns of Parliamentary Opposition, a Conservative Leader of the Opposition could still adapt its practices fundamentally. On going into opposition after an electoral defeat, it is always possible to argue that it is time to start afresh with a new system for Opposition. In the 1929–31 period, Baldwin replaced the full Shadow Cabinet with a smaller Business Committee, and a particularly secure Conservative leader might still be able to reduce the status of the Shadow Cabinet, and manage the affairs of the Opposition by means of less formal personal contacts with the chief whip, deputy leader and party

[1] Mackintosh, *The British Cabinet;* Crossman's Introduction to Bagehot, *The English Constitution.*

[2] P. Gordon Walker, *The Cabinet,* London 1970.

[3] Bagehot, *The English Constitution.*

chairman and deputy chairmen, all of whom the leader appoints. Even though complete abolition of the Shadow Cabinet is probably no longer possible for a Conservative leader, because of the need to appear ready for office with an alternative Cabinet, he could certainly still make major changes in the way that it operates, as its structure, composition, and procedures are still very much his personal responsibility.

In clear contrast, Labour's Shadow Cabinet is the creation of the PLP rather than of the party leader, and its composition and method of election is specified in the PLP's Standing Orders. A member of Labour's Parliamentary Committee has two roles, one as a Spokesman for a particular subject, selected by the party leader, and one as a member of the Parliamentary Committee, elected by the PLP. The leader can control him in the first role, although not in the second. There is thus a clear distinction between the two parties in their general front-bench arrangements in opposition. Nevertheless, it remains true for both parties that the system of Opposition Spokesmen that has developed since 1955 is very much subject to the personal control of the Leader of the Opposition. Although Leaders of the Opposition have created what amounts to Shadow Governments through the naming of a large number of official Opposition Spokesmen, the functions of these Spokesmen, unlike those of Ministers, are not defined by statute. Thus the Leader of the Opposition's freedom to determine the size, structure, and personnel of the Opposition team is much greater than that of the Prime Minister over the structure of government. There are, of course, practical limits to the freedom that the Leader of the Opposition enjoys in structuring his front-bench team, and although Opposition Spokesmen have no statutory powers, they now have a fairly well-established place in the organisation of the Opposition. In this respect the Leader of the Opposition today has less freedom than had Leaders of the Opposition in the nineteenth century, before the system of a Shadow Cabinet and Opposition Spokesmen had become part of the organisation of opposition. In the next two chapters the factors that go into the election and selection of the Opposition team will be considered.

4

The Election of Labour's Parliamentary Committee

THE LABOUR and Conservative Parties have each evolved basically different procedures for the formation of their front-bench teams in opposition. When the Conservatives are in opposition, the party leader selects the Consultative Committee and all the Spokesmen, and appoints them to their responsibilities. In the 1964–70 period, the Consultative Committee consisted of the leader, the deputy leader (apart from 1964–5 when no deputy leader was appointed), the party chairman, the leader, and deputy leader of the Conservative Peers, and a dozen to eighteen of the leading party figures in the Commons. The chief whip attended Consultative Committee meetings, but was not a full member. While Sir Alec Douglas-Home was party leader, the Committee had twenty-one or twenty-two members (including Douglas-Home himself, and the chief whip). Edward Heath reduced the number to eighteen or nineteen members in the 1966–70 Parliament, and to seventeen in the final session of the Parliament; he thus 'anticipated' the comparatively small Cabinet of eighteen members that he was to form when he became Prime Minister in June 1970. In direct contrast, Labour's Parliamentary Committee has a fixed number of members, and is elected by the PLP in a ballot at the beginning of each session. The other Spokesmen are selected by the leader, and he allocates the responsibilities to them and to Parliamentary Committee members alike, but the composition of the Parliamentary Committee is determined by a sessional ballot of the PLP. As well as representing a clear difference from Conservative practices in opposition, this

system contrasts with Labour's own (and Conservative) practice
in office. In its periods in office the Labour Party has come to
accept the basic conventions of Cabinet Government that were
established well before Labour emerged as a party of government. Thus all Labour Prime Ministers have personally appointed their Ministers in the same way as have Conservative
Prime Ministers, despite the demands that have been made in
the past that Ministers in a Labour Government should be
selected by more democratic procedures.[1] The practices surrounding the Shadow Cabinet, however, were, and still are,
much less firmly established than the conventions of office, so
that the Labour Party has been able to stamp its mould on
the Shadow Cabinet system. It was a Labour Leader of the
Opposition, for example, who introduced in 1955 the system
of Spokesmen that has been used by all subsequent Labour and
Conservative Leaders. Similarly, in all of its periods in opposition since 1922 Labour has retained its distinctive practice
of electing its Shadow Cabinet, although, of course, the Conservative Party has not followed this example.

The main features of the process of electing Labour's Parliamentary Committee will be examined in the rest of this
chapter, before looking in Chapter 5 at the factors that go into
the selection of Spokesmen by the Leader of the Opposition.
What are the arrangements governing the annual election of
the Parliamentary Committee? What factors do Labour MPs
consider when they are electing the Committee? How far does
the presence of an elected Shadow Cabinet represent a restriction on the power of a Labour Leader of the Opposition, and
in particular, what limitations does it place upon the party
leader's freedom to distribute the duties of Opposition Spokesmen? These general questions will be examined in the three
sections of this chapter.

Structure of the Parliamentary Committee of the PLP

Today, the Parliamentary Committee of the PLP consists of
nineteen members:

(1) the officers of the party (that is, the leader, deputy
leader, chief whip, and chairman of the PLP);

---

[1] See, for example, the 'Bradford Resolution', referred to above, p. 53.

(2) the leader (or in his absence, the deputy leader) and chief whip of the Labour Peers, together with a further representative of the backbench Labour Peers;

(3) twelve members of the Commons, elected by ballot.

The original Parliamentary Executive Committee of 1923 consisted of the leader, deputy leader and chief whip, plus twelve elected members. In 1925 the whip in the Lords was added to the Committee, and later the leader in the Lords and another representative of the Labour Peers were included, thereby raising the membership to eighteen. Apart from the small Committee formed in the 1931–5 Parliament,[1] membership remained at eighteen throughout the rest of Labour's inter-war and post-war periods in opposition, until in 1970 it was increased to nineteen through the addition of the chairman of the PLP. In opposition up to 1964, the leader chaired meetings of the PLP and of the Parliamentary Committee, but in 1970 it was decided to copy the party's practice in office and have a separate chairman to preside at PLP meetings, although the leader would continue to chair Parliamentary Committee meetings. As Prime Minister in the 1964–70 period, Harold Wilson attended PLP meetings, but these were chaired by Emanuel Shinwell and then by Douglas Houghton. They had been very effective and popular chairmen, and when the party went into opposition there was a strong feeling that the same arrangement should be retained. The fact that Douglas Houghton was available to fill the role probably helped to persuade MPs that the change from past practice in opposition was a desirable one. The change also freed the leader from what could be at times a difficult and onerous job. In the 1959–64 period Gaitskell had been criticised for his handling of some PLP meetings. Some of his critics felt that he used his power as chairman to call speakers who were favourable to his point of view, or (more subtly) to call those opponents of his who could be relied upon to present a case badly. Whether or not Gaitskell was guilty of such partiality, justice was not seen to be done. No change was attempted when Wilson succeeded Gaitskell in 1963, but with the return to opposition in 1970 the opportunity was taken to alter the system, and to elect a separate chairman

[1] See above, p. 58.

of the PLP. Douglas Houghton was duly elected, un-opposed, to this office in November 1970.

The election of the officers and Parliamentary Committee is covered by Standing Orders which were adopted at a meeting of the PLP on 8 July 1953, and were amended in July 1970.[1] The 1953 Standing Orders clarified, and in some cases altered, the practices that had applied previously. At the beginning of each session, the election of the officers takes place, although in most years in the 1951–64 period the serving members were not challenged.[2] This is followed by the election of the other members of the Committee, and the process is begun by the leader asking for nominations at a meeting of the PLP. In the 1924 ballot the nomination of candidates was not required, and ballot papers contained the names of all Labour MPs, so that the votes in that election were very thinly scattered.[3] Today the Standing Orders require that a candidate must be a member of the Commons, and must have a proposer and seconder from the Commons. Nomination forms are issued by the Labour whip's office, and must be signed by the candidate, and by his proposer and seconder. Once nominations have been made, withdrawals are not permitted. The Standing Orders make no provision for dealing with a situation where less than twelve candidates are nominated, but such an event is highly unlikely, and in most post-war years there have been thirty or forty candidates for the twelve places. The larger the number of candidates, of course, the greater will be the spread of votes, and the greater will be the chance of an 'outside' candidate being elected. Thus after there had been fifty-two candidates (virtually a fifth of the PLP) in the 1970 ballot, there were suggestions made by MPs that such large numbers of candidacies should be discouraged in future by requiring that each nomination be backed by a dozen sponsors, instead of merely a proposer and seconder.[4] This suggestion was not acted upon, but in 1971 the number of candidates fell to thirty-three without any formal restraints being imposed.

After nominations have closed, ballot papers containing the

---

[1] See Appendix C.
[2] For the 1971 timetable see Table 8.
[3] Cole, *Beatrice Webb's Diaries*, II, pp. 53–4.
[4] See *The Guardian*, 5 November 1970.

names of all the candidates are issued by the secretary of the PLP, and these must be returned within a week to a ballot box in the whip's room. The ballot is secret. In 1952 there were attempts by some of the Bevanite group to introduce greater openness into the PLP's affairs, but Attlee emphasised to Labour MPs that they were under no obligation to reveal to anyone how they had voted in the Parliamentary Committee ballot.[1] The ballot for the Parliamentary Committee and for the officers is confined to Labour members of the Commons. The party leader and the whip are entitled to vote, but the Labour Peers do not participate as they elect their own representative to serve on the Committee, along with their leader and whip. This process in the Lords takes place simultaneously with the ballots in the Commons. In the 1951–64 period, however, the leader, whip and representative of the Labour peers 'emerged' each year from the small band of Labour peers, and although in 1970 and 1971 formal nominations were sought, only one name was put forward for each post, so that ballots were again unnecessary.[2]

Before 1953 it was permissible to vote for any number of candidates, up to a maximum of twelve, and there was a tendency for members of groups or factions within the PLP, and especially the Bevanite group in the early fifties, to vote only for the two or three members of their group who were contesting the election. The PLP decided, however, that the principle involved in the election of the Parliamentary Committee was that of selecting a full team, not just one or two members of a team. Thus the practice of 'plumping' for three or four candidates was prohibited by the 1953 Standing Orders, which included a provision that all votes 'must record votes for as many Members as there are seats to be filled'.[3] In 1970, however, this requirement was ended, so that now, as before 1953, an MP is free to use all twelve of his votes, or just one or two as he pleases. Charles Pannell was prominent in persuading the PLP to drop the 'no plumping' rule in 1970. He pointed out that the party in 1970 was not divided into factions to the extent that it had been in the early nineteen-

---

[1] Dalton, *Memoirs*, III, p. 393.
[2] See Appendix A.
[3] 1953 Standing Orders, para. 3 (a).

fifties, and he argued that it was 'un-democratic' and pointless to ask MPs to use all twelve votes when they might wish to support only three or four candidates. Despite the end of the 'no plumping' rule, however, in the 1971 ballot MPs tended to use all or most of their votes, with the average number of votes cast being between nine and ten.

At the end of the week allowed for balloting, the votes are checked and counted by two assessors, who are appointed from the PLP and who serve for a full Parliament. The leading twelve candidates on the ballot are declared elected. In the election for the Committee in 1952, however, a two-ballot system was used, unlike any of the elections in the pre-war Parliaments, and unlike the elections in subsequent years. On the first ballot in 1952, only those who received 50 per cent of the votes cast were elected, and a second ballot was held a week later to fill the remaining places. On the first ballot, six of the candidates received the required 50 per cent of the votes and were thereby elected. On the second ballot, the proportion of votes received by each candidate altered slightly, but (as is shown in Table 7) the overall result was not affected, in that it was the top six of the unsuccessful first ballot candidates who were elected on the second ballot. The decision to use the two-ballot method in 1952 was taken by the PLP, against strong opposition from the Bevanites.[1] It seems that the scheme was devised specifically to exclude Bevan and his supporters from the Committee, through the combined votes of the anti-Bevanite majority on both the first and the second ballots. In the event, only three Bevanites (Bevan himself, Harold Wilson, and Geoffrey Bing) survived to the second ballot. Bevan was elected to the Committee, squeezing on in the final place, but Wilson and Bing were unsuccessful. The next year, the experiment with the two-ballot system was not repeated, although the 'no plumping' rule (referred to above) that was introduced in 1953 was designed to prevent the Bevan group from supporting only their own candidates.

Different procedures have been used over the years to deal with the situation produced by a tie for twelfth place. In the 1925 ballot there was a tie between Hugh Dalton and Arthur Ponsonby, and they drew lots to decide who would serve on

[1] See M. M. Krug, *Aneurin Bevan: Cautious Rebel*, London 1961, p. 172.

the Committee.[1] Dalton won, thereby commencing his many years of service on the Committee. In August 1931, when D. R. Grenfell and Molly Hamilton tied for twelfth place, both were declared elected, thereby giving the Committee an extra member for the short period up to the dissolution of Parliament in October 1931.[2] The Standing Orders now stipulate,

TABLE 7

Parliamentary Committee Ballots, November 1952

	First Ballot 19 Nov.		Second Ballot 27 Nov.
Griffiths	194	⎫	
Ede	189	⎪	
Gaitskell	179	Elected on	
Robens	148	the first ballot	
Dalton	140	⎪	
Callaghan	137	⎭	
Dr. Summerskill	130	155	⎫
Shinwell	124	150	⎪
Noel Baker	121	168	Elected on
Hall	113	162	the second ballot
Soskice	111	197	⎪
Bevan	108	137	⎭
Stokes	94	112	
Greenwood	93	123	
Herbison	92	129	
Wilson	91	116	
Williams	71	97	
Bing	71	97	

Source: The Times, 28 November 1952.

however, that in the event of a tie for twelfth place a second ballot shall be held, although this has not yet proved necessary.

If a vacancy occurs during a session, the runner-up in the previous ballot is co-opted on to the Committee. Thus, in April 1954, Harold Wilson was co-opted when Aneurin Bevan

[1] Dalton, *Memoirs*, III, p. 160.
[2] Ibid., p. 282.

resigned from the Committee. Similarly, in February 1956 Tom Fraser and Kenneth Younger joined the Committee when Hugh Gaitskell and James Griffiths became leader and deputy leader, in February 1963 Douglas Jay joined the Committee when Harold Wilson was elected leader, and in November 1970 William Ross became a member of the Committee when Douglas Houghton (who had come second in the ballot in July) became chairman of the PLP with an ex-officio place on

TABLE 8

Timetable of the 1971 Ballots for the PLP Officers and the Parliamentary Committee

12 Oct.	Nominations invited for the post of leader.
19 Oct.	Nominations closed: Harold Wilson declared re-elected unopposed.
26 Oct.	Nominations invited for the posts of deputy leader, whip, and chairman of the PLP.
4 Nov.	Nominations closed: Robert Mellish declared re-elected as whip, unopposed.
10 Nov.	Result of ballot for chairman and deputy leader: Douglas Houghton declared re-elected as chairman. Ballot for deputy leader indecisive.
17 Nov.	Result of second ballot for deputy leader: Roy Jenkins declared re-elected. Nominations invited for the Parliamentary Committee.
24 Nov.	Nominations closed for the Parliamentary Committee.
2 Dec.	Result of Parliamentary Committee ballot declared.

Source: *The Times* and *The Guardian* for the dates in question.

the Committee. In each of these cases, the co-opted member was subsequently re-elected to the Committee at the beginning of the next session. In October 1960, however, when Anthony Greenwood resigned from the Committee, Richard Crossman was co-opted on to the Committee for the few weeks until the ballot at the beginning of the new session, but he then declined to offer himself for re-election as a protest against Gaitskell's leadership.[1] In April 1972 three vacancies were caused through the resignation of George Thomson and Harold Lever from the Committee, and the election of Edward Short to succeed

[1] See below, p. 299, for details of Greenwood's and Crossman's protests.

Roy Jenkins as deputy leader.[1] Accordingly, Reg Prentice and John Silkin, who had been thirteenth and fourteenth in the 1971 ballot, were co-opted to the Committee, and a special ballot was held to decide whether Barbara Castle or Eric Heffer, who had tied for fifteenth place, would fill the other vacancy. In the special ballot Eric Heffer received 89 votes and Mrs Castle 111, and she thereby regained the place that she had lost in November 1971. Prentice was subsequently re-elected to the Committee in November 1972, but Silkin and Mrs Castle were defeated.

The whole annual process of electing the PLP's officers, and then the Parliamentary Committee, is clearly somewhat protracted, with a week for nominations and a week for balloting in each case. In the contests for the officers' posts, as many ballots are held as are necessary for one candidate to achieve an overall majority, and in 1971 it took two ballots, with a week for balloting in each case, for Roy Jenkins to achieve this in the contest for the deputy leadership. On occasions the procedures may be speeded up, and in the contest for the deputy leadership in April 1972 that was precipitated by Roy Jenkins' resignation, the nominating process and the two ballots were squeezed into less than a fortnight. Normally, however, these stages would cover three weeks. The election of the Parliamentary Committee is delayed until all the balloting for the officers' posts is complete, in case the unsuccessful candidates in these contests should wish to enter the Parliamentary Committee ballot. Thus in 1971 Michael Foot and Anthony Wedgwood Benn were defeated in the election for the deputy leadership, but were subsequently successful in the Parliamentary Committee ballot. In all, in 1971, the election of the officers and of the Parliamentary Committee spanned more than seven weeks, even though there was no contest for the leader's post (the precise timetable involved in 1971 being shown in Table 8). In any year in which there was to be a contest for the leadership, perhaps involving two or more ballots, followed by two or more ballots for one of the other officers' posts, virtually a quarter of the year could have elapsed before the PLP had completed its various annual ballots. The wheels of Parliamentary democracy indeed grind slowly.

[1] See below, pp. 288–9, for details of these resignations.

Voting Behaviour in Parliamentary Committee Ballot

What factors do Labour MPs consider when they are electing the Parliamentary Committee? One consideration would seem to be loyalty to the existing Committee, in that (as shown in Table 45, in Appendix D) in most years in the 1951–64 period the serving members of the Committee were re-elected. All in all, forty-one people were called upon to fill the eighteen places on the Committee in the thirteen years in opposition. Following both the 1955 and 1959 general elections, major changes took place in the composition of the Committee. Once the Committee membership was established in the first year or so of each Parliament, however, there were few subsequent changes for the rest of the Parliament, and there was thus quite a remarkable continuity of membership within each Parliament. During the 1951–5 Parliament a total of only twenty-one people filled the eighteen places; in the 1955–9 Parliament it was only twenty-five, and in the 1959–64 Parliament it was again twenty-five. James Callaghan served on the Committee continuously from 1951 to 1964, while Hugh Gaitskell, Sir Frank Soskice, and Harold Wilson each served for more than ten years. Of the eighteen members of the Parliamentary Committee in the 1963–4 session, thirteen had served since 1955, and one (James Callaghan) had served since 1951.

Further, such changes as did occur in the composition of the Committee in the 1951–64 period were mainly as a result of factors other than defeat in the annual ballot. Vacancies were caused by the deaths of Aneurin Bevan in 1960, Hugh Gaitskell in 1963, and Lord Lucan in 1964. Ten members of the Committee retired for age or health reasons (Clement Attlee, Herbert Morrison, William Whiteley, James Griffiths, Lord Jowitt, Chuter Ede, Hugh Dalton, Emanuel Shinwell, Richard Stokes, and Glenvil Hall). Aneurin Bevan resigned from the Committee in 1954 and did not seek re-election at the next ballot, although he did return to the Committee the year after that.[1] Similarly, Anthony Greenwood resigned from the Committee in 1960, at the height of the party's 'time of troubles' after the 1959 election setback, and chose not to seek

---

[1] See Krug, *Aneurin Bevan*, pp. 199–203.

re-election that year, and Richard Crossman, who filled Green-wood's place on the Committee for only a few weeks, also chose not to seek re-election. Sir Frank Soskice, Arthur Bottomley, and Alfred Robens ceased to be eligible for the Committee when they left Parliament for electoral or other reasons, while Lords Henderson, Faringdon and Listowel shared the representation of the Labour Peers among themselves more or less on an agreed basis.

Thus only on seven occasions in the 1951–64 period was a serving member of the Committee defeated in the ballot—Anthony Greenwood and Richard Stokes in 1952, Kenneth Younger in 1957, George Brown in 1958, Philip Noel-Baker in 1959, and Dr Edith Summerskill in 1957 and again in 1959. Of these, Greenwood, Stokes and Brown were later re-elected, while Dr Summerskill was re-elected after her 1957 defeat, but not after her 1959 defeat. Barbara Castle lost her place on the Committee in 1971, and again in 1972, after being elected back onto the Committee during the session. In general, however, in its annual review of the membership of the Committee, the PLP does not exhibit the characteristic which is seen as essential in a Prime Minister in the process of selecting and renewing a Cabinet—that of being a 'good butcher'. This further emphasises the clear distinction between, on the one hand, Labour's Parliamentary Committee in Opposition, *elected* by the PLP, and, on the other hand, an actual Cabinet *selected* by the Prime Minister, or a Conservative Shadow Cabinet *selected* by the Leader of the Opposition. Sentiment is undoubtedly one of the factors that influences votes in the annual Parliamentary Committee ballot, and to some extent this helps to explain the tendency for the serving members to be re-elected each year. In choosing and then revising his Cabinet a Prime Minister cannot afford to be too sentimental, but as a collective body electing a team for Opposition, the PLP would seem to be considerably less ruthless in its approach to serving members. To some extent, re-election is seen as a reward merely for being on the Com•mittee in the first place, and thereby working hard in the affairs of the PLP. One interviewed MP even suggested that it is an advantage to appear near the top of the alphabetical list of names on the ballot paper, as some MPs find it difficult to pass over any name without voting for it, and thus use up all their twelve votes early in the list. This may be a marginal factor in the voting, but in itself probably would not be enough to explain the failures of Mr Konni Zilliacus to secure election to the Committee in the 1955–9 Parliament.

Sentiment aside, the candidates who receive most consistent support in the ballot are those MPs who do their share, or more than their share, of the routine work of the Commons. As expressed by one MP in interview, those most likely to attract support are 'House of Commons people who work hard and are respected for that'. G. R. Strauss suggests that someone who failed to secure election to the Committee, or whose support dropped, would renew his activities in the House of Commons in an attempt to rally support: he would 'intensify his Parliamentary activities to restore his prestige among his colleagues'.[1] In interview, MPs also emphasised the importance of 'personal qualities', such as affability, approachability, and willingness to assist colleagues with constituency and other problems. In the 1951–64 period, G. R. Mitchison was perhaps typical of the sort of conscientious Parliamentary figure, who, as well as participating in the routine business of the House, was always helpful to backbenchers and to newcomers to Parliament. As a QC he was often asked to advise MPs on legal points, and both he and Sir Frank Soskice were perhaps untypical of the barristers and solicitors in the House in that they were prepared to devote a lot of their time to Parliamentary business in opposition. Their success in the Parliamentary Committee ballots in the 1955–9 and 1959–64 Parliaments was to some extent a reflection of this.

In contrast, many of the PLP's 'bright young intellectuals' in the nineteen-fifties and sixties were consistently unsuccessful in the annual ballot because they were resented by many MPs for not doing their fair share of work on the Standing and Select Committees of the Commons, or on the various backbench committees of the PLP. As a general election draws near, MPs might be more inclined to consider voting for potential Cabinet Ministers in the Parliamentary Committee ballot. Even in the November 1963 ballot, however, just a year before the party came to office, Roy Jenkins, Anthony Crosland,

[1] G. R. Strauss, 'The Influence of the Backbencher', *Political Quarterly*, 1965, p. 283.

Anthony Wedgwood-Benn, and George Thomson, as well as 'left-wingers' like Richard Crossman and Barbara Castle, were all unsuccessful in the Parliamentary Committee ballot, yet within two or three years all were prominent members of the Wilson Cabinet. Thus while the Parliamentary Committee ballot might represent an annual test of an MP's popularity with his colleagues, it clearly does not necessarily reflect the views of the PLP on the question of who are the promising young future Ministers within its ranks. At the beginning of a Parliament, as in 1951 and 1970, new MPs might be unfamiliar with the hard-working but unpublicised MP, and might therefore tend to vote for the well-known party figures, but this is less likely to happen as the Parliament proceeds. As some Labour MPs pointed out in interview, being a former Cabinet Minister might be an advantage in the ballot at the beginning of a period in opposition, but was a rapidly diminishing asset, as some ex-Cabinet Ministers discovered in the 1971 ballot. Other MPs in interview maintained that the party leaders who had performed most competently at the Despatch Box would be the ones to be supported in the subsequent Parliamentary Committee ballot, and that ex-Cabinet Ministers who were content to live off their Ministerial reputations, and did not make a spectacular impact in opposition, would soon lose support.

As in any election, those entering the Parliamentary Committee ballot do not necessarily expect to win, or even want to win. The purpose of participating in the election might be to gain publicity, measure the extent of personal popularity, build up support with a view to election on some future occasion, or 'show the flag' on behalf of some sub-group within the PLP. Candidates for the Parliamentary Committee are nominated as individuals, not as group representatives, but to some extent group loyalties affect the voting. With up to twelve votes at his disposal, the MP can afford to consider ideological, regional, or other group loyalties as the basis for at least some of his votes. Groups of personal friends will form around leading party figures, like the Bevan Group in the fifties, or Roy Jenkins' supporters in the 1970 and 1971 contests for the deputy leadership, while regional loyalties will affect the voting pattern to some extent. In the 1959–64 Parliament, the MPs from the north-east of England, for example, would tend to give one of their votes to Fred Willey, as a prominent member of their Area Group. The Scottish MPs supported Tom Fraser in the 1955–9 and 1959–64 Parliaments, and William Ross in 1970 and 1971, on the basis that it was desirable to have at least one Scottish MP on the Committee, and they sought to persuade the English MPs of the desirability of this also. The Welsh MPs have not needed to organise themselves to the same extent, however, as personalities like James Griffiths, Aneurin Bevan, and James Callaghan normally have been assured of places on the Committee because of the strength of their support among the PLP as a whole.

In the 1971 ballot the PLP was divided fairly clearly into pro-Common Market and anti-Common Market groups, as the Parliamentary Committee election came in the same month as the Parliamentary debate on the question of British entry into the EEC. Peter Shore, as a consistent anti-Marketeer, jumped from thirty-nine votes and thirty-first place in 1970, to 105 votes and eleventh place in 1971, almost certainly largely as a result of block support from anti-Marketeers, while the pro-Market forces rallied round their leaders in the ballot. In contrast, some prominent MPs very probably suffered in the ballot because they had vacillated on the issue, and thereby had lost the support of both camps.[1]

Of all the sub-groups within the PLP, however, 'the left' usually has been the most organised with regard to the Parliamentary Committee elections in the post-war period. The Bevanite group in the 1951–5 Parliament, the Victory for Socialism movement in the 1955–9 Parliament, the anti-Gaitskell faction after 1959, and the Tribune Group in the 1970 Parliament, all sought to organise themselves so as to achieve the maximum support for their group members in the ballot.[2] Indeed, in the 1951–5 Parliament in particular, the degree of organisation by the Bevan Group, and the extent of

[1] For press speculation about the 1971 ballot see *The Guardian* and *The Times*, 3 December 1971.

[2] The 'left wing' of the Labour Party, though generally easy to recognise, is difficult to define. The three groups or factions mentioned in the text represent possible definitions of 'the left' in the post-war period. See Haseler, *The Gaitskellites*, for an account of the conflict between 'left' and 'right' in the PLP in the 1951–64 period in opposition, and see Butler and

their unofficial whipping, was such that the PLP found it necessary to alter the procedures for the Parliamentary Committee ballot so as to counter the Bevanite tactic of 'plumping' only for their own handful of candidates.[1] In 1971 there was a Tribune 'ticket', although in spite of the abolition of the 'no plumping' rule it seems clear that Tribune Group MPs did not necessarily confine themselves to voting only for the names on the ticket. In the postwar period, however, 'the left' has been singularly unsuccessful in securing places on the Parliamentary Committee. Aneurin Bevan was normally assured of election because of his great prestige within the party, and after 1954 Harold Wilson invariably finished high in the ballot.

With these exceptions, however, members of left-wing groups did not command much support in the Parliamentary Committee elections, outside their own ideological faction. In the 1959–64 Parliament, the 'Gaitskellites' constituted a clear majority within the PLP, so that without having to resort to active campaigning or tactical planning, leading supporters of Gaitskell were normally assured of majority support in any clash with left-wing candidates in the Parliamentary Committee ballot. In interview, however, Labour MPs emphasised that there was no conscious attempt by the PLP to give to the leader the sort of Parliamentary Committee colleagues that he would wish: rather, the election of pro-Attlee and pro-Gaitskell Parliamentary Committees in the 1951–64 period, and the rejection in the main of left-wing candidates, was merely a natural reflection of the numerical strength of the pro-leadership group within the PLP in this period. Were it sufficiently cohesive and organised, the Trade Union Group of Labour MPs is large enough to dominate the ballot in any year, but it tends to divide itself into various sub-groups which are not able to deliver a solid block of votes for a particular candidate. In general, however, the trade-union-sponsored MPs, constituting the 'silent majority' of the PLP, tend to react against groups like the Bevanites in the 1950s, the anti-Gaitskellites in the 1960s, and the pro-Marketeers in the 1970s, who are seen

---

Pinto-Duschinsky, *The British General Election of 1970*, p. 4, for a comment on the Tribune group.

[1] See above, p. 114.

to be dividing the party against the official line of the PLP leadership.

The extent of planned group activity in connection with the Parliamentary Committee elections is easily exaggerated, however. There is little in the way of open canvassing or campaigning, either on a group or an individual basis, and in particular the candidates remain aloof from such activities. The electorate, of course, is small (between 250 and 300 in the 1951–1964 period, and under 300 in the 1970 Parliament) and other than in the first election of a new Parliament the leading candidates are well known personally to the majority of the members of the PLP. Campaigning is thus really unnecessary. The supporters of a particular candidate, in their day to day contacts in the House, might seek to make their colleagues aware that their man is seeking election, and is worthy of support, but formal lobbying does not take place. Indeed, in interview MPs suggested that formal and obvious campaigning by, or on behalf of, an excessively ebullient candidate would be much more likely to antagonise support than to gain it.

Some correlation might perhaps be expected between the Parliamentary Committee election placings and the results of the contests for the party leadership and deputy leadership. Certainly in the Committee elections of June 1955, Hugh Gaitskell came second and James Griffiths first, and during the course of the session, they were duly elected leader and deputy leader. Similarly, in the 1958 Committee elections Aneurin Bevan came top of the list, and in the next year he was elected deputy leader when Griffiths retired. In 1960, however, George Brown was elected deputy leader after being only eighth in the previous Committee elections, while in November 1962, some three months before being elected party leader, Harold Wilson came only third in the Committee placings behind James Callaghan and Sir Frank Soskice. Contests for the leadership and deputy leadership presumably involve much wider considerations than do contests for the Parliamentary Committee, so that the Committee elections do not necessarily form a reliable guide to the possible results of leadership contests.

Finally, the extent of the overlap of personnel between the Parliamentary Committee and the Labour Party's National

Executive Committee may be noted. The Labour Party NEC consists of twenty-eight members. The party treasurer, and the leader and (since 1953) the deputy leader of the PLP are ex-

TABLE 9

MPs Serving Concurrently on NEC and Parliamentary Committee 1951–64 and 1970

	1951	52	53	54	55	56	57	58	59	60	61	62	63	70	71
Attlee	+	+	+	+	+										
Griffiths	*	*	*	*	*	×	×	×							
Dr. Summerskill	*	*	*	*	*	*									
Morrison	*	×	×	×											
Dalton	*														
Bevan		*	*			*	*	*	×						
Gaitskell				*	*	+	+	+	+	+	+	+			
Wilson				*	*	*	*	*	*	*	*	*	+	+	+
Greenwood						*	*	*	*						
Callaghan							*	*	*	*	*		*	*	*
Brown										×	×	×	×		
Gunter										*	*	*	*		
Jenkins														×	×
Benn														*	*
Healey														*	*
Mrs Castle														*	
Mrs Williams														*	*
Total PC members on NEC	5	4	5	6	7	6	6	6	5	5	5	4	4	7	6
Total MPs on NEC	17	16	17	17	16	16	16	16	18	17	17	17	16	17	17

Source: Labour Party Annual Conference Reports for the years in question.

+ Served ex-officio as leader of the party.

× Served ex-officio as deputy leader of the party.

* Elected member of the Parliamentary Committee and the NEC.

Total membership of the NEC increased from twenty-seven to twenty-eight in 1953 and subsequent years by the inclusion of the deputy leader as an ex-officio member.

officio members. The other twenty-five members are elected at the annual conference in four 'constituencies' made up of the various classes of delegates to the conference. The four constituencies are the Trades Unions' Section (twelve members), the Socialist, Cooperative and Professional Organisations' Section (one member), the Constituency Organisations' Section (seven members), and the Women Members' Section (five members). MPs can be elected to the NEC through any of these sections, and theoretically it is possible for all members of the NEC to be MPs. Throughout the 1951–64 period, there were always sixteen to eighteen MPs among the twenty-eight members of the NEC, but of these MPs only a few were at the same time members of the Parliamentary Committee. Table 9 shows that in the 1951–64 period the overlap between the NEC and the Parliamentary Committee was never less than four but never more than seven. The Parliamentary Committee members never constituted a majority of the MPs on the NEC and never filled more than a quarter of the NEC places. The same general ratio applied in 1970 and 1971 also. Further, the overlap figures include the leader of the Parliamentary Party and, after 1953, the deputy leader, who are ex-officio members of the NEC, so that the number of MPs directly elected to both the NEC and the Parliamentary Committee was usually three or four, and never more than five, in any one year.

It is often suggested that an overlap of personnel between the NEC and the Parliamentary leadership has been a major reason for an absence of conflict between the Parliamentary and extra-Parliamentary sections of the Labour Party for much of its history. R. T. McKenzie, for example, discussing the party's history up to 1953, and referring specifically to the 1935–53 period, claims that '. . . this overlapping membership is of vital importance in accounting for the lack of friction during much of the period between the PLP and the NEC.'[1] In the 1951–64 period, however, even if it is agreed that on the whole there *was* an absence of friction between the NEC and the Parliamentary leadership, it was certainly not overlapping membership between the NEC and the Parliamentary Committee that was responsible for this. The Parliamentary Committee and the NEC are elected by different bodies, and the electorate in each case (the PLP on the one hand and the delegates to the Party Conference on the other), clearly apply different criteria in determining whom to select. The most

[1] McKenzie, *British Political Parties*, p. 416.

obvious result is the absence of left-wing figures from the Parliamentary Committee, in contrast to their not inconsiderable representation on the NEC in the 1951–64 period. Ian Mikardo, Barbara Castle, Richard Crossman, Tom Driberg, and Anthony Greenwood were elected to the NEC, through the Constituency Organisers' Section, throughout most of the 1951–64 period, and left-wing 'anti-leadership' figures commanded almost a monopoly of the seven Constituency Parties Section places on the NEC from 1953 onwards. Thus the composition of the NEC reflected the divisions of the PLP into left- and right-wing factions, while the Parliamentary Committee was almost exclusively a right-wing or pro-leadership-dominated body throughout the 1951–64 period.

Richard Crossman, as one who regularly failed to secure election to the Parliamentary Committee in the 1951–64 period, has argued that the PLP should abandon the practice of electing the Parliamentary Committee on the grounds that a Committee appointed by the party leader could be made more representative of the various groups within the PLP.[1] James Callaghan has also emphasised the extent to which the Parliamentary Committee was weakened in the nineteen-fifties because it was not representative of all the elements within the party.[2] Certainly, a secret ballot of three hundred MPs is likely to be a less effective means of securing a Committee that caters for minorities than is a process of selection by the leader, although this will depend on how far the leader feels he ought to go in accommodating the party's minority groups. As was noted earlier,[3] the principle of an elected Parliamentary Committee was established in the 1920s, when many Labour MPs were suspicious of the principles of 'Cabinet Government' and were anxious to emphasise a contrast between the practices of the democratic Labour Party and those of the more autocratic older parties. Today there is less concern among Labour MPs about these issues. Nevertheless, in interview Labour MPs pointed out that whatever the merits and demerits of the present system, the PLP is unlikely to agree to abandon a 'democratic' practice which gives MPs such a direct

[1] McKenzie, *British Political Parties*, p. 604.
[2] *The Times*, 5 December 1970.
[3] See above, p. 54.

control over the composition of their executive body. The question of whether an elected Parliamentary Committee can be truly representative of minorities will also depend on how clearly drawn are the divisions within the party. The bitter intra-party strife of the 1951–64 period was not apparent in 1970, for example, and one of the leading Tribune Group figures, Michael Foot, was elected to the Committee in sixth place in the 1970 ballot and second place in 1971. Further, the existence since 1955 of Spokesmen selected by the leader, as well as the Parliamentary Committee members elected by the PLP, has meant that minorities can be accommodated in the team as a whole, if not in the Parliamentary Committee. This, however, raises the broad question of the relationship between the elected Parliamentary Committee and the team as a whole in the allocation of Opposition duties, and this will be examined in the next section.

The Committee and the Front-Bench Spokesmen

To what extent does the presence of an elected Shadow Cabinet represent a limitation on the power and authority of a Labour Leader of the Opposition? Clearly, it is a disadvantage for him that the Shadow Cabinet with which he confers each week is a body that has been selected for him and not by him. He is denied the valuable patronage power of selecting the Opposition's 'committee of management', and it is possible for him to be faced with Committee colleagues who are hostile to him, and whom he is unable to dismiss from the Committee. The fact that the PLP chooses the Shadow Cabinet might reduce the tendency of MPs to quarrel with Shadow Cabinet proposals, but it certainly will not remove this tendency completely, and it is small compensation for the leader's loss of patronage power. The question is also raised of whether the existence of the elected Parliamentary Committee represents a limitation on a Labour leader's freedom to allocate the duties of Opposition. The factors that a leader has to consider when forming his team are numerous and complex, and the whole selection process is examined in detail in the next chapter. Under consideration here is only the one question of the extent to which the leader has to pay heed to the composition of the

Parliamentary Committee when he is allocating his duties, and the extent to which this represents a limit on his power as compared with a Prime Minister or a Conservative Leader of the Opposition.

Certainly, there now seems to be a 'convention of Labour Opposition', widely accepted by those Labour MPs who were interviewed, that those elected to the Parliamentary Committee will be allocated to some shadow duty. Thus Ray Gunter received his first post as a Spokesman (for Power) when he was elected to the Committee in 1960, while Peter Shore's election in 1971 was followed by his appointment as Spokesman for European Affairs (although, of course, he had held Cabinet office in the Wilson Government). To this extent, therefore, some of the members of the leader's team of Spokesmen are chosen for him, in a way that is not the case for the Conservatives in opposition. It may be, of course, that those who are elected to the Committee will be the most able members of the PLP, or those whom the leader would wish to appoint as Spokesmen. It was noted in the previous section, for example, that in the 1951–64 period the Parliamentary Committee tended to be composed of pro-leadership candidates, and in July 1970, as in October 1951, most of those elected to the Parliamentary Committee had been members of the Cabinet at the dissolution. As a period in opposition progresses, however, and an attempt is made to recruit new blood for the front-bench team, there is less likelihood that those elected to the Committee will necessarily be regarded by the party leader as desirable members of the team. Thus it is almost inevitable that at times the leader will be dissatisfied with the composition of the Committee. The bigger the team that the leader decides to appoint, of course, the easier it will be for him to accommodate the Parliamentary Committee members and still have plenty of places available for others. In 1970 there were sixty-six members of the team,[1] while in the 1955–64 period there were always forty to fifty members. With a team as big as that of

[1] That is, sixty Spokesmen in the Commons, plus the leader, chief whip, chairman of the PLP, and the three peers on the Parliamentary Committee, who do not have specific duties as Spokesmen in the House of Commons team. The three peers on the Committee are members of the House of Lords team (see Appendix A).

1970, the Parliamentary Committee members represent only a quarter or fifth of all the Spokesmen, so that the leader is still left with a considerable number of appointments for non-Committee members. The question remains, however, of whether Parliamentary Committee members are necessarily given the most important duties in the team. To what extent, then, did Attlee, Gaitskell, and Wilson appoint the Parliamentary Committee members to senior responsibilities?

In 1970 and 1971 the members of the Parliamentary Committee were all allocated to senior duties.[1] Thus even though Michael Foot had not been a member of the Wilson Government (although he had been offered Ministerial posts) he was made senior Spokesman for Power in July 1970. In the 1955–64 period, however, membership of the Parliamentary Committee did not always lead to the allocation of a senior front-bench responsibility. Philip Noel-Baker was a member of the Committee throughout the 1955–9 Parliament, but from November 1956 onwards he was merely an assistant Spokesman on Foreign Affairs. Similarly Denis Healey remained assistant Spokesman on Foreign Affairs, first of all to Bevan and then to Gaitskell, when he was elected to the Parliamentary Committee in 1959, although in 1961 he did become the senior Spokesman for Commonwealth and Colonial Affairs. G. R. Mitchison, though a Spokesman and a member of the Committee throughout both Parliaments, was from 1959 to 1963 only an assistant Spokesman on Treasury and Trade matters. While recognising that even a secondary responsibility for Foreign Affairs and the Treasury carries considerable authority and prestige, the fact remains that on these occasions Gaitskell allocated only assistant duties to Parliamentary Committee members.

Even allowing for the fact that the majority of the front-bench responsibilities must go to people not serving on the Committee, it was sometimes the case that important 'Cabinet rank' responsibilities were given to people who were not members of the Committee, while at the same time Committee members were allocated to less important duties. The determination of what are the most important responsibilities must

---

[1] The structure of the Opposition team, with the distinctions between senior Spokesmen and assistant Spokesmen, was outlined above, pp. 74–6.

vary from time to time, and from one party leader to another, but there are some subjects which are universally regarded as being of prime importance and of Cabinet status. Into this category (at least in the 1955–64 period) would go Foreign Affairs, the Treasury, Defence, Labour, and Power, and all were covered by Parliamentary Committee members through-out the 1955–64 period, and again in 1970. At the same time, Housing and Local Government, Home Affairs, Education, Colonies, Trade, and Scottish Affairs would also generally be included in this category in the 1955–64 period, but they were all at times held by people who were not members of the Parliamentary Committee.[1] Attlee gave Kenneth Younger responsibility for Home Affairs in July 1955, even though he had not been elected to the Committee in June 1955. Responsi-bility for Colonial Affairs (after 1961 this included responsi-bility for Commonwealth Affairs) was allocated to Committee members for the greater part of the 1955–64 period, but in a reallocation of duties that Harold Wilson made when he became leader in February 1963, this responsibility went to Arthur Bottomley, who was not a Committee member, and he retained it in November 1963, even though he remained out-side the Parliamentary Committee. Similarly, the Housing and Local Government responsibility was allocated to Committee members for most of the period, but in 1959 Michael Stewart was given this duty even though he was not on the Committee. Responsibility for Scottish Affairs was allocated to a Committee member (Tom Fraser) between 1956 and 1961, but Arthur Woodburn, James Hoy, and William Ross also served as senior Scottish Spokesmen for short periods when they were not mem-bers of the Committee. Education and Trade were handled by Committee members from November 1959 and February 1963 respectively, but before these dates were dealt with by people not serving on the Committee. Douglas Jay had the Trade responsibility from July 1955 onwards, but it was only in February 1963 that he became a member of the Parlia-mentary Committee.

[1] Some of the departmental areas referred to here in connection with the 1955–64 period (Labour, Housing and Local Government, Colonies) have since been absorbed into the 'Super-Ministries' created in recent years.

These, then, are all instances of important posts that would normally be of Cabinet status being allocated to people who were not Parliamentary Committee members. From these and from other instances in the 1955–64 period it is clear that election to the Parliamentary Committee did not necessarily result in promotion to a more significant responsibility, nor did ejection from the Committee necessarily involve demotion to a less significant responsibility. Fred Lee was 'promoted' from Labour to Power when he joined the Committee in 1959, but Kenneth Younger in 1956, Denis Healey in 1959, Michael Stewart in 1960, and Douglas Jay in 1963 retained the same duties when they became members of the Committee. Similarly, Dr Edith Summerskill retained her responsibility for Health when she lost her place on the Committee in 1957 and again in 1959, and she did not ultimately relinquish her duties until shortly before her elevation to the House of Lords. George Brown also retained his responsibility for Defence when he lost his Committee place in 1958, though, as with Dr Summerskill in 1957, his absence from the Committee was only for a year. In 1971 Barbara Castle was moved from Employment and Productivity to Social Security after losing her place on the Parliamentary Committee, but this was a 'horizontal' move rather than a demotion. Also, there had been fairly wide speculation about such a move long before her defeat in the ballot, and indeed it was her involvement with party policy in the industrial relations field that was seen as one of the likely reasons for her loss of votes in the ballot.

As an extension of this principle it may be noted that the annual changes in position within the Committee election lists had little or no apparent effect upon the allocation of responsibilities. It was noted above that the serving members were generally re-elected to the Committee, with only thirty-four people being involved in filling the eighteen places in the 1955–64 period, and only one serving member being defeated in 1971. This consistency, however, does not necessarily apply to the gradations within the Committee rankings, and (as is shown in Tables 44 to 46 in Appendix D) there are frequent changes in position in the election lists from year to year. There is no indication, however, that a high position on the list led to allocation to an important responsibility, or that a low placing led to a less significant duty. In the 1951–64 and 1970–1 periods there were twenty-two instances of movements of five or more places in the ballot from one year to another. Of these, seventeen led to no change at all in the responsibility, while on two other occasions a counter-effect was produced, James Callaghan in 1961 falling from first to seventh place but being 'promoted' from Colonial to Treasury Affairs, and G. R. Mitchison, also in 1961, falling from third to eighth place, but gaining additional responsibilities for Science and Works to add to his responsibility for Treasury matters. On two other occasions (Harold Wilson's rise from ninth to first place in 1961, and Fred Lee's fall from fifth to twelfth place in 1960) a change of responsibility did take place, but neither Wilson's change from Treasury to Foreign Affairs, nor Lee's change from Power to Labour could be described as 'promotion' or 'demotion'. Only in the case of G. R. Mitchison's fall from third to tenth place in 1959, accompanied by a demotion from senior Housing Spokesman to assistant Treasury Spokesman, is there any link between the loss of a senior duty and a fall in the election placings, and even here there is no indication that the change in duties came as a result of the change in Committee placings.

Thus the fact that Labour's Shadow Cabinet is elected by the PLP represents only a minor limitation on one vital aspect of a Labour Leader of the Opposition's power—his function of selecting Spokesmen. Although he is obliged to give some shadow duty to each Committee member, the most important duties are not necessarily allocated to Committee members. On occasions in the 1955–64 period when the Committee included those to whom the leader did not wish to give senior responsibilities, or when there were excluded from the Committee those to whom the leader did wish to allocate senior duties, he continued to distribute senior or assistant duties as he chose, regardless of the Committee's composition. The consequence of this, however, is that Labour's Parliamentary Committee may well contain Spokesmen with duties that would not normally qualify them for membership of either a Ministerial Cabinet or a Conservative Shadow Cabinet. The contrast between Labour's Shadow Cabinet and these other two bodies is thereby further emphasised.

One compensation for the leader for the fact that he does not appoint the Parliamentary Committee is that he cannot be held directly responsible for its deficiencies. In any conflict between the Parliamentary Committee and the rest of the PLP the leader can always point to the fact that the Labour MPs elected the Committee, and thus should accept its decisions. This, however, represents only a fairly minor debating point for a Labour leader, and certainly does not compensate him fully for the fact that he is not free to appoint his own Committee.

The election process attracts some publicity to the Opposition, and the annual movements up and down the 'league table' are commented on by the news media, particularly in a year like 1971 when the contest could be analysed in terms of 'pro-Marketeers versus anti-Marketeers'.[1] In this way, however, divisions within the party can be highlighted, while it is doubtful whether the 'democratic' aspect of the exercise is regarded by the electorate as being of any particular merit. Nevertheless, Labour's practice has the merit (if merit it is) of directly involving Labour MPs in the formation of their front bench. When in opposition the members of the PLP are able to participate annually in the process of electing their executive committee, while the Conservatives have theirs imposed upon them by the leader. If the Conservative MPs are dissatisfied with any member of the Consultative Committee, they can try to persuade the party leader to drop him from the Committee, but the ultimate power of 'hiring and firing' remains with the leader. Labour MPs, on the other hand, are able to remove a member from the Parliamentary Committee simply by withdrawing their votes from him at the next ballot. Thus the annual ballot provides a test of popularity for individual MPs, and also serves as something of a guide to the extent of the PLP's satisfaction with the performance of the Committee as a whole over the previous year. The rejection of all the serving members, and the election of an entirely new Committee, clearly would indicate an extreme level of PLP discontent with their leader's performance, and the ballot has never produced a result quite as swingeing as this. The election of Labour's

[1] See the comments in most of the national newspapers on 3 December 1971.

Parliamentary Committee, however, is only one aspect of the formation of an Opposition front-bench team, and in the next chapter the whole selection process will be examined in some detail.

5

The Selection of Opposition Spokesmen

Just as the selection of Ministers is the prerogative of the Prime Minister, so in opposition the selection of Spokesmen is the prerogative of the Leader of the Opposition. Only on very rare occasions will appointments be discussed by the Shadow Cabinet, and this is one of the factors contributing to the power of the Leader of the Opposition in relation to his colleagues. At the first PLP meeting of the 1970 Parliament Harold Wilson was questioned in general terms about the appointments that he intended to make to the team of Spokesmen, and there was some discussion about the form that the team should take, but there were no serious attempts to place restrictions on Wilson's personal choice. Normally, however, a Leader of the Opposition will not make his appointments without seeking advice from some of his senior colleagues. Individual members of the Shadow Cabinet might approach the leader informally to press the claims of particular backbenchers, or to suggest a reallocation of duties among the existing Spokesmen, and the leader will often consult with the deputy leader and chief whip. In making his first appointments on becoming party leader in 1956, for example, Hugh Gaitskell discussed matters with James Griffiths, the new deputy leader,[1] while the chief whip will usually be particularly influential in the allocation of backbenchers to their first duty. During the 1964 election campaign Sir Alec Douglas-Home had been in close touch with the chief whip and the party chairman, and after

[1] Griffiths, *Pages From Memory*, p. 134.

the election he consulted them about the nature of the arrangements to be made for Opposition. Other prominent party leaders may press the claims of their former PPSs or other backbench friends. In the appointment of assistant Spokesmen, the leader also normally will consult with the senior Spokesman involved as a matter of courtesy, and in the interests of harmony. When one of the junior Scottish Spokesmen resigned in April 1972, his post was left vacant on the advice of the senior Scottish Spokesman, William Ross.[1] When a Spokesman moves to a new duty, the leader will often seek his advice about a successor. Thus in 1959 Gaitskell asked G. R. Strauss to move from Transport to Aviation, and at the same time sought Strauss's advice on the suitability of Anthony Wedgwood Benn as his successor at Transport. When a group of Spokesmen are selected to cover one subject area, the leader may name the team, but leave the detailed allocation of responsibilities to the senior Spokesman. Thus in 1970, Labour's junior Scottish Spokesmen were named by Harold Wilson, after consultations with William Ross as the senior Scottish Spokesman, and all the Scottish Spokesmen then met together and divided the various categories of Scottish affairs (agriculture, education, development, etc.) among themselves. Similarly, because the Scottish Conservatives enjoy a degree of independence within the overall organisation of the Conservative Party, the senior Scottish Spokesman (Michael Noble and then Gordon Campbell in the 1964–70 period) will have more influence over the selection of his assistants than is the case with most other Conservative Spokesmen.

The general principle remains, however, that appointments are made by the Leader of the Opposition, and all the Leaders of the Opposition since 1955 have insisted on this. The invitation to serve as a Spokesman is generally given by the leader in person, although some contacts may be made by telephone, and some junior appointments may be passed on by the chief whip. The general procedure is less formal than that of the appointment of a Minister of the Crown. An Opposition Spokesman has no seals of office, and an appointment merely involves a public recognition of the man and the post by the

---

[1] See *Glasgow Herald*, 13 April 1972.

Leader of the Opposition. Some Spokesmen, in interview, commented on the extreme casualness of the whole process. For the most part, however, the leader sees the MP personally, and in 1970 Harold Wilson discussed almost all of his appointments at some length with the people involved. In selecting his Spokesmen, the Leader of the Opposition probably exercises a more strictly personal choice than does the Prime Minister in forming his Ministerial team. The Opposition team throughout the 1955–70 period was smaller than the Ministerial team, and thus could be more readily drawn from the ranks of MPs with whom the leader was familiar. Also, the Leader of the Opposition spends more time in the Commons than does the Prime Minister, so that he has a better chance of measuring the potential of his backbenchers. The extent of a leader's awareness of his backbenchers will vary from one leader to another, however. As a former chief whip, Edward Heath was particularly well informed about the personnel of the 1922 Committee, whereas in 1964 Sir Alec Douglas-Home's awareness of the less senior Conservative MPs was limited, as he had only recently joined the Commons from the Lords.

Nominally, the Leader of the Opposition has complete freedom of choice from among those MPs whom he regards as being sufficiently able, but in reality there are various practical factors that he has to consider. Opposition duties are less attractive than posts in government, and an MP who would happily accept any Ministerial job might be more discriminating about the Opposition duty he will take on. This will be particularly the case with the senior party figures, and the leader may be involved in more protracted negotiations in appointing Spokesmen than would be the case if he were a Prime Minister making Ministerial appointments. Thus in interview a number of MPs emphasised the contrast between the imperious manner in which a Prime Minister informed them that a specific Ministerial office was available, and the much less condescending way in which a Leader of the Opposition offered them a choice of a number of posts as Spokesman. Some fairly junior Spokesmen claimed to have turned down a particular post, and bargained for another, in a way that would not have been remotely possible in the case of a Ministerial appointment. One MP claimed to have told the leader that he was prepared to accept any one of three posts, and then left the leader to inform him later as to which one he wanted him to take on. Of course, some 'anti-establishment' MPs who would not wish to become part of a Ministerial machine might be more ready to take on a post in opposition. Michael Foot and Eric Heffer, for example, turned down offers of Ministerial posts in the 1964–70 period, but took on jobs as Spokesmen when Labour went into opposition in 1970. This, however, is not typical of the order of priorities of most MPs.

A Spokesman's duties involve a considerable amount of work and attendance in the House, for which no salary is paid. Some MPs may prefer to devote their time in opposition to activities outside Parliament, like Roy Jenkins and Anthony Crosland in the 1951–64 period.[1] The leader is likely to select as Spokesmen only those who are prepared to attend the House regularly. This does not mean that 'part-time' MPs are automatically excluded, but it does mean that MPs have to be prepared to work long hours if they wish to combine a shadow duty with a major outside interest. As with Ministerial appointments, the claims of some senior figures cannot be ignored, and some are in a position virtually to select their own duties. It is recognised that when a Prime Minister is forming his Government he has to ensure that the various elements within the party are represented. The British parties are coalitions of various 'groups, factions, and tendencies' and in the interests of party unity every Prime Minister has to balance the social, regional and ideological groups of the party. Thus after Harold Wilson had defeated George Brown in the ballot for the Labour Party leadership in 1963, he brought into the team Charles Pannell, who had served as Brown's campaign manager. Similarly, when Edward Heath became Conservative leader in 1965, he appointed a large number of Spokesmen, partly in order that he could heal any divisions in the party by including in the team MPs who had supported Enoch Powell and Reginald Maudling in the leadership contest. Having made this gesture of reconciliation, Heath was able to return to a small team of Spokesmen after the 1966 election, and John Biffen, Nicholas Ridley, and John Hay, who had all received

[1] See below, p. 186.

posts in 1965 after backing Powell's leadership bid, were then dropped from the team.[1]

In general, MPs attach rather less importance to the composition of an Opposition team than to that of a Ministerial team. At the same time, a Leader of the Opposition is often in an insecure position within his party, so that he still has to seek to placate the various groups and individuals upon whose support he depends. Thus Edward Heath included in his team in the 1965–70 period members of the 'right wing' Monday Club (such as Ronald Bell, John Peyton, Geoffrey Rippon), as well as members of more moderate bodies like PEST (Terence Higgins and Peter Emery) and the Bow Group (Paul Channon, Nigel Fisher, Maurice Macmillan). Similarly, in 1970 Harold Wilson's team included members of the Tribune Group such as Eric Heffer and Michael Foot, Cooperative MPs such as J. D. Mabon and Alfred Morris, and trade-union-sponsored MPs such as Roy Mason (NUM), John Silkin (TGWU), Ted Bishop (DATA), Richard Marsh (NUPE). Although it can never be clear whether someone is included on the grounds of ability, or because he 'represents' a group, it is certain that the Leader of the Opposition, like the Prime Minister, has to make his team fairly representative of the various elements within the party. The leader, therefore, may have to accept rather unwillingly some of his colleagues as Spokesmen. Because of Harold Wilson's standing in the party, for example, Hugh Gaitskell was obliged to include him in his team throughout his time as leader, even though their personal relations were cool. Similarly, Edward Heath tolerated Enoch Powell's maverick views on various aspects of party policy for some time before he eventually dropped him from the Shadow Cabinet in 1968.

Within these practical limitations, what factors does the leader consider in forming his team? What considerations determine the size and structure of the team, and does the Leader of the Opposition seek to match the government man for man? In recruiting Spokesmen what considerations, other than 'mere merit', does the leader take into account? To what extent are Spokesmen recruited on the basis of their Ministerial potential

[1] See Roth, *Enoch Powell*, pp. 331–2. Powell himself was 'promoted' by Heath from Transport to Defence as part of the process of reconciliation after the leadership contest.

as opposed to their skill as critics? To what extent are ex-Ministers asked to cover their old departments, and how far are backbenchers recruited into the team on account of their specific expertise in a particular subject? Are changes in the Opposition team made as frequently as they are in a Ministerial team, and what considerations cause a reallocation of duties? These questions will be examined in the subsequent sections of this chapter.

The Size of the Front-Bench Team

The first consideration for the Leader of the Opposition when he is making his appointments is how large a team he wishes to create. With the extension of the activities of the state in this century, Governments have tended to increase in size, although Edward Heath sought to halt this trend with a comparatively small Ministerial team in 1970.[1] Successive Prime Ministers have been faced with the problem of making the Ministerial team big enough to do the Government's work adequately, but small enough to operate as a reasonably cohesive unit. This is less of a problem in the case of the Opposition team. Fewer appointments need be made in opposition, and there are certainly no statutory requirements such as those which oblige a Prime Minister to make some appointments, but prevent him from exceeding a certain number.[2] Assuming that the Leader of the Opposition intends to continue with the post-1955 practice of naming official Spokesmen, there are perhaps two extreme courses that he could follow. At the one extreme, the leader could appoint a large team with as many Spokesmen as there are members of the Government in the Commons, so that each Minister and junior Minister would have a specific 'shadow'. In 1970 Harold Wilson made sixty-three appointments,[3] two *more* than the number of Ministers then serving in

[1] See F. M. G. Willson and D. N. Chester, *The Organisation of British Central Government*, London 1957; F. M. G. Willson ,'The Organisation of British Central Government 1955–61' *and* '1962–4', *Public Administration*, 1962, pp. 159–206 *and* 1966, pp. 73–101.

[2] Ministers of the Crown Act 1964 and Ministerial and Other Salaries Act 1972.

[3] This figure of sixty-three includes the Leader of the Opposition and the chief whip, but excludes the assistant whips. It also excludes the three

the Commons. The larger the team, the greater the leader's patronage power, but the greater the number of appointments he makes, the greater will be the number of MPs with hopes and expectations of office should the party come to power. Also, while the creation of a large team spreads the work load, it produces a somewhat unwieldy structure. At the other extreme, the leader could make a minimum number of appointments, with perhaps only one Spokesman for each department, or for each full Minister in the Government. This would involve about twenty appointments, so that with the chief whip and the party officers, the team would consist of twenty to twenty-five senior party figures. It would be compact, and could be easily coordinated. In the case of the Conservatives the appointments could even be contained within the framework of an expanded Consultative Committee, so that all members of the team could meet together on a regular basis. Such a small team, of course, would reduce the extent of the leader's patronage power, while the work load on each Spokesman would be considerable. The Spokesmen, however, could enlist the support of backbenchers from time to time to assist them with particular Bills or particular debates.

Since 1955 the size of the Opposition front-bench team has fluctuated considerably, but for most of the period Leaders of the Opposition have avoided both of these extremes. Generally, a senior Spokesman has been named to cover each department, together with one or two assistant Spokesmen for most departments, although apart from Wilson's 1970 team there have always been fewer Spokesmen than there were Ministers in the Commons.[1] As Figure H shows, the teams named by Attlee, Gaitskell, and Wilson in the 1955–64 period ranged only from forty to fifty members. In the 1964–70 period of Conservative Opposition there were rather greater fluctuations, and Heath experimented with a large team in the 1965–6 session, and then with a very small team after the 1966 election. Heath's 1965–6 team contained over sixty members, grouped around the various policy areas. The 'Treasury, Economic

---

peers who serve on the Parliamentary Committee and all the other Spokesmen in the Lords.

[1] For the definition of what constitutes 'the team' here and elsewhere see above, p. 76.

Affairs, and Trade Group', for example, consisted of Iain Macleod and Anthony Barber from the Consultative Committee, plus four other assistant Spokesmen. The 'Overseas Group', led by Sir Alec Douglas-Home, contained nine members, and the 'Defence Group' had five. Altogether the team consisted of the twenty-two members of the Consultative Committee, eight other senior Spokesmen outside the Committee,

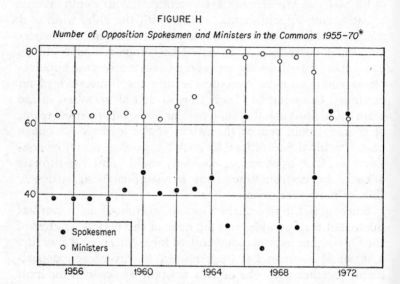

FIGURE H

Number of Opposition Spokesmen and Ministers in the Commons 1955–70*

* Excludes all Peers, assistant whips and Members of Her Majesty's Household

and thirty-four assistant Spokesmen (plus nine assistant whips). In contrast, the team that Heath formed in April 1966 consisted of only eighteen members of the Consultative Committee, plus ten other Spokesmen outside the Committee. By the end of the 1966–70 Parliament, however, Heath had reverted to a team that was much the same size as the 1955–64 Labour teams.

When Labour went into opposition in June 1970, Wilson at first named only twenty senior Spokesmen, but in December 1970, once the final shape of the Heath Government was known, he appointed a further number of assistant Spokesmen, raising the overall size of the team to sixty-six (sixty-three of them in the Commons). Like Heath's 1965–6 team, Wilson's Spokesmen were grouped around broad policy areas. Anthony Crosland, for example, headed a seven-man 'Environment Group', while Anthony Wedgwood Benn had five assistants in the 'Trade and Industry Group', and Denis Healey had four assistants to cover Foreign Affairs. Wilson's team more than matched the Government man for man, as in the 1970–1 session only sixty-two of Heath's Ministers were drawn from the Commons. The number of Spokesmen for Scottish Affairs, for example, exceeded the number of Scottish Ministers in the Heath Government, and even exceeded the number of Scottish Ministers there had been in the Labour Government at the dissolution. Consequently there was some feeling among Labour MPs that the team was too big, and that the leader was stretching his powers of patronage to their limit. Perhaps most logically a leader should appoint only a small team at the beginning of a Parliament, when he may be unaware of the capabilities of new MPs, and when the party's strategy for the Parliament may not be clear. He can then increase the size of the team as the Parliament progresses, ending up with a full Shadow Government as the election draws near. This was the conscious pattern that Edward Heath followed in the 1966–70 Parliament, so that by the fourth session of the Parliament he had evolved what amounted to a 'Government in exile' with which to face the electorate. The size of the team that Harold Wilson appointed on first going into opposition, however, would seem to preclude a similar pattern from emerging in the 1970 Parliament.

In comparing the size of Opposition teams in this way, of course, it must be remembered that the distinction between Opposition backbenchers and the front-bench team is much less clear cut than is that between Government backbenchers and Ministers. In the 1966–7 session, for example, when Heath experimented with a very small team of official Spokesmen, some of the former Scottish Spokesmen, and some future Spokesmen, performed front-bench duties without being digni- fied with the title of 'official' Spokesmen. Also in this session the vice-chairmen of the Conservative backbench subject groups acted as 'unofficial assistants' to the official Spokesmen in debates.[1] The scheme was abandoned, however, when the right-wing elements in the party captured some of the vice-chairmanships, thereby producing open disharmony between 'moderate' Spokesmen and 'right-wing' assistants (as when Sir Edward Boyle, the senior Education Spokesman, became teamed with Ronald Bell). Also, Spokesmen will often organise a team of backbenchers to assist them with the task of fighting a particular Bill: the Treasury Spokesman, for example, will invariably organise groups of backbenchers to concentrate on certain aspects of the annual Finance Bill.[2] More generally, backbenchers who are recognised as experts in a particular area will often be invited to come temporarily on to the front bench to open or close a particular debate for the Opposition. Michael Heseltine was 'blooded' in this way before being appointed as a Transport Spokesman in 1969, while in the 1959-64 Parliament George Darling often spoke for the Opposition on consumer affairs before eventually becoming a Spokesman in 1961. Such 'temporary assistant Spokesmen' will speak from the front bench on this one occasion and then return to the back benches. In the summer of 1970, before Harold Wilson had picked a full team of assistant Spokesmen, backbenchers were brought forward onto the front bench in order to assist the small group of senior Spokesmen who had then been appointed. In this way, Robert Hughes did much of the Opposition's work on the Hospitals (Scotland) Bill.

Such practices as these serve to involve a large number of backbenchers in front-bench activities without making them full members of the official team. It allows the work load to be shared, and it makes full use of the expertise of backbenchers. It also serves to break down the barriers that often exist between the front and back benches, and it enables the Leader of the Opposition to test the front-bench potential of anyone he may be considering for appointment as an official Spokesman. The process of 'flitting' between the front and back benches has been criticised, however, and Herbert Morrison argued that 'The Front Bench should be a recognisable Front Bench—not a haven of refuge or elevation . . .'[3] While it gives

---

[1] See below, pp. 301–7 for details of these groups and the Spokesmen's relations with them.   [2] See p. 255 for more comments on this practice.

[3] Morrison, *Government and Parliament*, p. 351.

expertise to a variety of MPs, it can produce inconsistencies and weaken confidence in the team. Also, a major difficulty in relying on backbench assistance is that in order to keep permanently up to date with the details of developments in Government policy, it is necessary to have a fixed responsibility for that subject area. Given enough time, of course, a backbencher could prepare himself to assist a Spokesman in a particular debate, but an Opposition attack often has to be prepared in a hurry, and this requires expert background knowledge. If only one Spokesman is assigned to cover a subject on a permanent basis, that Spokesman is likely to find himself fighting a lone battle from the front bench in an emergency debate because there are no backbenchers sufficiently well briefed to give him informed support.

The larger the official Opposition team, the fewer opportunities there will be for backbenchers to be used in this way. Thus with Heath's unusually small team in the 1966–7 session there were considerable opportunities for backbenchers to be used as temporary Spokesmen, while with the very large team formed by Wilson in 1970, the opportunities were less, as there were enough official Spokesmen to do the work. On the whole, however, Leaders of the Opposition since 1955 have avoided these two extremes and have sought to make some use of ad hoc backbench assistance, while at the same time maintaining a fairly large core of some forty or fifty official Spokesmen.

Horses for Courses

Having decided upon the size of the team that he wishes to form, what considerations determine the Leader of the Opposition's choice of personnel? Nominally he has a choice between two broad principles. On the one hand he can attempt to create a team which will perform well both in opposition and in the hoped-for future period in office. Alternatively, he can think in terms of two separate teams, one to be chosen on the basis of their skills as Parliamentary critics to serve in the current period in opposition, and an entirely different team to be selected only when the party comes to office, and on the basis of their Ministerial potential. In many ways the distinction between these alternatives is similar to that which exists between the tactics of American football and those of modern soccer. In soccer a team consists of the same eleven players throughout a match, with perhaps one or two substitutes: the team uses all eleven players in defence, and then mounts an attack with the same players (even down to the 1984 concept of 'the overlapping goalkeeper'). In American football, in contrast, a team fields its 'offence', skilled in the arts of passing and running, whenever it is on the attack, but when it is forced onto the defensive, the 'offence' leave the field to be replaced by the 'defence', who are skilled tacklers and blockers.

In terms of the Parliamentary and Ministerial 'game', many of the abilities required by a Minister are the same as those required by a Spokesman (as is discussed below),[1] but the skills are certainly not identical and are not necessarily found in the same person. In general, a middle-of-the-road 'consensus politician' will find it easier to adapt to office than to opposition, while for party militants, opposition will be much less inhibiting than will office. Again, an ex-Minister who has been conditioned by long years in office may be unable to acquire the degree of irresponsibility that is essential for effective opposition. The comment by A. J. Balfour, which was quoted in Chapter 1,[2] regarding the inversion of the roles of the Government and the Opposition, was an implied criticism of a system which assumes that (to quote Balfour further) ' . . . anyone who is competent to debate must be competent to administer, and anyone who is competent to administer must debate'.[3] Balfour was writing against the background of his experiences in the 1880–5 Parliament when Gladstone's Liberal Government met only ineffective opposition from the Unionist leaders. Sir Stafford Northcote, Richard Cross, and W. H. Smith had been very competent heads of departments in Disraeli's 1874–80 Government, but they were ineffective in opposition. They were so weak, in fact, that the 'Fourth Party' emerged among the ranks of the Unionist MPs in this Parliament, with Lord Randolph Churchill and A. J. Balfour seeking to put life into the Opposition.[4] Almost one hundred years later, Balfour's

---

[1] See below, p. 380.   [2] See above, p. 4.
[3] Balfour, *Chapters of Autobiography*, p. 141.
[4] For details see H. Gorst, *The Fourth Party*, London 1906; W. S. Churchill, *Lord Randolph Churchill*, London 1906 (2 vols).

comments remain valid, and are reflected in a similar plea from
a backbench Labour MP, Norman Atkinson, who, when
Labour returned to Opposition in 1970, called for

> bold and effective Parliamentary argument uninhibited by
> embarrassed ex-Ministers not willing to commit themselves
> in case they are again called upon to serve in the next Labour
> Government.[1]

It is equally the case, of course, that someone who has acquired
a reputation in opposition as a skilled Parliamentarian may be
unable to adapt to the role of being at the head of a department of state: vitriolic debaters of the James Maxton mould
will be excellent in opposition, but will be less at home with
the strictures imposed by a departmental responsibility. Thus,
while Lord Randolph Churchill (to keep the examples historical) was extremely successful in his 'Fourth Party' role in
opposition to the Gladstone Government in the 1880–5 Parliament, he was later considerably less successful in office.

The Leader of the Opposition can recognise this situation and
can apply the principle of American football when selecting
his team. Theoretically (and to mix the sporting parallels), he
can select 'horses for courses', surrounding himself with an
'offence' of savage critics to serve as Spokesmen in opposition,
but choosing an entirely different 'defence' of skilled adminis-
trators to serve as Ministers when the party comes to power.
For the most part, Leaders of the Opposition do not do this,
but adopt the principle of the soccer team, and select 'utility
players' who can serve competently both in opposition and in
office. Many MPs will accept a post in an Opposition team
only because they see it as a prelude to a Ministerial appointment. Thus a leader who was seen to be creating a team purely
to serve in opposition would have difficulty in finding MPs to
undertake responsibilities on those terms. More than this, however, as an alternative Prime Minister at the head of an office-
seeking Opposition, the Leader of the Opposition has to have a
team that is, and can be *seen* to be, made up of potential
Ministers. To a considerable extent his chances of gaining
office are dependent upon his ability to persuade the electorate
that he and his party are fit to govern, and to this end he has

[1] *Tribune*, 3 September 1970.

to put on show, and demonstrate, the abilities of a team of potential Ministers.

Many MPs, of course, will be equally competent in office and in opposition, and some who seem to be particularly at home in one role may do surprisingly well when they are called upon to fill the other role. Aneurin Bevan, for example, made his initial reputation as a debater and critic while a backbench MP in the 1935–45 Parliament, and many felt that although he was outstanding in opposition he lacked the skills necessary to be a successful Minister. In fact, he subsequently had an outstanding Ministerial career in the 1945–51 Attlee Government. The ideal Opposition Spokesman is perhaps the person who does possess all the qualities required by a Minister, together with those necessary to be an effective critic. This ideal figure, however, will not always be available, and undoubtedly there will be occasions when the Leader of the Opposition will be faced with the sort of direct choice described at the beginning of this section. Thus he has to be clear about his priorities, and in the absence of a sufficient number of good utility players he has to decide whether he is *primarily* concerned with selecting a team of prospective Ministers, or whether he is selecting Spokesmen on the basis of their skills as Parliamentary critics, regardless of their Ministerial potential (or lack of it).

A Shadow of the Past or a Cabinet of the Future?

To what extent, then, are Spokesmen recruited on account of their Ministerial potential? With very few exceptions the MPs interviewed for this study subscribed to the view that in selecting Opposition teams the prime concern of successive Labour and Conservative Leaders of the Opposition since 1955 has been to choose potential Ministers. In choosing his team in 1970 a major factor for Harold Wilson was the selection of Spokesmen who would not be too old for Ministerial office by the time of the next general election in 1974 or 1975. Leading Labour and Conservative Shadow Cabinet figures who had been close to Attlee, Gaitskell, and Heath suggested that, for them also, the prime concern had been the selection of potential Ministers, and only in very exceptional circumstances would they have given a post to someone they felt might do well in opposition, but was not Ministerial potential. The whole question of the transfer from opposition to office is looked at in Chapter 11 (including an examination of the precise extent to which Spokesmen did receive posts in the Labour Government in 1964 and the Conservative Government in 1970). In this section, however, the reverse process is being examined: that is, the question of the role played by ex-Ministers in the Opposition team, together with the extent of the recruitment of backbenchers into the team.

When a party first goes into opposition after losing a general election, there will probably be more former Ministers than there are Opposition posts to fill (unless, as in 1970, the leader chooses to appoint a very large team). Some former Ministers are likely to find themselves without duties in opposition, and there are unlikely to be many openings for backbenchers. There is the danger, however, that an Opposition front bench can all too easily seem to be (in Sir Winston Churchill's graphic phrase) ' . . . cumbered with the ancient and dreary wreckage of the late Administration'.[1] Churchill was referring to the Unionist front bench in the 1880–5 Parliament, but his own Shadow Cabinet in the 1945–51 period was composed almost exclusively of wartime Ministerial colleagues, many of them of advanced years. Normally, however, as a Parliament progresses some former Ministers will be dropped, thereby creating more opportunities for backbenchers to be brought into the team in preparation for the return to power. The Leader of the Opposition will probably be eager to infuse some new blood into the party hierarchy, especially if it seems, as perhaps in 1951 and 1964, that the party lost the election because the electorate regarded it as being led by old, tired, and jaded men. At the beginning of a new Parliament the leader will be conscious that a return to office is likely to be at least four years away, and that he has thus to look for Ministerial potential among younger members of the party. Also, from the leader's point of view a youthful team might be more responsive to his wishes than would older and longer-established colleagues, while a 'youth policy' also pushes into the background former Ministers who might otherwise be inclined to challenge the leader's position.

[1] Churchill, *Lord Randolph Churchill*, I, p. 121.

Thus in interview, MPs (both young and old) emphasised that after the appointments that the leader is obliged to make for one reason or another, he then gives a major priority to the recruitment of youthful Spokesmen. At the same time, of course, a lot of youthful appointments may produce a front-bench team that is largely unknown to the public, while well-known party figures languish in the background. The lack of well-known leaders can reduce the credibility of the Opposition as an alternative Government, and to some extent this happened in the 1966–70 Parliament, when a number of prominent Conservative former Ministers, such as Selwyn Lloyd, Derek Walker-Smith, Duncan Sandys, John Boyd-Carpenter and Ernest Marples, were without shadow duties. In interview a number of Conservative MPs maintained that too many experienced figures had been sacrificed in the desire to 'make way for youth' in the 1964–70 period. When it does face the electorate, the Opposition clearly has to avoid appearing either as 'yesterday's men', or as 'callow youths' lacking adequate experience of high office. A happy balance between youth and experience is ideal for an Opposition front-bench team, but this can be a very difficult balance to achieve. Of course, some former Ministers may have been defeated at the polls, while others may not have sought re-election. Some of those who do return to the Commons may prefer not to accept posts as Spokesmen. This may be because they seek a rest from official duties and prefer to pursue part-time activities outside the House, or because they are not attracted by the unpaid job of Spokesman, or perhaps because they are conscious of their age and feel that they should make way for younger men. Not all former Ministers, however, will be willing to 'make way for youth'. Although the Leader of the Opposition chooses the team, and theoretically can appoint and dismiss Spokesmen as he wishes, some senior figures can be difficult to remove. The leader's own position may be precarious, either as an election-losing former Prime Minister, or as a new and as yet insecure party leader, and he may be reluctant to risk antagonising old but influential members of his party. The number of newcomers that the leader wishes to introduce will also depend upon the ages of his former Ministers, the number of years they have spent in office, and the length of time the party has been in opposition. When Labour left office in 1951, many of the leading figures of the party had been in office since 1940, serving in the wartime Coalition Government, as well as in the post-war Attlee Government. Similarly, when the Conservatives went into opposition in 1964, the party had been in office for thirteen years, and many of the party leaders had held posts for most or all of the period. In both cases, however, it took two election defeats (1951 and 1955 for Labour, and 1964 and 1966 for the Conservatives) before many of the older figures left the team.

TABLE 10

Average Ages of the Front-Bench Teams 1951–70

	Shadow Cabinet	Team as a Whole
Labour 1951–64 and 1970		
Nov. 1951	56½	—
June 1955	56	53¾
Nov. 1959	54	52½
Oct. 1964	59¼	57¾
Dec. 1970	57	48
Conservatives 1964–70		
Oct. 1964	52½	50
Apr. 1966	48¼	47¼
June 1970	51¾	47¾

Source: Biographical information from Dod's *Parliamentary Companion* and The Times' *House of Commons*.

Table 10 indicates the average age of the members of the Opposition team at various points in the 1951–70 period. Edward Heath was successful in establishing and maintaining a fairly youthful team. Peter Walker was appointed to the Consultative Committee when he was only thirty-four, while Paul Channon, Charles Morrison, and Michael Heseltine became Spokesmen when they were respectively thirty-two, thirty-five and thirty-six. In October 1969 Heath appointed thirteen new Spokesmen. All but one were under fifty, and three were in their thirties. Thus even at the end of the 1966–70 Parliament, the average age of the Consultative Committee was just fifty-two, and of the team as a whole was forty-eight. In contrast, the average age of Labour's team in the 1951–64 period was usually in the high fifties, and in October 1964 it was particularly high. In December 1970 the average age of the Parliamentary Committee was much the same as in the 1951–64 period, but the team as a whole was much younger, with the average age being as low as that of Heath's team in the 1966–70 Parliament. Thus Heath in the 1966–70 Parliament, and Wilson in 1970, went further than did the Labour Leaders of the Opposition in the 1951–64 period in recruiting a youthful team. In this, however, a Labour Leader of the Opposition normally is limited by the generally older average age of the PLP than of the Conservative Party in Parliament,[1] which makes the youthful nature of Wilson's 1970 team all the more surprising.

A problem for a Leader of the Opposition is that the amount of front-bench potential among his young backbenchers in opposition may not be great. As is shown in Table 11, a party normally acquires its largest number of new MPs when it wins a general election, and thus goes into office. In Britain, general elections tend to be won and lost through the turnover of a comparatively small number of constituencies: most MPs represent safe seats which they retain even though the party may suffer an overall defeat through the loss of some marginal seats. What is more, for most MPs service in Parliament is regarded as a more or less permanent occupation, rather than merely a four- or five-year break from their main occupation, which is the case with Parliamentary service in some countries.[2] Most MPs wish to remain in Parliament, and for the most part their constituency associations oblige them by retaining them as their candidates at successive elections. The only ways in which a party acquires a large number of new MPs when it remains in opposition, are when it gains some seats without winning the election, as did the Conservatives in 1950, or when a large number of older MPs have vacated safe seats

[1] See The Nuffield Election Studies for comparative figures.
[2] For the situation in Canada, for example, see Thomas W. Casstevens and William A. Denham III, 'Turnover and Tenure in the Canadian House of Commons 1867–1968', *Canadian Journal of Political Science* 1970, pp. 655–61.

in favour of newcomers, as with Labour in 1970, when many of the MPs elected in 1945 had reached retirement age. The Opposition party can also expect to recruit some new MPs through by-elections, in which Governments invariably fare badly. Other than this, however, the Parliamentary party is unlikely to secure a large number of new recruits during a period in opposition. The Leader of the Opposition, therefore, will have to seek new faces for his front-bench team mainly from among the ranks of those who had remained on the back benches when the party was last in office.

TABLE 11

New MPs Elected at General Elections 1945–70*

	1945	1950	1951	1955	1959	1964	1966	1970
Labour	262†	37†	15	18	33	90†	69†	54
Conservative	76	120	41†	52†	74†	43	18	100†
Liberal	5	3	1	0	1	4	4	0
Other	2	1	1	2	0	0	0	2
Total	345	161	58	72	108	137	91	156

Source: The Times' *House of Commons* for the years in question.

* The figures include some former MPs returning to the House after a period out of Parliament.

† Indicates the party winning the election.

Even allowing for this, the overlap of personnel between the Attlee Government and the front-bench team throughout the 1951–64 period was quite remarkably high (see Table 12). Of the eighteen members of the Parliamentary Committee elected in November 1951, ten had been members of the Attlee Cabinet at the dissolution, three others had held Ministerial posts outside the Cabinet, and two had held junior Ministerial posts. Only three members of the Committee (Anthony Greenwood, Glenvil Hall, and Lord Shepherd) had been outside the Government at the end of Labour's period of office, and of these Glenvil Hall had been a member of the Government until May 1951, and Lord Shepherd had been a whip in the Lords.

Such an overlap might be expected in the first year or so in opposition, but what is more surprising is that the overlap remained high right through until 1964.

This general situation, and the problems involved, were highlighted by an incident involving Hugh Dalton and some of his Parliamentary Committee colleagues in 1955. On 31 May 1955, just after Labour's defeat in the general election, Dalton

TABLE 12

Overlap Between the Attlee Government in October 1951 and the Opposition Front-Bench Team of 1951–64

Status in October 1951		Opposition Team		
	Nov. 1951	June 1955	Nov. 1959	Oct. 1964
Cabinet Minister	10	7(9)	4(5)	2(3)
Minister Outside the Cabinet	3	3(8)	2(9)	2(4)
Junior Minister	2	4(17)	6(11)	8(11)
Backbencher	3	4(5)	5(18)	5(20)
Entered Parliament in 1951 or later	—	—(2)	1(6)	1(8)
Total	18	18(41)	18(49)	18(46)
Percentage Not Members of Attlee Govt. in Oct. 1951	16·7	22·2(17·7)	33·3(48·9)	33·3(60·8)

Source: Ministerial lists from *Hansard*.

The main figures relate to the Parliamentary Committee, and the figures in brackets to the front-bench team as a whole.

wrote to Attlee suggesting that the Parliamentary Committee contained too high a proportion of 'elderly' members.[1] In fact, five of the eighteen members of the Committee were then in their seventies (Attlee himself, William Whiteley, Chuter Ede, Emanuel Shinwell, and Lord Jowitt), and another six were in their sixties (Dalton himself, Herbert Morrison, Glenvil Hall, Philip Noel Baker, James Griffiths, and Lord Henderson). In his letter Dalton declared that

... It is essential, in my view, that, from the start of the new Parliament, there should be a much younger Shadow Cabinet.

[1] See Dalton, *Memoirs*, III, pp. 411–24.

> In the last Parliament this body . . . was becoming more and more a Shadow of the Past and less and less a Cabinet of the Future . . .[1]

He proposed that the older members should stand down to make way for younger men, although he specifically excluded Attlee from this, claiming that his continued leadership was essential for party unity. Attlee sent a sympathetic reply, but opposed the publication of the letter in the press. Dalton insisted on publication, however, and on 3 June it appeared in the *Daily Mirror*. In the next few days the *Daily Mirror* and other papers developed the story on the theme of 'Make Way for Youth'. On 6 June a meeting of the Parliamentary Committee was held, which Dalton later described in some detail.[2] At the meeting Shinwell and Chuter Ede revealed that they did not intend to seek re-election to the Committee, but they condemned Dalton's letter as a typically Daltonian publicity stunt.[3] Chuter Ede was particularly scathing, but James Griffiths and Hugh Gaitskell defended Dalton's initiative. When the elections for the new Committee were held on 23 June, Dalton, Ede, Shinwell, and Glenvil Hall did not seek re-election, and William Whiteley and Lord Shepherd retired as whips in the Commons and Lords. Over the subsequent eighteen months Attlee, Morrison, and Lord Jowitt also retired, so that by November 1956 only four members of the Committee were aged over sixty and only eight had been members of the Committee at the end of the 1951–5 Parliament.

This episode is an illustration of the sort of problem that can face a party in opposition, especially if its spell in opposition extends over two or three Parliaments. In the 1955–9 Parliament, Labour's Parliamentary Committee did come to look rather less like a 'Shadow of the Past', and the number of very elderly ex-Ministers on the Committee was reduced. Nevertheless, the infusion of 'new blood' without Ministerial experience was slow, and (as is shown in Table 12) even by October 1964 only a third of the Committee had not served in the Attlee Government, although the majority of those with Ministerial experience had served only as junior Ministers. Thus the PLP

[1] Ibid., p. 413.
[2] Ibid., p. 420.
[3] For Shinwell's account of the episode see Shinwell, *The Labour Story*, p. 199.

in *electing* the Parliamentary Committee, was slow to abandon former Ministers. More surprisingly, perhaps, among the front-bench team as a whole (that is, the Parliamentary Committee plus the other Spokesmen *appointed* by the Leader) the amount of new blood again was not particularly high. Of the original Spokesmen named by Attlee in July 1955, all except Green-wood and Mitchison were former Ministers, and although the number of former Ministers in the team declined, by 1964 they still constituted a clear majority among the team as a whole as well as among the Parliamentary Committee members. Even though those with Ministerial experience had served only as junior Ministers, the amount of Ministerial experience on the front bench was greater than might have been expected after a period of three full Parliaments in opposition. It may also be noted that in 1964, among those Spokesmen who lacked Ministerial experience, only eight had entered Parliament after 1951, reflecting the fact that (as shown in Table 11) at each of the general elections of the nineteen-fifties, the intake of new blood into the PLP was small.

A similar pattern emerges in the 1964–70 period of Conservative Opposition, and (as is shown in Table 13) in 1964 the overlap of personnel between Sir Alec Douglas-Home's Opposition team and his late Government was considerable. Eighteen of the twenty-one members of the Consultative Committee had held Cabinet posts at the dissolution. Of the three who had been outside the Cabinet, Martin Redmayne was chief whip in office and in opposition, and as such he is counted as a Consultative Committee member, although not as a Cabinet member. Iain Macleod and Enoch Powell had been members of Macmillan's Cabinet in October 1963, but had declined to serve in Douglas-Home's Cabinet. Nevertheless, they were included in the Consultative Committee in October 1964. Of the five members of the Douglas-Home Cabinet who were not included in the Consultative Committee, Henry Brooke, William Deedes, and Frederick Erroll retired to the backbenches after the election. Geoffrey Rippon and Anthony Barber were defeated at the 1964 election, but were re-elected to Parliament in 1965 and 1966, and subsequently joined the Committee. This overlap between the Douglas-Home Cabinet and the Consultative Committee continued under Heath's leadership. Following the 1966 election, the Committee did acquire something of a 'new look' with the addition of Lord Harlech and Peter Walker, who had not been members of Douglas-Home's Government. Nevertheless, former Ministers remained in a majority on the Committee throughout the 1964–70 Parliament. Even in June 1970, of the seventeen members of the Consultative Committee, only Peter Walker, Lord Balniel, and Iain Macleod had not been members of

TABLE 13

Overlap Between the Douglas-Home Government in October 1964 and the Opposition Front-Bench Team 1951–64

Status in October 1964	Oct. 1964	Opposition Team Apr. 1966	June 1970
Cabinet Minister	18(18)	11(11)	9(9)
Minister Outside the Cabinet	1(7)	1(3)	2(6)
Junior Minister	—(6)	2(6)	3(9)
Backbencher	2(3)	3(7)	3(14)
Entered Parliament in 1964 or later	—(—)	1(1)	—(8)
Total	21(34)	18(28)	17(46)
Percentage Not Members of Douglas-Home Govt. Oct. 1964	9·5(9·1)	22·2(28·5)	17·6(47·8)

Source: Ministerial lists from *Hansard*.

The main figures relate to the Consultative Committee, and the figures in brackets to the front-bench team as a whole.

Douglas-Home's Ministry, and Macleod, of course, had served in earlier Conservative Governments.

Taking the front-bench team as a whole, however, there was a considerably greater influx of 'new blood' from among the ranks of those who had been backbenchers in 1964, or who had entered Parliament only in 1964 or later. In 1964, Douglas-Home's front-bench team as a whole was like his Consultative Committee in the extent to which it was dominated by former Ministers. Under Heath, however, the proportion of new-comers among the Spokesmen increased, and by June 1970 the front-bench team was divided evenly between those with and those without Ministerial experience. Heath's team in 1970 still contained more former Ministers than did Wilson's team in 1964, but the Conservatives were only six years in opposition compared with Labour's thirteen.

With the return of Labour to opposition in 1970, a pattern emerged that was rather different from that of the 1951–64 period (see Table 14). In July 1970 the overlap between the late Government and the Parliamentary Committee was similar

TABLE 14

Overlap Between the Wilson Government in June 1970 and the Opposition Front-Bench Team in December 1970*

Status in June 1970	Opposition Team December 1970
Cabinet Minister	13(16)
Minister Outside the Cabinet	1(7)
Junior Minister	1(21)
Backbencher	4(21)
Entered Parliament in 1970	0(1)
Total	19(66)
Percentage Not Members of the Wilson Government in June 1970	21·1(33·3)

Source: Ministerial lists from *Hansard*.

* The appointments to the team were not completed until December 1970.
  The main figures relate to the Parliamentary Committee, and the figures in brackets to the front-bench team as a whole.

to what it had been when Labour left office in 1951. Of the twenty-one members of the Wilson Cabinet of June 1970, thirteen were elected to the Parliamentary Committee, and five others (Cledwyn Hughes, Roy Mason, Peter Shore, Michael Stewart, and George Thomas) were defeated in the ballot. Of the three other Cabinet members, John Diamond was defeated at the general election, Richard Crossman did not enter the Committee ballot, and Lord Gardiner did not contest the Lords' posts. Two of the other Committee members (Robert Mellish and Shirley Williams) had held non-Cabinet posts in

June, while the other four (Michael Foot, Douglas Houghton, Lord Champion, and Lord Beswick)[1] had been outside the Government. The senior duties were allocated to the Parliamentary Committee members and some other leading MPs soon after the Committee elections were over, but the 'second tier' appointments were not announced until December 1970. When the list did appear, however, it contained a large number of newcomers to the front bench. In all, a third of the team in December 1970 had not been members of the Government at the dissolution. This proportion of new recruits to the team was much higher than that in the Conservative team at the beginning of the 1964–70 period, and indeed was even higher than the proportion of new recruits included in the Heath team of April 1966, or the Attlee team of May 1955, after the parties had already spent one Parliament in opposition. For the most part, however, the new recruits to Wilson's team in 1970 were taking the place of former Ministers who had been defeated at the 1970 election (like John Diamond, Gerry Fowler, David Ennals, and Ben Whitaker), or who had not sought re-election (like James Hoy, Alice Bacon, and Eirene White). Because of this, and because he chose to appoint a large team, Wilson was able to recruit a good proportion of newcomers to the front bench without filling the backbenches with a large number of disgruntled former Ministers. There were, of course, some former Ministers who returned to the House at the election but did not receive posts in the Opposition team (including Peter Shore, Richard Crossman, Arthur Skeffington, John Mackie, and Charles Loughlin). Some of these, however, had indicated, publicly or privately, that they did not seek front-bench posts, so that again the process of recruiting new talent was made less painful than it might have been. It remains to be seen how far the recruiting process will be taken as the Parliament proceeds.

The Selection of Experts

To what extent are Spokesmen appointed on the basis of their expertise in the subject matter of their assigned topic? In

[1] Lord Beswick, however, as chief whip in the Lords, held a post in Her Majesty's Household.

the case of the ex-Ministers who are included in the team, this involves the question of whether they are asked to cover their old departments, while for newcomers to the front bench it involves the question of whether they are given responsibility for a subject in which as backbenchers they have established a particular expertise. There are certain clear advantages for the Opposition in having Spokesmen who were formerly Ministers in the departments they are covering. An ex-Minister normally will have a good knowledge of the working of his former department. Indeed, on first going into opposition he will probably be better informed than the Minister who has just replaced him, and in exchanges in the Commons he will be able to outshine the new Minister. This advantage over the Minister, of course, will not normally last more than six months or so, as the Minister begins to get on top of his job and the former Minister is denied the briefing of civil servants. Nevertheless, a former Minister will be able to retain the background information that he acquired in office. This information will be helpful to him in the preparation of his speeches in opposition, especially as the preparation will have to be done without the assistance of civil servants. Also, an ex-Minister will generally have a great number of personal contacts with pressure groups and influential individuals in the field in question, and this can prove invaluable in opposition. An ex-Minister's general knowledge of the way the department and its civil servants operate can also be highly useful as a means of detecting departmental errors on which the Opposition can capitalise.

At the same time, the role of a Spokesman is very different from that of a Minister, and (as is discussed elsewhere)[1] the required skills are not the same in each case. Success in one role neither guarantees nor precludes success in the other role, but even if the leader decides that a former Minister has the general qualities necessary to be a Spokesman, it may be that the specific qualities that made him an ideal Minister for a particular department may be superfluous in an Opposition Spokesman for that same department. A good negotiator, for example, may be successful as a Trade Minister or an Employment Minister, but in opposition he will have little chance to demonstrate his negotiating skills. The desirability of a Minister

[1] See below, p. 380.

covering his old department will also depend partly on how long he had held that particular Ministerial post. Former Ministers often seek a change of interest after years in one departmental area, and one of the positive advantages of opposition can be the opportunity that it gives to ex-Ministers to explore new subject areas, perhaps as a preparation for a subsequent Ministerial appointment in the new topic. Also, in making an appointment the leader has to consider the strengths and weaknesses of the Minister that a Spokesman will be facing. In some instances it may be desirable to confront a Minister with a Spokesman of contrasting style, while in other cases it may be better to match a Minister style for style. In 1966 Paul Dean was appointed Conservative Spokesman for Social Services partly because it was thought that his Parliamentary style would match that of the Social Security Minister (Richard Crossman), while in the same Parliament Peter Walker was made Transport Spokesman to some extent because it was thought that his abrasive approach would be effective in dealing with the Government's controversial transport policies, and in facing Barbara Castle as Minister of Transport. For such personality reasons the ex-Minister may not be the best person to face his departmental successor. More than this, however, it has to be recognised that expertise can be a distinct disadvantage in opposition. An ex-Minister can be *too* well informed to be a good critic, on the basis that 'many a good Opposition has been weakened by a knowledge of the facts'. This question, however, is considered more fully elsewhere.[1]

Much of the work of a department remains unaffected by a change of Government, so that an ex-Minister covering his old department may be called upon to lead the attack for the Opposition on policies that had been initiated when he was Minister. He may well have a lot of sympathy for the 'departmental point of view', and for the new Minister, grappling with administrative and policy problems that he himself had to face. Thus he may be loath to be 'disloyal' to his former civil servants by being critical of their work. In resisting attacks by the Opposition, a new Government can always point to the Opposition's failures in office, but Opposition criticisms can be made to appear particularly hypocritical if the former

[1] See pp. 201–4.

Minister is himself leading the Opposition's attack. This is
especially so if the Government can present the ex-Minister's
performance in office in an unfavourable light. Thus Reginald
Maudling, as Treasury Spokesman when the Conservatives
went into opposition in 1964, had difficulty in making credible
his attacks on the new Labour Government's economic policy.
As the ex-Chancellor of the Exchequer he was widely blamed
for the economic difficulties the Government had inherited,
and the reallocation of Opposition duties that took place in
February 1965 was precipitated largely by Maudling's own
desire to move away from his old department. Similarly, in the
1970–1 session, when Barbara Castle led the attack on the new
Conservative Government's Industrial Relations Bill, Conservatives were able to point to the difficulties she had encount-
ered in trying to deal with industrial relations when she was
Minister of Employment and Productivity.[1] For an ex-Minister
the tendency towards self-vindication can be overwhelming,
and this will be especially so if he is speaking regularly in
Parliament on his old department's affairs. Thus Roy Jenkins,
as the ex-Chancellor of the Exchequer, warned his colleagues
at the 1970 Labour Party Conference against becoming

> . . . superannuated spokesmen of the departments we then
> headed [in June 1970], explaining with all the dedicated irrele-
> vance of a Government in exile the exact minutiae of the policies
> we had then evolved.[2]

A fresh Spokesman, with no previous contacts with the department he is covering, is free from embarrassing commitments,
statements and errors made in office. In some circumstances, of
course, it may be embarrassing *not* to appoint a former Minister
to his old department, as this might be seen as an admission of
guilt. Also, responsibility for former policies will dissipate
through time. Nevertheless, it is clear that the experience and
expertise that former Ministers can bring with them into
opposition does not necessarily mean that it is desirable for
them to cover their former departments.

In July 1955 Attlee appointed most of his Spokesmen to

[1] For comments on this situation see *The Guardian*, 13 and 15 October
1970.
[2] *1970 Labour Party Conference Report*, p. 228.

duties which corresponded to the last Ministerial post that they had held (see Table 15), but under Gaitskell the former Ministers in the team acquired new responsibilities. By 1964 the vast majority of Spokesmen with Ministerial experience had Opposition duties which were different from the posts they had held in the Attlee Government. The same pattern emerged in the 1964–70 period. The majority of the ex-Ministers in Douglas-Home's team acquired in October 1964 the opposition duty equivalent to the last post they had held in

TABLE 15

Former Ministers Covering in Opposition the Departments in Which They Served at the Dissolution

| | Shadow Cabinet | Team as a Whole |
	(Percentages)	
Labour 1955–64 and 1970		
June 1955	64·3	70·6
Nov. 1959	27·8	22·6
Oct. 1964	16·7	6·5
Dec.	66·6	75·8
Conservatives 1964–70		
Oct. 1964	71·4	67·7
Apr. 1966	27·3	20·0
June 1970	14·3	20·0

Source: Ministerial lists from *Hansard.*

office, but in a major re-allocation of duties that took place in February, August, and October 1965, most of them were moved to duties unconnected with their former departments. By April 1966, of the twenty members of the front-bench team who had served in the Douglas-Home Government, only four held responsibilities which were the equivalent of their last Ministerial post, and in June 1970 the proportion remained the same (five out of twenty-four). In 1970, most of the ex-Ministers in Wilson's team were asked to cover their old departments, but if this period in opposition follows the pattern of the 1955–64 and 1964–70 periods, this situation will change drastically as the period in opposition proceeds. In both the 1955–64 and

1964–70 periods, the carry-over of personnel from power to opposition did *not* extend to the retention of former Ministerial duties: for the most part, the leaders were more concerned with preparing the next Ministerial team than with preserving the shape of the last one.

The associated question is how far backbenchers are recruited for the team on the basis of their knowledge of a particular subject. Undoubtedly, in many instances knowledge of the subject matter of the department to be covered will be one of the qualities sought in a new recruit to the front bench. It is often a good public relations exercise for an Opposition Spokesman, as for a Minister, to be identified with an influential group in the area of his responsibility. Thus Labour's Health Spokesmen have usually been doctors by profession, while the Agriculture Spokesmen of both parties have generally been farmers, or have at least represented farming constituencies. Charles Morrison's appointment as Conservative Spokesman for Sport came partly because, as chairman of the South West Regional Council for Sport, he was one of the few Conservative MPs with expertise in the administration of sport (although he gave up his membership of the Council when he accepted the 'political' post of Spokesman). An effective way for a backbencher to achieve recognition as a potential Spokesman is for him to exhibit a special knowledge of a particular subject through his activities in debates, question time, standing committees, and backbench subject groups. Backbenchers who served as PPSs to Ministers when the party was in office can have strong claims in opposition to appointment as Spokesmen for their old Ministers' departments. They will have some of the advantages of former Ministers without many of their disadvantages, in that as PPSs they will have acquired a certain expertise in the subject area of their departments, without being associated, in the eyes of the public, with responsibility for the departmental policies. What is more, the Ministers to whom they were PPSs may well be prominent party figures who are prepared to help their former assistants' careers by pressing for their appointment and promotion.

At the same time, when a backbencher is sought to fill a vacant post it is certainly not the case that the recognised expert will automatically be the one to be recruited, nor need a

potential Spokesman necessarily have any particular knowledge of the subject area to which he is to be assigned. Many
subject areas, of course, overlap to a considerable extent, while
the expertise of, say, an economist, can be applicable in a
number of posts. Nevertheless, there are a great many factors
other than expertise, which have to be taken into consideration
in the recruitment process. Many Spokesmen are recruited for
their general ability or influence within the party, rather than
for their specific expertise, and they may well be asked to deal
with subjects with which they are not particularly familiar.
Gregor Mackenzie, for example, had little specific knowledge
of Posts and Telecommunications before his appointment as
Spokesman for that subject in 1970. Thus comparative ignor-
ance of the subject will not necessarily prevent a backbencher
from being assigned to a particular duty.

Some indication of an MP's special interests can be obtained
by looking at the subjects in which he specialises in his Parliamentary activities,[1] and Table 16 provides some measure of
this for those backbenchers who were recruited into the front-
bench team in the 1955–64 and 1964–70 periods, and in 1970.[2]
The Table indicates the number of recruits for whom the topic
to which they were to be assigned was their main area of
activity in Parliamentary debates and questions in the session
immediately prior to their appointment. A total of twenty-
eight backbenchers joined the ranks of the Labour Spokesmen
in the 1955–64 period, and in the session preceding their
appointment only about a third of them specialised in the topic
to which they were to be appointed, to the extent of making it
their main area of activity on the floor of the House of Commons. Slightly more made it their main area of activity in
debates than was the case with questions, but on the whole,
specialisation in a topic did *not* precede appointment as Spokesman for that topic. The same is true of the backbenchers who
were brought into the team that Wilson formed on going into
opposition in 1970. With the Conservatives in the 1964–70
period, however, there was a closer relationship between an

---

[1] See Chapter 10 (and Appendix E) for a detailed consideration of
Spokesmen and their specialisations.

[2] By 'backbencher' here is meant someone who had not previously held
office as a Minister or as an Opposition Spokesman.

MP's specialisation in debates and questions and the post to which he was later to be appointed: of the thirty-three Conservative backbenchers involved, just over half specialised in their future duty in debates, and two-thirds did so in questions. This does not mean, of course, that the Conservative backbenchers knew they were soon to receive particular posts and therefore concentrated their activity on that subject (although a prospective Spokesman may be aware that he is in line for an appointment). Rather, it suggests that Edward Heath was inclined to assign particular posts to backbenchers who had

TABLE 16

Main Area of Parliamentary Activity of Backbenchers in the Session Before Their Appointment as Spokesmen

Main Area of Activity	Labour 1955–64 Questions	Labour 1955–64 Debates	Cons. 1964–70 Questions	Cons. 1964–70 Debates	Labour 1970 Questions	Labour 1970 Debates
Assigned Area	6	8	20	17	8	4
Other Area	22	20	13	16	9	13
Total	28	28	33	33	17	17

Source: Hansard Index (see Appendix E).

demonstrated a degree of specialisation in the subject. In so far as specialisation can be equated with expertise, therefore, Heath was more inclined to appoint experts as Spokesmen than were the Labour Leaders of the Opposition in the 1955–64 period and in 1970. This whole issue of front-bench specialisation, however, is looked at in more detail in Chapter 10.

The Re-allocation of Duties

What considerations govern the re-allocation of duties among the Spokesmen? The overall structure and composition of the team is normally reviewed at the beginning of each session, and major or minor changes may be made. In general, however, with the Opposition team, as with any team, the principle usually applied is that of leaving a winning combination unchanged. If the Government is doing badly, and the Opposition is capitalising on its errors and seems likely to win the next election, there is an incentive for the leader to maintain his successful combination without any major re-shuffles. Thus in 1963, when Harold Wilson became party leader at a time when an election was close, and Labour seemed well poised for victory, he made only a few minor changes in the front-bench team he inherited from Gaitskell. By the same token, however, if the party is not doing well in opposition, there is inevitably pressure on the Leader of the Opposition to make changes, except perhaps in the immediate run-up to an election, when in order to give an impression of confidence and stability, Opposition and Government alike have to settle for the combinations they arrived at earlier in the Parliament. Hugh Gaitskell regarded three or four years in one post as sufficient for a Spokesman, although this was not rigidly applied, and Douglas Jay retained connections with Trade and Treasury affairs continuously from 1947 to 1967, as a junior Minister, Opposition Spokesman, and then Minister.

As was noted in the previous section, soon after a party goes into opposition there is a tendency for former Ministers to be moved away from their old departments. Again, a second or third election defeat for the Opposition party, as for Labour in 1959 and the Conservatives in 1966, can produce a psychological need for major changes on the front bench, while in such an electoral reversal some Spokesmen may lose their seats, thereby making changes inevitable. Seven of Gaitskell's team in 1959, and eleven of Heath's team in 1966, did not return to the House after the election, and this was one of the factors that led Heath to reduce the overall size of his team by more than half after the 1966 election. Vacancies can also be caused by death, as with those of Aneurin Bevan in 1960 and Sir John Hobson in 1967. Other Spokesmen may retire of their own volition for age, health or other reasons. Anthony Wedgwood Benn left Gaitskell's team in 1961, just a year after joining it, when he was forced to leave the Commons over his Peerage issue. Lord Blakenham in 1965 and Miss Mervyn Pike in 1967 left the Consultative Committee for health reasons,[1] while in

---

[1] For the circumstances of Lord Blakenham's retirement see Young, *Sir Alec Douglas-Home*, p. 223.

1959 Tom Williams and Arthur Woodburn retired from the Labour team because of their age. A party in opposition is always liable to lose men of talent. In the 1955–64 period Kenneth Younger, Alfred Robens, George Chetwynd, Geoffrey de Freitas, Hilary Marquand, and Sir Lynn Ungoed-Thomas all gave up their Opposition duties in order to take up posts outside the House, as did Lord Harlech, R. A. Butler, and Sir Edward Boyle in the 1964–70 period, and Richard Marsh in 1971.

A Spokesman may resign or be dismissed for policy reasons. In March 1960 Gaitskell asked Richard Crossman to resign his responsibility for Pensions because of his opposition to the party's official defence policy, and in December 1960 Barbara Castle was not re-appointed as Spokesman for Public Building and Works, also because of her criticism of defence policy. In November 1960, Anthony Greenwood resigned from the front-bench team in protest against Gaitskell's leadership, and Enoch Powell was asked to resign from the Conservative team in April 1968, after his controversial immigration speech.[1] Spokesmen may be dismissed for less specific reasons. A number of Labour Spokesmen were dropped by Gaitskell in the re-shuffles of the 1959–61 period, because they were no longer seen as 'Ministers of the future'. Similarly, in October 1965, William Roots, T. G. D. Galbraith, James Ramsden, Julian Amery, Frederick Corfield, and Sir Peter Rawlinson were all asked to 'stand back' to make way for new talent, although Heath assured them that they would be almost certain of posts in any Government he might form.[2] In fact, Rawlinson, Ramsden, and Corfield returned to the Opposition team during the 1966–1970 Parliament. When Heath changed from a very large to a small team after the 1966 election, a number of Spokesmen were technically dropped, although most might have remained if Heath had continued with a large team, and some did return when the size of the team was increased again later in the Parliament.

In many respects a fairly rapid turnover of junior Spokesmen, as perhaps with junior Ministers, can be seen as a desirable

[1] See Chapter 9 for more details of these and other resignations in opposition.
[2] See *The Times*, 5 October 1965.

means of giving front-bench experience to a large number of MPs. Also, because of the nature of his role, a Spokesman is much less likely than is a Minister to be caught up in some special project that would collapse if he were to be moved to another post (although a Spokesman can get involved in detailed work on aspects of party policy). For the most part, however, Spokesmen are rather more secure in their posts than are Ministers. The Opposition can 'carry' a weak Spokesman much more easily than the Government can tolerate a poor Minister. The Leader of the Opposition's own position within the party is often precarious, and he may be unwilling to make enemies by dismissing a large number of Spokesmen. At the same time, the job of Spokesman is generally seen as less desirable than that of Minister, so there is less clamour among MPs for the replacement of the established team. Thus there were considerably fewer dismissals from the Opposition teams than from the Governments in the 1955–70 period.[1] Nevertheless, assistant Spokesmen who are seen as potential Ministers may gain rapid promotion to more senior responsibilities, as with Lord Balniel's promotion in 1967 from assistant Spokesman on Foreign Affairs to senior Social Services Spokesman, with a seat on the Consultative Committee. In the same way, Robert Carr moved from Overseas Development to Aviation in 1965, and then to Labour in 1967, with a place on the Consultative Committee from 1967 onwards, while Frederick Corfield was promoted from being assistant Spokesman for Trade and Power to being Aviation Spokesman in place of Carr.

For the most senior party figures, changes of duty are likely to involve moves to responsibilities of similar standing, in search of breadth of experience. As has been said of this type of re-shuffle, 'The stable remains the same; the horses are the same; but every horse is in a new stall.'[2] Thus Harold Wilson moved from Treasury to Foreign Affairs in 1961, as did Reginald Maudling in 1965. Between 1955 and 1964 George Brown

[1] For comments on the rate of Ministerial turnover in the Wilson Government, see A. King, 'Britain's Ministerial Turnover', *New Society*, 14 August 1966; 'Too Many Re-shuffles', *The Spectator*, 12 April 1968.

[2] Sir Henry Campbell-Bannerman's comment on a re-shuffle of Conservative Ministers in 1900, quoted in Asquith, *Fifty Years of Parliament*, II, p. 1.

was Spokesman on Agriculture, Supply, Labour, Defence, and finally Home affairs, with his longest tenure being five years as Defence Spokesman. In the same period, Patrick Gordon Walker moved from Commonwealth affairs to Home affairs, Treasury, Defence, and Foreign affairs. G. R. Mitchison also covered five subjects in the 1955–64 period, while James Callaghan and John Strachey each gained experience in four fields. These five, however, are untypical of the majority of Spokesmen in the breadth of experience they acquired. Even among those who served throughout the 1955–64 period, Douglas Jay covered only Treasury and Trade matters, and Arthur Creech Jones dealt with only Commonwealth and Colonial affairs. Similarly, Fred Willey, Tom Fraser, G. R. Strauss, James Griffiths, and Harold Wilson each covered only two areas. The emphasis was thus on depth of experience rather than breadth, and the same is broadly true of the Conservatives in the 1964–70 period. Throughout the period of Heath's leadership, Iain Macleod was Treasury Spokesman, and Joseph Godber was Agriculture Spokesman, while Gibson-Watt, Paul Bryan, and Robin Chichester-Clark retained their posts from October 1965 to June 1970. The vast majority of those who served as Conservative Spokesmen held only one or two posts, although Mrs Thatcher and Sir Keith Joseph each covered six areas, and Reginald Maudling, Anthony Barber, and Frederick Corfield each held four posts (with Barber and Maudling also serving respectively as party chairman and deputy leader for much of the period). In some cases the acquisition of such breadth of experience may be seen, as perhaps with Mrs Thatcher and Sir Keith Joseph, as a grooming of potential Cabinet Ministers who had not acquired wide experience in the previous period in office, but who required this experience to be able to participate in the Cabinet role of supervising all areas of policy.

In such changes of duty the initiative comes sometimes from the leader, and sometimes from the Spokesman. Gaitskell asked Reginald Paget to move from Navy to Army affairs in 1961, and G. R. Strauss's move from Transport to Aviation in 1960, and back again in 1961, came on Gaitskell's initiative. Similarly, Fred Lee's move to Labour in 1960, Alfred Robens' move from Foreign Affairs to Labour in 1956, Michael Stewart's move from Education to Housing and Local Government in 1959, and Fred Peart's temporary move from Agriculture to Science in 1960, and his move back again in 1961, were all at Gaitskell's request. Douglas Houghton's move from Pensions to the Treasury in 1963 was at Harold Wilson's request, in an attempt to strengthen the Treasury team. On the other hand, Miss Herbison's change from Scottish affairs to Pensions in 1962 came after she had asked Gaitskell to relieve her of Scottish duties, even if it meant going to the backbenches. Similarly, Tom Fraser's move from Scottish affairs to Power in 1961 was as a result of his own desire for a change. After the 1964 election Reginald Maudling sought a move from Treasury to Foreign affairs, and Sir Alec accommodated him when R. A. Butler gave up the post in 1965. There is no guarantee, of course, that the leader will comply with a Spokesman's request for a move, or that a Spokesman will accept a move that the leader wishes him to make. Both Reginald Paget and Geoffrey de Freitas declined to take over Agriculture in 1959, and the post eventually went to Fred Peart, who duly became Labour's Minister of Agriculture in 1964. George Brown did not become Foreign Affairs Spokesman in 1963, despite his well-known desire to have this post, and despite his prominent position within the party.[1] In contrast, in 1956 Gaitskell asked James Griffiths to give up the responsibility for Colonial Affairs in order that Aneurin Bevan might have the post after failing to defeat Gaitskell in the leadership contest.[2] In the re-allocation of duties, therefore, as in the initial appointment of Spokesmen, the degree of freedom enjoyed by the leader will depend a great deal on the extent to which he feels he must accommodate his colleagues for the sake of party unity.

Thus in relation to the Leader of the Opposition's personal authority, discussed in Chapter 3, his control over the selection of the Opposition team is restricted by various practical considerations. Among these are the claims of influential colleagues, the need to draw the team from the various groups within the party, the need to balance experienced ex-Ministers with young potential Ministers, and the unwillingness of some MPs when in opposition to devote themselves fully to Parliamentary

[1] George Brown, *In My Way*, London 1971, p. 84.
[2] See Griffiths, *Pages From Memory*, p. 134.

business. For a Labour Leader of the Opposition there is the additional factor, discussed in Chapter 4, that he has to give posts to the elected members of the Parliamentary Committee, although he does not necessarily have to appoint them to the most senior responsibilities. The Leader of the Opposition (Labour or Conservative) probably has less choice of personnel than has the Prime Minister, in that the posts he has to offer are less attractive than Ministerial posts. Apart from young backbenchers, eager for any post, his colleagues are likely to be less accommodating than they would be if he was distributing posts in government. At the same time, the Leader of the Opposition has more freedom than has the Prime Minister to decide the size of his team. There are no statutory provisions that require the Leader of the Opposition to make particular appointments, or any appointments for that matter, and the expectations of MPs and the public are vague as to the form of the front-bench arrangements in opposition. The Opposition teams, in fact, have varied considerably in size over the years, although the practice of 'flitting' between the front and back benches means that there is less of a clear cut division between Spokesmen and backbenchers than between Ministers and their backbenchers.

In this context, however, a further limitation on the leader's initiative may be noted. Since 1955 all Leaders of the Opposition have based their appointments on the Ministerial structure currently in existence, so that to a considerable extent, changes in the structure of the Opposition front-bench team follow from changes that are made in the Ministerial structure. The creation of a new department of state, or a new Ministerial post, is generally followed at once, or soon after, by an equivalent appointment in the Opposition team. In 1961, for example, the post of Chief Secretary to the Treasury was created in the Macmillan Government, and this was followed later by the appointment of Douglas Houghton to shadow this post for the Labour Opposition, although on this occasion there was a time lag as the Opposition was undecided as to the final form that the team should take in that Parliament. Similarly, when Harold Wilson created the post of Minister for Sport in 1967, Heath made the equivalent appointment of Opposition Spokesman for Sport. In 1964 Douglas-Home distinguished between

Treasury affairs and Economic affairs in his Opposition team, following the creation of the Department of Economic Affairs in the Wilson Government (although this distinction was terminated by the Opposition some time before the Department of Economic Affairs ceased to exist). Following the changes in the Whitehall machine in 1969, when the functions of the Minister of Technology were extended, and the new post of Secretary of State for Local Government and Regional Planning was created, the responsibilities of the Opposition Spokesmen were re-organised, with Sir Keith Joseph and Peter Walker acquiring new duties equivalent to the new Ministerial posts. Also, the appointment by Heath of a large number of new, young Spokesmen in October 1969 was partly in response to the large influx of 'new blood' into the Wilson Government earlier in 1969. Further, when they formed their Governments in 1964 and 1970, both Wilson and Heath made important changes in the Whitehall structure. Wilson, for example, created the Department of Economic Affairs and Ministry of Overseas Development, while Heath re-arranged some of the Ministries which had recently been created. Immediately prior to coming to office, however, neither Wilson nor Heath had used for the structure of their Opposition team the new Ministerial pattern that they were soon to create in office. Thus while a Leader of the Opposition may prepare for office by giving potential Ministers experience as front benchers in opposition, and while Spokesmen are, in fact, selected largely on the basis of their Ministerial potential, the duties to which they are allocated would seem to be determined by the structure of the existing Government, rather than by the Ministerial structure that the Leader of the Opposition plans to create when he comes to power. This suggests, perhaps, that the main concern of the team is that of 'shadowing' the existing Government—although this anticipates the detailed consideration of the activities of the Opposition, which will be undertaken in Part Three of the study.

part three

The Opposition
Team At Work

6

The Activities of
the Opposition

IT WAS noted in the introductory Chapter that the two ways in which an office-seeking Opposition can help to guard against bad government are by subjecting the activities of the established Government to scrutiny, and by posing as an alternative set of rulers. It was also noted, however, that either one of these functions could impede the successful execution of the other: in striving to pose as a statesmanlike body of potential Ministers, the Opposition leaders could inhibit their critical faculties, while the pursuit of a highly critical role in Parliament could damage the Opposition's image as a responsible alternative Government. Thus the way for the Opposition to attain office is not necessarily to indulge in vigorous resistance to the Government at every opportunity. There is certainly no direct correlation between vigorous Parliamentary criticism and the replacement of the Government by its critics: the Opposition's reward for unrelenting attacks on the Government may merely be the electoral verdict that it is effective in opposition but is not responsible enough for office. Given this, is it a greater sin for the Opposition to neglect its critical role in an attempt to pose as a statesmanlike body, than to indulge in unrelenting criticism at the expense of its image as an alternative Government?

Many would argue that the Opposition's prime duty is to emphasise its critical role, on the grounds that vigorous Parliamentary Opposition is a better safeguard against bad government than is the notion of alternating Governments. In the modern British context, the rejection of the value of alternating

Governments rests on two main arguments. The first is that the Conservative Party has had such a preponderant share of power this century, and especially since 1922 when Labour became its main rival, that in fact it is not possible to talk in meaningful terms of any 'regular' and 'natural' alternation of parties in office. In the early nineteen-sixties in particular, following three successive Conservative election wins, there was much comment to the effect that 'the electoral pendulum' had ceased to swing.[1] Governments that were guided by the opinion polls, and which had the ability to time elections and economic booms to coincide, were widely thought of as being incapable of losing general elections. Thus Professor Crick warned that, 'We are now in great danger of taking for granted the beneficent effects of a process that does not take place.'[2] The increased interest in Parliamentary reform in this period was partly a consequence of the view that as Governments had so many electoral advantages, it was necessary to have improved means of scrutinising their policies between elections.

The second basis for questioning the value of the notion of alternating Governments in Britain is that even when Conservative Governments are replaced by Labour Governments, the change in governmental output is only slight. Tweedledum replaces Tweedledee and proceeds to pursue similar ends by parallel means, following his predecessor in operating within a narrow front-bench consensus. This argument has been heard most recently in the context of the failure of the Wilson Government to 'build a Socialist Britain' in the 1964–70 period, although all the Labour Governments, to varying degrees, have been accused of 'betraying the Movement' by following 'Tory' policies. The Labour Party has long contained an element which has argued that more could be achieved through the 'purity' of uncompromising opposition from a solidly Socialist base, than through being in office surrounded by a hostile economic elite, a sullen civil service, an unsympathetic press, and sceptical foreign bankers.

[1] See, for example, G. N. Sanderson, 'The "Swing of the Pendulum" in British General Elections', *Political Studies*, 1966, pp. 349–60; Mackintosh, *The British Cabinet* (1962 edition), pp. 483–9; Abrams and Rose, *Must Labour Lose?*

[2] B. Crick, *The Reform of Parliament*, London 1964, p. 9.

Through these arguments the alternation of parties in office is sometimes presented as being less of a safeguard against bad government than is the subjection of those in power to rigorous scrutiny by a critical Opposition, even if it is a permanent or semi-permanent Opposition. The value of the alternation of parties in office, however, and the extent to which it occurs in Britain, are under-estimated by these arguments. In the first place, although the Conservatives have been more often in office than out of it this century, the periods of Conservative rule have been interspersed by Liberal, Labour, or Coalition Governments, and in half of the elections over the last fifty years the Government party has been defeated. Despite the many prophecies made in the early nineteen-sixties of per-manent Conservative rule, two of the three general elections since then have produced a change of Government, the Con-servatives were out of office for six years from 1964, and a major study of British voting behaviour has emphasised that the relationship between age and voting patterns could threaten the Conservatives' long-term electoral strength.[1] Further, even if it is conceded that a change of party in office in Britain does not produce major changes in the nature of Government policies (and it is very easy to exaggerate the extent of the similarities of Labour and Conservative Government policies), it can still be maintained that the alternation of Tweedledum and Tweedledee is much to be preferred to putting up with Tweedledum all the time. A change of men is some defence against arbitrary rule, even if the accompanying change of measures is only slight.

Thus the alternation of Governments should be encouraged. Even at the expense of critical Opposition, the leaders of the alternative Government should strive for office and should conduct themselves in such a way as to try to ensure their success at the next general election. A British Government that did not wish to remain in power, and thus did not fear the ultimate sanction of rejection by the electorate would have a vast freedom to ignore the effect that its policies were having on public opinion. By the same token, an Opposition which did not seek office, but was content with its role in opposition,

---

[1] Butler and Stokes, *Political Change in Britain.*

would offer no alternative Government to the electorate, and would pose no threat to the Government's retention of power. Thus, essential though the duties of the Opposition may be for the health of the political system, it is desirable that those in opposition should not be satisfied with that role as a staple diet.

In practice, the desire for office among Opposition leaders is likely to be an overwhelming one. For the most part, ambitious politicians accept the duties of an Opposition only because, for the time being at least, office is unattainable. The general distaste with which ambitious politicians regard a period in opposition was summed up well in interview by a former Labour Minister when he complained that, 'Returning to Opposition is basically frustrating: you are condemned to "gesture-politics" for four years.' There will be some MPs, of course, who will always prefer the freedom of opposition to the strictures of office, although such MPs generally will not be among the party's leaders. Again, there may be occasions when a party will feel that it is not quite ready for office. In 1924, for example, when Labour came to power very soon after becoming one of the two main parties, some Labour leaders felt that they had attained office too soon, and that they would have benefitted from more years as His Majesty's Opposition in order to gain more Parliamentary experience.[1] Labour's rapid rise to power was somewhat exceptional, but there may be more general occasions when a party will be quite thankful not to have the responsibility of office. During a particularly difficult economic or foreign crisis, for example, Opposition leaders will be happy to see their opponents being faced with awkward and potentially unpopular decisions. Such feelings, however, are based in large part on the assumption that the Government will make itself so unpopular in dealing with the crisis that its electoral defeat will be guaranteed, and its replacement by the Opposition will be assured.

Normally, then, Opposition leaders will be anxious for office. While acknowledging this, what are the compensations for a party that finds itself in opposition? How can it put its time in opposition to best use? To what extent should it seek to use

[1] For details of the 1924 Labour Government see R. W. Lyman, *The First Labour Government 1924*, London 1957.

the time to prepare for its next period in office? Precisely what
Parliamentary tactics should it adopt in order that it can have
the best chance of winning the next election? These questions
will be considered in this chapter, before looking at the particular activities of the Shadow Cabinet and individual Spokesmen in the rest of this part of the study.

The Compensations of Opposition

What compensations are there for a party in opposition? It is
easy to underestimate the extent to which the Opposition can
still influence Government policies. Although on major controversial issues the Opposition will set out to block the intentions of the Government, on other issues, and perhaps on the
majority of issues, the Opposition's concern will be to achieve
better government. The Opposition can help to improve legislation by pointing out deficiencies in the details of a Bill
during its passage through Parliament.[1] The often considerable
Ministerial experience of Opposition leaders can be important
in this respect. As well as co-operating with the Government
over legislation, the Opposition may be able to obtain concessions over legislative details by wearing the Minister down,
especially at a Bill's committee stage in the Commons. The
Government will often concede on one point in order to
obtain agreement on another, and in particular the Government may be prepared to bargain for Opposition support on
delicate issues like Rhodesia or Ulster.[2] Alternatively, the
Opposition can mount a publicity campaign against broader
aspects of Government policy, and by this means can perhaps
embarrass the Government sufficiently to force it to modify its
intentions. In this respect the more credible the Opposition as
an alternative Government, the more successful it is likely to
be in its attempts to persuade the electorate that its objections
to Government policies are well founded. Ultimately, of course,
the Government, through its secure majority and its control

[1] See R. L. Leonard and V. Herman, *The Backbencher and Parliament*,
London 1972.

[2] For a criticism of the 1964–70 Conservative Opposition's failure to
exploit its opportunities in this respect see S. Brittan, 'Some Thoughts on
the Conservative Opposition', *Political Quarterly* 1968, pp. 145–55.

of the Parliamentary timetable, retains the final word. Nevertheless, the Opposition has considerable bargaining power, which it can use to influence policy, so that its role is not entirely negative, and time spent in opposition is not devoid of creative opportunities. To some extent, therefore, the Opposition enjoys the powers traditionally ascribed to the Monarch —the power to warn, the power to advise, and the power to be consulted by the Ministerial team.

Being in opposition also has a number of practical compensations for former Ministers. Lord Palmerston, for example, was of the opinion that politics were 'an amusement, and not a labour, for those who are out of office'.[1] Certainly, a party that has been in power for a long period might welcome a spell in opposition to give its leaders a break from the physical and mental pressures of office. These stresses are considerable, and are undoubtedly greater today than in the nineteenth century, or in the period before 1939. After a long period before the public gaze, the comparative anonymity of opposition may be welcome. A former Minister will probably be glad of the opportunity to speak freely in public without every word being seized upon by the press. The excessively long hours that almost all Ministers now have to work must damage family life, and restrict areas of interest. Former Ministers have commented upon the difficulty of re-adjusting to 'normal' life, and of having to cope once again with such day to day problems as how to locate destinations after having been chauffeur driven everywhere in a Ministerial car. Thus, it seems, after thirteen years of Conservative Government, a number of ex-Ministers arrived late for the first Consultative Committee meeting in 1964 because '. . . they had not driven cars in London for years and forgot that meantime Brook Street had become one-way only.'[2]

When Labour left office in 1951, some of its leaders had held Ministerial office for eleven years, while by 1964 some Conservatives had held office continuously for thirteen years. On both of these occasions, there were indications that at least some Ministers welcomed a rest from office. This will not be true of all Ministers, of course. In the context of the 1945–51

[1] H. C. F. Bell, *Lord Palmerston* (2 vols), London 1966, I, p. 328.
[2] Young, *Sir Alec Douglas-Home*, p. 220.

period of Conservative Opposition, Harold Macmillan has commented that

> . . . Opposition in Parliament cannot be said to be a very enthralling affair. . . . For myself, I did not much enjoy the work, for my whole life has been directed, whether in business or politics, to trying to create rather than to destroy.[1]

On the other hand, Lord Woolton's reaction to the same period in opposition was that, 'Those of us who had been in the War Cabinet had benefited by a few years out of office—"out to grass"—in which our energies and our freshness had been restored.'[2]

Much will depend on the individual, and much will depend also on the circumstances. After long years in office, a short spell in opposition (such as the Conservatives have experienced on four occasions since 1918) may indeed be very welcome, always assuming that the period out of office does not extend beyond one or, at the most, two Parliaments. If, however, the period in office has been comparatively short, as was Labour's in 1924, 1929–31, and 1964–70 (although not 1940–51), the return to opposition will be less welcome. Again, for someone in his late fifties or sixties the return to opposition could mean the end of his Ministerial career, as he could well be seen as being too old for a Ministerial post by the time the party again secures office. He may thus have to reconcile himself to the fact that, although he is still far from being senile, he has probably made his last important Ministerial decision. A younger person, however, might see a spell in opposition as a benefit to his career, providing him with an opportunity to stake a claim to take over from an older colleague in some future Government.

Former Ministers can use a period in opposition to improve their personal financial positions by acquiring (or reviving) business interests. In the 1964–70 period, for example, many of the Conservative leaders acquired or developed business or professional interests which they combined with service in the Shadow Cabinet. Quintin Hogg returned to a legal practice, and Robert Carr, Lord Carrington, Anthony Barber, Sir Keith Joseph, Iain Macleod, and other Shadow Cabinet members

[1] Harold Macmillan, *Tides of Fortune*, p. 48.
[2] Woolton, *Memoirs*, p. 365.

developed their banking and industrial interests. In 1970 a number of Labour ex-Ministers also took up appointments in industry or the City. Other Opposition leaders may indulge in literary activities of one kind or another. In the 1945–51 period Sir Winston Churchill worked on his history of the second world war.[1] Harold Wilson and George Brown produced volumes of reminiscences soon after going into opposition in 1970,[2] as did Hugh Dalton in 1951.[3] In the 1951–64 period Roy Jenkins wrote biographies of Asquith and Dilke, as well as a study of the Parliament Bill crisis of 1910–11.[4] In this same period John Strachey, Anthony Crosland, and Richard Crossman produced books and pamphlets on the philosophy and practice of socialism.[5] In these several ways ex-Ministers clearly can put their time in opposition to good personal use.

As noted in Chapter 5, a spell in opposition provides a party with an opportunity to renew its personnel, replacing some of its older leaders with new talent in preparation for a further period in office. It is possible, of course, for a party to renew its personnel during the course of a long period in office. The 1951–64 period of Conservative Government saw four Prime Ministers, five Foreign Secretaries, and six Chancellors of the Exchequer, while of a total of 150 Ministers who held posts during Macmillan's spell as Prime Minister, only twenty served throughout the seven-year span. Part of the technique of selecting a Ministerial team is to achieve a blend of youth and experience, so that new talent is constantly being brought forward. This can prove to be a very difficult process, however, as exemplified by Harold Macmillan's 1962 attempt to revitalise his Cabinet by replacing a third of its members at one fell swoop. Thus as well as providing a rest for some leading party figures, a spell

---

[1] Sir W. S. Churchill, *The Second World War* (6 vols), London 1948–54.

[2] Lord George Brown, *In My Way*, London 1971; Harold Wilson, *The Labour Government 1964–70*, London 1971.

[3] Dalton, *Memoirs*.

[4] Roy Jenkins, *Sir Charles Dilke*, London 1958; *Mr. Balfour's Poodle*, London 1954; *Asquith*.

[5] See, for example, C. A. R. Crosland, *Britain's Economic Problems*, London 1953; *The Future of Socialism*, London 1961; *The Conservative Enemy*, London 1962; R. H. S. Crossman, *New Fabian Essays*, London 1952; *Planning For Freedom*, London 1965; John Strachey, *Contemporary Capitalism*, London 1956; *The End of Empire*, London 1959.

in opposition can also be a time to undertake a thorough over-haul of the leading ranks of the party, replacing some old leaders with new, younger ones, with the shock of election defeat tending to stimulate this process.

An election defeat also generally produces a self-analytical mood in a party, and the break from office provides the leisure for such a process of self-examination. In this respect the Opposition inevitably will be concerned with two separate things—firstly the process of *securing* office (which today means a general election victory), and then the process of *being* in office. Moreover, the Opposition will be concerned with these two things both in the *past* (its previous period of office and the general election that brought it to an end), and in the *future* (the next general election and the period in office that might follow it). Again, in its concern with its past governmental and electoral performance the Opposition can adopt a *self-critical* or a *self-justifying* stance, either defending and 'basking' in its record, or enquiring into what went wrong with its perform-ance. These alternative preoccupations of the Opposition (general election or period in office, past or future, self-justify-ing or self-critical) can be depicted as a six-fold classification as follows:

	Past		Future
	Self-justifying	Self-critical	
General Election	A1	A2	C
Period in Office	B1	B2	D

These options, of course, are not mutually exclusive, and a party in opposition will indulge itself in all of these exercises to some extent. Different emphases might be expected from the various sections of the party. Former Ministers, for example, might be particularly concerned with justifying their record in office, while party headquarters might concentrate on defending their handling of the election campaign. Backbench MPs or constituency workers may be critical both of the record in office and of the electoral machine, while young future Ministers may be especially anxious to direct attention to the policies and general attitudes that the party will adopt the next time that it is in office. As a consequence, consciously or unconsciously, various 'pressure groups' can emerge within the party, each seeking to direct the process of self-analysis along particular channels. Generally, however, a dominant mood will develop, either imposed from above by the preoccupations of the Leader of the Opposition or his senior colleagues, or else emerging from below through the prevailing attitudes of backbench MPs or the party outside Parliament. This dominant preoccupation is likely to change through time, and in this respect something of a 'natural' pattern might be expected to develop during the course of a Parliament: this progression will be discussed in the next section.

Opposition Preoccupations

In the first days and weeks in opposition a party strives to answer the question, why are we in opposition? A post-mortem on the election campaign is usual. The post-mortem might yield the view that the party's defeat was indeed due largely to electoral factors, such as the weakness of the constituency party organisations, the shortage of full-time agents, the lack of funds, the mis-handling of campaign propaganda, or the weakness of the campaign theme. In this case the party might undertake a detailed enquiry into its electoral machinery. After the 1955 election, for example, the Wilson Committee was set up to examine the Labour Party's electoral machinery,[1] and it came to the conclusion that the party was ' . . . still at the penny-farthing stage in a jet-propelled era.'[2] Reforms were proposed, but few were implemented. The Conservatives set up committees to find ways of improving their electoral machinery following their defeats in 1910, 1929, and 1945.[3] Although there was no parallel committee set up by the Conservatives in 1964 or 1966, the party chairmen (Edward du Cann and then Anthony Barber) did make a number of organisational reforms.[4]

[1] See R. T. McKenzie, 'The Wilson Report and the Future of the Labour Party Organisation', *Political Studies*, 1956, pp. 93–7.

[2] *Report of the Sub-Committee on Party Organisation*, Labour Party, 1955, p. 6.

[3] See Butler and Pinto-Duschinsky, *The British General Election of 1970*, p. 94.

[4] For a comment, see ibid.

Even if the post-mortem on the handling of the election attributes defeat largely to campaign factors, the party might still undertake an analysis of its record in office at the same time as attempting to improve its electoral machine. The party will certainly do this, however, if the electoral post-mortem produces the conclusion that the actual campaign was handled quite well, or even brilliantly, but that defeat was 'inevitable' because of things that had gone wrong in the year or so leading up to the election. In 1964, for example, this was to some extent the attitude that the Conservative Opposition adopted, looking for an explanation of its election defeat through questions such as whether the party became too complacent after three successive election victories in the nineteen-fifties, or whether the wrong leader had been chosen in 1963, or whether the party had failed to detect basic changes in public attitudes to policies like economic planning and regional development in the early sixties.[1] Similarly, in 1970 some commentators argued that the general election was 'lost' by Labour through the devaluation of the £ in 1967, or through the debacle over the attempted reform of industrial relations in 1969, and that as a consequence the actual election campaign was largely irrelevant.[2] It is clearly arguable whether these are correct interpretations of the reasons for the changes of Government in 1964 and 1970. Nevertheless, if sufficient members of an Opposition believe that factors such as these are responsible for the loss of office, then there will be great pressure for the party to indulge in a detailed re-examination of the mistakes of office.

Such a process of past-policy analysis might continue for the whole of a Parliament, and the party might tear itself apart in the process of recrimination. To some extent this was the fate of the Labour Party in the 1951-5 Parliament, when there were great disputes within the party over the question of whether the Attlee Government had been sufficiently 'Socialist' in its approach. Even if the Opposition avoids this extreme, its concern with its past mistakes can still provide ammunition for its political opponents by reminding the electorate of the party's

[1] For an analysis of the 1964 election see D. E. Butler and A. King, *The British General Election of 1964*, London 1965, especially Chapters I and IX.
[2] See Butler and Pinto-Duschinsky, *The British General Election of 1970*.

errors in office. Thus, unlike an examination of the weaknesses of the party's electoral machine, which is not particularly newsworthy, and is not likely to receive much public attention, a review of the mistakes of office can easily develop into a well publicised exercise in self-destruction. Clearly, therefore, the Opposition cannot allow the process to take too long, and it has to direct its attention to the more constructive question— how can we achieve a fruitful period in office in the future? In this, the first consideration is how to improve its electoral prospects. As well as seeking to strengthen its electoral machine, this will lead the party to a consideration of the tactics that it should adopt in Parliament and outside, in order to attract the most favourable publicity to itself, and to convince the electorate that the new Government is an inadequate one and should be replaced by the Opposition. Almost inevitably, there will be those within the party who will favour, as the means to success, uncompromising attacks upon the Government on every possible occasion, while others will argue for a more cautious approach to the new Government's policies. Clearly either approach involves dangers and difficulties (and these are considered in the next section).

The other aspect of the Opposition's concern with the future is the question of how best to prepare for the period in office that perhaps will follow the next general election. The post-mortem on the last period in office might yield the self-critical conclusion that the late Government made numerous major mistakes which must be avoided at all costs in the future. Such an attitude is likely to strengthen the Opposition's resolution to enter the next period of office well equipped with new ideas and policies. Thus in the 1945–51 period of opposition, the Conservatives, under R. A. Butler's stimulus, indulged in an analysis of general party attitudes, and produced numerous 'Policy Charters' as broad guides for a future Conservative Government. In the 1964–70 period Edward Heath, before and after he became party leader, encouraged a review of party policy on a more detailed basis than that undertaken in 1945–1951, and a wide range of policy groups was set up to examine various policy areas.[1] There can be, of course, an infinite number of interpretations of what *did* go wrong last time, and what

[1] See below, p. 264, for details of these 1945–51 and 1964–70 exercises.

should be done to avoid such errors next time. In very general terms, however, preparation for future office involves a broad choice between, on the one hand, researching into policies in detail, even down to the preparation of the small print of possible future legislation, or on the other hand, seeking to encourage among the electorate a general climate of opinion that will be favourable to the party's broad aims and general philosophy. Again, these alternatives are not necessarily mutually exclusive, but in opposition a debate often does develop within the party as to which approach should be adopted, or at least which approach should be given greatest emphasis (and this issue is considered later in this chapter).

Thus an ideal pattern of self-analysis can be envisaged for a party in opposition. In the first weeks in opposition it looks at its electoral performance and traces the weaknesses. When this enquiry is finished, or even before it is finished, it reviews its record in office, and after due debate at the various levels of the party, a consensus emerges regarding the past errors in office. Having completed its analysis of the mistakes that led it into opposition, the party moves on to consider what can be done to achieve a return to office, and what can be done to make the next period in government more successful than the last. In due course the party wins the general election and returns to power, having learned from the past and prepared for the future. Clearly, however, there are numerous factors which can prevent the emergence of such an orderly progression from stage to stage. In the first place, 'the Opposition' may not think and behave as a single, cohesive, rational unit. A common mistake of observers of the political scene is to assume that the behaviour of politicians and electors is much more deliberative and systematic than it actually is. In reality, Opposition party behaviour, like many other forms of political behaviour, may be extremely inconsistent and illogical. The Opposition may lack direction because the Leader of the Opposition and his principal colleagues in the Shadow Cabinet perhaps live from week to week, giving little thought to, or being unable to agree upon, an overall strategy for the party. Even if the leaders do produce an agreed strategy, they may be unable to impose this upon the party as a whole. Different sections of the party may have different preoccupations throughout the period in opposition, and each may come to conflicting conclusions about the nature of past errors and future remedies. Also, the various stages of self-analysis do not necessarily represent any rigid time-sequence of events. The examination of the record in office, for example, may well begin before the analysis of the election campaign is over. Indeed, a party does not need to wait until it leaves office before studying the reasons for the failure of any of its policies, and the post-mortem in opposition may merely be a continuation of analyses begun before the Government was dead. Again, the party may move on to the consideration of the future before the analysis of the past is complete, although in any situation it is generally advisable to be sure about the reasons for past failures before deciding how to run the course a second time.

It may be, of course, that as a result of examining its past performance (both its record in office and its handling of the election), the party may not move on to prepare for the future at all. It may decide, for example, that the record in office was excellent, and that the election campaign was handled magnificently, but that defeat was due to exceptional factors like unexpected and uncontrollable crises overseas, the machinations of foreign bankers, world trading conditions, a vicious press, or the perversity of the electorate, all of which were beyond the party's control. A self-justifying stance like this could lead to various attitudes in opposition. It could produce disillusionment with established institutions and procedures, and could lead the party down the path to revolutionary opposition. Alternatively, if it decides that it lost office merely because the electorate felt that it was 'time for a change', the party might be tempted to sit back and merely wait for the wind of change to blow it back into office. If it decides (rather less complacently) that defeat came because its otherwise excellent policies were distorted by a biased press and an irresponsible Opposition, the party might feel that the new Government should be subjected to similar treatment by an Opposition dedicated to the principle of 'oppose everything and propose nothing'.

Thus in any one of a number of ways a neat progression from stage to stage can be prevented. Nevertheless, something approaching the 'ideal' pattern might emerge during a spell in opposition. In this, therefore, and in the other ways considered in this section, a party can use the time in opposition to 'put its house in order', so as to be able to regain office, and to be in a position to make profitable use of office when it is attained. It remains an open question, however, just how long a party needs to spend in opposition in order to get the full benefit from such a process of self-analysis, or how long a party can spend in office at any one time without becoming tired and stale. If a party suffers a number of successive electoral defeats, and spends a decade or more in opposition, it can lose touch with the realities of office. Many of its talented members might fall away, it can become demoralised, and can find it difficult to retain its credibility, or to make a success of office when and if it is eventually attained. Equally, a Government that is able to retain office at successive elections, with little real challenge from the Opposition, can become excessively complacent, and can lose its responsiveness to outside pressures. At the other extreme, if two parties alternate in office after almost every election, as they did in Britain in the last thirty years or so of the nineteenth century, the parties when in opposition do not experience the full benefits that can flow from adversity, while the complacency that comes from an expected inevitable return to office inhibits the process of self-analysis in opposition. It is probably fair to say that had Labour won the general election of 1955, or the Conservatives that of 1966, each after only one short Parliament in opposition, they would have returned to office having 'learned and forgotten nothing'. Also, some aspects of a Government's policies can be geared to a four- or five-year Parliament, but others need a longer period in which to develop. Just one Parliament in office before returning to opposition does not allow time for longer term policies to bear fruit.

Clearly, there is no fixed number of years that constitutes the ideal time for a party to spend in or out of office. Much will depend on circumstances, and on the ability of a party and its leaders to adapt themselves to the responsibilities of office or to the challenges of opposition. In general, however, two election defeats and two Parliaments is perhaps the most desirable compromise between the two extreme situations described above. On this admittedly arbitrary basis, the 1951–64 period of Conservative Government and Labour Opposition was probably too long for all concerned, whereas the 1945–51 and 1964–70 periods of Labour Government and Conservative Opposition were somewhat closer to a happy balance between too long and too short a period between changes of Government. Regardless, however, of the length of time that a party spends in opposition, it will almost certainly be faced with disagreements within its ranks over two vital aspects of its behaviour and tactics while in opposition, namely, how vigorous and uncompromising an attitude it should adopt in its role as critic of the Government, and how much detailed work it should do on future policy in its role as a potential Government. These two questions will be considered in the next two sections.

Opposing the Government

'So soon as ever thou see'st him, draw; and, as thou drawest, swear horrible . . .' Sir Toby Belch's advice is often cited as the tactic that an Opposition should adopt in its confrontations with the Government. But are Opposition leaders wise to 'swear horrible' as soon as they see the whites of a Minister's eyes, or should they adopt a more moderate and statesmanlike approach, given that the Opposition's task is not merely to oppose the Government, but is also to seek to replace it? Because of the tendency of the British electoral system to produce a Parliamentary majority for one or other of the two main parties, and because of the strength of internal party discipline, Governments today normally are secure from overthrow between elections. While for some part of the nineteenth century Governments were liable to defeat in the House of Commons, Governments today are made and un-made at general elections rather than by Parliament. Thus the office-seeking Opposition has to conduct itself in such a way that at the next general election the electorate will regard it as a preferable alternative to the existing Ministry, and will accordingly vote it into office. At four elections since the war (1945, 1951, 1964, and 1970) the opposition party has succeeded in persuading the electors to 'throw the rascals out', and on the four other occasions (1950, 1955, 1959, and 1966) it has failed to do so. What happens on the floor of the House of Commons is only one of the factors that determine whether the Opposition can win an election, and it is currently fashionable to play down the extent to which Parliament today influences anything. It is undoubtedly the case that as important as, or more important than, Parliamentary party politics in determining election results are considerations like the state of the parties' election machines, the morale of their workers, the success of their publicity campaigns, the often accidental pattern of events between elections, and (perhaps most important of all) the timing of the election date. It is not intended here to attempt to assess the relative importance of Parliamentary politics and the many other factors that contribute to election results. The assumption that is being made, however, is that the way the Opposition party behaves in Parliament between elections has at least *some* effect upon its chances of transferring itself from opposition to office through a general election victory.

Given this assumption, how should the Opposition proceed so as to achieve electoral success?[1] There is, of course, much to be said for the view that every Government contains the seeds of its own destruction, and should be assisted along the path to electoral defeat by the constant exposure of its limitations. Indeed, one of the basic functions of Her Majesty's Opposition is to draw the attention of the public, and of the Government itself, to deficiencies in Ministerial policies, in the hope that the exposure of such weaknesses will lead to their remedy, either through remedial action by the Government, or through a change of Government at the next election. Governments invariably experience at least one particularly unpopular phase in every Parliament, when by-elections, local government elections, the opinion polls, and the bookmakers suggest that the Government's policies are being badly received. The temptation at such times is for the Opposition to capitalise on the trend in public opinion and 'attack, attack, attack' in order to push the Government further down the slope to destruction. The knock-about tactics involved in vigorous opposition are fairly easy to maintain, and frequent

[1] See H. J. Hanham, 'Opposition Techniques in British Politics (1867–1914)', *Government and Opposition*, 1966–7, pp. 35–48.

censure motions, regular divisions at the second and third reading of Bills, delaying tactics at the Committee stage, late sittings, and various other Parliamentary practices that the Opposition can use to fight the Government, are generally enjoyable for the participants (the Opposition participants, that is). Also, backbench MPs and party supporters generally urge uncompromising opposition at all times, as they tend to see virtually all Government actions in an unfavourable light, unlike less committed electors who are more discriminating in their attitude towards the Government. Further, regular outspoken attacks upon the Government enable the Opposition to attract publicity to itself. The news media are interested in 'action' rather than in 'opinion', and as the Government controls events in a way that the Opposition does not, there is a great temptation for the Opposition to try to attract news coverage to itself by all means possible, including dramatic and vigorous outbursts against the Government's 'villainy'.

For all of these reasons there is generally great pressure on the Opposition to 'swear horrible'. Uncompromising attack, however, has its limitations as a tactic for an Opposition to follow. In the first place, the Opposition has something of a responsibility 'in the national interest' to avoid unrestrained criticism. Ramsay MacDonald, for example, regarded opposition for its own sake as 'a crime against the state'.[1] He argued that opposition to legislation should not be carried beyond the Second Reading stage, and that after this the Opposition should concern itself with seeking to improve details within the broad principle of the measure, as 'The Opposition has no right to obstruct in the sense of making Parliament barren or unproductive.'[2] Many of the factors that were quoted earlier[3] as undesirable features of the British system of an official Opposition are all the more applicable if the Opposition leaders acquiesce to the demands of their more militant supporters for constant and uncompromising attacks upon the Government. The discouragement of Ministerial initiative, and the encouragement of Government secrecy; the highlighting of national

[1] Evidence to the 1931 Select Committee on Procedure (H.C. 161 of 1931, par. 29).

[2] Ibid.

[3] See above, pp. 27–9.

failures, and the playing down of national success; the cement-
ing of prejudices within the party and the electorate as a whole;
the often manufactured anger over issues on which the party
leaders are known to broadly agree—these features are all the
more likely to be characteristic of the British system if the
Opposition is especially militant in its tactics.

The recognition by Opposition leaders of the considerable
destructive and divisive powers that they possess can produce,
of course, a responsible approach to the use of these powers.
Even when this consideration does not influence Opposition
leaders, there are still other considerations of self-interest which
place some restrictions on Opposition attacks. Most important
of all, perhaps, vigorous Opposition might please party militants, but it does not necessarily gain support for the Opposition
among the electorate at large. The Opposition is clearly wise
to mount an all-out attack upon the Government on an issue
on which the Opposition has a particularly good case, and in
which the electorate is interested. There is a further incentive
if the Government seems likely to make concessions to the
Opposition's point of view. There is clearly less wisdom in
vigorous criticism, however, if the Opposition's case is weak,
the Government is firmly committed on the issue, and the
public is broadly sympathetic with the Government. Even in
such circumstances, of course, the Opposition may be pressed
to pursue its criticisms because its own particular supporters,
in or out of Parliament, expect the Opposition to put up some
sort of resistance to what they see as a partisan measure. The
Opposition has to preserve the loyalty of its militants upon
whose work and financial contributions it depends for a successful election campaign. At the same time, the Opposition
can only win an election if it succeeds in convincing a large
number of 'floating voters' that it is a reasonable and trust-
worthy alternative to the existing Government.

Thus the unenviable choice before the Opposition is often
that of following a militant line, which will be popular with
the party loyalists, or following a more moderate and 'statesmanlike' line which might add to its appeal as an alternative
Government with the less committed voters. To some extent
this was the Labour Opposition's dilemma over the Industrial
Relations Bill in the 1970–1 session. Among the electorate as

a whole there was undoubtedly a widespread feeling that 'something should be done about the unions', so that Labour's Parliamentary leaders might have been able to gain some electoral advantage by adopting a conciliatory attitude towards the Bill. A large section of the Labour Party, however, and particularly the unions themselves, were bitterly opposed to the measure, and the party was thereby obliged to mount an all-out Parliamentary attack on the Bill.

On occasions in the past, opposition to Government policies has been pressed to extreme lengths. In 1912, at a time when there were threats of civil war in Ireland over the home rule issue, the Leader of the Opposition, Bonar Law, was seen to be condoning armed resistance to the Liberal Government's policies when he declared publicly that

> I can imagine no length of resistance to which Ulster will go, which I shall not be ready to support and in which they will not be supported by an overwhelming majority of the British people.[1]

In the 1880-5 Parliament W. H. Smith's death was brought about largely by the strains imposed upon him as a Minister by the tactics of 'out and out opposition' practised by the Fourth Party,[2] while in the 1950-1 Parliament, when the Labour Government had a precarious majority and seemed likely to fall, the Conservative Opposition sought to wear the Government down physically through constant late-night sittings.[3] These, however, are exceptions to the general rule that the Opposition does not normally press its resistance to Government policies to physically damaging lengths. For the most part, such tactics are counter-productive, as they tend to arouse public sympathy for the Government's plight. The majority of the electorate is aware that no Government is wrong in everything that it does, and an Opposition that paints too black a picture of Government misdeeds risks destroying its own credibility.

---

[1] Quoted in Sir Harold Nicolson, *King George V: His Life and Reign*, London 1952, p. 199.

[2] For a comment see Hanham, *Government and Opposition*, 1966-7, pp. 39-40.

[3] See Hoffman, *The Conservative Party in Opposition 1945-51*, especially pp. 250-69.

Further, excessive criticism from the Opposition can serve to unite a Government party that might otherwise reveal internal divisions. Thus even in 1830 the Duke of Wellington cautioned his Tory colleagues against 'regular factious opposition' to the Reform Bill in case it served to cement the Whig Government together.[1] Indiscriminate attacks can all too easily seem like play-acting, whereas more occasional attacks can carry weight merely because they are selective. Uncompromising opposition is also artificial in a climate of consensus politics, when one Government's policies seem only marginally different from those of its predecessor. An Opposition which is faced by a Government with a clear ideological commitment, such as to increase public ownership, or reduce the welfare activities of the state, has an easier task than an Opposition facing a Government which has no clear ideological commitment, but which pursues policies based on pragmatic considerations. Thus the task of the Conservative Opposition in the 1945–51 period (faced with a Labour Government implementing a full programme of nationalisation), or of the Labour Opposition early in the 1970 Parliament (when the Conservative Government seemed to have taken a sharp turn to the 'right'), was easier than that of Labour and Conservative Oppositions in the 1951–70 period of 'Butskellism' and pragmatic politics. As one Conservative Research Department officer complained of the 1964–70 period, ' . . . it was much easier in 1945–51 when we at least had some socialism to attack.'[2]

The Opposition's tactics will be governed to some extent by the stage reached in the Parliament. In the first few weeks, or even months, of a new Government's life ex-Ministers and new Ministers often have difficulty in adjusting to their new role (as exemplified, perhaps, by the fact that Sir Alec Douglas-Home referred to Harold Wilson as 'the Prime Minister' on more than one occasion in the same day in the Commons in July 1970).[3] Although flushed with electoral success, the new Ministers are almost certainly less well informed than those they are succeeding. While this situation will soon alter, early

[1] Feiling, *The Second Tory Party*, p. 384.
[2] Quoted in Butler and Pinto-Duschinsky, *The British General Election of 1970*, p. 63.
[3] 805 H.C. Deb. 5s cols. 56 and 61.

Government mistakes can lead the Opposition to think that a rapid return to office is possible. At the same time, a new Government usually enjoys a 'honeymoon period' of several months in which the electorate is prepared to give Ministers a chance to demonstrate their abilities. Also, in the first year or so of a new Government's life, the electorate will still hold the old Government to blame for many aspects of current problems. In March, 1966, for example, a National Opinion Poll survey indicated that most of the electorate still blamed the Conservatives for the nation's economic problems, even though the Labour Government had then been in office for eighteen months.[1] In this situation Opposition attacks will be less effective than at a time when Government policies have patently failed to produce the desired ends. Nevertheless, early in a Parliament the Opposition is often compelled to indulge in vigorous criticism in response to the new Government's policies. In the confidence that stems from electoral success, a new Government may seek to implement controversial policies that it has been nurturing in opposition. Even if it does not actually present legislation, it may well make partisan statements of intent. The new Opposition then has little option but to state its objections in forthright terms, despite any claims by the Government that it has a clear 'mandate' to implement its policies.

Thus early in a Parliament the Opposition's task is to try to persuade the electorate that all is not well with the new Government, without drawing attention to its own failures in office. It is precisely at this time, however, that the Opposition is often tempted to seek to justify its own recent period in office, although this can merely serve to highlight its failures and distract attention from the mistakes being made by the new Government. The longer a Government remains in power, the fainter becomes the electorate's memory of the Opposition's previous record in office, and it becomes easier for the Opposition to blame the Government for current catastrophes. At the same time, although criticism of the Government becomes easier, the Opposition loses credibility as an alternative Government, as its front bench seems to be filled with a combination of old ex-Ministers, about whom the electorate has almost

[1] Quoted in Butler and King, *The British General Election of 1966*, p. 265.

forgotten, and young newcomers who have made little or no impact through the news media. Also, although late in a Government's life it can readily be held solely responsible for the nation's ills, such criticism can rebound on the Opposition when it comes to power itself, as it will then have to deal with problems that it condemned the old Government for failing to solve. Criticism has thus to be tempered with realism.

Thus because the Opposition's role is only temporary, it is all the more likely, and all the more advised, to be 'loyal' and 'responsible' in the manner in which it opposes. As a Privy Councillor, a potential Prime Minister, and often an ex-Prime Minister, the Leader of the Opposition is given access to secret Government information, and is consulted on major issues by the Prime Minister. A. J. Balfour often repeated the popular assertion that the function of the Opposition is to oppose, and in the days of the Fourth Party he had led many uncompromising attacks on the Gladstone Government.[1] In 1908, however, he accepted Asquith's invitation to join the counsels of the Committee of Imperial Defence, and this represented the most formal arrangement for contacts between a Leader of the Opposition and a Government that had been made up to that time.[2] In effect, Balfour was giving semi-official advice to the Government, and this clearly clashed with his own theories of uncompromising opposition. Bonar Law also served on the Committee of Imperial Defence, and in February 1913 he had confidential talks with Asquith over the Ulster crisis.[3] When Prime Minister in 1924 Ramsay MacDonald often sent Foreign Office papers to the Leader of the Opposition, Stanley Baldwin, in an attempt to achieve agreement on foreign policy.[4] MacDonald also consulted Baldwin in search of an all-party agreement on Ireland. Baldwin was anxious to preserve a Parliamentary consensus, although Churchill in particular resented his sympathy for the Government, and in 1929 MacDonald and Baldwin again sought to maintain front-bench unity over India policy.[5] In 1970 and 1971 the Prime Minister and the

[1] See above, p. 198.   [2] Young, *Arthur James Balfour*, pp. 263, 269.
[3] Beaverbrook, *Politicians and the War 1914–16*, I, p. 35; Chamberlain, *Politics From the Inside*, p. 605.
[4] Middlemas and Barnes, *Baldwin*, p. 268.
[5] Ibid., pp. 538–41; Young, *Baldwin*, p. 146.

Leader of the Opposition sought to maintain a degree of all-party agreement on the Ulster question. On this basis, on 18 October 1971, Harold Wilson and James Callaghan (then Opposition Spokesman on Home Affairs) requested and were immediately granted, consultations with the Prime Minister and the Home Secretary over allegations of brutality against internees in Ulster,[1] and when Wilson visited Ireland in November 1971 he was accompanied by a member of the staff of the Cabinet office.[2]

All opposition is not necessarily silenced by such co-operation between Ministers and Opposition leaders, as there are generally numerous groups or individuals outside the official Opposition who are not inclined to be 'responsible' in their attitude to Government policies. Indeed, the very existence of such unofficial and uncompromising critics can make it easier for the official Opposition to be statesmanlike in its attitude: the Opposition leaders can adopt a responsible stance on issues such as (recently) Ireland, law and order, or coloured immigration, in the knowledge that some of their backbench colleagues are likely to be less inhibited, and will make electoral capital for the party out of the issue. In this way the Opposition party can get the best of both worlds—a statesmanlike stance from the front bench, and political point-scoring from back benchers. Nevertheless, open co-operation with the Government has its dangers for the Opposition. The introduction of a salary for the Leader of the Opposition in 1937 was seen by many as giving him an obligation to the Government, and thereby emasculating him as an opposition figure. One Labour MP, Josiah Wedgwood, argued that ' . . . I had far rather it came from the party and from his friends than it should come from the Government and the Consolidated Fund . . .', and another, Ellis Smith, talked of ' . . . the bait which is always held out in order to obtain a compromise and create an atmosphere which will undermine the stand you are taking up.'[3] Ellis Smith's point was soon illustrated, as in December 1937 the Leader of the Opposition, Clement Attlee, was criticised by Conservative MPs when he returned from a visit to Spain and denounced the British policy of non-intervention in the

[1] See *The Times*, 19 October 1971.   [2] See *The Times*, 20 November 1971.
[3] 322 H.C. Deb. 5s col. 691; 323 H.C. Deb. 5s col. 634.

Spanish Civil War.[1] The Conservatives claimed that although Attlee was in opposition, he had an obligation, as a leading national figure, to defend the British Government abroad, and that this obligation was all the greater as he was a salaried officer of Parliament. Similarly, in 1969 Heath was criticised for speaking out against the Labour Government during a press conference on a visit to the USA.[2] The implication of the criticism was that although he was Leader of the Opposition, he was leading Her Majesty's *Loyal* Opposition, and thus had obligations of loyalty to national policy.

Defence, foreign affairs, and finance are subjects where 'the national interest' is frequently invoked, and where it is often desirable that the Opposition be made aware of the considerations behind a particular policy of the Government. This applies to all Opposition Spokesmen as well as to the Leader of the Opposition. It is clearly in the interests of the Defence Ministry, for example, that the Opposition Defence Spokesman be aware of the difficulties facing the military in particular situations, and the Opposition Spokesmen are often invited by the Defence Ministry to tour military establishments at home and abroad to gain first-hand experience of policy in action. Clearly, however, this can be inhibiting for an Opposition, and undoubtedly at times a Ministerial tactic is to 'flatter' an Opposition Spokesman by revealing to him confidential material which has the effect of undermining an Opposition line of attack. Thus on occasions a Spokesman will decline an invitation to be taken into a Minister's confidence, and will prefer to lead a full-blooded attack on Government policy without full knowledge of all the problems facing the Government. In the context of the 'Beeching cuts' in railway services in the nineteen-sixties, Labour Transport Spokesmen often declined the Minister's kind offer to reveal precisely why certain lines had to be closed, and no doubt the Opposition's attacks were all the more effective as a result. Similarly, in 1958, Hugh Gaitskell (then Leader of the Opposition) declined an invitation from Harold Macmillan to hold joint talks on defence policy. Gaitskell felt that such open co-operation could limit

---

[1] See 330 H.C. Deb. 5s col. 824. See also Max Beloff, 'The Leader of the Opposition', *Parliamentary Affairs*, 1957–8, pp. 155–62.
[2] See *The Times*, 28 and 29 May and 13 June 1969.

his Constitutional function of criticism, and might place him in a compromising position with backbenchers who were particularly militant on defence matters. Professor Max Beloff criticised Gaitskell's attitude on the grounds that the Opposition has a duty to the Crown to be co-operative and 'loyal' on matters like foreign policy and defence, and should look to the future when it might form the Government.[1] Beloff also argued that the Opposition should oppose whenever possible on the basis of maximum information.

In the past the most vigorous and outspoken Oppositions have invariably been Conservative Oppositions. In particular, much of the 1905–15 and 1945–51 periods of Conservative Opposition were marked by the ferocity with which the Liberal and Labour Governments' proposals were fought. To some extent this may be because these Governments were seeking to implement exceptionally controversial measures, like the constitutional and financial reforms of the 1905–15 period, and the nationalisation and social welfare programmes of the 1945–1951 period, or it may be that a 'left wing' Government will always arouse more controversy than will a 'conservative' one. Again, perhaps the Conservative Party, in its comparatively short and infrequent periods in opposition, will always react sharply when another party seems to be usurping its role as the country's natural rulers. Various people, however, have pointed to aspects of Labour Party organisation and attitudes as being likely to reduce the party's combativeness when in opposition. It has been argued, for example, that the outspoken militancy that many left-wing politicians exhibit outside Parliament is rarely maintained if they become MPs, as they are overawed by the seeming importance of their new role, and by the atmosphere and traditions of Parliament: they are rapidly socialised into the norms of moderate Parliamentary behaviour. The 'taming' of the Clydeside firebrands of the nineteen-twenties has been attributed to this factor.[2] Again, R. E. Dowse has argued that the size of the trade union element within the PLP produces docility.[3] He claims that

[1] See *The Times*, 29 April 1958.
[2] See R. K. Middlemas, *The Clydesiders*, London 1965, especially pp. 272–84.
[3] R. E. Dowse, 'The PLP in Opposition', *Parliamentary Affairs*, 1959–60, pp. 520–9.

trade unionists tend to be comparatively old, and therefore staid, by the time they obtain a Parliamentary seat, and that through their industrial background they are conditioned to seek their goals through slow and unspectacular negotiation, rather than through dramatic frontal assaults. Because of this (argues Dowse), and because they tend to see the Parliamentary battle as less significant than the extra-Parliamentary fight, they are comparatively restrained in their Parliamentary activities. Yet again, it may be (as Sir Ivor Jennings has argued)[1] that the Labour Party's particular need to prove to the British electorate that it is a respectable and responsible party, capable of forming a Government, means that its Parliamentary style has to be cautious and muted: as the respectability of the Conservative Party is rarely in doubt, it can more readily afford to behave in an outrageous manner when in opposition. Certainly, the longer a party spends in opposition, the greater its need to demonstrate that it is not merely a party of opposition, but that it can behave with the degree of responsibility that is looked for in Ministers and potential Ministers. All parties when in opposition, however, have to beware of behaving in such a way in their role as critics of the Government that they destroy their credibility in their other role as an alternative Government. The Opposition's more positive attempts to present itself as an alternative Government, by planning and advertising its strategy for office, are considered in the next section.

Preparing for Office

While in opposition, how far should a party go in attempting to prepare for its next period in office? In looking to the future should it work on the small print of possible future legislation, or is it better to undertake a more general and impressionistic review of party aims and philosophy? Although, as discussed in Chapter 7, both parties have elaborate machinery for studying policy issues when in opposition, it may be questioned whether it is indeed profitable for a party to use its time in opposition to plan in any detail the policies that it hopes to implement when it returns to power. There are, of course, invariably great

[1] Jennings, *Parliament*, p. 179.

pressures on party leaders to work on policy details in opposition. The shock of an electoral defeat, and the inquest that usually follows it, often produces a demand that the comparative leisure of opposition be used to examine past policy failures, and prepare detailed policy for the next period in office. R. A. Butler has argued that following their overwhelming electoral defeat in 1945, the Conservatives were obliged to indulge in a major and well-publicised review of their aims in order to convince the electorate that they had moved away from their 1930s attitudes.[1] With the Labour Party there is a tendency for electoral defeat to be followed by a period of introspection, and in the 1951–64 period the party's intellectual leaders indulged in great philosophical exercises. Ministers often complain that in government the inevitable concern with immediate problems prevents an appraisal of long-term policy aims, and that only in opposition can this be done effectively. A new Minister with policies prepared in detail in opposition can galvanise the civil service, and this can help the Minister to establish his influence in the department. Without clear ideas as to both ends and means, a new Minister will find it all the more difficult to impose his will on his civil servants when he arrives from opposition. A party that does come to office with clear-cut ideas of what it wants to achieve in both the short and the long run, and with specific policies worked out in detail, can begin implementing its proposals at once. Thus the introduction of Corporation Tax, and some of the other tax changes that the 1964 Wilson Government introduced in its first budgets, were prepared in opposition. Equally, the groundwork for Anthony Barber's budgets in 1970 and 1971 was done by Iain Macleod as Treasury Spokesman in the 1966–70 Parliament, and one interviewed Conservative MP argued that a major reason why Barber was selected to become Chancellor of the Exchequer on Macleod's death was because he was sympathetic with Macleod's aims and would expedite the implementation of tax changes that had been planned in detail in opposition. An unprepared Government can waste the first months, or perhaps years, of a Parliament. Lord George Brown has argued that before 1964 the Labour Party should have prepared in much greater detail

[1] Lord Butler, *The Art of the Possible*, London 1971, p. 133.

for the introduction of the Department of Economic Affairs.[1] Perhaps the classic example of lack of preparation, however, was the failure of the Labour Party before 1945 to make detailed plans for the implementation of its long standing nationalisation proposals. Thus when Emanuel Shinwell, as Minister of Fuel and Power in 1945, was called upon to nationalise the coal mining industry he had to start completely from scratch.[2] In contrast, the new Conservative Government in 1970 was able to introduce very quickly an Immigration Bill, and make changes in the organisation of the social services, because detailed work on these matters had been done in opposition.[3] It can be argued, of course, that any new Government will have definite views on how to tackle current problems: if this is the case, however, it is perhaps desirable that its prejudices at least be based on detailed information gleaned in opposition. The process of acquiring the information for a policy enquiry can bring the party into contact with important groups outside Parliament. One Conservative Spokesman, for example, claimed in interview that in the 1964–70 period his party benefited greatly from its contacts with economists, academics, and social welfare pressure groups, many of whom had previously been hostile to the party.[4]

The more detailed the changes that a party wishes to make, the greater the need for it to make plans in depth before coming to office: a party that is content largely to maintain the status quo, clearly has less need to prepare itself for office. For any party, however, the involvement of MPs and party activists in the process of re-thinking policies can help to combat the frustrations of opposition. Also, it can serve to educate the party in the theory and practice of policy making, and can reveal to those involved the problems of implementing particular party ideals. Thus in interview a number of Spokesmen suggested that one of their prime functions was to act as a catalyst for the Parliamentary and extra-Parliamentary party, stimulating a re-consideration of basic policies while in opposition. Some also argued that involving their colleagues in

[1] Brown, *In My Way*, p. 96.   [2] See Shinwell, *The Labour Story*, p. 182.
[3] For a comment see *The Times*, 29 June 1970 ('Takeover Problems').
[4] See also Butler and Pinto-Duschinsky, *The British General Election of 1970*, p. 67, for a comment on this.

debates on policy details at least prevented them from falling out over personalities or basic philosophy. A great 'policy exercise' can also be presented to the electorate as an indication that the party is prepared for office, and is aware of its responsibility as an alternative Government. In this way the work of policy committees can serve as the Opposition's equivalent of Royal Commission enquiries, indicating to the electorate that particular issues are 'under consideration', while at the same time postponing the need for clear commitments to be made. Compared with Royal Commissions, party policy committees have the added advantage that their reports do not necessarily have to be made public. Edward Heath favoured the idea of an Opposition going into great detail in the preparation of its policies for office on the grounds that

> . . . people today are so cynical and sceptical about the whole machinery of government that detail is needed to convince them that you really intend to carry out your promises.[1]

Thus before the 1970 general election Conservative leaders frequently claimed with pride that never before had an opposition party prepared itself for office with such detailed policies. In particular, attention was focused on the party's researches into the structure of government, in an attempt to encourage the view that a Conservative Government would be more 'efficient' than was the Wilson Government.[2] In their study of the 1970 election, however, Butler and Pinto-Duschinsky concluded that, in electoral terms, the party neither gained nor lost support as a result of the efforts to appear primed for office.[3] At the same time, many people undoubtedly felt that Labour lost the 1970 election partly because it failed to inspire the electorate by presenting new policies,[4] so that even early in the 1970 Parliament many Labour leaders were seeking to precipitate a major policy review within the Labour Movement. Roy Jenkins has since argued that Labour in opposition should concentrate on a fairly small, but well-defined, number

---

[1] See Butler and Pinto-Duschinsky, *The British General Election of 1970*, p. 66.

[2] Ibid., p. 68.   [3] Ibid., p. 92.

[4] See, for example, 'Mr. Wilson's Leadership', *Political Quarterly*, 1971, pp. 353–62.

of policy issues, and should strive to become clearly associated in the public mind with these specific objectives.[1] In this way (argued Jenkins) the party could best persuade the electorate of its readiness for office, with a clear sense of purpose and direction.

Thus there is a great temptation for a party in opposition to prepare the details of policies that it hopes soon to be able to implement. There are undoubted dangers in this, however. Great policy revisions in opposition can divide a party, as Labour found to its cost in the early nineteen-sixties, when major divisions emerged from Hugh Gaitskell's call for a re-thinking of party attitudes. Even if such divisions within the party are avoided, specific policy proposals provide targets at which the Government can aim. A century ago, when Gladstone, while in opposition, was pressed to reveal a detailed scheme for Irish home rule, he declared to Lord Rosebery that 'It is not the province of the person leading the party in opposition, to frame and produce before the public detailed schemes. . . .'[2] Disraeli was also aware of the limitations for a party in opposition of constantly having to pose as a responsible body with an alternative set of policies: he declared that

> The principle, now conveniently assumed by our opponents, that the Opposition is a body prepared to take office, and therefore bound to give its quasi-official opinion on the conduct of every department, seems to me to have no solid foundation, and is very injurious [to the Opposition][3].

More recently, Winston Churchill made much the same point, arguing that 'When an Opposition spells out its policy in detail . . . the Government becomes the Opposition and attacks the Opposition which becomes the Government. So, having failed to win the sweets of office, it fails equally to enjoy the benefits of being out of office.'[4] In accordance with this point of view, Churchill was somewhat suspicious of R. A. Butler's attempts to stimulate a re-thinking of Conservative principles during the 1945–51 period in opposition, and Churchill sought to

---

[1] BBC radio interview, reported in *The Guardian*, 27 May 1972.
[2] Morley, *Life of Gladstone*, II, p. 358.
[3] Monypenny and Buckle, *Life of Benjamin Disraeli*, IV, p. 405.
[4] Lord Butler, *The Art of the Possible*, p. 135.

keep the policy statements more vague than Butler and some others wished.[1]

Opposition policy proposals are invariably subjected to the question, 'why didn't you do it when you were in office?', or to the assertion that the Opposition is indulging in a purely theoretical exercise, far removed from the realities of office. Certainly, the Opposition lacks the advice of the civil service. Although, as is discussed in Chapter 8, a party in opposition can get assistance from its own Research Department, and from pressure groups, such advice is often one-sided, as not all interested parties will co-operate with the Opposition in the way they will with the Government. Policies made in opposition, without the benefit of 'the departmental point of view', thus can prove to be impractical or excessively partisan when office is attained. Thus in interview one Labour MP claimed that faced with a report from an NEC policy group he had to 'ignore it in a tactful manner', both as a Spokesman before 1964 and then as a Minister in the Wilson Government. The 1970 Industrial Relations Bill is perhaps an example of such a measure, designed, as it was, in opposition when party political pressures were strong.[2] The longer a party spends in opposition, and the more it loses touch with the realities of office, the more unreal and dangerous its attempts at policy making are likely to be. This is perhaps especially the case with the Labour Party, as even at the best of times ex-Ministers have only a limited role in the party's formal machinery for policy-making in opposition.[3] In some fields, of course, like education or agriculture, the factual information on which future policies have to be based is quite readily available. In other spheres, however, like defence, foreign affairs, or economic policy, much of the necessary information is available only from the department concerned. In these fields, detailed commitments made in opposition can be particularly embarrassing when the party achieves office and is faced with facts of which it was ignorant while in opposition. This was perhaps Labour's experience in the 1964–70 period, and in a post-

[1] Lord Butler, *The Art of the Possible*, p. 135.

[2] For a comment see *The Times*, 31 March 1970 ('Reform Hawks in the Ascendent').

[3] See below, pp. 267–72.

mortem on the Wilson Government's record, Professor A. H. Hanson concluded that 'The illusion that a party, having worked out a programme, can then proceed to a stage-by-stage implementation of it is now thoroughly shattered.'[1]

It is widely assumed, not least by Opposition MPs and supporters, that the Opposition has to have a clear policy, or at least 'a point of view', on every issue that emerges. Certainly, an Opposition that constantly declined to give a view on issues would damage its credibility as an alternative Government. At the same time, the Opposition is *not* the Government, and thus can reasonably point out that it should not be expected to have detailed policies for every issue that emerges. While on many occasions an effective tactic for the Opposition is to condemn the Government's actions, and at the same time present details of an alternative line of action, such an approach has many pitfalls. Opposition policies can quickly become out of date, especially if the Government anticipates the Opposition's intentions and changes its own policy accordingly. Alternatively, policies that are prepared and advertised in opposition can become 'pledges', which can quite quickly become 'broken promises' once the party comes to power. Thus soon after Labour came to power in 1964 Enoch Powell was able to attack the new Ministers on the basis that

> Within six weeks the brave new Government have run away from every one of the theses which they put forward in Opposition. They have adopted, with an exactitude that can only be stigmatized as plagiarism, the assertions of their political opponents.[2]

Specific commitments can also damage the Opposition's electoral prospects, and Labour's pledge to re-nationalise the iron and steel industry, after its de-nationalisation in 1953, remained as an often electorally embarrassing commitment throughout the rest of that long period in opposition. As was noted in the previous section, policy commitments cannot be avoided entirely, as to some extent a party cannot avoid making some pledges as part of its day-to-day comment upon the policies that the Government is pursuing. Thus Conservative commitments made before 1970 to give pensions to the over eighties,

[1] A. H. Hanson, 'The Future of the Labour Party', *Political Quarterly*, 1970, p. 385.   [2] Roth, *Enoch Powell*, p. 318.

and preserve the fee-paying principle in some Scottish schools, arose in this way. In these cases the commitments did not prove to be particularly embarrassing, as some action could be taken fairly easily when office was achieved. This, however, is a very different process from that of creating machinery with the specific objective of preparing and advertising detailed policies that the party intends to implement if elected. To some extent the Opposition can work quietly on its policy intentions without publicising the results of its enquiries. This will enable it to prepare for office without publicly committing itself. Such secrecy is difficult to maintain, however, and the Government and the press can seize on any 'leaks' there may be to present policy making behind locked doors as a somewhat sinister exercise. The speculation that developed in 1969 out of the Scottish Conservatives' silence over their policy on a Scottish Parliament perhaps illustrates this, as does the Conservative Government's embarrassment in 1971 over the revelation of proposals, made by a Spokesman in opposition, to dispose of the assets of the state-owned Upper Clyde Shipbuilders.[1] Even if policy is successfully worked out in secret, these proposals will still have been prepared without civil service advice, and because they are secret the electorate will be unaware that the party has prepared itself for office.

To some extent, therefore, the Opposition is bound to lose out. If it makes a lot of detailed policy, it may well be entering into commitments which will have to be altered when it meets civil service advice. If it makes no preparations, or works on policy in secret, it may be regarded by the electorate as being unprepared for office, with no new initiatives. On balance, the Opposition is probably best advised to err on the side of caution and to avoid making a lot of detailed preparations which might have to be modified or abandoned in face of the realities of office. Probably the most profitable approach for the Opposition is to seek to create among the electorate a general climate of opinion favourable to the broad aims of the party, rather than to specify the details of legislation it hopes one day to implement. Like any salesman, a political party has to create a basis of acceptance for the general nature and quality of its product. Thus its best tactic is to emphasise a 'glorious theme'.

[1] See *The Guardian*, 15 June 1971 and 19 October 1971.

In the 1945–51 period the Conservative Party in opposition sought, with some success, to encourage the attitude among the electorate that the state interfered in social and economic affairs to too great an extent, and that 'Conservative freedom' was a desirable alternative to 'Socialist controls'. Towards the end of the 1951–64 period in opposition the Labour Party was successful in persuading the electorate to accept the general proposition that more Governmental activity was necessary after a decade of social and economic stagnation. At the same time, in the 1966–70 Parliament the Government's incomes policy, and some of its other policies, perhaps failed because the party had not prepared either its own supporters, or the electorate in general, for what it was hoping to do.

A speech by Douglas Houghton in December 1970, on the Second Reading of the Industrial Relations Bill, is perhaps a model of the most profitable approach for an Opposition to take.[1] Houghton attacked the Government's proposals in the broadest possible philosophical terms. He made it clear that the Labour Party disagreed in principle with the approach embodied in the Government's proposals, but he avoided making any specific commitments as to what his party would do if returned to power. Above all he avoided any commitment to 'instant repeal' by a future Labour Government, although there were strong feelings in some sections of the party that such a pledge should be given. There are, of course, limits as to how far this can be taken. On occasions the Opposition will have to reveal the alternatives it offers, perhaps in detail, if it is to avoid seeming purely negative. If it is wise, however, the Opposition will confine such declarations of intent to the minimum, and as far as possible it will confine itself to encouraging public awareness of, and sympathy towards, its broad principles. This approach may well pay dividends electorally. More than this, however, if while in opposition a party can create a climate of public opinion broadly favourable to its own general philosophy, its activities when it does achieve office are likely to be all the more readily acceptable to the public. Thus a party's prospects of a successful period in office are probably best served by a spell in opposition devoted to emphasising the party's general approach to the problems of

[1] 808 H.C. Deb. 5s cols. 1143–52.

the day, rather than by working on the small print of possible future legislation: as expressed recently by Professor Crick, 'The real role of an Opposition is to prepare the public for the support its policies will need not just by casting their votes but by how they lead their lives. . . .'[1]

Thus, in facing the question, 'how can we achieve a successful period in office in the future?', the Opposition is probably best advised to resist the twin temptations of indulging in out-and-out opposition, and of preparing policies in detail. As has been argued in this and the preceding section of this chapter, its best overall strategy is to temper its criticisms of the Government with the moderation and statesmanship that is looked for in a potential Government, while preparing only in the most general terms for the broad theme that it hopes to emphasise when in office. Clearly, however, the Opposition's task is a difficult one, and the Opposition has to steer a very careful course between extremes. As a critic of the Government it has to please its own committed followers by making vigorous attacks upon 'the enemy', but it has also to make its criticisms seem fair and credible to less committed voters. If it is excessively responsible and cautious it will be ineffective as a critic: if it is too irresponsible, it risks losing electoral support by damaging its image as an alternative Government. As an alternative Government it has to acquire at least an aura of preparedness for office, without foreclosing its options before encountering the realities of power. It has to appear ready for office without presenting too many clear targets for the Government to ridicule as 'dangerous Opposition star-gazing'. It has to condemn Government actions without binding itself to too many pledges. It has to concern itself with the immediate situation, but it also has to look ahead to the next election, when it will be trying to persuade the electorate to promote it to office. It has to lead the attack upon what the Government is currently doing, but it has also to appear as the alternative Government, demonstrating that it is sufficiently responsible to do a better job than the current Ministry. In short, it has to 'conduct a war' against the Government while at the same time considering the problems that it will itself face in the task of 'post-war reconstruction'. In these ways the combination of the

[1] *Political Quarterly*, 1971, p. 361.

two basic functions that the Opposition performs (exposing Government deficiencies, and offering a choice of Government to the electorate) complicates the tactics of Opposition. The extent to which the Opposition is able to resolve these difficulties, and the extent to which it develops successfully a cohesive strategy, will be determined primarily by the members of the Opposition front-bench team. The way in which they approach their duties is considered in the next four chapters.

7

The Role and Organisation
of the Shadow Cabinet

LABOUR'S PARLIAMENTARY COMMITTEE and the Conservatives' Consultative Committee are popularly referred to
as the 'Shadow Cabinet', implying a direct comparison with
the actual Ministerial Cabinet. Clearly, however, the two
bodies perform very different functions.[1] While the Cabinet is
concerned with the immediate problems of government, and
the coordination of the work of the departments of state, the
Shadow Cabinet is concerned mainly with the tactical political
considerations of Parliamentary Opposition, and with the
management of the Parliamentary affairs of the Opposition
party. Very broadly, meetings of the Shadow Cabinet are concerned with four main types of business—Parliamentary tactics,
short term policy attitudes, day-to-day Parliamentary business,
and long-term party policy. The prime concern is with the
planning of the immediate tactics and organisation of the
Opposition in the Commons, and to a lesser extent in the
Lords. This involves deciding which items of business will be
opposed, whether the House will be divided, whether late
sittings will be forced, and so on. A major recurring item is the
use to which Supply Days will be put. The Opposition has at

---

[1] A background knowledge of the practices and procedures of the
Cabinet is assumed here. For details of the day-to-day working of the
Cabinet see P. Gordon Walker, *The Cabinet*, London 1970. For lengthier
studies of the role of the Cabinet see J. P. Mackintosh, *The British Cabinet*,
London 1962; H. Daalder, *Cabinet Reform*, London 1962; Sir Ivor Jennings,
Cabinet Government, London 1959.

its disposal twenty-nine[1] of these days, spread throughout the session, when it is allowed to select the subjects for debate. The Opposition will generally welcome the initiative that this procedure provides, although often a Supply Day will come at an inconvenient time for the Opposition, and it can be something of a problem for the Shadow Cabinet to select a suitably topical issue on which the Opposition has a good case.

The Shadow Cabinet will also decide who will speak for the Opposition in the week's debates, and who will lead the attack in Question Time. Generally, this is the first matter to be dealt with at Shadow Cabinet meetings, after which the whipping arrangements are considered. Many of the decisions as to who will speak in debates will be more or less automatic. The senior and assistant Education Spokesmen, for example, will normally open and close for the Opposition in an education debate, or the Agriculture Spokesmen in an agricultural debate. To some extent also the question of who will speak for the Opposition will be determined by the Government's own arrangements for the debate. A major speech by the Prime Minister almost certainly will be answered by the Leader of the Opposition, and the Chancellor of the Exchequer by the Treasury Spokesman, while a junior Spokesman will normally be selected to follow a junior Minister. In some instances, however, it is less obvious who should speak for the Opposition. A debate may cover more than one departmental area, and it may be decided to use the senior Defence Spokesman in a Foreign Affairs debate, or a Legal Spokesman to give weight to Opposition arguments on a technical subject. Also, a major debate covering two days will involve four major speeches for the Opposition (opening and closing speeches on each day), and it may be decided to use the party leader or the deputy leader for one of these speeches, or to bring forward a particularly competent backbencher as one of the principal Opposition speakers. Thus in the 1966–70 Parliament in debates on the Nigerian civil war, Edward Heath or Reginald Maudling, as party leader and deputy leader, would often open and close for the Opposition, rather than the Spokesman most directly concerned, while

---

[1] Four of the twenty-nine, however, are always given over to Defence debates, and four others are only half days, so that in effect the Opposition has only twenty-one full Supply Days at its disposal.

in the big Common Market debate of November 1971 Peter Shore and Douglas Jay were brought from the back benches to lead for the Labour Opposition (although the special circumstances of this particular debate are noted elsewhere).[1] These matters will be decided by the Shadow Cabinet.

As well as this purely organisational function, the Shadow Cabinet also determines the policy attitudes of the Opposition towards immediate issues, deciding the line to be taken in debates, the aspects of Government policy to attack, the current issues to be emphasised and those to be under-played, and the vigour with which the attack will be pressed. For every Opposition there is a time to be silent and a time to speak out, and successful opposition depends to a considerable extent on the Shadow Cabinet being able to judge which particular issues to attack most vigorously, and which to play down. While the detailed content of speeches will be left to the individual Spokesmen to decide, the Shadow Cabinet will lay down the broad strategy of the lines along which the Opposition's attack will be mounted.

The Shadow Cabinet is also responsible for managing the day-to-day administrative affairs of the Parliamentary party. In this, a lot of authority will be exercised by the chief whip or the leader, with the Shadow Cabinet becoming involved only when a major problem arises, such as a disciplinary issue. Nevertheless, the general political situation, the state of the party, the morale of Opposition MPs, or the nature of any discontent with the leadership will all be discussed at length at Shadow Cabinet meetings when the immediate business of making arrangements for the next week's business has been dealt with in full. Thus the agenda for Parliamentary Committee meetings contains as a regular item of business 'the political situation'.

Finally, the Shadow Cabinet concerns itself with long term party policy, producing policy statements and manifestos, and planning policies in anticipation of future office. Here, however, a clear and important distinction emerges between the two parties, in that with the Conservative Party policy-making in opposition is much more directly and exclusively a preserve of the Parliamentary leaders than is the case with the Labour

[1] See below, p. 388.

Party.[1] For Labour in opposition, the NEC retains ultimate constitutional responsibility for the formation of official party policy, and the sub-committees, working parties, and study groups that are set up by the NEC to examine aspects of policy are the centre of the party's long term policy making process. This does not prevent the Parliamentary Committee from discussing policy, and individually the Parliamentary leaders are still very much involved in the policy making process. Some Parliamentary Committee members serve on the NEC, and others may be coopted on to its policy committees, while the final form of the election manifesto is decided by joint meetings of the Parliamentary Committee and the NEC. Also, some of the party's commitments to policy ends merely 'emerge' through time as a result of the attitudes taken towards Government policies by the Opposition leaders in the day to day exchanges across the floor of the House. Thus the Parliamentary Committee and the individual Spokesmen are very much involved in the policy-making process, but the fact remains that for Labour in opposition the long term policy-making function is centred in the NEC rather than the Parliamentary Committee.

For the Conservative Party, on the other hand, the Parliamentary leaders retain direct control over the policy-making machinery, and it is the party leader, rather than any extra-Parliamentary body, that has final control over party policy. In this he consults with his Shadow Cabinet colleagues, and he or the Shadow Cabinet may ask Spokesmen to produce a review of policy in a particular area, or individual Spokesmen may take the initiative in submitting policy proposals for consideration at Shadow Cabinet meetings. In the 1964–70 period an extensive system of policy groups was set up, under the general supervision of the party's Advisory Committee on Policy, which was chaired by Edward Heath for most of the period. These Committees produced numerous policy documents which were duly considered by the Consultative Committee and rejected, amended and adopted, as the case might be.

Thus the nature of the relationship between the Shadow

[1] See below, pp. 261–72, for a more detailed discussion of the two parties' machinery for policy-making in opposition.

Cabinet and the policy-making process is different in each party, with the Conservative Consultative Committee being much more directly involved with policy than is Labour's Parliamentary Committee. For both parties, however, these' last two functions (long-term policy-planning and the day-to-day affairs of the Parliamentary party) are the least time-consuming of the Shadow Cabinet's activities, and by far the greatest part of the Shadow Cabinet's time is devoted to organising the Opposition's tactics and attitudes towards the immediate business of the week. Clearly, however, the amount of attention given to these matters in Shadow Cabinet meetings will vary from time to time, and from situation to situation. Immediately after an election defeat, the general state of the party's morale and organisation may be of some concern, and thus may take up a large part of the Shadow Cabinet's time. In a period of party disunity, such as Labour experienced in the mid-fifties and early sixties, disciplinary decisions may have to be taken by the Shadow Cabinet, and this may be very time-consuming. Long term policy is likely to be discussed less at the beginning than at the end of a Parliament, when, as a general election nears, there is a prospect of office. Thus in May 1970 there were a number of lengthy special meetings of the Conservative Shadow Cabinet to discuss the manifesto and the campaign arrangements for the 1970 general election. At any time in a Parliament the Shadow Cabinet may have to consider basic policy attitudes in face of the Government's legislative proposals, and special meetings of the Shadow Cabinet will be held purely to deal with long term policy. Nevertheless, for the most part the business and tactics for the next week in Parliament dominate the Shadow Cabinet's agenda, and among Shadow Cabinet members who were interviewed, estimates varied from two-thirds to three-quarters of Shadow Cabinet time being devoted to these day-to-day matters. The Ministerial Cabinet, of course, has to concern itself to some extent with Parliamentary tactics, business arrangements, and the affairs of the party. The time devoted to these matters, however, will be considerably less in Cabinet than in Shadow Cabinet meetings, as the Cabinet is clearly concerned with much more than these comparatively mundane matters. Similarly, although the Shadow Cabinet spends some time on the discussion of broad policy issues in preparation for office, this is very different from making decisions about the immediate affairs of government. To this extent, then, the title 'Shadow Cabinet' is a misleading one, implying too close a parallel to the real Cabinet. Labour's term 'Parliamentary Committee' is much more appropriate, as it describes accurately what the Shadow Cabinet really is—a committee to organise the day-to-day *Parliamentary* affairs of the party in opposition. Nevertheless, the term 'Shadow Cabinet' is a convenient shorthand, and thus is used here interchangeably with the more precise but cumbersome phrase 'Parliamentary Committee and Consultative Committee'.

Within this very broad definition of the Shadow Cabinet's functions, what are the details of its procedures and practices, and how do they compare with those of the Cabinet? Are the meetings held on the same regular basis as Cabinet meetings, and are they conducted on similar lines? What roles are performed by individual members of the Shadow Cabinet? Is there an 'Inner Shadow Cabinet', or a system of Shadow Cabinet committees, or a Shadow Cabinet Secretariat, mirroring the arrangements of the Cabinet? These matters will be considered in the following sections of this Chapter.

Meetings of the Shadow Cabinet

When and where does the Shadow Cabinet meet, and how are the meetings organised and conducted? The Shadow Cabinet is convened by the chief whip, at the request of the Leader of the Opposition, and in the past there was no certainty that meetings would be called with any regularity. In the 1905–15 period, the Conservative Shadow Cabinet met when the leader decided the situation required it, and on no fixed basis. Both Balfour and Bonar Law tried to avoid summoning it as far as was possible, because the party and its leaders were divided over the tariff question, the reform of the House of Lords, and the Irish home rule issue.[1] Similarly, in the brief 1924 Parliament the Conservative Shadow Cabinet met only infrequently, and at no fixed times,[2] while in the 1929–31 period Baldwin

[1] Fraser, *Joseph Chamberlain*, p. 307; Blake, *The Unknown Prime Minister*, p. 103; Chamberlain, *Politics From the Inside*, p. 527.
[2] Feiling, *The Life of Neville Chamberlain*, p. 114.

again avoided a regular routine of Shadow Cabinet meetings.[1] When the small Business Committee was formed in 1930, however, this body generally met weekly, although Baldwin sometimes broke the routine.[2] In the 1945–51 period, Churchill's Shadow Cabinet met regularly at 6.00 p.m. on Wednesdays, and the members also met for fortnightly lunches at the Savoy, at which political strategy and tactics were discussed.[3] Labour's Parliamentary Committee has always tended to have a much more regular routine. In the 1924–9 Parliament it met daily from Monday to Thursday, in order to discuss the business coming before the House that day.[4] Also in this Parliament the Parliamentary Committee often held an informal 'at home' to deal with policy and other general matters. In the 1931–5 Parliament the small Parliamentary Committee met each day for an hour before Question Time, to decide the tactics for the day's business, and these daily hour-long meetings continued when the Parliamentary Committee returned to its normal size in the 1935 Parliament.[5]

Since 1951 Labour and Conservative Shadow Cabinets have held regular meetings, whenever Parliament has been in session, at 5.00 p.m. on Wednesdays, with additional meetings at other times. The timing of the Wednesday meeting is significant, in that on Tuesday evenings the Government and Opposition chief whips meet to discuss the Parliamentary business for the next week. The Opposition whip states any objections that he may have to the Government's proposed arrangements, and these objections are then considered by the Government whip and the Leader of the House. On the Wednesday, the Opposition whip is told whether or not any concessions have been made in the light of his objections, and he duly reports on the revised arrangements at the Shadow Cabinet meeting on the Wednesday evening. Thus the Shadow Cabinet normally will hear the final details of the next week's business earlier than will the Cabinet, which usually does not meet until the Thursday morning. The Wednesday meeting is

[1] Macleod, *Neville Chamberlain*, p. 134.
[2] Ibid.
[3] Kilmuir, *Political Adventure*, p. 149.
[4] 1925 Labour Party Conference Report, p. 90.
[5] Attlee, *As It Happened*, pp. 77 and 81.

so timed that the Shadow Cabinet can decide on the tactics to adopt over the week's Business Questions, which are put by the Leader of the Opposition to the Leader of the House on the Thursday afternoon. The Parliamentary Committee at its Wednesday meeting would also decide on the line to be taken at the PLP meeting which is held on the Thursday evening. For the Conservatives, the 1922 Committee also meets on a Thursday evening, although apart from the chief whip, Consultative Committee members do not attend the 1922 Committee.

While the Cabinet normally meets in the morning, this would be less practical for the Shadow Cabinet because many Opposition leaders have part-time occupations which take up their mornings. Morning meetings of the Shadow Cabinet would also clash with the work of the Standing Committees of the House, in which Opposition leaders are more likely to be involved than are Ministers. At the same time, the evening meeting emphasises that the Shadow Cabinet is a *Parliamentary* device, and as such meets at a time of day when the House is sitting. The timing of Shadow Cabinet meetings for 5.00 p.m. is also convenient in that the front bench speeches in the day's debate will be completed by 5.00 p.m., and yet the meeting can be completed in time for dinner or other evening commitments. The meetings will usually last for an hour or so. Nominally there is no time limit, and for the most part Opposition leaders have more time at their disposal than have Cabinet Ministers. Even in opposition, however, there are some pressures of time, and party leaders will often have evening business in the House or elsewhere. In the 1964–70 period the Consultative Committee's Wednesday meeting had to be concluded by 6.15 p.m., as then the chief whip, the leader, and sometimes the deputy leader, attended the weekly meeting of the Conservative Business Committee in order to report the Consultative Committee's decisions regarding the next week's business.[1]

In addition to the regular Wednesday meeting, other meetings may be held from time to time. In the 1951–64 period the Parliamentary Committee sometimes had an extra meeting on a Monday or Tuesday evening to discuss a special policy or

[1] See below, p. 302, for the composition and role of the Business Committee in the 1964–70 period.

tactical matter. During the 1959–64 Parliament, for example, a series of extra meetings of the Parliamentary Committee was held to examine in depth the implications of the Macmillan Government's decisions to seek entry to the European Common Market, and on other occasions special meetings were held to deal with sudden domestic or foreign crises. In the 1970–1 session, however, there were only about half a dozen such special meetings. On 18 and 19 October 1971 the Parliamentary Committee met three times within twenty four hours to consider the vital question of whether the Opposition should follow the Government's initiative in allowing its supporters a free vote at the end of the crucial Common Market debate, and there were also special meetings on 17 and 22 November 1971, before and after the Leader of the Opposition's visit to Ulster. In the 1964–70 period the Consultative Committee also had additional meetings, and during the 1966–70 Parliament it met at 5.00 p.m. on most Mondays during the session to discuss policy matters. These Monday meetings of the Consultative Committee might last for two hours or more, as unlike the Wednesday meeting there was no Business Committee meeting to be attended. Extra Shadow Cabinet meetings mi ght be held just before a general election, or before Budget Day, while on 18 January 1971, the Parliamentary Committee held a day-long 'council of war' to review Labour's general strategy in opposition.

Normally the Parliamentary Committee and the Consultative Committee meet only when the House is sitting, although on rare occasions meetings may be held during the recess, and a meeting is usually held on the eve of a new session. During the recess in September 1970, for example, the Parliamentary Committee met to deal with post-election and pre-session matters. Normally, meetings are held in the Leader of the Opposition's room in the Commons, in surroundings which are considerably less awe-inspiring than the Cabinet room at 10 Downing Street. In the 1905–15 period Conservative Shadow Cabinet meetings were held most frequently at the home of Lord Lansdowne, then leader of the Conservative Peers,[1] and in the 1929–31 Parliament at least some of the

[1] Petrie, *Life and Letters of the Rt. Hon. Sir Austen Chamberlain*, I, pp. 196, 250 and 370.

meetings were held in the Conservative Party offices in Palace Chambers.[1] In very exceptional circumstances today, a meeting may be held away from the House, perhaps at the home of the leader, or at party headquarters. The first two ad hoc Consultative Committee meetings in 1964 were held at Sir Alec Douglas-Home's flat at Claridges and the Conservative Research Department,[2] while the Parliamentary Committee sometimes has met at Labour Party Conferences. In February 1970 there was a three-day gathering of the Consultative Committee, at the Selsdon Park Hotel, Surrey, at which party policy was discussed in a more leisurely and less formal way than is possible at Westminster during the session.[3] These, however, are exceptions to the general rule that the Consultative Committee and the Parliamentary Committee, as Parliamentary bodies, meet in the Palace of Westminster and when Parliament is in session.

In addition to the nineteen members of the Parliamentary Committee, its meetings are also attended by the secretary of the PLP. He serves as secretary to the Committee and is responsible for preparing minutes of the meeting. The General Secretary of the Labour Party also attends, and is invited to speak on any item affecting the party organisation as a whole. Similarly, Consultative Committee meetings are attended by a secretary to the Shadow Cabinet. In the 1964–70 period this was Sir Michael Fraser, who was at the same time deputy chairman of the party with a special responsibility for the work of the Research Department. In addition, the Director of the Conservative Research Department, Brendon Sewill (1965–70), attended Consultative Committee meetings as an observer, and the Leader of the Opposition's two PPSs, James Prior (1964–70) and Anthony Kershaw (1966–70), also sat in. The chief legal Spokesman, Sir Peter Rawlinson, also generally attended latterly, although, like the chief whip and the secretary, he was not a full member of the Committee.

Consultative Committee and Parliamentary Committee meetings alike are sometimes attended by Spokesmen who are not members of the Committee, in the same way that Ministers

[1] Birkenhead, *F.E.*, p. 521.
[2] Young, *Sir Alec Douglas-Home*, p. 220.
[3] *The Times*, 2 February 1970.

from outside the Cabinet are sometimes brought into Cabinet meetings when their work is under consideration. This is more likely to happen for the Parliamentary Committee than for the Consultative Committee, as almost all of the senior Conservative Spokesmen were members of the Committee anyway in 1964–70 period, and only rarely was it necessary for assistant Spokesmen to attend. The elected Parliamentary Committee, however, does not necessarily include all of Labour's senior Spokesmen, and thus non-members are summoned when policy areas are being dealt with, for which the recognised Spokesmen are outside the Committee. Thus in the 1970–1 session Mrs Judith Hart, as Spokesman on Overseas Aid, and Fred Mulley, as Transport Spokesman, attended the Parliamentary Committee when their subject was under discussion. If a senior Spokesman has to be absent from the Consultative Committee and his policy area is to be dealt with, an assistant Spokesman might be asked to attend in his place. This might also happen with the Parliamentary Committee, although it has to be remembered that the members of the Parliamentary Committee are elected as individuals, not because they are Spokesmen for particular policy areas. Just as senior civil servants sometimes attend Cabinet meetings, so outside experts and advisers are occasionally brought into Parliamentary Committee and Consultative Committee meetings. Many of the Parliamentary Committee's discussions on Labour's pensions plans in the 1959–64 Parliament, for example, were attended by the academics and others who were serving with the party research teams.

There is no fixed quorum for either the Parliamentary Committee or the Consultative Committee, and emergency meetings have been held with only a handful of senior figures present. A Shadow Cabinet meeting does not have the same priority for its members as does a Cabinet meeting, which takes precedence over all other commitments. Nevertheless, due notice, together with a reason, has to be given for absence from Shadow Cabinet meetings, and habitual non-attendance would not be tolerated. In the case of the Consultative Committee it would lead to dismissal from the Committee, although there is no recorded example of this happening. This, of course, would not be possible in the case of the elected Parliamentary

Committee, and the removal from the Committee of a non-attender would have to wait until the annual ballot, and even then would not be achieved if he maintained his popularity among Labour MPs.

The Shadow Cabinet in Action

How are Shadow Cabinet meetings conducted, and in style and atmosphere how do they compare with Cabinet meetings? Meetings of the Parliamentary Committee and Consultative Committee are altogether less formal than are Cabinet meetings.[1] There is some sense of occasion, and for meetings of the Consultative Committee in the 1964–70 period members waited outside the leader's room until they were invited to enter, but there is considerably less of an aura than surrounds Cabinet meetings. The members sit around an oblong table, in rather cramped conditions. At Consultative Committee meetings, the Director of the Research Department, and the Leader of the Opposition's PPSs, who attend the meetings as observers, sit back from the table, but the secretary and the chief whip sit at the table, even though they are not full members of the Committee. Apart from the leader, who, as chairman, occupies the middle seat on one side of the table, there are no specially allocated places, although, as in any regular gathering, members tend to gravitate towards the same seat each time. Discussions are more spontaneous than in Cabinet. The leader might suggest that X and Y should be heard first, but contributions do not have to be 'invited' in the way that they are in Cabinet meetings, and the whole process is much more conversational than in Cabinet. Lengthy contributions are tolerated more readily than they would be in Cabinet, although this clearly cannot be taken too far. Members are not referred to by their shadow titles, and, in the main, first names are used in discussions, and surnames in the minutes. The minutes, however, tend to be impersonal, and are a record of decisions made and arguments used rather than a verbatim record of individual contributions. Written notes, whether containing jokes, betting odds or state secrets, do not circulate to

[1] For accounts of the Cabinet at work see Gordon Walker, *The Cabinet*, pp. 99–158.

to the extent that they do at Cabinet meetings. The smallness of the table around which they sit perhaps encourages a conversational style, as does the fact that the meeting is essentially a party gathering without any civil servants being present. Further, the Parliamentary Committee with a fixed nineteen members, and the Consultative Committee with seventeen to twenty-two members in the 1964–70 period, have both been smaller than most Cabinets of recent years, and no doubt this also helps somewhat towards informality. In general, the pressure of time is considerably less acute than for Cabinet meetings, while the nature of the business being transacted is much less dramatic and urgent.

In interview, MPs who had served in both the Cabinet and the Shadow Cabinet emphasised the much greater sense of occasion and urgency that is associated with Cabinet meetings. Some maintained that a major factor in this is that, for the most part, the Shadow Cabinet is not in a position to control events, but can only react to initiatives that come from the Government. There is, of course, *some* urgency about Shadow Cabinet meetings, and Opposition leaders do not have unlimited time at their disposal. A Spokesman will often be asked to produce a policy statement dealing with a topical issue, which the Committee has then to approve or reject fairly quickly. Also, the Opposition often has to react quickly to Government decisions, and many Shadow Cabinet decisions regarding imminent Parliamentary business have to be taken at very short notice. In this respect, the Opposition is at a considerable disadvantage compared with the Government, which controls the Parliamentary timetable and can make its business arrangements for some weeks ahead, without necessarily informing the Opposition of the long-term arrangements. Thus life in opposition can be very hectic, with tactics, speakers and attitudes having to be decided upon very quickly. Nevertheless, in general, time pressures are less acute than for the Cabinet, and one of the advantages of being in opposition is that unpleasant or difficult issues can be shelved or ignored much more easily than when in office. Clearly, an Opposition which avoided all unpleasant decisions would leave itself open to ridicule, but there is considerably less pressure on the Opposition leaders than on Ministers to make final policy decisions within a given time period. As a result of all of these factors, the atmosphere in meetings of the Parliamentary Committee and Consultative Committee is much more relaxed and informal than in Cabinet meetings. At Parliamentary Committee meetings there might be an occasional show of hands to decide an issue, and the Committee's attitude to the controversial German rearmament issue in 1956 was decided by a vote.[1] The majority decision then became binding on the whole Committee, when it presented its view to the PLP. Such votes are exceptional, although as a generalisation it can be said that a vote is more likely at a Parliamentary Committee meeting than at a Consultative Committee meeting.

An essential aspect of the working of the Cabinet is that its proceedings are confidential,[2] and for the most part the same broad principle applies with the Shadow Cabinet. The Parliamentary party, of course, is informed of most of the decisions taken by the Shadow Cabinet. The 'general sense of the meeting' will usually emerge when the Parliamentary Committee presents its views to the PLP, and although the Conservative Consultative Committee does not meet with the 1922 Committee, there is a good liaison between the two bodies. In addition to this, individual members may reveal to their particular friends some of the details of the Committee's discussions. Within these limitations, however, a doctrine of Shadow Cabinet secrecy does operate, and it is considered improper to reveal what was said at Parliamentary Committee or Consultative Committee meetings. At times, the Prime Minister informs the Leader of the Opposition, and other Opposition Spokesmen, of classified information, particularly in the economic, defence, or foreign affairs fields. This can cause difficulties, as usually not all Shadow Cabinet members are Privy Councillors, and thus are not bound by the Privy Councillor's oath of secrecy. From this point of view there is perhaps a case for making all members of the Parliamentary Committee and Consultative Committee, members of the Privy Council. If this were done, however, it would in effect give the PLP the power to elect Privy Councillors when electing the

---

[1] See below, p. 309, for more details of this episode.
[2] See Gordon Walker, *The Cabinet*, pp. 167–71; Jennings, *Cabinet Government*, pp. 267–9.

Parliamentary Committee, and this might offend constitutional purists. In general, however, the sort of issue which is discussed at Parliamentary Committee and Consultative Committee meetings does not involve classified information or state secrets. The Shadow Cabinet is concerned primarily with party organisation and tactics in Parliament, and for this function there is less need for secrecy than is the case with Cabinet discussions over the affairs of government. The Shadow Cabinet, of course, also deals with Opposition policy, and here its deliberations need to be confidential. In this context, however, secrecy is required for reasons of party interest rather than constitutional considerations, and although Consultative Committee papers are marked 'secret', these are clearly party secrets rather than state secrets.

Shadow Cabinet secrecy, of course, is subject to the same limitations as Cabinet secrecy. Even in the eighteen-eighties Gladstone complained of ' . . . the incessant and incurable leakages of the late Cabinet . . .',[1] and today 'unattributable leaks' inevitably occur in opposition as in office.[2] In some respects the secrecy of Shadow Cabinet deliberations is more easily maintained than that of the Cabinet, because press, public, and party are less interested in Shadow Cabinet business, and are less likely to probe into its affairs. In a run-up to a general election, or in a time of crisis for an Opposition party, when more interest is taken in Opposition attitudes, leaks are rather more likely. Thus in the autumn of 1971 there was much comment in the press about the Parliamentary Committee meetings at which Labour's attitude and tactics over the Common Market issue were discussed.[3] In general, however, the maintenance of Shadow Cabinet secrecy is helped by the fact that for the most part its business is less newsworthy and less important than that of the Cabinet.

In interview some Shadow Cabinet members (Labour and Conservative) maintained that there was an excessive amount of secrecy surrounding Shadow Cabinet deliberations, and advocated less rigid rules. In the past, some Labour MPs have

[1] Garvin, *Life of Joseph Chamberlain*, II, p. 160.
[2] See, for example, *The Guardian*, 18 and 19 May 1971.
[3] See, for example, *The Guardian* and *The Times* in the week of 18 to 23 October 1971.

even called for the admission of the press to at least some Parliamentary Committee meetings.[1] Certainly, in so far as it is a function of party leaders in opposition to encourage policy discussions among the party and the public, there is a case for Shadow Cabinet deliberations being made less secret than they are, and for the Opposition leaders revealing more of their discussions on policy in the hope of stimulating interest among the party, press, and public. This, however, inevitably comes in conflict with the fear that Opposition parties often have of appearing to be divided over policy. Thus in 1970 the Conservative Consultative Committee did not reveal to its supporters its attitude towards the proposal for a Scottish Assembly, formulated by Sir Alec Douglas-Home's Constitutional Committee, because of the differences of opinion that were known to exist within the party on the issue.[2] This attitude is bound up with the British electorate's perhaps excessive attachment to the view that open policy disagreements among party leaders are an indication of unfitness for office.

The Shadow Cabinet has no equivalent to the elaborate Secretariat which serves the Cabinet. The Leader of the Opposition has his own personal secretarial staff, as described in Chapter 3, and secretarial arrangements exist for both the Parliamentary Committee and the Consultative Committee. Sir Michael Fraser was appointed deputy chairman of the party and secretary to the Consultative Committee by Sir Alec Douglas-Home in October 1964, and he retained these posts throughout the 1964–70 period of Conservative Opposition. From 1951 to 1964 he had been Director of the Conservative Research Department, and after 1964, as deputy chairman of the party, he had a special overall responsibility for the Research Department, although he was succeeded as its Director by Brendon Sewill. As secretary to the Consultative Committee Sir Michael Fraser helped the leader and the chief whip to prepare the agenda for its meetings, and was responsible for recording the minutes. He was also responsible for circulating any special papers required at the meeting, and had the resources of the Research Department at his disposal to prepare papers required for the Committee's deliberations. As an

---

[1] See Dalton, *High Tide and After*, p. 393.
[2] Young, *Sir Alec Douglas-Home*, p. 266.

authoritative figure within the party machine, he represented the interests and attitudes of the party organisation at Consultative Committee meetings. He would speak at meetings only when invited to do so, although when the party chairman was absent he would speak, as deputy chairman, on party matters.

The secretary of the PLP, who is appointed and paid by the NEC of the Labour Party, also acts as secretary to the Parliamentary Committee. Carol Johnson was secretary from 1943 to 1959, with Frank Barlow as his assistant for much of this time. When Carol Johnson was elected to Parliament in 1959, Frank Barlow succeeded him as secretary, although not 'as of right', as the post was advertised. The secretary attends Parliamentary Committee meetings, but does not join in policy discussions. He reports on correspondence, and on the general administrative affairs of the PLP, but apart from this he rarely joins in discussions. He serves as a link with the backbench groups, for which he also provides secretarial assistance, and he helps the chief whip to transmit subject group and general backbench attitudes to the Parliamentary Committee. He takes notes of the proceedings, and after the meeting he dictates the minutes to a typist. These are then circulated among the Committee members. After the meeting he will also inform non-Committee members of any decisions that affect them. His other duties as Secretary to the PLP are to deal with PLP correspondence, prepare the annual report of the PLP for the Party Conference, and generally serve as a link between the PLP and the NEC and Transport House.

The agenda for Consultative Committee meetings is decided by the leader, in consultation with the chief whip and the secretary, and is circulated to the members of the Committee before the meeting. The Parliamentary Committee now has the same practice, but in the 1951–64 period its arrangements were much less formal, and the agenda was not circulated before the meeting. For the regular Wednesday meeting of the Consultative Committee and Parliamentary Committee alike, the main item to be dealt with is the arrangements for the next week's business, although for this meeting the agenda will also always include the chief whip's report, House of Lords business, and a general item 'the political situation'. Because there is

less pressure of time at Shadow Cabinet meetings than at
Cabinet meetings, there is generally little difficulty in including
on the agenda, or raising under 'any other business', or the
'political situation', all the items with which members wish to
deal. Thus there is no real need for prior notice before an item
can be raised, apart, perhaps, from an informal word with the
leader or secretary before the meeting begins. The Prime
Minister's strict control over the agenda for Cabinet meetings,
and the power that he has to include or exclude particular
items, thus hardly applies to the Leader of the Opposition and
the agenda for the much more leisurely and informal meetings
of the Shadow Cabinet.

It was Conservative practice in the 1964–70 period to circulate to Consultative Committee members the minutes of the
previous meeting. This was not done for the Parliamentary
Committee in the 1951–64 period, but since 1970 Labour has
followed the Conservative pattern. Any papers that are to be
considered at the meeting will also be circulated beforehand.
A Spokesman may submit a report or statement of policy
which he has been asked to prepare, or which he wishes to
raise on his own initiative. Occasionally, a more general paper
on the conduct of business, or a comprehensive policy document
or manifesto, may be presented for consideration over a number
of meetings. Generally in this respect, however, Shadow Cabinet meetings are in marked contrast to Cabinet meetings, for
which a large amount of memoranda, policy documents, and
other written material is circulated beforehand, and is referred
to during the meeting. For the Consultative Committee and
the Parliamentary Committee, then, much more is done
through discussion, and much less through written papers and
memoranda, than is the case with the Cabinet.

Group and Individual Roles within the Shadow Cabinet

While the Shadow Cabinet is essentially a collective body,
bound by the principle of collective responsibility (as is discussed in Chapter 9), individual members of the Shadow
Cabinet will perform different roles. What are these roles? Do
groups and cliques emerge, and is there anything like a natural
hierarchy or a formal inner group? The Leader of the Opposition

is chairman of the Shadow Cabinet, and in this role he introduces the business and sums up discussions. In his absence the deputy leader will perform this function. As with any skilful chairman of a committee, the Leader of the Opposition can handle Shadow Cabinet meetings with sufficient caution to avoid being defeated on an important issue, or having to climb down in face of his colleagues' collective attitude. As chairman he can steer discussion along particular lines, and can extend the consideration of some issue so as to prevent or postpone the discussion of some other topic that he wishes to avoid. Also, his summing up of Shadow Cabinet discussions can be a valuable power, although in interview a number of Shadow Cabinet members commented on the leader's lack of authority in this respect, in comparison with that of the Prime Minister in Cabinet. This factor, of course, will always be conditional upon the personality and style of the particular individuals involved. Some items of business, particularly those dealing with the detailed aspects of the next week's business, might be delegated to the leader, chief whip and one or two others particularly concerned, to work out together, although in general, much less needs to be delegated to the leader in this way than is the case with the Cabinet. As long as he has close contact with the secretary, the Leader of the Opposition can 'adapt' the meeting's minutes to some extent, so as to make some points clearer, or other points seem more obscure, than they really are. This is obviously something that cannot be taken too far: no Leader of the Opposition, and no Prime Minister, can 'forge' the minutes, but he may be able to 'adjust points of detail' to his own advantage in a way that no other member of the Committee is able to do.

The other party officers also have particular roles within the Shadow Cabinet. In the Consultative Committee, the chairman of the party organisation will 'speak for the party', and will ensure that the views of the extra-Parliamentary organisation are taken into consideration.[1] For the Labour Party this role will be performed by the General Secretary of the party, who now is invited to attend Parliamentary Committee meetings, although he is not technically a member. Similarly, the chief

[1] For a comment on Anthony Barber's execution of this role, see Butler and Pinto-Duschinsky, *The British General Election of 1970*, p. 106.

whip, and also in the case of the Labour Party, the chairman
of the PLP, will provide the Shadow Cabinet with information
on the likely response of the backbench MPs to Shadow Cabinet
decisions. In many ways the chief whip is the central figure in
the Shadow Cabinet. While his place in the Cabinet is often
under-estimated, his role is even more significant in the Shadow
Cabinet, primarily concerned as it is with business matters. He
is personally responsible for the Opposition's whipping arrangements, although in this he will always take note of his Shadow
Cabinet colleagues' views. The chief whip also acts as the
official channel of communication between the Shadow Cabinet
and the Government, although for the Labour Party the chairman of the PLP also performs this function. As expressed by
one Labour MP in interview, the chief whip represents 'the
usual channels' (of communication with the Government), and
the Chairman of the PLP represents 'the unusual channels',
taking over if relations between the Government and Opposition whips become strained, as they did for a while in 1971
over the passage of the Industrial Relations Bill. The Chairman
of the PLP is also responsible for submitting the Shadow
Cabinet's recommendations to the meeting of the PLP. There
is no direct equivalent of the chairman of the PLP in the
Conservative Consultative Committee. In the 1964–6 Parliament, however, Selwyn Lloyd filled the post of 'Coordinator
of the Opposition in the House of Commons'. In this capacity,
he kept in touch with the Government and his own back
benchers on questions of House of Commons procedural reform, and, like the chairman of the PLP, he acted as a link
between the Shadow Cabinet and backbenchers, additional to
that provided by the whips and the Conservative Business
Committee.[1]

The Shadow Cabinet contains peers as well as members of
the Commons: the leader of the Labour peers, the chief Labour
whip in the Lords, and a representative of the backbench
Labour peers, are members of the Parliamentary Committee,
while the leader and deputy leader of the Conservative peers
were members of the Consultative Committee in the 1964–70
period. The peers are full and equal members of the Shadow
Cabinet, but inevitably they are concerned principally with

[1] See below, p. 302, for the role of the Conservative Business Committee.

House of Lords business. For both parties there is a Shadow
Cabinet convention that the peers will not take part in the
discussions about House of Commons business arrangements,
although on questions of policy, as opposed to purely business
matters, no such limitations apply. The House of Commons
members of the Shadow Cabinet may comment on the arrangements for business in the House of Lords, but the peers retain
the ultimate right to determine their own arrangements. They
do not slavishly follow their House of Commons colleagues.
Thus while a three-line whip was imposed on Labour MPs at
the end of the Common Market debate in October 1971, the
Labour peers were allowed a free vote.[1] Individual Spokesmen
in the Shadow Cabinet will be primarily concerned with their
own assigned areas of responsibility. Thus the Treasury Spokesman, as a potential Chancellor of the Exchequer, will be particularly interested in the potential cost of any policy proposals
being considered by his colleagues. This will be especially so
as an election nears, and the Opposition can be seen to be
committing itself to future action. Thus in the 1966–70 Parliament, all 'statements of intent' by Conservative Spokesmen,
which had financial implications, had to be approved by Iain
Macleod, the Treasury Spokesman. In general, however,
Shadow Cabinet members will be rather less likely than will
departmental Ministers in Cabinet to confine their contributions to their own assigned areas. For Ministers much more than
for Opposition Spokesmen, the pressures of work, and the
extent of their own specific departmental responsibilities, restrict both the ability and the desire to take an interest in policy
questions beyond their own area: as one ex-Cabinet Minister
has commented of the 1964–70 period of Labour Government,
'... Labour Ministers, with a few exceptions, locked themselves
up in Departments.'[2] In Opposition this is much less likely to
be the case, and Spokesmen who had served in both the
Shadow Cabinet and the Cabinet emphasised in interview that
Shadow Cabinet meetings are much more of an open forum
of debate than are Cabinet meetings, with members rising above
their own immediate responsibilities to comment on Opposition

[1] For more comments, see Appendix A.
[2] See Butler and Pinto-Duschinsky, *The British General Election of 1970*,
p. 1.

policy and tactics in general. One Shadow Cabinet member in particular argued that a major contrast between the two bodies was that in the Shadow Cabinet, members emerged as personalities to a much greater extent than in Cabinet, where contributions were always restricted by 'the departmental point of view'. Nevertheless, to some extent in Shadow Cabinet meetings, individual Spokesmen will inevitably emphasise their own particular responsibility.

Cliques or alliances may be formed by groups of Shadow Cabinet members who have common interests or a common outlook. Unlike Cabinet Ministers, however, Opposition Spokesmen are not defending departmental interests, nor are they competing for a share of Government expenditure, so that the alliances that emerge within the Cabinet for these purposes will not be reflected in the Shadow Cabinet. Also, there is no equivalent today, either in office or in opposition, to the 'country house cliques' of the nineteenth century, when, as part of the social round, groups of like-minded Ministers or Opposition leaders would gather to coordinate their activities. Nevertheless, groups and alliances will develop among Shadow Cabinet members of similar ideological standpoints, and in interview Shadow Cabinet members acknowledged that on occasions they had entered into alliances with like-minded colleagues in order to further, or to resist, particular policy proposals. They pointed out that this was particularly likely as an election drew near, and the party could be seen to be making commitments to expenditure in particular policy areas. Some MPs who had served on the Parliamentary Committee during Labour's internal conflicts of the 1950s, said in interview that occasionally they got the impression that groups of 'left-wing' or 'right-wing' Parliamentary Committee members had met in caucus before the full Committee meeting. For the most part, however, there were so few 'left-wing' members of the Parliamentary Committee in this period that regular ideological cliques could not develop. In the 1964–6 Parliament there was a clear division within the Consultative Committee between 'hawks' and 'doves' on the question of coloured immigration, and the Opposition's attitude to Government legislation in the field. The replacement of Sir Edward Boyle by Peter Thorneycroft as Home Affairs Spokesman in February

1965, was seen as a victory for the 'hawk' group on the Committee.[1]

In any committee there will be inevitably something of a hierarchy, or 'pecking order', with some members being more influential than others. In the case of the Cabinet, this is formally recognised through the official lists of Cabinet members that are published from time to time. In these lists the members of the Cabinet are presented in order of ranking, as determined by the Prime Minister, from the senior figures down to the most humble appointment (although a particular individual's weight within the Cabinet is not necessarily circumscribed by his current standing in the Cabinet 'league table').[2] With the Shadow Cabinet there is no equivalent to this official order of ranking. In the Parliamentary Committee the number of votes received in the annual ballot will contribute to a member's authority to some extent, but there is certainly no automatic relationship between the placings in the ballot and personal weight within the Committee. Factors like personality, Ministerial experience, and general status within the party are more likely to determine the nature of the Shadow Cabinet hierarchy. James Callaghan has recorded that when Labour went into opposition in 1951, Parliamentary Committee meetings were dominated very much by the senior figures like Attlee, Dalton, Morrison, and Chuter Ede.[3] As the youngest and Ministerially least experienced member of the Parliamentary Committee, Callaghan generally sat at the end of the meeting table, together with Alfred Robens and Anthony Greenwood, and they only occasionally entered into the discussions. In contrast, he claims that when Labour went into opposition in 1970, the Parliamentary Committee members were more uniform in age and experience, and that as a result there was much less of a clear hierarchy than there had been in 1951.

To some extent, no doubt, a Spokesman's influence with his

---

[1] Roth, *Enoch Powell*, p. 321.

[2] These lists appear regularly in the volumes of Hansard, and elsewhere, so that any Minister's movements up or down the Cabinet 'league' can be readily traced.

[3] James Callaghan, 'Fighting the Heath Government', *The Times*, 5 December 1970.

colleagues will depend on the shadow duty to which he has been appointed, with finance, foreign affairs, and defence being subjects of particular importance for an Opposition as well as a Government. The nature of this responsibility, however, will contribute rather less weight to a Spokesman's position than to that of a Minister, because a Spokesman does not have the support of a department of state behind him. Early in a period in opposition an individual's status may depend to some extent on the position he held in the late Government, although this is a factor which will decline in importance as the Parliament proceeds.

As well as having a natural hierarchy, a committee may contain a number of leading figures who constitute a powerful 'inner group' within the overall body. A Cabinet often contains three or four especially powerful Ministers who work particularly closely with the Prime Minister, meeting more regularly than the Cabinet as a whole, taking many of the more vital decisions, and thereby representing the 'inner core' of the Government machine. Ramsay MacDonald, for example, consulted with J. R. Clynes, Arthur Henderson, Philip Snowden, and J. H. Thomas more regularly than with any of his other Cabinet colleagues.[1] Similarly, Lord Halifax, Sir John Simon, and Sir Samuel Hoare were particularly influential in the 1937–40 Chamberlain Government, as were Ernest Bevin, Herbert Morrison, and Sir Stafford Cripps in the Attlee Government.[2] For the most part, such inner groups operate on an informal and un-official basis, but sometimes a Prime Minister might institute an Inner Cabinet on a more formal basis. In 1969, for example, Harold Wilson formed something of an Inner Cabinet, made up of six senior Cabinet Ministers with himself as chairman, as part of a general reorganisation of the Ministerial structure.[3]

To what extent does such an inner group emerge within the Shadow Cabinet, and is there anything that can be labelled

[1] See Gordon Walker, *The Cabinet*, p. 39.

[2] Ibid. For other comments on the Inner Cabinet concept see Mackintosh, *The British Cabinet*, pp. 162–6, and Jennings, *Cabinet Government*, pp. 253–5 and 292–3.

[3] Unfortunately this body was labelled the 'Parliamentary Committee', so that confusion has to be avoided between it and the Parliamentary Committee that is elected in opposition.

an 'Inner Shadow Cabinet'? Numerous examples can be cited
of informal inner groups within Shadow Cabinets in the past,
but there are fewer examples of the more formally constituted
'Inner Shadow Cabinet'. In this respect, therefore, Opposition
practice seems to mirror that of the Cabinet. The 'Shadow
Cabinets' of the eighteenth century, that were referred to in
Chapter 2, often had an 'inner circle'. The Prince of Wales'
Shadow Cabinet of 1747 had a nucleus of four who formed a
programme for the 1747 election, which was then approved by
a larger meeting of fourteen leading Tories.[1] In the seventeen-
sixties Rockingham's conciliabulum was in effect an 'Inner
Shadow Cabinet', which decided the attitudes and tactics for
the Rockinghamites in the Commons, and then presented its
views to a larger gathering of twenty or thirty colleagues.[2] In
the nineteenth century the ex-Cabinet often included an inner
group who had more authority than the other Opposition
leaders, and who met together on occasions. After 1846,
Gladstone, Herbert, and Graham formed a triumvirate within
the Peelite group,[3] while in the 1868–74 Parliament, Disraeli
consulted Gathorne-Hardy, Derby, Northcote, and sometimes
Cairns, as his closest colleagues. In January 1873, for example,
he summoned Gathorne-Hardy and Cairns to Hughenden for
discussions on party policy and tactics,[4] while the Conservative
manifesto for the 1874 election was produced, in effect, by
Disraeli, Gathorne-Hardy, and Cairns working together over
a weekend.[5] In general, Gladstone sought to avoid calling
meetings of the ex-Cabinet, as he preferred to meet his colleagues individually, or deal with the most senior of them
together, and throughout the 1886–92 Parliament Gladstone
met with Morley, Granville, and Harcourt much more frequently than with his other colleagues.[6]

In this century some of the most vital decisions facing
Opposition parties have been taken by a meeting of a small
inner group of leaders, rather than by the Shadow Cabinet as

---

[1] Feiling, *The Second Tory Party*, p. 36.
[2] Winstanley, *Lord Chatham and the Whig Opposition*, pp. 325 and 341.
[3] Morley, *Life of Gladstone*, I, p. 421.
[4] R. Blake, *Disraeli*, London 1966, p. 527.
[5] Monypenny and Buckle, *Life of Benjamin Disraeli*, V, p. 273.
[6] See, for example, Morley, *Life of Gladstone*, II, p. 505.

a whole. In 1914, the decision by the Unionist Opposition to support the Government in its attitude to the European crisis was taken by only a handful of the Unionist leaders (Balfour, Bonar Law, Austen Chamberlain, and Lord Lansdowne) at meetings at Lansdowne House on 1 and 2 August 1914.[1] In the first few months of the war, Bonar Law, Austen Chamberlain, and Lord Lansdowne kept in close touch with each other in order to manage Opposition affairs, and on 17 May 1915 these three met to discuss Fisher's resignation from the Government, and the possibility of the Unionists joining an all-party War Coalition under Asquith.[2] Not until the next day was the full Shadow Cabinet informed by Bonar Law that he had been invited to join a Coalition Government, and that he had decided to do so. Again, in August 1931 the decision that the Conservatives should join the National Government under Ramsay MacDonald was taken by Baldwin, after some consultation with Neville Chamberlain and the few Conservative leaders available in London over the weekend of 19 to 22 August.[3]

The Business Committee that Baldwin formed in March 1930 has been described by the biographer of one of its members as 'a sort of Inner Shadow Cabinet'.[4] It was set up because Baldwin wished to avoid calling meetings of the full Shadow Cabinet, which was badly divided over tariff policy and Indian independence. It had a fixed membership of Baldwin, Hoare, Churchill, Austen Chamberlain, Hailsham, Peel, and Stanley, and was intended originally to meet weekly, although Baldwin was later criticised for not summoning it often enough.[5] Thus of all the examples mentioned so far of 'inner groups' of senior Opposition leaders, Baldwin's Business Committee is the clearest example of a formal Inner Shadow Cabinet, having a fixed membership and a regular routine of meetings. It was not copied by Churchill in the 1945–51 period, nor by Douglas-Home or Heath in the 1964–70 period.[6] Nevertheless, Douglas-Home's Consultative Committee in 1964 was divided into

---

[1] Petrie, *Life and Letters of Sir Austen Chamberlain*, I, p. 370.
[2] Ibid., II, p. 21.   [3] Middlemas and Barnes, *Baldwin*, pp. 623–30.
[4] Feiling, *The Life of Neville Chamberlain*, p. 177.
[5] Macleod, *Neville Chamberlain*, p. 138.
[6] In the 1945–51 and 1964–70 periods of Conservative Opposition a

external and internal affairs sections, and the heads of these two sections (Reginald Maudling and R. A. Butler), together with Edward Heath as chairman of the Policy Committee, Selwyn Lloyd as Coordinator of the Opposition in the House of Commons, and Douglas-Home himself, constituted the nucleus of the Committee. Again, in the 1966–70 Parliament a nucleus was formed by Edward Heath as party leader, Reginald Maudling as deputy leader, Lord Carrington as leader in the Lords, William Whitelaw as chief whip, Anthony Barber as party chairman, Iain Macleod for financial affairs, Sir Alec Douglas-Home for external affairs, and Sir Michael Fraser as Secretary. Sir Michael Fraser kept in daily contact with the leader through a 9.15 a.m. telephone call to discuss general party business as well as Consultative Committee affairs, and each Tuesday morning in his flat Heath talked with William Whitelaw and Anthony Barber.[1] In general, however, although Heath tended to consult with some colleagues more than with others, the precise membership of his 'inner group' fluctuated through time, and from issue to issue, and the whole arrangement was very flexible and informal.

Labour in opposition has never had an arrangement for an Inner Shadow Cabinet quite as formal as Baldwin's Business Committee. Nevertheless in opposition in the nineteen-twenties, just as in the Labour Cabinets of 1924 and 1929–31, Labour's 'Big Five' were Ramsay MacDonald, J. R. Clynes, Arthur Henderson, Philip Snowden, and J. H. Thomas. It was these five who, at a dinner party at the Webbs' home immediately after the indecisive 1923 election, decided that Labour for the first time should attempt to form a Government.[2] Sidney Webb and Sir Patrick Hastings were also close to MacDonald, even though Hastings was never a member of the Parliamentary Committee, but the 'Fig Five' were the real inner group within the Parliamentary Committee.[3] In the

---

'Business Committee' was formed, but this was a large body made up of officers of the 1922 Committee and the backbench committees, together with junior Spokesmen. It was thus very different from Baldwin's small Business Committee. See below, p. 302 for an account of the working of the Business Committee in the 1964–70 period.

[1] Hutchinson, *Edward Heath*, p. 171.
[2] Snowden, *An Autobiography*, II, pp. 594–8.
[3] Cole, *Beatrice Webb's Diaries*, I, p. 233.

1931–5 Parliament, Attlee and Cripps were Lansbury's chief aides. They shared the Leader of the Opposition's room, and one of the three was always present on the Opposition front bench during debates.[1] As Leader of the Opposition in the 1951–6 period, Attlee would occasionally meet informally with some of his close colleagues, but he did not like meetings at the best of times, and he avoided even informal gatherings as much as possible. In the 1959 Parliament, Hugh Gaitskell often met with Roy Jenkins, Anthony Crosland, Douglas Jay, Patrick Gordon Walker, and other prominent 'Gaitskellites' at his home in Frognal Gardens, Hampstead. This, however, was not an inner group of the Parliamentary Committee, as not all of this 'Hampstead Set' were members of the Parliamentary Committee. Nevertheless, vital decisions were taken at these gatherings, indicating a highly personalised style of leadership from Gaitskell.

These, however, were essentially informal relationships, and no formal machinery existed. Despite the existence of an official Inner Cabinet in the Wilson Government after 1969, no equivalent Inner Shadow Cabinet was formed within the Parliamentary Committee when the party went into opposition in 1970. Harold Wilson, however, did establish the practice of a brief meeting with the deputy leader, the chairman of the PLP, and the chief whip at 3.00 p.m. on Mondays to Thursdays when the House was sitting. The purpose of the meeting was to discuss any tactical problems involved in the day's business, and the Spokesmen who were leading in the debates that day might also attend. Further, something of a natural Inner Shadow Cabinet is formed when Labour is in opposition by those MPs who are members of the NEC as well as of the Parliamentary Committee. In 1970 there were seven such MPs (James Callaghan, Anthony Wedgwood Benn, Denis Healey, Barbara Castle, Shirley Williams, Harold Wilson, and Roy Jenkins). The NEC, of course, consists of more than just MPs. Nevertheless, those MPs who do have places in both the Parliamentary and extra-Parliamentary centres of power constitute something of a natural inner group within the party, forming a link between the PLP and Transport House. They are also in an ideal position to rise above the details of the

[1] Attlee, *As It Happened*, p. 77; Cooke, *Life of Sir Stafford Cripps*, p. 136.

day-to-day management of Parliamentary business, with which the Parliamentary Committee is primarily involved, and form a small Parliamentary nucleus for the consideration of long-term strategy and policy. In the interests of the smooth working of the Labour Party organisation in opposition, therefore, there is perhaps a case for officially establishing this group as a formal Inner Shadow Cabinet, on the same lines as the Inner Cabinet that existed in the Wilson Government from 1969 onwards.

Shadow Cabinet Committees

To what extent does the Shadow Cabinet work through a system of sub-committees? In the post-1918 period the Government machine has evolved an increasingly sophisticated system of Cabinet committees for the various fields of policy.[1] These committees, composed of Cabinet and non-Cabinet Ministers, with a senior Cabinet Minister as chairman, have taken over much of the work that previously was carried out by the Cabinet as a whole. In his study of the Cabinet Patrick Gordon Walker has stated that

> The committee system puts a great strain upon Cabinet Ministers who spend much of their working day at committees. But it greatly relieves the burden on the Cabinet. Present-day business could not be transacted by the Cabinet, were not much of the work delegated to committees.[2]

Has there been any parallel development in opposition? On the whole, neither the Parliamentary Committee nor the Consultative Committee has developed a formal system of sub-committees. Each party, of course, has backbench 'subject groups' and 'area groups', and, as is described in Chapter 10, each party when in opposition sets up 'Policy Committees' to examine specific aspects of party policy. These various bodies, however, are in no sense sub-committees of the Shadow Cabinet. The pressure of work on the Shadow Cabinet is less than on the Cabinet, so that in opposition there is less need to delegate

---

[1] For an account of the Cabinet committee system see Gordon Walker, *The Cabinet*, pp. 40–8; Jennings, *Cabinet Government*, pp. 255–61; Mackintosh, *The British Cabinet*, pp. 510–18.

[2] Gordon Walker, *The Cabinet*, p. 48.

work through an elaborate system of committees. Also, much of the work of the Cabinet committees is concerned with reconciling the legislative and financial priorities of the various departments of state, and matching demands with resources. This vital aspect of the Cabinet committee system has no parallel in opposition. While there is undoubtedly a need for the coordination of effort among Opposition Spokesmen, much of this can be achieved by the Shadow Cabinet itself, or, in the comparatively relaxed atmosphere of opposition, through day to day personal contact in the House.

Nevertheless, there are many examples of committees of Opposition leaders being set up on an ad hoc basis to deal with specific problems, and even in the nineteenth century there were instances of committees being formed from the ex-Cabinet. In May 1880, for example, after the Liberal electoral triumph, a small committee was formed from the Conservative ex-Cabinet to see whether any aspects of Liberal Party organisation could usefully be copied by the Conservatives,[1] while in August 1889 Lord Rosebery proposed the creation of two or more committees of the Liberal ex-Cabinet to examine the Irish home rule issue in detail.[2] The 1906 Lord Lansdowne's memo to Balfour (referred to elsewhere),[3] concerning the Unionist Party's arrangements for opposition, included the suggestion that as well as a Shadow Cabinet, there should be set up sub-committees of the Shadow Cabinet for various policy areas. This proposal was not implemented, but in this period of opposition the Unionists did make some use of committees of the Shadow Cabinet. At the height of the Irish home rule crisis in February 1914, for example, following a Shadow Cabinet meeting at Lansdowne House at which the issue was discussed, a committee of the Shadow Cabinet was formed to look into the question of whether the Unionists should try to force a dissolution by amending the Mutiny Act in the Lords.[4] Again, in the inter-war years, Labour's Parliamentary Committee was sometimes divided into sub-committees. In 1927, for example, MacDonald appointed a policy committee to

---

[1] Monypenny and Buckle, *Life of Benjamin Disraeli*, VI, p. 576.
[2] Crewe, *Lord Rosebery*, I, p. 339.
[3] Newton, *Lord Lansdowne*, p. 353. See also above, p. 45.
[4] Chamberlain, *Politics From the Inside*, p. 605.

formulate a policy statement for the next election, after the Parliamentary Committee had turned down a programme drawn up by Arthur Henderson,[1] while in December 1928 the Parliamentary Committee set up a committee made up of Snowden, Webb, Shaw, and Graham to prepare the King's Speech for a new Labour Government.[2]

In the post-1945 period, various ad hoc groups of Parliamentary Committee or Consultative Committee members have been formed from time to time to deal with particular issues. Such groups are essentially informal, however, and are generally on the basis of 'Jim, Fred, and George' being asked to get together to look into a problem that cannot be settled at the full Committee meeting. Early in the 1970–1 session, for example, groups of Parliamentary Committee members looked into the arrangements for linking the PLP and Transport House, while in May 1971 a more formal 'think group' was set up, consisting of Harold Wilson, Roy Jenkins, James Callaghan, Ian Mikardo (a member of the NEC but not of the Parliamentary Committee), and Sir Harry Nicholas, the Labour Party General Secretary, to examine problems of party organisation.[3] A sub-committee of the Conservative Consultative Committee was formed in 1968 to draft an amendment to the Race Relations Bill that would accommodate the conflicting views that existed within the party about the Bill. Whether in office or in opposition the Conservatives at times set up a Steering Committee of senior party figures, chaired by the Party leader, for the central guidance of longer-term policy planning.[4] The policy document 'Make Life Better', and the 1970 election manifesto, were produced by the Steering Committee, assisted by members of the Research Department. This body is probably better classed as a committee of the Shadow Cabinet than as an 'Inner Shadow Cabinet', although it was made up of the senior figures of the Consultative Committee. In the 1966–70 Parliament, Lord Carrington, Sir Keith Joseph, and Robert Carr acted as a sub-committee to

[1] Dalton, *Memoirs*, p. 171.

[2] Ibid., p. 182.

[3] See *The Guardian*, 18 May 1971.

[4] See Butler and Pinto-Duschinsky, *The British General Election of 1970*, pp. 80–1. See above, p. 242.

coordinate the activities of businessmen who had volunteered to assist the Conservatives in their preparations for future office.[1] Similarly, in the 1970–1 session Labour's Parliamentary Committee set up an ad hoc 'action committee', consisting of Harold Wilson, Roy Jenkins, Robert Mellish, and Barbara Castle to plan the Opposition's tactics over the Industrial Relations Bill.

On another level, gatherings of senior and junior Spokesmen in related areas may take place from time to time, some on a fairly regular basis, to coordinate the work and tactics of opposition. When George Brown was Defence Spokesman from 1956 to 1961, he met with the Spokesmen for Admiralty, War, and Air regularly on Mondays during the session to coordinate defence attitudes. Brown was a member of the Parliamentary Committee for most of this period, and thus he represented the views of the other service Spokesmen at its meetings. In the 1966–70 Parliament Sir Alec Douglas-Home occasionally met with other external affairs Spokesmen, but such gatherings were essentially informal and irregular. The Conservative Spokesmen on Scottish Affairs also met together usually once per week in London to coordinate their activities. Since 1970, Labour's Scottish Spokesmen have met on a similar, though less regular, basis, while the Education Spokesmen have met together more or less weekly.

It must be emphasised, however, that all of these examples of Shadow Cabinet 'committees' or 'sub-units', merely represent ad hoc and generally informal arrangements. For the most part, neither the Parliamentary Committee nor the Consultative Committee has found it necessary to work through an elaborate system of sub-committees, so that this represents a fundamental contrast with the practice of Cabinet, which today depends so heavily upon a formal and extensive system of sub-committees for the transaction of its business. Nevertheless, the general organisation of the Shadow Cabinet is clearly based on Cabinet practices, and in recent years many aspects of Shadow Cabinet organisation have come to resemble Cabinet practices even more closely than in the past. In particular, the greater frequency of Shadow Cabinet meetings today compared with the pre-1914 and inter-war periods, and the more extensive

[1] Ibid., p. 89.

secretarial services provided for the Consultative Committee and Parliamentary Committee alike, have given the Shadow Cabinet a more regularised and formalised style. To some extent, however, the broad similarities between Cabinet and Shadow Cabinet *organisation* serve to cloak the fact that, as pointed out in the introduction to this chapter, the two bodies perform very different *functions*. Thus it needs to be re-emphasised here that while the business of the Cabinet is concerned with deciding major policy issues that face the departments of state, the Shadow Cabinet is basically a Parliamentary committee of management, whose time is taken up primarily with determining the Opposition's Parliamentary tactics and short-term Parliamentary attitudes.

As well as recognising this fundamental contrast between the functions of the Cabinet and Shadow Cabinet, it is also necessary to avoid exaggerating the similarities in the organisation and procedures of the two bodies. Despite the developments of recent years that were mentioned above, the Shadow Cabinet clearly still lacks much of the formality that surrounds the practices of the Cabinet. Indeed, in many ways existing Shadow Cabinet organisation is more akin to the way the Cabinet operated in the nineteenth century than to the way it functions today. The absence of a sophisticated system of sub-committees, the comparatively casual secretarial arrangements, the absence of any great number of Shadow Cabinet papers, the informal atmosphere, the comparatively unhurried conduct of business —all of these aspects of Shadow Cabinet organisation provide closer parallels with the organisation and structure of a pre-1914 Cabinet than of a contemporary Cabinet. Nevertheless, the organisation of the Shadow Cabinet has become considerably more formal over the last twenty years or so, and in this respect the patterns of opposition have come more and more to resemble those of office.

Within this general situation, however, there remain clear differences between the two parties. As well as the basic contrast that was emphasised in Chapter 4, between the formation of the Consultative Committee through selection by the party leader, and the formation of the Parliamentary Committee through election by the PLP, there is a clear difference between the two bodies in the amount of attention they devote to policy

formulation. Because of the Conservative leader's direct responsibility for long-term policy, in contrast to the situation in the
Labour party, where policy making machinery is centred on
the NEC, the Consultative Committee spends more time discussing the reports of policy committees than does the Parliamentary Committee. Also, in the general conduct of meetings,
Consultative Committee practices are somewhat more formal
and elaborate than are those of the Parliamentary Committee.
In these respects, therefore, the nature of Consultative Committee deliberations is closer to that of a Ministerial Cabinet
than is that of the Parliamentary Committee. This is not to
say, of course, that Conservative practices are a carbon copy of
those in office: as emphasised above, the crucial difference
between being in office and being in opposition means that,
for both parties, Shadow Cabinet organisation and behaviour
differs from that of the Cabinet in fundamental respects. For
Labour, however, this contrast is even more pronounced than
it is for the Conservatives. In this, then, as in other areas that
will be examined in the next three chapters, the transfer from
opposition to office produces greater changes in front-bench
organisation and behaviour for the Labour Party than for the
Conservatives.

8

Spokesmen as Parliamentary Critics and Policy Makers

THE TWO broad functions of an Opposition Spokesman are to organise and lead his party's attack upon the Government in his particular subject area, and to prepare and present the Opposition's alternative proposals. Thus as with the Leader of the Opposition, the Shadow Cabinet and the Opposition as a whole, each individual Spokesman is concerned partly with criticism and partly with preparation for future office. Within this broad definition of functions, however, an Opposition Spokesman has considerable freedom to interpret his role as he chooses. When appointing their Spokesmen neither Harold Wilson nor Edward Heath issued detailed instructions as to what the job involved, and, unlike a Minister, a Spokesman does not have civil servants to advise him as to his functions. Thus in interview a number of Spokesmen emphasised that they 'picked the job up as they went along', and consulted their more experienced colleagues where necessary. Generally the senior Spokesman for each subject will define the nature and extent of his junior colleagues' activities, but even here the extent of each Spokesman's freedom to interpret his role is probably greater than is the case in office. In the execution of his duties the Spokesman is involved with work in and out of Parliament, although it is the Parliamentary arena which is his main centre of activity. The amount of time that he spends in the chamber of the Commons, or in Committees, will vary from session to session, depending to a great extent on whether or not he is faced with legislation in his area. Outside Parliament the Spokesman will be involved with various elements in the party organisation, particularly the machinery that each party has for examining policy questions. Again, there is something of a distinction between the two parties here. The contrast that was noted in the previous chapter between Labour's Parliamentary Committee and the Conservative Consultative Committee over the question of the amount of time devoted to the discussion of policy documents is reflected also in the case of the role of individual Spokesmen in the two parties. The involvement of Conservative Spokesmen in their party's policy making machinery is much more direct than is the case with Labour Spokesmen, who may even be excluded from the NEC's committees working on projects in their subject area.

For Spokesmen of both parties, however, the Parliamentary arena is the centre of their daily activities, and it is the confrontation with the Government in the Commons that is the main aspect of their role. In this confrontation the Opposition suffers from the major disadvantage of not having the backing of the civil service. Each political party, of course, has its Research Department which can supply Spokesmen and backbenchers with political ammunition. Opposition MPs can also obtain information and assistance from other friendly sources, such as the business world, industry, or the Universities. Nevertheless, they cannot match the departmental resources upon which Ministers can draw. Thus Peter Shore has pointed out that there is

. . . a great gulf in the British political system between the Government and Opposition. It is the Government—and the Government alone—that has the inside story of events; the ready daily access to the Treasury, the Bank of England and the Foreign Office; the means of tapping and processing information that exists in the unofficial worlds of commerce and industry.[1]

Given this, the Parliamentary dice are loaded heavily in favour of the Minister. In more detail, then, precisely what duties does an Opposition Spokesman perform in and out of Parliament, just how far is he involved in his party's policy making machinery, and in these activities what sources of information are

[1] Peter Shore, *Entitled to Know*, London 1966, p. 9.

available to him? These matters will be considered in this chapter.

The Spokesman's Duties

G. R. Strauss has written that being a Spokesman involves, 'Studying the problems of the department, and, on all Parliamentary occasions, leading for the Party from the Front Bench.'[1] In debates in his subject area the Spokesman will open or close for the Opposition. Debating skill is thus at a premium, and above all the Spokesman must have the ability to attack effectively the Minister's policies and record. In Question Time the Spokesman will normally lead the questioning of the Minister. In this, as in all aspects of his role, the Spokesman's tactics and general approach will be governed to a considerable extent by the strengths and weaknesses of the Minister he is facing. A Minister whose performance at Question Time is poor will be an easy target for a sharp Parliamentarian, and part of the process of selecting an Opposition team is to pick the right Spokesman for a particular Minister. As each MP is limited to two questions per day, the Spokesman has to organise backbenchers to make a concerted attack, but he may raise supplementaries on his colleagues' questions.[2] After a supplementary from the Opposition front bench, however, the Speaker generally moves on to the next question, so the Spokesman has to take care not to intervene too soon, and thereby block contributions from his backbench colleagues. To plan such tactics, the backbench subject committees will often meet with the Spokesmen concerned the day before questions in their area are due.

The Spokesman will be required to scrutinise any Statutory Instruments that are within his subject area. As with Question Time, he will recruit backbench assistance for this task. In a session in which legislation is produced in his area, a Spokesman will be involved in a lot of detailed work on the terms of the Bill. As well as leading for the Opposition in the main debates at second and third readings, the Spokesman will be active at the

[1] Strauss, *Political Quarterly*, 1965, p. 284.
[2] For details of the procedure of Question Time see D. N. Chester and Nona Bowring, *Questions in Parliament*, London 1962.

Committee stage, where he will lead and coordinate the activities of his backbench colleagues on the committee. The committee stage of some major Bills, and some very minor Bills, is taken on the floor of the House. When a Bill is taken in a Standing Committee, one of the appropriate Spokesmen will generally be a member. This is a particularly vital aspect of a Spokesman's role. The frontal attack in a debate on the floor of the House, though spectacular, usually can be easily resisted by the Government. Constant niggling by the Opposition over legislative details in Standing Committee can be much harder to combat, and can be much more wearing for the Ministers concerned. As one Labour MP has written, 'Parliamentary Opposition is a kind of bloodless guerilla warfare in which the enemy is obstructed in committee, harassed at Question Time, and never beaten in set-piece battles.'[1] It should be noted here, however, that an Opposition Spokesman's role with regard to legislation will vary from one measure to another. On controversial legislation to which his party is violently opposed, his task will be to oppose the proposals by every means possible. On the more numerous non-controversial measures, however, his activities will be much more constructive, and he is likely to be involved in assisting the Minister to improve the details of the Bill at the Committee stage.[2] This aspect of a Spokesman's role is often under-estimated, as inevitably it is his more partisan activities that attract most comment in the press.

Table 17 shows the extent to which Spokesmen were members of Standing Committees in four sessions chosen from the 1955–70 period (two sessions of Labour Opposition and two of Conservative Opposition).[3] In the 1961–2 and 1965–6 sessions almost all of the Committees contained at least one Spokesman for the subject area of the Bill they were dealing with. The larger number of Committees without Spokesmen in the 1967–8 session can perhaps be explained by the smallness of the frontbench team in that session, together with the greater number of Bills dealt with in Standing Committee. Committees dealing

[1] Ray Fletcher, *The Guardian*, 15 July 1970.
[2] For a general comment on the constructive role of the Opposition, see above, p. 183.
[3] For the reasons for the selection of these particular sessions see Chapter 10 and Appendix E.

with measures which are likely to be passed without much debate might not contain any Spokesmen. In the 1967–8 session, for example, there were no Spokesmen on the Committee dealing with the Adoption Bill, but with this measure there was no dispute at the committee stage, which took just one minute to complete. In the case of the more important and more controversial Bills, however, the senior Spokesman will invariably be a member of the Committee. Thus in all four sessions shown in Table 17, the senior Spokesman in each case served on the Committees dealing with the major pieces of

TABLE 17

Spokesmen and Membership of House of Commons Standing Committees

Session	Number of Spokesmen in Team*	Number of Bills Taken in Standing Committees	Percentage of Committees Containing a) One of the Spokesmen for Subject	b) Senior Spokesman for Subject	c) Spokesmen for Other Subjects
1956–7	36	27	55·5	48·1	44·4
1961–2	39	30	96·7	73·3	50·0
1965–6	59	13	92·3	84·6	23·1
1967–8	30	55	50·9	38·2	5·4

Source: Hansard, Standing Committee Reports for the years in question.
* Excluding the leader, whip, and all peers.

legislation, such as the Rent Bill in the 1956–7 session, the Transport Bill in 1961–2, the Land Commission Bill in 1965–6, or the Prices and Incomes Bill and the Race Relations Bill in 1967–8. Sometimes all the Spokesmen for a subject will serve on a Committee dealing with a major measure. Thus all four Commonwealth and Colonial affairs Spokesmen served on the Standing Committee dealing with the South Africa Bill in the 1961–2 session, while the two Treasury Spokesmen and a Trade Spokesman served on the 1968 Finance Bill Committee. The vast majority of Spokesmen serve only on Committees dealing with Bills in their own subject areas, although some are active outside their assigned areas. Eric Fletcher, for example, while Home Affairs Spokesman in the 1961–2 Session, served on two Committees dealing with Local Government Bills, as well as on two Committees for Home Office Bills. In the sessions shown in Table 17, Conservative Spokesmen were less likely to serve on Committees outside their own area than were Labour Spokesmen, and this mirrors the greater levels of specialisation found among Conservative than Labour Spokesmen in other aspects of their Parliamentary activity examined in Chapter 10.

In the Standing Committees, or on the floor of the House, the Spokesmen will lead and coordinate the activities of their backbench colleagues. A Spokesman may form a team of backbenchers to fight a particular Bill or to examine a particular aspect of policy. Edward Heath, for example, as Treasury Spokesman, led team attacks against the 1965 Finance Bill,[1] and this helped to raise his popularity among Conservative MPs just before the party leadership became vacant. Douglas Jay and Harold Wilson organised similar groups to oppose Finance Bills in the 1951–64 period, and in the 1970–1 session Barbara Castle led a working party of MPs and outside experts against the Industrial Relations Bill.

Debates, standing committees and questions represent Spokesmen's main areas of activity in the House, but there are other aspects of Parliamentary procedure in which Spokesmen may be involved to some extent. Some Spokesmen are active in the Select Committees of the Commons, including the most recent subject committees created in the reforming zeal of the 1966–70 Parliament. Bernard Braine, for example, was Spokesman for Overseas Aid for part of the 1966–70 Parliament and he became vice-chairman of the Overseas Aid Committee when it was formed in 1969. Similarly, David Price served on the Technology Committee throughout the 1966–70 Parliament, while he was a Technology Spokesman. Dick Taverne and Joel Barnett, Treasury Spokesmen in the 1970–1 session, both served on the Expenditure Committee, and Barnett also served on the Public Accounts Committee. There is no automatic link, however, between Spokesmen and the appropriate Select Committee. In the three Parliaments of the 1960s only one Power Spokesman (Tom Fraser in the 1960–1 session) was a member of the Nationalised Industries Committee. The Agriculture Spokesmen did not serve on the Agriculture Committee in its

[1] For a comment see Butler and Pinto-Duschinsky, *The British General Election of 1970*, p. 69.

short life (1966–9), nor did the Home Office Spokesmen serve on the Race Relations Committee. In the 1959–64 Parliament, a number of Labour Spokesmen served on the Public Accounts and Estimates Committees, but the Treasury Spokesmen were rarely among these: Harold Wilson, while Treasury Spokesman, chaired the Public Accounts Committee, but he remained chairman when he became Spokesman for Foreign Affairs. Similarly, in the 1970–1 session Harold Lever chaired the Public Accounts Committee, even though he was European Spokesman, while Graham Page remained chairman of the Statutory Instruments Committee when he became Housing Spokesman in 1967. The Public Accounts, Estimates, and Statutory Instruments Committees, of course, are wide ranging bodies whose enquiries cover all the departments of state, so that a number of Spokesmen will follow their activities. In general, however, it may be noted that there is a convention of all-party co-operation on Select Committees, and it is assumed that Committee members, whether Opposition Spokesmen or not, will refrain from making use of Committee information for partisan purposes during the session in which the enquiry is being conducted.

The introduction of Private Members' Bills and the signing of Early Day Motions are devices widely used by MPs to draw attention to particular issues. They are primarily backbench devices, however, and Opposition leaders normally do not use them as a means of executing their role as Spokesmen. In the 1961–2 session, Roy Jenkins, while an Opposition Spokesman for Trade, made wide use of Early Day Motions as part of his activities for the pro-Common Market movement. Here, however, he was acting as a private member rather than as a Spokesman, and during the session he left the front bench in order that he might devote more time to the Common Market campaign. Similarly, although Spokesmen may occasionally present Private Members' Bills, they do so mainly in their capacity as constituency MPs or private members.[1] Between the wars the Labour Party in opposition sometimes used Private Members' Bills as a means of promoting official party policy, and in 1923 Willie Graham brought in the Prevention of Unemployment Bill, and J. H. Thomas the Workman's Compensa-

[1] For details of the procedure in Private Members' Bills, see P. A. Bromhead, *Private Members' Bills*, London 1956.

tion Bill as Private Members' Bills.[1] Since 1945, however, Opposition leaders have been much less likely even to participate in debates or votes on Private Members' Bills than was the case between the wars.[2] Nevertheless, Spokesmen sometimes enter the annual ballot for private members' time, and in the 1969–70 session Joseph Godber came fourteenth in the ballot, and in 1968–9 Sir Edward Boyle came twelfth, and Maurice Macmillan fourth.[3] All three duly introduced Bills, although none became law. Spokesmen can also use the other procedures available for the introduction of Private Members' Bills, but out of a total of 184 Private Members' Bills brought in during the 1968–9 and 1969–70 sessions, only ten were introduced by Spokesmen.[4] With six of the ten Bills the subject matter was within the Spokesman's assigned area, while the other four sprang from constituency or other interests.

Within his own party the Spokesman will maintain formal and informal contacts with backbenchers interested in his policy field. Conservative Spokesmen act as chairmen of the appropriate backbench subject groups, and although Labour Spokesmen do not necessarily chair their subject groups, they will generally attend meetings and maintain contacts with prominent members of the group. To some extent a Spokesman will provide an 'information service' for his backbench colleagues, briefing them on the details of his subject in preparation for debates, or even assisting his colleagues with constituency problems that touch on his subject. Here, however, the flow of information will be two-way, and the Spokesman will draw upon the knowledge of any backbenchers who are experts in his field. The Spokesman may be asked by the Leader of the Opposition to produce a statement on some aspect of policy, or he may take a policy initiative himself and seek to convert the party to his proposals. He may produce policy documents for submission to his colleagues. Reginald Paget, for example, while Navy Spokesman for part of the 1959–64 Parliament, did

[1] See Cole, *Beatrice Webb's Diaries*, I, pp. 9 and 13.

[2] Bromhead, *Private Members' Bills*, pp. 112–16.

[3] See I. F. Burton and G. Drewry, 'Public Legislation: A Survey of the Session 1968–9' and '1969–70', *Parliamentary Affairs*, 1969–70, pp. 154–83, 308–44.

[4] Ibid.

much to clarify and codify naval defence attitudes that the Labour Party had been developing over the years, but which until then had not been fully documented. During most sessions the Spokesman may have only a limited amount of time for these matters, although much will depend on whether or not he is faced at the time with a major piece of legislation in his area. The recess, however, and particularly the long summer recess, can be used for this purpose. In the Labour Party the NEC is the official medium through which policy is produced in opposition.[1] For day-to-day policy attitudes, however, and in the determination and organisation of Parliamentary tactics, Labour and Conservative Spokesmen alike use their own initiative, subject to the overall approval of the whips and the Shadow Cabinet.

These various Parliamentary activities can be very time-consuming. The Spokesman has to 'shadow' the Minister in literal terms, sitting opposite him in debates and in Question Time, and normally being present in the House when the Minister is liable to speak. He generally develops fairly close personal contacts with the Minister behind the scenes, and is often taken into the Minister's confidence. Unlike a backbencher who can pick and choose when he will attend debates, a Spokesman has to be in attendance in the House whenever his department's business is to be, or even *might* be, dealt with, and also invariably on Mondays when Ministerial statements may be made, and on Thursdays when the next week's business is announced. A number of Spokesmen, however, claimed in interview that they spent less time on the floor of the House than when they had been backbenchers, because their role as Spokesmen involved them in activities in committees of one kind or another. When not in the Chamber or in committee, the Spokesman often has to be in attendance in the Palace of Westminster, meeting backbenchers and others who are concerned with his subject, or preparing his speeches and doing his own research. The preparation of speeches can be very time-consuming, as unlike a Minister he has no civil servants to back him up. Most Spokesmen spend a lot of time in the library of the House of Commons preparing their own material. Although many Spokesmen are experts in their subjects when appointed,

[1] See below, pp. 267–72.

or soon become well acquainted with the subject matter, they have still to keep abreast of the details of current developments as contained in Bills, White Papers, and other reports. Douglas Jay, during the passage of the annual Finance Bill, would spend long periods in the House of Commons library, working on the details of the Bill, and on the Opposition's counter proposals, and Hugh Gaitskell made great use of the library for this purpose also. Some Spokesmen in interview acknowledged that because of the extent of their duties, they were obliged to abandon interests that they had pursued as backbenchers. Others claimed that they maintained many of their non-political activities, and as a consequence led much more hectic lives than they had done before becoming Spokesmen. Some pointed out that while the extent of a Minister's duties is widely appreciated, a Spokesman's tasks are often under-estimated by his constituents, fellow MPs, and colleagues outside the House, and that as a consequence Opposition MPs are expected to maintain activities for which they have no time once they become Spokesmen. Because of the extent of these duties, it is doubtful if more than a few Spokesmen fulfil their role as conscientiously as they should, and Spokesmen freely acknowledged this in interview.

Outside Parliament a Spokesman is widely regarded as the party's official mouthpiece in his particular policy area, and much of his work is of a 'public relations' nature. He may be called upon to make formal statements of policy and party attitudes, and the mass media look to a Spokesman for 'instant comment' about the affairs of the department that he is shadowing. In this sense the Spokesman becomes a press and television agent for his party. The news media are more likely to deal with an officially designated Spokesman than with an unofficial figure, and one of the effects of the use of Spokesmen's titles since 1955 has been to confer a certain status on Opposition leaders. Similarly, pressure groups will approach the official Opposition Spokesman in the same way that they approach the departments of state, but while a Minister has departmental officials to act as a buffer between pressure groups and himself, the Spokesman has to deal with these bodies directly. In interview one Spokesman pointed out that 'within hours' of being appointed Spokesman for a particular subject he was approached by the relevant pressure groups, all offering information in return for support for their cause. In this way pressure groups can be a very useful source of information for the Spokesman. Inevitably, the pressure groups will be most active and helpful as an election nears, and the Spokesman has a chance of becoming Minister.

Spokesmen will act as a link between the Parliamentary party and the party outside Parliament, and at the annual Conference and at regional and constituency gatherings he will be required to explain and defend the party's policies in his area. As experts in their own areas, Spokesmen have the task of informing MPs, and the party in general, of new developments in their field. When he was Defence Spokesman, George Brown was very conscious of the need to educate the party, in and out of Parliament, on defence matters. The performance of this educative role, however, will depend largely on the Spokesman's personality and relationship with the extra-Parliamentary party, and Patrick Gordon Walker, when Defence Spokesman, was rather less active in this direction than was George Brown. For Labour Spokesmen it is necessary to maintain contacts with the NEC and its policy sub-committees. This is easiest for those Spokesmen who have seats on the NEC. For this reason as much as any other Roy Jenkins' election in 1970 to the post of deputy leader of the party, carrying as it does a seat on the NEC, was seen as giving him greatly increased influence over policy-making in many fields outside his own main interest of the Treasury.

The nature and extent of a Spokesman's work load will vary from one time to another, depending on the topicality of his subject, whether a major piece of legislation is being introduced in his area, or whether the party is undertaking a major policy review in his area. Thus in any one session the work load is not evenly distributed among the members of the team. The nature, as well as the extent, of the work load will also vary from subject to subject. A Treasury Spokesman will have to deal each year with the time-consuming Finance Bill, whereas a Foreign Affairs Spokesman will be faced with less legislation, but may be involved in visits abroad. In the 1966–70 Parliament, for example, Sir Alec Douglas-Home visited a number of African countries, Enoch Powell, as Defence Spokesman, visited the

USA,[1] and Bernard Braine visited India in his capacity as Overseas Aid Spokesman. Some Spokesmen have duties which are so broad as to involve them closely in the work of their colleagues. The Treasury Spokesman, for example, has to consider the policy statements of his colleagues from a financial angle, in much the same way as the Chancellor of the Exchequer vets departmental estimates. This is especially important for the Opposition when it is preparing its programme for an election campaign, and the possible cost of its policies is likely to be challenged by the Government. The Spokesman on Law is also often required to fulfil a similar supervisory role, examining his colleagues' policy proposals from the legal standpoint. A policy document such as the Conservatives' 'Fair Deal At Work', produced in the 1966–70 Parliament, clearly had numerous legal implications which took it beyond the scope of the Spokesmen on labour relations. Similarly, Labour's Working Party on the Industrial Relations Bill in the 1970–1 session included Ronald King Murray, one of the legal Spokesmen. The Foreign Affairs Spokesman is also often required to consider the impact on foreign relations of policies in financial, trading and other spheres. Thus the position of Spokesmen as members of a team is emphasised.

Spokesmen and Policy-making

What role do Spokesmen play in the process of policy-making in opposition? There are various ways in which party policy is produced during a period in opposition. In forming its plans for the immediate business in Parliament, the Shadow Cabinet and individual Spokesmen, often at very short notice, have to decide the 'line' that the party will adopt. In this way, many policy commitments merely 'emerge', almost by accident, from the day-to-day Parliamentary battle. Repeated criticism by Spokesmen of a Government's failure to achieve a certain annual house building figure, for example, carries the implication that the Opposition, when in office, will achieve or exceed the figure. Whether a particular Opposition 'line' becomes a 'pledge', and thus a 'policy', will often depend (as expressed by one MP in interview) 'largely on the amount of noise with which a

[1] For an account of this trip see Roth, *Enoch Powell*, p. 341.

Spokesman's comments are received by the House'. With the most important of the immediate issues, the official party attitude will be decided at the weekly meeting of the Shadow Cabinet, or at a special meeting if a crisis should emerge suddenly. On the less important matters the individual Spokesman will decide the attitude that he, as the official party representative, will take towards the issue. Thus in the 1971 session the Opposition's attitude to the location of the third London airport was worked out and presented by the senior Spokesman concerned. Regardless of who decides the party's stance, however, once a Spokesman has given expression to a particular point of view which attracts publicity, the Government, the Opposition's own supporters, and the electorate in general, see the Opposition as being committed to that stance, and it is likely to be accused of being inconsistent and untrustworthy if it ignores such commitments.

At another level, the Leader of the Opposition, or some other senior party figure, may take a major personal initiative in a currently topical issue. In November 1971, for example, Harold Wilson, on returning from a visit to Ireland, produced a fifteen point plan for a long-term solution of the Irish problem.[1] It was welcomed as a significant new contribution to the Ulster debate, and was regarded as the approach that a Labour Government would take to the problem. Again, in May 1968, Edward Heath committed the Conservative Party to examining the possibility of creating a Scottish Parliament. This proposal met with a mixed reception from the party, and a committee under Sir Alec Douglas-Home was set up subsequently to examine the various forms that such a Parliament could take.[2] In any period of opposition there will be a number of such occasions when the Parliamentary leaders will commit the party to a particular stand on major issues. Thus at various times during 1971 and early 1972 the Leader of the Opposition, or Spokesmen, committed a future Labour Government to establish a Development Authority and set up a Development Bank for the regions, create Public Investment Boards, re-transfer (without compensation) air routes from BUA and Caledonian to BOAC and BEA, re-establish the Industrial Reorganisation Corporation,

[1] See *The Guardian*, 26 November 1971.
[2] See below, p. 307.

abolish museum charges, and repeal the Housing Finance Act.[1] Other sections of the party also may make declarations of which the Parliamentary leaders do not necessarily approve, but on which the party is seen to have committed itself. Thus during 1971 Labour's NEC or the annual Conference called for the restoration of free school milk, the provision of security of tenure for tenants in furnished property, of a major reform of the National Health Service and of private medical practice, the repeal of the Industrial Relations Act, and the elimination of immigration quotas based on race or country of origin.[2]

As well as having policy emerge directly from the Parliamentary leaders, both parties have machinery outside the strictly Parliamentary organisation for the review of party attitudes. Whether the Opposition party is wise to indulge in a great policy revision exercise in opposition is debatable (as was discussed in Chapter 6), but both parties do so to some extent. In each of their four periods in opposition since 1918 the Conservatives have established such machinery. After the 1923 election, according to J. C. C. Davidson,

> . . . Baldwin spent his entire time—and kept his 'shadow cabinet' exercised—in drawing up plans for the next occasion when the Conservative Party was in power. All the great measures of 1924 to 1926 were devised then.[3]

This claim as to the extent of the policy review is perhaps extravagant, as the Conservatives were in opposition for only nine months on this occasion. Nevertheless, policy-making machinery was established, with a Policy Secretariat (the forerunner of the modern Research Department) being set up. Committees of MPs were also formed for each policy area, generally chaired by the appropriate ex-Minister. Neville Chamberlain was involved with the committees for municipal reform and national insurance, and these committees' efforts did lead to legislation by the 1924–9 Government, when Chamberlain was Minister of Health.[4] Again, in the 1929–31

---

[1] See 1971 *Labour Party Conference Report*, pp. 43–7 and *The Guardian*, 9 March 1972, for a fuller list and a comment ('Benn's Secret Blueprint').
[2] Ibid., and *The Guardian*, 11 and 22 February 1972.
[3] James, *Memoirs of a Conservative*, p. 192.
[4] Feiling, *The Life of Neville Chamberlain*, p. 115.

period of Conservative Opposition committees of MPs were formed for each policy area, mostly chaired by ex-Cabinet Ministers.[1] The Policy Secretariat had lapsed when the Conservatives returned to office, but it was revived in 1929, with Neville Chamberlain as its chairman, and in 1930 it moved to the present Conservative Research Department's headquarters in Old Queen Street. In this period its function was described, somewhat idealistically, as being '. . . to investigate economic and other problems free from any political bias, and with the sole object of obtaining the true facts on which a policy can be based.'[2] It is clearly not the function of any political party's research department to be 'free from any political bias', as party leaders in opposition need to be supplied with the maximum number of highly 'political' bullets to fire at the Government. In fact the Policy Secretariat serviced the various policy committees that had been set up in 1929, and helped the committees to produce various policy reports, including one on the then controversial tariffs issue.[3]

When the Conservatives returned to Opposition in 1945, a major review of party policy was again undertaken, largely under the inspiration of R. A. Butler. He re-organised the Research Department and used its resources to assist various committees that were set up to examine different aspects of Conservative policy.[4] These committees produced documents such as 'The Industrial Charter', 'Agriculture Charter', 'Imperial Policy', 'Scottish Control of Scottish Affairs', and 'Policy for Wales', and they were eventually all drawn together into the general policy statement 'Right Road for Britain', which was published in the summer of 1949, and which, in abbreviated form was the Conservative manifesto for the 1950 general election. Backbench MPs and figures from outside Parliament were involved with the work of the committees to some extent, but for the most part the members of the Shadow Cabinet were the dominant figures on the committees. The

[1] Macleod, *Neville Chamberlain*, p. 134.
[2] James, *Memoirs of a Conservative*, p. 338.
[3] Macleod, *Neville Chamberlain*, p. 134.
[4] For a detailed analysis of this process see J. D. Hoffman, *The Conservative Party in Opposition 1945–51*, pp. 118–97; Butler, *The Art of the Possible*, p. 145.

1945–51 policy documents were in no sense draft legislation, which Conservative Ministers could implement when they achieved office. Nevertheless, their basic themes of the need for the Conservative Party to accept the welfare state and the mixed economy and avoid a return to pre-war policies, undoubtedly helped to set the mood of the Conservative Government in the 1951–64 period, and it is largely through his work on the Industrial Charter and other documents that R. A. Butler is credited with 'civilising' the Conservative Party in the postwar period.

After 1964 the Conservatives once again undertook a general review of policy, with an elaborate system of committees supervised by the party's overall Policy Advisory Committee, which functions whether the party is in office or in opposition.[1] For most of the 1964–70 period the Policy Advisory Committee was chaired by Edward Heath (who had succeeded R. A. Butler as chairman in 1964), with Sir Edward Boyle as vice-chairman, but in 1968 Reginald Maudling took over as chairman and Lord Jellicoe as vice-chairman. The Policy Advisory Committee is made up of twenty-five or so members. The chairman and deputy chairman are appointed by the leader. Seven members are elected to represent the Parliamentary Party, and eight are elected by the executive committee of the National Union. Some party officers are ex-officio members. In opposition the Advisory Committee would meet every month or so. The chairman of the Committee appointed the members of the various policy committees, of which nineteen were set up in the 1964–5 session. The number was later increased to thirty, with one for each broad policy area, such as Economic Policy, Education, Balance of Payments, and so on. Some groups, like Agriculture, divided into sub-committees. Membership of the Policy Committees was not made public, but was generally divided more or less equally between MPs and outside experts from the business world and the universities: on the Arts Group, however, there were twice as many outsiders as Parliamentarians. The senior Spokesman for the subject usually served as chairman of the committee, and was always very influential in its deliberations.

[1] For more comments on these bodies see Butler and Pinto-Duschinsky, *The British General Election of 1970*, pp. 68–9; Hutchinson, *Edward Heath*, p. 134.

The officers of the appropriate backbench subject committees were generally members. The policy committees in the 1964–70 period produced a number of reports and proposals, including studies of industrial relations, housing, taxation, east-of-Suez policy, agriculture, social services, and international treaty obligations.[1] Heath himself served as chairman of the Economic Policy Group for much of the 1966–70 period, and was thus particularly influential in its work.

Some of the committees' reports were incorporated in the party's official policy documents, and 'Putting Britain Right Ahead', produced in 1965, and 'Make Life Better', in 1968, were largely amalgams of various such reports.[2] The actual manifesto for the 1970 general election, however, did not contain detailed comment on the party's policy proposals.[3] Each committee sat for as long as was necessary for it to produce a report, and then went into abeyance. The reports were in the form of recommendations to the leader, who retains ultimate control for policy. Thus they were confidential, although some were later published in the form of policy documents like 'Fair Deal at Work', dealing with industrial relations, and pamphlets like 'A New Style of Government', dealing with the machinery of Whitehall.

The Parliamentary leaders are in a position to accept or reject the work that the committees do. In the consideration of the reports the nominal 'chain of command' was that the policy committee concerned made its recommendations to the Policy Advisory Committee, which accepted, rejected or modified the proposals. They then passed on to the leader, who discussed them with his senior colleagues individually, and at meetings of the Steering Committee and the Shadow Cabinet. The leader retained final responsibility, although the influence of the particular Spokesman concerned normally would be considerable, especially if, as was usual, he was chairman of the committee. In the case of the 'east of Suez' policy that emerged in the 1964–1970 period, for example, the principle was worked out at Shadow Cabinet level, but the detailed implications were left to the Spokesmen concerned. The Spokesman's influence would be all

[1] Butler and Pinto-Duschinsky, *The British General Election of 1970*, p. 80.
[2] Hutchinson, *Edward Heath*, p. 150.
[3] Butler and Pinto-Duschinsky, *The British General Election of 1970*, p. 150.

the greater if he were also a member of the Consultative Committee, and if his personal relations with the party leader were
close. Ultimately, however, the party leader, in consultation
with the Consultative Committee, retained final control over
policy in opposition as in office.

Thus the Conservative policy committees act as advisory
bodies on policy issues, but the Spokesmen, the Consultative
Committee, and above all the party leader, remain in command
of the policy-making process. The situation within the Labour
Party when it is in opposition is somewhat different, and the
Parliamentary leaders do not have so direct a control over the
policy-making process in opposition.[1] When Labour is in office,
policy is made by Ministers and civil servants. In opposition,
however, the NEC presides over the process of studying long-
term policy options, and the Parliamentary Spokesmen do not
necessarily have any particularly privileged position in this
machinery. In the view of some members of the Labour Party
there always has been, and there always should be, a clear
division of responsibility when Labour is in opposition, with the
Parliamentary leaders being responsible for the Opposition's
role as a day-to-day critic of the Government in Parliament, and
the NEC being responsible for preparing the Opposition's
policies as the alternative Government. Over the years, the
trend has been away from such a clear demarcation of duties,
and towards closer links between the Parliamentary leaders and
the NEC's policy-making machinery, but the practice as well as
the theory of Labour Party organisation in this respect remains
somewhat different from that of the Conservative Party.

The structure of the NEC's policy-making machinery is complex. Domestic affairs are the concern of the Home Policy Sub-
Committee of the NEC, while the International Committee
covers foreign and defence policy. Both of these bodies set up
various committees, working parties and study groups to examine in depth aspects of policy, although in general, domestic
affairs lend themselves more to policy group enquiries than
do defence and foreign affairs. The committees, which are

[1] The subject has been well debated. See McKenzie, *British Political
Parties*, pp. 521–31; S. Rose, 'Policy Decision in Opposition', *Political
Studies*, 1956, pp. 128–38 (and a rejoinder by R. T. McKenzie, *Political
Studies* 1957, pp. 176–82).

serviced by the Labour Party Research Department, produce reports which are considered by the Home Policy or International Sub-Committee as the case may be, and if they are approved they are passed on to the NEC. If accepted by the NEC, the recommendations are submitted for consideration by the party as a whole at the annual conference, and may be included in the party's election manifesto, or in other official policy documents. A number of such policy committees are set up each year by the NEC, and some remain in operation for a number of years. The Old Age and Security Study Group, for example, deliberated for most of the 1955–9 Parliament and all of the 1959–64 Parliament.

With the return to opposition in 1970 the Home Policy Committee decided to undertake a major review of policy, and at a special Home Policy Committee meeting in October 1970 the general research strategy for the Parliament was worked out.[1] In April 1972 the first of a series of Labour Party 'green papers' was produced. It dealt with citizenship and immigration policy, and was a product of the Immigration Study Group's work over the previous eighteen months.[2] In May 1972 there was an all day meeting of the NEC and the Parliamentary Committee to discuss the policy document 'Priorities in Government', which had been drawn up on the basis of the proposals that had emerged from the policy groups in the 1970–2 period.[3] This policy document was made public in July 1972,[4] with the intention that it be debated within the party and then revised in time for the 1973 party conference.

The general composition of the sub-committees and study groups of the NEC in operation in the last session of the 1959–64 Parliament and the first session of the 1970 Parliament is shown in Table 18. Each committee (or 'study group' or 'working party') is made up of a core of NEC members, of whom the majority are normally MPs, together with additional co-opted members from Parliament or outside. Thus in the pre-1964 period Roy Jenkins, Anthony Crosland (who were not then members of the Opposition team), and Professors Kaldor and

[1] 1971 *Labour Party Conference Report*, p. 43.
[2] See *The Guardian*, 15 April 1972.
[3] See *The Guardian*, 20 May 1972.
[4] See *The Guardian*, 7 July 1972.

TABLE 18

Study Groups, Sub-Committees and Working Parties of the Labour Party NEC 1963–4 and 1970–1

Committee	Total	MPs	Spokesmen†	Chairman
		Membership		
1963–4 Session				
Air Transport*	8	5	2	F. Lee‡
Commonwealth Immigration	9	8	1	A. Greenwood
Crime Prevention*	16	9	1	Lord Longford
Disarmament*	13	9	4	P. Gordon Walker‡
Finance and Economic Policy	19	10	3	I. Mikardo
Local Government	19	11	3	A. Skeffington
Science and Industry	21	9	1	R. H. S. Crossman‡
Security and Old Age	31	14	1	R. H. S. Crossman
Supply of Teachers	16	8	2	R. H. S. Crossman
1970–1 Session				
Agriculture	22	8	2	Lady White
Finance and Economic Policy	21	13	3	R. Jenkins‡
Industrial Policy	28	14	6	J. Chalmers
Science and Education	37	9	3	Miss Lestor‡
Social Policy	22	10	4	W. Simpson
Regional, Local Govt.	32	17	7	F. Allaun
Immigration	12	7	0	T. Driberg
Common Market	14	9	2	D. Healey‡
Capital Shares	15	8	0	T. G. Bradley
Discrimination Against Women	18	5	3	Mrs Bellerby
Higher Education	18	3	0	G. Rhodes
South African Trade	8	5	2	A. Cunningham
Overseas Development	14	6	1	Mrs Hart‡
Scale and Purpose of Military Spending	5	2	1	F. Allaun
European Security	10	5	1	D. Healey‡
Commonwealth	5	4	1	T. Driberg

Source: 1964 and 1971 Labour Party Conference Reports.

* Indicates joint committee of NEC and PLP (for which the chairman need not be an NEC member), rather than a sub-committee or study group of NEC.

† That is, Spokesmen for the area covered by the committee.

‡ Indicates that the chairman was Spokesman for that subject.

Balogh worked on the NEC committees' taxation studies, while Peter Townsend and Professor R. M. Titmuss were members of the Old Age and Security Study Group.

In the pre-1964 period the Spokesmen did not necessarily become members of committees dealing with their subject. In 1970, however, in an attempt to improve links between the Parliamentary leaders and the NEC policy committees, it was decided that the PLP could appoint representatives to the committees, and in practice those appointed are generally the appropriate Spokesmen.[1] Even so, a Spokesman is unlikely to be chairman of a committee dealing with his subject. The chairman has to be a member of the NEC, so that this rules out many of the Spokesmen. Thus in 1970 Edward Short, the senior Education Spokesman, was a member of the NEC's Education and Science Committee, but the Committee was chaired by Joan Lestor, who was only an assistant Education Spokesman, but was an NEC member. Even when a Spokesman is a member of the NEC, however, it does not necessarily follow that he chairs a committee covering his subject. Thus James Callaghan was Treasury Spokesman in the 1963–4 session, but Ian Mikardo was chairman of the Finance and Economic Policy Sub-Committee. Similarly, Mrs Eirene White was an Education Spokesman in 1963–4, but Richard Crossman chaired the Supply of Teachers Study Group. Crossman was also chairman of the Old Age and Security Study Group throughout the Parliament, but he served as Spokesman on Pensions only from October 1959 to March 1960. In the 1970–1 session Barbara Castle was a member of the NEC's Industrial Policy Committee, but although she was the senior Spokesman on the Industrial Relations Bill, and was an NEC member, the committee was chaired by a trade unionist, Jim Chalmers.

Thus the role of Conservative Spokesmen as chairmen of their party's policy committees is only rarely repeated in the case of Labour Spokesmen with the NEC's committees. Although a Spokesman who also serves on the NEC may be closely involved in the policy study machinery, this will be through his role as an NEC member rather than through his role as a Parliamentary Spokesman, and Spokesmen who are not members of the NEC have no assured role in the NEC's

[1] *1971 Labour Party Conference Report*, p. 42.

various committees. Again, because the policy committees report to the NEC, rather than directly to the leader and the Parliamentary Committee, only those Parliamentary Committee members who also serve on the NEC will be in a position to examine the policy committee reports at first hand, before they are made public. This is clearly a major contrast with the situation in the Conservative Party, where the control of the Parliamentary leaders over the policy reports is direct and exclusive.

At the same time, the importance of the contrast between the two parties' practices can be exaggerated. Some senior Labour Spokesmen who had served on NEC committees claimed in interview that although they were not chairmen this did not necessarily inhibit their role in the committees' deliberations. They pointed out that the chairman's job was to report to the NEC on the committee's work, but that this did not necessarily mean that he had a dominant influence in the committee's work. They argued that as former Cabinet Ministers their own influence on the committee was considerable, although, presumably, the longer the party spends in opposition the less weight ex-Ministers will carry in such situations. Again, machinery exists to coordinate the views of the Parliamentary Committee and the NEC on major issues. Labour's election manifesto is framed at joint meetings of the Cabinet and the NEC when Labour is in office, and of the Parliamentary Committee and the NEC when in opposition. Spokesmen who are members of either the Parliamentary Committee or the NEC will be in a strong position to influence the content of the document, although Spokesmen who had been in this position claimed in interview that they had less influence over the manifesto's content than would Ministers when the party was in power. Joint meetings of the NEC and the Parliamentary Committee are also held at least annually, and in May 1971 a two-day gathering discussed policy and general organisational matters.[1] Also, joint committees from the NEC and PLP are formed from time to time to look at policy matters. They are made up of members selected by the NEC and by the Parliamentary Committee, and here the position of the Spokesmen is somewhat stronger than on the purely NEC committees.

[1] See *The Guardian*, 18 May 1971.

In 1970 some concern was expressed within the context of the Home Policy Sub-Committee of the NEC over the nature of the relationship between the NEC and the Parliamentary leaders. Some members sought to achieve closer links than had existed in previous periods of Labour Opposition, and to this end it was decided (as noted above) that if they were not otherwise members, Parliamentary Spokesmen would be co-opted on to the NEC policy committees dealing with their subject areas. As a further possible development along the same lines some Labour MPs in interview argued that even when a senior Spokesman was not an NEC member he should become at least joint chairman, or vice-chairman, of any NEC committees in his subject area. In 1971 there was set up a 'liaison committee' (or 'think group'), made up of four or five leading party figures, with the function of keeping the NEC and the Parliamentary Committee in touch with each other. Despite this innovation there is still something to be said in favour of the six or seven MPs who serve on both the NEC and the Parliamentary Committee being constituted into a formal Inner Shadow Cabinet.[1] Even with such a development, however, there would remain as a characteristic feature of the Labour Party's organisation in opposition the somewhat artificial division of functions between the NEC, responsible for studies of long-term policy, and the Parliamentary Committee, responsible for immediate Parliamentary attitudes and tactics. In this respect, then, a clear difference exists between the organisation of the Labour and Conservative parties in opposition.

The Opposition Civil Service

Opposition Spokesmen require a supply of factual information if they are to perform their role effectively. This is perhaps especially so if they are involved in the work of planning party policy and future legislation. Even in their day-to-day role as critics of the Government, however, they have to be well informed if they are to be convincing. Without the support of civil servants, how can Spokesmen obtain the factual information and reliable opinions that they require? The political parties have their own Research Departments which, as one of

[1] See above, p. 244.

their functions, service the Spokesmen: as party bodies they are particularly useful in providing ammunition for the party political battle in Parliament. In the 1964–70 period, Sir Michael Fraser, as deputy chairman of the Conservative Party, and secretary to the Consultative Committee, was in overall charge of the Conservative Research Department, with Brendon Sewill in day-to-day control as Director of the Department. In this period the Research Department was staffed by some thirty research officers, with a further twenty-five or thirty clerical and other staff. The Department was divided into five broad sections (Economic, Home, External, Constitutional and Library, and Research), with each section sub-divided into policy areas with a research officer responsible for each one. Each Spokesman had the services of a research officer, although some officers served more than one Spokesman.

When the Conservatives are in office, the Research Department acts as a channel of communication between the party organisation and the Parliamentary leaders, but in periods of Conservative opposition it combines a party political and an 'Opposition Civil Service' function.[1] In office or in opposition it undertakes research on long-term party policy, and it prepares information publications, and electoral and other general propaganda. When in opposition, the Department provides the Spokesmen, the backbench groups, and the MPs in general, with Parliamentary briefs for debates and for questions to Ministers. It provides more detailed briefs for the teams of MPs who, under a Spokesman's leadership, lead the attack upon a particular Bill. Special briefs are also provided for party leaders when they require them, as for visits abroad or to the regions. This Parliamentary briefing, and then long-term policy planning, are seen as the Department's main functions in opposition. In all of its work, priority is given to assisting Consultative Committee members, then the other Spokesmen, and then the backbench MPs and party groups. Thus backbenchers get better service from the Research Department when the party is in office than when it is in opposition, in that Ministers, unlike Spokesmen, have a more limited need for the Department's services.

[1] For the various sources of information available to MPs see A. Barker and M. Rush, *The Member of Parliament and His Information*, London 1970.

In all of its work the Department's role is not merely passive, and it often initiates work on long-term and short-term policy, the results of which a particular Spokesman or the Consultative Committee can accept or reject. Some Spokesmen will be more inclined to call on the Department's services than will others: a newly appointed Spokesman will generally need more assistance than will a former Minister, and a Spokesman who at some time worked in the Research Department will be particularly aware of its value. The number of such Spokesmen is generally quite high, and of the front-bench team in the 1964–70 period, Reginald Maudling, Iain Macleod, Enoch Powell, Lord Balniel, Gordon Campbell, Richard Sharples, Michael Alison and Paul Dean had all previously served in the Department. A Spokesman in charge of a particularly topical issue, such as labour relations or law and order in the 1966–70 Parliament, will make great use of the Department.[1] In general, however, legal issues do not lend themselves to research into facts and figures, whereas economic policy does require factual research. The Department is probably strongest in such subjects, as this tends to be the background of its research officers, and the economic section was often quoted by Spokesmen in interview as being the most effective in the Department in the 1964–70 period.

Since 1948 each research officer has dealt with all aspects of his topic, from short-term briefing to long-term policy. This system produces consistency within a policy area, and, according to R. A. Butler, keeps long-term theorising in touch with short-term realities.[2] It also reduces costs, in that a larger staff would be required if the Research Department were to be divided into separate sections for day-to-day matters and longer-term planning. For these reasons the present system was adopted in 1948 and has been retained since then. The system, however, has been criticised: for example, Paul Dean, as an assistant director of the Research Department 1957–64, and a Social Services Spokesman 1969–70, has argued for separate sections

[1] See, for example, The Times, 9 March 1970 ('Instinct for Law and Order') for a comment on the influence and sources involved in policy making in the sphere of law and order. See also The Times, 20 November 1969 for general comments on the Research Department's work.

[2] Butler, The Art of the Possible, pp. 138–42.

for long-term planning and for short-term briefing.[1] He claims that under the existing structure, the broad policy picture does not emerge, as each research officer is concerned only with his own immediate area. He claims also that long-term policy is subordinated to short-term briefing, and that long-term policy will be neglected until a separate section is created for this purpose. It has been estimated, for example, that in the 1964–70 period only about 25 per cent of the research officers' time was devoted to research on long-term policy.[2] This, it may be noted, is in direct contrast to the situation within the Labour Party, where (as is discussed below)[3] a major complaint among Spokesmen is that in their day-to-day Parliamentary tasks they are not well served by their Research Department, because it subordinates Parliamentary briefing to work on long-term policy.

In the 1964–70 period there were other Conservative Party bodies which supplied the Spokesmen with information. In 1962 an organisation was set up in Edinburgh to serve as a Scottish Central Office, and the research section of the office was expanded after 1964.[4] It was concerned solely with research into Scottish affairs and was used extensively by the Scottish Spokesmen. The Conservative Political Centre is concerned primarily with long-term thinking on the broad issues of Conservative philosophy, rather than with the briefing of Opposition Spokesmen. Nevertheless, it was of some assistance to Conservative Spokesmen in the 1964–70 period by revealing the views of party activists and sympathisers, and by producing factual information which could be used in attacks upon the Government. The Public Sector Research Unit was created when the party went into opposition in 1964.[5] Ernest Marples directed its operations, assisted by David Howell, MP, and Mark Schreiber of the Research Department. Its function was to plan how the structure of Government could be streamlined when the Conservatives returned to power. It was thus primarily concerned

[1] Paul Dean, 'A Look at the Conservative Research Department', *Crossbow*, Vol. XI, No. 41, pp. 16–17.

[2] Butler and Pinto-Duschinsky, *The British General Election of 1970*, p. 89.

[3] See p. 277.

[4] For changes in the organisation of the Scottish party in this period see D. W. Urwin, 'Scottish Conservatism: A Party Organisation in Transition', *Political Studies*, 1966, pp. 144–62.

[5] Hutchinson, *Edward Heath*, p. 178.

with future office, but it provided some information for Spokesmen, as with the Opposition's call for a 'war on waste' in the
departments of state. The Conservative Systems Research
Centre was also set up during the 1964–70 period, with a
primary concern with future office, but with some side benefits
for the Spokesmen. Its function was to analyse the implications
of policy proposals and options by computer methods, and, by
the systematic analysis of economic and social data, estimate
the long-term effects of future Conservative Government's overall plans.[1] It thus reflected Edward Heath's desire to be up to
date in the use of sophisticated computer methods in preparation for office. Its value to Conservative Spokesmen was limited,
but it did provide the Treasury Spokesmen with authoritative
data with which to attack the Finance Bills and the Labour
Government's economic strategy.[2]

These bodies supplemented the service provided for the
Spokesmen by the Conservative Research Department in the
1964–70 period. It seems clear that Conservative Spokesmen,
and Conservative MPs in general, receive a better service from
their Research Department than do Labour MPs and Spokesmen from theirs, although even some Conservative Spokesmen
in interview maintained that they received excellent clerical
service from the Department, but little more than this.[3] One
pointed out that for his subject (a large departmental area) he
had the services of a young research officer and the share of a
typist, so that the service he received was bound to be limited.
Nevertheless, in their study of MPs' sources of information,
Anthony Barker and Michael Rush found that among MPs as a
whole, 80 per cent of Conservatives and 18 per cent of Labour
MPs saw their party headquarters as a source of information
and briefing.[4] Among Conservatives, 91 per cent were satisfied
with the service they received, and 9 per cent were dissatisfied,
while among Labour MPs 40 per cent were satisfied and 50 per
cent were dissatisfied (with 10 per cent 'don't knows'). The

---

[1] See Butler and Pinto-Duschinsky, *The British General Election of 1970*,
p. 83.

[2] See *The Times*, 26 May 1970 ('Computer Aids Tory Planning').

[3] See also the similar comment in Butler and Pinto-Duschinsky, *The
British General Election of 1970*, p. 89.

[4] Barker and Rush, *The Member of Parliament and His Information*, p. 234.

majority of Labour MPs are probably more self-sufficient in these matters than are Conservative MPs, partly because so many Conservatives are only part-time MPs. Also, the Labour Party Research Department has a smaller staff and a smaller budget than its Conservative counterpart. Currently, Labour's Research Department has a staff of about a dozen research assistants, with eight or so clerical staff and half a dozen library staff. The size of the department has changed little since 1951, whether in office or in opposition. It is headed by the Secretary (at present Terry Pitt), who is responsible to the Home Policy Sub-Committee of the NEC. The NEC's International Department is separate from the Research Department, and has its own staff of four or five research assistants. As one of its functions the International Department prepares briefs for the Foreign and Commonwealth and Defence Spokesmen, but even the combined resources of the Research Department and the Overseas Department fall short of those of the Conservative Research Department.

The main factor behind the Research Department's comparatively poor service to Labour MPs and Spokesmen, however, is that it is geared more to long-term policy planning than to Parliamentary briefing. It is the servant of the NEC, not of the PLP, and as such its main concern is with extra-Parliamentary matters. It was formed in 1932 because some Labour leaders saw the 1929–31 Labour Government as having been 'deceived' by the Civil Service, and the creation of a Research Department was seen as a means by which a future Labour Government could be freed from sole dependence upon Civil Service sources of information. It was thus regarded essentially as a means of assisting the party when next it was in office. Ever since then its main concern has been with the broad issues of policy in preparation for future office, rather than with the day-to-day needs of Opposition Spokesmen. Thus each research assistant is in charge of one of a dozen or so policy areas, such as the nationalised industries, the regions, private industry, and so on, but these divisions do not mirror the departments of state or the PLP's subject groups, and the research assistants are not linked directly with any Parliamentary Spokesmen.

Today the Research Department's main functions are to produce general party literature and major policy statements (like

'Challenge to Britain' in 1953, and 'Signposts For The Sixties' in 1961), and to service the various sub-committees and special study groups set up by the NEC to plan future policy. In 1970 it was decided that the Research Department should service the Parliamentary Committee,[1] and in interview some Committee members acknowledged that this had produced distinct improvements on the pre-1964 situation. The Department will also provide some briefs for other Spokesmen, subject groups, and backbench MPs, although a Spokesman will be referred to the source of information rather than presented with a fully prepared brief. Spokesmen who are members of the NEC tend to make more use of the Department's services than do other MPs, and in the 1959-64 Parliament, Harold Wilson, George Brown, and James Callaghan often sought the Department's assistance. Even here, however, the initiative tends to come from the Spokesmen, rather than the Department preparing and offering briefs on its own initiative. If the Research Department were to do more to serve the Spokesmen in their day-to-day functions as Parliamentary critics, this would involve more expenditure and additional staff to enable the research officers to continue with what they see as their main function of working on long-term policy projects.

Other Sources of Information

Given the limitations of the party Research Departments, what other sources of information are available to Spokesmen? Some Spokesmen can be quite self-reliant in this respect. Former Ministers, for example, who are covering their old departments, will have less need to gather information than will Spokesmen who have come into contact with a department for the first time. For some subjects, like defence, much information is secret and cannot be 'researched' by anyone outside the Ministry. In some other subjects, like finance, information is more readily available, and here the problem for the Spokesman is that he has to work on his own with little assistance in analysing the large quantity of material that does come his way. Spokesmen gathering information on their own can use the libraries of the House of Commons and the House of Lords and other specialist

[1] For a comment, see *1971 Labour Party Conference Report*, p. 37.

libraries.[1] Some Spokesmen have personal research assistants
to do basic research for them, while all can make use of their
backbench colleagues, on the basis that the House of Commons
contains experts on most conceivable subjects. The party's subject groups can be helpful in this respect, and sponsored MPs
can make use of the facilities of their sponsoring bodies. The
National Union of Mineworkers, the Transport and General
Workers Union, and the Co-operative Movement have small
research departments covering their own areas of interest, and
these are available to Spokesmen as well as to backbench MPs.
A Spokesman may form his own research group, and Norman
Wylie, for example, when Scottish Legal Spokesman in the
1966–70 Parliament, set up a Conservative Legal Committee in
Edinburgh, made up of QCs, to advise him on legal topics. The
Muir Society of Scottish Labour Lawyers can provide a similar
service for Labour's Scottish Spokesmen.

The studies carried out by the various policy committees and
study groups of the NEC of the Labour Party, and the Conservative Party's policy committees of MPs and outside experts,
can also yield information that Spokesmen can use. Some
Spokesmen have close contacts with specialist organisations,
which will be useful sources of information. Ernest Davies, a
Labour Transport Spokesman from 1956–59, was a Joint
Chairman of the Roads Study Group, and as such could
readily gain advice and facts on transport problems. Enoch
Powell, while Conservative Defence Spokesman, was a member
of the Institute of Strategic Studies, and Kenneth Younger, a
Labour Foreign Affairs Spokesman in the 1955–9 Parliament,
was prominent in the Institute of International Affairs, and
eventually became its Director after leaving the front bench.
Conservative Spokesmen very often have close contacts in the
business world, and in the 1964–70 period a number of execu-
tives from industry and the City advised the Conservatives on
managerial problems. In July 1967, for example, the Conservatives held an 'Economics Seminar' at Church House to discuss
tax reforms and the question of sterling parity, at which a
number of outside economic advisers were present.[2] Groups of

---

[1] See Barker and Rush, *The Member of Parliament and His Information*,
pp. 285–353, for details of the library's organisation and work.

[2] Hutchinson, *Edward Heath*, p. 182.

ex-civil servants, led by Sir Con O'Neill, the former Permanent Secretary at the Foreign Office, advised the Conservatives on the possible reform of the Diplomatic Service,[1] and in the autumn of 1969 a seminar was held, attended by top industrialists and leading Opposition Spokesmen, on the machinery of government.[2] Some of these advisers subsequently received posts in Whitehall when the Conservatives came to power.

Pressure groups will seek out the Spokesman and provide him with probably an excess of information, and his problem is really that of sifting and absorbing the material. The National Farmers Union and the Agricultural Workers Union, for example, will advise the Agriculture Spokesman, just as they advise the Minister, and Agriculture Spokesmen will invariably develop close contacts with these bodies. The British Iron and Steel Federation briefed all Conservative MPs, and not just the Spokesmen, on the case against steel nationalisation in 1964, and the Road Hauliers Association briefed Peter Walker, then Conservative Transport Spokesman, on the 1967 Transport Bill.[3] An MP's mail contains much material which would be useful to Spokesmen, and to the Research Departments, but much is lost because only a few MPs have research assistance or a filing system that enables the information to be preserved. Some MPs, however, do make a point of sifting pressure-group literature and passing on the more valuable material to the appropriate Spokesman or to the party Research Department.

Foreign embassies can provide information on foreign affairs, and in these sorts of contacts, the fact that the Spokesman has an official title and status within the Opposition party will be helpful to him in his approaches. The Spokesmen, like all MPs, can also obtain some information from general sources such as constituents' letters, radio and television, books, journals and the press. Denis Healey, when Labour's Defence Spokesman before 1964, kept his own files of press cuttings on defence matters.[4] In the nineteenth century the London clubs were

[1] See *The Times*, 21 July 1967. See also *The Times*, 17 November 1970.
[2] See *The Times*, 17 November 1969.
[3] Barker and Rush, *The Member of Parliament and His Information*, pp. 87 and 252.
[4] Ibid., p. 245.

centres for the transfer of information, and although this is not true to anything like the same extent today, much information can be gathered in social contact in the lobbies and bars of the Commons.

Parliamentary and departmental publications like Green or White Papers, or Select Committee Reports, can be used by conscientious Spokesmen prepared to spend time on their own research. Information can also be obtained from Ministers through Parliamentary questions. For purely factual material, questions for written answer are more suitable than questions for oral answer, but a Minister will probably object to an excessive use of this procedure, and less formally the Spokesman can approach the Minister personally or by letter. A Minister might offer unsolicited information, often in the interests of maintaining a common front-bench approach on some vital aspect of foreign or economic policy, although the dangers of this for the Opposition have been discussed above.[1] Civil servants may provide a Spokesman with purely factual information to save him the laborious job of gathering the material on his own. The extent of formal contacts between the Spokesmen and the civil service will vary from department to department, depending on the attitude of the Minister. Some Ministers will be more accommodating than others, perhaps depending on their own experience when in opposition. For the most part, however, the civil service goes to great pains to avoid 'political' contacts with the party in opposition. After the 1964 election Sir William Armstrong, then Permanent Secretary at the Treasury, cut off contacts between the departments of state and the Conservative Research Department, and the Spokesmen themselves will normally avoid public contacts with civil servants. Margaret Herbison, for example, did not know personally the civil servants in the Pensions Ministry before she became Minister in 1964, despite the work she had done in the pensions field while in opposition. Reginald Maudling deliberately dropped his Treasury connections when he left office in 1964, so as not to embarrass his former civil servants. Other ex-Ministers might not be so scrupulous, however, and may seek to make use of contacts in their former department. Social contacts may be preserved, but even at this level some Spokesmen

[1] See above, pp. 201-4.

and some civil servants prefer not to be seen fraternising with 'the enemy'.

While Spokesmen can obtain some factual information from the departments, there is a limit to the amount and type of information that a Minister will be prepared to allow his department to reveal. Also, if a Spokesman were to abuse such a privilege, the supply of information would cease. Any Opposition Spokesman, when he makes a visit abroad, can obtain a briefing from Foreign Office Ministers or officials, and defence matters are also seen as something of a 'special case' in this regard. Also, it is recognised that Opposition Privy Councillors are given certain privileges regarding access to information. Some MPs object to Opposition front benchers receiving favoured treatment in these various matters: Michael Foot, for example, has deplored the fact that '. . . there should be a kind of first and second-rate citizenship in the House of Commons about the information which can be obtained from the Civil Service.'[1] Nevertheless, there is a very good case for Opposition Spokesmen, as potential future Ministers, having increased access to departmental information. Certainly, when a general election is imminent the Prime Minister will authorise official contacts between the civil service and Opposition leaders in order that formal preparations can be made for a possible change of Government. In these matters much of the initiative will come from the senior civil servants themselves, who clearly have a vested interest in securing as smooth a transfer of power as possible.

In the summer of 1964, Sir Alec Douglas-Home authorised contacts between Labour Spokesmen and the departments they were covering. Even before this, George Brown had talks with the Treasury about the possible creation of a Department of Economic Affairs by a Labour Government.[2] Sir Eric Roll and Sir Donald MacDougall were approached about the possibility of their joining such a department. Even though the Cabinet learned of these preparations, no action was taken because it was realised how essential it was to have prior consultation about a change as major as the creation of a new key Ministry. In July 1964 Harold Wilson was invited to dine with Sir

[1] 800 H.C. Debs. 5s cols. 253.
[2] Brown, *In My Way*, pp. 96–8.

Laurence Helsby, then Joint Permanent Secretary at the Treasury, and Labour's plans for office were discussed. Sir Alec Douglas-Home was aware of, and approved of, this consultation, although, as he was anxious that it should not be made to appear that the Conservatives had conceded the inevitability of electoral defeat, he made the stipulation that the Opposition should not seek to make political capital out of the episode.[1]

Again, before the 1970 election, Harold Wilson authorised contacts between Conservative leaders and the departments. Edward Heath and his leading colleagues began seeking such contacts in the autumn of 1969, but on 21 April 1970 there was a suggestion in the *Daily Express* that the Government was imposing something of a 'gag' on civil servants by restricting the access of Opposition leaders to the departments. In a statement in the Commons, Harold Wilson vigorously denied that he or the Head of the Civil Service had imposed any such restriction, and the Opposition did not offer any specific instances.[2] Earlier in the Parliament, in 1968, a consultancy firm, which had been engaged by the Conservative Party to study certain departmental methods of work, was denied access to the departments. Also in 1968, Ernest Marples, as head of the Conservative Public Sector Research Unit, had been denied permission to interview certain top civil servants about departmental organisation, and when he later sent a lengthy questionnaire to the Permanent Secretaries he was informed that the information he required could best be obtained through Parliamentary Questions. Accordingly, on 25 July 1969, Marples put down for written answer a long list of questions dealing with departmental policies in the awarding of contracts.[3] These somewhat exceptional approaches apart, the general level of co-operation between civil servants and Opposition leaders in 1969 and 1970 seems to have been much the same as operated in 1964, although there were complaints from the civil service in 1970 that the Conservatives had not consulted them enough when drawing up their plans for office.[4]

It is not necessary, of course, for civil servants to have formal

[1] Harold Wilson, *The Labour Government 1964–70*, London 1971, p. 4.
[2] 800 H.C. Debs. 5s cols. 244–7.
[3] 787 H.C. Debs. 5s cols. 504–608.
[4] Butler and Pinto-Duschinsky, *The British General Election of 1970*, p. 89.

contact with Opposition leaders for them to know what they plan to do if they come to power. An Opposition party usually reveals its major plans before an election, and indeed fights the election, to some extent at least, on its proposed reforms. Thus before the 1964 election, the public, and the civil servants in the Ministry of Power, were aware that a Labour Government would create a number of new departments of state, and would take steps to nationalise the iron and steel industry.[1] Similarly, the Treasury knew of Labour's plans for a Corporation Tax and a Capital Gains Tax, and the Ministry of Pensions knew of Labour's social services plans. In 1970 the Ministry of Employment and Productivity was aware of the detailed proposals that the Conservatives had announced for the reform of industrial relations, and the policy statement 'Fair Deal at Work' was eventually used as the basis for possible legislation. The Treasury was equally aware of the Conservatives' interest in a Value Added Tax. Thus departments can make contingency plans on the basis of what they and the public know of the Opposition's electoral promises, and in 1964 the Ministry of Power had a rough draft of a Steel Nationalisation Bill ready for the new Labour Government, although obviously with the controversial details, like the compensation clauses, left blank.

Despite any fleeting contacts that might be established between Opposition leaders and civil servants, and despite the various other sources of information that are available to the Opposition, a Spokesman remains at a distinct disadvantage as compared with a Minister of the Crown. Thus Peter Shore's observation, quoted at the beginning of the chapter, needs to be re-emphasised: there *is* 'a great gulf in the British political system between the Government and Opposition'. Possible ways of strengthening the Opposition's position in this respect will be considered in the concluding chapter. It may be noted here, however, that although the Opposition team has now acquired many of the trappings of office, there still remain basic differences between Spokesmen and Ministers, not least in the matter of their sources of information. More generally, it was noted in Chapter 5 that a major consideration for the Leader of the Opposition in the selection of Spokesmen was the recruitment of future Ministers. In Chapter 7, however, it was pointed out

[1] Wilson, *The Labour Government 1964–70*, pp. 4, 8.

that the Shadow Cabinet devoted the bulk of its time to the management of the affairs of opposition rather than to the preparation for future office, and in this chapter it has been shown that although the individual Spokesmen may be future Ministers, the bulk of their time is taken up with the business of Parliamentary Opposition rather than with work on future policy. The general picture is thus re-affirmed of the Shadow Cabinet and the team of Spokesmen being primarily a device to improve the effectiveness of the Opposition as a critic of the Government, rather than a means of preparing the party for a future period in office. The contrast between the appearance and the practice of the Opposition team is thereby emphasised. In the next two chapters more detailed aspects of the Spokesman's role will be examined.

9

Spokesmen and Their Parliamentary Colleagues

It is clear from the preceding two chapters that the environment in which a Spokesman operates is a complex one. Parliament is the centre of his activities, and most of his working day will be spent in the Chamber of the Commons, or in committee, or in various other parts of the Palace of Westminster in contacts with his Parliamentary or other colleagues. In Parliament his chief 'enemy' is the particular Minister, or Ministers, whose department he is covering, but his attacks will also be directed at the Government in general, and at the Government's Parliamentary supporters. The Spokesman will have a somewhat ambivalent attitude towards the civil servants who support the Minister, and the pressure groups who seek to influence Government policies. On the one hand he will see them as part of the governmental machine that it is his duty to attack, but at the same time he will rely upon civil servants and pressure groups to some extent as sources of information. The Spokesman's principal 'allies' will be the other Spokesmen who are covering his subject, or associated subjects, but he will also be involved with many of the Spokesmen for other subjects, and with his party's back-bench MPs. Outside Parliament, he will come in contact with various parts of his party organisation, including the Research Department as a source of information (although with the reservations that were noted in the previous chapter), and the party officers, activists, and sympathisers who serve on the committees that examine party policy in opposition.

Thus an Opposition Spokesman is essentially a member of a

team. The senior members of the team will meet together in the Shadow Cabinet, and there seek to coordinate the efforts of the team as a whole. In order to organise opposition in his subject area, a senior Spokesman will meet with his assistant Spokesmen, in some instances on a regular weekly basis. Occasionally, gatherings of the whole front-bench team may be held, in order to prevent the assistant Spokesmen from feeling too remote from the party leadership, although such gatherings are likely to be held only once or twice a session. All Labour Spokesmen, however, attend the weekly meeting of the PLP, which provides another opportunity for regular contact with their front and backbench colleagues, while at some time or other most Opposition MPs will be involved with many of the tasks that the Spokesmen perform. In the broadest sense, therefore, the Opposition team can embrace most or all of the party's MPs, so that there is a clear contrast with the situation in the Government party, where the distinction between Ministers and backbenchers is much more firmly drawn. More than this, in a still broader sense, the Opposition team extends to the sections of the party outside Parliament that provide assistance and support for the Spokesmen. Again, although they are in no sense members of the team, the individuals, pressure groups, and departments of state, from which the Spokesmen receive advice and information, are all part of the general 'support system' of the Opposition team.

Most of these relationships have been touched on in previous chapters. There remains to be considered here, however, the nature of the Spokesman's relations with other members of the front-bench team, and with backbench MPs. What is the precise nature of these relationships? How far does the principle of collective responsibility apply among members of the Opposition team, and to what extent do resignations and dismissals from the team occur in opposition as in office? What machinery exists within each party to link the Opposition team with their backbench colleagues? These questions will be considered in this chapter.

Spokesmen and Collective Responsibility

To what extent are Opposition Spokesmen bound by the principle of collective responsibility? An Opposition team, like a Ministerial team, seeks to present a united front to Parliament, the party, and the electorate, on the basis that 'unity is strength'. In office the principle of collective responsibility demands that Ministers must accept their share of the credit or the blame for Government policies.[1] They may criticise these policies in the secrecy of Cabinet discussions, or in private talks with other Ministers, but they must refrain from public criticism. If they are not prepared to abide by these restrictions they must resign. The same broad principle applies in the case of the Shadow Cabinet, although the pressures for resignation in

TABLE 19

House of Commons Division on the Principle of Common Market Entry 28 October 1971, Voting of Labour MPs

	Parl. Comm.	Other Spokesmen	Other Labour MPs	Total Labour MPs
Voted for the motion	5	18	46	69
Abstained	2	2	16	20
Voted against the motion (in accordance with the whip)	9	26	163	198

Source: 823 H.C. Debs, 5s col. 2211.

face of a breach of unity of the team apply less rigidly in opposition than in office. For the Labour Opposition in the 1970 Parliament the issue was brought to a head through the divisions within the Parliamentary Committee and the front-bench team, and within the PLP as a whole, and the extra-Parliamentary party, over the question of the party's attitude towards the European Common Market. On 28 October 1971, in the division at the end of the marathon debate on the Conservative Government's Common Market policy, a large proportion of the Parliamentary Committee and the Spokesmen outside the Committee were among the eighty-nine Labour MPs who defied a three-line whip and either voted in

[1] For comments on the operation of the principle of collective responsibility in office, see Gordon Walker, *The Cabinet*, pp. 30–5; Jennings, *Cabinet Government*, pp. 277–89; Mackintosh, *The British Cabinet*, pp. 520–4.

favour of the principle of British entry into the EEC, or else abstained. The pattern of the voting of Labour MPs in the division is shown in Table 19. Among the 'rebels' who voted in favour of entry were the deputy leader of the party (Roy Jenkins), the chairman of the PLP (Douglas Houghton), the senior Opposition Spokesman on Europe (Harold Lever), and the former 'Minister for Europe' in the Wilson Government (George Thomson). There were demands for their resignations from their positions in the front-bench team, but, at this stage, they declined. Roy Jenkins, however, declared that he would have resigned from the deputy leadership if the annual election for the post had not been imminent,[1] and Harold Lever seriously contemplated resigning his post as European Spokesman.[2] A few weeks later, at the beginning of the new session, Roy Jenkins and Douglas Houghton were re-elected to their posts, and the other Parliamentary Committee rebels were all re-elected to the Committee.[3] None of the rebellious senior Spokesmen were dropped from the team when the appointments for the new session were announced, although six assistant Spokesmen who had been among the rebels in November were dropped when there was a re-organisation of 'second tier' duties in January 1972.[4] The controversy within the party continued, however, and in April 1972, soon after the Shadow Cabinet had decided to support the demand for a national referendum on the question of British entry to the Common Market, a group of pro-Marketeers resigned from the front-bench team.[5] Roy Jenkins resigned as deputy leader and Treasury Spokesman, and George Thomson and Harold Lever resigned from the Parliamentary Committee and from their posts as Spokesmen. Dick Taverne, David Owen, and Lord Chalfont also gave up their posts as junior Spokesmen. J. Dickson Mabon, although not a pro-Marketeer, also resigned his front-bench post in protest at the manner in which the whole episode had been handled by the party leader. In addition, Roy Hattersley and Mrs Shirley Williams wrote to

[1] See *The Guardian*, 30 October 1971.
[2] See *The Guardian*, 23 October 1971.
[3] See below, Table 46.
[4] See *The Times*, 21 January 1972.
[5] See *The Times*, 11, 12 and 13 April 1972.

Harold Wilson pointing out that although they had decided not to resign from the front-bench team, they had considerable reservations, as pro-Marketeers, about the Shadow Cabinet's attitude to the whole European issue, and they indicated that they might feel obliged to resign at some later date.

Thus after the prominent front-bench rebels had escaped largely unscathed in the autumn of 1971, a number of voluntary resignations followed six months later. The whole episode is particularly noteworthy in face of some of the assumptions about collective responsibility among Opposition leaders. While many party leaders in the past have bemoaned the lack of pressures for unity in opposition, it has generally been thought that dissent among Shadow Cabinet members was much less likely to lead to resignations than was the case with the real Cabinet. A. J. Balfour, for example, complained to Austen Chamberlain in July 1911, that after the Parliament Bill issue,

> The shadow Cabinet showed irreconcilable differences of opinion. Had it been a real Cabinet one of two things would have followed. Either the dissentient minority would have resigned, or they would have silently acquiesced in the decision of the majority. There could, of course, be no question, in the case of a shadow Cabinet, of resignation. There certainly has been no silent acquiescence.[1]

Much more recently, Harold Macmillan has also pointed to differences between Government and Opposition in this respect: in 1969 he observed that

> One of the advantages of office is that however divided internally on any issue, short of total break-up or the resignation of particular Ministers, the Government must present an unbroken front. With an Opposition this is not so. Without responsibility there is not the same pressure for unanimity.[2]

Outside observers have made similar assumptions.[3] Certainly, while there may be practical political reasons for maintaining a united front in opposition as in office, the Constitutional doctrine which underlies collective responsibility among

---

[1] Petrie, *Life and Letters of Sir Austen Chamberlain*, I, p. 285.
[2] Macmillan, *Tides of Fortune*, p. 77.
[3] See, for example, R. J. Jackson, *Rebels and Whips*, London 1968, p. 189.

Ministers does not apply in opposition. Also, some Ministers resign from the Government 'for the good of the department', when they feel that a particular Government policy decision is damaging to their departments' interests. Shadow Ministers, however, are not at the head of departments of state, and they do not have a 'departmental point of view' to defend, so that their attitude and reaction to particular policies is purely personal. Again, the duties of Spokesmen are not defined by statute, and for the most part the job is advisory. A Spokesman might feel tempted to give up his responsibility if his advice on some aspect of future policy were to be ignored, or if the leader refused to give approval to a proposal to which the Spokesman was particularly committed. Such a situation, however, is much less likely to lead to dissent and resignation than the sort of situation that can arise in office, when a decision to which the Minister and his department are committed is reversed by the Cabinet. In general, firm policy decisions are not being made in opposition, so that life in opposition contains fewer 'moments of truth' than does life as a Minister, and resignation situations are less likely to emerge. As one Conservative Spokesman expressed it in interview

> One of the advantages of Opposition is that you don't *have* to make decisions: if an issue is too awkward you can shelve it or fudge it, and nobody really cares.

Clearly, there are limits to this, and in 1971 the Labour Opposition was forced to face up to major decisions over the Common Market issue. Nevertheless, the basic point remains.

An Opposition post is often seen as a step towards Ministerial office, and just as Ministers may be deterred from resignation by career considerations, so dissent in opposition may be overcome by ambition for possible future office when the party next holds power. In general, however, Spokesmen have less to lose through resignation than do Ministers, in that they are not giving up a salary or treasured departmental project, and on the whole a career is probably less badly damaged in the long run by resignation in opposition than by resignation in office. 'Tactical resignation'[1] (that is, a resignation to bring an

---

[1] Phrase used by R. K. Alderman and J. A. Cross, *The Tactics of Resignation*, London 1967.

issue into the open) is less feasible in opposition than in office because a resignation in opposition does not immediately affect policy, and in general the Shadow Cabinet receives less publicity than does the real Cabinet. Further, a party in office is expected to fulfil electoral pledges, and one reason for a Ministerial resignation can be if the Cabinet decides not to implement a policy for which a Minister feels a particular commitment and responsibility. The Opposition, however, is not in a position to implement pledges, and although the Opposition has to abide by the broad lines of party policy, Spokesmen can have much greater freedom of expression than can Ministers. As expressed by R. K. Alderman and J. A. Cross, the principle of collective responsibility will apply less rigorously in opposition than in office because '. . . a Shadow Cabinet is concerned, so to speak, with policy in the abstract, not with the translation of policy into immediate governmental action.'[1]

Thus the Labour leaders who felt reservations about Britain's application to join the Common Market were more ready to express their doubts *after* they went into opposition in 1970 than they had been when in office. On first going into opposition, of course, some ex-Ministers may retain some of the inhibitions of office, while as an election nears, policy speculation by Opposition leaders may be interpreted as specific commitments. Also, if a specific alternative to current Government legislation is being advocated, the Opposition has to be clear and united. For the most part, however, in the discussion in opposition of possible future policies it is reasonable for conflicting views to be tolerated. There is a clear distinction between disagreements being revealed by a Government which is about to implement a particular policy, and speculative discussion by Opposition leaders on some aspect of future policy. Indeed, Opposition leaders perhaps have a duty to educate their party followers, and the public in general, about policy options, and thus should not be discouraged from expressing controversial views in order to stimulate discussion. There is much more room for variety in attack than in defence: in office, policies have to be defended, and the Government

---

[1] Alderman and Cross, *The Tactics of Resignation*, p. 75.

has to be collectively committed to this end, but the Opposition can attack the Government's policies and record from many angles.

For all these reasons, departure in public from official Opposition policy has sometimes been tolerated on the part of Shadow Cabinet members, and on occasions it has even seemed that the principle that applies in opposition is that of 'collective irresponsibility' rather than collective responsibility. During the 1929–31 Parliament, for example, there were clear divisions within the Conservative party over tariff policy, and L. S. Amery warned his Shadow Cabinet colleagues that he would have to dissent publicly from the official Conservative policy of opposing food taxes.[1] On 7 February 1930 Amery spoke in public in defence of food taxes, only two days after Baldwin had supported the contrary policy. Lord Linlithgow, in a letter to *The Times*, called upon Baldwin to dismiss Amery from the Shadow Cabinet for so blatant a rejection of the principle of collective responsibility, but Baldwin said that because of Amery's long-standing commitment to the cause of tariff reform there was no question of his being dismissed. Amery, however, records that Baldwin made it clear that, '. . . the latitude accorded to me was personal and did not apply to other colleagues.'[2] Later in 1930 Amery was dropped from the Shadow Cabinet, after he had publicly supported the 'Empire Crusade' of Lord Beaverbrook and Lord Rothermere, against Baldwin's wishes, but he rejoined the Shadow Cabinet in March 1931.

In the 1935–9 period defence was a divisive issue within the PLP, and in the Parliamentary Committee Hugh Dalton was one of a minority who fought for a tougher attitude towards defence policy.[3] In the summer of 1936, at meetings of the Parliamentary Committee, he urged that the party should call for greater military expenditure, but he received little support from his colleagues. Nevertheless, he was allowed to argue his minority view before the PLP, thus producing a clear breach

[1] Amery, *My Political Life*, III, p. 23. See also Feiling, *The Life of Neville Chamberlain*, p. 171; Garvin and Amery, *Life of Joseph Chamberlain*, VI, pp. 1019–22.

[2] Amery, *My Political Life*, III, p. 23.

[3] Dalton, *Memoirs*, II, pp. 88, 133.

in the principle of collective responsibility.[1] More recently, in July 1958, George Brown, then Defence Spokesman, abstained from voting on an Opposition motion which disapproved of the sending of British troops to Jordan. He subsequently offered to resign his Defence duty, but Gaitskell declined the offer.[2] In the 1966–70 Parliament, Sir Keith Joseph abstained over the second reading of the 1965 Race Relations Bill, and Iain Macleod was allowed to dissent over the Commonwealth Immigration Bill in 1968, both as concessions in the face of the official collective attitude of the Conservative Consultative Committee. In Macleod's case, he had written an article in *The Spectator*, outlining his views on the Bill, a few days before the Consultative Committee framed its collective attitude. He was consequently allowed to dissent from the official line on the grounds that he had already committed himself publicly on the issue.

Thus Labour's Common Market rebels in October 1971 had a number of respectable precedents to support their action in going against the official Opposition line on a major policy issue. Like Amery in 1930, and Dalton in 1936, they could argue that in opposition they were justified in standing by their strongly held, and long held, principles without being obliged to resign from the team. At the same time, too many open disagreements on policy matters will weaken the Opposition's electoral credibility, as Labour found to its cost in the nineteen-fifties. Thus a united front has to be maintained in public to some extent, particularly when an election seems near. With the Conservative Party especially, there is a strong commitment to 'the team', and to the principle of maintaining unity of word and deed in face of the enemy, whether in office or in opposition. Also, in both parties, while the party leader might at times be inclined to tolerate independence of mind among his leading colleagues, backbenchers and the party outside Parliament may exert pressure for rebels to be brought to heel. In order to maintain the morale of the party faithful, and to preserve their confidence in their leaders as likely election winners, a degree of unity has to be maintained. In opposition, therefore, collective responsibility in the

---

[1] Dalton, *Memoirs*, II, p. 133.
[2] See *The Times*, 18 and 22 July 1958.

interests of the party replaces to some extent the constitutional
basis of collective responsibility in office. Thus, one Labour
MP in interview revealed that on becoming a Spokesman he
even felt obliged to withdraw his name from a Private Member's
Bill that he had previously sponsored, as the terms of the Bill
were contrary to official party policy. Despite Balfour's
complaint, quoted above, about the lack of acceptance of
collective responsibility in his Shadow Cabinet, F. E. Smith,
then an outspoken backbencher, was reluctant to join the
Shadow Cabinet in 1910, because he felt that 'It is their gain
and not mine if I join their shadow cabinet—they clip my
wings and make me responsible for their policy.'[1] Similarly,
when Hugh Dalton was elected to the Parliamentary Committee
in 1925, he felt that his style would be cramped, as he would
have to accept responsibility for the Committee's decisions.[2]
For much the same reason Josiah Wedgwood, James Maxton,
John Wheatley, and George Lansbury threatened not to seek
election to the Parliamentary Committee in 1925, although
in the end only Maxton carried out the threat.[3] Thus even
though freedom of dissent is greater for Opposition leaders
than for Ministers, it is recognised that there are limits to the
amount of dissension and controversy that can be tolerated in
opposition.

Resignations and Dismissals

Given the situation described in the previous section, to
what extent do dismissals and voluntary resignations from the
team occur in opposition? Because Labour's Parliamentary
Committee is elected, a Labour Leader of the Opposition
cannot dismiss a dissentient member. The members of the PLP
can withdraw their support from him at the next ballot, and
the leader can terminate his appointment as a Spokesman,
but between ballots a Labour leader cannot enforce a resignation from the Parliamentary Committee. This is not the case

[1] Birkenhead, *F.E.*, p. 150.
[2] Alderman and Cross, *The Tactics of Resignation*, p. 71.
[3] R. E. Dowse, *Left in the Centre: The ILP 1893–1940*, London 1966,
p. 119; C. V. Wedgwood, *The Last of the Radicals: Josiah Wedgwood*,
London 1951, p. 154.

with the Conservative Consultative Committee, however, and
as with the practice in government, a Conservative leader can
dismiss any member of the Committee who is seen to breach
the principle of collective responsibility. Thus in 1968 Enoch
Powell was dismissed from the Consultative Committee. On
20 April he made a speech in his constituency in which, in
colourful language, he pointed to the possibility of racial
conflict in Britain in the future, and advocated that coloured
immigration into Britain should be reduced to 'negligible
proportions', with financial aid being made available to
encourage repatriation. The next day Heath wrote to Powell,
condemning the speech as 'racialist in tone and liable to
exacerbate racial tensions', and informing him that he was
dismissed from the Consultative Committee.[1] Powell, of
course, had a long history of independence of thought and
action as an MP. In June 1950 he was among six MPs who
ignored a three-line whip and abstained in a Commons vote
because he opposed Conservative policy towards European
unity, and in June 1958 he resigned from his post at the
Treasury, together with Peter Thorneycroft and Nigel Birch,
when the Cabinet would not authorise cuts that he felt to be
necessary in public expenditure.[2] Along with Iain Macleod he
declined to serve in Sir Alec Douglas-Home's Government in
1963, although he did accept a post as Spokesman when the
party went into opposition. As Defence Spokesman under
Heath he expressed some views which were out of line with
the attitude of his colleagues, and in particular he criticised
the continuation of Britain's military presence 'east of Suez'.
In the 1966–8 period Heath had private discussions with him
about the need for collective responsibility among Consultative
Committee members. He had been rebuked at a Consultative
Committee meeting in February 1967 after making controversial statements, outside Parliament, about Welsh affairs
and industrial policy, as well as immigration.[3] Before making
his immigration speech in April 1967, Powell did not inform
Heath or Quintin Hogg, who, as Home Affairs Spokesman,

[1] *The Times*, 22 April 1968. For a full account of the episode see Roth,
Enoch Powell, pp. 349–61.

[2] See Jackson, *Rebels and Whips*, p. 145.

[3] Roth, *Enoch Powell*, pp. 335 and 346.

was the Consultative Committee member responsible for Conservative immigration policy. This, combined with his record of dissent, the policy advocated in his speech, and the highly emotional terms in which it was expressed, led Heath to dismiss him from the Consultative Committee and relieve him of his duties as a Spokesman. No doubt Heath's reaction was governed to a large extent by fear of the emergence of the sort of splits that the Conservatives had experienced in opposition under Baldwin, and by the thought that had he not dismissed Powell, Quintin Hogg would probably have resigned from the team.[1]

In opposition, as in office, anyone who is in open disagreement with his colleagues may, of course, choose to resign, without waiting to be disciplined by the leader. Labour's Common Market rebels were certainly not the first Opposition leaders to follow such a course. Disraeli condemned such resignations in opposition: he declared that

> I am opposed to all secessions from the front bench of an Opposition. They never are happy in their results, and are always imputed to unworthy motives or looked on as a coup de théâtre.[2]

Thus he prevailed upon Sir James Pakington to refrain from formally withdrawing from the Conservative ex-Cabinet in 1857 over the party's education policy. Winston Churchill and Aneurin Bevan, however, were both involved in controversial resignations from the Shadow Cabinet. Churchill resigned from Baldwin's Shadow Cabinet in 1931, after conflict over the party's trade and India policies.[3] Churchill felt that the Conservative Opposition should have attacked more vigorously the Labour Government's policy of granting dominion status to India, and his resignation came three days after the Labour Government, with Baldwin's approval, had released Gandhi from prison. His resignation almost caused a major split in the Conservative ranks, although Baldwin managed to hold things together. Nevertheless, Churchill's resignation led to his exclusion from the National Government in August 1931,

---

[1] Ibid.

[2] Monypenny and Buckle, *Life of Benjamin Disraeli*, IV, p. 63.

[3] Middlemas and Barnes, *Baldwin*, p. 585; Winterton, *Orders of the Day*, p. 170; Templewood, *Nine Troubled Years*, p. 48; James, *Churchill*, p. 198.

and he remained out of office until 1939. Thus Duff Cooper claims that Churchill's resignation in opposition was '. . . the most unfortunate event that occurred between the two wars. It reduced Winston Churchill to impotence for ten years . . .'[1]

Aneurin Bevan resigned from the Parliamentary Committee in April 1954, after a period of stormy relations with the Labour leadership. In all, he participated in more than half of the rebellions against the whip in which Labour MPs were involved in the 1951–5 Parliament,[2] but he was elected to the Parliamentary Committee in November 1952, and for a while he was comparatively conformist. On 13 April 1954, however, in a Commons debate on the Conservative Government's policy in the Far East, he criticised the concept of collective security in South East Asia, despite the fact that, on behalf of the PLP, Attlee had spoken in favour of the Government's policy.[3] Many Labour MPs saw this as a direct challenge to Attlee's leadership, and at a meeting of the PLP Attlee openly rebuked Bevan. The next day Bevan announced his resignation from the Parliamentary Committee.[4] One of Bevan's biographers argues that his resignation was a calculated move, as Bevan wanted to be free from the restrictions that membership of the Committee imposed upon him.[5] Whether or not this was the case, Bevan remained critical of official party policy, and after he ignored a three-line whip and abstained in a division on defence policy in March 1955, the whip was withdrawn from him. It was restored after only forty days, however, after an apology from Bevan, when a general election was imminent. Bevan also regained his place on the Parliamentary Committee at the beginning of the new Parliament in June 1955, and although he was unsuccessful in his bids for the party leadership and deputy leadership in 1956, he eventually became deputy leader of the party in 1959.

In this same period of Opposition, Anthony Greenwood also resigned from the Parliamentary Committee. He gave up his

[1] Duff Cooper, *Old Men Forget*, London 1953, p. 171.

[2] Jackson, *Rebels and Whips*, p. 137.

[3] See above, p. 69, for the significance of this in relation to the introduction of the system of official Spokesmen in 1955.

[4] For an account of the row within the Parliamentary Committee see Dalton, *Memoirs*, III, p. 393.

[5] Krug, *Aneurin Bevan*, p. 202.

place on the Committee soon after the stormy 1960 Labour Party Conference at Scarborough, as a protest against Hugh Gaitskell's leadership, and he announced that he would not seek re-election to the Committee in the annual ballot which was only a few weeks away.[1] In 1962 and 1963 he did seek re-election, but without success.

With the introduction of the system of official front-bench Spokesmen in 1955, the question was raised of the extent to which the principle of collective responsibility should apply to the team as a whole, as opposed to just the Parliamentary Committee or the Consultative Committee. The issue was put to the test early in the 1959–64 Parliament, in a dispute between Hugh Gaitskell and Richard Crossman, who had been appointed Pensions Spokesman after the 1959 election. In December 1959 Crossman co-sponsored an Early Day Motion condemning the supply of tactical nuclear weapons by NATO to West Germany, and then in March 1960 he was one of forty-three Labour MPs who abstained on an official Opposition defence motion.[2] This led Gaitskell to write to him telling him that he would have to accept official party defence policy if he was to remain a Spokesman. Crossman left the front-bench team as a result, and in a reply to Gaitskell's letter he complained that too rigid an interpretation of collective responsibility was being applied to the team as a whole.[3]

In interview a number of MPs argued that with regard to collective responsibility rather more flexible rules should apply to Spokesmen outside the Parliamentary Committee and Consultative Committee than to Committee members. They maintained that while the Committee had to retain something of a united front before the party and the public, more freedom could be accorded to the other Spokesmen. In practice, however, a number of junior Spokesmen, in addition to Richard Crossman in 1960, have resigned or been dismissed from the team because they were seen as being out of step with the team as a whole. In November 1960 Barbara Castle supported Harold Wilson in his challenge to Gaitskell's

---

[1] See *The Times*, 13 October 1960.
[2] Jackson, *Rebels and Whips*, pp. 176–8.
[3] See *The Times*, 3, 4 and 15 March 1960.

leadership, and declined to seek election to the Parliamentary Committee, although in previous years her attempts to secure election to the Committee had not been successful. As a consequence, Gaitskell did not reappoint her as Spokesman for Works in the new session. Similarly, Nigel Fisher, while a Conservative junior Commonwealth Spokesman, voted in favour of the Labour Government's Rhodesian Oil Sanctions Order in 1966. Heath did not re-appoint him to the team after the 1966 election, and no doubt his earlier rebellion was a factor in this. Again, as was noted in the previous section, some of the junior 'Common Market rebels' were dropped from the Labour team in 1972, although it was not specified whether their dismissal was because of their rebellion, or because of more general factors.[1]

In the 1959–60 Parliament, Christopher Mayhew, as a junior Spokesman, was involved in a 'semi-resignation'. During the 1961–2 session he served as Information Services Spokesman and also as an assistant Foreign Affairs Spokesman. In July 1962 he resigned his responsibility for Information Services after the Labour Party had given support to the Pilkington Committee Report on the future of broadcasting.[2] He retained his Foreign Affairs responsibility, however, and thus remained a member of the front-bench team. For more general reasons, Angus Maude resigned his job as Spokesman on Colonial Affairs under Edward Heath in January 1966. In an article in *The Spectator* Maude described the Conservative Opposition as 'a meaningless irrelevance', and he returned to the back benches after serving as a Spokesman for only a year.[3]

Thus members of the Shadow Cabinet and Spokesmen outside the Shadow Cabinet have resigned because of specific disagreements over Opposition policy attitudes, and also for more general reasons. Also, party leaders have dismissed Shadow Cabinet members and other Spokesmen following specific and general disagreements on policy and other matters. The closer a general election, the more sensitive the party leader is likely to be about seeming disunity in his team's

[1] For press speculation see *The Guardian* and *The Times*, 21 January 1972.
[2] See *The Times*, 30 July 1962.
[3] See *The Times*, 19 January 1966; and Hutchinson, *Edward Heath*, pp. 176–7.

ranks. Thus in January 1970, Paul Bryan was replaced as principal Spokesman on Broadcasting by Lord Carrington, although he was allowed to remain as an assistant Spokesman under Lord Carrington.[1] Bryan had embarrassed the Opposition leaders by advocating a scheme for a hundred local commercial radio stations, without first consulting the Consultative Committee. Clearly, Opposition Spokesmen are members of a team in which, for the practical reasons discussed earlier in this section, a reasonable degree of unity of purpose and outlook has to be preserved. Nevertheless, it is clear that the principle of collective responsibility applies less rigidly in opposition than in office, and that, despite the eventual outcome of Labour's Common Market rebellion, dismissals and resignations from the team are much less likely to occur in opposition than in office. As Amery and Dalton discovered in the nineteen-thirties, and the Labour Common Market rebels in October 1971, much more latitude can be accorded to Opposition leaders than to Ministers, so that in this respect there is a significant difference between Government and Opposition.

Spokesmen and their Backbench Colleagues: the Conservative Party

While both parties in opposition recognise the Spokesmen as the Parliamentary spearhead of their attack upon the Government, effective Parliamentary Opposition requires co-operation between Spokesmen and backbenchers. Unlike Ministers, however, Spokesmen, other than the party leaders, do not have Parliamentary Private Secretaries, so that this important channel of communication between the front and back benches does not operate in opposition. What machinery does exist to link Spokesmen and their backbench colleagues, and what is the nature of their relationship? In the 1964–70 period the Conservative and Unionist Private Members Committee (the 1922 Committee) met regularly at 6.00 p.m. on Thursdays, although generally for no more than thirty minutes at a time. Membership of this body is open to all Conservative backbench MPs. In opposition this includes Spokesmen outside the Consultative Committee, but excludes

[1] See *The Times*, 19 March 1970.

Consultative Committee members. A senior backbench figure serves as chairman (this was Sir William Anstruther-Gray in the 1964–6 Parliament and Sir Arthur Vere Harvey in the 1966–70 Parliament). The regular business that comes before the 1922 Committee is the arrangements for the next week's Parliamentary business, and reports from the party groups. Although Consultative Committee members are not members of the 1922 Committee, they may attend its meetings in order to 'observe', and on occasions a member of the Consultative Committee may be specifically invited to attend a meeting in order to comment on a particular topic of current interest that is within his policy area. In this way, 1922 Committee meetings can serve as a sounding board for backbench attitudes to party policy. On the whole, however, the 1922 Committee meetings are not used to hold great policy debates. Although disquiet may be voiced about aspects of party policy or business arrangements, only very rarely is the Committee used as a forum in which to attack Consultative Committee decisions, and unlike the practice of the PLP, the views of the Consultative Committee are not presented in the 1922 Committee for formal approval.

The chief whip attends all 1922 Committee meetings, and he serves as a link between the front and back benches. He explains to the backbenchers the Consultative Committee's decisions on policy and business, and he conveys the views of the backbenchers to the Consultative Committee. The fact that he attends Consultative Committee meetings, without being a full member, is seen as a symbolic expression of his role as a link between the party leaders and the backbenchers.

In the 1945–51 and 1964–70 periods of Conservative Opposition a large Business Committee was formed, which served as a further link between the Consultative Committee on the one hand, and the junior Spokesmen and the backbench MPs on the other.[1] In the 1964–70 period it was made up of those Spokesmen who were not members of the Consultative Committee, together with the officers (that is, the vice-

---

[1] It should not be confused with the small 'Business Committee' that Baldwin formed in the 1929–31 period of Conservative Opposition, or the 'Unionist Business Committee' that was formed in 1915. See p. 241 and Appendix A.

chairman, secretary, and in some cases the treasurer) of the backbench committees. It supplemented the 1922 Committee, and in some respects was a rival to it. It met weekly at 6.15 p.m. on Wednesdays, after the meeting of the Consultative Committee, and the whip and the leader or deputy leader attended to report on the decisions of the Consultative Committee regarding the next week's business. Theoretically the Consultative Committee's proposals were discussed, and the Business Committee voiced possible objections to the arrangements. On Wednesday evening it was still possible to alter the arrangements for the next week's business, whereas by Thursday evening, when the 1922 Committee met, the arrangements had been announced to the House. In fact, the Business Committee proved to be a fairly deferential body, the meeting was usually brief, and only very occasionally was criticism voiced of the arrangements that the Consultative Committee had made. As a consequence, some Conservative junior Spokesmen commented in interview that they often felt out of touch with Consultative Committee decisions, for which, nevertheless, they were held to be collectively responsible.

In most recent sessions, in office or in opposition, there have been about fifteen to twenty Conservative backbench committees, although some of these also set up sub-committees. The committees for the Conservatives' last session in office, together with their chairmen, are shown in Table 20. The frequency of the meetings would largely depend on the chairman, but in the 1964–70 period most groups met once a week for up to an hour, with membership open to all who cared to attend. For most subject groups there were up to ten 'hard core' attenders, with perhaps twenty or so less frequent attenders, but for some meetings attendance would be much more than this. At times of overseas crisis, for example, the Foreign Affairs committee would be attended by most Conservative MPs, while the Finance committee was always well attended at Budget time. For perhaps one in three meetings guest speakers would be invited, especially to the Foreign Affairs and Defence committees, and for a particularly attractive visitor the attendance would be higher than normal. About a third to a half of backbenchers did not attend any of the committees, and most of the rest would attend only two or three with any regularity. As most of the committees met weekly, their timing often conflicted. In the 1969–70 session, for example, the Scottish Unionist Members Committee met on Wednesdays at 4.00 p.m., the Education committee at 4.15 p.m., and the Defence committee at 5.00 p.m., so that a Scottish MP who was interested in education and defence would have

TABLE 20

Conservative Backbench Subject Committees 1969–70 Session

Committee	Chairman*
Agriculture	Joseph Godber
Arts and Amenities	Paul Channon
Aviation	Frederick Corfield
Broadcasting and Communications	Paul Bryan
Defence	Geoffrey Rippon
Education	Mrs Thatcher
Employment and Productivity	Robert Carr
Finance	Iain Macleod
Foreign and Commonwealth Affairs	Sir Alec Douglas-Home
Health and Social Security	Lord Balniel
Home Affairs	Quintin Hogg
Housing and Local Government	Peter Walker
Legal Committee	Sir Peter Rawlinson
Public Building and Works	Robin Chichester-Clark
Trade and Industry Coordinating Committee	Sir Keith Joseph
Trade	Nicholas Ridley
Power	Sir John Eden
Technology and Science	David Price
Transport	Peter Walker

Source: H. Mitchell and P. Birt, *Who Does What in Parliament* (No. 1).
* In each case the senior Spokesman acted as Chairman of the group.

difficulty in attending all three. At any one meeting however, attendance would be fluid, with some joining and some leaving the meeting as it proceeded. A committee would usually hold a special meeting the day before its subject area was due to come up in Question Time, and tactics for supplementary questions were worked out in advance with the Spokesmen concerned.

In addition to the subject committees there were also the

area groups for Scotland, Ulster and the English regions, open to the MPs for the area. The Scottish Unionist Members Committee was formal and regular in its activities, but the Ulster and English regional groups were more casual, and met less regularly than the subject committees. The function of the regional groups, as described by one Conservative MP, was to 'coordinate regional interests': only in the case of the Scottish Members Committee, however, was there any direct link between Spokesmen and a committee. Also, special back-bench study groups were set up from time to time to examine current topics in more detail than was possible in the weekly subject committee meetings. In the 1966–70 Parliament, for example, special committees were formed to prepare Conservative Party attitudes towards the Redcliffe-Maud and Wheatley Reports on local government reorganisation.

These various committees comprise a complex structure with which the Spokesmen have to keep in touch if they are to retain the confidence of the backbench MPs. In the 1945–50 Parliament the chairmen of the backbench committees were elected, but in the 1950–1 Parliament, when office seemed near, Churchill appointed the chairmen. Harold Macmillan, for example, was appointed chairman of the Housing Committee, and this served as his introduction to the subject for which he was to become Minister in 1951. In the 1964–70 period the senior Spokesmen served as chairmen of the appropriate committees, but the vice-chairman, secretary and sometimes a treasurer, were elected. The vice-chairman had some claim to be regarded as an influential voice in his policy area, and in the 1966–7 session, when Heath appointed only a small number of official Spokesmen, this gave the vice-chairman of the groups the role of unofficial assistants to the Spokesmen.[1] Apart from this, however, being an officer of the groups did not carry any special front-bench status. The selection of the officers took place in the first week of the session. Often there was not a contest, and the vice-chairman and secretary 'emerged' from among the regular attenders, but on occasions there would be a contest, and then voting was open to all the Conservative MPs, and not just the regular

[1] See above, pp. 145–6, however, for the complications that this experiment caused.

attenders of the committee concerned. For the most important committees, an election was often contested on an ideological basis.[1] In the 1966–70 Parliament, for example, the Home Affairs and Education committees were particularly important because of topical issues in those fields, and their offices were usually closely contested, with lobbying before the election. For the most part, however, the officers of the committees were re-elected each session, and were more permanent in their roles than were the Spokesmen. Oscar Murton, for example, served as secretary and then vice-chairman of the Housing and Local Government Committee throughout the 1964–70 period, whereas a number of Spokesmen covered the subject in this period. This continuity provided by the officers of the committees is thus somewhat analogous to that of civil servants in relation to Ministers.

Essentially, the committees provided an opportunity for backbench MPs to make known to the Spokesmen their views on policy. In interview some Conservative MPs maintained that the committees were rather more influential in opposition than in office, but that the difference was only slight. As in office, their role was to seek to influence, but not to direct. Like a Minister, a Spokesman would 'take note' of opinions and dissent expressed at committee meetings, although he was in no way subject to the committee's control. Each committee had the services of a Research Department officer, but the committees certainly were not 'policy committees' in the sense that they decided party policy, and the party's leaders remained in control of this. Votes were not taken, and this would be pointless because attendance was on such an irregular basis. At the same time, one of the whips attended each committee meeting, forming a channel of communication between the front and back benches, and enabling the chief whip to judge the relationship that existed between the Spokesman and his committee. It also enabled the chief whip to note the expertise of any backbenchers who might be regarded as future Spokesmen, and the committees thus served as one of the arenas in which an aspiring Spokesman would seek to make his presence felt.

In general, Conservative back benchers are probably as

[1] For a comment see Butler and Pinto-Duschinsky, *The British General Election of 1970*, p. 75.

deferential towards their Spokesmen in opposition as they are towards Ministers when they are in power. This is not to say, of course, that the Spokesmen ride rough-shod over back-benchers: Spokesmen will invariably take heed of backbench opinions as expressed at meetings of the 1922 Committee or subject committees, or in chance social encounters. Thus there are examples, as revealed by Conservative MPs in interview, of 'behind-the-scenes' backbench pressure resulting in changes in party policies and attitudes. The disquiet felt by many Conservative MPs, and constituency activists, about the Value Added Tax was made known to Iain Macleod, as the Treasury Spokesman, during the 1966–70 Parliament, and this led to a softening of the party's commitment to this policy prior to the 1970 election. Similarly, in 1969 and 1970, official Opposition commitments towards the Common Market were seen by many MPs as being excessively firm, and in a speech he delivered in Paris in May 1970, Heath's attitude towards the Common Market issue was rather more guarded than it had been previously, partly as a result of backbench pressure.[1] Similarly, Sir Alec Douglas-Home's Commission to enquire into the question of Scottish devolution, was set up largely as an act of conciliation after Scottish Conservative backbenchers had reacted against Heath's 'Perth Pledge' in 1968, when largely on his own initiative he had committed the party to some form of Scottish Parliament.[2] Thus Conservative Spokesmen have to take note of the views of backbenchers if they are to retain their confidence. Although there is no procedure in the 1922 Committee or the subject committees to oblige the party leaders to accept backbench wishes, the smooth working of the Conservative Party in Parliament, like the smooth working of the British Constitution, depends upon 'two-way deference', with those at the top paying heed to the views of those whom they are leading.

Spokesmen and their Backbench Colleagues: the Labour Party

To what extent does the situation that was described in the previous section apply also in the case of the Labour Party?

[1] See *The Times*, 6 May 1970.
[2] See *The Times*, 20 May 1968, and 8 July 1968. See also Young, *Sir Alec Douglas-Home*, p. 266.

Basically, the same broad principles govern the relationship between Spokesmen and backbenchers in both parties. There are, however, contrasts in important points of detail, and in general Labour Spokesmen do not enjoy the same automatic status within the structure of the PLP as that enjoyed by Conservative Spokesmen in relation to the 1922 Committee. In opposition the PLP has a regular weekly meeting on Thursdays at 7.00 p.m. to consider the arrangements made by the Parliamentary Committee for dealing with the next week's Parliamentary business. Additional meetings may be held from time to time to discuss special matters. The Chairman of the PLP acts as convener, and decides when such special meetings are required. Unlike the practice of the 1922 Committee, PLP meetings are attended by members of the Parliamentary Committee, who sit together on a platform at the end of the large committee room where the meetings are held. In the periods of Opposition before 1970 the party leader acted as chairman at the PLP meetings, but when the party went into opposition in 1970 the office of chairman of the PLP was separated from that of party leader.[1] In 1924 a move was made to copy the 1922 Committee practice and exclude the party leaders from PLP meetings, but this was not implemented,[2] and the Parliamentary leaders remain present and active at PLP meetings. The PLP thus has no need for a 'Business Committee' such as that used by the Conservatives to link the Consultative Committee with the 1922 Committee. While the Parliamentary Committee members' presence at PLP meetings may help them to influence the course of the meeting, it means that they are there as targets to be attacked on any controversial issue. Decisions made by the Parliamentary Committee are submitted for approval at PLP meetings, and although this approval is invariably forthcoming, the Parliamentary leaders are frequently criticised and called upon to justify their decisions to an extent not found with the Conservative Party, and to an extent not found when Labour is in office. In turn, the PLP meeting can make recommendations for the Parliamentary Committee to consider.

As noted in the previous section, in discussions at PLP

[1] See above, p. 112.
[2] See Cole, *Beatrice Webb's Diaries*, II, p. 54.

meetings the Parliamentary Committee members maintain a united front, on the principle of collective responsibility, and in any votes the Committee members will vote together. Votes at PLP meetings are rare, however, and generally the 'sense of the meeting' emerges without any recourse to a show of hands. Nevertheless, on perhaps half a dozen occasions in a session a vote may be taken on particularly vital issues when the sense of the meeting is not clear. Thus at the PLP meeting on 19 October 1971, three votes were held, including one of 140 votes to 111 against the principle of a free vote at the end of the Common Market debate in the Commons.[1] Subsequently, the chief whip and the Parliamentary Committee decided to act in accordance with this PLP recommendation. On another crucial occasion, in February 1954, the PLP decided by a majority of only nine votes to support the Parliamentary Committee's recommended policy of favouring German re-armament.[2] The nine-vote majority for the Parliamentary Committee's motion was achieved only because all of the Parliamentary Committee members, bound by the principle of collective responsibility, cast their votes in support of the motion, even though at the Parliamentary Committee meeting at which the recommendation was framed, the members had been clearly divided. If voting at PLP meetings was by secret ballot rather than by a show of hands, the solidarity of Parliamentary Committee voting could not be enforced, although there does not seem to be any great pressure within the PLP for such a change.

In this context it may be noted that while meetings of the Conservative 1922 Committee are restricted to members of the Commons, meetings of the PLP are attended by Labour peers. The peers do not comment on purely House of Commons business matters, and thus did not take part in the vote, referred to above, on the whipping arrangements for the Common Market division in the Commons. On broad policy questions, however, and matters affecting the party as a whole,

[1] The voting figures, though nominally secret, were reported in the press the next day.
[2] See Haseler, *The Gaitskellites*, p. 128. For an account of the whole issue see S. Rose, 'The Labour Party and German Rearmament', *Political Studies* 1966, pp. 133–43.

they do speak and vote as full members of the Committee. Thus, if they chose, the hundred or so peers who take the Labour whip would be in a position to swamp PLP meetings, or at least could play a decisive role in some of their deliberations. In fact, very few peers do attend PLP meetings, and in recent sessions there have been no more than about half a dozen in attendance on most occasions. Even the meetings in October 1971 at which the Common Market issue was debated at length, were attended by no more than ten to twelve peers. Nevertheless, the peers could hold the balance on some issues, and, theoretically at least, it would be possible for a Labour Leader of the Opposition to 'pack' the Labour benches in the Lords with life peers who could be relied upon to attend PLP meetings, and support the leadership there. A Labour leader, however, is unlikely to attempt any such nineteenth-century style 'politics of the peerage', and such a practice would almost certainly be counter-productive, alienating MPs who might otherwise be sympathetic towards the leadership on a particular issue.

Before 1970, in office or in opposition, the PLP generally had twenty or so subject groups, mirroring the departments of state, but in November 1970 the number of groups was reduced from twenty to sixteen, matching the departmental structure evolved by the Heath Government. A number of the groups, however, set up sub-committees, and the Environment group, for example, had a total of nine sub-committees or working parties. There are also the area groups, with the Welsh and Scottish groups being rather more active and influential than the English regional groups. The subject groups for the 1970–1 session, and their chairmen, are listed in Table 21. From the comments of Labour and Conservative Spokesmen who were interviewed, it is clear that the PLP groups devote more time to the discussion of policy, as opposed to tactical and business matters, than do the Conservative groups. Also, although the broad organisational arrangements are similar to those for the Conservative groups, there are some significant differences in detail. The PLP groups, for example, are not serviced by a Research Department officer in the way that the Conservative groups are. They meet less frequently than the Conservative subject committees (usually monthly as opposed to weekly), and unlike the Conservative practice, each PLP group has an official membership, with each Labour MP limited to a maximum of three groups. Only group members can vote in contests for the offices of the group, but attendance at group meetings is open to any MP. The appropriate Spokesman from the House of Lords, and

TABLE 21

PLP Subject Groups 1970–1 Session

Group	Chairman
Aviation Supply	William Rodgers*
Defence	Sir Geoffrey de Freitas
Economic and Finance	Dick Taverne*
Education and Science	Edward Short*
Employment	Barbara Castle†
Environment	Arthur Blenkinsop
Europe	Harold Lever†
Food and Agriculture	John Mackie
Foreign and Commonwealth	Denis Healey†
Health and Social Security	Mrs Williams†
Home Office	Arthur Davidson
Overseas Aid	Mrs Hart†
Parliamentary Affairs	Michael English
Post Office	Ivor Richard†
Power and Steel	Alexander Eadie
Trade and Industry	Anthony Wedgwood Benn†

Source: Mitchell and Birt, *Who Does What in Parliament* (No. 3).

* Indicates the chairman was an assistant Spokesman for the subject.

† Indicates the chairman was the senior Spokesman for the subject.

any other interested peers, can also attend, although in fact they rarely do so.

While the senior Conservative Spokesman for each subject automatically becomes chairman of his committee, the chairmen of the PLP subject groups are elected by the group members. The senior Spokesman, or one of his assistants, may be elected chairman of his group, but there is nothing automatic about this: just as the Leader of the Opposition is not chairman of the PLP, so many Labour MPs feel that the Spokesmen should not be chairmen of the groups. In the 1951–64 period, for example, the Transport group usually elected as chairman someone with a railway background, and although G. R. Strauss was Transport Spokesman for almost the whole of the 1955–64 period, he did not serve as chairman of the group. In the 1970–1 session, as Table 21 indicates, more than half of the groups were chaired by senior or assistant Spokesmen, and it is probably fair to say that in this session the senior Spokesmen who did not become chairmen of their subject groups were excluded only because they wished to be. Thus Hugh Jenkins had served as chairman of the Posts and Telecommunications group during much of the period when Labour was in office, but in 1970 the senior Spokesman for the subject, Ivor Richard, became chairman, with Hugh Jenkins (still a backbencher) as vice-chairman. In the nineteen-fifties, however, when the PLP was divided over policy issues, this was not the case, and Spokesmen sometimes sought and failed to secure the chairmanship of their group. A powerful backbench figure would sometimes emerge as chairman of a subject group, and would pose as something of a rival to the Spokesman in that subject. In such cases relations between the Spokesman and the group would be strained, and sometimes on policy questions there would be conflicting approaches from the Spokesman and the group. The defence group, for example, was often controlled by the pacifist left-wing of the party, and was thus dubbed the 'No Defence Committee' by the official Defence Spokesmen, whose influence in the group was negligible. There is perhaps less likelihood of this situation arising in the currently more united PLP.

Spokesmen often refer policy and tactical questions to the backbench groups for comment, and the Spokesmen will seek to draw upon the expertise of the groups' members. Pressure of time, however, often prevents adequate soundings being taken of backbench opinions. Even if the Spokesman is elected to be chairman of his subject group, there is still less likelihood of the subject group deferring to his wishes than is the case with the Conservatives when in opposition. In general, Labour Spokesmen have less influence within their subject groups than is the case with their Conservative counterparts, and the PLP is almost 'aggressively democratic' in refusing to accept un-questioningly the authority of a Spokesman, whether or not he is chairman of his group. In this, as with the place of the Shadow Cabinet at Parliamentary party meetings, the difference between the two parties is clear. The contrast could become even more pronounced, as in 1970 some Labour MPs demanded for the groups a much more powerful place in the PLP's affairs than had been the case in previous periods of Labour Opposition. It remains to be seen how the relationship between Spokesmen and the groups will develop.

Thus, while there is in a party in government a sharp distinction between the Ministers of the Crown and the rest of the party in and out of Parliament, in opposition the distinction between the Spokesmen and 'the rest' is much more blurred: as stressed at the beginning of the chapter, the official Spokesmen are merely the spearhead of the Opposition's attack upon the Government. Further, in opposition the front-bench team is managing *party* affairs, not affairs of government. For both parties when in opposition, therefore, the involvement of the party leaders with their backbench and extra-Parliamentary colleagues is much more direct than is the case when the party is in office. Within this general situation, however, it is clear from this Chapter and Chapter 8, that there are significant differences of detail between the two parties as regards the power and status of the Spokesmen in the party organisation in and out of Parliament. In Chapter 8 it was noted that Conservative Spokesmen are much more directly involved than are Labour Spokesmen with the machinery through which their party reviews its policy in opposition. The senior Conservative Spokesmen are almost invariably chairmen of the policy committees, and the Research Department officer who is attached to the policy committee will also serve the Spokesmen for that subject. In contrast, Labour Spokesmen are only rarely chairmen of the NEC policy committees, and only since 1970 have they been guaranteed places on the committees. As revealed in this Chapter, there are also contrasts between the two parties with regard to the relationship between the Spokesmen and their backbench colleagues in Parliament. Members of the Conservative front-bench team enjoy a particularly prestigious position within the party's Parliamentary machinery. The leader and the members of the Consultative Committee remain aloof

from the deliberations of the 1922 Committee; the decisions
of the Consultative Committee do not have to be submitted
to the 1922 Committee for approval or discussion; in general
the Spokesmen are held in as much awe by backbench MPs
and the party rank and file as are Conservative Ministers when
the party is in office. In contrast, the Labour Leader of the
Opposition and his Shadow Cabinet attend PLP meetings,
and in the periods in opposition before 1970 the Leader served
as chairman of the PLP; Labour Spokesmen are not necessarily
chairmen of the backbench subject groups, nor do they receive
the same amount of assistance from their Research Department
as do Conservative Spokesmen. Thus within the broad picture
of the role of Opposition Spokesmen there are discernible
differences between the two parties' arrangements. What will
be considered in Chapter 10 is whether the behaviour of
Labour and Conservative Spokesmen differs in the particular
matter of the extent to which, in their Parliamentary activities,
they choose to specialise in their assigned subjects.

10

Spokesmen and their Parliamentary Subject Specialisations

THE HOUSE OF COMMONS is the centre of an Opposition Spokesman's activities. How seriously do Spokesmen take their Parliamentary duties, and, in particular, to what extent do they concentrate upon their assigned subjects in their Parliamentary activities? In their participation in the business before the House of Commons, Ministers of the Crown concentrate almost exclusively on their own departmental affairs. Only rarely will a Minister speak in a debate on a subject that is outside his own area. At Question Time he will rarely or never be drawn into exchanges on any topic outside his own field, and he will attend only such Select or Standing Committees as are dealing with topics within his departmental area. In their Parliamentary activities, therefore, Ministers practise virtually complete specialisation. To what extent do Opposition Spokesmen follow this Ministerial pattern of behaviour? Are they like Ministers in the extent to which, in their Parliamentary activities, they concentrate on their assigned duties, or do their contributions in Parliament range over a number of subject areas, additional to their assigned area? Less subject specialisation might perhaps be expected of Opposition Spokesmen than of Ministers, if only because Opposition duties are less time-consuming than are those of a Minister. Although a Spokesman's duties now take up more time than they did in the past, most Spokesmen still have rather more time than do Ministers to look beyond their own immediate areas of concern. Also, it is impossible always to compartmentalise policies: defence policy, for example, can involve those responsible for Foreign and Commonwealth affairs, and Finance, as well as the specific Defence Spokesman or Minister. In office, however, one Minister has to assume responsibility for a Bill or a policy statement, even though it may encroach on to the territory of some of his colleagues, whereas the opposition to a Bill or a policy can come from a number of Spokesmen, as there need not necessarily be only one line of attack. In Question Time a Spokesman may be drawn into supplementary exchanges on some controversial issue, or on some subject that touches only incidentally on his own area. A Minister, however, in answering questions deals only with his own subject, and will rarely or never be drawn into supplementary exchanges in another Minister's area. Again, a Spokesman, like all MPs outside the Government, may use debates and Question Time to raise constituency issues that are outside his own immediate subject area. A Minister's constituency matters, on the other hand, will be dealt with by means of behind-the-scenes contacts with his Ministerial colleagues.

For these practical reasons the level of specialisation among Opposition leaders would not normally be expected to be as high as that among Ministers. More than this, however, one of the major compensations of being in opposition has often been thought to be the freedom that it gives to ex-Ministers to spread their interests over a number of separate policy areas, thereby acquiring a breadth of experience that is denied to them in office, when they are restricted within the narrow confines of a specific departmental responsibility. Thus many people condemned the introduction of the system of official Spokesmen in 1955. The advantage of being able to take an interest in a wide range of subjects in opposition would be lost (they argued) if former Ministers were given responsibility for specific policy areas in opposition. Harold Macmillan has since echoed these fears, claiming that it is detrimental to a party in opposition to have its leaders cast into watertight subject compartments. For Macmillan, the main compensation for being out of office was the opportunity it offered former Ministers to diversify their interests: says Macmillan, 'Out of office let them wander free and unencumbered. This at least was Churchill's plan.'[1] Equally, however, the defenders of the post-1955 system of official Spokesmen argue that it has produced more effective opposition, with Spokesmen becoming experts in their assigned areas, and thus becoming better able to face Ministers on equal terms across the floor of the House. They argue that in the modern world the Opposition has to be highly organised, professional, and specialised if it is to be at all convincing, either as a critic or as an alternative Government. The whole issue, therefore, is bound up with the question of the relative merits of the 'specialist' and the 'generalist' within the Parliamentary context today.

Thus to what extent are Opposition Spokesmen cast into watertight subject compartments, and what evidence is there of this in their activities in Parliament? Over the years has there been any change in the level of specialisation among members of the Opposition front bench, and in particular has there been any change in behaviour since the introduction of the system of official Spokesmen in 1955? Does the level of specialisation vary from one form of Parliamentary activity to another, perhaps being greater in debates than in questions, and greater in oral questions than in written questions? Are there any differences in this between senior and junior Spokesmen, or between Spokesmen with Ministerial experience and those without? What is the relationship between degree of specialisation and level of activity? In all of these matters are there any differences between the two parties? Some light can be thrown on these questions by examining the performance of Opposition front benchers in debates and questions in the House of Commons, as reflected in the entries in the Hansard Sessional Index. This is attempted in the following pages, by the method that is outlined in Appendix E.[2] Those who are unwilling to work through the detailed analysis that is contained in the next three sections should turn to the final section of the chapter (p. 350) which discusses the causes and consequences of the general patterns of behaviour revealed by the analysis.

[1] Macmillan, *Tides of Fortune*, p. 44.
[2] See below, p. 473. I am grateful to L. W. Bear, the current editor of Hansard, for discussing with me some of the problems involved in analysing Hansard and its Index.

Index of Specialisation 1900–70

Has there been any change in the level of subject specialisation among members of the Opposition front bench this century? Table 22 shows the Index of Specialisation among Opposition leaders in various sessions this century.[1] In each case the figure is a composite

TABLE 22

Index of Specialisation 1900–70

Session	Main Topic (%)
1908	37·1
1910	55·2
1912	57·2
1923	31·8*
1924	48·3
1926	40·9*
1929–30	50·1
1932–33	26·3*
1937–38	40·2*
1947–48	36·4
1950–51	41·1
1952–53	54·6*
1956–57	63·4* (59·8)*
1961–62	58·1* (60·0)*
1965–66	83·8 (67·4)
1967–68	78·9 (77·8)

Source: (for this and all the tables in this chapter): *Hansard* Sessional Index for the years in question.

The main figures relate to the Shadow Cabinet, and the figures in brackets relate to the front-bench team as a whole (that is, the members of the Shadow Cabinet, plus the other Spokesmen).

* Indicates the figures for Labour Oppositions: other figures relate to Conservative Oppositions.

one for the Shadow Cabinet as a whole, with an additional figure for the front-bench team as a whole in the sessions after 1955. The figures are percentages, and they reflect the proportion of their Parliamentary debating and questioning activity

[1] See Appendix E, p. 473, for the way in which the 'Index of Specialisation' was calculated, and the basis on which the sessions were selected.

that the Opposition leaders devote to their main area of activity, as measured by the number of entries in the Hansard Sessional Index. Table 22 indicates that over the 1900–70 period there was an increase in both parties in the level of specialisation. In this, the period is divided by the changes of Government in 1951 and 1964. Before 1951, all of the Labour figures, and all but two of the Conservative figures, were on or below 50 per cent: in the 1951–64 period, on the other hand, all the figures were above 50 per cent, and in the 1964–70 period the figures were above 75 per cent. The 1900–70 period can thus be divided into three 'plateaus', with the 1900–51 figures generally being below 50 per cent, the 1951–64 figures fluctuating around 60 per cent, and the 1964–70 figures reaching in excess of 75 per cent.

Almost all of the figures (Labour and Conservative) before 1951 were between 30 per cent and 50 per cent. The particularly low Labour figure in 1932–3 is largely a reflection of the fact that in the 1931–5 Parliament, after Labour's debacle in 1931, there were very few experienced Labour MPs, so that the front benchers had to spread their activities more widely than usual. The high Conservative figures in 1910 and 1912 are largely a reflection of the exceptionally high level of concentration on the House of Lords reform and Irish home rule issues in these sessions. In most sessions, of course, there is one topic which attracts more attention than others, but in 1910 the reform of the Lords, and in 1912 the issue of Irish home rule, dominated the Parliamentary time-table to a particularly great extent (as is discussed below).[1]

Within the overall pattern it may be noted that period by period the Conservatives have shown a higher level of specialisation than Labour. The Labour figures from the 1951–64 period were all above the pre-1951 norm of both parties, but were not as high as the Conservative figures of the 1964–70 period. This fits in with the generally greater tendency towards specialisation among Conservative Spokesmen than among Labour Spokesmen in their activities on Select and Standing Committees, as noted in Chapter 8. In the sessions since 1955 (when a figure can be obtained for the front-bench team as a whole, as well as for the Shadow Cabinet) the two Conservative figures

[1] See p. 331.

for the team as a whole are higher than the two Labour figures by as much as 8 per cent and 17 per cent. In three of the four sessions, the level of specialisation is higher for the Shadow Cabinet than for the team as a whole, although apart from

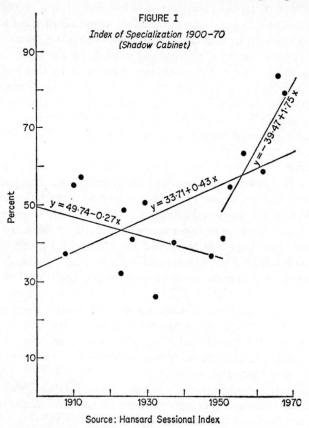

FIGURE I

Index of Specialization 1900–70
(Shadow Cabinet)

$y = 49.74 - 0.27x$

$y = 33.71 + 0.43x$

$y = -39.47 + 1.75x$

Source: Hansard Sessional Index

1965–6 the difference between the two figures is only 2 per cent or 3 per cent.

The Shadow Cabinet figures of Table 22 are depicted graphically in Figure I, with trend lines for the 1900–70, 1900–50, and 1950–70 periods being shown separately.[1] The

[1] In the equation $y = a + bx$, let a stand for the level of specialisation at the beginning of the period under consideration (1900), x for the unit of one session, and b for the annual rate of increase in specialisation.

trend line for the 1900–50 period indicates a *decline* in the level of specialisation, largely as a result of the contrast between the comparatively high levels of specialisation among the Balfour, Bonar Law, and Baldwin Shadow Cabinets in the 1908–31 period, and the lower level of specialisation among Churchill's Shadow Cabinet after 1945. In the 1950–70 period, on the other hand, the trend line is steeply upwards. This emphasises the sharp contrast between Conservative behaviour in the 1964–70 period and that in earlier periods of Conservative Opposition. It may also be noted that in the 1950–70 period the variation about the trend line was less than in the period before 1950,[1] so that the level of specialisation is much more predictable in the period since 1950 than in the pre-1950 period.

Will the level of specialisation vary from one stage of a Parliament to another? One of the problems that arises from selecting only one middle session in each Parliament is that an MP's behaviour in the sessions just before or just after a general election may be different from that in the middle sessions of a Parliament. Thus the sessions shown in Table 22 may not be representative of the other sessions of those Parliaments. Some MPs served as Spokesmen throughout the 1955–64 and 1964–70 periods, which are the main periods of concern here, and thus provide a means of comparison over the whole period. In the 1955–64 period of Labour Opposition there were twelve such MPs, and in the 1964–70 period of Conservative Opposition there were seven. The performance of these Spokesmen in each session of the period is examined in Tables 23 and 24, to see if the level of specialisation was markedly different in the middle session of a Parliament than in other sessions.

It is clear from both Tables that the figures for the middle sessions of the four Parliaments are neither exceptionally high nor exceptionally low, and the highest figures for each Spokesman in each Parliament are not concentrated in the middle session. In general, in the Labour sessions different Spokesmen produced different patterns of increasing or static levels of specialisation. Douglas Jay's Index of Specialisation was uniformly high, and all but one of his figures were above 70 per

---

[1] In Figure I, $r^2 = 70.5$ per cent for the 1950–70 period, compared with 30.2 per cent for the 1900–70 period as a whole, and 18.0 per cent for the 1900–50 period.

TABLE 23

Index of Specialisation: Labour Spokesmen who served throughout the 1955–64 Period

Spokesman	1955–6	1956–7	1957–8	1958–9	1959–60 (percentages)	1960–1	1961–2	1962–3	1963–4
Brown	41·4	76·1	92·4*	85·6	72·7*	27·7	31·6	36·5	16·4
Callaghan	16·7	47·0	57·7	72·7*	61·3	33·3	64·4*	59·4	47·7
Creech-Jones	100·0*	89·6	97·6	93·0	88·2	85·7	100·0*	46·1	33·3
Fraser	64·8	67·8*	51·9	51·5	44·4	77·6*	46·3	40·5	41·9
Miss Herbison	57·5*	33·3	32·5	31·9	66·3*	64·8	65·9	56·4	36·7
Jay	92·3*	76·9	90·7	87·7	59·9	86·5	81·6	72·8	88·7*
Lee	60·3	43·2	56·6	83·9*	72·7	38·8	56·8	61·9	78·4*
Mitchison	64·9	64·3	53·4	80·4*	71·6*	45·6	51·0	69·1	30·3
Stewart	48·4	35·3	38·6	49·0*	52·3	63·9	60·0	89·7*	85·6
Strauss	76·1*	65·9	66·7	73·2	62·2	85·7	94·2*	89·8	92·8
Gordon Walker	66·4*	75·9*	62·7	43·5	56·3	59·2	40·6	51·7	69·3*
Willey	67·6	50·3	53·1	36·6	69·3	38·4	68·5	52·7	72·2*
Average	64·8	65·9	57·7	73·2	66·3	59·2	64·4	59·4	69·3

* Indicates each Spokesman's highest figure of the Parliament.

cent, and most were above 80 per cent. With Margaret Herbison, on the other hand, all the figures were below 70 per cent, and four of the nine were below 50 per cent. Arthur Creech Jones' first seven figures were all in excess of 80 per cent, but his last two figures were below 50 per cent. Similarly, George Brown's figures declined from 1957–8 onwards, although this is explained in part by the fact that he was deputy leader of the party during most of the 1959–64 Parliament, with consequently wide-ranging responsibilities. For the most part, however, the sessional variations in the Labour Spokesmen's figures

TABLE 24

Index of Specialisation: Conservative Spokesmen who served throughout the 1964–70 Period

Spokesman	1964–5	1965–6	1966–7	1967–8	1968–9	1969–70
			(percentages)			
Carr	76·8	77·6*	64·2	77·8	92·0	94·7*
Godber	79·2	100·0*	82·2	95·5	84·6	98·5*
Hogg	59·3*	31·4	57·4	79·9	94·6	96·9*
Joseph	57·9	97·1*	70·1	100·0*	95·7	97·0
Macleod	32·6	80·6*	85·0	88·7	90·8*	89·8
Mrs Thatcher	67·6	88·9*	90·6	83·9	100·0*	97·9
Wood	71·2	89·7*	92·4	67·8	70·0	92·9*
Average	67·6	88·9	82·2	83·9	91·9	95·9

* Indicate each Spokesman's highest figure of the Parliament.

do not follow any clear pattern, although it is clear that the 1956–7 and 1961–2 sessions were *not* exceptional. For the Conservatives, on the other hand, the variations from session to session are less marked, and after the 1964–5 session, only two figures (Quintin Hogg's figures in 1965–6 and 1966–7) fall below 64 per cent.

One general tendency in all four Parliaments covered in Tables 23 and 24 is that the figures are somewhat higher in the final session of the Parliament than in the other sessions, perhaps indicating an inclination towards increased specialisation when a general election seems likely. In the short 1964–6 Parliament all but one of the seven Conservative Spokesmen had higher figures in the second session than in the immediate post-election session. The generally lower figures for the 1964–5 session than for any other of the Conservative sessions may indicate an initial 'rush to freedom' on going into opposition, after the inhibitions of Ministerial office, or it may merely indicate a slowness in developing patterns of behaviour in opposition. Alternatively, it may be that the accession of Edward Heath to the party leadership towards the end of 1964–5 was followed at once by a new style of opposition behaviour, with a greater level of specialisation among the Spokesmen. This question, however, is discussed in more detail in the concluding section of the chapter. On the whole, both Tables confirm the overall picture of Table 22 and Figure I (and of Table 25 and Figure J below), that the Labour figures fluctuate around 60 per cent to 65 per cent, while the Conservative figures, after the 1964–5 session, jump to a new plateau in excess of 80 per cent.

Does the level of specialisation vary from one form of Parliamentary activity to another? Tables 22, 23 and 24 were concerned only with a general Index of Specialisation, but in Table 25 this is broken down into separate indexes for debates, oral questions and written questions in the sessions since 1945 (before 1945 the Hansard Sessional Index did not distinguish between these different forms of activity).[1] The general picture of increasing specialisation that emerged in Table 22 is reflected in Table 25, in that for all three forms of activity there was a clear trend towards greater specialisation, with, for the most part, each figure being higher than that for the preceding session. In most sessions, for the Shadow Cabinet and for the team as a whole, debating was the most specialised form of activity, and in all sessions written questions were the least specialised. Many MPs, including Spokesmen, use written questions for raising constituency matters, and this might explain the lower level of specialisation in this form of activity. It may be noted, however, that in many ways questions put down for written answer are the truest guide to an MP's real interests and motivations. Participation in the oral Question Time is restricted by the fact that particular Ministers are required to answer oral questions only at certain times in the session, and participation in debates

[1] For this and other methodological problems see Appendix E.

is governed by the nature of the business before the House at any given time in the session. There are virtually no restrictions on the putting down of questions for written answer, however, so that participation in this form of activity is purely spontaneous (although it should be remembered that some of the questions which receive a written answer were originally put down for oral answer, but were not reached in the time available in Question Time).[1]

TABLE 25

Index of Specialisation: Debates, Oral Questions and Written Questions

Session	Debates	Oral Questions (%)	Written Questions (%)
1947–48	44·6	27·3	15·6
1950–51	49·6	44·2	23·8
1952–53	61·1*	49·2*	34·5*
1956–57	64·6* (61·9)*	62·5* (63·9)*	60·2* (51·7)*
1961–62	60·7* (60·6)*	74·2* (66·9)*	49·4* (53·7)*
1965–66	87·4 (78·3)	84·1 (70·9)	77·3 (54·5)
1967–68	78·7 (77·2)	80·6 (82·9)	72·3 (60·4)

The main figures relate to the Shadow Cabinet, and the figures in brackets to the front-bench team as a whole.

  * Indicates the figures for Labour Oppositions: other figures relate to Conservative Oppositions.

The higher level of specialisation in debates than in oral or written questions to some extent may be consequent upon the level of preparation that is necessary for most debating contributions. Question Time is well attended, and invariably lively, and a Spokesman may be drawn into a spontaneous supplementary question on a topic outside his main area of interest. An interjection in a debate, of course, might also be spontaneous, but a lengthy debating contribution requires more studied preparation than does a brief supplementary in Question Time, or a written request for information. A Spokesman,

[1] See Chester and Bowring, *Questions in Parliament,* for details of these procedures.

or any MP, might be expected to confine such prepared contributions to his own main area of interest. Also, debates, much more so than questions, are used to make formal statements of party attitudes and policies, and these will be made by one of the Spokesmen for the subject concerned.

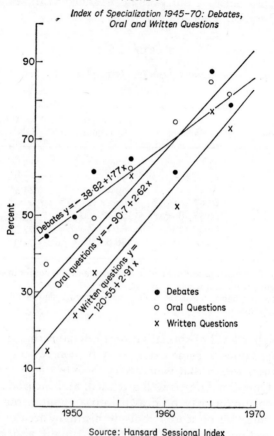

FIGURE J

Index of Specialization 1945–70: Debates, Oral and Written Questions

Source: Hansard Sessional Index

The figures from Table 25 are depicted graphically in Figure J, with the trend lines indicating the clear increase in specialisation in all three forms of activity over the 1945–70 period as a whole. The trend lines for oral questions and for written questions are almost parallel, and are steeper than the trend line for debates. In all three cases, the variations about the trend lines are slight.[1] Thus it can be seen from Table 25 and Figure J, even more clearly than from Table 22 and Figure I, that the trend towards greater specialisation began *before* 1955: that is, the introduction of the system of official Spokesmen followed from, rather than preceded, an increase in the level of specialisation among Opposition front benchers. It may well be, of course, that once the system of official Spokesmen was introduced, it reinforced the trend towards specialisation, and it may be that without the Spokesmen system the behaviour of Opposition front benchers would not be as specialised as it has been in recent years. Nevertheless, the general trend towards increased specialisation had emerged before 1955, with this trend being particularly pronounced, as shown in Table 25 and Figure J, in the case of oral and written questions.

While concentrating on one main topic, do Spokesmen divide the rest of their time over a lot of subject areas, or do their activities range only over two or three areas? Clearly, Spokesman X who devotes 70 per cent of his time to one topic, and 30 per cent to another single topic, is more 'specialised' in his behaviour than is Spokesman Y, who also devotes 70 per cent of his time to one topic, but spreads the remaining 30 per cent of his time over eight or nine other areas. Thus as a further measure of specialisation, the number of separate policy areas in which Spokesmen participate can be examined. Table 26 shows the average number of subject areas covered by the Spokesmen in the various sessions under consideration. In each case the figure is achieved by totalling the number of policy areas covered by each Spokesman in a session, and then dividing this figure by the number of Spokesmen involved. In the three sessions before 1955, the members of the Shadow Cabinet, on average, spoke in debates covering five or six different areas. Since then, however, they have tended to make their contributions in fewer and fewer areas, and in 1967–8 the average figure was just 3·1. In the short session of 1965–6, the figure was even lower at 2·2. There is a similar trend for questions, except that in 1967–8 the trend is reversed. In all four sessions since 1955, for debates

---

[1] In Figure J, for oral questions $r^2 = 94·1$ per cent, for writter questions 86·0 per cent, and for debates 82·3 per cent.

and for questions, the Shadow Cabinet participated in fewer areas than did the team as a whole, and in general the trend towards participation in fewer policy areas is more pronounced for the Shadow Cabinet than for the team as a whole.

In the first five sessions, for the Shadow Cabinet and the team as a whole, the figures were no different for debates than for questions, but in the two Conservative sessions since 1964,

TABLE 26

Average Number of Policy Areas covered by Front Benchers in Debates and Questions

Session	Number of Spokesmen	Debates	Questions
1947–8	13	5·5	5·7
1950–1	11	5·6	5·4
1952–3	13	6·0*	5·7*
1956–7	12 (35)	4·6* (4·6)*	4·7* (6·3)*
1961–2	13 (39)	4·5* (5·1)*	4·3* (5·3)*
1965–6	16 (58)	2·2 (2·4)	2·9 (6·0)
1967–8	15 (28)	3·1 (4·1)	5·2 (6·2)

The main figures relate to the Shadow Cabinet, and the figures in brackets relate to the front-bench team as a whole (that is, the members of the Shadow Cabinet, plus the other Spokesmen).

* Indicates the figures for Labour Oppositions: other figures relate to Conservative Oppositions.

the degree of specialisation was greater for debates than for questions. The trend lines are indicated in Figure K, and this contrast between debates and questions emerges clearly.[1] Figure K and Table 26 thus confirm the general trends of the earlier Tables, and reveal a pattern of increased specialisation, as reflected in participation in fewer and fewer different policy areas. This emphasises further the particularly marked contrast between Conservative behaviour before 1951 and after 1964.

To what extent do Spokesmen make their assigned duty their main area of activity? The preceding Tables are all based on front

[1] In Figure K, the variations about the trend line are less for debates than for questions: for debates $r^2 = 79 \cdot 2$ per cent, and for questions $42 \cdot 2$ per cent.

benchers' main area of activity, but in the sessions since 1955 it is possible to distinguish between a Spokesman's main area of activity and his assigned area. It might be expected that usually the two will be equated, but there may be some

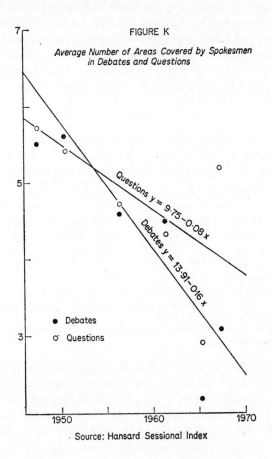

FIGURE K

Average Number of Areas Covered by Spokesmen in Debates and Questions

Questions $y = 9.75 - 0.08x$

Debates $y = 13.91 - 0.16x$

● Debates
○ Questions

Source: Hansard Sessional Index

Spokesmen who will concentrate their activity on some subject other than their assigned duty: an Education Spokesman, for example, with ambition to be a future Foreign Secretary, might devote more time to foreign affairs than to his education duty. This is examined in Table 27, which shows the proportion of Spokesmen who made their assigned duty their main area of activity in the sessions under consideration.[1] The percentages are uniformly high, with none lower than 82 per cent, indicating that only a very small proportion of the Spokesmen concentrated on anything other than their assigned duty. The proportion concentrating on their assigned duty is higher in the two Conservative sessions than in the two Labour sessions, indicating, perhaps, a greater willingness among the Conservative Spokesmen to take their assigned duties seriously. In each session the figure in the debates column is higher than in the questions column, indicating that if a Spokesman is going to

TABLE 27

Main Topic related to Assigned Duty

Session	N	Proportion of Spokesmen whose Main Topic was also their Assigned Duty		
		Debates	Questions	Total
1956–7	12 (36)	91·7* (85·7)*	91·7* (85·7)*	91·7* (85·7)*
1961–2	12 (42)	92·3 (82·0)	84·6 (82·0)	84·6 (89·7)
1965–6	15 (36)	93·7 (96·5)	87·5 (82·7)	100·0 (82·7)
1967–8	17 (30)	100·0 (100·0)	100·0 (96·4)	100·0 (100·0)

The main figures relate to the Shadow Cabinet, and the figures in brackets relate to the front-bench team as a whole (that is, the members of the Shadow Cabinet, plus the other Spokesmen).

* Indicates figures for Labour Oppositions: all other figures relate to Conservative Oppositions.

concentrate on a topic other than his assigned duty, he is marginally more likely to do so through questions than through debates. In only one instance (debates in the 1965–6 session) is the figure for the Shadow Cabinet lower than for the team as a whole, suggesting that junior Spokesmen are rather more likely to stray beyond their assigned areas than are members of the Shadow Cabinet.

Thus the over-riding feature of Table 27 is the very high proportion of Spokesmen who do concentrate their main activity in their assigned areas, especially in the sessions of Conservative Opposition. This emphasises an essential difference between the behaviour of Opposition leaders today and

[1] See also Tables 34, 35 and 36 below.

in the 'pre-Spokesmen era' before 1955. It was noted at the beginning of the section that the 1910 and 1912 sessions stood out from the other sessions of the period because their Index of Specialisation was almost as high as that of the more recent sessions. In the 1910 and 1912 sessions, however, the high figures were a product of the fact that a number of MPs concentrated on the issues that dominated the timetable in those two sessions (House of Lords reform in 1910 and Irish Home Rule in 1912). This was possible in sessions before 1955 because the Opposition leaders were not assigned to cover particular areas, and thus a number of them could specialise in the major issues of the session. Today, on the other hand, only one or two Spokesmen would be assigned to cover a particular topic, no matter how vital it might be, and the other Opposition leaders would have their own assigned duties. Thus, paradoxically, in the 1910 and 1912 sessions the high Index of Specialisation was a direct result of the *absence* of assigned jobs for Opposition Spokesmen, whereas today, as Table 27 shows, the high Index of Specialisation is achieved in combination with Spokesmen concentrating on their own assigned duties.

Degree of Specialisation and Level of Activity

In the preceding section certain clear conclusions emerged. In the Parliamentary activities of Opposition front benchers there has been a general increase in the level of subject specialisation in this century, with the trend emerging most clearly in the early 1950s, *before* the introduction of the system of official Spokesmen in 1955. Increasingly, however, Spokesmen have made their assigned duties their main areas of activity. Of the three forms of Parliamentary activity that were examined, written questions was in each case the least specialised, and debates was usually the most specialised, although by the 1960s oral questions had 'caught up' with debates in the degree of specialisation. Thus the contrast in behaviour between 1947–8 and 1967–8 is greater for oral and written questions than for debates, because even in 1947–8 debates were a fairly specialised form of activity in comparison with questions. In 1967–8, however, the difference in the degree of specialisation between the three forms of activity was only slight. In any given period the level of specialisation was higher for Conservative than for Labour front benchers, although in many ways the most dramatic feature of the Tables is the contrast between Conservative behaviour before 1951, and Conservative behaviour in the 1964–70 period.

So far, however, no attempt has been made to relate these changes in degree of specialisation to the level of activity, although clearly the relationship between the two is essential to a proper understanding of the situation. In effect, the increased level of specialisation could be the result of any of three possible changes in the way Spokesmen apportion their time:

1. Increased specialisation could be a result of Spokesmen increasing their activity in their main area, while at the same time maintaining their previous level of activity in other areas. In this case the greater specialisation would be accompanied by an overall increase in the spokesmen's level of activity.

2. Greater specialisation could result from Spokesmen spending no more time on their main subjects, but merely reducing their activities in their fringe interests. In this case the Spokesmen's overall level of activity would decline as the degree of specialisation increased.

3. Increased specialisation could result from a combination of an increase in activity in a Spokesman's main area, and a decrease in activity in other areas. In this case the increased specialisation might not involve any change in the overall level of activity, if the increase in time spent on the main topic is matched precisely by the decrease in the time spent on other topics.

Which of these possible changes of behaviour has accompanied the growth of front-bench specialisation? In the period in which the level of specialisation has grown, has the overall level of Spokesmen's activity increased, declined or remained static? In general, is there a simple relationship between level of activity and degree of specialisation, or has there been an increase in specialisation among active and inactive Spokesmen alike? Tables 28 and 29, and Figure L, present data on these questions.

Has there been any change in the level of activity among Opposition Spokesmen in the period since 1955? In order to measure the extent of the activity of the Opposition team over several sessions, it is not enough merely to compare the total number of references in each session. The number of Spokesmen involved has varied over the period, and the sessions have varied in length. To obtain a figure which is comparable with figures in other sessions, therefore, it is necessary to produce a figure which represents the number of references per Spokesman per day.

TABLE 28

Level of Activity in Main Areas compared with Other Areas

Session	Number of References per Spokesman per Day		
	A Total	B Main Area	C Other Area
1947–8	0·88	0·35	0·53
1950–1	0·84	0·38	0·46
1952–3	1·09*	0·61*	0·48*
1956–7	0·82* (0·70)*	0·52* (0·43)*	0·30* (0·27)*
1961–2	0·72* (0·77)*	0·44* (0·47)*	0·38* (0·30)*
1965–6	0·61 (0·64)	0·52 (0·45)	0·09 (0·19)
1967–8	0·67 (0·64)	0·53 (0·50)	0·14 (0·14)

The main figures relate to the Shadow Cabinet, and the figures in brackets relate to the front-bench team as a whole (that is, the Shadow Cabinet plus the other Spokesmen).
* Indicates figures for Labour Oppositions: all other figures relate to Conservative Oppositions.

This is done by dividing the number of references for the Shadow Cabinet, and for the team as a whole, by the number of days in the session, and again by the number of Spokesmen involved. Even this method will provide only a rough guide: Parliamentary days are not of uniform length, as late sittings occur more frequently in some sessions than in others. Nevertheless, this method does permit some broad comparisons to be made over a number of sessions, as is done in Table 28.[1]

[1] In this, however, it is not possible to compare the pre-1945 sessions with those since 1945, because in the Hansard Index the degree of detail recorded and the method of presentation is different after 1945 from what it was before 1945. 100 references in the 1926 Index, for example, do not reflect the same level of activity as 100 references in the 1956–7 Index. This prevents a comparison of the level of activity before and after 1945, although it does not prevent a comparison of the degree of specialisation, as 60 references on one topic out of a total of 100 references produces an Index of Specialisation of 60 per cent, before and after 1945 alike.

Column A in Table 28 shows the overall number of references per Spokesman per day in the sessions indicated. It reveals a clear decline in the overall level of activity of Shadow Cabinet members in the post-war period, with the three figures before 1955 all being higher than the four figures since then. This is

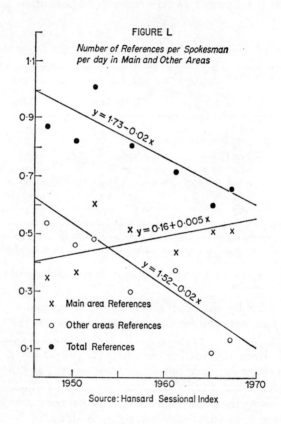

FIGURE L

Number of References per Spokesman per day in Main and Other Areas

Source: Hansard Sessional Index

reflected also in the figures for the team as a whole since 1955, with the two Conservative figures being lower than the two Labour figures. In two of the post-1955 sessions (1956–7 and 1967–8) the Shadow Cabinet was more active than the team as a whole, and in the other two sessions the reverse was the case. Thus, while the trend in the Index of Specialisation Tables is towards greater *specialisation*, the clear trend revealed in Column A of Table 28 is towards a decline in the *level of activity* among the Spokesmen.

In Columns B and C, the overall level of activity figure is broken down into separate figures for the Spokesmen's main area of activity and for the other areas. In Column B (the 'main area of activity' column), there is little difference between the figures since 1951, so that in this period Opposition front benchers (Labour and Conservative) have maintained roughly the same level of activity in their main area of interest. In the two sessions *before* 1951, however, the Conservative leaders were less active in their main area of activity than has been the case *since* 1951. In Column C, which shows the level of activity in areas other than the Spokesmen's main area, the figures show a fairly steady fall from one session to another, and it is this which underlies the overall decline in the level of activity. The trends for the Shadow Cabinet in the three columns of Table 28 are indicated in Figure L.

Over the period since 1951, then, the Opposition leaders have spent only a little more time on their main area of interest, but they have gradually spent less of their time on their other areas of interest. Thus it is the second of the three possibilities referred to at the beginning of this section that has led to the increased specialisation over the period: greater specialisation has resulted from a clear decline in Spokesmen's fringe activities, rather than from any marked increase in activity in their main subject. In this there is almost certainly a connection with the other aspects of the Spokesman's job, which were discussed in Chapter 8. In interview, many Spokesmen pointed out that their duties involved work in committee, or away from the House, and that the more seriously they took these duties, the less time they had to devote to their fringe interests on the floor of the House. A lot of Conservative Spokesmen in particular attributed the extent of their specialisation to a lack of time for other interests. Many pointed out that the business of achieving a respectable income in opposition could be a very time-consuming business, while many of the younger Conservative Spokesmen claimed that when they were not involved with work in the House on their assigned subject, their time was taken up, particularly in the 1966–70 Parliament, with the work of the policy committees. It is this work load outside

F.B.O.—M

Parliament that has contributed heavily to the decline in activity in Spokesmen's fringe areas in Parliament, which in its turn has produced the increase in the Index of Specialisation over the period.

Within each session is there necessarily a simple relationship between the most active Spokesmen being the least specialised, and the least active being the most specialised? At the extreme, someone who makes only one contribution in a session will inevitably have an Index of Specialisation of 100 per cent. At the other extreme, someone who contributed on each day of the session would be bound to have a very low Index of Specialisation, as in the course of a session the Parliamentary timetable ranges over all departmental areas. These extremes apart, however, there is no automatic link between a low level of activity and a high degree of specialisation, or between a high level of activity and low specialisation. Even four contributions in a session would produce an Index of Specialisation of only 25 per cent if each contribution was in a different subject area. Equally, it is possible for a Spokesman to achieve a high level of activity without moving outside his assigned area, although the precise extent of the opportunities for participation will vary, depending on factors like the size of the team, the length of the session, the nature of the subject, and its topicality.

Thus with the exception of subjects like Sport or Arts and Amenities, which are outside the departmental mainstream, it is possible for an Index of Specialisation of 100 per cent to be based on a very high level of activity, while an Index of Specialisation of 10 per cent could possibly be based on only ten contributions in a session. How does this work out in practice? Is there any difference in the degree of specialisation achieved by Spokesmen of differing activity levels? This can be tested by grouping the Spokesmen in each session according to the extent of their activity. The degree of specialisation can then be compared from one activity level to another, as well as from one session to another. This is done in Table 29. As in Table 28, the level of activity is measured by the number of references recorded per day. The number of Spokesmen in each group in each session is indicated, together with the overall Index of Specialisation for the members of each group. With the Shadow Cabinet, if not with the team as a whole, the

TABLE 29

Index of Specialisation Related to Level of Activity

Session	Activity Groupings (Average Number of References per Day)					Total
	0–0·39	0·40–0·59	0·60–0·79	0·80–0·99	1+	
Shadow Cabinet						
1947–8	30·2 (3)	26·5 (2)	66·4 (1)	78·2 (1)	35·3 (6)	36·4 (13)
1950–1	56·4 (3)	62·3 (1)	54·3 (2)	30·8 (2)	38·8 (3)	41·1 (11)
1952–3	50·0 (2)	36·0 (3)	—	—	56·5 (8)	54·6 (13)
1956–7	50·9 (1)	51·1 (3)	73·0 (4)	28·9 (1)	62·8 (3)	63·4 (12)
1961–2	73·8 (3)	52·1 (2)	59·1 (4)	31·6 (1)	89·2 (3)	58·1 (13)
1965–6	91·0 (7)	84·8 (2)	71·5 (3)	69·7 (2)	81·7 (2)	83·8 (16)
1967–8	93·4 (2)	79·3 (5)	85·9 (3)	66·2 (4)	88·2 (1)	78·9 (15)
Team as a whole						
1956–7	68·4 (8)	56·1 (8)	62·4 (8)	41·5 (4)	62·1 (7)	59·8 (35)
1961–2	59·2 (11)	62·3 (6)	66·9 (7)	42·6 (4)	48·3 (11)	60·0 (39)
1965–6	72·6 (19)	71·8 (10)	70·1 (9)	62·3 (10)	60·6 (10)	67·4 (58)
1967–8	88·4 (6)	76·6 (11)	77·6 (4)	71·2 (4)	76·5 (3)	77·8 (28)

The figures in brackets indicate the number of Spokesmen in each activity group.

number of Spokesmen involved in each category is small, so that a 'freak' performance by one Spokesman can disrupt an otherwise clear pattern. Nevertheless, clear trends can be detected in the figures in Table 29. In the first place, the overall decline in the level of activity over the 1945–70 period, that was noted in Table 28, is reflected also in Table 29 in that in the first three sessions most Spokesmen fall into the two most active categories, whereas in the more recent sessions most of them fall into the less active categories. The main feature of Table 29, however, is that the Index of Specialisation figures show greater and more consistent changes in the vertical columns (which measure the time scale) than in the horizontal columns (which measure the activity level). Within each of the activity groups, the Index of Specialisation tends to increase from one session to another, with the highest figures being found, for the most part, in the two most recent sessions.

Thus the pattern of increased specialisation through time that is found in the Shadow Cabinet as a whole, is found also in *each* of the activity categories. Within each session there are some variations from one activity group to another, but these are not consistent, and the highest specialisation figures are not necessarily found in the least active categories. Certainly, in some sessions, and most clearly in the 1965–6 session, the Index of Specialisation tends to fall slightly as the level of activity rises, and in the 1965–6 and 1967–8 sessions, for the Shadow Cabinet and for the team as a whole, the highest figures are found in the least active group. In most cases, however, the difference between the most and least active groups is slight, and in the 1965–6 and 1967–8 sessions in particular, specialisation is high regardless of the level of activity. Where exceptionally high and exceptionally low figures do occur, as with the contrasting figures of 78 per cent and 26 per cent in 1947–8, and 73 per cent and 28 per cent in 1956–7, it is certainly not simply a case of a low level of activity producing a high Index of Specialisation, or a high level of activity producing a low Index of Specialisation. Thus Table 29 confirms the overall decline in the level of activity, but shows that specialisation is not merely a product of a low level of activity, and that specialisation has increased through time at each level of activity.

Individual Spokesmen and their Specialisations

The implications of the general conclusions of the preceding sections need to be considered in detail. Before doing this, however, it will be profitable to examine some related questions. So far, attention has been focused on the Shadow Cabinet and the team as a whole as collective units, but aspects of the behaviour of individual Spokesmen also need to be considered. To what extent is a Spokesman's degree of specialisation determined by the nature of the topic to which he is assigned, on the basis that some subjects provide more opportunities for specialisation than do others? How quickly do backbenchers who join the team achieve a high level of specialisation? Does a newly appointed Spokesman achieve a high level of specialisation even in his first year on the front bench, or does specialisation in a topic perhaps pre-date appointment as Spokesman for that subject? Similarly, does a Spokesman who is moved to a new post immediately change his specialisation, or does specialisation precede rather than follow from such a change of duty? In these matters are there any differences between the two parties, or between the Shadow Cabinet members and the other Spokesmen, or between questions and debates? Data on these questions are presented in Tables 30 to 37.

To what extent is a Spokesman's degree of specialisation governed by the nature of topic to which he is assigned? It was noted in Table 27 that for the majority of Spokesmen their assigned duty was also their main area of activity. Some subjects, however, like foreign affairs or economic affairs, are allocated more time on the floor of the House than are subjects like Sport or Public Building and Works. In any given session a Foreign Affairs or Treasury or Defence Spokesman has more opportunity to specialise than has a Spokesman for Public Building and Works, or for Sport, or Welsh affairs. Within this, however, the amount of Parliamentary time devoted to a particular department will vary to some extent from one year to another, depending on factors such as the topicality of the subject, the vulnerability of the Minister, and the extent and nature of the legislation that is introduced in the subject area. It was noticeable in Table 23 that there were some fluctuations in the degree of specialisation among the individual Labour Spokesmen in different sessions of the 1955–64 period. It may be that these fluctuations were caused to some extent by changes from one session to another in the Spokesmen's assigned duties. If specialisation does vary to some extent from subject to subject,

TABLE 30

Index of Specialisation by Subject Area

Subject Area	1956–7*	1961–2*	1965–6	1967–8
External Affairs				
Foreign Affairs	76·8	52·5	58·0	93·6
Colonies/Comm./Overseas Development	53·8	67·4	51·1	66·2
Defence/Aviation/ Disarmament	73·5	45·4	68·1	72·6
	70·0	52·3	62·4	74·2
Home Affairs				
Home Office/Welsh Affairs	50·0	76·9	40·3	68·8
Agriculture	55·2	60·9	65·5	95·7
Education/Science	22·7	41·8	81·6	82·9
Soc. Services/Health/Pensions	33·6	38·5	56·5	77·1
Housing/Local Govt./Public Building & Works	61·1	41·9	69·7	57·1
	47·2	51·2	62·5	69·6
Finance and Industry				
Treasury/Trade	67·9	61·7	67·1	85·3
Transport/Technology	65·2	59·2	67·6	85·2
Labour	39·8	44·1	27·2	77·8
Power	36·8	46·3	90·3	83·7
	58·0	57·9	56·7	84·2
Miscellaneous				
Law	32·3	100·0	51·7	100·0
Post Office	28·0	23·8	54·9	90·3
Scotland	58·7	69·7	67·4	75·0
Others	—	35·6	31·4	82·6
	44·8	45·8	58·7	84·6
Median	53·8	52·5	58·0	82·9
Team as a whole	59·8	60·0	67·4	77·8

* Indicates sessions when Labour was in opposition: other sessions the Conservatives were in opposition.

this will not affect the overall level of specialisation among the Shadow Cabinet or the team as a whole, as all subject areas are represented in the team in any one session. It might, however, affect an individual Spokesman's level of specialisation if he is moved from Foreign Affairs to Public Building and Works, or from Sport to Defence.

In Table 30 an Index of Specialisation for each of four broad policy areas (External Affairs, Home Affairs, Finance and Industry, and Miscellaneous topics) is shown for each of the four post-1955 sessions. For most subject areas more than one Spokesman was involved, so that the figure shown is a composite one for the several Spokesmen in each case.[1] The figures show that some subjects tend to have a generally higher level of specialisation than do others. All but one of the External Affairs figures, for example, are above 50 per cent, and all of the Treasury, Trade, Transport, and Technology figures are in the region of 60 per cent or above. The Scottish Affairs and Agriculture figures are also in excess of 50 per cent in each session. On the other hand, Education, Social Services, Labour, Post Office and Power all have figures below 50 per cent for the two Labour sessions, although in the two Conservative sessions the figures are much higher. All the figures in the two Conservative sessions, in fact, are uniformly high, regardless of subject, whereas in the two Labour sessions there are much greater variations from one subject to another. Nevertheless, even allowing for the tendency for some subjects to have a higher Index of Specialisation than others, the main feature of Table 30 is the extent to which the level of specialisation in any subject area varies from one session to another. This suggests that for the most part the level of specialisation is determined as much by the attitude of the individual Spokesman concerned as by the nature of the subject.

How quickly do backbenchers who are given front-bench duties adapt to the role of Spokesmen? Does specialisation in an assigned area precede or follow from an appointment in that area, and does a newly appointed Spokesman achieve a high level of specialisation even in his first year on the front bench? It was noted

[1] This figure was calculated by the same method used in earlier Tables to achieve a composite figure for the Shadow Cabinet and team as a whole: see Appendix E.

in Chapter 5 that Edward Heath was more inclined to appoint 'experts' as Spokesmen than were the Labour Leaders of the Opposition of the 1955–64 period. Table 16 in Chapter 5 indicates that only about a third of the backbench recruits to the Labour team in the 1955–64 period were specialists (as measured by their Parliamentary activity prior to their appointment) in the topic to which they were assigned, whereas for the Conservatives in the 1964–70 period the proportion was over half. Table 31 incorporates Table 16, and extends the analysis

TABLE 31

Specialisation in Assigned Area Before and After Appointment as Spokesman

| Main Area of Activity | Labour 1955–64 | | | | Conservatives 1964–70 | | | |
| | Before Appointment as Spokesman[a] | | After Appointment as Spokesman[b] | | Before Appointment as Spokesman[a] | | After Appointment as Spokesman[b] | |
	Ques.	Debs.	Ques.	Debs.	Ques.	Debs.	Ques.	Debs.
Assigned Duty	6	8	21	21	20	17	32	30
Other Areas	22	20	7	7	13	16	1	3
Total	28	28	28	28	33	33	33	33

[a] That is, in the last session as a backbencher.

[b] That is, in the first session as a Spokesman. For those who became Spokesmen in the middle of a session, their performance is examined in that session before and after the appointment.

by examining the extent to which, in their first session as Spokesmen, the new recruits to the team in the 1955–64 and 1964–70 periods specialised in their assigned subjects. Of the Labour recruits, a quarter continued to concentrate on some topic other than their assigned duty in their first session as Spokesmen. Of the Conservative recruits, however, virtually all immediately made their assigned topic their main area of activity. Thus more Conservative than Labour backbenchers concentrated on their future topic before appointment, and more Labour than Conservative Spokesmen continued to concentrate on areas other than their assigned duty after their appointment.

In Tables 32 and 33, two sessions are looked at in more

detail (1961–2 for Labour, and 1967–8 for the Conservatives), and the performance before and after appointment is examined of all those backbenchers who became Spokesmen at the beginning of these sessions. Six backbenchers became Labour Spokesmen for the first time at the beginning of the 1961–2 session. Table 32 shows the proportion of their questioning and debating time that they devoted to their assigned topic in the 1961–2 session (their first session as Spokesmen), and also in the 1960–1 session (when they were still backbenchers).

TABLE 32

Index of Specialisation: Labour Backbenchers Appointed as Spokesmen in 1961–2 Session

Spokesman	Topic	1960–1[a]		1961–2[b]	
		Ques. %	Debs. %	Ques. %	Debs. %
Cronin	Aviation	9·7	0	56·5	63·1
Darling	Trade/Agriculture	53·6	36·1	68·2	65·2
Fletcher	Home Affairs	30·4	44·2	39·3	74·6
Hoy	Scotland	82·3	65·2	78·6	15·0
Ross	Pensions	30·8	12·4	27·3	7·7
Willis	Admiralty	24·1	12·9	25·9	9·5

[a] That is, last session as a backbencher.
[b] That is, first session as a Spokesman.

Different patterns of behaviour emerge for the different Spokesmen. For John Cronin, appointment as Aviation Spokesman produced at once a marked increase in specialisation in his assigned duty. For George Darling and Eric Fletcher, appointment as Spokesmen also produced something of an increase in the proportion of their time devoted to their assigned duty, but they devoted a fairly large proportion of their time to that topic even before they were appointed as Spokesmen. James Hoy, on the other hand spent most of his time on Scottish affairs while still a backbencher, and appointment as Scottish Spokesman did not change markedly his level of specialisation. Similarly, but perhaps surprisingly, for William Ross and George Willis appointment as Spokesmen did not change the proportion of their time spent on their assigned duty, in that they continued to spend more time on other subjects than on their assigned topic.

A rather clearer pattern emerges in Table 33, which lists the seven backbench MPs who became Conservative Spokesmen at the beginning of the 1967–8 session. In all the cases but one, appointment as Spokesman meant that at least half of their time, and in most cases at least three-quarters of their time, was devoted to the assigned duty in both debates and questions.

TABLE 33

Index of Specialisation: Conservative Backbenchers Appointed as Spokesmen in 1967–8

| Spokesman | Topic | 1966–7[a] | | 1967–8[b] | |
		Ques. %	Debs. %	Ques. %	Debs. %
Braine	Colonies/Comm.	1·3	0·6	86·9	91·7
Channon	Arts/Amenities	0·6	26·4	75·7	90·5
Higgins	Trade	47·4	84·2	74·0	83·3
Jenkin	Treasury	18·4	54·2	83·7	87·6
Macmillan	Health	66·1	33·9	65·2	93·3
Morrison	Sport	1·0	0	81·5	40·0
Page	Housing/Land	85·0	45·9	88·6	59·5

[a] That is, last session as a backbencher.
[b] That is, first session as a Spokesman.

The one exception is Charles Morrison, who devoted more than 80 per cent of his questioning activity to his assigned topic (Sport), but only 40 per cent of his debating activity. His debating activity was restricted to only two speeches on Sport, which, of course, is only rarely the subject of debate. With four of the seven (Terence Higgins, Patrick Jenkin, Maurice Macmillan, and Graham Page) promotion to the front bench was 'anticipated' by a fairly high level of activity in the assigned area in the session preceding the appointment. As was discussed in Chapter 5 this does not mean that these backbenchers knew they were to be appointed as Spokesmen for particular subjects, and as a consequence devoted most of their time to those subjects in preparation for their future role (although backbenchers may sometimes learn that they are in line for a particular post). The more likely explanation is that in these four cases it was the policy of Edward Heath to select as Spokesmen those who had already exhibited their expertise in the subject. In the other three cases, however, there was a major change in behaviour from one session to the next. Each spent only a negligible proportion of his activity on his future topic in 1966–7, but spent more than three-quarters of his time on his topic once he became Spokesman (although Morrison's exception to this has been noted). Thus in some of the individual cases shown in Tables 32 and 33, specialisation in a topic preceded appointment as Spokesman for that topic, but when it did not, the appointment was usually followed by 'instant specialisation' in the assigned topic. This pattern, however, was much more pronounced for Conservative than for Labour Spokesmen.

How quickly does specialisation emerge when a Spokesman is involved in a change of duty? Does allocation to a new responsibility produce an immediate change in specialisation, or does specialisation in a topic perhaps precede rather than follow from appointment as a Spokesman for that topic? Table 34 summarises the performance of those Spokesmen who were involved in a straight switch of duties in the 1955–64 and 1964–70 periods.[1] It shows how many Spokesmen concentrated on their future duty in the session before the change was made, how many concentrated on their old duty in the session after the change was made, and how many concentrated on their current duty in each case. There were forty-two Labour Spokesmen involved in such changes in the 1955–64 period, and thirty-two Conservatives in the 1964–70 period. In both periods the majority of the Spokesmen concentrated on their current topic. In other words, they did not anticipate a change by concentrating on their future topic, and after the change they dropped the old topic and applied themselves at once to their new duty. Some did not conform to this pattern, however, especially among the Labour Spokesmen. *Before* the change,

[1] This does not include changes from a post as Spokesman to one of the party offices (whip, leader, etc.), or vice versa. Changes that merely involved the addition of new duties to existing duties are also excluded.

some Labour Spokesmen concentrated on their future topic, but none of the Conservatives did this. *After* the change, some Labour Spokesmen continued to specialise in their old topic, but only one of the Conservatives did this, and then only in debates and not in questions.

In Tables 35, 36, and 37, this question is looked at in more detail. In Table 35 are listed the thirteen Labour Spokesmen who were involved in a straight switch of duties at the beginning or the end of the 1961–2 session. It shows the proportion of

TABLE 34

Specialisation in Assigned Area, Before and After Change of Duty

Main Area of Activity	Labour 1955–64				Conservatives 1964–70			
	Before Change of Duty[a]		After Change of Duty[b]		Before Change of Duty[a]		After Change of Duty[b]	
	Ques.	Debs.	Ques.	Debs.	Ques.	Debs.	Ques.	Debs.
Current Post	34	32	36	33	32	28	30	28
Future Post	3	4			0	0		
Past Post			3	7			0	1
Other	5	6	3	2	0	4	2	3
Total	42	42	42	42	32	32	32	32

[a] That is, in the last session for the old duty.

[b] That is, in the first session for the new duty. For those who changed duty in the middle of a session, their performance is examined in that session, before and after the change of duty.

questioning and debating time devoted to their old and new topic, before and after the change of duty. As in Table 32, different patterns emerge for different Spokesmen. Harold Wilson was Treasury Spokesman in the 1960–61 session, and two-thirds of his questioning time and three-quarters of his debating time were devoted to Treasury matters: none of his time was given to Foreign Affairs. At the beginning of the 1961–2 session, however, he ceased to be Treasury Spokesman and was appointed Foreign Affairs Spokesman, and although he did not abandon Treasury affairs entirely, he devoted more than half of his time to his new topic. This pattern emerges even more clearly with Ray Gunter and Denis Healey, while George Brown, James Callaghan, Fred Lee, and John Strachey also achieved a clear change-round in their interests with their new appointment. Reginald Paget and Fred Peart, on the

TABLE 35

Index of Specialisation: Labour Spokesmen involved in a Change of Duty at Beginning or End of 1961–2 Session

Spokesman	Topic	1960–1 Ques. %	1960–1 Debs. %	1961–2 Ques. %	1961–2 Debs. %	1962–3 Ques. %	1962–3 Debs. %
Brown	Defence	46·4*	22·3*	0	23·5		
	Home	14·3	0	52·4*	27·8*		
Callaghan	Colonies	42·3*	26·0*	8·9	2·6		
	Treasury	2·1	18·5	17·9*	55·5*		
Fraser	Scotland	100·0*	75·5*	37·5	36·8		
	Power	0	0	25·0*	48·3*		
Gunter	Power	75·0*	85·7*	0	23·1		
	Labour	0	0	100·0*	65·4*		
Healey	Foreign	84·4*	84·0*	25·0	12·5		
	Colonies/ Comm.	0	0	75·0*	87·5*		
Lee	Labour	65·0*	30·8*	13·3	0		
	Aviation	10·0	0	66·7*	51·7*		
Paget	Admiralty	47·2*	20·7*	5·3	0		
	War	20·7	42·5	81·6*	87·9*		
Peart	Science	86·7*	20·0*	6·7	0		
	Agriculture	0	58·7	86·7*	92·7*		
Strachey	Aviation	65·2*	0*	15·0	2·3		
	Colonies/ Comm.	8·7	0	55·0*	58·1*		
Walker	Home	80·0*	57·7*	0	53·3		
	Defence	0	5·6	81·3*	33·3*		
Wilson	Treasury	66·7*	76·2*	17·2	8·3		
	Foreign	0	0	58·6*	55·0*		
Miss Herbison	Scotland			88·6*	55·8*	68·6	44·3
	Pensions			0	0	21·4*	37·1*
Ross	Pensions			27·3*	7·7*	10·1	4·6
	Scotland			52·3	31·9	72·1*	52·8*

* Indicates a Spokesman's current duty.

other hand, 'anticipated' their change of duty to some extent, in that in the 1960–1 session they spent considerably more debating time, although not more questioning time, on their future topic than on their current topic.

A different pattern emerges for William Ross and Margaret

TABLE 36

Index of Specialisation: Conservative Spokesmen involved in a Change of Duty at Beginning or End of 1967–8 Session

Spokesman	Topic	1966–7		1967–8		1968–9	
		Ques. %	Debs. %	Ques. %	Debs. %	Ques. %	Debs. %
Lord Balniel	Foreign	77·8*	93·5*	0	0		
	Social Services	5·9	0	79·8*	79·0*		
Carr	Aviation	68·4*	54·9*	6·1	0		
	Labour	19·7	35·4	82·9*	70·7*		
Corfield	Power/ Trade	63·7*	85·1*	3·3	5·1		
	Aviation	6·9	0	89·1*	82·0*		
Wood	Colonies/ Comm.	96·9*	79·5*	0	16·7		
	Foreign	0	7·7	68·7*	66·7*		
Mrs Thatcher	Treasury	79·3*	93·3*	0	13·0		
	Power	0	0·8	90·0*	78·3*	0	0
	Transport			0	0	100·0*	100·0*
Rippon	Housing/ Land			86·5*	45·4*	6·0	10·0
	Defence			0	0	82·0*	83·3*
Walker	Transport			82·5*	95·0*	13·9	0
	Housing/ Land			2·5	3·9	86·0*	81·4*

* Indicates a Spokesman's current duty.

Herbison. At the end of the 1961–2 session they exchanged posts (Pensions and Scotland), but in each session they both spent more time on Scottish affairs than on Pensions, regardless of their officially assigned duty. Similarly, Tom Fraser changed from Scottish affairs to Power at the beginning of the 1961–2 session, but continued to spend more than a third of his time on Scottish affairs. This, combined with the patterns for Hoy, Ross, and Willis in Table 32, suggests that regardless of their officially assigned topic, Scottish MPs much more so than English and Welsh MPs, spend much or most of their time on their own regional affairs.

A much more clear-cut pattern emerges in Table 36, which lists the seven Conservative Spokesmen who were involved in a straight switch of duties at the beginning or end of the 1967–8 session. Like Table 35, it shows the proportion of questioning

TABLE 37

Index of Specialisation: Mrs Thatcher

Session	Assigned Topic[a]	Oral Questions %	Written Questions %	Debates %	Total %
1964–5	Pensions	82·3	47·6	73·3	67·6
1965–6	Housing/Land	100·0	72·7	100·0	88·9
1966–7	Treasury	91·7	20·0	93·3	90·6
1967–8	Power	93·3	80·0	78·3	83·9
1968–9	Transport	100·0	—[b]	100·0	100·0
1969–70	Education	100·0	—[b]	96·7	97·9

[a] In each session her assigned topic was also her main area of activity.

[b] In the 1968–9 and 1969–70 sessions she asked no written questions at all.

and debating time devoted to the old and new topics in the two sessions. In each case, the Spokesmen spent at least half of their time, and in most cases more than three-quarters of their time, on their assigned topic, achieving a complete change of emphasis with the change of duty. Lord Balniel, for example, as Foreign Affairs Spokesman in 1966–7, spent almost all of his time on Foreign Affairs. He did not speak in any Social Service debates, and asked only 5 per cent of his questions in this area. In 1967–8, however, when he changed to Social Services, he spent well over three-quarters of his time on his new topic, and did not speak or question at all in Foreign Affairs.

The pattern is much the same for the other six Spokesmen, including Mrs Margaret Thatcher, who provides the most dramatic example of 'instant specialisation' in the 1964–70 period. She served as a Spokesman throughout the two Parliaments, and was involved in a change of duty at the beginning of each session. She thus had six different duties in six years, and of all the Conservative Spokesmen she gained the most varied experience in the period of Opposition. Table 37 shows Mrs Thatcher's Index of Specialisation for each session. It shows that with each change of duty she achieved an immediate change of specialisation, dropping at once her old duty, and concentrating on her new assignment. In each of the six sessions her current duty was her main area of activity, and her overall Index of Specialisation, in all but the 1964–5 session, was above 80 per cent. Thus, despite being involved in six changes of duty, Mrs Thatcher achieved immediate and almost complete specialisation throughout the six-year period.

Patterns of Behaviour

Mrs Thatcher's devotion to her assigned duties is fairly typical of the Parliamentary behaviour of Conservative Spokesmen in the 1964–70 period, and it emphasises the remarkable degree of specialisation achieved by Opposition Spokesmen in recent years. Of course, even the very high Index of Specialisation for Mrs Thatcher and other Conservative Spokesmen in that period does not quite reach the level of specialisation achieved by Ministers. Unlike most Ministers, few Spokesmen have an Index of Specialisation of 100 per cent, and for the Spokesmen who do, the figure is generally associated with an exceptionally low level of activity. Nevertheless, the general level of specialisation among Spokesmen in the 1951–70 period, and particularly in the 1964–70 period, is still very high. More particularly, the contrast with the years before 1951 is very marked, indicating a major change over the years in the way that Opposition leaders apportion their time on the floor of the House. This contrast with earlier Parliaments is even more dramatic in view of the fact that today there exists a large frontbench 'team', with a number of Spokesmen covering each subject. Before 1955 a former Minister might take a special interest in his old department, but in doing so he would not have the assistance of any official 'assistants'. Today, however, the senior Spokesman for each subject has one or two assistant

Spokesmen who share in the tasks of opposition. The greater the number of Spokesmen involved, the less the work load of each one, and the less the need or the opportunity to specialise.[1] In this respect, some Labour MPs in interview argued that the team formed in 1970 was too big, and that with most subjects there were too many assistant Spokesmen 'hanging about, waiting for the chance to contribute something on their assigned subject'. Also, it is remarkable that the level of specialisation for oral questions has increased despite the changes that have taken place over the years in the procedure of Question Time.[2] In the earlier years of this century there were few restrictions on the way Question Time was organised, and it was possible for an MP to question a particular Minister on almost any day. Today, however, Ministers appear in Question Time on a strict rota, and some Ministers appear only three or four times in a session. Thus an Education Spokesman who wishes to concentrate his oral questioning activity upon the Ministry of Education has only a limited number of occasions during the session when he can do so, so that his ability to specialise is limited. Specialisation has *increased*, therefore, despite certain organisational factors which might be expected to *reduce* an MP's ability to concentrate his activities in one particular area.

What has caused the increased specialisation and what are its consequences? In the preceding sections it was noted that the Shadow Cabinet was invariably more specialised in all three forms of activity than was the team as a whole, and also that the Conservatives were more specialised than Labour in any given period. In interview a number of Spokesmen (junior and senior, Labour and Conservative) argued that as the principal Spokesman was more likely to be in the public eye than were his assistants, there was more pressure on him to exhibit 'Ministerial' patterns of behaviour, including a high level of specialisation in his assigned area. On the other hand, some other Spokesmen argued that the highest level of specialisation was most likely from comparatively junior MPs who were filling their first posts as assistant Spokesmen, and were anxious to

---

[1] See *The Guardian*, 28 November 1970, for the problem in this respect caused by the size of the Labour team in 1970.

[2] See Chester and Bowring, *Questions in Parliament*, for details of these changes. See also P. Howarth, *Questions in the House*, London 1956.

establish their command over their subject. It might be, of course, that the differences between junior and senior Spokesmen, and between Labour and Conservative Spokesmen, are related to the proportion of former Ministers in an Opposition team. Because Labour's Parliamentary Committee is elected, there is a tendency for it to contain more MPs without Ministerial experience than is the case with the appointed Conservative Shadow Cabinet. Conservative Shadow Cabinets have been based largely on the composition of the 'late Cabinet', and since 1915 the Conservatives have not been in opposition for long enough periods for many back benchers to work their way on to the Shadow Cabinet, although Heath's attempts to rejuvenate his team were discussed in Chapter 5.

It is questionable, however, in what way prior experience as a Minister will affect performance on the Opposition front bench. On the one hand it might be that former Ministers might be inclined to specialise to an almost Ministerial extent, having acquired the habit of single-mindedness whilst a Minister. On the other hand, Cabinet Ministers, theoretically at least, are required to rise above their own immediate departmental affairs and concern themselves with all aspects of Government policy. Also, the longer serving Ministers, whether in the Cabinet or not, will normally have had experience in various posts, and thus will have acquired varied knowledge of the departments of state. In the nineteen-fifties and 'sixties there was a tendency for Ministerial re-shuffles to occur more frequently than in the past,[1] with Ministers consequently spending less time in one post, and thus being less likely to become single-minded, than used to be the case (although Edward Heath seems to have reduced the number of Ministerial re-shuffles). Again, a general factor contributing towards specialisation in opposition is that, unlike a Minister, a Spokesman has no staff to feed him advice and information, and has to devote a lot of time to doing research for himself. In this respect, however, an ex-Minister, with the background knowledge acquired through years in government, will have an advantage over his junior colleagues, and will have more time to roam beyond his assigned area. Moreover, if a controversial issue arises, someone with past Ministerial experience in that

[1] See above, p. 171, footnote 1.

area may be tempted to give the House the benefit of his experience, even if he is Spokesman for another subject. Iain Macleod, for example, spent eight years in the Cabinet in the 1951–64 period, and got experience of the Ministry of Health, the Ministry of Labour, and the Colonial Office. Despite the

TABLE 38

Index of Specialisation: Members of the Shadow Cabinet without any Ministerial Experience Compared with Shadow Cabinet and Team as a Whole

Session[a]	All Members of the Shadow Cabinet		Members of the Shadow Cabinet without Ministerial Experience	
	N	Index of Specialisation	N	Index of Specialisation
1912	9	57·2	1	48·8
1923	13	31·8*	12	31·9*
1926	13	40·9*	5	31·0*
1929–30	16	50·1	1	34·8
1932–3	8	26·3*	4	25·9*
1937–8	10	40·2*	3	45·3*
1956–7	13 (35)	63·4* (59·8)*	2 (2)	66·2* (66·2)*
1961–2	13 (39)	58·1* (60·0)*	4 (16)	60·4* (53·3)*
1965–6	— (58)	— (67·4)	— (23)	— (59·6)
1967–8	13 (20)	78·8 (77·8)	2 (7)	84·7 (79·1)

a Excluded are those sessions when all the members of the Shadow Cabinet were former Ministers.

The main figures relate to the Shadow Cabinet, and the figures in brackets relate to the front-bench team as a whole (that is, the members of the Shadow Cabinet, plus the other Spokesmen).

* Indicates the figures for Labour Oppositions: other figures relate to Conservative Oppositions.

depth and breadth of knowledge he must have acquired, however, he still devoted 80 per cent or more of his Parliamentary time to his assigned topic of Treasury affairs in the 1966–70 Parliament. Similarly, at various times in the 1951–64 period, Quintin Hogg had Ministerial responsibility for Education and Science, the Admiralty, Sport and North-East affairs, but he nevertheless had a very high Index of Specialisation for most of the 1964–70 period.

It is dangerous, of course, to draw too many conclusions from these two isolated examples. In Table 38 an attempt is made to present a more general picture by comparing the Index of Specialisation of Spokesmen with Ministerial experience with those without. In seven of the sessions shown in Table 22, the Shadow Cabinet was composed entirely of former Ministers, and these sessions have been excluded from Table 38.[1] In the other nine sessions, when there was a mixture of those with and those without Ministerial experience, no clear pattern emerges. In two of the three Conservative sessions (1912 and 1929–30), the former Ministers were more specialised than the others, but in 1967–8 they were less specialised. In three of the six Labour sessions (1926, 1932–3 and 1961–2), ex-Ministers were more specialised than the others, but in the other three sessions they were not. In 1923 J. R. Clynes was the only former Minister in the Parliamentary Committee, and his Index of Specialisation was lower than that of the Shadow Cabinet. In the four sessions since 1955, when it has been possible to look at the team as a whole as well as at the Shadow Cabinet, the figures are equally inconclusive. In two of the sessions, the Index of Specialisation for the ex-Ministers was higher than for the others, and in the other two it was lower. Thus there is no regular pattern, and apart from the 1932–3 session, the balance between those Spokesmen with and those without Ministerial experience is too uneven to make more detailed comparisons profitable.

In itself, therefore, this is not sufficient to explain the greater degree of specialisation among Conservative than among Labour Shadow Cabinets. An alternative explanation might be that the greater level of Conservative specialisation merely reflects the traditional assumption that there tend to be more 'part time' MPs in Conservative than in Labour ranks. It may be, in other words, that Conservative Spokesmen, with many interests outside Parliament, have less time and inclination to participate in Parliamentary business, and thus attend only in order to perform required duties. Certainly, in interview, some Conservative Spokesmen argued that far from regarding their subject area as their own private responsibility, they would welcome any assistance, front-bench or backbench, that would

[1] That is, 1952–3 for Labour, and 1908, 1910, 1924, 1947–8, 1950–1, and 1965–6 for the Conservatives.

lighten their own work load. At the same time, some claimed that not all of their colleagues shared this attitude, and that some were unreasonably resentful of 'encroachments' into their areas.

Another possible explanation of Labour's generally lower levels of specialisation might be that Labour MPs have a greater inclination for the role of Opposition than have the Conservatives, perhaps as a result of Labour's greater experience of Opposition, or perhaps merely as a natural consequence of left-wing politics. It may be that Labour Spokesmen are more prepared to participate in debates and questions beyond their own assigned areas, whereas Conservative leaders are less willing to devote time to Parliamentary affairs in opposition, merely because they minimise the significance of Parliamentary Opposition. Again, it may be that Labour MPs tend to be outspoken and somewhat self-indulgent, giving expression to their views regardless of whether the issue is within their assigned area, whereas Conservatives are more willing to defer, and give the floor to whichever colleague has been formally assigned to express the party view. Yet again, the Conservatives have had more experience of office than of opposition in this century, and it may be that when they are in opposition they tend to copy the habits of office, including an almost Ministerial degree of specialisation in debates. In particular, it may be that three consecutive election victories and thirteen years of office between 1951 and 1964, served to reinforce the Conservative view that they were 'the natural ruling party', and that in their brief spells in opposition they should conduct themselves as if they were still in office. Pressures from the party outside Parliament may contribute towards this. Certainly, as discussed in Chapters 8 and 9 the general structure and organisation of the Conservative Opposition team tends to copy Governmental arrangements much more closely than does Labour's, and it may be that this is reflected also in the behaviour of Spokesmen in the House.

None of these factors, however, explain the much higher level of specialisation among Conservative leaders in the 1964–1970 period than among Conservative leaders in the 1945–51 period. It was noted above that the increased specialisation among Labour leaders preceded, rather than followed from, the introduction in 1955 of the system of official Spokesmen. It may be the case, however, that once it was established, the system itself encouraged specialisation even further, so that the greater specialisation in 1964–70 than in 1945–51 may have been produced to some extent by the Conservative acceptance of the system of Spokesmen that Labour introduced. More generally, the increased specialisation may be merely a reflection of the trends of the age, in which emphasis is placed upon the 'specialist' and the 'expert' rather than the 'generalist' or the 'layman'. Certainly, many of the aspects of modern life and politics that were mentioned in Chapter 2 as contributing to the introduction and retention of the system of official Spokesmen, might also be likely to encourage specialisation by the Spokesmen once the system was established. Thus specialisation among Spokesmen may be part of a general trend towards specialisation in various aspects of Parliamentary behaviour, with the increased interest in specialist committees in the Commons in the nineteen-sixties being another facet of this.

Yet again, it may be that the high level of specialisation may be a reflection of the philosophy and style of a particular party-leader. Certainly, it was shown above that for the seven Conservative Spokesmen listed in Table 24, the Index of Specialisation was lower in the one session (1964–5) in which Douglas-Home was leader, than in the other sessions of the 1964–70 period (although, as was discussed above, the low figures for the 1964–5 session perhaps can be explained in other ways).[1] Heath certainly did not issue instructions to his Spokesmen that they had to specialise in their assigned topics at the expense of other subjects, but a leader can nevertheless set the 'style' for his colleagues to follow. In the 1965–70 period the Conservative Party was left in no doubt as to the importance that the leader attached to the merits of 'professionalism', and to the need for a future Government to appear well prepared for office, with evident expertise. General commitments to the principle of specialisation (Parliamentary or otherwise) will vary from one personality to another, and a party leader is always tempted to select Spokesmen who share his own philosophy. Thus in interview a number of Conservative MPs suggested that when selecting his team Edward Heath favoured MPs who would be

[1] See above, p. 324.

likely to confine their activities to the subject area of their assigned duty, and a major problem with Enoch Powell was that he did not fit readily into this pattern of behaviour.[1] To a considerable extent Heath's style of 'professionalism' implies an emphasis on specialisation, the delegation of tasks to the expert, and the rejection of the concept of the 'amateur layman': thus it is often Heath's practice as Prime Minister in Question Time to refer a questioner to a more 'appropriate' Minister for a fuller answer. This is perhaps part of a general tendency for him to apply rigidly the principle of a clear-cut division of responsibilities within his team, whether as Prime Minister or as Leader of the Opposition. This general attitude to the role of members of a team clearly contrasts with Sir Winston Churchill's philosophy for opposition in the 1945–51 period, which rejected the need for Opposition leaders to specialise. Churchill's theme, as Harold Macmillan has pointed out, was to 'let them wander free'.[2] Under Heath, however, Conservative Spokesmen did not 'wander free', but concentrated very firmly on their assigned topics.

Whatever the reason for the increased specialisation, the effect has been to produce a more single-minded group of Opposition leaders. A qualification should be noted here, however. The tables in this chapter merely reflect levels of specialisation in activities on the floor of the House of Commons, and a high level of specialisation in Parliament might be accompanied by activities outside Parliament which are spread over a number of subject areas. Thus in interview many Spokesmen who recognised a need to specialise in one subject in the Commons, argued that they should be free, and regarded themselves as being free, to dabble in other subjects away from the House.[3] Indeed some Spokesmen revealed that when asked by the leader to take on a particular duty they did so only on the understanding that their speeches outside the House at least did not have to be confined to their assigned area. Nevertheless, Spokesmen who made this point still acknowledged

[1] For a comment see Hutchinson, *Edward Heath*, p. 174.
[2] Macmillan, *Tides of Fortune*, p. 44. See above, p. 65. For a comment on Churchill's views, see Hutchinson, *Edward Heath*, p. 172.
[3] For Enoch Powell's commitment to this view see Roth, *Enoch Powell*, p. 316.

that if they were to be making a speech outside the House in another Spokesman's area, they would inform the Spokesman concerned, as a matter of courtesy, and would confirm that the sentiments they were to express were not contrary to recognised party policy. Thus even in their utterances outside the House, Spokesmen recognised the principles of individual and collective responsibility.[1]

In the privacy of Shadow Cabinet meetings, of course, Opposition leaders can 'wander free' over all policy areas, and indeed such a committee can only operate effectively if the members are prepared to take an active interest in policy and organisational matters outside their own immediate areas of responsibility. The more that Shadow Cabinet members concentrate on their assigned areas in their Parliamentary activities, however, the narrower their outlook is likely to become, and the more the Shadow Cabinet will come to operate as a body of twenty or so individuals, each bound up in his own specialisation. The dangers of this happening with the Shadow Cabinet are considerably less than in the case of the Cabinet, as the work load of an Opposition Spokesman is considerably less than that of a departmental Minister. Nevertheless, the same general principle can be seen as applying to both bodies.

In so far as a Spokesman's activities are dominated by his assigned duties, his other activities, including his constituency duties, would seem to have to suffer. While a Minister can have his constituency problems dealt with by his Ministerial colleagues, and thus will not have to raise them in the House, a Spokesman is like backbench MPs in having to use Parliamentary channels as the ultimate means of publicising a constituency problem. Thus the increase in specialisation, accompanied by a decline in the level of activity in debates and questions, can be interpreted as a decline in the amount of time devoted to constituency duties. This, of course, will vary to some extent from subject to subject, and in some instances constituency interests might coincide with a Spokesman's official duties. A Pensions Spokesman can combine his duties as a Spokesman with activity on behalf of any constituents with pensions problems. Similarly, a Spokesman on Power who

[1] See above, Chapter 9 for details of the application of the principle of collective responsibility in opposition.

represents a mining constituency (like Tom Fraser in the 1959–1964 Parliament or Michael Foot in the 1970–1 session) will be able to combine the interests of his constituency with his official Opposition duties. The duties of a Foreign Affairs or Commonwealth Spokesman, on the other hand, are unlikely to coincide with constituency interests. Clearly, however, MPs can pursue constituency affairs away from the floor of the House, and concentration on Commonwealth affairs in debates and questions can be accompanied by assiduous efforts on behalf of constituents through personal contacts with Ministers and civil servants. Some Spokesmen pointed out that faced with an important constituency problem outside their assigned area, they would ask the relevant Spokesman to raise it in the House on their behalf, which he would generally do with a passing reference to the MP and the constituency involved. Also, many Opposition Spokesmen, as senior figures in Parliament, and perhaps as ex-Ministers, will have more contacts with Ministers and civil servants than will most back benchers, and through their familiarity with the Westminster and Whitehall 'corridors of power' they may be more effective than backbenchers in dealing with constituents' problems. Nevertheless, purely in terms of activity on the floor of the House, a Spokesman's increased concentration on official Opposition duties would seem to lead in most cases to a reduction of activity in constituency matters.

Too rigid an application of the principle of specialisation can waste the talent of leading party figures, confining their activities to the one subject area, which in any one session may offer only limited opportunities for Parliamentary activity. Each session tends to be dominated by one or two particular issues, generally determined by the Government's legislative priorities, so that Spokesmen who are not involved with the session's main issues will have a comparatively quiet Parliamentary year. Thus a number of Labour Spokesmen complained that in the 1970–1 session they were prevented from taking a leading part in the Parliamentary fight against the Industrial Relations Bill because this task became the preserve of Barbara Castle, as the senior Spokesman for Employment, and her 'team' of assistant Spokesmen and backbench MPs. Despite the fact that the committee stage of the Industrial

Relations Bill was taken on the floor of the House, half of the Parliamentary Committee failed to contribute even an interjection at any stage during the Bill's slow passage through the Commons, and Barbara Castle's contributions accounted for 89 per cent of the total for Parliamentary Committee members (measured, as with the other calculations in this chapter, by the numbers of references credited to each person in the Hansard Index). In interview, one Labour Spokesman who deplored the general trend towards greater specialisation, contrasted the situation with regard to the Industrial Relations Bill, to that of the party's campaign against the Trade Disputes Bill in 1927, when debating duties were shared among most of the party's leading figures, with all the members of the Parliamentary Committee, and not just a group of official Spokesmen, being active in the fight at one stage or another. To some extent, therefore, the modern principle of 'one Spokesman one job' means that the talents of the senior MPs may not be fully used in any one session.

The reduction by Opposition leaders of their activity outside their main area has produced a pattern of Opposition frontbench behaviour which is closely parallel to that of Ministers. The overall effect is to create the image of a professional, single-minded group of Opposition leaders, who take their assigned duties very seriously, and who behave increasingly like an alternative team of Ministers. It can be argued that this single-minded approach to Opposition has produced a betterinformed Opposition team, and also a better-informed House of Commons, through confrontations between a Minister and an Opposition Spokesman who is dedicated to his assigned duty. Whether such single-mindedness in opposition is the best preparation for Ministerial office, however, is another matter. It can be argued that a high level of specialisation by Spokesmen in opposition will indeed lead to more 'professional' government, in that, assuming the Opposition comes to power, Ministers will have acquired in opposition a depth of knowledge of their subject. Any *depth* of knowledge acquired by specialisation in opposition, however, can be applied in office only if Spokesmen receive the Ministerial posts that they covered in opposition. If a Spokesman is appointed to some other post, either initially or in a Ministerial re-shuffle, his lack of *breadth* of experience in opposition will severely limit his knowledge of his new subject. Paul Bryan, for example, was a Post Office Spokesman throughout the 1966–70 period, and in 1967–8 had an Index of Specialisation of 85 per cent. In 1970, however, he was appointed to a post in the Department of Employment and Productivity, whose affairs he had not covered in opposition. Similarly, Maurice Macmillan received a post at the Treasury in 1970, after specialising on Health and Social Services in opposition (to an extent of an Index of Specialisation of almost 100 per cent in 1967–8), while Lord Balniel received a Defence post in 1970 after concentrating (79 per cent in 1967–8) on Social Services. In this situation, far from being an expert, the new Minister will know less about his Ministerial area than if he had spread his interests in opposition and had acquired breadth of experience rather than depth. These and other aspects of the transfer from Opposition to office, however, will be examined more fully in the concluding chapter.

part four

Conclusion

11

From Opposition to Office

'PUT ME on earth again, and I would rather be a serf in the house of some landless man, with little enough for himself to live on, than king of all these dead men that have done with life.'[1] Thus, in *The Odyssey*, Achilles addressed Odysseus when they met in Hades. Had Achilles been an Opposition Parliamentary Spokesman his plea might have been: 'Put me in office again, and I would rather be a humble junior Minister, with some minor governmental role to perform, than a leading Shadow Cabinet figure in an Opposition team made up of "yesterday's men".' Opposition figures are nothing if they are not ambitious for office. As was pointed out in Chapter 1, and as has been emphasised throughout this study, Her Majesty's Opposition is essentially Her Majesty's Alternative Government, eager for office. Despite the several compensations of being in opposition that were discussed in Chapter 6, few MPs see time spent in opposition as preferable to time spent in government. Certainly, the chief desire of Opposition front-bench MPs is, like Achilles, to elevate themselves to their former glories. In their desire for office, however, the Opposition leaders have to be patient, in that today their ambition is likely to be achieved only at a general election, probably towards the end of a full Parliament. Should the Opposition party win the election, however, the actual process of transferring from Opposition to office is a very rapid and somewhat scrambled process, of which the 1970 replacement of the Wilson Labour Government by the Heath Conservative Government was fairly typical.

Shortly after 2.00 p.m. on the afternoon of Friday, 19 June,

[1] Homer, *The Odyssey* (translated by E. V. Rieu), Penguin Classics edition, London 1946, p. 184.

the day after polling day in the 1970 election, Harold Wilson
conceded defeat by asking for an audience with the Queen
when the Conservatives won their 315th seat, assuring them
of an overall majority in the Commons. The Queen was at
Ascot, but returned to Buckingham Palace where Harold
Wilson tendered his resignation and handed over the seals of
office at 6.25 p.m. Edward Heath was sent for, as leader of the
victorious Conservative Party, and at his audience with the
Queen at 7.00 p.m. he kissed hands and thereby assumed office
as the eleventh Prime Minister of the century.[1] Wilson, mean-
while, returned to 10 Downing Street, where he and his wife
collected their immediate belongings and left by the back door
to spend the night with friends, deprived as they were of a home
as well as a job. Prime Ministers sometimes refer to the benefits
of 'living over the shop', but this is clearly a disadvantage when
both have to be abandoned together. Heath duly returned to
Downing Street, and entered by the front door after making
a very brief speech to the waiting crowds. After sending for his
pyjamas and toothbrush from his flat at the Albany, he spent
his first night in his new job in his new home. Over the next
few days removal vans completed the physical transfer from
office to opposition, and from opposition to office, with the
triumphant Conservative supporters in Downing Street alter-
nately cheering and jeering the activities of the removal men,
depending on whether they were moving belongings into or
out of Downing Street.

Thus the implementation of 'the electoral will' in Britain is
characterised by almost indecent haste. Within twenty-four
hours of the polls closing, the outgoing Prime Minister has to
abandon his home and office, and this is done without any
public expression of gratitude to him for services rendered. The
outgoing Prime Minister does not even need to wait for all the
results to be declared before acknowledging his defeat and
tendering his resignation. Technically, he has lost the election
as soon as the Opposition party secures a majority of the seats
in the Commons. Today, of course, thanks to the wonders of
psephology, the winning party in a general election normally can
be identified within an hour or so of the polls closing. Thus in

[1] See above, pp. 78–9, for the Constitutional rights and obligations of
the Leader of the Opposition in this respect.

1959 Hugh Gaitskell, as Leader of the Opposition, acknowledged that Labour had lost the election in a memorable television interview four hours after the polls had closed, when three-quarters of the results were still to come.[1] Defeated Prime Ministers, and the Monarch, require more positive evidence of the electoral will, and in 1964 Sir Alec Douglas-Home acknowledged defeat only at the point when Labour secured a majority of the seats, and in 1970 Harold Wilson followed the same principle. Nevertheless, on these occasions the formal transfer of power was achieved within twenty-four hours of the polls closing, and Cabinet appointments were announced within a further twenty-four hours.[2]

Thus an incoming Prime Minister is pitched at once from conducting an exhausting election campaign as Leader of the Opposition, to serving as Prime Minister after only the barest of preparations. In 1970 the change of Government was followed by a short sitting of Parliament, and then a summer break, which afforded some opportunity for the new Government to ease into office. When, however, an election is held in the autumn, which is more usual than a spring election, the change of Government is followed at once by a full session of Parliament without any transitionary period at all. The precipitous nature of the implementation of the will of the people, therefore, provides no opportunity for immediate preparations for office. Theoretically, however, the problems that could arise from such a rapid transfer of power are eased in two respects by the existence of a Shadow Government. Firstly, a new Prime Minister can use those who served on the front bench in opposition as the basis of his Ministerial team, and secondly, service in the Opposition front-bench team can provide some preparation for the responsibilities of office. This, of course, raises the basic questions of the extent to which service as an Opposition Spokesman *is* a preparation for Ministerial Office, and also the extent to which Opposition Spokesmen *do* receive Ministerial posts when the new Prime Minister forms his Government. These two points will be examined in the next two sections of this chapter.

[1] See Butler and Rose, *The British General Election of 1959*, p. 189.
[2] See Butler and King, *The British General Election of 1964*, p. 291, and Wilson, *The Labour Government 1964–70*, p. 1.

The Overlap between Opposition and Office 1964 and 1970

When a party comes to power, to what extent are Ministerial posts given to those who served as Spokesmen in opposition? In the transition from opposition to office only the leader can be certain of the post he will fill. The Leader of the Opposition moves into the post of Prime Minister as a constitutional right, and then proceeds to select his Ministerial team. He is free to select or reject those who have served as Spokesmen in opposition: thus Winston Churchill is reported to have remarked at the end of the last Shadow Cabinet meeting of the 1945–51 period of Conservative Opposition, 'We shall meet again soon in happier circumstances—some of us!' When the Leader of the Opposition appoints his Spokesmen, he does not guarantee them Ministerial office in the department that they are covering, or in any other post. It is evident from interviews with Spokesmen that Leaders of the Opposition in the 1955–70 period made it clear to their Spokesmen that the appointment carried no obligations on either side: someone who was given an Opposition duty should not necessarily expect a Ministerial post, and at the same time, because someone accepted an Opposition duty in a particular area it did not necessarily follow that he was prepared to accept a Ministerial responsibility in the same area. Indeed, early in the 1970–1 session Harold Wilson formally emphasised this at a meeting of the PLP. Nevertheless, there are certainly 'great expectations' on both sides. A Leader of the Opposition, in selecting his team of Spokesmen, undoubtedly looks principally for recruits who can be seen as Ministerial potential. What is more, he can legitimately assume that most MPs wish to achieve Ministerial office, and that if someone is willing to undertake unpaid and comparatively unglamorous duties in opposition, he will also be prepared to undertake Ministerial duties unless perhaps for health, age, or similar reasons an MP found Opposition responsibilities acceptable, but not the more arduous Ministerial duties.[1] For their part, the vast majority of Spokesmen undoubtedly expect that they will receive some Ministerial office when the party comes to power. Even though Opposition duties are given 'without strings attached', and

[1] See above, p. 147, for a comment on this.

even though few Spokesmen would publicly *admit* to having expectations of office, most of them expect to achieve the 'substance of their shadows'. Most of them undoubtedly regard years spent on the Opposition front bench as preparation for a Ministerial post in the particular area that they covered in opposition, and earlier it was noted that Lord Morrison and Lord Balfour subscribed to the view that in practice the creation of official Opposition Spokesmen would hamper the Prime Minister's freedom of appointment should the party come to power.[1]

To what extent, then, were Opposition Spokesmen given Ministerial posts when the Labour and Conservative Governments were formed in 1964 and 1970? Following Labour's victory at the general election of 15 October 1964, Harold Wilson assumed office as Prime Minister and announced his Government appointments over the next few days. Despite previous declarations that he favoured the principle of a small Cabinet,[2] Wilson's original 1964 Cabinet contained twenty-three members, which compared with the fixed number of eighteen members in the Parliamentary Committee in the 1951–64 period. Thirteen of those who served on the Parliamentary Committee during the 1963–4 session received Cabinet posts in October 1964. Of the other five Parliamentary Committee members, Fred Willey and G. R. Mitchison received posts outside the Cabinet, while Lord Alexander (who was almost eighty) and Lord Listowel were excluded from the Government. Lord Shepherd remained as whip in the Lords, but this did not give him a place in the Cabinet. Thus there was a coincidence between the view of the PLP as to who should be *elected* to the Parliamentary Committee in November 1963, and the view of Harold Wilson as to who should be *appointed* to his Government in October, 1964. Of the senior party figures, James Callaghan had been Treasury Spokesman from 1961 onwards, while Patrick Gordon Walker had been Foreign Affairs Spokesmen since February 1963, and they duly became Chancellor of the Exchequer and Foreign Secretary respectively. Douglas Jay, Denis Healey, and Ray Gunter also

[1] See above, p. 66.
[2] See, for example, Norman Hunt, *Whitehall and Beyond*, London 1964, p. 26.

received Cabinet posts that were equivalent to their 1963–4 Opposition duties, but the other seven Parliamentary Committee members who joined the Cabinet received posts unconnected with their duties in the 1963–4 session. Among these, George Brown, then deputy leader of the party, had been given a wide-ranging responsibility over Home affairs from 1961 onwards, and in October 1964 he became First Secretary of State and Minister of Economic Affairs, with the task of creating the new Department of Economic Affairs.

The 1964 Wilson Cabinet also included ten who had not served on the Parliamentary Committee in the 1963–4 session, but it must be remembered that the Parliamentary Committee had a fixed membership of eighteen (now nineteen), while Wilson chose to extend his Cabinet to twenty-three members. At the same time, the Cabinet posts to which Barbara Castle, Frank Cousins, Anthony Greenwood, Lord Gardiner, and Lord Longford were allocated had no counterpart among the Opposition duties, while Frank Cousins and Lord Gardiner had not been eligible for posts in opposition, as they entered Parliament only in 1964. The five other members of the Cabinet had all previously been Spokesmen, but had not been members of the Parliamentary Committee in the 1963–4 session. It may be noted that two members of the Cabinet, James Griffiths and Patrick Gordon Walker, had also been members of Attlee's Cabinet in 1951, and Wilson himself had been in the Attlee Cabinet until his resignation in 1951. Two other members of the 1964 Cabinet, George Brown and Sir Frank Soskice, had held Ministerial posts outside the Cabinet in 1951, and seven others (James Callaghan, Tom Fraser, Douglas Jay, Michael Stewart, Herbert Bowden, Fred Lee, and Arthur Bottomley) had been junior Ministers in October 1951. These twelve, then, forming a majority of the Cabinet, spanned the thirteen years of Opposition between the Attlee and Wilson Labour Governments, and gave the Wilson Cabinet a greater level of Ministerial experience than might have been expected after so long in opposition.

Turning to the front-bench team as a whole, it is clear that the overlap of personnel between the 1963–4 Opposition team and the 1964 Government was not very pronounced. In the first place, not all of those who served as Spokesmen in the

1963–4 session received posts in the Government. Despite the fact that Wilson made over ninety Ministerial appointments (with eighty-three of them going to members of the Commons), eight of the forty-five members of the Labour front-bench team at the dissolution did not receive jobs. Lords Alexander, Listowel, and Shepherd have been referred to above. In addition,

TABLE 39

Former Spokesmen holding Ministerial Posts in the Wilson Government 1964–70, and the Heath Government in July 1970 and April 1972 (percentages)

	Nov. 1964	Wilson April 1966	June 1970	Heath July 1970	April 1972
Former Spokesmen holding Ministerial Posts that were:					
Equivalent to their last Opposition duties	40·5	28·6	7·1	54·3	40·4
Equivalent to a former Opposition duty	7·1	—	4·8	8·7	2·1
In the same broad area as their last or former duty*	16·7	23·8	11·9	15·2	19·1
Unrelated to any Opposition duty	35·7	26·2	16·7	21·7	25·5
Former Spokesmen dropped from the Government	—	21·4	59·7	—	12·7
N	42	42	42	46	47

Source: Ministerial Lists from *Hansard*.
* See p. 372 for an explanation of this category.

Arthur Creech Jones left Parliament in 1964, while R. T. Paget, G. R. Strauss, John Cronin, and Philip Noel-Baker were overlooked by Wilson for age or other reasons. To the thirty-seven members of the Government who had been Spokesmen during the 1963–4 session, may be added a further five (Roy Jenkins, Barbara Castle, Anthony Wedgwood Benn, Anthony Greenwood, and Harold Finch) who had held Opposition duties prior to 1963, but who had not been in the team in the 1963–4 session. In all, therefore, forty-two of the Ministers appointed in October 1964 had experience as Opposition Spokesmen, but as is shown in Table 39, less than half of these received posts in departments that they had covered in opposition. Seventeen received the Ministerial post which corresponded to their Opposition duty in the 1963–4 session, and three others received posts that they had shadowed at some time prior to 1963. The other twenty-two, however, received posts in departments that did not correspond to any duties that they had held in opposition.

Thus some of the Opposition Spokesmen were overlooked in the formation of the Government in October 1964, and most of those who were included went to departments that they had not covered in opposition. Further, those who did receive posts in areas in which they had been Opposition Spokesmen, did not necessarily keep them for long. By the beginning of the new Parliament in April 1966, almost a quarter of the former Spokesmen had been dropped from the Government. Of the thirty-three who remained, twenty-one were in posts in which they had no specific Opposition experience. By June 1970, at the end of the period of Labour rule, but still less than six years after the party had come to power, well over half of the former Spokesmen had been dropped. Of the seventeen who did remain, only five (Denis Healey, Willie Ross, Roy Jenkins, Richard Crossman, and Wilson himself) had posts that they had previously covered in opposition. All in all, out of the forty-two former Spokesmen who had joined the Government in 1964, only twenty-three had at some time during the 1964–6 and 1966–70 Parliaments held posts that they had covered when in opposition.

Some of the former Spokesmen who were not given posts in departments that they had covered in opposition, were at least allocated to related departments. George Thomson, for example, who was a Colonial affairs Spokesman in opposition, went to the Foreign Office as a junior Minister in October 1964. He was thus in a department that he had not covered in opposition, but he was working in the same broad area of 'external affairs'. Even on such a broad categorisation of the areas of governmental activity, however, the overlap between opposition and office is not very marked. In 1964 and 1966, a third of the former Spokesmen in the Government held posts which were not even in the same broad area as any duty they had held in opposition, while by 1970 the proportion was between a third and a half.

Thus not all of those with experience as Spokesmen in opposition received posts in the Government in 1964. Those who did get jobs did not necessarily receive them in departments which they had covered, and most of those who did receive posts in their own areas were soon moved into other posts in which they did not have Opposition experience. This general lack of carry-over from opposition to office is further emphasised by Table 40, which shows the number and proportion of the House of Commons members of the Cabinet and the Government as a whole who had experience as Opposition Spokesmen.[1] In November 1964, most of the Cabinet and half of the MPs in the Government as a whole had been Spokesmen when in opposition. After this, however, the influx of new blood into the Government was such that the former Spokesmen constituted just over a third of the MPs in the Government in April 1966, and under a quarter by June 1970, although they remained in a clear majority in the Cabinet. Of course, in opposition neither Gaitskell nor Wilson had attempted to match the number of Conservative Ministers exactly, and at any one time there were always more Conservative Ministers than there were Labour Spokesmen.[2] Further, when he formed his Government in 1964, Wilson made a record number of appointments, so that there were inevitably more Government posts to dispose of than there were former Spokesmen to fill them. Nevertheless, the point illustrated in Table 40 is that even though the former Spokesmen constituted a clear majority of the Government in November 1964, by April 1970 they constituted only a minority. Thus in the main, those who had led the party in opposition had been replaced by newcomers who had served only as backbenchers up to 1964, or who had entered Parliament only in 1964 or later.

[1] As indicated in Table 40, these figures relate only to members of the Commons: the peers in the Government and the Shadow Cabinet are excluded from the calculations. Also, here, as throughout this study, Ministerial numbers exclude the assistant whips and the members of Her Majesty's Household. See above, p. 76.

[2] See Figure H., p. 144.

To what extent was this pattern repeated when the Conservatives came to power in 1970? There was a greater initial carry-over of responsibilities from opposition to office in 1970 than had been the case in 1964, and even after the first major Government reshuffle in April 1972 the carry-over was still high. Heath announced his Cabinet appointments on 20 June 1970, and of the seventeen members of the Consultative Committee in the 1969–70 session, fifteen received Cabinet posts.

TABLE 40

Former Spokesmen as Proportion of MPs in the Wilson Cabinet and Government 1964–70, and the Heath Cabinet and Government July 1970 and April 1972*

Former Spokesmen as a Proportion of	Nov. 1964		Wilson April 1966		June 1970		Heath July 1970		April 1972	
	N	%	N	%	N	%	N	%	N	%
Cabinet	18	85·7	18	85·7	12	63·1	15	93·7	14	93·3
Government as a whole	42	50·6	33	39·7	17	22·7	48	74·2	47	68·1

Source: Ministerial Lists from *Hansard.*

* These figures relate only to members of the Commons: the Peers in the Government and in the Shadow Cabinet are excluded from the calculations. Also, here, as throughout this study, Ministerial numbers exclude the assistant whips, and the members of Her Majesty's Household.

The two who were excluded were Joseph Godber and Lord Balniel, who were given posts as Ministers of State outside the Cabinet. In addition to the fifteen Consultative Committee members, Cabinet posts went to Michael Noble (who had been a member of the Committee until January 1969), Peter Thomas (who had been a legal Spokesman in 1965–6, but had been outside Parliament from 1966 to 1970), and James Prior (who had been Heath's Parliamentary Secretary in opposition and thus had generally attended Consultative Committee meetings). Two of the key figures in opposition received the Ministerial posts they had shadowed throughout the 1966–70 Parliament —Sir Alec Douglas-Home the Foreign and Commonwealth

Office, and Iain Macleod the Treasury, although Macleod's death in July took Anthony Barber to the Treasury. Quintin Hogg, who had been Home Affairs Spokesman, became Lord Chancellor, and the Home Office went to Reginald Maudling, who had been deputy leader without any specific departmental duty in the 1969–70 session. The chief whip in opposition, William Whitelaw, became Leader of the House of Commons and Lord President of the Council.

The overlap between the Shadow Cabinet and the Cabinet was thus more complete in 1970 than in 1964. Although most of Labour's 1963–4 Parliamentary Committee received posts in Wilson's Cabinet in October 1964, the Cabinet also contained ten who had not served on the Parliamentary Committee in the 1963–4 session. In 1970, however, Heath's Cabinet was almost a carbon copy of his 1969–70 Consultative Committee in terms of size, composition and the duties to which its members were allocated, although unlike Wilson, Heath was free in opposition to determine the size and composition of his Shadow Cabinet. Similarly, of the front-bench team as a whole in the 1969–70 session, forty-one of the forty-six received posts in the Government. The five who did not were Bernard Braine, James Ramsden, Charles Morrison, Robin Chichester-Clark, and Ian MacArthur, who all returned to the back benches. Of the forty-one Spokesmen who joined the Government, twenty-five were given posts in the departments that they had covered during the 1969–70 session, and four others were given posts in departments that they had covered prior to 1969. The vast majority of the Spokesmen, therefore, received posts in which they had specific experience in opposition, although of these twelve, Lord Carrington (Defence) and Joseph Godber (Foreign and Commonwealth Affairs) had also previously had Ministerial experience there. In addition to the Spokesmen who had served in the 1969–70 session, seven Government posts in 1970 went to Spokesmen who had served at some time during the 1964–70 period, but had not been members of the team in the 1969–70 session. Only one of these, however, went to a department that he had covered at some time as a Spokesman.

Thus in all, the Ministry that Heath formed in June 1970 contained forty-eight who had been Spokesmen at some time

during the 1964–70 period, thirty of them with posts in departments they had covered at some point. Forty-six of the forty-
eight were MPs, and they constituted three-quarters of the
MPs in the Government. There was thus a much greater carry-
over of personnel *and* of responsibilities from opposition to office
in June 1970 than there had been with Labour in October 1964
(as shown above in Tables 39 and 40). This may be a mani-
festation of the 'Heath style of professionalism', with the high
level of specialisation by Spokesmen on their assigned duties
in opposition, as noted in the preceding Chapter, being followed by the appointment of these 'experts' to the equivalent
Ministerial posts. It may also be noted that the Conservative
Spokesmen who were included in the Government in 1970
were considerably younger, on average, than their Labour
counterparts in the 1964 Government—the average age being
forty-seven in 1970 compared with fifty-seven in 1964. Presumably, therefore, the Conservative Spokesmen are in a position to
remain in the Government for a longer period of time than did
Labour's former Spokesmen after 1964, thus maintaining the
overlap between opposition and office more clearly than in
the 1964–70 period. Certainly, two years after the Heath
Government came to power, the proportion of Spokesmen who
had been dropped or moved away from the departments they
had covered in opposition, was much smaller than was the case
after two years of the Wilson Government's life.

In comparing the 1964 and 1970 transitions to power, however, it should be remembered that in October 1964 Harold
Wilson had been Leader of the Opposition for only eighteen
months. When he succeeded Gaitskell in 1963 he inherited a
well established team of Spokesmen, at a time when a general
election was expected within a few months. Wilson made very
few changes in the team in February 1963, but this may well
have been in order to avoid possible strife at a time when a
general election was imminent. He may have tolerated an
Opposition team with which he was not entirely happy, in the
knowledge that after the election, win or lose, he could make
whatever new appointments he chose. In June 1970, in contrast, Edward Heath had been Leader of the Opposition for
almost five years, and he had been able to build up a team
gradually as the 1966–70 Parliament proceeded. Had the Con-

servatives come to power in 1966 instead of 1970, the carry over of personnel from opposition to office might not have been so pronounced. In March 1966 Heath had been leader of the party for less than a year, and he had not had a proper chance to select an opposition team that carried his own stamp. By 1970, however, he had been able to gather carefully a team for the election that was bound to come in 1970 or 1971. Also, in 1966 the team was much bigger than in 1970 (sixty-four members as opposed to forty-six), and thus it would have been more difficult to accommodate all the Spokesmen and still have Ministerial posts for any other MPs or Peers it was desired to bring into the team. Further, someone who has served long years in opposition might be too old for an extended and successful career as a Minister. By 1964 Labour had been in opposition for thirteen years, and some of Labour's Spokesmen had served on the Parliamentary Committee, or in some other capacity in the team, for all or most of the period, and were too old to remain long in office. As noted above, the average age of the Labour front-bench team at the end of the period in opposition was fifty-seven, and a quarter of the team were in their sixties or seventies.[1]

Nevertheless, it is clear from the accession to power in 1964, and even in 1970, that there is certainly no automatic carry-over of personnel or responsibilities from opposition to office. In the 1955–70 period there were always fewer duties allocated in opposition than in office, as a Leader of the Opposition does not normally try to cover the Government 'man for man', although in the 1970–1 session Harold Wilson's Opposition team actually exceeded the number of Ministers in the Commons. Edward Heath's comparatively small Ministerial team of seventy-one in 1970 was still more than half as big again as the Opposition team that he had prior to the election. Of course, a Prime Minister may wish to give Ministerial posts to MPs who had declined jobs in opposition. Michael Noble, for example, left the Consultative Committee in January 1969 in order to concentrate on his business interests, but he was willing to accept a Cabinet post in June 1970. Also, a Prime Minister has to allocate some Ministerial posts to peers, and in 1970 four full Ministers and seven junior Ministers were drawn from

[1] See above, p. 153.

the Lords. He may also wish to give posts to some of those who have just entered Parliament, or to bring into the Government people from outside Parliament. Thus in 1964 Wilson recruited Lord Chalfont and Lord Gardiner to his Government through life peerages in the Lords, and brought Frank Cousins into the Commons and the Government through a by-election. Similarly, in his first set of Ministerial changes in October 1970, Heath brought John Davies into the Cabinet even though he had entered Parliament only in June. The need to balance in the Government the various elements of the party may also lead to the inclusion of some who had not served in the Opposition team, where the need for such a balance is less marked.

Even allowing for these factors, it would still have been possible for Harold Wilson in 1964 and Edward Heath in 1970 to allocate Ministerial duties to all of the Spokesmen had they so wished, and still have had posts left over for those who had not served in opposition. A Prime Minister, however, may choose to overlook some Spokesmen when he is forming his Government, or to give them posts initially, but drop them fairly early in the Government's life. It may be that in October 1964 Harold Wilson was reluctant to overlook those who had been elected regularly to the Parliamentary Committee in the 1959–64 Parliament, but was less concerned about dropping them from the Government having once given them the 'reward' of a spell in office. Also, many of these older figures were the only Labour MPs with any previous Ministerial experience, and thus had to be included in the Government, if only initially, in order to give it some weight. James Griffiths was appointed Secretary of State for Wales in 1964, at the age of 74, but it was understood that his task was merely to establish the new Welsh Ministry, and that he would retire after about a year. Accordingly, he left the Government after the 1966 election.[1]

All Prime Ministers have periodic re-shuffles of their Ministerial team in order to promote some Ministers, remove others, bring new talent into the team, and keep alive the Ministerial hopes of backbench MPs. Such re-shuffles occur in Britain much more frequently than in most comparable countries. In the 1955–70 period, Ministers served for an average of just

[1] Wilson, *The Labour Government 1964–70*, p. 219.

two years in any one post (compared with an average of three years in the 1900–14 period).[1] Also, in Britain a Ministerial promotion generally involves a move to another department, unlike the pattern in American government, where promotion is more likely to be within the same department.[2] Given this, Spokesmen who served faithfully in opposition may be dropped from the team, or at least may be moved from the departments they covered in opposition.

Sometimes very early in the life of a new Government, a Prime Minister will re-shuffle his Ministers in order to make way for some bright, young, new MPs, who, after a few months in the House, have exhibited sufficient potential to justify a Ministerial post. Studies of Ministerial careers suggest that, for the most part, some sort of backbench apprenticeship has to be served before promotion to the Treasury bench is secured.[3] Nevertheless, rapid promotion to Ministerial office can be achieved, especially if, as is usually the case, the infusion of new blood into the Parliamentary party during the period in opposition was slight, and the greatest influx of talent came in the election which brought the party to power. In these circumstances, some of the older Ministers, who may well have served long years in opposition, may be dropped. Thus long-serving Labour Spokesmen like Tom Fraser, James Griffiths, and Lord Mitchison left the Labour Government after less than eighteen months, and MPs elected only in 1964, like Edmund Dell, David Ennals, Roy Hattersley, and Mrs Shirley Williams, were given Ministerial posts. Although most of Labour's 1963–4 Parliamentary Committee were given Government posts in October 1964, only eleven remained in the Government in 1966, and only four in 1970.

Much more generally, however, poor appointments can be

---

[1] R. Rose, 'The Making of Cabinet Ministers', *British Journal of Political Science*, 1970–1, p. 408.

[2] Ibid.

[3] See P. W. Buck, *Amateurs and Professionals in British Politics 1918–59*, London 1963; P. W. Buck, 'MPs in Ministerial Office 1918–55 and 1955–9', *Political Studies* 1961, pp. 300–6; P. W. Buck, 'The Early Start to Cabinet Office 1918–55', *Western Political Quarterly*, 1963, pp. 624–32; F. M. G. Willson, 'Routes of Entry of New Members of the British Cabinet 1868–1958', *Political Studies*, 1959, pp. 222–32; F. M. G. Willson, 'Entry to the Cabinet 1959–68', *Political Studies*, 1970, pp. 236–8.

tolerated much more readily in opposition than in office, and it may be felt that someone who had revealed himself to be barely adequate as a Spokesman should not be risked in a Ministerial appointment. Again, someone who is very successful as a Spokesman does not necessarily succeed as a Minister. It is necessary now, therefore, to consider in more detail just how far service as a Spokesman is a preparation for Ministerial office.

Spokesmen and Ministers

It is possible for a party in opposition to prepare itself for office by deciding upon its policy objectives, and planning these in detail. As was suggested in Chapter 6, however, concentration while in opposition on the small print of future legislation carries with it more pitfalls than rewards. A party in opposition is probably best advised to avoid working on the details of future policy, and concentrate instead on creating a climate of opinion among the electorate favourable to the general philosophy that it intends to follow when it comes to power. In other respects, however, service as an Opposition Spokesman might be expected to provide a general training for life as a Minister. To what extent is this the case in fact? Just how far is service as an Opposition Spokesman a good preparation for Ministerial office?

Clearly, there are some immediate and very practical differences between the roles of Spokesmen and Ministers. Unlike the Minister, the Spokesman's status and responsibilities are not governed by statute. He is not paid a salary, other than his salary as an MP, and many Spokesmen have part-time occupations additional to their Parliamentary duties. The Spokesman has no department to run, and he does not have to prepare legislative details. The House of Commons is the main forum of his activities, whereas for a Minister it represents only one part of his work. The skills required for being a good Spokesman are mainly Parliamentary in nature, and service as a Spokesman does not provide training in how to preside over a department of state. The Spokesman is essentially a partisan figure, operating in a framework in which all of his colleagues are party figures. The Minister operates in rather less of a party political setting, surrounded as he is by non-partisan civil servants. It has been estimated that in an average Ministerial working week of seventy hours, when Parliament is sitting, Ministers spend in the order of fifty hours in Parliament, in Cabinet or Cabinet Committee meetings, or in personal meetings with other Ministers, pressure group leaders or other essentially 'political' figures.[1] For these activities, service as a Spokesman can be something of a useful preparation, but for the remaining fifteen to twenty working hours of a week, spent in a departmental office context, experience in opposition is likely to be less valuable. As was noted in Chapter 8 a Spokesman will have some dealings with the departments of state in the course of his duties, although formal contacts are restricted. Although a Spokesman will have more Civil Service contacts than will most backbenchers in opposition, knowledge of how the Government machine works is probably as well obtained through service on the Public Accounts Committee or the Estimates Committee, as through service as a Spokesman.

Ministers have to deal with a vast amount of paperwork, and thus they have to be highly skilled in reading and absorbing material quickly. Opposition Spokesmen will handle a certain amount of paper work, but their role demands primarily oral skills. Because a Spokesman has no departmental duties, he is required to spend less time than a Minister on visits away from London, although, of course, Scottish and Welsh Spokesmen are exceptions to this. Also, when Parliament is not sitting, a Spokesman's duties are greatly reduced, whereas a Minister's departmental duties are continuous. Thus a Spokesman's annual work load is considerably less than that of a Minister, and in terms of volume of work there is probably much more of a contrast between Ministers and Spokesmen, than between Spokesmen and most backbenchers. At the same time, while most Ministers probably work equally hard, the time and effort devoted to the job of Spokesman will vary considerably from man to man and job to job. A Spokesman for the Treasury or Foreign Affairs, for example, will have much more work than a Spokesman for Sport, or Arts and Amenities. Also, because so many Spokesmen do have outside jobs, their combined

[1] B. W. Headey, forthcoming study of the roles of Cabinet Ministers.

Parliamentary and extra-Parliamentary activities may add up
to a working day as long as that of a Minister.

A Spokesman is more likely than a Minister to look beyond
his own subject, and to take an interest in his colleagues' activities. Cabinet Ministers, of course, have a general responsibility
for all aspects of Government policy, and some do concern
themselves with a wide range of subjects beyond their own
immediate departmental duties. Nevertheless, a Minister's
Parliamentary and public utterances will be confined almost
exclusively to his own departmental area, whereas a Spokesman
will at times move beyond his own area of responsibility to
speak, in and out of Parliament, on other subjects. The extent
to which the degree of specialisation among Spokesmen has
increased over the years was emphasised in the previous chapter. It was also noted, however, that few Spokesmen have as
yet reached quite the same level of single-mindedness as have
Ministers, and outside the House a Spokesman still has more
freedom to express a personal point of view than has a Minister.
No doubt this is partly because an Opposition Spokesman's
views are seen as being somewhat less significant than those
of a Minister, at least as far as press and public are concerned.
The job is certainly less prestigious than that of a Minister of
the Crown, and in and out of Parliament an Opposition Spokesman is likely to be treated with rather less deference than is
a Minister. This is probably especially true for Labour Spokesmen, as much of the Conservative Party's traditional deference
towards its leaders applies in opposition as much as when the
party is in office. A Labour Spokesman, however, is not likely
to be accorded the same respect as is a Labour Minister by
backbenchers, the NEC, the annual party conference, or the
constituency parties, and he is obliged to pay more attention
to their views than is a Minister. Because a Spokesman's duties
are centred on the Palace of Westminster, he is more accessible
to his backbench colleagues than is a Minister, and he is also
more likely than a Minister to come into regular personal contact with his front-bench colleagues, and with his leader.

A Minister has his department as a base from which to
operate, and a personal staff to assist him. With the improvement in House of Commons accommodation in recent years,
most Spokesmen now have a room in the House in which to

work and keep papers, but a Spokesman is unlikely to have more than a secretary by way of staff. He has thus to be more self-reliant than a Minister. Because he has to do so much research work for himself, the Spokesman may become better informed about his subject area than is the Minister, whose information is gathered for him, and whose speeches are often prepared by civil servants. An essential aspect of the technique of being a successful Minister is the ability to delegate to his junior Ministers and civil servants. A senior Spokesman may be aided by an assistant Spokesman, and he will be able to call on backbenchers to assist him in debates and questions, but the bulk of the duties of opposition he has to perform himself. The extent of a Spokesman's knowledge of his subject, however, will vary from one individual to another, and one subject to another, and while there are considerable sources of information available to a Spokesman in areas like Education or Agriculture, in Defence or Foreign Affairs much information is available only to the Minister.

These, then, all represent practical differences between the roles of Spokesmen and Ministers. Despite these factors, there are ways in which experience as a Spokesman can be useful to a Minister. In this a distinction can perhaps be made between specialist knowledge gained in opposition, and a more general training in front-bench techniques. The general level of expertise among Spokesmen almost certainly grew during the nineteen-sixties, as Spokesmen came more and more to specialise in their assigned areas. Many would argue that this would prove to be extremely valuable if the Spokesman became a Minister. In the 1966–70 Parliament, for example, the Conservative Spokesmen achieved very high levels of specialisation in their assigned duties, and then in June 1970 most were appointed to the departments they had covered in opposition. This can be seen as a very 'positive' approach to a period in opposition, using it as preparation for office, with knowledge acquired from specialisation in the comparative leisure of opposition being carried over in the transfer from opposition to office, always provided that, unlike the 1964–70 period of Labour Government, Ministers retain their posts for a number of years. Clearly, in so far as expertise in his departmental area is seen as desirable in a Minister, service as an Opposition

Spokesman in his subsequent Ministerial area will be a definite recommendation in a Minister's background. In this context, however, it should be remembered that service as an Opposition Spokesman does not necessarily *develop* expertise, as the MP is very often an expert in the subject for which he is appointed Spokesman. Certainly, for backbenchers being given their first appointment, prior expertise in the subject is often an essential requirement. Nevertheless, no matter how well informed a backbench MP may be about the subject, service as a Spokesman can perhaps add to this by giving close contact with legislative and administrative details. In interviews, a number of Spokesmen pointed out that having to speak regularly on a subject in the critical atmosphere of the House of Commons, can 'concentrate the mind wonderfully'. Being recognised as an official Spokesman can also lead to contacts with the press, pressure groups, and other outside bodies which might not be so readily available to a backbencher.

Thus prior service as a Spokesman can provide a Minister with expertise and contacts which he can use to advantage while in office. This is perhaps particularly valuable in a major area like defence, where continuity of policy is normally desirable. It is less valuable in a department like the Home Office, which is responsible for a wide range of varied subjects. Equally, if a new Minister wishes to introduce a major policy change in any department within a short period of coming to office, expertise that he developed in opposition will be valuable to him in his task of persuading his departmental and Cabinet colleagues of the merits of his proposal. If, however, as a Minister he is content to choose between various policy options presented by his civil servants, the qualities of the 'intelligent layman' may be of more value than those of the 'expert'. Thus just as there are reservations, noted in Chapter 10, about the merits of specialisation among Opposition Spokesmen, there is also clear disagreement about the desirability of a Minister possessing a particular expertise in his Ministerial field. One study of Cabinet Ministers and their attitudes to their job, found that of fifty or so Ministers and former Ministers interviewed, roughly half regarded expertise as a desirable quality in a Minister, while half favoured the principle of the Minister being an 'intelligent layman'.[1] Clearly, for those who argue that the layman makes the best type of Minister, service as an Opposition Spokesman in a particular field is no recommendation for Ministerial office in that field. Indeed, far from being a recommendation, it will be regarded as a major disqualification.

It was noted in Chapter 5 that former Ministers do not always make good Spokesmen for their old departments, as they can be embarrassed in opposition by things that they said and did in office. The same principle applies in the transfer from opposition to office, as rash statements made in the comparative freedom of opposition often rebound on a party when it is faced with the realities of office. This can be especially so when a former Spokesman, after years spent in opposition criticising a particular departmental policy, finds that he is obliged to follow much the same policy when he becomes the Minister in charge of that department. The Government as a whole is damaged by any accusation that its actions in office are different from its words in opposition, but if a particular 'broken promise' can be laid at the door of the Minister actually covering the topic in question, the criticism is all the more telling. A former Spokesman who is given Ministerial responsibility for a department with which he had no official dealings when in opposition is less likely to be haunted by ghosts from his past than is someone who becomes Minister in a department that he covered in opposition.

Thus, just as in opposition there is much to be said for giving to ex-Ministers duties which are unrelated to their former departments, there are advantages in giving to former Spokesmen Ministerial duties which are unconnected with the tasks they performed in opposition. Further, whatever the merits of the 'layman versus expert' argument, expertise gained in opposition is of little value to the Spokesman if he is appointed to a post other than the one he has been covering, or if, after an initial appointment in the department he has shadowed, he is moved to a new department in a Ministerial re-shuffle. While in the transfer from opposition to office in 1970 most Spokesmen were given posts in departments that they had covered in opposition, there was still a third or so of the Spokesmen who received posts unrelated to the Opposition

[1] I am grateful to B. W. Headey for providing this information.

duty they had held. For Labour in 1964 this proportion was more than a half, while almost all of those who did receive in 1964 the Ministerial post they had been covering in opposition, were moved to other posts in the various re-shuffles of the 1964–70 period.

It is very easy, therefore, to exaggerate the extent to which service as an Opposition Spokesman provides an MP with particular expertise that he can subsequently use in office. Nevertheless, there are a number of other more general ways in which service as a Spokesman can provide a useful training in some Ministerial arts, regardless of the post that is held. There is a sense in which an MP is always 'in opposition', as even when his party is in office, and he holds a Ministerial post, much of his activity involves opposing his civil servants and challenging the departmental point of view. Thus the critical approach that an Opposition Spokesman has to adopt in his attacks on the Government can be something of a general training for office, preparing him for the task of persuading his civil servants that a particular policy is practical after all, despite all the excellent departmental arguments why it cannot be done. Also, regular confrontations with a Minister across the floor of the House will develop debating and other Parliamentary skills, and of course this will be valuable whichever post is obtained in office. Changes of oratorical style are required in the transition first of all from the party platform to the House of Commons, and then from the back benches to the front bench. In this, the responsibility of speaking from the Opposition front bench can serve as something of a preparation for the Treasury Bench. Those who move into Ministerial office straight from the freedom of the back benches may take some time to adjust to the single-mindedness that is required of them in their new role. Those who first serve as Opposition Spokesmen, however, are likely to have less difficulty in making this adjustment, especially in view of the degree of specialisation that, as revealed in the previous chapter, is now achieved by Opposition Spokesmen. Some financial responsibility has to be exercised in opposition, especially when the Opposition party seems likely to come soon to office, so that the Spokesman has to learn to be cautious in the commitments into which he enters. A Spokesman, of course, has to attack the Government at times with a degree of irresponsibility, and an excessively cautious Spokesman will not be effective in opposition. A distinction has to be made, however, between attacks on Government policies, in which the Spokesman has to be outspoken in order to be effective, and promises of future action, on which the Spokesman has to be much more cautious. Service as a Spokesman, as a bridge between the back benches and a Ministerial post, can thus help to develop a certain degree of circumspection, essential for any Minister.

A Minister has to be a 'specialist in public pleading', and like a lawyer with a client, he has to be competent as a salesman on behalf of his department. To some extent the oratorical skills required for this function can be learned in opposition. Although a Spokesman is concerned with attack (criticising the Government's record), and the Minister is primarily concerned with defence (defending that record), the techniques involved in debating well, and being able to score points in debates and in Question Time, are similar in many respects.

Thus being a member of an Opposition front-bench team will give something of a grounding in the basic Parliamentary skills which all Ministers have to possess. The ability of a Minister to defend his department, and to 'sell' its legislative priorities to his party and the public, and then pilot them through Parliament, represents his 'eleven plus' in which he must qualify before he can be a success in his ' "O" and "A" levels' in the broader aspects of the Ministerial role. Ministers who lack Parliamentary experience can often succeed in wartime, as did Lord Woolton, Sir John Anderson, and Ernest Bevin in the 1940–5 period, when the normal Parliamentary battle is suspended.[1] It can be much more difficult to cope with Parliament in peacetime, however, as was discovered by Ernest Bevin in 1945, Frank Cousins in 1964, and John Davies in 1970. To some extent, of course, it is possible to 'get the feel of the House' as a backbencher, but there still remains a distinction between the techniques required by backbenchers and front benchers, and in interview a number of Spokesmen emphasised this strongly. Service on the Opposition front bench will also give some introduction to the discipline of office, including the need to accept the collective view, and to be

[1] For a comment on the wartime situation see Appendix A.

collectively responsible for policies outside one's own immediate sphere of responsibility. By serving in the Opposition 'team' the Spokesman will learn about his colleagues' attitudes, and will thus be better able to anticipate how they might react to different situations in government. A Minister's civil servants are particularly well aware of the importance for the department of the Minister being able to win political battles in the Cabinet, or in party or Cabinet Committees, and Shadow Cabinet experience can be something of an advantage here. Pressure groups tend to seek out Opposition leaders, and thus a Spokesman will acquire much more experience than will a backbencher in dealing with these bodies, and getting the most out of such contacts. In these dealings he will learn who is important and who merely seems important, and this will serve him well in office.

Thus an Opposition Spokesman does gain general experience in being a front bencher, with all that this involves in being conciliatory in dealings with backbench colleagues, and guarded in dealings with pressure groups and the press. Although he acquires no experience in a Minister's departmental role, a Spokesman's activities do provide preparation for a Minister's Parliamentary and 'public relations' roles, and, if the Spokesman is a Shadow Cabinet member, for his Cabinet role. Assuming that he has not already acquired this experience as a Minister in some previous period in office, his experience as an Opposition Spokesman will give him some indication of the realities of political leadership, and of the problems involved in translating desired policy into acceptable political terms in a Parliamentary and party context. This can be, and has to be, learnt 'on the job' by any Minister who has not served as a Spokesman: the great advantage for a new Minister of having had front-bench experience in opposition, however, is that he can come to his Ministerial job with some of the necessary skills already acquired, and thus with clear benefits, particularly in the vital first weeks in office.

Towards a More Formal Opposition

Despite the several ways in which prior service as an Opposition Spokesman can be advantageous to a Minister, it has to be emphasised that being a member of the Opposition front-bench team remains basically different from being a member of the Ministerial team. Although the Shadow Government is an alternative Government, and *looks* like an alternative Government, the activities in which it indulges are *fundamentally* different from those of the Government. The full significance of this seemingly obvious fact is often under-estimated, and it is necessary to re-emphasise the basic distinction that exists in British politics between the Government and 'the rest', with 'the rest' embracing Opposition leaders, back-bench MPs of all parties, pressure groups, the press, and the many groups and individuals who comment upon Government activities. The Government alone is responsible for taking action in defence of the national interest: 'the rest' are merely on the outside looking in, criticising and seeking to influence those in power. Certainly, the Opposition leaders are different from 'the rest of the rest', in that they hope soon to replace the established Ministers, but as long as they remain in opposition they, like the rest of society, are 'mere mortals' and can only look on and comment while the Government alone takes action.

While accepting this fundamental distinction in roles between Government and Shadow Government, however, one of the clearest trends described in this study has been the overall tendency for Opposition front-bench practices to become more formal and sophisticated in the post-1945 period, and thereby to come to resemble those of office more closely. The clearest example of this has been the use since 1955 of formal titles for Opposition Spokesmen, with an official list of 'Shadow Government' members being made available to party, press, and public. Within this post-1955 pattern, the general structure of the team has gradually become more elaborate, with distinctions now being drawn between 'senior', 'deputy', 'assistant', and 'temporary' Spokesmen, and with the distinction also being made between the 'party Spokesman', and the 'House of Commons Spokesman', if the party's recognised expert in a particular field is a member of the Lords. The practice of paying a salary to the Leader of the Opposition, additional to his salary as an MP, has now extended to the Opposition Leader in the Lords, the Opposition chief whip in each House, and two assistant whips in the Commons. The Opposition salary bill, paid by the state, now amounts to some £30,000 a year. The secretarial provision that the Opposition party makes for its Shadow Cabinet has become more extensive, and in recent years both Labour and Conservative Leaders of the Opposition have had a 'Private Office' of up to ten clerical and administrative assistants, paid for by the party. The physical comforts of the Leader of the Opposition have increased in other ways also, and he is now provided with a car and a chauffeur. As well as these organisational changes, the Parliamentary behaviour of Opposition front benchers has come to resemble more closely that of Ministers in the important matter of the extent to which they concentrate their activity in their assigned subject areas.

In this context, however, it has to be emphasised that the influence of any particular party leader will be extremely important in determining patterns of organisation and behaviour in opposition. This study has been concerned primarily with the years 1951–72. In this time only Clement Attlee, Hugh Gaitskell, Harold Wilson, Sir Alec Douglas-Home, and Edward Heath served as Leader of the Opposition, and of these Sir Alec Douglas-Home served for less than a year. For the most part, therefore, the system and practices that have been described in this study reflect the leadership of only four men. With different Leaders of the Opposition somewhat different patterns might well have emerged, and this should be borne in mind before too firm conclusions are drawn about Opposition front-bench practices in general. The Leader of the Opposition, of course, lacks powers that contribute to the Prime Minister's dominant place in the Government team, and he is much less of a 'Presidential' figure, and much more of a 'first among equals', than is the Prime Minister. Nevertheless, the Leader of the Opposition has one clear advantage over the Prime Minister: his freedom to alter the structure of the Opposition team is greater than the Prime Minister's ability to re-structure the machinery of government. To some extent, certainly, a Prime Minister can adapt Government structure to meet the Ministerial needs of the moment and his own concepts of governmental organisation, but in general the structure of government is much more difficult to mould than is the structure of the Opposition team. There are no statutory provisions governing the Opposition front bench, a change of structure merely involves individuals and not departments of state, and party, Parliamentary and public expectations are vague as to the form that an Opposition team should take. Thus, much more readily than with the structure of government, the pattern of organisation and behaviour in opposition can be determined by the current party leader. In 1955 when Attlee introduced the system of official Spokesmen, he changed the nature of front-bench organisation quite fundamentally. Since 1955, the size of the team has varied considerably from time to time, and leader to leader, with Wilson's team since 1970 being much bigger than Attlee's and Gaitskell's team in the last period of Labour Opposition. Again, the level of subject specialisation achieved by Conservative Spokesmen under Edward Heath's leadership was markedly greater than that achieved in the previous period of Conservative Opposition, when Winston Churchill's attitude to specialisation was to 'let them wander free' over a number of subjects.

As these examples indicate, the Leader of the Opposition has considerable freedom to mould the shape and style of the Shadow Government (although the election of Labour's Parliamentary Committee clearly represents a major exception to this). While acknowledging the importance of the attitudes of particular Leaders of the Opposition, the general point remains that Opposition front-bench practices have become gradually more formal and sophisticated over the post-war period. A major consequence of this has been to increase the similarities in appearance between the Opposition and Government front-bench teams. The Opposition's appearance as an alternative Government has been strengthened, and the credibility of its 'office-seeking' role has been improved. How far, then, has the trend towards greater elaboration in Opposition front-bench organisation been merely 'window dressing' to emphasise to the electorate that the Opposition is a 'Government in waiting' operating already in conditions similar to those of office? Undoubtedly, this factor is not unimportant. Appearances *do* matter in the Opposition's attempts to persuade the electorate that it is a credible alternative

Government. To this end it is advantageous for Shadow Cabinet meetings and 'decisions' to be publicised by the media, and for the Shadow Cabinet to be photographed occasionally, sitting at work, as if ready to move en bloc into the Cabinet Room at 10 Downing Street. Similarly, the announcement of appointments to, or removals from, the Opposition 'team', the appearance of Opposition leaders alongside their Ministerial rivals in television programmes, and the publicity given to visits to foreign capitals by the Leader of the Opposition or his senior colleagues, all serve to reinforce the image of the Opposition as an alternative Government, poised to take over the reins of office.

In these ways, much of the seeming pretentiousness of Opposition front-bench organisation in fact fulfils an important image-building function. It is also the case to some extent that the nature of the Opposition party's organisation merely reflects a desire by former Ministers to create something approaching the organisational style to which they became accustomed while in office—rather like a deposed and decaying aristocracy seeking in exile to re-live former glories. Equally, there might be a tendency for ex-Ministers, and young, potential Ministers, to overdramatise the role of the Shadow Cabinet and Opposition Spokesmen, and to exaggerate the amount of time and effort required for Opposition functions to be performed adequately, in an attempt to relieve the frustrations and boredom of 'the waiting months' between general elections. Undoubtedly, a major problem for men accustomed to working twelve to eighteen hours a day on the affairs of Government, can be that of finding something to do with their time in opposition. Many former Ministers, of course, take up activities of one kind or another away from Parliament, and this, combined with their Parliamentary duties, can produce an extremely busy life. For some, however, the comparative leisure of opposition can encourage the over-elaboration of the tasks that they do have to perform as Opposition front benchers.

While acknowledging this, however, the existing level of sophistication of Opposition front-bench arrangements is more than merely 'window dressing', and is more than just a result of Opposition leaders seeking to give their role an exaggerated importance. A degree of elaborate organisation is necessary in order to manage the affairs of a large Parliamentary party that is seeking to examine the complex activities of a modern Government. In interview a number of Shadow Cabinet members maintained that a Shadow Cabinet meeting once a week was the very minimum level of consultation necessary in order to manage party affairs and determine current Parliamentary tactics. They argued that without at least this level of consultation by Opposition leaders, the affairs of the Parliamentary party, and the business of Parliamentary Opposition, would suffer through lack of direction. In this respect it has to be remembered that the Shadow Cabinet is a much less active body than the Cabinet, in that it meets only once or twice a week as a rule (whereas the Cabinet usually meets at least twice), its meetings usually last no more than an hour (while Cabinet meetings usually last two hours or more), and it delegates very little to sub-committees (whereas the Cabinet is at the centre of a web of sub-committees). Thus the Opposition leaders spend considerably less time in formal consultation than do Ministers. Again, the existence since 1955 of a Shadow Government, as well as a Shadow Cabinet, is partly a response to the increasingly complex and technical nature of the activities of government. If the Opposition is to perform effectively its role as scrutineer and critic of the Government, it is necessary today for it to have a recognised team of experts, capable of competing with the Minister with his vast departmental backing. Far from being merely an ostentation, the appointment of a Shadow Government made up of Spokesmen covering all policy areas, is to a large extent a practical device to help the Opposition to perform its role effectively in the modern world of 'big government' and technical government.

Thus as well as increasing its credibility as a potential Government, the greater sophistication of Opposition front-bench organisation has been designed to improve the Opposition's ability to perform its role as a Parliamentary critic. Without these developments, this aspect of the Opposition's role would be executed in a much less professional manner than it is today. Nevertheless, there is undoubtedly room for further developments along the same lines, to strengthen further the Opposition's hand in the Parliamentary battle. The Opposition remains at a distinct disadvantage in its confrontations with a Government that is backed by a vast Civil Service machine that provides guidance on the whole range of activities of the modern state. Both the quantity and the technicality of legislation has so increased in recent years that Opposition leaders are much less able to be self-sufficient than was the case earlier in the century. While the modern system of a Shadow Cabinet and Opposition Spokesmen has evolved partly in response to this situation, there is undoubtedly room for further developments along the same lines. There is much to be said, for example, in favour of the provision for Opposition Spokesmen of better sources of information and more research assistance than exist at present. One possibility would be to establish a senior civil servant within each department with the function of acting as a liaison officer with the Opposition. In interviews a number of Spokesmen claimed that it would be a considerable advantage for them to have an official point of contact with the departments they were covering. Such an official need not become an Opposition spy, but could serve as an information officer, through whom requests for information could be made. The more direct the contacts between the Opposition and the established departments of state, of course, the greater is the danger of civil servants becoming schizophrenic, with their primary duty to their Ministers being challenged to some extent by their need to be fair to the Opposition. At present, however, civil servants provide information for the House of Commons Select Committees on a fairly regular basis, so that the creation of closer contacts with the Opposition Spokesmen would be merely an extension of this sort of function. Civil servants' inhibitions about contacts with Opposition leaders might be eased if all members of the Parliamentary Committee and Consultative Committee were made members of the Privy Council, and were thereby subject to the oath of secrecy. This might limit the sort of information that Spokesmen could use in the Parliamentary battles, but access to this information could be valuable when Spokesmen were preparing plans for future office. Another way round the problem would be to create a special department of state to service the Opposition, thereby providing a small 'Opposition Civil Service', financed out of public funds, and answerable to the Leader of the Opposition. A number of Spokesmen favoured such an innovation, although they acknowledged that it was an unlikely development in the immediate future.

Barker and Rush, in their study of MPs' sources of information, argue that Spokesmen have less need for research assistants than have backbenchers, as they have the resources of their party's Research Department behind them.[1] This may be true of Conservative Spokesmen, but it is clearly less true of Labour Spokesmen, who are not so well served by Transport House. Thus the creation by the Labour Party of a separate 'Parliamentary Research Department' or 'Centre for Labour Studies' was advocated by some Labour Spokesmen in interview. Such a body would cover the specifically Parliamentary needs of Labour MPs and Spokesmen, and would thereby free the Transport House Research Department to concentrate on its work on long-term policy.[2] Even Conservative Spokesmen, despite all their assistance from the Research Department, would no doubt also benefit from the provision of free secretarial and clerical assistance, together with the services of one or more research assistants, constantly on call in the House, who could do something to counter-balance the Minister's team of Parliamentary Private Secretaries and personal assistants within the Ministry. Some Conservative Spokesmen pointed out in interview that although their young Research Department officers were efficient and conscientious, they often lacked specifically Parliamentary political instincts, and that personal research assistants were called for, located in Parliament. The Joseph Rowntree Social Service Trust has recently given grants of £2,500 to the Labour and Liberal Parties to provide assistance for MPs[3] (the Conservatives, as the government party, did not take up the offer directly, although some help was given to the PEST group). Such schemes, if more money were available, could provide research assistance for at least some Spokesmen.

[1] *The Member of Parliament and His Information*, pp. 326–32.
[2] For conflicting views of this proposal see letters in *The Guardian*, 11 and 14 October 1971.
[3] For a comment see *The Guardian*, 2 November 1971.

The Leader of the Opposition has his own small private office staff, paid for by the NEC in the case of a Labour leader, and by Central Office in the case of a Conservative leader. This function could perhaps be better financed by Parliament, and this would free the Leader from obligations to his party, and would give him greater freedom in the use he made of his private office staff. The material lot of individual Spokesmen could also be improved. Among the office accommodation in the Palace of Westminster there is a 'Shadow Cabinet corridor', where Consultative Committee or Parliamentary Committee members have offices, and where some of the Leader of the Opposition's staff is located. At present, however, not all Spokesmen who are outside the Shadow Cabinet have sole use of an office. In interview, a number of Spokesmen complained that the inadequacy of the existing office accommodation reduced their efficiency. They pointed out that they had to store files and records at home, and for interviews had to rely on the general interview rooms, bars, or corridors of the Commons. There is much to be said for automatically allocating office space to Spokesmen on appointment, as a base from which to operate.

The duties of some Spokesmen, such as those concerned with local government or regional development, involve travel within the United Kingdom if the job is to be carried out effectively. Other duties, like defence and foreign affairs, involve travel abroad if the Spokesman is to be fully up to date. For the Leader of the Opposition and very senior party figures, the party will meet the cost of tours at home and abroad, and sometimes the departments of state will finance a trip by an Opposition Spokesman, as it is in their interests that the Opposition should be well informed, and perhaps obligated to the Government. Many of the travelling and other expenses incurred by Spokesmen, however, are not met by the party or anyone else. All such 'occupational expenses' could perhaps justifiably be met by Parliament, thus giving the Spokesmen more independence in the performance of their duties. In the Canadian Federal Parliament the Opposition parties receive grants, paid out of Parliamentary funds. The minor parties benefit from this, as well as the main Opposition party, although the size of the grant that a party receives is roughly in proportion to the number of its MPs. In Sweden and West Germany also, direct state subsidies are paid to the parties, partly in order to free them from dependence upon their traditional paymasters. As in Canada, the size of the grant is determined by the extent of the party's electoral support. While the wisdom of this particular aspect of the system can perhaps be questioned, the general principle of the Canadian, Swedish and German schemes could be introduced profitably in Britain.

As a further step, a Spokesman could be paid a salary higher than that of a backbench MP. One of the proposals that is sometimes canvassed as an alternative to a flat increase in an MP's salary is the payment of a bonus to those MPs who are particularly active in the House, in committee work and the like. The difficulty with such a scheme is that of finding a satisfactory formula for deciding which MPs merit a bonus award. If, however, the principle is seen as viable, then Opposition Spokesmen could be among those worthy of such payment for special services. Although the job of a Spokesman is by no means as time-consuming as that of a Minister, to do the job conscientiously involves a considerable amount of time and effort. Thus one Conservative ex-Minister revealed that he gave up his job as a Spokesman because he found it '. . . too much of a chore without the help of civil servants and the use of a car, and without any great financial rewards.' When a party goes into opposition the former Ministers often seek part-time employment outside Parliament, partly because the drop in salary from that of a Minister to that of a MP is quite marked. Thus a former Minister may find that he will have his duties as an MP, a part-time occupation outside Parliament, and his duties as an Opposition Spokesman. The payment of a salary differential for service as an Opposition Spokesman would enable MPs to concentrate upon their duties full-time, without the need for outside occupations. As well as the Leader of the Opposition, the Opposition Leader in the Lords, the Opposition chief whip in each House, and two assistant whips in the Commons now all receive salaries.

The payment of a salary to the Spokesmen, or at least to the members of the Consultative Committee or the Parliamentary Committee, would be a desirable and logical further step.

While it may not always be easy to feel personal sympathy for 'deprived' ex-Ministers, having to live in opposition without an official car, and with a reduced salary, it is in the interests of an effective Parliamentary system for Opposition leaders to be able to devote themselves fully to their Parliamentary duties, without the distractions of a part-time job outside Parliament. The argument, of course, is not that Opposition leaders should receive higher salaries because they were used to a certain income as a Minister, but is that they should receive a salary that will enable them to give their Opposition duties their undivided attention. Thus in return for the payment of a salary differential, a Spokesman, like a Minister, would have to undertake to abandon any outside employment.

The payment of grants, salaries, bonuses, or expenses, the provision of secretarial, clerical, and research assistance, and the improvement of contacts between Spokesmen and the departments of state, could lead to a more efficient performance of the tasks of an Opposition, and could increase the attraction of service as an Opposition Spokesman. Such reforms would help to redress the balance between the Opposition and the Government. It is one aspect of the reform of Parliament that has not been explored in any depth, but which clearly is worthy of consideration. Two fundamental objections, however, are always advanced against such proposals. The first is that it is illogical to expect the Government to assist materially the attempts of the Opposition to probe Ministerial deficiencies. In 1937, during the passage through the Commons of the Bill to provide a salary for the Leader of the Opposition, the Conservative MP, P. C. Loftus, maintained that:

> Surely, it is almost absurd to pay an individual to do everything he possibly can, as is his duty as Leader of the Opposition, to criticise and hinder the work of the King's Government, carried out by the King's paid servants. That is an anomaly.[1]

This argument is invariably raised when any further attempts are made to formalise the machinery of opposition, and it reflects Otto Kirchheimer's observation, quoted to preface the book, as to the 'eternal paradox' of the notion that '. . . impedi-

[1] 323 H.C. Debs. 5s col. 632.

ments to political action may be wholesome and are therefore to be protected.' The situation is neither anomalous nor paradoxical, however, once the principle is established that a 'loyal' opposition is concerned only with 'limited' resistance within agreements on the basic features of the political system. Once it is recognised that the Opposition is concerned not with pulling the system down, but with improving it, the encouragement of its activities is not only logical, but highly desirable.

The second fundamental objection is that no matter how logical and desirable the toleration of a loyal Opposition may be, the system has various undesirable side-effects which are emphasised by any reforms designed to make the Opposition's position stronger. Undoubtedly, the encouragement of an official Opposition does carry with it a number of disadvantages for the political system. As discussed in Chapter 1, the presence of an Opposition, ready to pounce, can encourage secrecy and discourage enterprise on the part of Ministers. It can stimulate artificial divisions over policy, and this sham warfare can serve to discredit all politicians and the whole political system. The constant highlighting of Government failures also can encourage the view that all Governments are incurably incompetent, and that there exists a situation of permanent national crisis and failure.

These factors are limitations on the desirability of a system which includes an official Opposition within Parliament which at one and the same time can be 'loyal' to the Crown, but extremely 'disloyal' to the Crown's current Ministers. These limitations clearly have to be included in any balance sheet of the strengths and weaknesses of the British system. The great merits of the principle of an official Opposition, of course, are that it serves to keep the Government up to the mark, and it provides an alternative Government 'in the wings', ready to take over should the electorate seek a change. These major benefits (it is argued here, at least) outweigh the other factors referred to above: once the value of an official loyal Opposition is accepted, the Government has to reconcile itself to the paradox and the disadvantages of assisting its critics to some extent, in order that the constitutional role of the Opposition can be fulfilled most effectively. As has been suggested in this study, the increased formalisation and professionalisation of Opposition front-bench arrangements represent attempts to strengthen the Opposition in the two aspects of its role. On the one hand they serve to increase the efficiency of the Opposition as a critic of the Government, and on the other they enable the Opposition to pose more convincingly as an organised, cohesive 'Government in waiting'. Despite the claims of those who see a fundamental anomaly in the concept of an official, publicly financed Opposition, further changes to increase the similarities in the structure and organisation of the Government and the Opposition should be welcomed as being likely to benefit the British political system as a whole, through the more effective performance of the twin functions of Her Majesty's Loyal Opposition.

Appendices

APPENDIX A

Coalitions, Liberals, and Peers

THIS STUDY has centred on the role, organisation and behaviour of the Opposition front bench in the House of Commons in the 'normal', modern, peacetime situation of Labour–Conservative two-party conflict. Only passing references have been made to the nature of Parliamentary Opposition in wartime, or to the role of the Liberal Party over the last fifty years as the 'third party', or 'second Opposition', in the Commons, or to the role of the Opposition front bench in the House of Lords. In this Appendix some brief comments are offered on these three topics, which are only incidental to the main themes of the book, but which are of interest within the general context of Parliamentary Opposition in Britain.

Parliamentary Opposition in Wartime

In times of national emergency, and especially in wartime, Parliamentary Opposition becomes particularly difficult. In major crises such as the two world wars this century, or even in rather lesser crises, like Suez in 1956 or Northern Ireland more recently, there is clearly a role for a critical Opposition to play. In such situations as much as, or more than, in more settled times, there is a need for Government inefficiency to be revealed and attacked, in and out of Parliament. At the same time, in emergency situations great emphasis is normally placed on national unity, so that those who dare to criticise the Government's handling of the crisis are readily condemned for 'rocking the boat' or 'lining up with the enemy' or 'stabbing the troops in the back'. The general tendency for a Parliamentary Opposition, even in peacetime, to appear carping and generally unpatriotic, is greatly increased in wartime or in crisis situations. In major crisis situations, therefore, those in opposition are often faced with a choice between attempting to preserve the 'normal' Parliamentary confrontation between the Government and a hostile Opposition, or, in the interests of national unity, seeking to suspend party conflict through the creation of a Coalition Government for the duration of the crisis. In the two world wars of this century Coalition Governments eventually were formed, although the single-party Governments in power at the outbreak of war remained in office for almost a year before a Coalition came into being. In the first few months of war, therefore, Opposition MPs (Unionist in 1914 and Labour in 1939) were brought face to face with the dilemma of how to react to the national emergency: should they maintain a normal, critical role, in order that the Government's mistakes be revealed, and the war pursued as efficiently as possible, or should they refrain from criticism in the interests of national unity? On each occasion different elements within the Opposition party came to conflicting conclusions.

With the outbreak of war in 1914 the Asquith Liberal Government remained in office, and the Unionist Shadow Cabinet continued to meet,[1] but something of a general political truce was agreed upon by the party leaders. Contacts between the Government and the Opposition became closer, and Asquith consulted Bonar Law before the actual declaration of war.[2] Lord Lansdowne, the Unionist Leader in the Lords, was also taken into the confidence of the Cabinet, and he became chairman of the important Manpower Committee.[3] A compromise was reached over the issue of Irish home rule, which had divided the country in the period up to the outbreak of war; the Unionists agreed not to press resistance to the Home Rule Bill in the House of Lords, while for its part the Government agreed that the measure would not be implemented until after the war, and that the question of

---

[1] Beaverbrook, *Politicians and the War*, I, p. 51.
[2] Ibid., p. 38.
[3] Newton, *Lord Lansdowne*, p. 442.

Ulster would then be reviewed.[1] Bonar Law was conscious of the need to give the Government every support in its handling of the war situation, but some of his more militant colleagues called for vigorous attacks upon the Government's handling of the war. Walter Long, in particular, argued that a silent Opposition was pointless, and that either there should be a normal, vigorous Opposition, or else a Coalition Government should be formed.[2] A Unionist Business Committee was formed in January 1915 by those who shared Walter Long's views.[3] Initially, the Business Committee comprised a group of some twenty-five Unionists who were opposed to Bonar Law's policy of co-operation with the Government, but eventually a majority of Unionist MPs joined its ranks.[4] It had a small executive committee, with Walter Long as its chairman. The Business Committee sought to stir up unrest over the crisis caused by the shortage of munitions in the Spring of 1915, despite Bonar Law's attempts to play the issue down at first.[5] At a Shadow Cabinet meeting on 14 May 1915, however, Bonar Law and the other leading Unionists decided to adopt a more critical approach in Parliament in an effort to make the Government more active.[6] It was largely as a consequence of the munitions crisis, and its effects on Government–Opposition relations, that Asquith decided to re-organise the Government into a Coalition made up of most of the leading Liberals and Unionists, and some Labour MPs. In 1916 Asquith was replaced as Prime Minister by Lloyd George, but the Government remained a Coalition for the remainder of the war.

Similar disagreements over tactics between 'hawks' and 'doves' among Opposition MPs, emerged at the beginning of the second world war. For the first nine months of the war, when military incidents were only sporadic, the Chamberlain Conservative Government stayed in office, and Labour remained in opposition. The PLP agreed to support the

---

[1] Petrie, *Life and Letters of Sir Austen Chamberlain*, pp. 5 and 14.

[2] Beaverbrook, *Politicians and the War*, I, p. 93.

[3] For a list of the original members, see Petrie, *Walter Long and His Times*, p. 188.

[4] Petrie, *Life and Letters of Sir Austen Chamberlain*, p. 18.

[5] Beaverbrook, *Politicians and the War*, I, p. 93.   [6] Ibid., p. 113.

Government in its conduct of the war, and the Government undertook to keep the Opposition well supplied with information.[1] To this end, Labour's Parliamentary Committee members were linked to particular Ministers, with, for example, A. V. Alexander covering the Admiralty, H. B. Lees-Smith the War Office, and Hugh Dalton the Air Ministry.[2] Some Labour MPs, however, including Herbert Morrison, argued from the very outbreak of war that the PLP should not support the Chamberlain Government, but should work to secure its resignation in order that a more dynamic leadership could be obtained.[3] At various times during the first few months of the war the Parliamentary Committee considered this question without ever coming to a clear decision to withdraw support from the Government.[4] In the spring of 1940, however, hostilities broke out in earnest, and the British military expedition to Norway ended in failure. The Chamberlain Government was forced to resign, and Winston Churchill formed a Coalition Government made up of leading Conservative and Labour figures, together with some Liberals and non-party men. The Coalition remained in office until the end of the war in Europe, although an election was held in 1945 before the final defeat of Japan.

Thus for much the greater part of the two wars, Coalition Governments were in office in Britain. Coalition Governments have also operated in peacetime on two occasions this century —1918–22, when the Lloyd George Wartime Coalition Government was extended into the post-war period, and for a year from August 1931, when the MacDonald National Government was formed to deal with the economic crisis.[5] During the lives of these two peacetime Coalition Governments, however, something like a 'normal' Opposition existed in the Commons. In 1918 Lloyd George's Coalition was backed by Coalition Unionists, Coalition Liberals, and a handful of Coalition Labour. Most Labour MPs, however, remained opposed to the Government, together with the Asquithian Liberals, the Irish party, and various other groups. Thus the

---

[1] Dalton, *Memoirs*, II, p. 272.   [2] Ibid.   [3] Ibid., p. 282.
[4] Ibid., p. 297; Morrison, *An Autobiography*, p. 172.
[5] See A. J. Beattie, 'British Coalition Government Re-visited', *Government and Opposition*, 1966–7, pp. 3–34.

usual basic division of the Commons into the Government party and the main Opposition party was replaced by a division into the Coalition Government and various anti-Coalition groups, although between them these anti-Coalition elements made up almost a third of the Commons. In 1931 all but a handful of Labour MPs remained in opposition to the National Government, and functioned as a 'normal' Opposition, although after the general election in October 1931 there were only fifty-two Labour MPs.

Thus the wartime Coalitions have better claims to be regarded as truly all-party Governments than have the Coalitions of 1918–22 and 1931–2. Even in wartime, however, the union was far from complete. In 1915 and 1940 the parties retained their distinct organisational structures, in and out of Parliament, and preserved their own whipping arrangements. Also, although in both world wars the three main parties agreed to observe a by-election truce (whereby the party holding the seat was not opposed by the other main parties), minor party and independent candidates continued to oppose candidates who supported the Coalition Government. In such by-elections, the electorate still had something of a choice between the Coalition Government candidate and 'the rest'. Further, within Parliament there were various groups and individuals who regarded themselves as being in opposition to the Government, and who subjected its activities to searching enquiry. Writing of the eighteenth-century attempts to create Ministries 'of all the talents', Ionescu and de Madariaga point out that, 'Efforts to construct a government composed of the best men regardless of party failed, since an opposition automatically formed against whoever was in power'.[1] The same general point can be made about the wartime attempts to create all-party coalitions. In May 1915, Henry Chaplin, as a senior and respected Unionist figure who had not joined the Coalition Government, served as a nominal Leader of the Opposition, asking the Business Questions, and speaking second on formal occasions.[2] More critical opposition, however, came from various 'pressure groups' of MPs and peers.

---

[1] G. Ionescu and I. de Madariaga, *Opposition*, London 1968, p. 52.
[2] Lord Oxford and Asquith, *Memories and Reflections* (2 vols), London 1928, I, p. 177.

Lord Milner led a 'Forward Party' in the Lords, and Sir Edward Carson a 'Unionist War Committee' in the Commons.[1] These two bodies campaigned for a more vigorous war policy. L. S. Amery was also prominent among the Conservative MPs opposed to the Coalition Government's handling of the war, and he called for the formation of a War Policy Cabinet.[2] Amery, Milner, and Carson were regular attenders at a dinner group of seven or eight prominent Unionists outside the Government who were highly critical of the Government's handling of the war.[3] This Unionist 'ginger group' became increasingly hostile to Asquith during 1916, and in particular Milner pressed for the introduction of conscription. Largely as a result of his vigorous opposition to the Asquith Government, Milner was awarded a Cabinet post when Lloyd George became Prime Minister in December 1916.[4]

Thus even with the formation of an all-party Coalition in 1915, 'ginger groups' or 'pressure groups' remained in both Houses of Parliament, performing the role of scrutineers and critics of the Government's war policies. With the resignation of Asquith as Prime Minister in 1916, and the departure of some of his supporters from their Ministerial posts, the Liberal Party divided into 'Asquithian' and 'Lloyd Georgian' camps, with the Asquithian Liberals constituting an Opposition group in Parliament. They sat on the Opposition benches, Asquith served as Leader of the Opposition, and Herbert Samuel became chairman of the new Select Committee on Expenditure in 1917.[5] Asquith was not in favour of vigorous, critical opposition to the Coalition, and he did not vote against any Government proposal until May 1918, eighteen months after becoming Leader of the Opposition. He has recorded that, as a consequence, some of his colleagues found him 'unduly fainthearted and mealy-mouthed'.[6] When he did oppose the Government, however, in the 'Maurice debate' in May 1918, on the military situation on the western front, he

[1] Gollin, *Proconsul in Politics*, p. 307; Beaverbrook, *Politicians and the War*, II, p. 87.

[2] Amery, *My Political Life*, II, p. 67.

[3] Ibid., p. 81.

[4] Gollin, *Proconsul in Politics*, p. 370.

[5] Jenkins, *Asquith*, p. 464; Lord Samuel, *Memoirs*, London 1945, pp. 1–8.

[6] Oxford and Asquith, *Memories and Reflections*, II, p. 167.

was bitterly attacked for being unpatriotic, and in the 1918 general election Liberals who had voted with Asquith at the end of the Maurice debate were similarly condemned out of hand.[1]

In the second world war, as in the 1915–16 period, groups of MPs maintained criticism of the all-party Coalition Government. In May 1940 the PLP decided that an 'Administrative Committee' should be formed, made up of those members of the Parliamentary Committee and of the 'second eleven' who were not given posts in the Government.[2] This Administrative Committee, which held its first meeting on 23 May 1940, operated throughout the war years, and fulfilled the same broad functions as the peacetime Parliamentary Committee. H. B. Lees-Smith and F. W. Pethick-Lawrence were the only Privy Councillors serving on the Administrative Committee in 1940, and Lees-Smith was elected to serve as acting chairman of the PLP.[3] Like Henry Chaplin in 1915, Lees-Smith occupied the Leader of the Opposition's seat in the Commons, put the weekly Business Questions on Thursdays, and generally performed the duties of a Leader of the Opposition, although the payment of the Leader of the Opposition's salary was suspended during the lifetime of the Coalition.[4] Pethick-Lawrence acted as his deputy, and served as chairman of the Public Accounts Committee.[5] When Lees-Smith became ill in December 1940, Pethick-Lawrence succeeded him, until he in turn was replaced by Arthur Greenwood when he left the Government in February 1942.[6] As soon as the Coalition was formed, Lees-Smith had talks with the Speaker, and with Conservative Privy Councillors who were not in the Government, about the occupancy of the Opposition front bench. The Speaker quoted Erskine May to the effect that 'The front bench on the Opposition side, though other members may sit there, is reserved for leading Members of the Opposition who

[1] C. L. Mowat, *Britain Between the Wars*, London 1955, p. 3.

[2] Dalton, *Memoirs*, II, p. 332; Shinwell, *The Labour Story*, p. 165. See above, p. 58, for comments on the nature of the 'second eleven' at this time.

[3] Dalton, *Memoirs*, II, p. 332.

[4] See above, p. 82, footnote 3.

[5] Brittain, *Pethick-Lawrence*, p. 117.

[6] Ibid.

have served in the offices of State'.[1] The Speaker maintained that this was flexible enough to allow ex-Ministers and 'a few prominent back benchers' to share the bench. Accordingly, Conservative Privy Councillors outside the Government and members of Labour's Administrative Committee both occupied the Opposition front bench for the life of the Coalition.[2]

As in 1915, however, the general arrangements made in 1940 were not approved of by the more militant MPs, as they felt that Lees-Smith had been chosen to serve as a nominal Leader of the Opposition only because he would be unlikely to be a vigorous critic of the Government.[3] James Maxton argued that he should have filled Lees-Smith's post, as the ILP members were the only genuine opponents of the war.[4] Emanuel Shinwell was also critical of the arrangement, although he had little support among the members of the PLP, most of whom were prepared to accept a muted Opposition for the duration of the war.[5] Shinwell has since commented on the wartime situation that 'On the Labour side mild criticism came only from Pethick-Lawrence, Arthur Woodburn, and James Griffiths, with rather more forceful criticism from Aneurin Bevan and myself.'[6] Harold Macmillan has also acknowledged that Bevan and Shinwell among Labour MPs, the Earl Winterton among the Conservatives, were the only real and persistent Parliamentary critics that the Government had to face.[7] They scrutinised and criticised the Government through debates and questions, but more particularly through new Parliamentary institutions, like the Select Committee on National Expenditure, and the Scrutiny Committee (the forerunner of the Statutory Instruments Committee).

Thus Opposition in Parliament was not silenced during the lifetime of the wartime Coalition Governments. In May 1940 the Speaker of the House of Commons observed that 'It cannot be said that there is now an Opposition in Parliament in the hitherto accepted meaning of the words; namely, a party in

[1] 361 H.C. Debs. 5s col. 27. See above, p. 56.
[2] Griffiths, *Pages from Memory*, p. 69.
[3] Shinwell, *The Labour Story*, p. 165.
[4] Griffiths, *Pages from Memory*, p. 69.
[5] Shinwell, *The Labour Story*, p. 165.   [6] Ibid., p. 164.
[7] Macmillan, *Tides of Fortune*, p. 65.

Opposition to the Government from which an alternative Government could be formed.'[1] Nevertheless, in 1940, as in 1915, there remained within Parliament various groups and individuals who constituted, in effect, a 'non-office-seeking opposition'. Their role was that of a critical pressure group, rather than an alternative Government; they performed one of the vital functions of opposition (that of scrutinising and criticising those in power in order to keep them on their toes), without performing the other function (that of posing as an alternative set of rulers). To some extent, therefore, their role was a reversion to that played by Parliament in the seventeenth century and earlier, before the constitutional developments of the eighteenth century produced the modern concept of the role of an Opposition being combined with that of an alternative Government.

The Liberal Party in Opposition

Like the Parliamentary critics of the Wartime Coalition Governments, the Liberal Party has long had the status of a 'non-office-seeking Opposition'. Although the party may still have dreams of attaining office at some time in the future, in reality for many years it has been doomed to a seemingly permanent place on the Opposition side of the House. The last Liberal Government in Britain left office on 25 May 1915, when Asquith's Liberal Ministry gave way to a Coalition. Liberals, of course, held posts in the Coalition Governments under Asquith and Lloyd George in the 1915–22 period, and also in the Coalition Governments that were formed in 1931 and 1940, but an exclusively Liberal Government has not existed since May 1915. Further, since 1922 the Liberals have been relegated to the status of third party in the Commons, or 'second opposition party'. In the 1920s, and perhaps the 1930s, the Liberal leaders could enjoy reasonable hopes that the party would regain its position as a party of government. Since 1945, however, the Liberals have had no real prospects of office. The number of Liberal MPs elected at general elections since 1945 has ranged from six to twelve, and even with by-election gains there have been no more than thirteen

[1] 361 H.C. Debs. 5s col. 28.

Liberal MPs in the House at any one time. Thus, with never
more than 2 per cent of the seats in the Commons, the status
of the Liberal Party in Parliament in the post-war period has
been fundamentally different from that of the main Opposition
party, which, as emphasised throughout this study, is essentially office-seeking *and* office-attaining. In view of this, how
does the organisation and behaviour of the Parliamentary
Liberal Party compare with that of the main Opposition
party?

It was noted in Chapter 6 that recent experience of office,
and the hopes and prospects of future office, could act as a
restraining influence upon the main Opposition party, causing
it to be 'responsible', and often excessively cautious in its
approach to Government policies. Unlike the main Opposition
party, however, the Liberal Party, in the formulation of its
attitudes, is not hampered by 'ghosts' from previous periods in
office, and is not restricted by the possibility of having to form
a Government and thereby have to justify comments made in
opposition. Further, it has been argued that 'Minor parties
whose vocation is the propagation of opinions can afford unpopularity; major parties cannot.'[1] Is the Liberal Party,
therefore, in a position to be unrestrained in its criticisms of
Government policies, and in its advocacy of sweeping alternatives? Undoubtedly, on many occasions the Liberals have
been noticeably more willing to advocate 'extreme' solutions to
problems than have the Government or the main Opposition
party. In 1965, for example, the Liberals advocated the use
of military force to assist in the crushing of the Rhodesian
rebellion, when both the Labour Government and the
Conservative Opposition rejected this course. Again, throughout the 1960s the Liberals were more outspoken in their
criticisms of American involvement in Vietnam than were
either of the other parties, in office or in opposition. For the
most part, however, the Liberal Party behaves in no less
restrained a manner than do the two office-seeking parties.
There are various reasons why this should be so. In the first
place, the Liberal Party, despite its radical stance on some

[1] Giuseppe di Palma, 'Disaffection and Participation in Western
Democracies: the Role of Political Oppositions', *Journal of Policies*, 1969,
p. 990.

social issues, is essentially a moderate, middle-of-the-road party, and its MPs are responsible men. A Communist or 'Poujadist' party in the same Parliamentary position as the Liberals might be less likely to operate within an all-party consensus. At the same time, however, any minor party, be it Communist, Poujadist, or Liberal, that is without recent experience of office, and has no immediate prospects of office, is very susceptible to accusations of being irresponsible and out of touch with the realities of office. Extreme policies such as the halving of income tax, or the doubling of Government expenditure, might pay electoral dividends in the short term, but a minor party that constantly advocated such policies would soon have its credibility destroyed by the main parties. The very fact, therefore, that the Liberal Party is free from direct responsibility for government means that it has to be at pains to show that it is a responsible party. Thus the tag of 'Bomber Thorpe' that was attached to the Liberal leader after his advocacy of the use of even limited military forces in the Rhodesian situation, undoubtedly proved embarrassing. Although the Liberal Party's role in Parliament is a subordinate one, it is certainly not the case that it has 'nothing to lose'. It wishes to improve, and at the very least maintain, its Parliamentary strength, but with the exception of Orkney and Shetland, its current seats are held by precarious majorities, and it cannot afford to antagonise the all-important moderate electoral opinion.

For electoral considerations, then, the Liberal Party has to appear credible and responsible as a Parliamentary force. As well as these factors, however, there is a more general pressure upon the Parliamentary Liberal Party, especially from its own activists and supporters, to organise itself and conduct its Parliamentary affairs as though it still had the status of a party of Government. Particularly in face of the party's past glories, many Liberals feel the need to 'keep up with the Joneses', and adopt the general stance of a party with Ministerial pretensions. Today, with only a handful of MPs, the Liberals cannot follow the organisational patterns of the two main Parliamentary parties. For a while in the 1920s, however, the Liberals continued to function as a party expecting soon to return to office, with a Shadow Cabinet meeting regularly.

The Asquith Liberals remained outside the Lloyd George Coalition Government that continued in office after the 1918 election, and Asquith held a number of 'conclaves' with his senior colleagues to prepare for future office.[1] Sir Edward Grey, Walter Runciman, Sir Donald Maclean, and Lord Crewe were generally among those regularly attending these gatherings. Even after 1922, when Labour had replaced the Liberals as the main Opposition party, and the Liberals no longer provided the Leader of the Opposition, Asquith continued to call Shadow Cabinet meetings. With the break-up of the Coalition Government in 1922, there was something of a reconciliation between Asquith and Lloyd George, and both wings of the party were represented in the Liberal Shadow Cabinet under Asquith's leadership in the 1922–6 period.[2] Conflict continued at this level, however, and at one Shadow Cabinet meeting in May 1924 Asquith and Lloyd George clashed over the question of the attitude the party should adopt towards the Labour Government's electoral reform proposals.[3] There was a further major clash between the two men in May 1926, when Lloyd George dissented from the official Liberal attitude of condemning the general strike.[4] Lloyd George spoke in public in support of the strike, and Asquith criticised him for breaching the collective responsibility of the Shadow Cabinet, which Asquith equated with that of an actual Cabinet.[5]

Later in 1926, following Asquith's retirement through ill health, Lloyd George became overall party leader, but unlike Asquith he was reluctant to institute a regular system of Shadow Cabinet meetings.[6] Similarly, Sir Herbert Samuel (who led the party 1931–5) and Sir Archibald Sinclair

[1] Jenkins, *Asquith*, pp. 490–2; Lord Oxford and Asquith, *H.H.A.: Letters to a Friend*, London 1933, p. 196.

[2] Jenkins, *Asquith*, p. 512.

[3] T. Wilson, *The Downfall of the Liberal Party 1914–35*, London 1968, p. 296.

[4] F. Owen, *Tempestuous Journey: Lloyd George, His Life and Times*, London 1954, pp. 704–6; Spender and Asquith, *Life of Lord Oxford and Asquith*, II, pp. 361–71; Oxford and Asquith, *Memories and Reflections*, II, p. 236; Samuel, *Memoirs*, London 1945, p. 195.

[5] See *The Times*, 2 June 1926. See above, p. 287, for other comments.

[6] Mowat, *Britain Between the Wars*, p. 348.

(1935–45), rarely summoned formal gatherings of their leading colleagues, although some such meetings did occasionally take place.[1] Since 1945 the number of Liberal MPs has fluctuated between five and thirteen, and these have been small enough numbers to allow the party's Parliamentary affairs to be dealt with at gatherings of all Liberal MPs. Thus a Parliamentary executive committee has been unnecessary. At present, the Parliamentary Liberal Party holds a regular meeting at 5.30 p.m. on Wednesdays whenever Parliament is in session. As well as the six MPs, the leader and whip of the Liberal peers also attend, together with any of the other thirty or so Liberal peers who choose to do so. The meeting is also generally attended by some figures from outside Parliament, like the head of the Research Department and other party officials. In all, there are generally about fifteen persons present. The meeting is chaired by the party leader, or in his absence, by the whip in the Commons. The main item dealt with at each meeting is the next week's Parliamentary business, and the coordination of attitudes and tactics in the two Houses. After the meeting, the six MPs often meet together alone in order to deal with purely House of Commons matters, and the Liberal peers also generally meet together the next day.

Despite their remoteness from prospects of office, the Liberals follow the practice of the other two parties and give MPs the title of 'Spokesmen' for particular subjects. Each of the Liberal MPs has a subject or subjects in which he specialises, and for which he is regarded as the party's principal Parliamentary Spokesman. In effect, therefore, all Liberal MPs are front benchers, and when David Steel was elected in a by-election in 1965 he at once became Liberal Spokesman on Labour affairs. Thus the leader has no choice of members for his team, although he does determine which topics will be allocated to each MP. Technically, it is possible for a Liberal MP to resign from his responsibility, but such an event clearly would cause considerable difficulties for such a small Parliamentary group.

As well as the general desire to follow the practices of the main Opposition party, the very fact that there are so few Liberal MPs means that they need to divide the Parliamentary

[1] See, for example, Samuel, *Memoirs*, p. 276.

work load among themselves on a fairly strict basis. The volume and nature of the business before Parliament means that the individual Liberal MPs cannot master the details of all subjects, and yet the party is expected to have a point of view on every subject. Often at very short notice Liberal MPs themselves need guidance on how to respond to, and vote on, the details of legislation, and this guidance has to come from some 'expert' within the ranks of the Parliamentary party. The mass media look for statements of official party attitudes from the Liberals as well as from the two main parties, and if the Liberals are to attract publicity they have to be able to provide informed comment at short notice. Liberal Party supporters also look to their MPs as authoritative sources of information, and as guides on policy questions.

To meet these various demands, the small band of Liberal MPs have to specialise. Before 1964 the allocation of MPs to particular subject areas was very informal and flexible, and no official lists of names and duties were issued to the press. When Liberal representation rose to nine in 1964, however, and to twelve in 1966, more formal arrangements were made, and these were announced to press and public. Each MP was given a particular responsibility for one subject area, and was accorded the title of Liberal Party Spokesman for that subject. As well as this prime responsibility, most Liberal MPs also had a subordinate responsibility for another subject or subjects, so that most topics were covered by two or three of the dozen or so MPs. The allocation of responsibilities during the last session of the 1969–70 Parliament is shown in Table 41. The party leader was not given any specific area to cover, but, like his Labour or Conservative counterpart, was left free to roam over all subject areas. After the 1970 election, when Liberal representation once again fell to six, the MPs continued to specialise in particular subjects, but, as in the 1959–64 Parliament, the allocation of these responsibilities was not made public. For the Liberal peers, however, an official list of Spokesmen was again published, with the duties for the new Parliament being the same as those listed in Table 41 for the 1969–70 session.

In this same general context it may be noted that in May 1972 the Ulster Unionists announced that in future each of seven Unionist MPs at Westminster would specialise in particular aspects of Ulster affairs. They claimed that this division of responsibilities had been made necessary by the abolition of Stormont, and the resultant increase in the work

TABLE 41

Liberal Party Spokesmen in the Commons and the Lords
1969–70 Session

House of Commons

Peter Bessell	Trade, Transport, Regional Planning
James Davidson	Defence
Jo Grimond	Constitutional Reform, Scotland
Emlyn Hooson	Law, Agriculture, Wales
Russell Johnston	Foreign Affairs
Wallace Lawler	Housing, Home Affairs
Eric Lubbock	Power, Local Govt., Home Affairs, Health & Social Security, Science & Technology
Alasdair Mackenzie	Agriculture, Posts & Telecommunications
John Pardoe	Education, Health & Social Security
David Steel	Commonwealth, Overseas Aid
Richard Wainwright	Treasury
Michael Winstanley	Broadcasting, Health & Social Security, Home Affairs, Employment & Productivity

House of Lords

Lord Amherst	Aviation
Lord Amulree	Health
Lord Beaumont	Education
Lord Byers	Finance, Overseas Dev.
Lord Foot	Home Affairs
Lord Gladwyn	Defence, Foreign Affairs
Lord Henley	Agriculture
Lord Norwich	Arts
Lord Rochester	Industrial Relations
Lord Wade	Housing, Transport

Source: Mitchell and Birt, *Who Does What in Parliament* (No. 1).

load of Ulster MPs at Westminster. This action also served to emphasise the semi-independent status of the Ulster Unionists within the Conservative Party at a time when they felt increasing reservations about the Government's Ulster policies.

The Liberal MPs are served by a small band of clerical and administrative assistants. The whip has a secretary who takes the minutes at a weekly party meeting, and performs other clerical and administrative duties for the Parliamentary party. The Liberal peers have a similar assistant. These officers are paid for by the party, as is the staff of the small Research Department, which provides individual MPs and peers with such briefings and assistance as its limited financial resources will allow. There is also a Research Officer attached to the whip's office who is financed by the Rowntree Trust.[1] The leader of the party has a political adviser and an administrative assistant, both paid for privately. As discussed earlier, there is a good case for the Liberals, and the larger parties, being given a state grant to meet the administrative costs of running a Parliamentary party. There is also a case for a salary being paid to the Liberal leader and whip in each House, in line with the practice in Canada where, for some years, a salary has been paid to the leaders of minor parties as well as to the Leader of the Opposition.

The small Liberal representation in the Commons means that many key party figures are in the Lords, or are outside Parliament altogether. It is perhaps surprising, therefore, that the leader of the Liberal Party is selected by the MPs alone, with the peers and the extra-Parliamentary party having no part at all in the process. Unlike the Conservative Party procedure whereby a meeting of Conservative MPs, peers, candidates, and executive members of the National Union has to approve the MPs' choice of leader, the Liberal MPs' choice does not even have to be ratified by any organ of the extra-Parliamentary party, and unlike the Labour Party practice, the Liberal leader is not subject to annual re-election. The presence of key party figures outside Parliament, however, does mean that the extra-Parliamentary party occupies a major place in the machinery for supervising party policy. For the past twenty-five years or so there has existed within the Liberal Party structure a committee made up of MPs and party figures from outside Parliament which has had the function of supervising the broad field of Liberal Party policy, and of linking the small Parliamentary party with the party outside Parliament. It has been known at different times as the Grand Committee, the Liberal Party Committee, and (currently) the Standing Committee, and its

[1] See above, p. 395.

composition has varied from time to time.[1] Although in some official Liberal party publications this body has been referred to as the party's 'Shadow Cabinet',[2] the majority of its members inevitably are drawn from outside Parliament, and its role is more akin to that of the Conservative Party's Advisory Committee on Policy, or Labour's NEC, than to either party's Shadow Cabinet. Currently, the Standing Committee has some twenty members. The leader and whip in each House are ex-officio members, and there are representatives of the Scottish, Welsh, and Ulster parties. Twelve other members are elected by the MPs, Parliamentary candidates, and the Liberal Council, and up to three others can be co-opted. The chairman is an MP, and is selected by the party leader: Richard Wainwright became chairman in 1969, but when he was defeated at the 1970 general election he was replaced by John Pardoe.

The prime function of the Standing Committee is that of supervising Liberal Party policy. It reconciles conflicts within the party on policy matters, and as well as issuing its own policy statements it oversees the work of the Liberal Party's 'policy advisory panels'. These exist for most policy fields. Like the Conservative policy groups, or the policy committees of Labour's NEC, their function is to examine party attitudes, and produce recommendations for policy documents. The panels are appointed by the party leader, in consultation with his colleagues on the Standing Committee and the party Executive Committee. They are composed primarily of Liberal activities and experts from outside Parliament, although MPs and peers will generally be members of panels for subjects in which they specialise. For the most part, the chairmen are drawn from outside Parliament, and in recent years Professor Keith-Lucas has been chairman of the Machinery of Government panel, and A. D. C. Peterson of the Education Panel. The chairmen acquire considerable status within the party as authoritative figures in their field. Normally they will keep in close touch with the MP who is responsible for covering their subject in the Commons.

Thus the Liberals adopt some of the aspects of the 'Shadow Government' organisation of the two main parties, like the

---

[1] See J. Rasmussen, *The Liberal Party*, London 1964, pp. 80–4, for the post-war history of these bodies.

[2] Ibid., p. 83.

creation of policy panels to review party policy, and, when numbers make it feasible, the naming of MPs and peers as official Spokesmen for particular policy areas. The Liberal MPs also generally behave in Parliament with the degree of moderation and responsibility that is associated with an office-seeking party. Clearly, however, the Liberal Party is *not* now a party of government. Its small Parliamentary representation, the consequent presence of many influential party figures outside the Commons, its remoteness from experience of office, or from real prospects of office, clearly distinguish the Liberal Party from the Labour and Conservative parties. This is reflected most obviously in the fact that the size of the Parliamentary party means a Parliamentary executive committee is unnecessary, while by the same token some machinery (currently the Standing Committee) has to be created to link the small band of MPs with the many important party figures outside the House of Commons. Nevertheless, the modern Liberal Party remains as an example of a 'second Opposition party' that, while not an alternative Government, copies some of the organisational patterns of the two main parties in order that it can more effectively perform its role as a second Parliamentary critic of the Government of the day.

The Opposition Front Bench in the House of Lords

Although in practical terms the role of the House of Lords is now subordinate to that of the Commons, and the press and public take only a passing interest in its deliberations, the Upper House still represents an arena in which the Opposition can perform its functions.[1] The House of Lords contains a considerable number of men and women of ability whose talents can be used by Government and Opposition alike, and indeed the Conservative and Liberal parties are numerically stronger in the Lords than they are in the Commons. In every Government

[1] For a general review of the role of the House of Lords, see P. A. Bromhead, *The House of Lords and Contemporary Politics*, London 1958. See also B. Crick, 'What Should the Lords be Doing?', *Political Quarterly*, 1963, pp. 174–84; P. G. Henderson, 'Legislation in the House of Lords', *Parliamentary Affairs*, 1967–8, pp. 176–7; J. R. Vincent, 'The House of Lords', *Parliamentary Affairs*, 1965–6, pp. 475–85.

some Ministers are drawn from the Lords, and departments that do not have Ministers there are represented by members of Her Majesty's Household or by senior party figures. Thus there is a recognisable and organised Government front bench which the Opposition has to match if it is to be effective. The Government issues Ministerial statements and generally explains and defends its policies in the Lords as well as the Commons, so that the Opposition also is expected to present its point of view in both Houses. Legislation that originates in the Commons must pass through the Lords, and with controversial measures the Opposition will normally welcome this further chance to present its objections, and perhaps wrest concessions from the Government. Major Bills that have been delayed in the Commons often reach the Lords only late in the session, and the Government may concede points in the Lords in order to prevent further delays. Again, the Opposition in the Lords can play a constructive role, helping Ministers to improve the numerous non-controversial Bills that originate in the Lords, or the equally numerous Bills that pass too quickly through the Commons. On one day each week the Opposition selects the topics for debate in the Lords, and these general debates, together with those initiated by the Government, provide a further outlet for Opposition attitudes.

Because of these various considerations, the Opposition has to organise itself in the Upper House. What Opposition front-bench arrangements have the parties evolved? For both the Labour and Conservative parties when in opposition the front-bench team in the Lords consists of the officers (that is, the leader of the peers, deputy leader, whip, and, for Labour, a representative of the backbench peers), together with Spokesmen for particular subjects and assistant whips. Labour's officers are elected by and from those hundred or so peers who currently take the Labour whip. In the 1951–64 period, however, when there were few Labour peers, the posts were filled more or less on an agreed basis, so that ballots were unnecessary. When Labour returned to Opposition in 1970, nominations were invited for the posts, but in each case only one nomination was received. Thus Lord Shackleton became leader, Lord Shepherd deputy leader, Lord Beswick chief whip, and Lord Champion the representative of the Labour peers. In 1971 all four officers were again unopposed. The leader, whip, and backbench representative serve as ex-officio members of the Parliamentary Committee, with the deputy leader standing in for the leader if he is unable to attend. The officers of the Conservative peers are not elected, but merely 'emerge' through the same process of informal consultations that the Conservatives used to use to produce a leader in the Commons. In the 1964–70 period, Lord Carrington as leader of the Conservative peers, and (in turn) Lords Dilhorne, Harlech, and Jellicoe as deputy leader, served as members of the Consultative Committee. For a short while there was also a third peer on the Committee, when in the first few months after the 1964 general election Lord Blakenham served as party chairman, with a place on the Committee.

For each party, the leader in the Lords, and *not* the overall party leader, selects the Opposition Spokesmen. There was some discussion among Labour peers in 1970 about the possibility of electing a dozen or so peers to serve as Spokesmen, but the idea was not seriously canvassed. In selecting the Spokesmen, the leader in the Lords may have informal consultations with the party leader, or with the other officers in the Lords, or his Parliamentary Committee or Consultative Committee colleagues, but the final choice is his alone. To this extent, then, the Opposition teams in the two Houses are separate entities. Thus when Lord Chalfont, as one of Labour's Common Market rebels, resigned his post as Foreign and Defence Spokesman in April 1972,[1] his letter of resignation was sent to the Labour leader in the Lords, Lord Shackleton, not to Harold Wilson. In the 1951–64 period of Labour Opposition the allocation of duties among the Labour peers was very informal and flexible, and the arrangements were not made public. In the 1964–70 period, however, the Conservatives made more formal arrangements, and official lists of Spokesmen were published. When labour returned to opposition in 1970, it was decided to follow the more formal pattern that the Conservatives had adopted, and an official list of Labour Spokesmen in the Lords was published. Those peers appointed to serve as Conservative Spokesmen in the 1969–70 session, and as Labour Spokesmen in the 1970–1 session, are listed in Tables 42 and 43, and it can be seen

[1] See above, p. 289.

that in each case the team in the Lords was small in comparison with the number of Spokesmen generally appointed in the Commons. Some peers are given broad areas of responsibility.

TABLE 42

Conservative Opposition Spokesmen in the House of Lords 1969–70 Session

Lord Carrington*	Leader
Lord Jellicoe*	Deputy Leader
Earl St Aldwyn	Chief Whip
Lord Aberdare*	Education, Wales
Lord Belstead†	Agriculture, Education, Transport
Earl Bessborough†	Foreign & Comm., Overseas Dev., Power, Technology
Baroness Brooke	Health, Social Security
Lord Brooke	Home Affairs
Viscount Colville	Housing & Local Govt., Law
Lord Denham	Housing & Local Govt., Post Office
Lord Derwent	Employment & Productivity, Home Affairs
Lord Drumalbyn	Trade, Scotland, Health, Social Security, Employment & Productivity
Earl Dundee	Scotland
Lord Erroll	Civil Aviation, Economic Affairs
Earl Kinnoull	Trade, Power, Technology
Lord Lansdowne	Foreign & Comm., Overseas Dev., Home Affairs
Lord Lothian*	Scotland
Lord Mowbray	Home Affairs, Public Building & Works
Lord Newton	Housing & Local Govt., Post Office
Lord Nugent	Agriculture, Transport
Lord Sandford*	Education, Overseas Dev., Health, Social Security, Employment & Productivity
Lord St Oswald	Defence, Transport, Technology, Public Building
Lord Thurlow	Defence
Lord Windlesham*	Civil Aviation, Economic Affairs

Source: Mitchell and Birt, *Who Does What in Parliament* (No. 1).

* Indicates received a Government post in 1970.

† Indicates received a Government post in one of the departments covered in opposition in the 1969–70 session.

In the 1970–1 session, for example, Lord Chalfont covered two major departments while Lord Beswick, as well as being the whip, dealt with three major subjects. In the 1964–70 period the Conservatives generally had two Spokesmen for each subject area, although many of the Spokesmen were allocated to more than one subject. Thus in the 1969–70 session Lord Drumalbyn and Lord Sandford each had duties ranging over five departments.

The House of Lords sits for fewer days and for shorter hours

TABLE 43

Labour Opposition Spokesmen in the House of Lords 1970–1 Session

Lord Shackleton	Leader (and Spokesman on general matters)
Lord Shepherd	Deputy Leader (and Spokesman on Transport, Foreign & Commonwealth, Overseas Development)
Lord Beswick	Chief Whip (and Spokesman on Treasury, Air Transport, Law and Order)
Lord Champion	Representative on Parliamentary Committee (and Spokesman on Transport and Agriculture)
Lord Brown	Board of Trade
Lord Caradon	United Nations & Colonial Affairs
Lord Chalfont	Foreign & Commonwealth, Defence
Lord Delacourt Smith	Technology, Power, Employment & Productivity
Lord Diamond	Technology, Power, Employment & Productivity
Lord Gardiner	Law
Lord Greenwood	Regional Planning, Environment
Lord Hughes	Scottish Affairs
Lord Kennet	Housing, Local Govt., Environment
Lady Lee	Arts
Lady Llewelyn-Davies	Broadcasting
Lady Phillips	Education & Science, Welsh Affairs, Pensions, Consumer Affairs
Lady Serota	Health, Home Office
Lord Strabolgi	Overseas Dev., Public Building, Housing & Local Govt., Health, Post Office, Arts
Lord Wilson	Scottish Law
Lord Winterbottom	Public Building & Works, Defence

Source: Mitchell and Birt, *Who Does What in Parliament* (No. 3).

than does the House of Commons. The work required from the team as a whole in the Lords will thus be less than in the Commons, although as most of the small band of Spokesmen have wide-ranging duties, their individual work loads will be at least as great as those of House of Commons Spokesmen. As well as the official Spokesmen, however, other peers will be brought down to the front bench at times to lead for the Opposition in subjects in which they are particularly well qualified. The same thing, of course, happens in the Commons to some extent, but much more of this is done in the Lords. Each party has a number of very able and experienced peers who attend the House only infrequently. While they are not prepared to serve as official Spokesmen, and thereby be required to attend the House regularly, they are prepared to attend for some debates, and thus form a large band of potential 'temporary Spokesmen'.

The general principles involved in the selection of Spokesmen in the Lords will be broadly similar to those that apply in the Commons, although there will be some differences in detail. For the most part, there will be less competition for posts in the Lords. Most of those who become Spokesmen in the Lords are mature former Ministers who are prepared to continue to serve the party in the comparative obscurity of the Upper House. Of the twenty Labour peers shown in Table 43, for example, fourteen had been members of the Wilson Government in June 1970, and three others had held posts as members of Her Majesty's Household. Two of the nineteen. were in their seventies, and the average age was just over fifty-eight. For the Conservative peers in Table 42, the average age was a little under fifty-three. To some extent this contrast in the ages of the two teams reflects differences that were noted as existing between Labour and Conservative teams in the Commons.[1] In the Lords, however, the difference is perhaps accentuated by the fact that the Conservatives can call upon the services of a number of young heirs to hereditary titles (like Lord Belstead, Lord Windlesham, Viscount Colville, and Earl Kinnoull, all under forty in 1970), whereas Labour's representation in the Lords is mainly made up of Life Peers, who are invariably mature public figures by the time they enter the Lords.

With the exception of young peers like the four referred to above, however, only rarely will a peer be recruited into the team on the basis of his as yet untapped Ministerial potential, and few Spokesmen in the Lords will have prospects of an extended Ministerial career should the party come to power. Of the twenty-four Conservative peers in Table 42, only eight received Ministerial posts in June 1970, and only two of these

[1] See above, p. 153.

went to departments that they had been covering in the 1969–70 session, despite the breadth of subjects covered by most Spokesmen. For the most part, unlike the situation in the Commons, there will be few peers clamouring to begin a front-bench career in opposition, and the leader's problem is more likely to be that of recruiting a sufficient number of able peers who are willing to devote their time to being official Spokesmen. Equally, once appointed, few peers will seek moves to more substantial duties as part of a process of building a career, and although some peers will retire for age or health reasons, few will have to be dismissed from the team in order to make way for emerging talent (other than when the creation of a new batch of peers, perhaps after a general election, brings a lot of able men into the Lords). In general, the leader in the Lords will have to pay less attention than his counterpart in the Commons to making the team representative of factions within the party. The press, public, and party outside Parliament pay less attention to the composition of the team than is the case with the Commons team, and in any case, groups and cliques are not as evident in the Lords as they are in the Commons. For the most part, within a party in the Lords there is much less of a 'power struggle', either between individuals or between groups, than is the case in the Commons. Thus in selecting the Spokesmen the leader in the Lords is subject to less pressure, and has to do less of a balancing act with personalities and factions, than his Commons counterpart. Much more so than in the Commons, therefore, Spokesmen will be selected on the basis of a combination of their personal ability and their availability.

The coordination of the activities of the Spokesmen in the Lords is achieved through regular meetings. On Thursdays the House of Lords assembles at 3.00 p.m., instead of the normal meeting time of 2.00 p.m., in order to allow the parties to meet in caucus. At present, the fifteen or so members of the Labour front-bench team gather together at 1.30 p.m. on Thursdays, and then all the Labour peers assemble at 2.15 p.m. The 1.30 p.m. meeting is something of a 'peers Shadow Cabinet', although unlike the Shadow Cabinet in the Commons it is attended by all the Spokesmen, together with the whips and officers, so that usually more than twenty peers will be involved. At the meeting the matters dealt with are much the same as those at Parliamentary Committee meetings. The main recurring item is the next week's business, and in particular the issues to be raised on the one day each week when the Opposition determines the business in the Lords. General party issues and organisational matters will also be covered, and the peers who serve on the Parliamentary Committee report on the previous evening's meeting. The 1.30 p.m. meeting can only be brief, however, as at 2.15 p.m. all the Labour peers meet together and hear the recommendations that emerge from the Spokesmen's meeting. In the 1964–70 period, the Conservative Spokesmen had a similar weekly gathering, although meetings of all Conservative peers were not so regular.

Because their duties are so wide ranging, Spokesmen in the Lords normally will be content to confine their activities to their assigned areas. As the team is so small, however, Spokesmen for related, or even un-related, subjects will help each other out in particularly important debates to a greater extent than is the case in the Commons. In the Lords there are no backbench subject groups, although under the guidance of the Spokesmen, ad hoc committees of Opposition peers may be formed from time to time to fight a particular Bill, and in opposition or in office the Scottish Unionist Peers meet together occasionally as an 'area group'. Individual peers may be involved in the work of the backbench subject groups in the Commons, and in 1970 Lord Kennet, the Environment Spokesman in the Lords, became vice-chairman of the PLP's Environment Group. Some peers may also be involved in the work of the machinery of policy committees that each party creates in opposition, and for the Conservatives specific arrangements are made to include two peers on the Advisory Committee on Policy.

In Governments today the senior Minister in each department is generally drawn from the Commons, although in some cases he comes from the Lords, and the department is represented in the Commons merely by junior Ministers. In 1970, for example, Lord Carrington was made Secretary of State for Defence, and in the Commons the Defence Ministry was represented by a Minister of State and Parliamentary Under-Secretaries. In opposition it is rarely specified whether it is the Commons or the Lords Spokesman who is the party's principal authority. Generally the Spokesman in the Commons is seen as having more prestige and authority than his counterpart in the Lords, although in 1970 Baroness Lee was given the status of being the Labour Party's principal Spokesman on the Arts, with the Spokesman in the Commons (Andrew Faulds) being officially designated as her assistant. The party leaders in the Commons do not try to dictate to the peers on tactics and attitudes, and in opposition Labour and Conservative Peers alike retain their independence of action. To some extent, the passage of legislation through the Lords must produce a continuation of the battles of the Commons. A major function of the House of Lords, however, is to deal with matters that the House of Commons has not had time to cover adequately, so that often the Spokesman in the Lords will have to formulate the party's attitude on aspects of legislation not dealt with in the Commons. With issues that have been covered in the Commons, a good Spokesman in the Lords will avoid merely repeating points that have been made at length in the Commons.

In October 1971, for the vote on the principle of British entry into the EEC, a three-line whip was imposed on Labour MPs in the Commons, but the Labour peers were allowed a free vote.[1] In contrast to the line taken in the Commons, the Labour whip in the Lords (Lord Beswick), although himself an anti-Marketeer, argued in a letter to *The Times* that '. . . though I believe it to be profoundly mistaken to accept the commitments of EEC membership, I should consider it utterly repulsive to have anyone vote with me on this issue if they had consistently expressed themselves in favour of entry.'[2] This issue, of course, was somewhat exceptional, because of its importance and the controversy that it aroused within each party, and also because it is unusual for both Houses to be considering an issue simultaneously. Nevertheless, House of Lords procedure differs from that in the Commons in various respects, and as a result whipping arrangements in the two Houses inevitably will differ. It is a well-established convention of House of Lords procedure, for example, that only very rarely is there a division on the second reading of Bills, so that vigorous resistance to a Bill at every stage in the Commons cannot always be mirrored in the Lords.

[1] See above, p. 288, for comments on the situation in the Commons.
[2] *The Times*, 9 October 1971.

Because peers have no constituents, and because House of Lords activities attract only limited attention from the press and the party outside Parliament, an independent line can be tolerated more readily from a Spokesman in the Lords than in the Commons. Also, because a Spokesman in the Lords is less likely than a Commons Spokesman to be starting a front-bench career, there is less pressure for him to conform to the strict party line for career reasons. Nevertheless, if a Spokesman in the Lords does wish to make a personal comment that clashes with party policy, he will normally make his contribution from the back or cross-benches. Thus Lord Chalfont and Lord Diamond, who both argued in favour of the principle of British entry into the EEC in the Common Market debate in October 1971, spoke from the back benches on this occasion. For the Opposition to appear credible, however, it has to prevent frequent and major differences of attitude from developing between its Spokesmen in the two Houses. When a department's Ministerial team is drawn from both Houses, coordination between the Lords and Commons Ministers can be achieved within the department. In opposition, however, there is no such daily point of contact between Spokesmen for a particular subject in each House, and coordination has to be achieved by other means. Neither party has any formal machinery, other than that provided by the weekly Shadow Cabinet meeting, but individual Spokesmen will generally make some informal and ad hoc arrangements for keeping in touch with their counterpart in 'the other place'. Much will depend on the individuals concerned, but on controversial issues some consultations will normally take place in an effort to coordinate the Opposition's attitude in the two Houses. In the case of Ministerial statements, which are made simultaneously in each House, contact will generally take place on the day in question, perhaps by telephone or over lunch. With Bills that come from the Commons the Spokesman in the Lords has access, through Hansard, to the attitudes his colleagues adopted in the Commons, and normally he will study at least the committee stage deliberations. The Party Research Department can help to coordinate attitudes in the two Houses by providing information and assistance for Spokesmen in the Lords as well as the Commons, although generally the peers make less use of the Research Department than do the MPs.

At another level, the peers who serve on the Parliamentary Committee or the Consultative Committee act as a link between the teams in the two Houses. The three Labour peers who serve on the Parliamentary Committee, together with the deputy leader, meet together from time to time on an informal basis. On first going into opposition in 1970 they met regularly at 4.15 p.m. on Wednesdays, before the 5.00 p.m. Parliamentary Committee meeting, but this practice has since been abandoned in favour of more casual and irregular meetings. At Parliamentary Committee meetings they convey the attitudes of the Labour peers, but their contributions are certainly not restricted to House of Lords matters. They are full members of the Committee, and although they refrain from commenting on purely House of Commons business arrangements, they contribute freely on policy questions, or on general party matters. Traditionally, the Conservative peers have played a more influential role in their party's affairs than have Labour peers, although of the Labour team in the Lords in 1970, Lord Shackleton, Lord Gardiner, Lord Diamond, Lord Greenwood, and Lord Beswick were experienced former Cabinet Ministers. In this, however, as with the general constitutional position of the House of Lords, it is the role of the Commons and its members that is the dominant one in the Parliamentary balance of power.

APPENDIX B

The Cross-National Context

THIS HAS been a somewhat insular study, confined almost exclusively to the British experience. While the book may be none the worse for that, it needs to be emphasised that the pattern of party organisation and behaviour that has been described here is not necessarily replicated in other political systems. Clearly, the organisation and behaviour of out-of-office groups will vary according to the basic constitutional framework in which they operate. Most obviously, basic differences will exist as between Parliamentary systems, in which the executive has to have the confidence of the legislature, and Presidential systems, in which executive and legislature are elected independently of each other, and the executive holds office whether or not it has a majority in the legislature. Thus the American Presidential system provides a major contrast with the British concept of Parliamentary Opposition. The physical separation of President and Congress means that in America there is no direct confrontation between 'the Government' and 'the Opposition' across the floor of the legislature. There is no Leader of the Opposition, Shadow Cabinet, or Shadow Government as they are understood in Britain. Various potential Presidential candidates emerge from time to time, but an official 'alternative President' appears only a few months before a Presidential election, when the non-incumbent party holds its Convention. Congress performs the continuing function of opposing Presidential policies. Within Congress there are leaders of the majority and minority parties in each House, and individual Senators and Representatives, especially the chairmen of Senate or House committees, may become recognised as the leading opponents of particular aspects of Presidential policy. None of

these figures, however, fills the role performed by the Leader of
Her Majesty's Opposition in Britain—that of leading critic of
the incumbent government, and also head of an alternative
government.

The institutions of opposition, then, will be very different as
between Presidential and Parliamentary systems. Most constitutional systems fall into one or other of the Presidential or
Parliamentary moulds (although the nature of executive–
legislative relations in Switzerland and the French Fifth Republic, perhaps places them in a separate 'hybrid' category). Under
the general label of 'Parliamentary' systems, however, clear
distinctions exist as between those in which Ministers are required to be members of the legislature, and those in which they
are not. In Britain and Canada, constitutional convention
demands that Ministers serve in the legislature, and in New
Zealand, Australia, and India this requirement is enshrined in
a written constitutional provision. In direct contrast, the con-
stitutions of Norway and the Netherlands specifically require
that members of the legislature cannot serve as Ministers, while
in Italy and West Germany the constitution merely provides
that Ministers *may* be members of the legislature (and in
practice some Ministers are members and some are not).

Where Ministers are not members of the legislature, many of
the features of the British Shadow Government system, that
have been described in this book, clearly will not be evident. In
considering the role of Opposition Spokesmen in Chapter 8
emphasis was placed on the regular physical confrontation
between a Minister and his 'shadow' across the floor of the
House of Commons, while in Chapter 9 attention was focused
on the questions of the extent to which service on the Opposition
front bench is a preparation for office, and the extent to which
Opposition Spokesmen receive Ministerial posts once their
party comes to power. Such considerations clearly are largely
irrelevant in situations where Ministers are drawn from outside
the legislature.

As well as differences in the organisation and behaviour of
opposition parties that result from such basic legal constitutional
considerations, differences will also exist between one Parliamentary system and another according to the prevailing pattern
of government–opposition party relations. Clear contrasts with

the British pattern are provided, for example, by Belgium, where the opposition parties invariably face a coalition government, and by Sweden, where minority governments are not uncommon. Even in countries which share the British tendency for majoritarian governments, there can be found contrasts with the particular British situation–as in India, where the parties do not alternate in office, or Canada, where the second party is challenged by a third party of increasing strength, or New Zealand, where the situation of two-party dominance is even more firmly established than in Britain.

In this general context three of the more important factors governing the nature of government–opposition relations will be:[1]

(a) the party composition of the government (whether the government is based upon a single party or a coalition);
(b) the party make-up of the opposition benches (whether there is one dominant opposition party or several);
(c) the regularity of the movement of parties between opposition and office.

In the following sections of this Appendix an attempt is made to produce a general classification of Parliamentary systems according to these three factors, so that the British pattern of Parliamentary relationships that has been described in this book can be seen in a broad cross-national context.

Composition of the Government

In competitive party systems, the government benches can be occupied by a coalition, a single-party majority government, or a single-party minority government. These broad categories could be sub-divided, and distinctions could be drawn (as in Figure B in Chapter 1) between different types of coalitions, or between 'small' and 'overwhelming' government majorities. For the purposes of this analysis, however, a three-way division is adequate. On this basis countries can be grouped as follows,

---

[1] These three factors are the same as those used as the basis for Figure B in Chapter 1.

according to the type of government situation they have experienced most often in the post-war period:[1]

Single-Party Majority	Single-Party Minority	Coalition
United Kingdom	Sweden	West Germany
Northern Ireland	Eire	Netherlands
New Zealand		Switzerland
South Africa		France (4th Rep.)
Australia		France (5th Rep.)
Canada		Luxembourg
Norway		Austria
India		Belgium
Japan		Finland
		Italy
		Iceland
		Denmark

Listed are the sixteen Western European countries that have Parliamentary systems and competitive party systems, together with Australia, Canada, New Zealand, South Africa, India, and Japan. Northern Ireland is listed separately from the United Kingdom, and here and later is referred to as a 'country', although its status is clearly different from the others. The French Fourth and Fifth Republics are listed separately, and Switzerland is also included, although, as mentioned above, the Swiss and the Fifth Republic constitutional provisions mean that they are 'hybrid' rather than strictly 'Parliamentary' systems. For the most part, the period covered is the quarter-century 1945–70, although in some cases, such as Japan and West Germany, the period is shorter because of the delay in establishing a post-war constitution and holding elections for the legislature. In this period some countries have experienced only one type of situation, and thus are easily classified. Many other countries, however, have experienced more than one type of

[1] The information as to the party composition of governments was obtained primarily from J. Blondel, 'Party Systems and Patterns of Government in Western Democracies', *Canadian Journal of Political Science*, 1968, pp. 180–203 (especially pp. 201–3). Blondel's data were brought up to date, and extended to other countries, through information from *Keesings Contemporary Archives*. Electoral data were obtained from D. W. Urwin, *Elections in Western Nations 1945–1968*, University of Strathclyde Occasional Paper 1969, and from *Keesings Contemporary Archives*.

situation, and they are classified according to the situation that has prevailed for the greater part of the period. Thus while Sweden since the war has experienced periods of coalition, single-party majority, and single-party minority government, it has had more years of minority government than of either of the other two, and it therefore appears in the minority government list. A classification on this basis may not reflect a country's most recent experience. Norway, for example, has been ruled by a minority Labour Government since 1965, although for much the greater part of the 1945–70 period the Labour Party had a clear overall majority in the Storting. The use of a classification based on a country's most recent experience, or based on a longer or shorter time-scale than the one used here, would produce some changes in the lists.

Perhaps the most obvious feature of the classification is the general tendency for the continental European countries to experience coalition government, and the Anglo-Saxon countries to experience single-party majority government. Japan and India also fall into the single-party majority category, while the Scandinavian countries are distributed among all three categories. Also illustrated is the comparative rarity of the minority government situation: where no one party secures an overall majority in the legislature, a coalition tends to emerge rather than a minority government. The broad tactics of opposition will be different in each of these circumstances. Faced with a coalition government, the strategy of the opposition parties may be, as in a two-party situation, to seek to replace the government en bloc, by defeating it in Parliament or in a general election. Equally, however, the opposition leaders may seek merely to weaken the government, or destroy it by stealth, by detaching one or more of the partners from the coalition. Yet again, the opposition leaders may seek to join the coalition, rather than destroy or weaken it. Thus in Finland in the 1950s and '60s the Liberals and the Conservatives alternated between office and opposition, sometimes opposing and sometimes serving in the Agrarian-dominated coalition government. With a 'grand coalition' of all the principal parties, those outside the coalition may be so weak as to make the Parliamentary contest an uneven one, as in Austria in the 1950s and '60s. Certainly, when the coalition is an all-party coalition, as with the British wartime coalitions, groups of MPs who remain antagonistic to the government will not be an alternative government in any sense, although, as noted in Appendix A, they will still be able to perform the other opposition role of being hostile critics of those in power.

Given strong internal party discipline, as in the British parties today, an opposition party that is faced by a single-party government with a majority big enough to withstand by-election setbacks, has little choice but to wait patiently until the government seeks re-election. In this situation the attitudes and tactics described in this book are likely to emerge. Where, however, there is loose party discipline, an opposition party's outlook is likely to be governed to a large extent by the knowledge that between elections it might be able to detach from the support of the government a sufficient number of MPs to deprive it of a majority. Similarly, when the government has only a very narrow majority, or when a minority government is sustained only by the support of another party, the opposition parties are unlikely to wait patiently for the Parliament to run its full course but are likely to try to wear the government down, or, in the case of a minority government, seek to detach one of the parties from its support of the government. Thus in Britain in 1951 the Conservatives won an 'early' general election after the Labour Government had striven for twenty months to survive on a small overall majority, while in 1924 the minority Labour Government was defeated at the election that was called when the two out-of-office parties had combined to defeat the Government in the Commons. The strength of an opposition party's position in such circumstances should not be exaggerated, however. The British Labour Government elected in 1964 with a majority of only four, survived for eighteen months and then secured a big increase in its majority when an election was held, while the Asquith Liberal Government survived for almost five years after losing its overall majority in 1910, and even then was only terminated when an all-party wartime coalition was formed. In Sweden and Eire, minority governments have survived for long spells in the post-war years, although in most countries where elections fail to produce overall party majorities, coalitions are more likely to emerge than single party minority governments.

Types of Opposition Situation

A clear distinction exists between a situation where the opposition benches are occupied by only one party, and a situation where two or more parties share the opposition benches. In this latter case, a further distinction can be made between a situation where one of the out-of-office parties is clearly dominant, in the sense of being numerically much stronger than any of the others, and one where the out-of-office parties are fairly evenly balanced. In Britain the opposition side of the Commons quite clearly is dominated by the main opposition party: throughout the post-war period the main out-of-office party (be it Labour or Conservative) has held at least 90 per cent of the seats on the opposition side of the House. In India, on the other hand, there have usually been twenty or so parties ranged in opposition to the ruling Congress party, with no single party holding more than about 15 per cent of the opposition seats. These two examples are of clear-cut situations, but in many countries the position is less obvious. In order to provide a basis for a general classification, it is necessary to arrive at a working definition of 'dominance' in this context. For the purposes of this classification, then, an opposition party is defined as dominant when it commands two-thirds of the seats held by the out-of-office parties. Thus in South Africa the United Party is defined as being 'dominant' among the out-of-office parties because in the post-war period it has usually held well over two-thirds of the opposition seats in the House of Assembly. In Fifth Republic France, on the other hand, the Socialists have been the principal opposition party, but they have held only about half of the opposition seats and thus are not 'dominant' as defined here.

This definition of dominance is quite clearly arbitrary, and there is no particular significance in the use of thirds, rather than halves or any other fraction, as the basis of the measure: other measures, and other general definitions, could be used which would result in countries being classified differently. On the basis of the definition of dominance that is used here, however, the countries that were listed in the previous section are re-classified below according to the predominant situation on the opposition benches of their legislature in the 1945–70 period:

Single-Party Opposition	Multi-Party Opposition with One Party Dominant	Multi-Party Opposition with No Party Dominant
Australia	United Kingdom	Netherlands
New Zealand	South Africa	Switzerland
West Germany	France (4th Rep.)	Belgium
Austria	Iceland	Denmark
	Luxembourg	Northern Ireland
	Italy	France (5th Rep.)
	Eire	Canada
		Norway
		India
		Japan
		Finland
		Sweden

Single-party oppositions are rare: only four countries fall into this classification, and of these only in New Zealand did the situation apply throughout the 1945–70 period. Further, among the countries with two or more parties in opposition, only a third share the British pattern of one of these parties being dominant (as defined here). The clear distinction that emerged in the previous section between the patterns of government in the Anglo-Saxon and continental European countries is not reflected in this classification. The Anglo-Saxon countries are distributed among all three categories, and although the majority of the European countries are in the 'no party dominant' column, some are placed in the other categories. Where there are a number of out-of-office parties without any one being dominant, the British concept of *the* Opposition, and *the* Shadow Government, clearly does not apply. In a multi-party situation there exist, in effect, a number of mini-oppositions, and perhaps a number of mini-Shadow Governments. The basic confrontation of government and opposition is complicated by the existence of several minor confrontations between the various opposition parties, and opposition leaders have to consider not only the activities of the government, but also the policies, tactics, and strength of those with whom they share the opposition benches. Thus in Eire in the post-war period, Fine Gael has had to concern itself not merely with seeking to draw support away from the ruling Fianna Fail, but also with preventing Labour from usurping Fine Gael's role as the second main party. Similarly, in Canada the Conservative Party's role as the main alternative to the dominant Liberals has been challenged in recent years by the growing New Democratic Party. In such situations the government can seek to divide and rule the forces of opposition by exploiting differences that exist between the out-of-office parties.

In a multi-party situation in which no party is in a particularly dominant position, the preoccupation of party leaders might be expected to be with building and maintaining alliances on which an alternative government can be based. In particular, when there has been a long spell without a change of government, the leaders of normally antagonistic opposition parties may be forced into an unholy alliance in an attempt to create a credible alternative to the long established government. In Sweden, for example, the several 'bourgeois' parties have sought recently to coalesce in an attempt to end the long reign of the Social Democrats, while in France the various forces of the left have long sought to overcome their differences in order to break the electoral dominance that the Gaullists have enjoyed in the Fifth Republic. In a multi-party opposition in which one of the parties is clearly dominant, there is less need for that party's leaders to think in terms of alliances, although they will still have to glance over their shoulders from time to time in order to assess the activities of the minor parties. Where there is only one party in opposition, as in New Zealand in the post-war period, the leaders are spared these complications, and can pose as a single-party alternative government without worrying about potential rivals in opposition. In this situation the task of opposition party leaders is not one of building alliances, but of maintaining internal party unity so as to be able to face the government as a cohesive force.

Movement of Parties between Opposition and Office

With the question of the regularity of the movement of parties between opposition and office, there is a fundamental difference between single-party governments and coalitions. In a coalition situation the party or parties that make up the core of the coalition may remain unchanging, while other parties move into and out of the coalition quite regularly. Thus in the Netherlands the Catholic Party has been at the centre of all governments since the war, but the overall composition of the coalition has fluctuated as the Liberal, Labour, Christian Historical Union, and Anti-Revolutionary parties have all moved into and out of office. In this way the 'stability' of one party being in office continuously can be accompanied by the 'instability' of frequently changing coalitions. In countries like Britain, on the other hand, where single-party majority governments are the norm, access to office is dependent upon an 'everybody out' situation, with the replacement of the Prime Minister and all his Ministers by an entirely new team. In other words, in single-party government situations it is possible to talk in terms of one alternation of parties in office, but in coalition situations one has to talk in terms of the movement of parties into and out of fluid governmental alliance systems.

Where there is regular movement into and out of office, as there has been in Britain and most of the coalition countries of western Europe in the post-war period, opposition leaders will have had some experience of government. They will probably tend to assume that past patterns will be repeated, and that they will soon be returned to office. Their approach to their role as an alternative government, and in particular to the making of practical preparations for office, is likely to be different from that of opposition party leaders in a situation like that of Northern Ireland, where the long periods of one-party dominance have meant that opposition leaders have been denied experience of office. Again (as noted in Chapter 6) regular movement of parties between office and opposition can give party leaders a respite from the burdens of government without their losing touch with governmental realities. Where there is only limited movement, however, those out of office can become removed from the practicalities of office. The longer a party spends out of office, the harder will become the task of persuading the electorate that it has the experience and the competence to enable it to govern, and the harder it will be for it to make the necessary adjustments in its own attitudes if office eventually is achieved.

Thus the extent to which parties have access to office will have a fundamental effect upon their patterns of behaviour.

Problems are involved, however, in attempting to devise a meaningful measure of the extent of the movement of parties between office and opposition. There is no problem, of course, with countries that experience no movement at all, as with Japan, where the Liberal-Democrats have ruled throughout the post-war period, or India, where Congress has ruled since independence. In some other countries, there is only irregular movement between office and opposition, as measured by almost any standard. In South Africa, for example, there has been only one change of party in office in the post-war period, with the National Party gaining power in 1948 and remaining in office ever since then. At the other extreme, Belgium has experienced regular movement, again by almost any definition, in that it has been ruled by a variety of coalition and single-party governments in the post-war period, with, until 1962, none holding office for more than four years at a time. Few countries, however, fall into such clear moulds as these, and as with the question of single-party dominance, there is no universally accepted measure of regularity of movement of parties into and out of office. One possible measure is the average period of time that governments remain in power in particular countries. Jean Blondel applied such a measure for the 1945–65 period to seventeen western countries with Parliamentary systems.[1] The average duration of their governments during this period was as follows (the figures representing years per government):

Australia 7·0	Norway 3·3	Denmark 2·1
Canada 5·2	Eire 3·0	Belgium 1·2
Sweden 5·0	Austria 2·3	Finland 1·0
New Zealand 4·4	Luxembourg 2·3	Italy 0·9
United Kingdom 3·3	Iceland 2·3	France 0·7
Germany 3·3	Netherlands 2·2	

[1] Blondel, *Canadian Journal of Political Science*, 1968, pp. 180–203. An alternative means of expressing the same broad measure is merely to count the actual number of changes of government that took place in a given period, and grade the countries accordingly. For this measure applied to a slightly larger group of countries than that used by Blondel, and with the time period extended to 1970, see M. Taylor and V. M. Herman, 'Party Systems and Government Stability', *American Political Science Review*, 1971, pp. 28–37.

Bottom of the stability league were France, Italy, Finland, and Belgium, all with an average life of post-war governments of about a year. Top of the league was Australia with a seven-year average life, while other Anglo-Saxon countries, Canada and New Zealand, were also high in the list with a four- or five-year average government life. Blondel pointed out, however, that ' . . . governmental stability is much lower everywhere than is intuitively felt. . . . Few countries keep governments with the same political base and the same head for as many as four years (one U.S. Presidential term) and only the Australian, Canadian, and Swedish governments show the same stability as that of the United States executive'.[1] This approach, however, does give a somewhat exaggerated impression of the extent of opposition parties' access to office, because of the definition that is used to determine a government's life. Blondel defined a single period of government as being one in which (a) there was no change of Prime Minister, and (b) there was no change in the party basis of the government's support.[2] Thus although in the 1951–64 period Britain had thirteen years of unbroken Conservative rule, on the basis of Blondel's definition there were four periods of government in these years, as four separate Conservative Prime Ministers held office. In strict constitutional terms, of course, a new British government does come into existence with a new Prime Minister, but the changes of Conservative Prime Minister in the 1951–64 period made no difference to the Labour Party's access to office, other than in the indirect way in which a change of Prime Minister increased or reduced the Government's chances of retaining power at a later general election. As the concern here is primarily with the chances of out-of-office parties moving into power, another measure needs to be found which would give a truer impression of the extent to which opposition parties have access to office. One alternative would be to ignore occasions when there was merely the replacement of one Prime Minister with another from the same party, and count only those occasions when there was a change in the party basis of the government. On this basis Blondel's data for the 1945–65 period can be re-assessed, and the countries re-grouped as

[1] Blondel, *Canadian Journal of Political Science*, 1968, pp. 190–1.
[2] Ibid., p. 190.

follows (the figures again representing years per government, but on the revised definition of a government's life):

Austria 21·0	New Zealand 5·3	Iceland 3·0
Australia 10·5	Eire 4·2	Belgium 2·6
Canada 7·0	Netherlands 4·2	France 2·3
United Kingdom 7·0	Luxembourg 4·2	Italy 1·9
Norway 7·0	Denmark 4·2	Finland 1·9
Sweden 7·0	West Germany 3·4	

Most countries retain much the same position in this second list as they held in the Blondel's original list. The bottom four in each list are the same, while Canada and Australia are among the three most stable in each list. There are some changes in position between the two lists, however, and most notable is the case of Austria. The 'grand coalition' of Socialist Party and People's Party remained in power without a break in the 1945–65 period, although there were a number of different Prime Ministers in these years. Thus with no changes at all in the party composition of the government, Austria appears as the most stable of the countries in this second list, whereas it was placed half-way down the list that took account of changes of Prime Minister as well as of party composition. On the same basis, Britain (where the Conservatives were led by four Prime Ministers in their 1951–64 period in office) is placed slightly higher in the second list than in the original, while with Germany (where one Christian Democrat Prime Minister presided over a variety of coalitions between 1949 and 1963) the reverse is true.

Thus the second list gives a somewhat truer picture of the extent of opposition parties' access to office than does Blondel's original list. Even this second measure, however, gives a misleading impression of the extent to which parties share office. One party, for example, might come to power on two or three occasions in a given period, but each time lose office very quickly; another party might come to power on a similar number of occasions, but each time retain office for a long spell. New Zealand has had two periods of Conservative Government and two periods of Labour Government since 1945, but each spell of Labour Government has been comparatively short, and in all, the Conservatives have held office for about four-fifths of the post-war period. Counting the number of changes of government, therefore, has clear limitations as a means of assessing the extent to which government and opposition roles are shared by the parties. An alternative measure, which would avoid these limitations, would be to calculate the total number of years in which any one combination of parties has held office in a given period. On this basis a broad three-way classification is presented below. The countries listed, and the period covered (1945–70), are the same as in the two previous sections.

No Movement of Parties Between Office and Opposition	*Irregular Movement*	*Regular Movement*
India	Australia	U. Kingdom
Japan	New Zealand	W. Germany
Switzerland	South Africa	Luxembourg
Northern Ireland	France (5th Rep.)	Netherlands
	Austria	Iceland
	Canada	Italy
	Norway	Belgium
	Eire	Denmark
	Sweden	Finland
		France (4th Rep.)

The basis of the three categories is as follows:

(a) where one party in the case of single-party governments, or one combination of parties in the case of coalition governments, has held office throughout the period, the country is classified as experiencing *no movement* of parties between office and opposition;

(b) where one party in the case of single-party governments, or one combination of parties in the case of coalition governments, has held office for at least two-thirds of the period, but not for the whole period, the country is classified as experiencing *irregular movement* of parties between office and opposition;

(c) where no party in the case of single-party governments, or no one combination of parties in the case of coalition governments, has held office for two-thirds of the period, the country is classified as experiencing *regular movement* of parties between office and opposition.

Thus Canada is classified as experiencing 'irregular movement', as although the Liberals and the Conservatives each held office for spells in the 1945–70 period, the years of Liberal government amounted to more than two-thirds of the period. Britain, on the other hand, is classified as experiencing 'regular movement' as neither the Conservative nor the Labour years in office amounted to two-thirds of the 1945–70 period. Luxembourg is also classified as experiencing regular movement, even though the Catholic Party has been in office throughout the period. The Catholic Party, however, has been only one partner in a multi-party coalition, the overall membership of which has fluctuated considerably, with no single combination of parties holding office for as much as two-thirds of the period. It can be argued, perhaps, that this gives a false impression of the amount of basic change that takes place in coalition governments in Luxembourg and some other countries. It should be borne in mind, however, that the situation is being examined from the standpoint of the out-of-office parties, and what is being sought is an assessment of the extent to which they have prospects of office, even if it is only as temporary and minor parties in a coalition that has an unchanging core of parties. As with the definition of single-party dominance that was used in the previous section, there is no special significance in the use of thirds as the basis of the distinction between regular and irregular movement between opposition and office. The use of a different fraction would produce some changes in the classification as between the middle and right-hand columns, although, of course, the left-hand column represents an exclusive category.

The vast majority of countries experience some movement of parties into and out of office. The consistency of the domination of office by the Congress Party in India, or the Liberal-Democrats in Japan, or the Unionists in Northern Ireland, is unusual and remarkable. Even more remarkable, perhaps, is the maintenance throughout the period of the Swiss Coalition, consisting of a four-party alliance of Socialists, Radicals,

Catholic-Conservatives, and Farmers, Traders, and Citizens. The countries that do experience some movement of parties into and out of office divide equally between the regular and irregular movement categories (on the basis of the definitions that are used here). With the exception of Britain, the Anglo-Saxon countries all fall into the irregular movement category, together with Norway, Sweden, Austria, and France (Fifth Republic). The regular-movement category is occupied by the other continental European countries, plus the 'off-shore islands' of Iceland and Britain. With the exception of Britain the countries in the regular-movement category all experience coalition governments, while in the irregular-movement category all the countries except France (Fifth Republic) experience single-party governments.

This leads on to the question of the general relationship that exists between the three factors that have been examined in this Appendix, and in particular to the United Kingdom's place in the overall pattern. Figure M depicts this pattern, combining the classifications that have been used here for the types of government situation and opposition situation and the movement of parties between office and opposition.[1] A twenty-four-cell framework is produced, allowing for the fact that a single-party minority government, by definition, cannot be combined with a single-party opposition. With regard to the movement of parties into and out of office, a clear contrast emerges between the countries with coalition governments and those with single-party governments. Britain is alone among the eleven countries with single-party governments in falling into the regular movement category, whereas among the twelve coalition government countries, only France (Fifth Republic), Austria, and Switzerland are *not* in this category. This emphasises still further the remarkably cohesive nature of the Austrian grand coalition of the 1950s and '60s, and the even more remarkably well-knit structure of the Swiss coalition throughout the period. In France, of course, the Gaullists have had an overall majority in the Assembly for most of the time

[1] The categories shown in Figure M are basically the same as those that were used in Figure B in Chapter 1 to place the British post-1945 pattern into an historical context, although there are some differences between the two figures in the amount of detail in the classifications.

FIGURE M

Patterns of Government–Opposition Relationships in Western Parliamentary Systems 1945–70

Government situation	Regularity of movement of Parties between Office and Opposition			Opposition situation
	Regular	Irregular	No Movement	
Single-Party Majority		Australia New Zealand		Single Party
	Britain	South Africa		Multi–Party with one Party Dominant
	Canada Norway		India Japan Ulster	Multi–Party with no Party Dominant
Single-Party Minority				Single Party
		Eire		Multi–Party with one Party Dominant
		Sweden		Multi–Party with no Party Dominant
Coalition	West Germany	Austria		Single Party
	France 4th. Rep. Iceland Italy Luxembourg			Multi–Party with one Party Dominant
	Belgium Denmark Finland Netherlands	France 5th. Rep.	Switzerland	Multi–Party with no Party Dominant

since 1958, and the Fifth Republic is classed as a coalition system only because the Gaullist-dominated government has also contained a small proportion of Conservatives and (for a four-year spell) Radicals. Nevertheless, the lack of movement of parties into and out of office in the Fifth Republic is clearly out of line with the predominant continental coalition pattern, just as the extent of the movement into and out of office in Britain is out of line with the predominant pattern of the Anglo-Saxon single-party government countries.

Britain and Switzerland represent the two extreme points in the overall pattern. The Swiss experience of coalition government, multi-party opposition without any opposition party being dominant, and no movement of parties between opposition and office, contrasts in each respect with the British pattern of single-party majority government, 'almost single-party' opposition, and regular movement of parties between opposition and office. A number of countries have one of these characteristics in common with Britain: six have the same opposition classification as Britain, eight have the same government classification, and nine experience regular movement between opposition and office. Five countries share two characteristics with Britain. South Africa is like Britain in having single-party majority governments and multi-party opposition with one party dominant, but in South Africa the movement of parties between opposition and office is much less regular than is the case in Britain. Italy, France (Fourth Republic), Iceland, and Luxembourg are in the same opposition category as Britain, and have regular movement of parties between opposition and office, but they have coalition governments rather than the British pattern of single-party governments.

Thus the British pattern of Parliamentary relationships can be seen within a cross-national framework. The brief and general observations that have been made here serve to indicate that the post-war British pattern of single-party majority governments, 'one-and-a-half-party' opposition, and regular movement of the two main parties into and out of office, which has formed the basis for the themes of this book, reflects only one rare type of Parliamentary situation. Quite clearly, the expectations and attitudes of leaders of out-of-office parties will vary from country to country, and from time to time, according to the prevailing pattern of government–opposition relations. The three factors examined in this Appendix certainly do not represent the only variables that will affect this pattern. Also of vital importance will be considerations like the 'distance' between government and out-of-office parties as represented by the size of the government's Parliamentary majority; the extent of internal party cohesion; the amount of consensus within the system and the willingness of parties to co-operate with each other (whether in office or in opposition); the nature and extent of contacts between Government and out-of-office parties, and the degree to which exclusion from office necessarily excludes a party from participation in the policy-making process; the number and strength of anti-system parties and the extent of their opposition to the Constitution. In this Appendix, then, only the tip of the iceberg has been examined: there clearly remains considerable scope for detailed empirical cross-national analysis of the patterns of organisation and behaviour in opposition that emerge from the wide variety of party relationships that are to be found in Parliamentary systems.

APPENDIX C

Standing Orders for the Election of the Officers of the Parliamentary Labour Party

THESE STANDING ORDERS for the election of the officers of the PLP were adopted at a meeting of the PLP on 4 November 1970. They modified Standing Orders which had been in operation since July 1953.

1. *The Officers*

When the Parliamentary Labour Party is in Opposition the officers shall be the Leader, the Deputy Leader, the Chief Whip and the Chairman. The Chairman, or in his absence, the Chief Whip shall preside over all meetings of the Parliamentary Party.

2. *The Parliamentary Committee*

The executive authority of the Parliamentary Labour Party in Opposition shall be vested in the Parliamentary Committee which shall be composed of:

(a) the four officers of the Parliamentary Party;
(b) twelve Members of the Parliamentary Party having seats in the House of Commons;
(c) the Leader and the Chief Whip of the Labour Peers and one member of the Party having a seat in the House of Lords.

3. The Officers and members of the Parliamentary Committee who have retained their seats in the House of Commons shall retain their respective positions in a new Parliament until fresh elections can take place.

4. *Elections*

At the commencement of, or immediately before, each Session, as may be found convenient, the Parliamentary Party shall proceed to the election of the four officers and the Parliamentary Committee.
 (a) The Officers:
    (i) The Sessional election of the Leader, Deputy Leader, Chief Whip and Chairman shall be conducted in the following manner, that is to say, by notice given to all Members of the Party with seats in the House of Commons that nominations are to be received and by ballot votes thereafter, if such are necessary.
    (ii) Wherever more than one nomination is made for any one of the four offices then ballot papers shall be issued immediately, and if there are more than two candidates for any one position, eliminating votes shall be taken until one candidate has an absolute majority.
 (b) The Parliamentary Committee:
    The 12 Commons Members of the Committee shall be elected in accordance with the following procedure:—

    (i) nominations shall be invited by Notice given to all members of the Party with seats in the House of Commons;
    (ii) if more than twelve nominations are made ballot papers shall be issued immediately;
    (iii) ballot papers must not record more votes than there are places to be filled;
    (iv) the 12 candidates receiving the highest number of votes shall be declared elected but in the event of a tie for the last place a further ballot shall be taken to decide which of the candidates concerned shall fill the remaining place;

    (v) any casual vacancy during the session shall be filled by the member obtaining the highest vote of the unsuccessful candidates in the last Sessional ballot for the Committee, but if two or more members have received an equal number of votes for the 13th place in that ballot, a further ballot shall be taken to decide which of these members shall fill the vacancy.

5. *Nominations*

No nominations, whether for the officers or the Parliamentary Committee, shall be made without the consent of the candidate.

6. It shall be for the Party Meeting to agree upon time-tables for elections within the Parliamentary Labour Party, whether for the officers or the Parliamentary Committee; and only members with seats in the House of Commons shall be entitled to vote in the ballots for the election of the officers and the 12 Commons Members of the Parliamentary Committee.

7. *The Labour Peers*

The election of the Leader of the Labour Peers, the Deputy-Leader of the Labour Peers, the Chief Whip of the Labour Peers, and of the Labour Peer to represent Members of the Party in the House of Lords on the Parliamentary Committee, shall be conducted in such manner as the Labour Peers may determine, provided that any such determination shall be in accordance with the principles contained in these Standing Orders.

8. *The Parliamentary Labour Party*

When a Parliament has been dissolved, those Members of the Parliamentary Party at the time of the dissolution shall be mpowered to act, if necessary, until such time as the results the following General Election have been declared.

9. These Standing Orders shall not apply when the Party is in Government.

Source: 1971 *Labour Party Conference Report,* pp. 102–3.

APPENDIX D

Parliamentary Committee Ballot Results and Lists of Opposition Spokesmen

THIS APPENDIX contains the results of the ballots for the Parliamentary Committee in the periods of Labour Opposition since 1923, and lists of Labour and Conservative Spokesmen since 1955. For Tables 44, 45, and 51 the numbers indicate the placings in the ballot, and the following symbols are used for the officers' posts:

L   party leader
D   deputy leader
W   chief whip
C   chairman of the PLP

LL leader of the Labour Peers
LW chief whip in the Lords
LR representative of
        backbench labour peers

For Tables 46 to 50 party officers who did not serve as subject Spokesmen are excluded. An asterisk indicates a member of the Parliamentary Committee or Consultative Committee. A dash indicates no change from the preceding column.

Source: Butler and Freeman, *British Political Facts*, pp. 104–5, for Table 44; *The Times* and *The Guardian* for the dates in question for Tables 45 to 51.

TABLE 44

Results of the Parliamentary Committee Ballot 1923, 1924–9 and 1931–9

	Feb. 1923	Dec. 24	Dec. 25	Dec. 26	Dec. 27	June 28	Nov. 31	Nov. 32	Nov. 33	Nov. 34	Nov. 35	Nov. 36	Nov. 37	Nov. 38	Nov. 39
Lansbury	2	1	10	9	10	*									
Snowden	1	3	1	1	1	*									
Thomas	4	4	3	5	5	*									
Wheatley	8	5													
Adamson	9		11	11	8	*									
Webb	10		9	10	9	*									
Johnston	3			4	4	*					3	2	3	6	
Shaw	11		7		12	*									
Davies	12														
Jowett	6														
Morel	5														
Shinwell	7												10	11	9
Graham		8	2	2	3	*									
Smillie		2	5	7											
Trevelyan		7	6	8	11	*									
Maxton		6													
Roberts		12													

Wedgwood	9												
Walsh		8											
Lees-Smith	11	4	6	6	*				9	11	8	8	5
Dalton		12	3	7	*				2	3	5	3	10
Henderson	10		12	2	*								
Cripps					1	2	1	2	1				4
Grenfell					2	2	1	2	5	4	4	4	4
Hicks					4	3	3	5	10	4	11	4	
Jones					7	7	4	6	11	8			12
Lunn					5	4	6	4	12				
Maclean					6	6	7	7					
Williams					3	5	5	3	7	7	6	7	3
Alexander									7	5	1	2	1
Morrison									4	1	1	1	8
Pethick-Lawrence									8	9	9	9	6
Clynes									1				
Noel-Baker									10	12	12	10	11
Pritt									12				
Benn											7	5	2
Hall												7	
Lawson													12

There is no record of the placings in the ballot in 1928, although all serving members were re-elected (see Dalton, *Memoirs*, I, p. 180).

TABLE 45

Results of the Parliamentary Committee Ballot 1951–64

	Nov. 1951	Nov. 52	Nov. 53	Nov. 54	June 55	Nov. 56	Nov. 57	Nov. 58	Nov. 59	Nov. 60	Nov. 61	Nov. 62	Nov. 63
Attlee	L	L	L	L	L								
Gaitskell	3	3	2	1	2	L	L	L	L	L	L	L	
Wilson				12a	5	1	1	2	1	9	1	3	L
Morrison	D	D	D	D	D								
Griffiths	1	1	9	2	1	D	D	D					
Bevan		12			7	3	3	1	D				
Brown					8	10	9		8	D	D	D	D
Whiteley	W	W	W	W									
Bowden					W	W	W	W	W	W	W	W	W
Ede	5	2	6	9									
Dalton	8	5	5	4									
Shinwell	11	11	11	7									
Hall	2	10	12	11									
Callaghan	7	6	4	10	3	5	5	5	2	1	7	1	2
Robens	4	4	7	6	4	2	6	7	4				
Dr Summerskill	10	10	8	5	6	9		11					
Noel-Baker	9	8	10	8	9	8	10	10					
Greenwood	12				10	6	7	8	6				

Table of committee membership (rotated layout; values are ballot positions for Members and L L / L R / L W codes for Peers):

Name	1	2	3	4	5	6	7	8	9	10	11	12	13	14
Stokes	6				11	7	4	4	3	2	2	2	2	4
Soskice		7			12	4 11b	2	3	10	3	8	7	7	12
Mitchison			3	3		12b								
Younger						6	8	12	6	9	11	6	5	6
Fraser						11	12	6	9	11	12	8	11	5
Gordon Walker						12	9							
Bottomley														9
Lee						5	12	12	12	12	11	11	10	9
Willey						11	6	5	11	11	5	4	9	10
Healey						12		4	5		4	5	8	7
Stewart								7	4	6	7	6	10	8
Gunter								10	7	4	10	8	10	3
Houghton										3		3	4	11c
Jay					LL									
Lord Jowitt	LL	LL	LL	LL	LL	LL	LL	LL						
Lord Alexander	LR	LR	LR	LR	LR	LR	LR	LR	LR	LR	LR	LR	LR	LR
Lord Henderson				LR	LR	LR	LR	LR	LR	LR	LR	LR	LR	LR
Lord Faringdon			LR											
Lord Listowel	LW	LW	LW	LW	LW	LW	LW	LW	LW	LW	LW	LW	LW	LW
Lord Shepherd	LW	LW	LW											LW
Lord Lucan	LW	LW	LW	LW	LW	LW	LW	LW	LW	LW	LW	LW	LW	LWd

a Co-opted in April 1954, and re-elected in November 1954.
b Co-opted in February 1956, and re-elected in November 1956.
c Co-opted in February 1963, and re-elected in November 1963.
d Lord Lucan died in January 1964, and was replaced by Lord Shepherd.

TABLE 46

Labour Opposition Front-Bench Spokesmen 1955–9 Parliament

	July 1955	February 1956	November 1956	November 1957	November 1958
Agriculture	Williams	—	—	—	—
Fisheries & Food	Brown*	Champion	—	—	—
	Willey	—	—	—	Beswick
Aviation	Brown*	—*	—*	—*	—*
Colonies	Griffiths*	Bevan*	Callaghan*	—*	—*
Commonwealth	Creech Jones	Creech Jones	—	Bottomley*	—*
Defence	Gordon Walker	—*	Brown*	—*	—*
Admiralty	Stokes*	—*	—	—	—
Air	Callaghan*	De Freitas	—	Steele	—
War	Strachey	Strachey	—	—	—
Education	Stewart	Miss Herbison	—	—	—
	J. Edwards				
	Stewart				
Foreign	Robens*	—*	Bevan*	—*	—*
	Younger	—*	—*	—*	—*
Health	Summerskill*	—*	Noel-Baker*	—*	—*
	Blenkinsop	—*	—*	—	—*
Home	Younger				
	De Freitas	Greenwood*	—*	—*	Gordon Walker*
					—*

Housing & Local Govt.	Mitchison*	—*	—	—*	—*
Labour	Lindgren				
	Bevan*	Brown*	Robens*	—*	—*
Law	Lee				
	Ungoed-Thomas		Soskice*	—*	—*
Pensions	Marquand				Miss Herbison
	Steele				
Post Office	N. Edwards				
	Hobson				
Power (& Atom. Eng.)	Callaghan*	—*		—*	—*
	Noel-Baker*	Neal	Robens*		
	Woodburn				
Scotland	Fraser	—*	—*	—*	—*
	Miss Herbison				
Transport	Strauss	Davies			
Treasury & Trade	Wilson*	—*	—*	—*	—*
	Gaitskell*	Gordon Walker	—*	—*	—*
	Jay				
	Bottomley				
Works	Greenwood*	—*	—*	—*	J. Edwards —*

TABLE 47

Labour Opposition Front-Bench Spokesmen 1959–64 Parliament

	November 1959	November 1960	November 1961	December 1962	February 1963
Agriculture	Peart	De Freitas	Peart	—	—
Fisheries & Food	Willey*		Darling	—	—
Aviation	Strauss	Strachey	Lee*	—*	—*
	Chetwynd		Cronin		
Colonies	Callaghan*	—*	Healey*	—*	Bottomley
	Creech Jones				
	Thomson				
Commonwealth	Marquand		Strachey		
Defence	Brown*	—*	Gordon Walker*	—*	Healey*
Admiralty	Steele	Paget	Willis		
Air	De Freitas	Mulley	—		
War	Strachey	Mayhew	Paget		
Education	Greenwood*	Willey*	—*	—*	—*
	Mrs White				
Foreign	Bevan*	Gaitskell*	Wilson*	—*	Gordon Walker*
	Healey*	—*	Mayhew		
	Noel-Baker				
Health	Summerskill			—*	—*
	Robinson				
Home	Gordon Walker	—*	Brown*		—
	Miss Bacon				

Housing & Local Govt.	Stewart	—*	Fletcher *	—*	—*
	Hughes				
	McColl				
Labour	Robens*	Lee* —*	Gunter* *	Gunter* —*	—*
	Prentice				
Law	Ungoed-Thomas	—*	—*	—*	—*
	Soskice*				
Pensions	Crossman	—*	Ross *	Miss Herbison —*	Mitchison*
	Houghton				
Post Office	N. Edwards	Williams —*	Ross *		
	Williams				
Power (& Atom. Eng.)	Mason	Gunter* —*	Fraser* *	—*	—*
	Lee*				
	Finch				
Scotland	Fraser*	—*	Hoy *	Ross	
	Miss Herbison				
Transport	Benn	Strauss	—*	—*	—*
	Mellish				
Treasury & Trade	Wilson*	—*	Callaghan* *	Houghton* —*	Houghton* —*
	Mitchison*	—*	—*		
	Jay				
	Jenkins		Darling		
Works	Mrs Castle		Mitchison* *	Pannell	Pannell *
	Griffiths				
Wales			Mitchison*		Pannell
Science	Peart	Peart	Mitchison* *	Crossman	Crossman
Information			Mitchison* —*		
Disarmament			Mayhew	Noel-Baker	

TABLE 48

Conservative Opposition Front-Bench Spokesmen 1964–6 Parliament

	October 1964	January/February 1965	August 1965	October 1965
Agriculture	Soames*	Redmayne*	Godber*	—* Scott Hopkins
Aviation	Maude	—	—	Carr/Stainton
External Affairs			Douglas Home*	—*
Foreign Affairs	Butler*	Maudling*	Soames*	—* Balniel/Tweedsmuir
Commonwealth & Colonies	Sandys* Amery	—* —	Selwyn Lloyd*	Maude/Fisher
Overseas Development	Carr	—	—	Chattaway
Defence	Thorneycroft*	Soames*	Powell*	—* Beamish/Bell Eden/Ridley
Education & Science	Hogg*	Boyle*	—*	—* Hill/Price
Home Affairs	Boyle*	Thorneycroft*	—*	—* Goodhart Sharples
Housing & Land	Boyd-Carpenter* Corfield	—* —	—* —	—* Page/Hay Mrs Thatcher
Social Services	Joseph*	—*	—*	—* Howe

Health	Wood	—	—	—
Pensions	Mrs Thatcher	—*	—	Longbottom
Labour	Godber*	—*	Joseph*	Joseph*/Tiley; Van Straubenzee
Law	Hobson	—	—	—
Post Office	Rawlinson; Miss Pike	Rootes; Rawlinson	—	Thomas; Bryan/Gibson-Watt
Power	Peyton	—	—	—
Public Buildings & Works	Ramsden	—	—	McNair-Wilson; Chichester-Clark; Channon
Scotland	Noble*	—*	—*	—*; Campbell/Stodart; MacArthur/Wylie
Technology	Marples*	—*	—*	—*; Biffen
Transport	Powell*; Galbraith	—*	Redmayne*	—*; Webster
Economic Affairs	Heath*			
Treasury	Maudling*	Heath*	Macleod*	—*; Jenkin/Walker
Trade	Du Cann	Barber*	—*	—*; Clark/Emery
Steel	Macleod*	—*	Barber*	Gibson Watt
Wales	Joseph*	—*	Thorneycroft*	—
Special Duties	Selwyn Lloyd*	—*/Hogg*	Sandys*/Hogg*	Sandys*/Hogg*

F.B.O.— Q

TABLE 49

Conservative Opposition Front-Bench Spokesmen 1966–70 Parliament

	Apr. 1966	Feb. 1967	Sept. 1967	Apr. 1968	Nov. 1968	Oct. 1969
Agriculture	Godber*	—*	—*	—*	—*	Stodart —*
Aviation	Carr	—*	Corfield —*	—*	—*	—*
Foreign Affairs	Douglas Home*	—*	Wood —*	—*	—*	Wood/Lambton —*
	Balniel	—*				
Commonwealth & Colonies	Maudling*	—*	Braine —*	Douglas Home* —*	Maudling* —*	Braine/Lambton —*
	Wood					
Defence	Powell*	—*	Ramsden —*	—*	Rippon* —*	—*
Education & Science	Boyle*	—*	—*	—*	—*	Mrs Thatcher* —*
						Van Straubenzee
Home Affairs	Hogg*	—*	—*	—*	—*	—*
Housing & Land	Rippon*	—*	Page —*	—*	Walker* —*	Carlisle —*
Social Services	Miss Pike	Balniel* —*	—*	—*	—*	Chataway —*
Health			Macmillan			Dean —*

Labour	Joseph*	Carr*	—*	—*	—*	Smith
Law	Hobson	—	—	Rawlinson	—	—
Post Office	Bryan	—	—	—	—	—
Power	Barber*	Joseph*	Mrs Thatcher*	—*	Eden	Joseph*
Public Bldg. & Works	Corfield Chichester-Clark	—	—	—	—	—
Scotland	Noble*	—*	—*	—*	—*	Campbell* Buchanan-Smith MacArthur/Wylie
Technology	Price	—	—	—	—	—
Transport	Walker*	—*	—*	—*	Mrs Thatcher*	Joseph*/Ridley Walker* Heseltine Alison
Treasury	Macleod* Mrs Thatcher	—*	—*	—*	—*	—*
Trade	Barber*	Joseph*	—*	—*	—*	Higgins/Ridley
Wales	Corfield Gibson Watt	Higgins	—	—	—	—
Arts		Channon	—	—	—	—
Special Duty	Barber*		—	—	—	—
Sport		Morrison	—	—	—	—

TABLE 50

Labour Opposition Front-Bench Spokesmen 1970 Parliament

		July/Nov. 1970	Jan. 1972	April 1972
Agriculture		Hughes	Peart*	—*
		Barnes	Buchan	—
Civil Service		Sheldon	—	—
Defence		Thomson*	—*	Hattersley
		Morris	—	—
		Owen/Walden	Owen/Maclennan	Judd
Education		Short*	—*	—*
		Miss Lestor	—	—
		Williams	Moyle	—
Employment		Mrs Castle*	Callaghan*	Prentice
		Heffer	—	—
		Rose/Walker	Prentice/Walker	Walker
Environment		Crosland*	—*	—*
		Freeson/Marsh	Freeson	—
		Silkin/Howell	— —	— —
		Mulley/Bradley	— —	— —
Europe		Lever*	Shore*	—*
Foreign Affairs		Healey*	—*	Callaghan*
		Hattersley/Foley	— —	Roberts
		Lyon/Roberts	— —	Richard
Health &	Social Sec.	Mrs Williams*	Mrs Castle	—*
		Morris/O'Malley	— —	— —
		Dr Summerskill	—	—
Home Affairs		Callaghan*	Mrs Williams*	—*
		Morgan	Fraser	—
		Rees	—	
Law		Jones	—	—
		Silkin	—	—
		King-Murray	—	—
Overseas Dev.		Mrs Hart	—	—
Parl. Affairs		Peart*	Foot*	—*
Posts & Telec.		Richard	—	
		Mackenzie	—	—
Scotland		Ross*	—*	—*
		Buchan/Carmichael	— —	— —
		Mabon/Maclennan	Mabon	
Trade &	Industry	Benn*	—*	—*
		Mason/Varley	— —	— —
		Dell/Rodgers	Williams/Booth	— —
		Foot*	Lever*	
		Bishop/Millan	— —	— —

TABLE 50—*continued*

	July/Nov. 1970	Jan. 1972	April 1972
Treasury	Jenkins*	—*	Healey*
	Barnett	Walden/Barnett	Barnett/Gilbert
	Taverne	—	Walden/Sheldon
Wales	Thomas	—	—
	Edwards	Morgan	—
Arts	Faulds	—	—
Northern Ireland			Rees

TABLE 51

Results of the Parliamentary Committee Ballot 1970–2

	July 1970	Nov. 1971	Nov. 1972
Wilson	L	L	L
Jenkins	D	D[c]	
Short	9	1	D[d]
Houghton	4	C[a]	C
Mellish	W	W	W
Callaghan	1	4	5
Healey	2	12	6
Crosland	3	8	3
Benn	5	10	11
Foot	6	2	4
Mrs Williams	7	3	2
Lever	8	7[c]	9
Peart	10	6	8
Thomson	11	9[c]	
Mrs Castle	12		f
Ross		5[b]	7
Shore		11	12
Prentice			1[e]
Silkin			e
Rees			10
Lord Shackleton	LL	LL	LL
Lord Beswick	LW	LW	LW
Lord Champion	LR	LR	LR

[a] Elected chairman in August 1970, and re-elected in November 1971.
[b] Co-opted in August 1970, and re-elected in November 1971.
[c] Resigned in April 1972.
[d] Elected deputy leader in April 1972, and re-elected in November 1972.
[e] Co-opted in April 1972: Prentice re-elected in November 1972, but not Silkin.
[f] Elected after special ballot in April 1972, but defeated in November 1972.

APPENDIX E

A Note on Sources
and Methods

As MENTIONED briefly in the introductory chapter, the information on which this study is based was obtained from a variety of sources. There is a wealth of political biographies and autobiographies, some of which provide information on past practices in opposition. These were used particularly for the history of the Shadow Cabinet, and to provide historical background to contemporary practices. Secondary sources, such as the standard works on Parliament, the Cabinet, the political parties, and the theory of opposition, also provided much background material. The main concern of the study, however, has been with the period since 1951, and for this the main source of information has been interviews with MPs and party officials. Press reports are also invaluable for more recent events, and the Index to *The Times* newspaper provides something of a guide to the quantity of press coverage given to Ministers and Opposition leaders. The opinion polls also provide information on public attitudes towards the Leader of the Opposition and his party. *Hansard* and its Index, Select and Standing Committee reports, and other Parliamentary papers offer a guide to the Parliamentary activities of MPs. The methods used in tapping some of these sources are discussed below.

The Interviews

The greater part of the information on contemporary practices was obtained from eighty non-attributable interviews with MPs, peers, party officials, and officers of Parliament. I am extremely grateful to them for giving me their time, and for being willing to talk about their experiences. I am grateful also to the Nuffield Foundation for the financial assistance that made possible the necessary visits to London. To have attempted to talk to all those MPs who had served in the Parliamentary Committee and the Consultative Committee in the 1951–71 period, or who had served as official Opposition Spokesmen in either House after 1955, would have involved up to 300 interviews. It was neither practical nor necessary to undertake such an exercise, given that the object of the interviews was to draw on the experience of leading Labour and Conservative MPs, and thereby build up a picture of Opposition front-bench organisation and behaviour in the period: a scientifically precise sampling of opinion was not being sought. Thus those selected for interview were chosen on a more or less haphazard basis, although an attempt was made to draw from the various broad categories of Spokesmen. Most of the interviews were obtained through a direct written request to the person concerned, but some were arranged through other MPs, and Tom Steele, Rt. Hon. George Thomson, and Rt. Hon. William Whitelaw, when he was Opposition chief whip, were very helpful in this respect.

In all, 108 requests for interview were made.[1] Twelve MPs refused, and five did not reply. Ninety-one positive replies were received, but in eleven cases a mutually convenient time and place could not be arranged, which is one of the difficulties involved in doing research on Parliament from a northern base. Of the eighty interviews that did take place, fifty-four were with Labour or Conservative MPs or peers who were serving, or had previously served, as Opposition Spokesmen. A further three were with Liberal MPs or peers who had served as Spokesmen, fourteen were with Labour or Conservative backbench MPs, one was with the editor of *Hansard*, and eight were with Conservative, Labour, or Liberal party officials (and two of the backbench MPs also previously had served as party officials).

[1] For a sound analysis of the problems involved in elite interviewing, see Lewis A. Dexter, *Elite and Specialized Interviewing*, Evanston, Illinois, 1970. See also Theodore Caplow, 'Dynamics of Information Interviewing', *American Journal of Sociology*, 1956–7, pp. 165–71; Peter K. Manning, 'Problems of Interpreting Interview Data', *Sociology and Social Research*, 1967, pp. 302–16; David Grey, 'Interviewing at the (Supreme) Court', *Public Opinion Quarterly*, 1967, pp. 285–9.

As well as being divided on party lines, Spokesmen can be grouped, very basically, according to whether or not they have served in the Shadow Cabinet (the Parliamentary Committee or the Consultative Committee), whether or not they had Ministerial experience before serving as Spokesmen, and whether or not after serving as Spokesmen, they were subsequently appointed to Ministerial posts. These broad categories of Spokesmen, and the number of interviewed Spokesmen of each party in each group, can be depicted as follows (the main figures relate to Conservative Spokesmen, and the figures in brackets to Labour Spokesmen):

Shadow Cabinet Members 10(16)	Former Ministers 9(11)	Future Ministers 3(9)
		Not Future Mins. 6(2)
	Not Former Mins. 1(5)	Future Ministers 1(5)
		Not Future Mins. –(–)
Spokesmen Outside Shadow Cabinet 15(13)	Former Ministers 10(8)	Future Ministers 7(1)
		Not Future Mins. 3(7)
	Not Former Mins. 5(5)	Future Ministers 2(2)
		Not Future Mins. 3(3)

These, of course, are only very general and very basic groupings. As well as the standard sociological categories, based on age, sex, education, occupation, and so on, Spokesmen can be further sub-divided into groups according to considerations such as, for example, whether or not the ex-Ministers (or future Ministers) covered in opposition the departments in which they served (or were to serve) as Ministers; whether or not the ex-Ministers had Cabinet experience; whether or not they had served in more than one period in opposition, or under more than one Leader of the Opposition; whether or not they had been involved in a change from one Opposition duty to another; whether or not they had resigned, or been dismissed from the team, after involvement in some dispute. The interviewees included representatives from each of these several sub-categories.

The interviews were held during 1970 and 1971, and spanned the change of Government in June 1970. Most of the Labour

MPs and officials who were interviewed had experience of both the pre-1964 and the post-1970 periods in opposition. The opposition experience of most of the Conservative figures, however, was restricted to the 1964–70 period, although some had been in Parliament in the 1945–51 period. About three-quarters of the interviews took place in London, and the vast majority of these were at Westminster, in MPs' offices, or in interview rooms or other parts of the Palace of Westminster. A number of the Scottish MPs were interviewed in Glasgow or Edinburgh, or in their constituencies.

The length of the interviews varied, and depended primarily upon the amount of time that the interviewee was prepared to spend. The longest was over two hours, and the shortest was just ten minutes. The bulk of them, however, lasted between thirty minutes and an hour. It is arguable whether, for studies such as this, a few very lengthy interviews would be more profitable than a large number of shorter ones. Certainly, a day-long session with a leading party figure would probably yield more than would ten or so fifty-minute interviews with different MPs, although the ideal pattern perhaps would be to balance a few depth interviews with a number of shorter ones. Clearly, however, even in the comparative leisure of opposition, few, if any, leading MPs could afford to devote hours to any single academic researcher, especially in face of the large and growing number of interviewers who now descend on Westminster. As it was, some MPs were prepared to devote two hours or more to the interviews, which was a very generous allocation of their time.

A standard questionnaire was not used, as what was being sought in the interview was the comment and opinion of 'top people', rather than a mass of statistical data. The format of the interviews was thus governed by the assumption that the most valuable information would be achieved by encouraging the interviewee to talk as freely as possible about what he saw as relevant to the subject. To this end, initial questions were mainly open-ended, and the nature of the follow-up questions and promptings varied from one interview to another. Some precise factual questions had to be asked, of course, especially in the early interviews, in order to gather information about each party's structure and organisation in opposition, but such purely factual questions were less necessary in the later interviews.

As well as broad questions about the general role of the Opposition, the Shadow Cabinet, the Leader of the Opposition, and individual Spokesmen, the interviewees were asked questions appropriate to their own particular experience. Thus those Spokesmen who had also served as Ministers were asked to comment on the differences and similarities between the two roles. Those who had been recruited into the team from the back benches were asked about the manner of their appointment, how they thought they had attracted attention to themselves on the back benches, what they were told about the role of Spokesmen when they were appointed, and how they adapted to their new role. Spokesmen who had served in the Cabinet as well as the Shadow Cabinet were asked to compare the working of the two bodies, and those who had served in the Shadow Cabinet under successive Leaders of the Opposition were asked to compare their style and performance. Those who had resigned or been dismissed from a post in opposition were asked about the circumstances of the episode, and how it compared with Ministerial resignations and dismissals. The backbench MPs were questioned about their attitudes to Spokesmen as opposed to Ministers, and about the place of Spokesmen in the machinery of the Parliamentary party. Labour back benchers were asked about the annual ballots for the PLP's officers and Parliamentary Committee, and about the factors that determined their voting preferences in these elections. The party officers were questioned about the role of the party Research Departments, and about the general relationship between the Parliamentary leaders and the extra-Parliamentary party. As no one has yet served both as a Labour and a Conservative Spokesmen, comparison of the two parties' practices and attitudes could only be achieved indirectly. Thus as well as being asked about their own party's system, MPs were asked to comment on particular aspects of their opponents' practices (although a surprisingly large number of MPs were uninformed and uninterested in how their opponents managed their affairs in opposition). The longer-serving MPs were asked to compare Opposition techniques and performance when they first entered Parliament with what they are today.

Interviews which seek long answers to largely spontaneous questions, as opposed to the rigid format of a multi-response questionnaire, involve problems about the recording of answers during the interview. The use of a tape-recorder during the interview could solve many problems, but even if the interviewee did not object in principle to being recorded on tape, his answers would almost certainly be less frank than they would otherwise be. Equally, of course, he might be put off by constant frantic note-taking during the interview, while the more time the interviewer spends making notes, the less time he has to think about his follow-up questions. In the event, a tape-recorder was not used, but some notes were taken during the interview (other than in the few interviews when staccato answers prevented this), and these were written up immediately after the interview.

One consequence of the emphasis on general, open-ended questions in the interviews was that many responses were not strictly relevant to the subject, and former Ministers in particular often tended to stray into accounts of their years spent in office. Such digressions yielded a vast amount of interesting and valuable information about Government, and added greatly to the interviewer's overall understanding of the British political system, but were off the main theme of the enquiry. Nevertheless, the desire of some former Ministers to talk about Government rather than about Opposition is in itself a comment on the nature of Her Majesty's Opposition, and reinforces a major theme of the whole study—that Opposition leaders are 'office-seeking' and are concerned with their former and future periods in office as well as with their current role in opposition.

Index of Specialisation

It is possible to obtain a measure of an MP's degree of specialisation in his activities on the floor of the House of Commons by examining the entries in the Hansard Sessional Index. This process was used as the basis of an examination of the Parliamentary behaviour of Opposition leaders at various points in time, the results of which are presented in Chapter 10. Each contribution by an MP in debates or questions is recorded beside his name in the Sessional Index, and these contributions are divided into the various subject areas of education, foreign affairs, housing, and so on. It is thus possible to see how many subject areas an MP's Parliamentary activity covered in the session. It is also possible to measure the extent to which his activity was concentrated in one main subject area, for no matter how many different areas he may cover, an MP normally has one main field in which he is more active than in others. An 'Index of Specialisation' can be calculated, based on the extent to which an MP's activity is concentrated in one area. This can be done for any MP, but the concern here, of course, is with the members of the Shadow Cabinet and other Opposition leaders at various points in time.

In effect, the Index of Specialisation will measure how closely an MP's *main* area of activity comes to being his *sole* area of activity. This can be calculated as follows:

1. counting the number of references beside an MP's name in the Hansard Sessional Index in the session in question;
2. counting the number of these references which applied to the area in which he was most active;
3. calculating the second number as a percentage of the first number.

For example, George Wyndham had a total of 119 references to his name in the 1908 Sessional Index. Of these, fifty-two were in his main area of activity, which was Army Affairs, and the other sixty-seven were spread over several topics. His Index of Specialisation is thus fifty-two as a percentage of 119, or 43·7 per cent. Although this represents less than half of his Parliamentary contributions in that session, there was no other single topic which attracted more than this proportion of his time. Similarly, in the same session, Henry Chaplin had a total of seventy-one references, thirty of them relating to Agriculture, and forty-one scattered over several policy areas. His Index of Specialisation was thus 42·2 per cent, or thirty as a percentage of seventy-one.

When calculations have been made for each member of the Shadow Cabinet, a composite figure for the Shadow Cabinet as a whole can be achieved as follows:

1. counting the total number of references of each member of the Shadow Cabinet;

2. counting the total number of main-topic references of each member of the Shadow Cabinet;

3. calculating the second number as a percentage of the first.

Thus in 1908, the total number of references for the members of the Shadow Cabinet was 1,055, and the total number of main-topic references of the members of the Shadow Cabinet was 392. The Index of Specialisation for the Shadow Cabinet as a unit, therefore, was 37·1 per cent, and this is the figure which appears for that session in Table 22 in the text.

An alternative means of arriving at a figure for the Shadow Cabinet as a whole would be to take the average of each Shadow Cabinet member's Index of Specialisation (that is, totalling the percentage figure of each member of the Shadow Cabinet and dividing it by the number of people involved). Another alternative would be to take the median percentage (that is, the middle figure when the various Indexes of Specialisation are ranked in order). Both of these methods give equal weight to each person's Index of Specialisation, whereas when the total number of references are used as the basis, the most active members of the Shadow Cabinet contribute more to the figures from which the average is calculated than do the less active members. The relationship between the level of activity and the degree of specialisation is a complex one, and is examined in more detail in the text. In so far as the prime concern is with the Shadow Cabinet *as a unit*, however, a percentage derived from the total of each person's references is more appropriate than either the median figure or the average of the individual percentages. For this reason, the method used throughout is that of the percentage derived from the total figures. The accompanying table shows for six sessions the results achieved by the three different methods of arriving at an average figure.

Alternative Methods of Achieving a Percentage for the Shadow Cabinet	Session					
	1908	1910	1912	1923	1924	1926
Percentage Derived from Total Figures*	37·1	55·2	57·2	31·8	48·3	40·9
Median Percentage	43·7	46·1	57·9	30·5	50·8	44·4
Average of the Percentages	48·1	47·5	58·4	34·5	50·2	49·1

* This is the method used in the text.

In four of the six sessions the highest figure was produced by averaging the percentages, while the lowest figure was produced in four cases by taking the percentage derived from the total figures. Thus the method used in the text perhaps produces rather lower figures than would be achieved by the other methods, although the difference will be only marginal.

In Table 22 in the text one session has been taken for all but two of the Parliaments this century. The 1900–6 Parliament is excluded because in this Parliament the Liberal Opposition did not have an identifiable Shadow Cabinet, and the 1919–22 Parliament is excluded because for most of this Parliament the Liberal 'rump' and the small Labour Party shared the role of official Opposition, and neither party had an identifiable Shadow Cabinet. Apart from the 1910 and 1924 Parliaments, which lasted only one session, and the 1929–31 Parliament, which was complicated by a change of Government during the second session, the second or third session was selected for each Parliament. The first session of a Parliament was avoided so that the Opposition party could 'settle down' into the new Parliament, and so far as possible, the final 'pre-election' session of a Parliament was avoided, although, of course, it was not possible to avoid this in one- or two-session Parliaments. A possible objection is that this does not distinguish between sessions in the middle of a Parliament and sessions just before or just after an election, when MPs' behaviour may be different. To some extent, however, this problem is dealt with in Tables 23 and 24 in the text, which for some Spokesmen cover all the sessions in the 1955–64 and 1964–70 periods.

In the sessions before 1945, the Hansard Sessional Index did not distinguish between a member's contributions through debates and his contributions through oral and written questions. Since 1945, however, oral and written questions and debates have been listed separately in each MP's entry. Thus in post-1945 sessions it is possible to break down the general Index of Specialisation into separate indexes for debates, oral questions and written questions, and this has been done in Table 25 in the text. Further, since the introduction of official Spokesmen in 1955, it has been possible to calculate a figure for the front-bench team as a whole, as well as for the Shadow Cabinet. It has also been possible since 1955 to distinguish between a

Spokesman's main area of activity and his assigned Opposition duty. In *most* cases the two are the same, and Spokesmen are usually most active in their assigned subject. In *some* cases, however, Spokesmen are more active in a subject other than their assigned duty, and this distinction is presented in Table 26 in the text.

The references upon which the Index of Specialisation is based represent the following things:

1. The figure for *debates* represents the number of separate occasions when the Spokesman intervened in debates. A lengthy speech that is broken up into several sections by interruptions will appear in the Index as several short contributions, and thus will count as several references. It thus represents a general level of activity, rather than a precise number of speeches made or columns filled.

2. The figure for *oral questions* represents the number of separate occasions when the Spokesman intervened in Question Time, to put a question or a supplementary. Like the figure for debates, it represents a general level of participation in Question Time, rather than the actual number of questions put down on the order paper.

3. The figure for *written questions* represents the number of written answers that the Spokesman received. The questions may have been put down for written answer, or may have been put down for oral answer but were not reached in the time available in Question Time and thus were given a written answer.

4. In Table 22, the figures are for the *total* number of references for debates and oral and written questions.

In questions, most references are single-column entries, as the format of Question Time is such that contributions have to be brief. In debates, on the other hand, some entries cover a number of columns. A lengthy speech of several columns, perhaps opening or closing a major debate, or at the Second Reading of a Bill, will invariably be subjected to numerous interjections. When this happens, the speech appears as several entries in the Index, and thus will count as several references. A lengthy *uninterrupted* speech, on the other hand, appears as only one entry. Few speeches are un-interrupted, of course, as only very dull or very grave contributions are listened to without being broken up by interjections of one kind or another. Thus this potential distortion is not a major disadvantage in the method. Nevertheless, an alternative method of calculation would be to exclude entirely single-column references in debates, and count only references of two or more columns. This would have the effect of giving extra weight to the more studied type of contribution that is implied in a speech of more than one column. Another alternative would be to count the number of *columns* rather than the number of *references*. This would distinguish more precisely between a single-column entry, and one of several columns, and it would give full weight to lengthy speeches that are uninterrupted.

These alternative methods, however, could only be used for Parliaments over the last forty-five years, as before 1928 the Hansard Index did not always specify the number of columns in a contribution. For example, before 1928, a reference to column 568 might indicate a single-column contribution, or a contribution that began at column 568 but continued for several columns. Thus methods based on excluding single-column entries, or counting the number of columns, cannot be used for the longer historical comparisons. They can be used if the analysis is restricted to the post-1928 period, although they would still be an imprecise measure: a single-column entry may refer to a speech filling a full column, representing a contribution of two or three minutes or 400 words, or merely a one word interjection. Similarly, a two-column entry may be one line at the foot of one column, and half a line at the top of the next column. Also, counting the number of columns is more time-consuming than counting the number of references, so that fewer cases can be dealt with in a given amount of time.

The accompanying Table indicates the Index of Specialisation for the Shadow Cabinet in debates in three sessions, using the three different methods. On the whole the three methods produce much the same overall results, and it is clear that the method used in the text does not greatly overstate or understate the level of specialisation.

In all of the Tables, 'Shadow Cabinet' means for the Labour party the Parliamentary Committee, and for the Conservatives the Consultative Committee in the sessions since 1964, and the

Balfour, Bonar Law, Baldwin, and Churchill Shadow Cabinets
in the sessions before 1951. In every case the peers have been
excluded, as this study relates primarily to the House of Commons. Also, the Leader of the Opposition and the chief whip are
excluded from the calculations as they do not have duties as
departmental Spokesmen. In the sessions since 1955, the 'front-
bench team as a whole' means the Shadow Cabinet plus the
other Spokesmen outside the Shadow Cabinet.

	Session		
Alternative Methods of Measuring	1946–7	1950–1	1952–3
Specialisation in Debates		Percentages	
(Shadow Cabinet)			
Counting all References*	44·6	49·6	61·1
Counting only References of two or			
more Columns	45·5	52·3	61·3
Counting Columns	50·7	47·1	59·3

* This is the method used in the text.

In all of the calculations in the Tables, a 'subject area', or a
'policy area', or 'topic', or 'area of interest', means an area
covered by a department of state, with a separate category for
Parliamentary business. Some departmental areas have changed
over the years, and new departments have come into existence
and others have been abolished. Since 1945, for example,
British relations with India have been covered at different times
by the India Office, the Dominion Office, the Commonwealth
Office, and (now) the Foreign and Commonwealth Office. In
each session, however, the departments then in existence are the
ones used as the basis for this classification, and in most sessions
this has meant a total of some fifteen or sixteen subject areas.
There is thus a minimum level of specialisation: an MP who
devoted his time equally among all of the fifteen or sixteen possible policy areas would have an Index of Specialisation of
about 6 per cent. An MP who devoted all of his time to one area
would have an Index of Specialisation of 100 per cent, so that
the possible range in any one session will be from 100 per cent
to about 5 per cent or 7 per cent. Most references can be readily

classified into departmental areas, but some are obscure. In the obviously doubtful cases, the debate or question can be traced in Hansard to see which departmental Minister was involved, but there is always a margin of error with references that seem logically to apply to one department, but which in fact apply to another.

This method of studying the behaviour of MPs clearly has a number of limitations. Two particular objections may be noted. Firstly, merely counting the number of contributions that an MP makes does not measure the quality of a Parliamentary performance, or the care and time that goes into the preparation of the different speeches or questions. Some contributions may be more subtle, more learned, and more weighty than others, and a Spokesman may spend a lot of time preparing speeches in his own field but little or no time in preparing contributions of the same length on a topic outside his own field. Secondly, while an MP's activity in the House will generally reflect his main interests, this need not always be the case. It has to be emphasised, therefore, that this study is concerned with only one aspect of a Spokesman's activity, and although participation in activities in the Chamber of the Commons is a vital aspect of a Spokesman's duties, it is by no means the only aspect. As was discussed in Chapter 8, a Spokesman spends considerable time on organisational matters, such as coordinating the activities of backbench MPs in attacks on the Government. In any session in which the Government is presenting a Bill in his subject area, a Spokesman will be involved in a great deal of work at the Committee stage (although, of course, this might be taken on the floor of the House and thus would appear in the Sessional Index used for this enquiry). As well as leading the attack on the Bill, the Spokesman will have the task of coordinating the efforts of his party colleagues. Some Spokesmen will be involved in the work of the Select Committees, and they will all be expected to attend meetings of the party's appropriate backbench committees, with Conservative Spokesmen, and some Labour Spokesmen, serving as chairmen of these bodies. Also, much of the Spokesman's time is taken up with work away from Parliament altogether, building up contacts with outside bodies. Thus the floor of the House is only one area in which Spokesmen operate, and the amount of specialisation there is not necessarily the final guide to the overall proportion of time that a Spokesman devotes to his assigned topic. There are some comments, however, on the specialisation of Spokesmen in relation to Select and Standing Committees in Chapter 8.

Regardless of its limitations, this means of studying the activities of MPs clearly has considerable scope for development. The behaviour of MPs as reflected in their level of activity, their specialisation and the different policy areas they cover, can all be examined over several sessions, and in time, a comprehensive picture can be built up of the behaviour of different groups of MPs in different time periods.[1] As a social science tool, then, this method of analysing the Hansard Sessional Index has considerable potential. The analysis that is presented here represents a limited attempt to examine in some detail over several sessions only one aspect (degree of specialisation) of the behaviour of just one section of the House of Commons—the leading figures of Her Majesty's Opposition.

The Index to The Times

The Index to The Times newspaper provides a guide to the amount of journalistic coverage given to particular events, issues or individuals. Beside a person's name in the Index is a list of all the dates, together with the page and column references, on which he was mentioned in The Times in the period covered by that Index. A count of the number of references thus produces a measure of the amount of coverage a person received in a particular period. This was done for the Cabinet and Shadow Cabinet for the years 1961 and 1968, and for the 1964, 1966 and 1970 general election campaigns, in an attempt to compare the amount of publicity received by Ministers and Opposition leaders in both election and non-election situations. The results are presented in Tables 5 and 6 in the text. The years 1961 and 1968 were selected as middle years of the 1959–

---

[1] For other comments on the use of the Hansard Index, see M. Franklin, *Using Computers to Analyse the Activities of Members of Parliament*, University of Strathclyde Occasional Paper, Glasgow 1971. For other quantitative studies based on the Index, see R. Oakley and P. Rose, *The Political Year 1970* (and *1971*), London 1970 (and 1971); Craig, *The Political Companion* (quarterly); R. L. Leonard and V. Herman, *The Backbencher and Parliament: a Reader*, London 1972.

1964 Parliament (Conservative Government) and the 1966–70 Parliament (Labour Government). In the case of the three general elections, the calendar month up to polling day was used as the time period. One volume of *The Times* Index covers a two-month period, so that the figures for 1961 and 1968 represent the totals for the six volumes for the year in each case. In the Index a distinction is made between references to Parliamentary questions, statements or speeches, and references to non-Parliamentary coverage, such as speeches in the country or abroad, interviews given to *The Times*, or articles written for *The Times*, or other newspapers. Coverage that includes a photograph is also indicated. Comparisons could be made, therefore, between an MP's Parliamentary coverage and his extra-Parliamentary coverage. For the purposes of the enquiry made in this study, however, merely a general measure of coverage was sought, so that all the Parliamentary and non-Parliamentary references were lumped together in the calculations. In the calculations for the three general election campaigns, of course, there were few Parliamentary references, as Parliament was dissolved at the beginning of the campaign.

Unlike the Hansard Index, the Index to *The Times* does not provide a precise measure of a level of activity, but merely gives a measure of the amount of coverage given to a particular individual or subject by one newspaper. Also, the Index (like the Hansard Index) provides a purely quantitative measure. It gives information on the number of references to a subject, but it does not indicate the amount of space given to a story, or the prominence or size of headline that it received. At the same time, as each reference includes the page and column in which the story appeared, a distinction could be drawn, if desired, between 'front page' coverage and other coverage, although this was not felt to be necessary for the purposes of this enquiry. *The Times*, for good or ill, is not typical of the whole of the British press. Thus the coverage given by *The Times* is not necessarily an indication of the level of interest shown by Fleet Street as a whole. Nevertheless, in the case of major events, or particularly topical individuals, the quantity, if not the quality or style, of coverage in *The Times* probably will reflect that of the popular press to at least some extent. Finally, it may be noted that in *The Times* Index the subject matter of each reference is given, so that it is possible to assess the range of subjects in which a person was reported as speaking, in and out of Parliament. Thus an Index of Specialisation could be calculated on the basis of a person's Parliamentary and extra-Parliamentary references. Although this was not attempted in this study, it represents a possible further means of examining the behaviour of MPs. As noted above, however, this would not provide a precise measure of a person's activity, but would only be an indication of *The Times*' coverage of that activity.

The Gallup Political Index

Findings of the Gallup Poll, which are published monthly by Social Surveys (Gallup Poll) Limited in the Gallup Political Index, were used to compare the popularity ratings of the parties and the party leaders over the last decade.[1] The data are presented graphically in Figures A, F, and G in the text. In each case the percentages on which the graphs are based represent an average for a three-month period. For the most part Gallup use a quota sample, generally with about a thousand respondents. During election campaigns they also use random samples. In some months, such as just after a general election, surveys are not published, and in these cases the quarterly average is based on only one or two months' polls. On the other hand, in some months Gallup may publish more than one poll. In these cases the poll that is published closest to the middle of the month is the one that is used here. The monthly issue of the Index normally contains figures for previous months, to provide comparisons with the current month's poll. Some inconsistencies emerge through this practice, however, and the original figures which appeared in, say, the January issue, may not be the ones that are subsequently quoted for that month in the February, March and April issues. Such variations may represent inaccuracies, or it may be that in months when more than one survey was taken, the two sets of figures are interchanged.[2] In any case, for the purposes of this enquiry the figures that are

[1] For comments on some of the problems involved in using the Gallup Political Index, see Goodhart and Bhansali, *Political Studies* 1970, pp. 43–106.

[2] See ibid., pp. 49–52, for more detailed comments on this problem.

taken for any month are those that appeared in the original Index for that month.

The question asked by Gallup to test voting intention is 'If there were a General Election tomorrow, which party would you support?'. During an election campaign the question becomes 'If you vote, which candidate will you support?'. In surveys since 1963, the initial question is followed by a further question to the undecided respondents: 'Which would you be most inclined to vote for?'. After this follow-up question, those who are still undecided are eliminated from the calculations, and a final set of figures is presented in which the party scores are adjusted to add up to 100 per cent. It is these final figures that are used as the data for this enquiry.

In the case of the party leaders the questions used are, 'Are you satisfied or dissatisfied with Mr X as Prime Minister?', and, 'Do you think Mr Y is or is not proving a good leader of the Z party?' (although for a while after a change of Government these questions are re-phrased slightly). Unlike the enquiry as to voting intention, these are not followed up by any further questions to the undecided respondents. Thus in the case of the Prime Minister, the figures used for the graphs represent the percentage satisfied with his performance, and in the case of the Leader of the Opposition they represent the percentage who think he is proving to be a good leader of his party. As pointed out in the text, therefore, it should be remembered that while the question on voting intention requires the respondent to make a choice between the parties, the questions on the leaders' performance permit of the same answer in each case: those who are satisfied with the performance of X as Prime Minister may also regard Y as a good leader of his party. The same is true of the parallel questions asked by the National Opinion Polls: 'Are you satisfied with X as Prime Minister?', and, 'Are you satisfied or dissatisfied with Y as Leader of the Opposition?'. The Harris Poll, on the other hand, in assessing the party leaders, presents the respondent with the same direct choice as in the voting intention enquiry by asking, 'Who would you like to see as Prime Minister, X or Y?'. This factor should be borne in mind when assessing the Gallup data that are presented in the Figures in the text.

Bibliographical Note

Over the past decade or so an increasing amount has been written on the theory and practice of political opposition, and on Parliamentary Opposition in particular. The appearance of the journal *Government and Opposition* in 1965 symbolises the increased interest in this subject. It contains articles and book reviews of all aspects of political opposition. In addition, a number of book-length studies of political opposition have appeared in recent years. Among the most useful of these are, Rodney Barker (ed.), *Studies in Opposition*, London 1971; R. A. Dahl, *Political Oppositions in Western Democracies*, New Haven 1966; and Ghita Ionescu and Isabel de Madariaga, *Opposition: Past and Present of a Political Institution*, London 1968.

On the Leader of the Opposition there are two useful articles, M. Beloff, 'The Leader of the Opposition', *Parliamentary Affairs*, 1957–8, pp. 155–62, and D. E. McHenry, 'Formal Recognition of the Leader of the Opposition in Parliaments of the British Commonwealth', *Political Science Quarterly*, 1954, pp. 438–52, while Austin Mitchell's *Government by Party*, London 1966, contains an interesting interview with the then Leader of the Opposition in New Zealand. There is no book-length study of the Leader of the Opposition, however, or of the contemporary working of the Shadow Cabinet.

The history of the Shadow Cabinet is dealt with in D. R. Turner, *The Shadow Cabinet in British Politics*, London 1969, and, in passing, in John P. Mackintosh, *The British Cabinet*, London 1968. A. S. Foord, *His Majesty's Opposition*, London 1964, deals with the evolution of loyal Opposition in Britain, and provides insights into the leadership of Opposition in the eighteenth century. Useful studies of parties in that period are J. W. Derry, *The Regency Crisis and the Whigs 1788–9*, London 1963, K. Feiling, *The Second Tory Party 1715–32*, London 1959, G. Kitson Clark, *Peel and the Conservative Party 1832–41*, London 1929, A. Mitchell, *The Whigs in Opposition 1815–30*, London 1967, M. Roberts, *The Whig Party 1807–12*, London 1965, and D. A. Winstanley, *Lord Chatham and the Whig Opposition*, London 1966. There are also a number of books and articles on the Labour and Conservative parties in opposition in the post–1945 period: S. Haseler, *The Gaitskellites*, London 1969, J. D. Hoffman, *The*

Conservative Party in Opposition 1945–51, London 1964, S. Brittan, 'Some Thoughts on the Conservative Opposition', *Political Quarterly*, 1968, pp. 145–55, R. E. Dowse, 'The PLP in Opposition', *Parliamentary Affairs*, 1959–60, pp. 520–9, H. Hanson, 'The Future of the Labour Party', *Political Quarterly*, 1970, pp. 375–386, R. Hornby, 'Parties in Parliament 1959–63: The Labour Party', *Political Quarterly*, 1964, pp. 240–8, and J. Enoch Powell, '1951–9 Labour in Opposition', *Political Quarterly*, 1959, pp. 336–43.

Compared with most aspects of British politics, however, the role of Opposition front benchers has received little direct attention, and for the most part the subject has been dealt with only in passing in the general studies of the Cabinet, Parliament and the political parties. There is no shortage, of course, of such general books and articles, and no attempt is made here to list them all: only mentioned are those that contain more than just a passing reference to some of the themes of this study. Comments on Shadow Cabinet organisation are provided in some of the major works on the Cabinet like Sir Ivor Jennings, *Cabinet Government*, London 1969, John P. Mackintosh, *The British Cabinet*, London 1968, and P. Gordon Walker, *The Cabinet*, London 1972. The standard books on Parliament deal with the general functions and activities of Her Majesty's Opposition. Particularly valuable in this respect are R. Butt, *The Power of Parliament*, London 1967, B. Crick *The Reform of Parliament*, London 1964, Sir Ivor Jennings, *Parliament*, London 1969, Lord Morrison, *Government and Parliament*, London 1959, P. G. Richards, *Honourable Members*, London 1964, and H. V. Wiseman, *Parliament and the Executive*, London 1966.

More specific aspects of the role of Opposition Spokesmen are dealt with in the following books on Parliamentary behaviour: R. K. Alderman and J. A. Cross, *The Tactics of Resignation*, London 1967, A. Barker and M. Rush, *The Member of Parliament and His Information*, London 1970, P. A. Bromhead, *Private Members' Bills*, London, 1956, D. N. Chester and Nona Bowring, *Questions in Parliament*, London 1962, and R. J. Jackson *Rebels and Whips*, London 1968. The following articles on Parliament also touch on aspects of the role of Spokesmen: R. K. Alderman, 'Parliamentary Party Discipline in Opposition: The PLP 1951–1964; *Parliamentary Affairs* 1967–8, pp. 124–36, H. Berrington,

'Partisanship and Dissidence in the Nineteenth Century House of Commons; *Parliamentary Affairs* 1967–8, pp. 338–74, Paul Dean, 'A Look at the Conservative Research Department', *Crossbow*, Oct–Dec. 1971, pp. 16–17, A. Junz, 'Accommodation at Westminster', *Parliamentary Affairs*, 1959–60, pp. 100–13, and G. R. Strauss, 'The Influence of the Backbencher: A Labour View', *Political Quarterly* 1965, pp. 277–85.

Of the many works on the political parties, the most valuable for party organisation and behaviour in opposition are A. Beattie (ed.), *English Party Politics*, London 1970 (2 vols.), R. Blake, *The Conservative Party From Peel to Churchill*, London 1970, and R. T. McKenzie, *British Political Parties*, London 1963. The Nuffield Election Studies of 1951, 1964, and 1970 provide some insights into the process of transferring from opposition to office, as do R. Rose 'The Making of Cabinet Ministers', *British Journal of Political Science*, 1970–1, pp. 393–414, and Peter Shore, *Entitled to Know*, London 1966.

The role of the Opposition in the House of Lords is dealt with generally in P. A. Bromhead, *The House of Lords and Contemporary Politics*, London 1958, and in B. Crick 'What Should the Lords be Doing?', *Political Quarterly* 1963, pp. 174–84, and P. G. Henderson, 'Legislation in the House of Lords', *Parliamentary Affairs* 1967–8, pp. 176–7. Information on the Liberal Party's role since it ceased to be one of the two main parties is contained in J. Rasmussen, *The Liberal Party*, London 1964, and Trevor Wilson, *The Downfall of the Liberal Party 1914–1935*, London 1966.

These several books and articles all have some bearing on the themes of this study. There remain a vast number of biographies, autobiographies and memoirs of political figures which are invaluable as sources of information about the development of Opposition practices over the past two centuries. Many of these have been referred to in footnotes in the text, particularly in Chapter 2. For a comprehensive list of political biographies and autobiographies, however, see the bibliography in R. M. Punnett, *British Government and Politics*, London, second edition, 1971, pp. 484–90.

Index of Names

(References to names in Tables are not included)

Aberdeen, Lord (4th Earl), 40
Adamson, W., 62, 80
Alderman, R. K., 292
Alexander, A. V. (1st Earl), 369, 371, 406
Alison, M. J. H., 274
Amery, H. J., 170
Amery, L. S., 61, 293, 294, 301, 408
Anderson, Sir J. (Lord Waverley), 51, 52, 387
Anstruther-Gray, Sir W. J. (Lord Kilmany), 302
Apter, D. E., 3
Armstrong, Sir William, 281
Asquith, H. H. (Lord Oxford and Asquith), 16, 44, 61, 80, 82, 91, 186, 201, 241, 404, 405, 406, 408, 409, 411, 414, 436
Assheton, R. (Lord Clitheroe), 51
Atkinson, N., 149
Attlee, C. R., 58, 59, 60, 63, 65, 68, 69, 70, 81, 82, 84, 87, 88, 89, 91, 114, 119, 124, 131, 132, 143, 150, 153, 155, 156, 157, 158, 161, 164, 165, 189, 202, 203, 238, 239, 243, 298, 370, 390, 391

Bacon, Miss A., 161
Bagehot, Walter, 105, 108
Balcarres, Lord (Earl of Crawford), 46, 47, 49
Baldwin, S. (1st Earl), 45, 48, 49, 50, 51, 57, 61, 84, 90, 91, 201, 221, 222, 241, 242, 293, 297, 321, 479
Balfour, A. J. (1st Earl), 4, 43, 45, 46, 47, 49, 66, 73, 82, 84, 85, 89, 91, 92, 148, 201, 221, 241, 245, 290, 295, 321, 369, 479
Balniel, Lord, 159, 171, 274, 349, 361, 374
Balogh, Professor, T., 270
Barber, A. P. L., 144, 158, 172, 185, 188, 206, 242, 375
Barker, A., 276, 395

Barlow, F., 232
Barnett, J., 255
Beaverbrook, Lord, 21, 293
Beeching, Lord, 203
Bell, R. M., 141, 146
Beloff, Professor M., 204, 205
Belstead, Lord, 425
Benn, A. W., 118, 122, 138, 145, 169, 243, 371
Beswick, F. (Life Peer), 161, 421, 423, 428, 430
Bevan, A., 23, 24, 69, 88, 97, 100, 114, 115, 119, 122, 123, 124, 125, 131, 150, 169, 173, 297, 298, 410
Bevin, E., 92, 239, 387
Bhansali, R. J., 104
Biffen, W. J., 140
Bing, G. H. C., 115
Bingham, G. C. P. (see Lord Lucan), 119
Birch, N. C., 296
Birkenhead, Lord (see Smith, F. E.)
Bishop, E. S., 141
Blakenham, Lord (see Hare, J. H.)
Blondel, Professor J., 441, 442, 443
Bottomley, A. G., 59, 120, 132, 370
Bowden, H. W. (Lord Aylestone), 370
Boyd-Carpenter, J. A., 152
Boyle, Sir E. C. G., 146, 170, 237, 257, 265
Braine, Sir B. R., 255, 261, 375
Brodrick, W. S. J. (Lord Midleton), 47, 60
Brooke, H. (Life Peer), 158
Brown, G. A. (Life Peer), 59, 88, 100, 120, 125, 133, 140, 171, 173, 186, 206, 247, 260, 278, 282, 294, 323, 347, 370
Bryan, P. E. O., 172, 301, 361
Buchan-Hepburn, P. G. T. (Lord Hailes), 51
Butler, D. E., 100, 103, 104, 208
Butler, R. A. (Life Peer), 51, 170, 173, 190, 206, 209, 210, 242, 264, 265, 274

Cairns, H. (1st Earl), 240
Callaghan, L. J., 59, 88, 119, 123, 125, 128, 134, 172, 202, 238, 243, 246, 270, 278, 347, 369, 370
Campbell, G. T. C., 138, 274
Campbell-Bannerman, Sir H., 44, 89, 90
Carr, L. R., 171, 185, 246
Carrington, P. A. R. (6th Lord), 185, 242, 246, 301, 375, 422, 427
Carson, Sir E. H. (1st Lord), 408
Castle, Mrs B. A., 118, 120, 122, 128, 133, 163, 164, 170, 243, 247, 255, 270, 299, 300, 359, 360, 370, 371
Chalfont, Lord (see Gwynne-Jones, A.)
Chalmers, J., 270
Chamberlain, A. N., 50, 239, 241, 263, 264, 405, 406
Chamberlain, J., 82
Chamberlain, Sir J. A., 47, 48, 49, 50, 61, 85, 241, 290
Champion, A. J. (Life Peer), 161, 421
Channon, Sir H., 50, 52
Channon, H. P. G., 141, 153
Chaplin, H. (1st Viscount), 46, 82, 91, 407, 409, 474
Cherwell, Lord (see Lindeman, F. A.)
Chesterfield, Lord (see Stanhope, P. D.)
Chetwynd, G. R., 170
Chichester-Clark, R., 172, 375
Churchill, Lord R. H. S., 148, 149
Churchill, W. S., 8, 16, 23, 45, 49, 50, 51, 52, 59, 62, 65, 69, 70, 81, 84, 89, 90, 91, 97, 98, 99, 105, 151, 186, 201, 209, 222, 241, 297, 298, 316, 321, 357, 368, 391, 406, 479
Clarke, Sir E., 61
Clynes, J. R., 53, 54, 57, 58, 87, 239, 242, 354
Colville, J. M. A. (4th Viscount), 425
Cooper, A. D. (Lord Norwich), 298
Corfield, F. V., 170, 171, 172
Cousins, F., 370, 378, 387
Crawford, Earl (see Balcarres, Lord)
Crewe, Lord, 414
Crick, Professor B., 180, 214
Cripps, Sir R. S., 58, 239, 243
Cronin, J. D., 343, 371
Crookshank, H. F. C. (1st Viscount), 51
Crosland, C. A. R., 121, 140, 145, 186, 243, 268
Cross, J. A., 292
Cross, R. (1st Viscount), 148

Crossman, R. H. S., 108, 117, 120, 122, 128, 160, 161, 163, 170, 186, 270, 299, 372
Curzon, G. N. (1st Lord), 48

Dalton, H. J. N. (Life Peer), 62, 115, 119, 156, 157, 186, 238, 293, 294, 295, 301, 406
Darling, G., 146, 343
Davidson, Sir J. C. C. (1st Viscount), 263
Davies, E. A. J., 279
Davies, J. E. H., 378, 387
Dean, A. P., 163, 274
Deedes, W. F., 158
de Freitas, Sir G. E., 170, 173
Dell, E. E., 379
de Jouvenel, B., 31
de Madariaga, Isabel, 407
Derby, Lord (14th Earl), 41
Derby, Lord (15th Earl), 240
Diamond, J., 160, 161, 429, 430
Dilhorne, Lord (see Manningham-Buller, Sir R. E.)
Dilke, Sir C., 186
Disraeli, B. (Lord Beaconsfield), 27, 41, 148, 209, 240, 297
Dodington, G. B. (Lord Melcombe), 37
Douglas-Home, Sir A. F. (Lord Home), 45, 55, 70, 81, 84, 85, 89, 91, 92, 96, 97, 104, 106, 110, 137, 139, 144, 158, 159, 165, 173, 174, 199, 225, 231, 241, 242, 247, 260, 262, 282, 283, 296, 307, 356, 367, 374, 390
Dowse, R. E., 204
Driberg, T. E. N., 128
Drumalbyn, Lord (see Macpherson, N. M. S.)
du Cann, E. D. L., 188
Duncannon, Lord (see Ponsonby, J. W.)

Ede, J. C., 119, 156, 157, 238
Eden, Sir A., 50, 51, 52, 63
Edmondson, J. C. (Lord Sandford), 424
Edwards, C., 58
Elliot, W. E., 51
Emery, P., 141
Ennals, D., 161, 379
Errol, F. J. (1st Lord), 158

Faringdon, Lord (see Henderson, G. G.)
Faulds, A. M. W., 428

Finch, H. J., 371
Fisher, H. A. L., 241
Fisher, N., 141, 300
Fletcher, Sir E. G. M., 254, 343
Foord, Professor A. S., 36
Foot, M. M., 118, 129, 131, 140, 141, 161, 282, 359
Fowler, G., 161
Fraser, Sir M., 225, 231, 242, 273
Fraser, T., 59, 117, 123, 132, 172, 173, 255, 348, 359, 370, 379

Gaitskell, H. T. N., 69, 70, 81, 88, 89, 91, 94, 97, 98, 101, 106, 112, 117, 119, 123, 124, 125, 131, 137, 138, 141, 143, 150, 157, 165, 169, 170, 172, 173, 203, 204, 209, 243, 259, 294, 299, 300, 367, 373, 376, 390, 391
Galbraith, T. G. D., 170
Gandhi, M. K., 297
Gardiner, G. A. (1st Lord), 160, 370, 378, 430
Gathorne-Hardy, G. (Lord Cranbrook), 41, 240
Gibson-Watt, J. D., 172
Giffard, H. S. (see Lord Halsbury), 91
Gladstone, W. E., 40, 41, 42, 43, 44, 60, 61, 148, 149, 201, 209, 230, 240
Godber, J. B., 172, 257, 374, 375
Goodhart, C. A. E., 104
Graham, Sir J. (2nd Lord), 40, 240
Graham, W., 57, 62, 246, 256
Granville, Lord (see Leveson-Gower, G.)
Greenwood, Anthony W. (Life Peer), 88, 117, 119, 120, 128, 155, 158, 170, 238, 298, 370, 371, 430
Greenwood, Arthur, 82, 87, 91, 409
Grenfell, D. R., 58, 62, 116
Grey, C. (2nd Earl), 44
Grey, Sir Edward (1st Viscount), 414
Griffiths, J., 58, 117, 119, 123, 125, 137, 156, 157, 172, 173, 370, 378, 379, 410
Gunter, R. S., 130, 347, 369
Gwynne-Jones, A. (Lord Chalfont), 289, 378, 422, 423, 429

Halifax Lord (see Wood, E. F. L.)
Hall, G. H. (1st Viscount), 59
Hall, W. G., 119, 155, 156, 157
Halsbury, Lord (see Giffard, H. S.)
Hamilton, Lord G. F., 60
Hamilton, Mrs M. M., 116

Hanson, Professor A. H., 211
Harcourt, Sir W. G., 42, 44, 82, 240
Hare, J. H. (Lord Blakenham), 169, 422
Hare, W. F. (Lord Listowel), 120, 369, 371
Harlech, Lord (see Ormsby-Gore, Sir W. D.)
Harmsworth, H. S. (Lord Rothermere), 21, 293
Harris, J. H. (Lord Malmesbury), 41
Hart, Mrs J. C. M., 226
Hartington, Lord, 41
Harvey, Sir A. V., 302
Hastings, Sir P., 242
Hattersley, R. S. G., 74, 75, 289, 379
Hay, A. W. G. P. (Lord Kinnoull), 425
Hay, J. A., 140
Healey, D. W., 74, 75, 131, 133, 145, 243, 280, 347, 369, 372
Heath, E. R. G., 45, 70, 81, 85, 86, 88, 89, 90, 91, 95, 96, 97, 98, 99, 101, 102, 103, 106, 110, 139, 140, 141, 142, 143, 144, 145, 147, 150, 153, 154, 158, 159, 160, 161, 168, 169, 170, 172, 174, 175, 190, 203, 217, 219, 241, 242, 250, 255, 262, 265, 266, 276, 283, 296, 297, 300, 305, 307, 310, 324, 342, 345, 352, 356, 357, 365, 366, 374, 375, 376, 377, 378, 390, 391
Heffer, E. S., 118, 140, 141
Helsby, Sir L., 283
Henderson, A., 53, 54, 57, 58, 82, 87, 91, 239, 242, 246
Henderson, G. G. (Lord Faringdon), 120
Henderson, W. W. (1st Lord), 120, 156
Hennessy, D. J. G. (Lord Windlesham), 425
Herbert, S., 240
Herbison, Miss M. M., 59, 173, 281, 323, 348
Heseltine, M. R. D., 146, 153
Higgins, T. L., 141, 344
Hoare, Sir Samuel (Lord Templewood), 239, 241
Hobson, Sir J. G. S., 169
Hogg, Q. M. (Lord Hailsham), 100, 185, 241, 296, 297, 353, 375
Hope, V. A. J. (Lord Linlithgow), 293
Horne, Sir R. S. (1st Viscount), 61

Houghton, A. L. N. D., 112, 113, 117, 161, 173, 174, 213, 289
Howell, D. A. R., 275
Hoy, J. H., 132, 161, 343, 349
Hughes, C., 160
Hughes, R., 146
Hurd, D. R., 98

Ionescu, Professor G., 407

James, R. R., 90
Jay, D. P. T., 117, 132, 133, 169, 172, 218, 243, 255, 259, 321, 369, 370
Jellicoe, G. P. J. R. (2nd Earl), 265, 422
Jenkin, C. P. F., 344
Jenkins, H. G., 312
Jenkins, R. H., 118, 121, 122, 140, 164, 186, 208, 209, 243, 246, 247, 256, 260, 268, 289, 371, 372
Jennings, Sir I., 78, 79, 205
Johnson, C. A., 232
Johnston, T., 62
Jones, A. C., 172, 323, 371
Joseph, Sir K., 172, 175, 185, 246, 294
Jowitt, Sir W. A. (1st Viscount), 119, 156, 157
Joynson-Hicks, Sir W. (Lord Brentford), 49, 50, 61
Judd, F. A., 98

Kaldor, Professor N., 268
Keith-Lucas, Professor B., 419
Kennet, Lord (see Young, W.)
Kershaw, J. A., 98, 225
Kinnoull, Lord (see Hay, A. W. G. P.)
Kirchheimer, Professor O., 398

Lansbury, G., 57, 58, 62, 87, 91, 92, 243, 295
Lansdowne, Lord (see Petty-Fitz-maurice, H. C. K.)
Law, A. B., 45, 46, 47, 48, 82, 84, 85, 88, 91, 198, 201, 221, 241, 321, 404, 405, 479
Lawson, J. J. (1st Lord), 59
Lee, F., 133, 134, 172, 347, 370
Lee, Miss J. (Life Peer), 428
Lees-Smith, H. B., 82, 91, 406, 409, 410
Lestor, Miss J., 270
Lever, N. H., 117, 256, 289
Leveson-Gower, G. (Lord Granville), 43, 240
Lindeman, F. A. (Lord Cherwell), 52

Linlithgow, Lord (see Hope, V. A. J.)
Listowel, Lord (see Hare, W. F.)
Lloyd, J. S. B., 67, 152, 235, 242
Lloyd-George, D. (1st Earl), 61, 80, 93, 405, 406, 408, 411, 414
Lloyd-Graeme, P. (Lord Swinton), 51
Loftus, P. C., 398
Long, W. H. (1st Viscount), 43, 48, 61, 66, 85, 405
Longford, Lord (see Pakenham, F. A.)
Loughlin, C. W., 161
Lowell, A. L., 13
Lucan, Lord (see Bingham, G. C. P.)
Lyttelton, O. (Lord Chandos), 51, 63

Mabon, J. D., 141, 289
MacArthur, I., 375
MacDonald, J. R., 53, 54, 56, 57, 62, 80, 84, 86, 87, 90, 91, 196, 201, 239, 241, 242, 245, 406
Macdougall, Sir D., 282
MacGregor, J., 98
Mackenzie, J. G., 167
McKenzie, R. T., 127
Mackie, J., 161
Mackintosh, J. P., 108
Maclean, Sir D., 80, 82, 414
Macleod, I. N., 144, 158, 159, 172, 185, 206, 236, 242, 274, 294, 296, 307, 353, 375
Macmillan, H., 51, 63, 65, 72, 104, 106, 158, 174, 185, 186, 203, 224, 290, 305, 316, 357, 410
Macmillan, M. V., 141, 257, 344, 361
Macpherson, N. M. S. (Lord Drumalbyn), 424
Malmesbury, Lord (see Harris, J. H.)
Manningham-Buller, Sir R. E. (Lord Dilhorne), 422
Marples, A. E., 152, 275, 283
Marquand, D. I., 76
Marquand, H. A., 170
Marsh, R. N., 141, 170
Mason, R., 141, 160
Maude, A. E. U., 300
Maudling, R., 85, 86, 96, 140, 164, 171, 172, 173, 217, 242, 265, 274, 281, 375
Maxton, J., 149, 295, 410
Maxwell-Fyfe, D. P. (Lord Kilmuir), 51
May, Sir T. Erskine, 10, 409
Mayhew, C. P., 29, 300
Mellish, R. J., 160, 247

Midleton, Lord (see Brodrick, W. S. J.)
Mikardo, I., 128, 246, 270
Mill, J. S., 3
Milner, Sir A. (1st Viscount), 46, 408
Mitchison, G. R. (Life Peer), 121, 131, 134, 158, 172, 369, 379
Morley, John (1st Viscount), 44, 240
Morris, A., 141
Morris, C. R., 98
Morrison, C. A., 153, 166, 344, 345, 375
Morrison, H. S. (Life Peer), 65, 66, 67, 72, 73, 87, 88, 119, 146, 156, 157, 238, 239, 369, 406
Morrison, W. S. (Lord Dunrossil), 51
Mosley, Sir O. E., 20
Mulley, F. W., 226
Murray, R. King, 261
Murton, H. O., 306

Nicholas, Sir H. R., 246
Noble, M. A. C., 138, 374, 377
Noel-Baker, P. J., 120, 131, 156, 371
Northcote, Sir S. (Lord Iddesleigh), 148, 240

O'Neill, Sir C. D. W., 280
Ormsby-Gore, Sir W. D. (Lord Harlech), 159, 170, 422
Owen, D. A. L., 289

Page, R. G., 256, 344
Paget, R. T., 172, 173, 257, 347, 371
Pakenham, F. A. (Lord Longford), 370
Pakington, Sir J., 297
Palmerston, Lord, 184
Pannell, T. C., 114, 115, 140
Pardoe, J., 419
Peart, T. F., 173, 347
Peel, Sir R., 39, 40, 240
Peel, W. R. W. (1st Earl), 241
Peterson, A. D. C., 419
Pethick-Lawrence, F. W. (1st Lord) 62, 82, 91, 409, 410
Petty-Fitzmaurice, H. C. K. (Lord Lansdowne), 45, 46, 47, 48, 84, 224, 241, 245, 404
Peyton, J. W. W., 141
Pike, Miss I. M. P., 169
Pinto-Duschinsky, M., 103, 208
Pitt, T. J., 277
Ponsonby, A. A. W. H. (1st Lord), 115
Ponsonby, J. W. (Lord Duncannon), 39

Powell, J. E. 85, 86, 98, 100, 140, 141, 158, 170, 211, 260, 274, 279, 296, 297, 357
Prentice, R. E., 118
Price, D. E. C., 255
Primrose, A. P. (Lord Rosebery), 60, 82, 209, 245
Prior, J. M. L., 98, 225, 374

Ramsden, J. E., 170, 375
Rawlinson, Sir P. A. G., 170, 225
Redmayne, Sir M. (Life Peer), 158
Richard, I. S., 312
Ridley, N., 140
Rippon, A. G. F., 141, 158
Robens, A. (Life Peer), 120, 170, 172, 238
Rockingham, C. W. (2nd Marquis), 38, 39, 240
Roll, Sir Eric, 282
Roots, W. L., 170
Rosebery, Lord (see Primrose, A. P.)
Ross, W., 117, 123, 132, 138, 343, 348, 349, 372
Rothermere, Lord (see Harmsworth, H. S.)
Runciman, W. (1st Viscount), 414
Rush, M., 276, 395
Russell, Lord John, 39, 41

Salisbury, Lord (5th Marquess), 51, 63
Samuel, Sir H. L. (1st Viscount), 408, 414
Sandford, Lord (see Edmondson, J. C.)
Sandys, D., 152
Schreiber, M., 275
Sewill, B., 225, 231, 273
Shackleton, E. A. A. (Life Peer), 421, 422, 430
Sharples, R. C., 274
Shaw, T., 246
Shepherd, G. R. (1st Lord), 155, 157
Shepherd, M. N. (2nd Lord), 369, 371, 421
Shinwell, E., 24, 62, 112, 119, 156, 157, 207, 410
Shore, P., 123, 130, 160, 161, 218, 251, 284
Short, E. W., 117, 270
Silkin, J. E., 118, 141
Simon, Sir J. A. (1st Lord), 57, 239
Sinclair, Sir A. H. M. (Viscount Thurso), 414

Skeffington, A. M., 161
Smith, E., 202
Smith, F. E. (Lord Birkenhead), 48, 49, 295
Smith, W. H., 148, 198
Snowden, P. (1st Viscount), 54, 57, 62, 239, 242, 246
Soskice, Sir F. (Lord Stow Hill), 119, 120, 121, 125, 370
Spencer, C. (Lord Sunderland), 37
Stanhope, P. D. (Lord Chesterfield), 37, 39
Stanley, O. F. G., 51, 63, 241
Steel, D., 415
Steele, T., 469
Steel-Maitland, Sir A. H. R. D., 46
Stewart, R. M. M., 67, 132, 133, 160, 172, 370
Stokes, D., 100, 105
Stokes, R. R., 119, 120
Strachey, J. S., 172, 186, 347
Strauss, G. R., 121, 138, 172, 252, 312, 371
Stuart, J. G. (1st Viscount), 51
Summerskill, Dr Edith, 120, 133
Sunderland, Lord (see Spencer, C.)
Swinton, Lord (see Lloyd-Graeme, P.)

Taverne, D., 255, 289
Thatcher, Mrs M. H., 172, 349, 350
Thomas, J. H., 54, 57, 239, 242, 256
Thomas, P. J. M., 374
Thomas, T. G., 160
Thomson, G. M., 117, 122, 289, 372, 469
Thorneycroft, G. E. P. (1st Lord), 237, 296
Thorpe, J., 413
Titmuss, Professor R. M., 270
Townsend, Professor P., 270
Townshend, C., 37

Ungoed-Thomas, Sir A. L., 170

Wainwright, R. S., 419
Walker, P. E., 153, 159, 163, 175, 280
Walker, P. Gordon, 108, 172, 243, 244, 260, 369, 370

Walker-Smith, Sir D. C., 152
Walpole, Sir R., 37, 39
Webb, Mrs B. (Lady Passfield), 56
Webb, S. J. (Lord Passfield), 57, 242, 246
Wedgwood, J. C. (1st Lord), 58, 202, 295
Wellington, Duke of, 39, 199
Wheatley, John, 62, 295
Wheatley, Lord, 305
Whitaker, B. C. G., 161
White, Mrs E., 161, 270
Whitelaw, W. S. I., 242, 375, 469
Whiteley, W., 119, 156, 157
Willey, F. T., 123, 172, 369
Williams, Mrs S. V. T. B., 160, 243, 289, 379
Williams, T. (Life Peer), 62, 170
Willis, E. G., 343, 349
Wilson, J. H., 28, 59, 68, 69, 70, 81, 84, 88, 89, 91, 92, 97, 98, 99, 102, 103, 104, 105, 106, 112, 115, 117, 119, 122, 124, 125, 130, 131, 132, 134, 137, 138, 139, 140, 141, 142, 143, 144, 145, 146, 147, 150, 154, 160, 165, 167, 169, 171, 172, 173, 174, 175, 180, 186, 188, 199, 202, 206, 208, 210, 211, 239, 243, 244, 246, 247, 250, 255, 256, 262, 278, 282, 283, 289, 290, 299, 346, 365, 366, 367, 368, 369, 370, 371, 372, 373, 375, 376, 377, 378, 390, 391, 422, 425
Windlesham, Lord (see Hennessy, D. J. G.)
Winterton, Earl (Lord Turnour), 51, 410
Wood, E. F. L. (Lord Halifax), 239
Woodburn, A., 59, 132, 170, 410
Woolton, Lord, 51, 185, 387
Wylie, N. R., 279
Wyndham, G., 474

Young, W. (see Lord Kennet), 427
Younger, K. G., 117, 120, 132, 133, 170, 279

Zilliacus, K., 121

Subject Index

Accommodation at Westminster, 382
Admiralty, First Lord of, 61, 353
Adoption Bill 1967, 254
Agricultural Workers Union, 280
'Agriculture Charter', 264
Agriculture Committee, 255
Agriculture, Minister of, 62
Australia, 78, 434, 438–9, 441–4, 447
Austria, 434–5, 438, 441, 443–4, 446–7

BEA, 262
Belgium, 433–4, 438, 441–4, 447
Bevanite group (in PLP) 23–4, 114–15, 122–4
BOAC, 262
Bow Group, 23, 141
'Bradford Resolution', 53
British Caledonian Airways, 262
British Iron and Steel Federation, 280
British Union of Fascists, 20–1
BUA, 262
Business Committee
    1915,   405
    1930–1,   50–1, 222, 241–2
    1945–51,   51
    1964–70,   223, 302, 308
'Butskellism', 199
By-elections, 12, 13, 378

Canada, 78, 396–7, 432–4, 438–9, 441–445, 447
Carlton Club, 39, 85
Carlton House, 38
Centre for Labour Studies, 395
'Challenge to Britain', 278
Chancellor of the Exchequer, 5, 61–2, 164, 186, 206, 217, 236, 369, 375
Chief Whip
    Conservative, 110–12, 137–8, 158, 222–5, 232, 302–3, 375
    Labour, 54, 56–8, 114, 222–5, 235, 369, 421
    Liberal, 419

General, 218, 390
Child Poverty Action Group, 21
Clydesiders, 23, 204
Coalition Governments
    1915–18, 16, 404–11, 436
    1918–22, 406, 411
    1931, 11, 59, 241, 406–7
    1940, 8, 11, 16, 185, 404–11, 436
    Abroad, 433–6
    General, 15–18, 433–6, 441, 447
Colonies, Secretary of State, 353, 375
Committee of Imperial Defence, 201
Common Market (see European Economic Community)
'Common Market rebels' (Labour Party), 123, 135, 288–92, 294, 297, 300–1, 422
Commonwealth Immigration Bill 1968, 294
'Conciliabulum', 38, 240
Conservative Governments
    1900–5, 46–7
    1922–4, 49
    1924–9, 12, 263
    1935–40, 239, 405–6
    1951–64, 52, 158–61, 165, 184, 194, 283, 296, 355
    1970, 144–5, 151, 175, 199, 207, 212, 365, 374–9, 425–6
Conservative Legal Committee, 279
Conservative Party (see also Spokesmen, etc.)
    Advisory Committee on Policy, 219, 265–7, 427
    Attitude to Opposition, 6–9, 14–15
    Backbench groups, 68, 145–6, 303–7
    Chairman, 110, 172, 232–4, 242
    Comes to office, 1970, 283–5, 365–7, 374–9
    Conference, 29
    Consultative Committee role, 216–49
    Discipline, 293–4, 296–8
    Evolution of Parliamentary organisation, 6, 36–53, 60–5, 70–3

Conservative Party—*cont.*
  Meetings of 1922 Committee, 223,
    301–3
  Policy making, 219–20, 262–7
  Research Department, 94, 225, 263–
    264, 272–5, 306, 395
  Selection of Leader, 84–6, 88–93
Conservative Political Centre, 275
Conservative Systems Research Centre,
  276
Consolidated Fund, 78, 202
Consultative Committee (*see* Shadow
  Cabinet)
Co-operative Movement, 279

Daily Express, 21, 283
Daily Mirror, 157
Defence, Secretary of State, 427
Denmark, 434, 438, 441, 443–4, 447

Early Day Motions, 256, 299
Economic Affairs, Secretary of State,
  175, 370
Education Bill 1906, 46
'Electoral pendulum', 7–8, 10–13, 180–
  182, 193–4
'Empire Crusade', 21, 293
Employment, Minister of, 162, 353, 361
Estimates Committee, 256, 381
European Economic Community, 21,
  32, 123, 224, 230, 236, 256, 288,
  291–2, 294, 307, 309–10, 428–9
'Ex-Cabinet' (*see also* Shadow Cabinet),
  5, 35, 40–5, 54–5, 297, 352
Expenditure Committee, 255, 408, 410

'Fair Deal at Work', 261, 266, 284
Finance Bills
  1909, 47
  1971, 76
  1968, 254
  1965, 255
Finland, 434–5, 438, 441–4, 447
Foreign Affairs, Secretary of State, 186,
  329, 369
Forward Party (1915–16), 408
'Fourth Party' (1880–5), 23, 148–9, 201
France, 432, 434, 437, 438–9, 441–4,
  446–8
Front-bench seating arrangements, 9–
  10, 56–7, 67, 409–10

'Gaitskellites', 124
Gallup Poll, 12, 103–6, 483–4

General Elections
  1895, 44
  1906, 44–5, 53, 82
  1910, 53, 188
  1918, 53, 80, 82, 86
  1922, 53, 80, 86, 87
  1923, 49, 84, 242
  1924, 84
  1929, 49, 84, 188
  1931, 10, 58, 83, 87, 91, 319
  1935, 58, 87
  1945, 10, 50, 84, 105, 155, 188, 194,
    206
  1950, 52, 154–5, 194
  1951, 10, 78, 84, 153, 194
  1955, 119, 153, 188, 193–4
  1959, 10, 78, 105, 119, 169, 194, 299,
    367
  1964, 78, 84, 89, 100, 102, 153, 158,
    173, 188–9, 194, 281, 367, 416, 422
  1966, 90, 102, 105, 153, 158–9, 169–
    170, 188, 193–4, 416
  1970, 78, 84, 89–90, 102–3, 105, 155,
    161, 189, 194, 208, 220, 246, 366–7
General Strike (1926), 414

Hansard, 468–9, 473–82
Harris Poll, 484
Health, Minister of, 61, 263, 353
Her Majesty's Opposition (*see also*
  Leader of the Opposition, Shadow
  Cabinet, etc.)
  Analysis of past failures, 188–90
  Characteristics of, 9–20
  Electoral appeal, 180–2, 197–8
  Limitations of, 27–32, 196–7
  Parliamentary tactics, 194–205, 214–
    215
  Preoccupations, 187–94
  Preparing for office, 190–4, 205–15
  Responsible opposition, 201–14
  Role of, 4–5, 25–6, 30–2, 179–83,
    365–6, 398–400
Home Affairs, Secretary of State, 375
Honours List, 96
Hospitals (Scotland) Bill 1970, 146
Housing and Local Government,
  Minister of, 175
Housing Finance Act 1972, 263

Iceland, 434, 438, 441, 443–4, 446–8
Immigration Bill 1970, 207
'Imperial policy' 264

Independent Labour Party, 53, 410
'Index of Specialisation', 97–8, 313–61,
    373–81
India, 60, 201, 261, 433–5, 437, 438,
    441, 443–5, 447
'Industrial Charter, The', 264
Industrial Relations Bill 1970, 197, 210,
    213, 235, 255, 261, 263, 359–60
Industrial Reorganisation Corporation,
    262
Institute of International Affairs, 279
Institute of Strategic Studies, 279
Interviews (with MPs), 468–73
Ireland (*see also* Northern Ireland)
    General, 99, 262
    Home Rule issue, 42–3, 46, 48, 198,
        201, 245, 319, 331, 404
    Opposition in, 434, 436, 438, 441,
        443–4, 447
    Secretary of State, 61
Irish Party, 18, 24, 406
Italy, 432, 434, 437, 438, 441–4, 447–8

Jacobites, 20
Japan, 406, 434–5, 438, 441, 443–5, 447
Jordan, 294
Joseph Rowntree Social Service Trust,
    395, 418

Labour Governments
    1924, 8, 182, 185, 239, 242
    1929–31, 8, 57, 83, 87, 185, 239, 242,
        277
    1945–51, 8, 59, 150, 153, 155–8, 165,
        185, 198–9, 204, 207, 239, 370
    1964–70, 8, 25, 145, 151, 160–1, 164,
        175, 185, 194, 199–200, 203, 206,
        210–38, 244, 283–4, 300, 365, 369–
        373, 375–9, 425
Labour Party (*see also* Parliamentary
    Committee: Election, Spokesmen,
    etc.)
    Administrative Committee (1940),
        409
    Attitude to Opposition, 6–9, 14–15,
        180
    Backbench groups, 68, 146, 310–4
    Comes to office 1964, 283–5, 369–73
    Conference role, 267–8
    Discipline, 298–300
    Election of Leader, 86–92, 94
    Evolution of Parliamentary organisa-
        tion, 6, 53–61, 63–73

    General Secretary, 225, 234, 246
    Meetings of PLP, 287, 307–10
    NEC, 94–5, 219, 232, 243, 260, 267–
        272
    Parliamentary Committee's role,
        216–49
    PLP chairman, 80, 86, 112–13, 235,
        289, 308
    Policy making, 219, 267–72
    Research Department, 94, 268, 276–
        278, 395
    PLP secretary, 225, 232
    'Second eleven', 58
    Subject specialisation, 350–6
    Trade unions, 21, 141, 279
Leader of the Opposition (*see also*
    Shadow Cabinet, Opposition
    Spokesmen etc.)
    As Party Leader, 80–4, 95
    Constitutional role, 78, 94, 365–7
    Electoral coverage, 102–3, 107
    Emergence, 84–8
    House of Lords, 81–2, 84, 421–9
    Opinion poll rating, 103–7
    Overthrow, 91–3
    Patronage, 66, 95–7
    Power, 93–9, 390–2
    Private office, 98–9, 390, 396
    Public appeal, 100–7
    Role in Shadow Cabinet, 97, 234
    Room at Westminster, 77, 224–5
    Salary, 77, 202, 389
    Status, 77–84, 99, 107
    Tenure in post, 89–90
    Wartime, 408–10
'Leicester House Opposition', 37, 39
Liberal Party
    Decline, 18, 411–12
    Election of Leader, 418
    Opposition role, 24, 412–20
    Parliamentary organisation, 413–
        418
    Policy-making, 419–20
    Research Department, 418
    'Shadow Cabinet', 418–19
    Splits, 408, 414
Library (of House of Commons), 258–9,
    278–9
Local Government Bill 1961, 255
London Airport issue, 262
Lords, House of
    Caucus meetings, 430
    Collective responsibility, 428–9

Lords, House of—*cont.*
  Coordination with Commons, 426, 429
  Institutional Opposition, 22, 420
  Leader of Opposition, 79–80, 82
  Opposition organisation, 76, 421–30
  Peers in Shadow Cabinet, 56, 235–6, 421–9
  Reform issue, 25, 47, 290, 319, 331
  Role of Spokesmen, 422–6
  Subject specialisation, 427–8
Luxembourg, 434, 438, 441, 443–5, 447–8

'Make Life Better', 246, 266
Manpower Committee (1914), 404
Maurice Debate (1918), 408–9
Medieval Parliament, 4, 411
Ministerial and Other Salaries Act 1972, 77
Ministerial Salaries Act 1957, 77–8
Ministerial Salaries Consolidation Act 1965, 77, 79
Ministers of the Crown Act 1937, 77, 79–80
Monarch, 78–9, 366–7
Monday Club, 23, 141
Muir Society, 279
Munitions Crisis (1915), 405

National Farmers Union, 280
Nationalised Industries Committee, 255
National Opinion Poll, 200, 484
National Union of Mineworkers, 141, 279
National Union of Public Employees, 141
NATO, 299
Netherlands, 432, 434, 438, 440–1, 443–4, 447
'New Style of Government, A', 266
New Zealand, 432–4, 438, 441–4, 447
Nigerian Civil War, 217
'No Defence Committee' (PLP), 312
Northern Ireland
  General, 99, 183, 202, 224, 403, 417
  Opposition in, 434, 438, 440, 443, 447
Norway, 432, 434–5, 438, 441, 443–4, 446–7
Nuffield Foundation, 469

'Odyssey, The', 365
Opinion polls, 13, 103–6, 483–4

Opposition (*see also* Her Majesty's Opposition)
  Backbench, 23–5
  Compensations of, 183–8
  Direct action, 21
  'Disloyal Opposition', 20
  Institutional Opposition, 22
  In wartime and crises, 403–11
  Minor party, 24, 411–20
  Patterns of Government–Opposition relations, 15–20
  Patterns and tactics abroad, 431–49
  Pressure group, 21–2
  Revolutionary, 14–15, 20–1, 30, 192
  Value of, 3–4
Opposition Spokesmen: role (*see also* Shadow Cabinet)
  Attractions of job, 139–40
  Backbench committees, 257–8, 303–307, 310–14
  Civil Service contacts, 281–4, 394–5
  Committee work, 253–6
  Compared with Ministers, 380–8
  Constituency issues, 68, 316, 359
  Debates, 252, 258, 318–61
  Dismissals, 295–6, 300–1
  Duties in Parliament, 250–9, 331–9
  Duties outside Parliament, 250, 259–261
  Early Day Motions, 256
  Finance, 185–6, 396–8
  Hours of work, 184–6
  Parliamentary Party meetings, 301–303, 307
  Policy-making role, 261–72
  Pressure groups, 259–60, 279–80
  Private Members Bills, 256–7
  Question Time, 252–3, 258, 318–61
  Resignations, 289–94, 297–301
  Sources of information, 272–85, 395–6
  Subject specialisation, 254–5, 315–61
Opposition Spokesmen: selection (*see also* Shadow Government system)
  Age factor, 152–4, 157–8
  Backbench recruitment, 151–5, 159–161, 166–8
  Former Ministers, 148–52, 155–68, 385
  Future Ministers, 149–57, 368–79
  Group representation, 141–2
  Influence of MPs on Leader, 137–9
  Leader's difficulties, 139–42

Number of Appointments, 142–7, 377–8
Place of Parliamentary Committee members, 130–4
Promotions, 171–2
Re-allocation of duties, 168–73, 345–350
Overseas Aid Committee, 255
Overseas Development, Minister of, 175

Parliamentary Commissioner (Select Committee), 9
Parliamentary Committee: election (see also Shadow Cabinet, Opposition Spokesmen)
Casual vacancies, 116–18
Continuity of membership, 119–20, 133–4
Group tactics in ballot, 115, 122–5
House of Lords members, 114, 421–2
Members as Spokesmen, 129–36
Merits of system, 118, 128–9, 134–5
'No plumping' rule, 114–15
Overlap with NEC, 125–8
Standing Orders, 113–14, 116, 450–2
Structure, 111–13
Voting behaviour, 119–29
Parliamentary Private Secretaries, 76, 98, 138, 301
'Partial Cabinets', 108
Peelites, 40
Peers (see Lords, House of)
Pensions (and Social Security), Minister of, 163, 281
PEST (Pressure for Economic and Social Toryism), 23, 141, 395
Pilkington Committee Report, 300
'Policy for Wales', 264
Poujadist Party, 413
Power (and Fuel and Power), Minister of, 207
Preparing for office
Expertise gained in Opposition, 383–388
Policy-making machinery, 263–72
Recruiting front benchers, 149–57, 186
Shadow Cabinet's role, 219–21
Wisdom of policy-making, 205–14
Press Lords, 21
Prevention of Unemployment Bill 1923, 256
Prices and Incomes Bill 1968, 254

Prime Minister
Appointment of, 78–9, 81, 84
Change of, 26–7, 78–9
Dealings with Opposition, 199–203, 282–4
'Inner Cabinet', 239
Opinion poll rating, 105–9
Power and security, 88–103, 390
Press coverage, 100–3
Question time, 357
Selects Ministers, 66, 120, 137–40, 186, 238, 365–79
'Shadowed' by Leader of the Opposition, 217
'Priorities in Government', 268
Private Members' Bills, 256–7, 294
Progress Trust, 23
Proportional representation, 18
Public Accounts Committee, 255–6, 381
Public Investment Boards, 262
Public Sector Research Unit (Conservative Party), 275, 283
'Putting Britain Right Ahead', 266

Question time (House of Commons) 5, 58, 80, 217, 222–3, 253, 258, 283, 304, 315–16, 324–51, 357, 387, 407, 409, 476–7

Race Relations Bill 1968, 246, 254, 294
Race Relations Committee, 256
Redcliffe-Maud Commission Report, 305
Reform Bills 1830–2, 39, 199
Rent Bill 1956, 254
Rhodesia (UDI), 183, 300, 412
'Right Road For Britain', 264
Road Hauliers' Association, 280
Roads Study Group, 279
Rockinghamites, 38, 240
Rowntree Trust (see Joseph Rowntree)
Royal Commissions, 208

Scotland, Secretary of State, 62
Scottish Assembly (Conservative proposal,) 231, 262, 307
'Scottish Control for Scottish Affairs', 264
Scottish Nationalism, 14
'SEATO' incident, 69–70, 298
Select Committees (see also Public Accounts, Estimates, etc.), 72, 121, 281, 319, 469, 480–1

Selsdon Park Conference, 225
Senate (Roman), 4
Shadow Cabinet
    Agenda, 23–2
    Business, 216–21
    Cliques, 237
    Collective responsibility, 287–301
    Committees, 244–7
    Conduct of meetings, 227–33, 393
    Eighteenth century, 36–9, 56, 240
    Evolution, 36–59
    Frequency of meetings, 45–6, 51, 74,
        221–4, 393
    Inner Shadow Cabinet, 74, 238–44
    Membership, 46–8, 51
    Nineteenth century, 38–44, 60–5,
        240–1, 245
    Peers, 56, 235–6, 421–9
    Secrecy, 229–31
    Secretary, 225, 231–3, 242, 273
    Venue, 224–5
    Visitors to meetings, 225–6
Shadow Government System
    Criticism of, 65–9, 398–9
    Evolution, 5, 59–65, 111, 316
    Flexibility, 108–9
    Leader's control over, 389–90
    Reform, 389–99
    Structure, 74–7, 108, 174–5, 390–1
    Value, 64, 70–3, 389–99
Shelter, 21
'Signposts For The Sixties', 278
Sinn Fein, 80
South Africa, 434, 438, 441, 443–4,
    447–8
South Africa Bill 1961, 254
Spanish Civil War, 203
Speaker (of House of Commons), 56–7
    77, 80, 409–10
Spectator, The, 294, 300
Spokesmen (see Opposition Spokesmen)
Sport, Minister of, 174, 353
Standing Committees (of Parliament),
    121, 253, 319, 468, 481
Stanleyites, 40

Statutory Instruments Committee, 9,
    256, 410
Stormont, 10, 417
Suez crisis, 403
Sunday Times, 100
Supply Days, 9, 216–17
Sweden, 397, 433–6, 438–9, 441–4,
    446–7
Switzerland, 432, 434, 438, 443–8

Technology Committee, 255
Times, The, 101–3, 293, 428, 468, 481–3
Trade Disputes Bill 1927, 360
Transport and General Workers Union,
    141, 279
Transport Bill 1967, 280
Transport, Minister of, 163
Treasury bench, 56, 386
Treasury, Chief Secretary to, 75, 174
Tribune Group, 24, 123–4, 129, 141
Tribunes (Roman), 4, 31

Unionist Party (Northern Ireland), 10,
    416–17, 445
Unionist War Committee, 408
Upper Clyde Shipbuilders, 212
USA
    Separation of powers, 22
    Presidential elections, 105
    General, 99, 148–9, 203, 261, 379
    Constitution, 431–2
USSR, 99

'Victory for Socialism', 123
Vietnam War, 412

Wales
    Secretary of State, 378
    Welsh Nationalism, 14
West Germany
    397, 432, 434, 438, 441, 443–4, 447
Wheatley Commission Report, 305
Whip (see Chief Whip)
Wilson Committee 1956, 188
Workman's Compensation Bill 1923,
    256